The Journals and
Miscellaneous Notebooks
of
RALPH WALDO EMERSON

RALPH H. ORTH   *Chief Editor*

LINDA ALLARDT   RONALD A. BOSCO

HARRISON HAYFORD   DAVID W. HILL

GLEN M. JOHNSON   SUSAN SUTTON SMITH

Editors

The Journals and
Miscellaneous Notebooks
of
RALPH WALDO EMERSON

VOLUME XV

1860–1866

EDITED BY

LINDA ALLARDT   DAVID W. HILL

RUTH H. BENNETT
ASSOCIATE EDITOR

THE BELKNAP PRESS
OF HARVARD UNIVERSITY PRESS

Cambridge, Massachusetts
and London, England
1982

Library of Congress Cataloging in Publication Data (Revised)

Emerson, Ralph Waldo, 1803–1882.
  Journals and miscellaneous notebooks.

  Bibliographical footnotes.
  Vols.   accompanied by separate "Emendations and departures from the manuscript," by the editors.
  CONTENTS; v. 1. 1819–1822.—v. 2. 1822–1826.—v. 15. 1860–1866.
  1. Emerson, Ralph Waldo, 1803–1882—Diaries. 2. Authors, American—19th century—Biography. I. Gilman, William Henry, 1911–1976 ed.
PS1631.A3   1960   818'.303 [B]   60-11554
ISBN 0-674-48470-3 (v. 8)   AACR1
ISBN 0-674-48478-9 (v. 15)

Preface

This volume has been a collaborative effort: all three editors shared in the labor, although Linda Allardt, as the senior editor, is responsible for the final form of text and notes. Linda Allardt and Ruth H. Bennett each did one collation from photocopy, as did David Hill for Journals WAR and FOR; Mrs. Bennett did manuscript collation, research, and annotation for Journals DL and GL, Professor Hill for WAR, FOR, and the Pocket Diaries, and Professor Allardt for VA, KL, HT, and the Pocket Diaries. An additional manuscript collation was done by J. E. Parsons. Professors Hill and Allardt wrote the Foreword, and Mrs. Bennett the Chronology.

With the completion of this volume Mrs. Bennett leaves the Emerson journals for other challenging research. An incomparable researcher, she began as a volunteer on the project seventeen years ago and worked closely with chief editor William H. Gilman until his death in 1976, quietly taking on more and more of the difficult work of the volumes edited in Rochester. When something baffled everyone else, it was Mrs. Bennett who—usually within only a few days—appeared waving the half-sheet on which she had recorded the previously unfindable fact. Her impressive knowledge of Emerson's writings, published and unpublished, and the calm and unassuming brilliance of her editing earned her the respect of her fellow editors; her personal qualities have earned our affection.

The editors wish to thank a number of institutions and persons for help of various kinds. The Ralph Waldo Emerson Memorial Association has continued to provide regular grants-in-aid which have been indispensable to the progress of the edition. The work of all three editors was supported by a grant from the National Endowment for the Humanities. Professor Hill was aided by an Andrew W. Mellon Foundation fellowship awarded by the University of Rochester, which

v

also continued its generous support of the Emerson center in Rochester.

Special thanks are due to David Mycoff for dedicated accuracy in checking and researching notes, to Anne Boyle for checking and typing notes, to Marian Bodian for typing the text, to Richard V. Bennett for research, and to Anne Laskaya and Sarah Bulgatz for assistance on the index. Professor William H. Gilman guided the early planning for this volume up to the time of his death.

For other assistance and courtesies, thanks are due to Miss Marte Shaw, Professor William H. Bond, and others of the staff of Houghton Library; the staffs of Widener Library, Rush Rhees Library of the University of Rochester, the Penfield Library of the State University of New York College at Oswego, and the Concord Public Library; Professor Wallace E. Williams; Professor Albert Von Frank; Douglas E. Wilson; Professor Joel Myerson; and Professors Rowland L. Collins, George Ford, James Carley, and Frederick Locke of the University of Rochester.

Unless otherwise noted, translations of classical quotations are from the Loeb Classical Library, published by Harvard University Press.

The four illustrations are reprinted by permission of the Ralph Waldo Emerson Memorial Association, and by permission of the Houghton Library, Harvard University.

All the editors named on the edition title page have responsibilities of various kinds for the edition as a whole. The Chief Editor has the primary responsibility for the edition and for certification of individual volumes.

R.H.O.

Contents

Illustrations

Foreword to Volume XV

The Civil War was an immediate and pervasive presence in Emerson's life between October 1860 and February 1866, the period when he used these journals. He felt the losses, fears, angers, and frustrations that come to those who believe in a cause they are too old to fight for, but his public position as a man of letters on the antislavery side brought him experiences denied to all but a few Northerners. During a lecture trip to Washington in 1862 he met Lincoln and senior members of his administration and heard them analyze and chat about the war, diplomacy, and each other. The next year he was fascinated by his work as a member of the Board of Visitors to West Point, where he found young men apparently ready by character and training to meet the demands that the battlefield would soon make on them. In his reading and writing he kept coming back to his conception of the war as a catalytic agent that forced the full emergence of the individual and national characters he had studied for years in his ongoing critique of nineteenth-century civilization in America and Europe. "The war searches character," he wrote, "& acquits those whom I acquit, whom life acquits, those whose reality & spontaneous honesty & singleness appear." The war was above all a national cause, a dedication of America to its true nature. Of the Emancipation Proclamation he wrote, "It seems to promise an extension of the war. For there can be no durable peace, no sound Constitution, until we have fought this battle, & the rights of man are vindicated."

In his visit to the nation's capital in January and February of 1862, Emerson was taken to see Lincoln, Secretary of State Seward, Secretary of the Treasury Chase, the British ambassador Lord Lyons, and other major governmental figures, and heard them gossip about, discuss, and excuse themselves from responsibility for events such as the Mason and Slidell affair, the shortage of shallow-draft vessels on a coastal raid off North Carolina, and Seward's spectacularly undiplomatic remark to a member of the British cabinet who visited the United States in 1860. Seward made enough of an impression on Emerson to entice him to Episcopal services, where, he said, "I had the old wonder come over me at the Egyptian stationariness of the English Church." In his two meetings with Lincoln at the White House, Emerson—who had not expected much from the Midwesterner—found him "frank, sincere, well-meaning . . . not vulgar, as described"; a conscientious man "with a lawyer's habit of mind" well suited to lead the nation in the dangerous years ahead.

Impressions of West Point were of a different sort. Emerson's fascination with the cadets whom he examined in June 1863 came in part from his belief in individual character as an agent of moral force, but also from the anxieties for the youth of the North that he shared with other fathers, uncles, and family friends of young men. In rough notes he said of the cadets, "Your ways inspire lively curiosity. I tho[ugh]t 2 days suff[icien]t. I could willingly spend twenty, & know the power & hope & career of each youth." These young men and their training became part of his vision of the war as cleanser of the nation, a force that made genuine heroes out of young men who otherwise might lack purpose and goal. He developed this strain in his thought in many passages headed "Uses of the War." One such entry said, "A benefit of War is, that the appeal not being longer to letter & form, but now to the roots of strength in the people, the moral aspect becomes important, & is urgently presented & debated." At the beginning of Journal WAR he quoted Jean Paul Richter's *Titan:* "Vesuvius stands in this pastoral poem of Nature, & exalts everything, as War does the Age."

But Emerson neither forgot those who died nor allowed himself to surrender his realism about the fragility of the link between his moral cause and the Union cause. In a remarkable passage headed "Negro Soldiers" he outlined in uncharacteristically passionate and ungrammatical language his fears that political emancipation might not produce that moral emancipation which alone would justify the sacrifice of the young men of Massachusetts: "Do you think such lives as this city [&] state have yielded up already, the children of this famed city, the children of our public schools, the children of Harvard College, the best blood of our educated counties, objects of the most romantic hope and love, poets and romancers themselves . . . that these precious young men . . . are given up to bring back into the Capitol of Washington the reckless politicians who had reeled out of it with threats to destroy it, or came back into it to rule again[?] Never."

Later in the same series of passages he tried to answer a question that troubled those Northern abolitionists who found themselves unable to accept blacks as the equals of the whites who had died in order to end slavery: "Perhaps only [the Negro's] period is larger, & his return to light requires a better medium than our immoral civilization allows." The ultimate results of the war were decades, perhaps generations, away, and he realized that he would never live to see them; but the struggle revivified his lifelong faith in the regeneration possible to humanity both individually and in the social mass.

To borrow the title of an 1839–40 lecture series, "The Present Age" dominated Emerson's lecture topics in the first half of the 1860s. Even in "Essential Principles of Religion," which he presented on March 16, 1862, Emerson talked about the moral sentiment exercising itself as character on the battlefield and in the halls of government. At the end of a discussion of the political motives that led Lincoln to delay the Emancipation Proclamation, Emerson linked spiritual force and details of political calculation: "Moral tendency is the regnant West wind, resulting from the astronomic motion of the planet." The topics of "The Celebration of the Intellect" (June 10, 1861), "Courage" (February 15, 1863), "The Scholar" (July 22, 1863), "Perpetual Forces" (November 18, 1862), and "Character" (January 1, 1865) were as closely connected to the war as "Civilization at a Pinch" (April 23, 1861), "American Nationality" (November 12, 1861), "The Emancipation Proclamation" (October 12, 1862), and "The Fortune of the Republic" (December 1, 1863). During 1862 and 1863 Emerson's reading and writing turned on his concern for the underlying endurance of the nation, whose strength lay, he thought, in the moral strength of people who enacted the "perpetual force" of the moral sentiment in their lives. To this end he amassed and used in his lectures anecdotes of character from eighteenth-century France, martial tales from the Napoleonic wars and the Viking era, Persian and Confucian advice to rulers, the Hindu scriptures, and the classical writers to demonstrate how spiritual purpose had worked through (and sometimes in spite of) its human agents.

Because of the limitations placed on the lecture circuit by the war, Emerson did not attempt a full lecture series during most of this period. One series was actually interrupted by the beginning of the war: "Life and Literature," which he had begun in Boston on April 9, 1861. On April 12 Fort Sumter was fired on, and Emerson responded by inserting "Civilization at a Pinch" into the series eleven days later. No other series followed until the end of 1864. The same pressures may have had something to do with the number of lecture readings Emerson gave during the war years (about thirty a year) in comparison to that of the previous decade (almost sixty a year). He read between twenty-five and twenty-eight different lectures (although in a few cases title changes may not reflect substantial changes in matter), twenty-one of which were written during these years. In addition to the lectures named above, familiar titles from this period include "Immortality," "The Scholar," "Social Aims," and "Resources."

His lecturing twice took him through upstate New York and Ontario on his way to the Middle West, where he spoke in Chicago and Milwaukee in 1863 and 1865. During the rest of the war years almost all of his lecturing was done in New England and New York State, with the notable exception of his presentation of "American Civilization" at the Smithsonian Institution in Washington on January 31, 1862. Lectures to college audiences were a summer event, at Tufts in 1861, Dartmouth and Waterville Colleges in 1863, Middlebury in 1864, and Ripley Female College and Williams in 1865. The very special occasion of the "Harvard Commemoration Speech" that same summer closed the war era in Emerson's lecturing.

Much of Emerson's reading during this period was directed by the war. Among the military biographies and memoirs he read were the *Private Diary . . . in the Campaigns of 1812, 1813, 1814* of Sir Robert Wilson, Herbert Randolph's biography of Wilson, the *Commentaries* of Marshal Montluc of France, and Henry Bruce's *Life of General Sir William Napier.* What he said of his reading in the *Tagebücher* of Friedrich von Gentz was true of much of his reading in military and diplomatic history: "Gentz's Diary inevitably translates itself into American war." In addition to much reading in British, Continental, and ancient history, he explored contemporary analyses of the slavery crisis and the Civil War by Americans, Englishmen, and Frenchmen. Perhaps his interest in the relationship between intellectual and political liberty led him to read widely in the *Denkwürdigkeiten und Vermischte Schriften* and *Tagebücher* of the German liberal K. A. Varnhagen von Ense.

His interests in literary society and French culture brought Emerson back to the works of the prolific critic and literary historian C. A. Sainte-Beuve again and again. Emerson drew many anecdotes, estimates of character, and judgments about writers and statesmen from Sainte-Beuve's *Causeries du lundi, Nouveaux lundis, Portraits de femmes,* and *Portraits littéraires.* He quoted from Renan's *Essais de morale et de critique* and *Vie de Jésus* both in the original and in English translation. At the center of his reading interests in French and German was his growing sense that American writers needed to discover and define their place as part of a literary community that included Europe as well as England.

One of the important uses to which Emerson put his skill in French and German was to make up for his lack of knowledge of the language in which much of his favorite poetry was written. He compared English translations of Saadi's *Gulistan* with translations into German by K. H. Graf and those in Joseph von Hammer-Purgstall's *Geschichte der schönen Redekünste Persiens.* His German allowed him to draw material from the only available European translation of Saadi's *Bostan,* while he translated many Persian aphorisms from Chardin's *Voyages . . . en Perse et autres lieux de l'Orient.* He explored a new translation of an old acquaintance: the traditions, sayings, and biography of Confucius in the first volume of James Legge's *Chinese Classics.* He continued his reading in the religious classics of India, most notably in the *Upanishads,* from which he drew a long series of passages in Journal GL.

Matthew Arnold sent him his polemical *On Translating Homer* and *On Translating Homer: Last Words.* He read Arnold's *Merope* and discovered William Blake and his sayings about the imagination through Gilchrist's *Life.* One of his least rewarding reading experiences was Jane Austen's *Pride and Prejudice,* which, with *Persuasion,* led him to characterize her work as "vulgar in tone, sterile in invention, imprisoned in the wretched conventions of English society," and so concerned with marriage that her novels were " 'the nympholepsy of a fond despair', say rather, of an English boardinghouse."

As far as his own works were concerned, *The Conduct of Life* appeared in December 1860 just as Emerson began to use these journals. Though Emerson published no new book during the war, Ticknor and Fields kept his writing before the public, issuing five editions of the *Poems,* four of *Essays: Second Series,* two of *Essays: First Series,* and three each of *Representative Men, English Traits,* and *The Conduct of Life.* He published new articles and poems in *The Atlantic Monthly* and allowed Moncure Conway to republish some earlier pieces in the last few issues of his short-lived revival of *The Dial.* He contributed a preface to a new edition of an old favorite, Francis Gladwin's translation of the *Gulistan* of Saadi. His writing in these years for the lecture circuit prepared the way for the late harvest of publications in *Society and Solitude* and those collections that James Elliott Cabot helped him prepare. Lists in Journals GL and FOR, apparently made in response to requests for another book from James T. Fields, show that Emerson thought very carefully about new collections; essays on these lists form the core of his own later selections for *Society and Solitude* and those for the volume of *Miscellanies* that Cabot edited the year after Emerson's death.

The deaths of friends, relatives, and associates—Arthur Hugh Clough in the autumn of 1861, Thoreau the next May, his aunt Mary Moody Emerson a year later, and Hawthorne in May 1864—led Emerson to reread his correspondence with them and, where possible, to read their journals not only as a way of mourning them but also in an effort to retrieve the life now lost. While Clough's death led Emerson to think of other losses, Thoreau's illness and death led him to savor the man as he found him on his sickbed and later in the journals Emerson read. Now the differences between the two men seemed insignificant, and Emerson saw vividly the unique worth he celebrated so well at the end of the essay "Thoreau." A month after Thoreau's death, Emerson wrote, "Henry T. remains erect, calm, self-subsistent, before me, and I read him not only truly in his Journal, but he is not

long out of mind when I walk, and, as today, row upon the pond."
The next spring he felt the sadness and loneliness of his aunt's life,
particularly when no one else at her funeral was interested in the journals in which Emerson had found so much that brought her back to
life.

Emerson now called himself "a decorous old gentleman" dragged
out of his home into the "juvenile" trade of lecturing; he complained
about old age, lamented his occasional slowness of memory, and
dreamed that he had fallen asleep in the middle of lecturing. But he
also listed the benefits of old age, including "the general views of life
we get at 60 when we penetrate show & look at facts." With the Yankee temper that had always been his, he knew the need to husband his
resources against the inevitable encroachments of age. There were
ideas he could yet have, lectures to be written and delivered, books
that the public would gladly receive from a man whose value as writer
and philosopher had long been recognized. He had the rewards of
companionship in the Saturday Club, and the pleasure of seeing his
young son Edward Waldo cross the threshold into adulthood. Above
all, he saw his country emerge from the carnage of internecine war
ready, if its resolve did not fail it, to assume the position of moral lead-
ership in the family of nations that had been part of its promise from
the beginning.

Volume XV includes DL, GL, WAR, VA, FOR, and KL,
printed as journals; HT, clearly a topical notebook; and Pocket Diaries
for 1861, 1863, 1864, and 1865; but it becomes increasingly difficult
to apply the editorial distinction between regular journals and notebooks in this period. Emerson began DL at the start of the lecture
season in October 1860, while using CL as a journal; he continued to
use DL for notes, quotations, and at times for journal entries until
early 1866. GL, begun in January 1861, follows CL in the sequence of
regular journals. Emerson began WAR, perhaps as a topical notebook, in January 1862, and used it until early 1864; meanwhile he
used VA from February 1862 to March 1863, and FOR ("Forces &
Forms") from the beginning of 1863 to the spring of 1864; he may
have added notes in the fall of 1864 for the "American Life" lecture
series. During the summer of 1864 he used HT for notes on Thoreau

and DL for journal entries; he used KL heavily from September 1864 through the lecture season until May 1865, then probably used DL as a regular journal again until he began Journal LN early in 1866.

Editorial technique. The editorial process follows that described in volume I and the slight modifications introduced in subsequent volumes of the edition. In volume XV there is relatively little erased pencil writing, but in each case every effort has been made to recover the text. Use marks in the journals and notebooks comprising volume XV have been carefully described, transcriptions and expansions of passages have been recorded, and uses in *Society and Solitude, Letters and Social Aims,* and other published works have been noted where possible, often with help from the locations supplied by Edward W. Emerson in the manuscripts.

In the manuscripts, Emerson's topical headings are sometimes underlined, sometimes set off by a rule or by enclosing straight or wavy lines; unless he seems to have intended something more than marking to identify the matter as a heading, the various forms are interpreted by setting the heading in italics. When the text is quoted in the notes, no silent emendations are made; hence there are occasional variations between notes and text.

As in volumes XI–XIV, Emerson's own cross references to his other journals can be located through the use of Appendix I, which indicates where all of the journals published up to the volume in hand appear in the Harvard edition. Because the edition carries Emerson's manuscript pagination as well as its own, the reader can easily locate any cross reference to a journal already printed.

Numbering of "Fragments on Nature and Life" and "Fragments on the Poet and the Poetic Gift" follows that assigned by Edward Emerson or by George S. Hubbell, *A Concordance to the Poems of Ralph Waldo Emerson.*

A list of silent emendations has been prepared; copies are to be deposited in the Rush Rhees Library of the University of Rochester, the Library of Congress, Houghton Library, Huntington Library, and Newberry Library. The following statement describes the silent or mostly silent emendations. These range from numerous—as with punctuation of items in a series, supplying periods at the ends of sentences if the next sentence begins with a capital, or expansion of contractions—to occasional, as with supplying quotation marks, dashes, or parentheses missing from intended pairs.

Emendation of prose. A period is silently added to any declarative sentence lacking terminal punctuation but followed in the same paragraph by a sentence beginning with a capital letter. If a declarative sentence lacking a period is followed by a sentence beginning with a small letter, either a bracketed semicolon is supplied, or a bracketed period is supplied and the small letter is silently capitalized. In the second instance the reader will automatically know that the capital was originally a small letter. If a direct question lacking terminal punctuation is followed by a sentence in the same paragraph beginning with a capital the question mark is silently added. Punctuation of items in a series, since Emerson habitually set them off, is silently inserted. Small letters at the beginning of unquestionable paragraphs or of sentences that follow a sentence ending with a period are silently capitalized. Where indispensable for clarity a silent period is added to an abbreviation. Quotation marks, dashes, and parentheses missing from intended pairs have been silently supplied; so have quotation marks at the beginning of each of a series of quotations. Apostrophes have been silently inserted or normalized in possessives and contractions. Superscripts have been lowered and double or triple underscorings have been interpreted by small or large capitals. Common Emersonian contractions like y^t for *that,* y^e for *the, wh* for *which, wd* and *shd* for *would* and *should,* and *bo't* for *bought* are silently expanded. His dates have been regularly normalized by the silent insertion of commas and periods.

Emendation of poetry. On the whole, Emerson's poetry has been left as it stands in the manuscripts; apostrophes and some quotation marks have been supplied, in accordance with the rules for emending prose, but only where Emerson's intention was unmistakable.

Certain materials are omitted, either silently or with descriptive annotation; these will not be reported in the list of emendations. Omitted silently are slips of the pen, false starts at words, careless repetitions of a single word, and Emerson's occasional carets under insertions (assimilated into the editor's insertion marks). Underscoring to indicate intended revisions is not reproduced. Omitted, but usually with descriptive annotation, are practice penmanship, isolated words or letters, and miscellaneous markings.

CHRONOLOGY 1860–1866

1860: November 4–28, Emerson delivers four lectures in Boston and Concord; November 6, Lincoln is elected President of the United States; December 2–29, Emerson lectures in nine cities and towns in Massachusetts, and in Concord and Nashua, N.H.; December 8, *Conduct of Life* is published in Boston.

1861: January 6–15, Emerson lectures in Boston, Mass., and in Elmira, Owego, Hornellsville, Cortland, Alfred, and Buffalo, N.Y.; January 24, he attempts to speak at the Massachusetts Anti-Slavery Society meeting in Boston, but is shouted down; February 3–24?, he lectures in Boston, South Danvers, and Gloucester, Mass., in New Haven, Conn., and in Augusta and Portland, Maine; February–May, he lectures to classes of ladies in Boston; April 2, he lectures in New Bedford, Mass.; April 9–May 15, he delivers the six lectures in the new "Life and Literature" series in Boston; April 12, Confederates fire on Fort Sumter and the Civil War begins; June 2, Emerson lectures before the Parker Fraternity in Boston; July 10, he lectures at Tufts College, Somerville, Mass.; July 16, Edward Emerson is accepted at Harvard College; July 21, the Confederate victory at the First Battle of Bull Run sobers the North; September 27, Emerson lectures at the Teachers' Convention in Yarmouth, Mass.; October 27 and November 12, he lectures at the Parker Fraternity in Boston; November 13, Arthur Hugh Clough dies; November 27–December 29, Emerson lectures in Salem, Cambridgeport, Concord, and Boston, Mass., and possibly in Portland, Maine, and New Bedford and Lynn, Mass.

1862: January 2–21, Emerson, in need of money, lectures in Concord, Worcester, Lowell, Charlestown, Chelmsford, and New Bedford, Mass.; January 31, he lectures at the Smithsonian Institution, Washington, D.C.; February 1–3, Charles Sumner introduces Emerson to President Lincoln, Secretary of State Seward, and other cabinet members, as well as the British Ambassador; February 2, he attends church with Seward and has a second visit with Lincoln; February

7–25, he lectures in Brooklyn, N.Y., and in Boston, Lowell, and Lynn, Mass.; March 16 and April 13, he lectures at the Parker Fraternity in Boston; May 6, Henry David Thoreau dies; May 9, Emerson delivers the funeral speech for Thoreau in Concord; May 12, Edward Emerson leaves Concord on an extended western trip; June, Emerson reads Thoreau's manuscript journals; June 29, he delivers a lecture on Thoreau at the Music Hall in Boston; August 29–30, Federal forces are repulsed at the Second Battle of Bull Run; September 22, President Lincoln issues the preliminary Emancipation Proclamation; September 29, Emerson seeks a commission for his nephew Charles Emerson; October 6, Edward Emerson returns from his western trip and a week later leaves for Harvard; October 12, Emerson lectures on "The Emancipation Proclamation" before the Parker Fraternity in Boston; November 12 and 18, he delivers two lectures, one of them "Perpetual Forces," before the Parker Fraternity in Boston; November 19–December 30, he repeats "Perpetual Forces" ten times at Salem, Concord, Charlestown, Lynn, New Bedford, Manchester, Cambridgeport, Fall River, and Worcester, Mass., and Albany, N.Y., and lectures again in Boston and Cambridgeport.

1863: January 1, Lincoln issues the Emancipation Proclamation; Emerson reads the "Boston Hymn" at the Music Hall in Boston; January 5, a fire forces him to evacuate the American House in Niagara Falls at 3 A.M.; January 5–27, he delivers twelve lectures in Toronto, Canada, Rochester and Buffalo, N.Y., Cleveland, Ohio, Detroit and Ann Arbor, Mich., Milwaukee and Racine, Wis., Chicago, Ill., and Indianapolis, Ind.; February 3–25, he lectures in Pittsburgh, Pa., Gloucester and Boston, Mass., and Montreal, Canada; March 3, he lectures before the Social Circle in Concord; March 20, he speaks in Boston at the fund-raising meeting for Colonel Robert Gould Shaw's Negro regiment; April 12, he delivers three lectures in Portland, Maine; May 1, Emerson's aunt, Mary Moody Emerson, dies at the age of eighty-nine; June 1–?, as a member of the Board of Visitors, he inspects the United States Military Academy at West Point; July 1–3, a Federal victory at Gettysburg marks a turning point in the war; July 22, Emerson delivers "The Scholar" at Dartmouth College, and repeats it August 11 at Waterville College in Maine; September–October, he confers with Sophia Thoreau and publisher James T. Fields about publishing Thoreau's remaining works; September 20, he lectures in Portland, Maine; November 19, Lincoln delivers the Gettysburg Address; December 1–30, Emerson delivers "The Fortune of the Republic" in Boston, Feltonville, Newburyport, Concord, and Manchester, Mass., and in Brooklyn, N.Y.

1864: January 5–February 9, Emerson repeats "The Fortune of the Republic" in Worcester, Lynn, Cambridgeport, Salem, and Taunton, Mass., Augusta and Bangor, Maine, and North Bennington, Vt.; January 27, he is elected to the American Academy of Arts and Sciences; February 22, he speaks at the Concord Fair; February 29, William E. Emerson, Jr., Emerson's nephew, dies; March 9, Grant is put in command of the Northern forces; April, Emerson serves with Lowell and Holmes on a Committee of Arrangements for the Saturday Club's celebration on April 23 of the three hundredth anniversary of Shakespeare's birth; May, he receives $550 from Ticknor and Fields for "blue and gold" editions of the *Essays* and *Poems;* May 23, he attends Hawthorne's funeral and burial in Sleepy Hollow Cemetery; August 9, he lectures at Middlebury College, Vt.; November 2, he lectures on education before a convention of teachers in West Chester, Pa.; November 5–20, he delivers a speech in honor of William Cullen Bryant at the Bryant Festival in New York City, and possibly three Sunday lectures before the Parker Fraternity in Boston; November 8, Abraham Lincoln is reelected President of the United States; November 27–January 1, 1865, Emerson delivers the six lectures in the new "American Life" series in Boston, and lectures in Waltham, Concord, and South Danvers, Mass.

1865: January 3?–20, Emerson lectures in Connecticut, Massachusetts, Vermont, New York, Ohio, and Pennsylvania; January 23–February 4, he delivers the "American Life" series in Milwaukee and Chicago; February 7–28, he lectures in Erie, Pa., Lawrence, Feltonville, and Springfield, Mass., and Hartford, Conn.; February 17–March 24, he repeats the six "American Life" lectures in Worcester, Mass.; March 8 and 15, he lectures in Lynn, Mass.; March 21, he speaks before the Social Circle in Concord, and March 27? before the Ladies' Social Club in Boston; March 28–April 18, he delivers four lectures at the Harrison Square Church in Boston; March 29, he lectures in Haverhill, Mass.; April 9, Lee surrenders at Appomattox;

April 15, President Lincoln dies; April 19, Emerson speaks at funeral services for Lincoln in Concord; May, he is appointed to the planning committee for Memorial Hall at Harvard; June 26, he lectures at Ripley Female College in Poultney, Vt.; July 21, he delivers the "Harvard Commemoration Speech" at Cambridge; July 31, he addresses the Williams College Adelphi Union in Williamstown, Mass.; September 21, he speaks at the Middlesex Agricultural Exhibition in Concord; October 3, Edith Emerson is married to Colonel William H. Forbes; October 17–24? Emerson delivers the "American Life" series in Amherst, Mass.; October 22, he delivers two lectures in Florence, Mass.; November 7–14, he repeats the "American Life" series in Williamstown, Mass.; November 15–December 12, he lectures in North Adams, Mass., Concord, N.H., Rutland, Vt., and Albany, Morrisania, West Troy, and Coxsackie, N.Y.; December 15–22, he delivers three lectures for the Brooklyn Fraternity Course and three more at the New England Congregational Church in Brooklyn, N.Y.; December 27, Henry James, Sr., lectures in Concord and is Emerson's guest.

1866: January 3 and 4, Emerson lectures in Salem and Concord, Mass.; January 11–February 27, on an extensive western tour, he delivers twenty-seven lectures, mostly from the "American Life" series, in cities and towns in Pennsylvania, Ohio, Indiana, Illinois, Iowa, Wisconsin, Michigan, and New York.

SYMBOLS AND ABBREVIATIONS

⟨ ⟩	Cancellation
↑ ↓	Insertion or addition
/ /	Variant
‖ . . . ‖	Unrecovered matter, normally unannotated. Three dots, one to five words; four dots, six to fifteen words; five dots, sixteen to thirty words. Matter lost by accidental mutilation but recovered conjecturally is inserted between the parallels.
⟨‖ . . . ‖⟩	Unrecovered canceled matter
‖msm‖	Manuscript mutilated
[ ]	Editorial insertion
[. . .]	Editorial omission

[ ]	Emerson's square brackets
⌞ ⌟	Marginal matter inserted in text
[ ]	Page numbers of original manuscript
n	See Textual Notes
∧	Emerson's symbol for intended insertion
[R.W.E.]	Editorial substitution for Emerson's symbol of original authorship. See volume I, plate VII.
*	Emerson's note
epw	Erased pencil writing
☞ ☜ 𝕴	Hands pointing

ABBREVIATIONS AND SHORT TITLES IN FOOTNOTES

CEC	*The Correspondence of Emerson and Carlyle.* Edited by Joseph Slater. New York: Columbia University Press, 1964.
J	*Journals of Ralph Waldo Emerson.* Edited by Edward Waldo Emerson and Waldo Emerson Forbes. Boston and New York: Houghton Mifflin Co., 1909–1914. 10 vols.
JMN	*The Journals and Miscellaneous Notebooks of Ralph Waldo Emerson.* Ralph H. Orth, Chief Editor; Linda Allardt, Ronald A. Bosco, Harrison Hayford, David W. Hill, Glen M. Johnson, Susan Sutton Smith, Editors (volume I edited by William H. Gilman, Alfred R. Ferguson, George P. Clark, and Merrell R. Davis; volumes II–VI, William H. Gilman, Alfred R. Ferguson, Merrell R. Davis, Merton M. Sealts, Jr., Harrison Hayford; volumes VII–XI, William H. Gilman, Alfred R. Ferguson, Harrison Hayford, Ralph H. Orth, J. E. Parsons, A. W. Plumstead; volumes XII–XIII, William H. Gilman, Alfred R. Ferguson, Linda Allardt, Harrison Hayford, Ralph H. Orth, J. E. Parsons, A. W. Plumstead; volume XIV, Ralph H. Orth, Linda Allardt, Harrison Hayford, J. E. Parsons, Susan Sutton Smith; volumes XV–XVI, Ralph H. Orth, Linda Allardt, Ronald A. Bosco, Harrison Hayford, David W. Hill, Glen M. Johnson, Susan Sutton Smith). Cambridge: Harvard University Press, 1960–
L	*The Letters of Ralph Waldo Emerson.* Edited by Ralph L. Rusk. New York: Columbia University Press, 1939. 6 vols.
Lectures	*The Early Lectures of Ralph Waldo Emerson.* Volume I, 1833–1836, edited by Stephen E. Whicher and Robert E. Spiller; volume II, 1836–1838, edited by Stephen E. Whicher, Robert E. Spiller, and Wallace E. Williams; volume III, 1838–1842, edited by Robert E. Spiller and Wallace E. Williams. Cambridge: Harvard University Press, 1959–1972.

Life   Ralph L. Rusk. *The Life of Ralph Waldo Emerson.* New York: Charles Scribner's Sons, 1949.

W   *The Complete Works of Ralph Waldo Emerson.* With a Biographical Introduction and Notes, by Edward Waldo Emerson. Centenary Edition. Boston and New York: Houghton Mifflin Co., 1903–1904. 12 vols. I—*Nature Addresses and Lectures;* II—*Essays, First Series;* III—*Essays, Second Series;* IV—*Representative Men;* V—*English Traits;* VI—*Conduct of Life;* VII—*Society and Solitude;* VIII—*Letters and Social Aims;* IX—*Poems;* X—*Lectures and Biographical Sketches;* XI—*Miscellanies;* XII—*Natural History of Intellect.*

PART ONE

The Journals

$\mathcal{DL}$

1860–1866

Emerson began Journal DL in October 1860, using it concurrently with Journal CL until January 19, 1861, and with GL, WAR, VA, FOR, and KL between January 1861 and May 1865. He continued to use DL until February 1866, shortly before he began Journal LN.

The covers of the copybook, of marbled brown, red, and blue paper over boards, measure 17.0 × 21.4 cm. The spine strip and protective corners on the front and back covers are of tan leather. "1860", "1861", "1863", and "1864–5–6" are written on the front cover; "DL" is written on the upper right leather corner of the front cover.

Including flyleaves (1–2, 295–296), there are 296 unlined pages measuring 17.4 × 20.6 cm. Twenty-three pages were misnumbered and corrected: 1⟨1⟩2–1⟨4⟩5, 12⟨0⟩2, 13⟨3⟩2 (written and corrected in pencil), 13⟨5⟩4, 16⟨2⟩3, 19⟨2⟩1, ⟨278⟩218, 23⟨0⟩2, 23⟨1⟩3, 23⟨6⟩5, 2⟨23⟩36, 23⟨4⟩8, ⟨237⟩240, ⟨238⟩241, ⟨239⟩242 (written in ink, corrected in pencil), 24⟨0⟩3, 24⟨1⟩4 (in ink, corrected in pencil), 24⟨2⟩5, 25⟨7⟩6, and 27⟨7⟩9. Most of the pages are numbered in ink, but thirty-two are numbered in pencil: 1, 3, 5, 7, 9, 22, 27–30, 32–34, 44, 46, 50, 52, 62, 64, 66, 68, 69, 84, 86, 87, 108, 110, 132, 142, 230, 280, and 288. Pages 38, 58, 67, and 270 are numbered in pencil overwritten in ink. Twenty-two pages are unnumbered: 2, 23, 35, 41, 45, 47, 51, 63, 65, 109, 113, 152, 153, 189, 195, 205, 229, 255, 269, and 294–296. Forty-seven pages are blank: 12, 21–24, 28–30, 32, 35, 41–42, 44–48, 50–51, 54, 57, 62–66, 69–70, 73–76, 86, 109, 112–113, 144, 153, 205, 220, 223, 285, 288, and 292–295. The gathering containing pages 135–165 is loose.

[front cover]   DL

1860
1861
1863
1864-5-6

[front cover verso] [Index material omitted]

3

[1]   *DL*   October 1860

At mihi succurrit pro Ganymede manus.[1]

[Martial, *Epigrams*, II, xliii]

[2] Lectures

American Life
    1. Education
    2. Social Aims   ↑x↓
    3. Resources   ↑x↓
    4. Table-Talk
    5. Books ↑& Culture   x↓
    6. Character[2]

      Country-Life
↑x↓ Success.
↑x↓ Clubs.
      Third-Estate in Literature, or Criticism.
↑x↓ Classes of Men
      Courage
      Works & Days

⟨Cl⟩Morals

Genius
[3] Art.
Boston
Poetry.
Fortune of the Republic
Forces
Doctrine of Leasts
The People's Books.
        or

---

[1] "But my own hand is Ganymede to serve me." See *JMN*, XIII, 4.

[2] "Character" is struck through diagonally in pencil. The "x" marks and "& Culture" are added in pencil. Emerson gave these six lectures in his "American Life" series in Boston, from November 27, 1864, to January 1, 1865. See *L*, V, 399.

Books for the People

Subjects

Greatness ⎫ ↑see ⟨H⟩KL↓[3]
Eloquence ⎭
Bohemian.
↑Affirmative &↓ Negative ↑including Temperament↓
Being & Seeming
High Culture
How imaginative are all values!
History, ↑See *Old Index*↓[4]
Hospitality, *DL* 6

[4] For the first topic, "American Life," the Lecture might draw on
⟨Ameri⟩ "Anglo American"
        "Fortune of the Republic"
        "American Nationality"
        "Boston"
        "Forces"
        "Waterville oration" 1863

[5] *Subjects.* John Potter, Worthington, Ohio, writes to the N.Y. Farmers' Club, about hedges, & concludes,
"I sometimes think ministers could do a vast deal of good by urging their hearers to pay more attention to making their homes attractive."

[6] Hospitality looks like a good title. The hospitality of manners is so vital
        hospitality of mind so diverse in men.
hospitality over nationality
hospitality in the Arabs. Le Grand Desert[5]

---

[3] The brace and "see ⟨H⟩KL" are in pencil.
[4] Emerson may refer to Index II, pp. [161]–[162], headed "History" (and copied into Index Major, pp. [143]–[144]).
[5] Melchior Joseph Eugène Daumas and Ausone de Chancel, *Le Grand Dèsert, ou itinéraire d'une caravane du Sahara au pays des nègres, royaume de Haoussa* (Paris, 1848).

[7] *Michel Angelo.*

In 1540, Francesco d'Ollanda, miniature painter in the service of King of Portugal, visited Rome, & saw there Michel Angelo, as well as Vittoria Colonna. His Ms. Journal was discovered by Count Raczynsky in Lisbon. Grimm uses a French translation of this.

———

↑It seems that the ⟨book⟩manuscript cannot now be found in Lisbon library and Count Raczynsky is believed to be a liar.↓[6]

[8]   "Me you call great: mine is the firmer seat,
The truer lance: but there is many a youth
Now crescent, who will come to all I am,
And overcome it; & in me there dwells
No greatness, save it be ⟨a⟩some far off touch
Of greatness to know well I am not great:
There is the man."

↑*Tennyson*↓ ["Elaine," ll. 445–451][7]

[9] The Memorabilia of philosophy are:
Plato's doctrine of Reminiscence

Berkeley's Ideal World

Socrates' interpretation of the Delphian oracle,
Σοφὸς Σοφοκλῆς, σοφώτερος Εὐριπίδης,
Ἀνδρῶν τε πάντων Σωκράτης σοφώτατος;[8]
and Tennyson's use of it in *"Elaine,"* [ll. 445–451] see *Idyls,* p. 150[–151][9]

[10] "Dance" of Plotinus

[6] For this and the preceding entry, see Herman Friedrich Grimm, *Leben Michelangelo's,* 2 vols. (Hannover, 1860–1863), II, 358–373 and note 86, p. 586. This work is in Emerson's library.

[7] *Idyls of the King* (Boston, 1859), pp. 150–151; in Emerson's library. The quotation is struck through in pencil with a vertical use mark.

[8] "Wise is Sophocles, wiser Euripides,
But of all men Socrates is the wisest" (Ed.). See *JMN,* I, 209, and IV, 421.

[9] "Socrates' interpretation . . . p. 150" is struck through in pencil with a vertical use mark. The diacritical marks on the Greek words are added in pencil. A hand sign following "p. 150" points to the lines from Tennyson written on the lower third of p. [8].

Doctrine of Absorption
⟨indent⟩Nir⟨w⟩vana
Greek saying, that the soul is absorbed into God as a phial of water
broken in the sea
Plotinus's saying[10]
↑Heraclitus said "War is the father of all things."
"A dry light makes the best soul."↓[11]

[11] Like can only be known by like. *Heraclitus.*

"Nec sentire deum nisi qui pars ipse deorum est."[12]

————

Ne te quaesiveris extra.[13] [Persius, *Satires,* I, 7]

————

Natura in minimis existit. ↑Aristotle↓[14]

————

Hunger & thirst after righteousness. [Matt. 5:6]

————

Kingdom of God cometh not by observation [Luke 17:20]
⟨indent⟩is received as a little child [Luke 18:17]

Xy[*Christianity*], *pure deism.*

————

[10] " 'Dance' of Plotinus" is struck through in pencil with two diagonal use marks, and "Doctrine of . . . saying" with two vertical use marks. For " 'Dance' of . . . Nir⟨w⟩vana", see *JMN,* XIV, 321 and 337. "Greek saying, . . . sea" is used in "Poetry and Imagination," *W,* VIII, 14; see also *JMN,* V, 77. For "Plotinus s saying", see p. [13] below.

[11] "Heraclitus said . . . things.' ", struck through in pencil with five diagonal use marks, is used in "Harvard Commemoration Speech, July 21, 1865," *W,* XI, 341. For both quotations, see *JMN,* VI, 306.

[12] "Only if man be himself the infinite, can the infinite be known by him." For this and the preceding quotation, see *JMN,* VI, 144.

[13] "Look to no one outside yourself." Used as the epigraph to "Self-Reliance," *W,* II, 43. See *JMN,* VII, 181.

[14] See Francis Bacon, *The Works* . . . , ed. Basil Montagu, 3 vols. (Philadelphia, 1850), I, 188, "Advancement of Learning": "Aristotle noteth well, 'that the nature of every thing is best seen in its smallest portions.' " The quotation, struck through in pencil with three diagonal use marks, is used in "Swedenborg," *W,* IV, 104 and 114, and "Works and Days," *W,* VII, 176. See *JMN,* XI, 17, 390, and 393.

God considers integrity not munificence. *Socrates*[15]

———

[1⟨1⟩2] [blank]
[1⟨2⟩3]   *Imagination*
"Names, countries, nations, &⟨c⟩ the[n] like, are not at all known to those who
are in heaven; they have no idea of such things, but of the realities signified
thereby." [Emanuel] *Swedenborg* [*Heavenly*] *Arcana*[. . . , 12 vols. (Boston,
1837–1848)] II. p. 9.

———

↑"apparent imitations of unapparent natures"
———   *Zoroaster*   [cited in *U* 144]↓

Plotinus says of the heavens,
"There however every body is pure, (transparent), and each inhabi-
tant is as it were an eye." p. 365[16]

[1⟨3⟩4]   *like*
Note our incessant use of the word, [like a pelican pecking her breast
to feed her young] [like a horse always at the end of his
tether]   [Athens wh⟨o⟩ich ⟨has⟩ has lost her young men is like a year
without a spring.][17]

The mind in conversation is perpetually provoked to see how all things
reflect or [1⟨4⟩5] image her momentary thought.

[15] "Kingdom of . . . *Socrates*" is in pencil. For "Hunger & . . . *Socrates*", see *JMN*,
VI, 183, 184, and 179.
[16] " 'Names, countries, . . . p. 365" is struck through in pencil with a vertical use
mark. "apparent imitations . . . *U* 144]", and the two rules above and below it, are in
pencil; this and the preceding quotation are used in "Poetry and Imagination," *W*, VIII,
19–20. For " 'There . . . an eye.' ", see *Select Works of Plotinus* . . . , trans. Thomas Taylor (London, 1817); in Emerson's library.
[17] "Athens wh⟨o⟩ich . . . spring." is struck through in pencil with a diagonal use
mark. With "Note our . . . spring.", cf. "Poetry and Imagination," *W*, VIII, 11–12.

Whenever this resemblance is real, not playful, & is deep, or pointing at the causal identity, it is the act of imagination: if superficial, & for entertainment, it is Fancy.

↑↑probably↓ printed in "Social Aims"↓[18]

[16]   Images
Block of marble. M. Angelo's first sonnet[19]

[17] *Merlin*

↑printed in "Social Aims &c"↓[20]
"Never other person will be able to discover this place for anything which may befall, neither shall I ever go out from hence, for in the world there is no such strong tower as this wherein I am confined; and it is neither of wood, nor of iron, nor of stone, but of air, without anything else, & made by enchantment so strong, that it can never be demolished while the world lasts, neither can I go out, nor can [18] any one else come in, save she who hath inclosed me here."

> Southey: *Morte d Arthur*
> Vol 1. p. xlvii[21]

[19]   ↑printed in "Success."↓
     I have always one saw to say, & never get it rightly said. It is that if you work at your task, it signifies little or nothing that you do not yet find orders or customers. The time which your mate or *rival*[n] (to use the profane word) spends in hastily finishing his ordered task, hastily & for the market, not ideally, you spend in preparation & experiments, ⟨of⟩ essential steps to your real knowledge & efficiency. He has

---

[18] "probably printed . . . Aims' " is in pencil. With "Whenever this . . . Fancy.", struck through in pencil with two vertical use marks, cf. *JMN*, IX, 107, and "Poetry and Imagination," *W*, VIII, 28–29.

[19] For Emerson's translation, see "Sonnet of Michel Angelo Buonarotti," *W*, IX, 298, and *JMN*, XIV, 222–223. The first five lines in English and the first four lines in Italian are used as epigraphs to "Michel Angelo," *W*, XII, 213 and 214.

[20] Added in pencil.

[21] Sir Thomas Malory, *The Byrth, Lyf, and Actes of Kyng Arthur . . . and . . . Le Morte Darthur*, with an introduction and notes by Robert Southey, 2 vols. (London, 1817). The quotation, struck through in ink with two diagonal use marks in the shape of an X on p. [17] and two diagonal use marks on p. [18], is used in "Poetry and Imagination," *W*, VIII, 61–62.

thereby sold his picture, but you have raised yourself into a higher school of artists, whose prices are [20] enormously enhanced over the other.[22]

Dr Rimmer wishes ↑"↓to make a statue which will not be bought.↑"↓[23]

"Cathmore dwelt in the wood to avoid the voice of praise." ↑*Ossian*↓[24]

[21]-[24] [blank]

[25]   Stories agreeable to the human mind [AC 294, CL 115]

———

Pindar & his customer [Σ 106-107]

———

Sigurd & Eystein [VS 5-7]

———

Time   "The little grey man" [N 26-27]

———

Pied piper, Menetrier de Meudon [CD 37], Oriental story in Tholuck, Orpheus.

Gyges' Ring   Fortunatus' Cap, Aladdin's Lamp

Wandering Jew
Transmigrations of Indra
Seven sleepers
Thawed Tune [RS 182]
[26] Solomon & the Spectre   S [Σ 1][25]

———

[22] "I have . . . artists," struck through in ink with a discontinuous vertical use mark and in pencil with a vertical use mark, is used in "Success," *W*, VII, 294–295.

[23] William Rimmer (1816–1879) was a sculptor, painter, and physician in Chelsea and East Milton, Massachusetts. The quotation marks are added in pencil.

[24] James Macpherson, *The Poems of Ossian* (Boston, 1857), p. 403. This volume is in Emerson's library.

[25] "Pindar & his customer" is struck through in pencil with one vertical and one diagonal use mark; the anecdote is used in "The Man of Letters," *W*, X, 253–254. Both use marks were extended through "Sigurd & Eystein"; see p. [71] below. "Time . . . man' " is in pencil. "Pied piper . . . Thawed Tune" is struck through in pencil with a discontinuous vertical use mark; with "Stories . . . mind" and "Pied piper . . . Tune", cf. "Quotation and Originality," *W*, VIII, 186–187. For "Pied piper . . . Meudon," see "Eloquence," *W*, VII, 65. For Tholuck, see *L*, V, 28. For "Solomon & the Spectre", see "Tragedy," *Lectures*, III, 105–106, and *JMN*, XII, 312.

[27]²⁶   I ⟨a⟩care not where I am or go
        Or if my task be high or low
        Work to /cover/hide/, or proudly show
        Or if ⟨my⟩ my mates shall be my peers
        Or only ⟨transient⟩ ↑rare met↓ travellers
        ⟨Or⟩ whether I pace the shoplined street
        Or lofty square where statesmen meet
        ⟨O'erlooking⟩ ↑Eyeing↓ the city at their feet
        With secret pride to rule the town
        And ⟨county⟩ shire on which the dome looks down.

[28]–[30] [blank]
[31]   Metaphysical.
⟨Ranking.⟩ Thoughts rank themselves.
Currents.

Pace

Divining. *TO* 54   Plutarch²⁷
Never was any discovery by observation that had not already been
   divined by somebody, as Leibnitz, the Zoophytes
                      Newton, the combustibility of diamond,
                      Kant, the asteroids,
                      Digby, the law of color,
                      Van Helmont the sex of plants.

"Ὃ χρή ὀε νόειν νόου ἄνθει."²⁸

----

²⁶ Page [27] is in pencil. "hide", "rare met", and "Eyeing" were probably added,
and "Or" canceled, later.
    ²⁷ In Notebook TO, p. [54], Emerson quotes a passage from *Plutarch's Morals* and a
reference to Journal E, p. [7] (*JMN*, VII, 270), where the same quotation occurs.
    ²⁸ This quotation, in pencil, is from Ralph Cudworth, *The True Intellectual System of
the Universe*, ed. Thomas Birch, 4 vols. (London, 1820), II, 71, where it is translated as
"[God who] cannot be apprehended otherwise than by the flower of the mind." See *JMN*,
VI, 179. With "Never was . . . somebody," above, cf. "Progress of Culture," *W*, VIII,
222.

[32] [blank]

[33]   *Idealism*

Viasa, Berkeley,

Doubt whether matter an appendix to my will or my will to matter.

_____

more hurt by the base, & burlesque, & inconvenient, than by reason.

_____

See "Nature" in my Encyclopedia p 189[29]

"The severe schools shall never laugh me out of the philosophy of Hermes, that this visible world is but a picture of the invisible, wherein, as in a portrait, things are not truly, but in equivocal shapes, & as they counterfeit some real substance, in that invisible [34] fabric." *Sir Thomas Browne*[30]

[35] [blank]

[36][31]   Historical

_____

When the doctrine of free trade was broached?

_____

"All men are born free & equal"

_____

[37]   Historical

Eras.

When the 47th proposition of Euclid was demonstrated.

When Thales measured the pyramid by its shadow.

When Kepler announced his 3 laws.

When Newton declared the law of gravity.

↑Dalton's Atomic Theory.↓

When the Doctrine of Idealism was first taught.

The doctrine of Correspondences.[32]

[29] *"Idealism . . .* p 189" is in pencil. Viasa, or Vyāsā, is the author or "arranger" of the Indian epic, the *Mahābhārata.*

[30] *Religio Medici*, I, 12. See *The Works of Sir Thomas Browne*, ed. Geoffrey Keynes, 6 vols. (London, 1928–1931), I, 17.

[31] Page [36] is in pencil.

[32] "Daltons Atomic Theory." is in pencil. Similar lists of these historical eras appear in Notebook S (Salvage), p. [137], Index Major, p. [143], and *JMN*, IX, 231–232.

Schelling. "All difference is quantitative."[33]

[38] Clarendon's portraits
    De Retz's[34]

———

Condé at St Antoine [AZ 156]
———

Earl of Caernarvon's speech   *T* 57[–58]
———

Old English laws from Harleian Miscellany,   *T* 85

    [39] In 1215, were 1115 castles in England.
———

Measure of civilization is the perfection of iron-manufacture.[35]
———

    Building of Rome
    First Olympiad

[40]   Historical Pairs   *AC* 284

[41]–[42] [blank]
[43]   *Classic & Romantic.*
↑See LO 281   *SO* 75,82,   FOR 124↓
                        ↑*SO* 74↓
        Greeks οξεις επινοησαι   *RS* 101
———

    Menander had finished his play all but the verses.

———

___33___ *"Schelling ... quantitative.'"* is in pencil. See *JMN,* XIII, 302, and John Bern-
hard Stallo, *General Principles of the Philosophy of Nature* . . . (Boston, 1848), p. 222. For
this quotation and the list above, see "Literature," *W,* V, 242.

___34___ Page [38] is in pencil. Edward Hyde, 1st Earl of Clarendon, *The History of the
Rebellion and Civil Wars in England,* 6 vols. (Boston, 1827) and *The Beauties of Claren-
don, Consisting of Selections from His Historical and Moral Works* (London, n.d.) are in
Emerson's library. Emerson borrowed Jean François Paul de Gondi, Cardinal de Retz,
Memoirs of the Cardinal de Retz, 3 vols. (Philadelphia, 1817) from the Boston Athenaeum
in 1854.

___35___ For "In 1215 . . . England.", see *JMN,* XIV, 402. With "Measure of . . . iron-
manufacture.", cf. "The Superlative," *W,* X, 178.

[44]–[48] [blank]
[49]   Romaic Poems
      Lochinvar[36]
      Charon

[50]–[51] [blank]
[52]   *Hegel.*

Seyn	Being;	the Universal
Daseyn	So-being;	the particular
Fursichseyn	self-ness;	the singular

↑figurate conceptions↓

Vorstellung	↑"Conception" "Imagination" "Assocn of Ideas"↓
Begriff	↑pure notions↓

Inhalt	*In*tent, the filling,
Gehalt	*Con*tent

Anschauung   Perception

[53] The Aristotelian formula—

	Form,	Matter,	Actualization
	$\delta\upsilon\nu\alpha\mu\iota s$	$\upsilon\lambda\eta$	$\epsilon\nu\tau\epsilon\lambda\epsilon\chi\epsilon\iota\alpha$
	Begriff	Urtheil	Schluss
	Acorn,	⟨E⟩elements,	Oak

Dr Stirling
see *Secret of Hegel*
Vol 1. p 204[37]

[54] [blank]
[55]   *Sentences.*
Aristotle's dying speech. See below, 67

[36] "Lochinvar" is in pencil.

[37] The entries on pp. [52]–[53] are taken from James Hutchinson Stirling, *The Secret of Hegel: Being the Hegelian System in Origin, Principle, Form, and Matter*, 2 vols. (London, 1865); for "Inhalt . . . *Con*tent," see *ibid.*, I. 136. See Emerson's discussion of Stirling's book in his letter of January 7, 1866, to Carlyle, *CEC*, p. 547.

Rabelais
Tiberius'
Plotinus's Dance

[56]³⁸ Hobbes   on laughter
                         life of man see *T* 26, 50,

        Hooker
        Milton

[57] [blank]
[58]   Negative

____

Vulgar people show much acuteness in stating exceptions. *G* 58

____

Intellect in the Bohemian a piratical schooner cruising in all latitudes for his own pot. *K* 54 [actually *U* 137]

____

↑I hate the malignity of American Governments. AB 63↓
Democratic Party wish to destroy everything, & would tear down God, if they could, out of heaven.

"Barbarians destroy & create nothing. The glory of the people of Athens consisted in the exercise of creative power."³⁹ *AZ* 95 [actually 94]

[59] Lord Hervey says of Sir Robert Walpole; "He had more warmth of affection & friendship for some particular people than one could have believed it possible for any one who had been so long raking in the dirt of mankind to be capable of feeling for so worthless a species of animals." *Memoirs of the reign of George II.* [2 vols. (London, 1848)] Vol 1. p 23

"I am afraid he is one of those disconsolate preachers," said poor Joshua Ellis,—

____

³⁸ Except for "Hobbes", p. [56] is in pencil.
³⁹ James Augustus St. John, *The History of the Manners and Customs of Ancient Greece,* 3 vols. (London, 1842), I, xii; in Emerson's library.

Beware of the minor key!

↑See *DL* 255↓

[60] When Napoleon asked Laplace why there was no mention
of God in the "Mécanique ⟨"⟩Celeste,"— "Sire, je n'avais pas besoin
de cette hypothèse."[40]

You perceive the theory?—
But the facts contradict it.—
↑So much↓ ⟨T⟩the worse for the facts. ⟨—⟩

"In 1837, the same Academy [the Faculty of Medicine in Paris,] offered a
prize of 3000 francs to any one who could read through a board. No one
gained the prize" Büchner, *"Force & Matter"* [1864,] p. 153

[61] Thoreau's page reminds me of Farley,[41] who went early
into the wilderness in Illinois, ⟨&⟩ lived alone, & hewed down trees, &
tilled the land, ⟨& pleased himself⟩ but retired again into newer country
when the population came up with him. Yet, on being asked, what he
was doing⟨,⟩? said, he ⟨w⟩ pleased himself that he was preparing the land
for civilization.

[62]–[66] [blank]
[67][42]   Aristotle
Λογου αρχη, ου λογος, αλλα τι κρειττον[43]

Poetry is something more philosophical & excellent than history

[Action comes less near to vital truth than description. *Plato*][44]

[40] Friedrich Karl Christian Ludwig Büchner, *Force and Matter*, trans. J. Frederick
Collingwood (London, 1864), p. 52. Emerson borrowed this work from the Boston Athenaeum August 19–September 18, 1865.
[41] Perhaps Frederick A. Farley, who resigned the pastorate of the Westminster
Congregational Church in Providence in 1840. See *JMN*, VIII, 100.
[42] Page [67] and "causa . . . ⟨ca⟩mei!' " on p. [68] are in pencil.
[43] "The first principle of reason is not reason, but something better" (Ed.). See
JMN, VI, 144 and 186.
[44] This and the preceding quotation come from D. K. Sandford's "Greek Philosophy
of Taste," in the *Edinburgh Review*, LIV (Sept. 1831), 48. See *JMN*, VI, 173.

———

The hand is the instrument of instruments, & the mind is the form of forms.[45]

———

Ε τεχνη εστι λογος του εργου ανευ υλης.[46]

———

"Foede in hunc mundum intro⟨ov⟩avi, anxie vixi, perturbatus egredior, [68] causa causarum, miserere ⟨ca⟩mei!"[47]

Intellect is the science of metes & bounds.[48]

———

All men of genius are melancholy.[49]

———

Entelecheia
    reality   ↑See *supra* p 52↓
    completeness[50]

———

[69]–[70] [blank]
[71]   *Readings.* ↑Transferred to ↑*ST*↓ p 55↓
From Demosthenes [T 20–21, 23]   ↑⟨V⟩↓
Chief Justice Crewe's opinion [T 49]
Paganini [T 51]
Sigurd & Eystein [VS 6–7]
Mme. ⟨de⟩ Récamier [T 24]
Conclusion of the Mahabarat.
Troilus[n] & Cressida.

———

[45] Bacon, *The Advancement of Learning,* bk. V; see *The Works of Francis Bacon,* ed. James Spedding et al., 15 vols. (Boston, 1860–1864), IX, 63. See *JMN,* VI, 186.

[46] Attributed to Aristotle in Cudworth, *The True Intellectual System of the Universe,* 1820, I, 336, and translated "Art is . . . the reason of the thing without matter." See *JMN,* VI, 213–214.

[47] "In sin and shame was I born, in sorrow have I lived, in trouble I depart; O! thou Cause of causes, have mercy upon me!" (Ed.). See *JMN,* VI, 328, where Emerson calls it "Aristotle's farewell."

[48] This sentence is used in "The Scholar," *W,* X, 263. Cf. *JMN,* VI, 329, and VIII, 377.

[49] Cf. *JMN,* XIII, 336, and "Immortality," *W,* VIII, 331.

[50] "Entelecheia . . . completeness" and the two rules above and below it are in pencil.

Saint Anthony's address to the fishes. [TU 106]
_____

Gibbon's Autobiography
_____

Portia, uxor Bruti.
_____

Hamlet's Soliloquy
_____

Makaria
_____

Lord Clarendon's Portraits[51]
_____

[72]   Readings
_____

Thomas Taylor's naïvétés
_____

Characteristics of Goethe
_____

Synesius
_____

Ben Jonson's Masques & Songs
_____

Saadi at Kuaresin[52]

[73]–[76] [blank]
[77]   *Genius*[n]
At Mrs Hooper's, 23 February, we had a conversation on Genius, in which I enumerated the traits of Genius.

[51] "Transferred to . . . 55" and "V" are in pencil. "Sigurd & Eystein" is struck through in pencil with four diagonal use marks; "Hamlet's Soliloquy" is struck through in pencil with two diagonal use marks. All but "Paganini" and "Lord Clarendon's Portraits" occur in *JMN*, XIV, 320–322. For Clarendon, see p. [38] above. See also *JMN*, VI, 337, 338, and 327, and Pocket Diary 16, pp. [114] and [121] below.
[52] "Readings" and "Thomas Taylor's naïvétés" are in pencil. "Saadi at Kuaresin" is struck through in ink with two diagonal use marks.

1. love of truth
    distinguished from *talent*, which Mackintosh defined *"habitual facil-
ity of execution."*[53]

2. Surprises; incalculable

3. ⟨I⟩Always the term Genius, when used with emphasis, implies [78]
imagination, use of symbols
figurative speech

4. creative. advancing leading by new ways to the ever-new or infi-
nite↑.↓[54]

Coleridge said, "its accompaniment is the carrying the feelings &
freshness of youth into the powers of manhood."[55]
Most men in ↑their↓ life & ways make us feel the arrested development; [79] in Genius, the unfolding goes on,—perfect metamorphosis, & again, new metamorphosis.
↑And every soul is potentially Genius, if not arrested.↓

5. Moral. Genius is always moral.

And finally, my definition is, Genius is a sensibility to the laws of the
world.[56] ↑things make a natural impression on him,—belong to us as
well.↓
Quoted Pindar, & ⟨Raphael⟩ Lessing concerning Raphael without
hands.[57]

and read from [Goethe's] "Notes to the Westostlichen Divan."

[53] This quotation is used in "Powers and Laws of Thought," *W*, XII, 47.
[54] The period is added in pencil.
[55] *The Friend*, sec. II, Essay I, Postscript. See *JMN*, VI, 195.
[56] With "Genius is . . . moral.", cf. "The Sovereignty of Ethics," *W*, X, 185. "Genius is . . . world." is used in "Powers and Laws of Thought," *W*, XII, 42.
[57] Lessing, *Emilia Galotti*, I, iv. For this and quotations from Pindar, see *JMN*, XIV,
121–122.

[80] talked of Browning
                Burke
                Bettine
                Burns
                Moliere
                Father Taylor
and read ⟨P⟩Saadi's Persian Boy

All its methods are a surprise. When the Indian Mythology taught the people that when Brahma should come the deep should be a ford to him, they little suspected that the sailor was predicted who should make of the barrier the road of nations.
↑See Balloons *DL* 125   and Borrow of Menai↓[58]

[81]   Genius.
I should have added, but did not, the Catholicity of Greek mythology,—"that's nae for naething neither," & read the passage from [Schiller's] Wallenstein, under the head of Veracity of Genius.

[82]   Classic & Romantic
            at Mrs Parkman's[59]

---

    read ⟨Saadi's Persian boy⟩
                    ↑See supra
                    P. 43↓[60]

[83]   Doctrine of Leasts.
at Mrs Parkman's, May 25, 1861

Should have cited, but did not, Swedenborg's saying, "To construct a philosophy, is nothing more than to give the best attention to the operations of one's own mind."

[58] "See Balloons . . . Menai" is in pencil. For the Menai, see George H. Borrow, *Wild Wales: Its People, Language and Scenery,* 3 vols. (London, 1862), and Journal VA, p. [282] below.
[59] "Mrs Parkman" may be Caroline Hall Parkman (1794–1871), widow of Boston preacher Francis Parkman and mother of the historian by the same name. See *L,* V, 243 and 536.
[60] "See supra P. 43" is in pencil.

Swedenborg said, "Touch apprehends the surfaces of parts; taste & smell, the surfaces of parts of parts."

[84] "All the sanguineous forces of the heart are counted out singly, or, if one may use the expression, man by man, in the lungs."

Swedenborg

"Everything is a series, & in a series." *Swedenborg.*

The circles of substances involve corresponding circles of all their accidents.

[85] "Hell itself may be contained within the compass of a spark."

Thoreau.[61]

Use the low style. Build low. ↑Mr↓ Downer said the "snuggeries" in Dorchester kept their tenants; the ⟨gay⟩ airy houses on the hills soon lost them.[62]

↑I have heard that↓ Col. Wainwright, (was it, or what ⟨f⟩gay gentleman?) took Allston out to ride one day; Allston painted ⟨on⟩ ↑out of↓ that ride three pictures.[63]

———

———

Faraday's subjects were, a tea-kettle, a chimney, a fire, soot, ashes, &c.

———

Nature's low fare system   *CO* 147

———

↑Back to GL p 168↓[64]

[61] See *The Journal of Henry D. Thoreau*, ed. Bradford Torrey and Francis H. Allen, 14 vols. (Boston, 1949), I, 19. Emerson mentions "Mr Thoreau's MS. Journal, now on my table" in a letter to his son, written a month after Thoreau's death (May 6, 1862); see *L*, V, 278–279.

[62] See *JMN*, XIII, 25.

[63] See "Inspiration," *W*, VIII, 291. The insertions are in pencil.

[64] "Back to . . . 168" is in pencil. For the two preceding entries, see *JMN*, XII, 598 and 597.

[86] [blank]
[87] 1863
    June 11—   Notes for Discourse at Waterville.[65]

A scholar is a collector of finer coins than the numismatologist, of finer shells than the Conchologist.

'Tis fair to say that the ideal of any people is in their best writers & artists—   ↑*LI* 19↓
A man is to be judged by his best⟨.⟩↑: for he knows the difference as well as you do.↓[66]

The costliest benefit of books is, that they set us free from themselves also.[67]

                       ↑Books
                  see next page↓

[88] A.W. Schlegel quotes Duclos's remark, that "few distinguished works have been produced by any but authors by profession."

The Gauss-&-Pierce theory of books—*BL* 114   *VO* 173
      ↑See *infra* p. 106, Rimmer.↓

Goethe, the pivotal man of the old & new times: he shuts up the old, he opens the new. ↑LI 121↓[68]

See Nala's exchange of his skill in horses, for Rituparna's skill in dice & in numbers.[69]

---

[65] Emerson's discourse on August 11, 1863, at Waterville College, Maine, given as "The Scholar," was printed in 1883 as "The Man of Letters" to distinguish it from the 1876 oration, "The Scholar."

[66] "*LI* 19" is in pencil, overwritten in ink; ": for he . . . do." is in pencil.

[67] A vertical line in pencil is drawn in the left margin beside this sentence. See *JMN*, XIV, 349.

[68] "See *infra* . . . Rimmer." is in pencil; see also p. [20] above. "LI 121" is in pencil, overwritten in ink. For "Goethe, the . . . new.", see *JMN*, XI, 430.

[69] See *Mahābhārata. Nala and Damayanti, and Other Poems*, trans. Henry Hart Milman (Oxford, 1835), pp. 67–68, and Journal VA, p. [70] below.

Books. Ste. Beuve's History of Port Royal?

[89] The Emperor of Austria says, that, knowing too much only gives people the headach[e].[70]

Ernest Renan finds, that Europe twice assembled for exhibitions of industry, & no poem graced the occasion, & nobody remarked the defect.[71] &c &c   *FOR* 66

Concentration indicates control of thoughts, holding them as lanthorns to light each other & the main fact.—[72]
A guiding star to the arrangement & use of facts is in your leading thought.

[90] The deep book,—no matter how remote the subject,—alone helps.   *VA* 272

Treason of Scholars. They are *par excellence* ⟨fre⟩ idealists, & should stand for freedom, justice, & ⟨beneficent⟩ public good.[73]

⟨Niebuhr's divination returned to him⟩[74]

[91][75] There is no unemployed force in nature
                              See Substance & Shadow[, 1863,]
                              H James p 237[76]

---

[70] See *JMN,* XIV, 283.

[71] Ernest Renan, *Essais de morale et de critique* (Paris, 1860), pp. 356–357. Emerson received this book from Charles Eliot Norton in October, 1862 (see *L,* V, 293), and borrowed it from the Boston Athenaeum February 16–April 6, 1863. The sentence is used in "The Man of Letters," *W,* X, 245.

[72] A vertical line in pencil is drawn in the left margin beside this sentence.

[73] "Treason of . . . good." is used in "The Man of Letters," *W,* X, 254.

[74] For "Niebuhr's . . . him", in pencil and partially erased, see *JMN,* XIII, 396, and "Inspiration," *W,* VIII, 282.

[75] Page [91] is in pencil.

[76] Henry James, *Substance and Shadow: or Morality and Religion in Their Relation to Life: An Essay upon the Physics of Creation* (Boston, 1863), paraphrased. This volume is in Emerson's library. Two short vertical lines are drawn in pencil in the left margin beside "There is . . . force in". The sentence, struck through in pencil with a vertical use mark, is used in "The Man of Letters," *W,* X, 248.

By life we have been dipped into evil, we know new means, the whole armory of man.

↑Sailor knows how to make a ford of the sea.↓[77]

Angels stand foot to foot with devils   H[enry]. J[ames]. [*Substance and Shadow,* 1863,] p 248

―――

Inspiration of modern history, [*ibid.,*] p 243[78]

―――

I do not wish you to be a perpetual prey & victim, but an armed & complete man[.]

―――

――――

Crabbed age & youth cannot live together

Men ⟨of 4⟩ over forty are no judges of a new book, said *Dr. K.*↑*irkland.*↓[79]

[92] "I defended," says Varnhagen, "the essence of Wilhelm Meister, but I say so only after Goethe & Rahel,—that pure loveliness, & right good will are the highest manly prerogatives, before which all energetic heroism (kraftige Heldenthum) with its lustre & ⟨fame⟩ renown must recede." Vol. 1. p. 84.[80]

―――

Heart, head, hand. "To give the feminine element in life its

―――――――

[77] "Sailor knows . . . sea." is used in "Resources," *W*, VIII, 144; see p. [80] above.
[78] For the quotation, see pp. [92]–[93] below.
[79] Two short vertical lines are drawn in pencil in the left margin beside "I do not . . . be a". "I do . . . man" is struck through in pencil with a vertical use mark, extended through "Crabbed age . . . K.↑irkland.↓" With the first sentence, cf. "The Man of Letters," *W*, X, 250–251, and the lecture "Public and Private Education," *Uncollected Lectures,* ed. Clarence Gohdes (New York, 1932), p. 13. For "Crabbed age . . . together", see Shakespeare, "The Passionate Pilgrim," XII, l. 1. "Men ⟨of 4⟩ . . . book," is used in "The Man of Letters," *W*, X, 254–255. Dr. Kirkland is John Thornton Kirkland (1770–1840), president of Harvard (1810–1828).
[80] Karl August Ludwig Philipp Varnhagen von Ense, *Tagebücher von K. A. Varnhagen von Ense,* 14 vols. (Leipzig, 1861–1870). Emerson withdrew this volume from the Boston Athenaeum March 5–April 6, 1863. "pure loveliness . . . recede.' " is used in "Character," *W*, X, 121.

hard-earned but eternal supremacy of the masculine element: has been
the secret [93] inspiration of all past history."
                    Henry James. [*Substance and Shadow,* 1863,] p. 243[81]

"There is no enforced or arbitrary authority existing in heaven, since
no angel in his heart acknowledges any one superior to himself but
(the Lord) God alone."[82]
                    Swedenborg, ap *Henry James,* [*ibid.,*] p. 36

Wherever one is on trial, two are on trial. The examiner is instructed,
whenever the pupil is examined.[83]

[94]   ↑*Friendship.*↓
The sublime point ↑in experience↓ is the sufficient man. Cube this
value by the meeting of two who ⟨perfectly⟩ understand & support
each other, & you have organized Victory.[84]

———

Buonaparte called the Ecole Polytechnique "the hen that laid him
golden eggs."

In Prussia in 1836(?) Professor Stendler in Breslau, the sanscrit
scholar, was displaced, because it was discovered, that, [95] ten years
ago, he belonged to the Burschenschaft.
                    See *Varnhagen* [von Ense], [*Tagebücher,* 1861,] I. 34.

———

Pray for the Advent of the Lawgiver, for the Stoic,
chalybeate waters,

[81] " 'only after . . . recede.' " on p. [92], struck through in ink with a vertical use
mark, and " 'To give . . . history.' ", struck through in ink with one vertical use mark and
in pencil with another on p. [92], and in ink with three vertical use marks on p. [93], are
both used in "Character," *W,* X, 121.

[82] Two vertical lines in pencil are drawn in the left margin beside "There is . . . arbitrary". The quotation is used in "Progress of Culture," *W,* VIII, 227.

[83] Four vertical lines in pencil are drawn in the left margin, two beside "Wherever
one . . . two" and two beside the entire entry. "cf [Journal] NY-76" is written in pencil,
probably by someone other than Emerson, following this entry.

[84] "in experience" is in ink over the same in pencil. Two vertical lines in pencil are
drawn in the left margin beside "sufficient man . . . understand." The paragraph is used in
"Progress of Culture," *W,* VIII, 225–226.

Now we are falling abroad with levity, and the very clergy lend themselves to the decomposing process.

See Henry James [*Substance and Shadow,* 1863,] p. 238

"But why, Socrates, need we consider the opinion of the generality of men, who say anything that occurs to them?," says Protagoras.

Bohn's Plato. vol. 1, p. 284[85]

[96] In the College, it is complained, money & the vulgar respectability have the ↑same↓ ascendant as in the city. What remedy? There is but one,—namely, the arrival ⟨of young men or a young man⟩ of genius, which instantly takes the lead, & makes the fashion. ↑At Cambridge,↓ E. Everett, ⟨&⟩ Buckminster, John Everett, ⟨&⟩ Lee, and Edward & Charles Emerson, each in their turn, gave vogue to literary taste & eloquence in their [97] classes.[86]
"Stand by your order."[87]

↑Thoreau↓

"Herndon says of the Amazon Country, 'There is wanting an industrious & active population who know what the comforts of life are, & who have artificial wants to draw out the great resources of the Country,'—But what are the 'artificial wants' & 'the great resources' of a country? Surely not the love of luxuries, like the tobacco & slaves of his native ↑(?)↓ Virginia, or that fertility of soil which [98] produces these. The chief want is ever a life of deep experiences, that is, character, which alone draws out the great resources of Nature. When our wants cease to be chiefly superficial & trivial, which is commonly meant by artificial, & begin to be wants of character, then the great

---

[85] *The Works of Plato. A New and Literal Version, Chiefly from the Text of Stallbaum* . . ., 6 vols. (London: H. G. Bohn, 1848-1854), in Emerson's library.

[86] Joseph S. Buckminster (1784-1812) was an eloquent Unitarian minister; John Everett (1801-1826) was Edward Everett's brother; Charles Carter Lee (1798-1871), a Southerner, graduated from Harvard in the class of 1819; Edward and Charles Emerson were Emerson's brothers.

[87] For this sentence, used in "The Man of Letters," *W*, X, 251 and 251-252, see *JMN*, XIII, 133 and 385.

resources of a country are taxed & drawn out, & the result, the staple production, is poetry."

H.D. Thoreau MS Journal. June 1854, p. 265[88]

[99] It is claimed for the clergy that it is the planting of a qualified man in every town, whose whole business is to do good in every form.

———

Il n'y /a/est/ que le matin en toutes choses.[89]

↑as Alexander Henry↓[90]

—— ↑ ————————————————————————↓

↑1863↓ Self-help. At West Point,[91] the chamber was in perfect order; the mattrass on the iron bedstead rolled up into a scroll. "Who makes your bed?" "I do." "who brings you water?" "I do." "Who blacks your boots?" "I do."

↑See (better to this point) Roederer's account of Napoleon↓[92]

⟨Protagoras⟩ ↑Hippias Minor↓ in Plato.
Learn to ride, to ha⟨nes⟩rness your horse,—'tis worth a journey over the Plains: to row,[93] to fish, to shoot, to leap a fence, to dance.

[100] Then do not look sourly at the Club which does not choose you: For is not their loss equal to yours? And every highly organized person knows the value of the social barriers, since the best society has often been spoiled to him by the intrusion of bad companions. He ⟨therefore⟩ of all men would keep the rights of exclusion sacred, and feel that the

---

[88] See *The Journal* . . . , 1949, VI, 335–336.
[89] This proverb is used in "Inspiration," *W*, VIII, 286.
[90] These three words, and the long rule below them, are added in pencil.
[91] In June of 1863, Emerson went to West Point as an appointed member of a committee of visitation to the United States Military Academy.
[92] "See (better . . . Napoleon" is enclosed on three sides with one straight and one curving line in ink. See *JMN*, XIII, 313.
[93] "Self-help. . . . boots?' 'I do.' " and "Hippias . . . to row," are used in "The Man of Letters," *W*, X, 251, and "Public and Private Education," in Gohdes, *Uncollected Lectures*, 1932, pp. 13–14.

exclusions are in the interest of the admissions,—though they happen ⟨for⟩at this moment to thwart his wishes.[94]

↑Is not this page already printed?
1876↓[95]

[101] ——
It is impossible to extricate oneself from the questions in which our age is involved. You can no more keep out of politics than out of the frost.

——

Nature says to the American, I understand mensuration & numbers. I have measured out to you by weight & tally the powers you need. I give you the land & sea, ↑the↓ forest ↑&↓ ⟨&⟩the mine; ↑the↓ elemental forces; nervous energy, & a good brain. See to it that you hold & administer the continent for mankind.   ↑See next page↓[96]

[102]   ↑By kinds↓ I keep my kinds in check,
          I plant the oak, the rose I deck

——

Uses of the War
We do not often have a moment of grandeur in these hurried ⟨&⟩slipshod lives. *FOR* 115

——

Now Education itself is on trial.

We will not again disparage America↑,↓ now that we have seen what men it will bear. *GL* 386[97]

---

[94] This paragraph, struck through in pencil from "the Club" to "they happen" with a vertical use mark, is used in "Social Aims," *W*, VIII, 90–91.

[95] The rule and "Is not . . . 1876" are in pencil.

[96] Emerson struck "It is . . . involved." through in pencil with a diagonal use mark, then extended it vertically to the bottom of the page. For "You can . . . frost.", see *JMN*, V, 63–64, where it is attributed to Webster. "Nature says . . . mankind." is used in "The Man of Letters," *W*, X, 249–250. "See next page" is added in pencil.

[97] "Uses of . . . *GL* 386" is struck through in pencil with a diagonal use mark. Two vertical lines in pencil are drawn in the left margin beside "Now Education . . . trial." "We do not . . . lives." and "We will not . . . bear." are used in "The Man of Letters," *W*, X, 257. The latter is also used in "Harvard Commemoration Speech, July 21, 1865," *W*, XI, 345. The comma after "America" is added in pencil.

from p. 101

I compute the curve of the rainbow, the ebb & flow of ⟨the sea⟩ waters, the recoils of forces, the errors of planets, & the balance of attraction & recoil, the ellipse of the moon,[98]

[103] The war was to him a new glass to see things through.

↑What sort of a universe were it, if you omit the earths?↓ —All sky & no stars.[99]

Courage! ↑"↓God himself prefers atheism to fear,↑"↓ thought T.↑horeau.↓[100]

———

What business have you ⟨to stand⟩ on that side?　　See *NO* 83

———

The ⟨wonder⟩ ↑miracle↓ of men is, that the reason of things comes to my side moulded into a person like myself, & full of universal relations.

———

The Dance. *Plotinus* [*Select Works* . . . , 1817, p.] 84.[101]

———

[104] "But Cathmore dwelt in the wood to avoid the voice of praise."[102]

———

But what do you exist to say?[103]

[98] "I compute . . . moon," struck through in pencil with a diagonal use mark, is used in "The Man of Letters," *W*, X, 250.

[99] "The war . . . through." is written in ink over "The war ↑was to him↓ || . . . || see things through" in erased pencil. "All sky . . . stars." is used in "Powers and Laws of Thought," *W*, XII, 45.

[100] Cf. *The Journal* . . . , 1949, II, 468, paraphrased. The original is quoted in "Thoreau," *W*, X, 483; a different paraphrase is used in "Perpetual Forces," *W*, X, 87. The quotation marks are added in pencil overwritten in ink.

[101] See pp. [10] and [55] above.

[102] The quotation is struck through in pencil with a vertical use mark. See p. [20] above.

[103] See *JMN*, XIII, 265.

In Dante, the hypocrites.
In Europe nations talking thro' their noses.

New generation better than the last. We have had peace & its disablings. *FOR* 114

Cotton but one of 200 000 plants[104]

The Arabs measure distance by horizons, & ⟨we m⟩scholars must.

[105] Go into the school, the college, & see the difference of faculty. Some who lap up knowledge as a cat laps milk, and others very slow blockheads, ⟨all "‖ . . . ‖"⟩

"Every thing is a series, & in a series."[105]

↑*Rhetoric*↓[106]
Rivarol said of Dante, "il se tient debout par la seule force du substantif et du verbe, sans le secours de l'adjectif."[107]

⟨M⟩It was Saurin[108] who proposed ⟨as⟩ to the Academy the inscription on the bust it erected to Molière, Rien ne manque à sa gloire, il manquait à la notre.

[106] Dr Rimmer ⟨would f⟩ ↑wishes to↓ make a statue which will not be bought. ↑*à la Gauss & Pierce*↓[109]

[104] Cf. "The Fortune of the Republic," *W*, XI, 512.
[105] See p. [84] above.
[106] *"Rhetoric"* is added in pencil.
[107] A vertical line in pencil is drawn beside "Rivarol said . . . l'adjectif.' ", and the entry is marked for insertion on p. [104], following "But what . . . say?", by converging lines in ink. Emerson's source may be Charles Augustin Sainte-Beuve, "Rivarol," in vol. V of *Causeries du lundi,* 15 vols. (Paris, 1851–1862); Emerson borrowed this volume from the Boston Athenaeum September 16–October 31, 1863.
[108] Bernard-Joseph Saurin (1706–1781), French dramatic poet.
[109] Two vertical pencil lines are drawn in the left margin beside "Dr Rimmer . . . bought."; see also p. [20] above. "*à la . . . Pierce*" is added in pencil. For Karl Friedrich Gauss and Benjamin Peirce, see *JMN,* XIV, 166, and p. [88] above.

"There are periods when something much better than happiness
& security of life is attainable." *Niebuhr.*[110]
His divination, *NO* 44[111]

"Mathematics," said Copernicus to the Pope, "are written for Mathematicians."[112]

Good Thoughts in Bad Times

———

[107]   *Scholar's Rules*

Read proudly⟨.⟩ ↑of that which is yours: it seems that the man was your
ancestor & ⟨wrote⟩ ↑anticipated↓ your thought.↓
Stand by your order.
Live by your strength, not by your weakness——[113]
By method, not by multitude or mass,

———

If not by genius, then by sympathy.

———

The truth is in the minorities[114]

———

Affirm and affirm.[115]

———

[110] This quotation, from *The Life and Letters of Barthold Georg Niebuhr* . . . , trans.
Susanna Winkworth, 3 vols. (London, 1852), II, 361–362, is used in "American Civilization," *W*, XI, 299. See *JMN*, XIII, 395.
[111] See also p. [90] above.
[112] Sir David Brewster, *Memoirs of the Life, Writings and Discoveries of Sir Isaac
Newton*, 2 vols. (Edinburgh, 1855), I, 257–258. See *JMN*, XIV, 82.
[113] "of that . . . thought.", enclosed on three sides by wavy lines, is added in ink to
the right of "Read proudly⟨.⟩" For "Stand by . . . order.", see p. [97] above. For "Live
by . . . weakness——", used in "The Man of Letters," *W*, X, 247, see *JMN*, VIII, 243 and
IX, 200; "The Scholar," *W*, X, 274; and "Instinct and Inspiration," *W*, XII, 80. With
"Read proudly⟨.⟩", cf. "The Scholar," *W*, X, 288.
[114] With this sentence, cf. "Progress of Culture," *W*, VIII, 216.
[115] See *JMN*, XIII, 319, and "Instinct and Inspiration," *W*, XII, 78.

Conscience of Intellect, see *V* 109, *U* 109, *R* 68 J ⟨10⟩ 95, *IT* 9,
"For Gods are to each other not unknown."
↑Homer↓ Odyssey, v. 79.[116]

over ☞

[108]   ↑See *IM* 73, Φβ 5, 17,↓
                          Scholar.
"ne pratique ↑pas toutes↓ ses maximes, mais il maxime toutes ⟨s⟩les pra-
tiques." *Guizot*[117]

Men ride on a thought as on a horse which plunges madly. *NO* 47

———

Shop of power. *CO* 240

———

Wholes & details   *NO* 262, 269,

———

A diamond merchant[118]

———

[109] [blank]
[110]   Quotation & Originality[119]
⟨J⟩Hudibras says;
       "Like words congealed in Northern air:"[120]
hence came Munchausen's; & Hudibras had it from ⟨Lucian,⟩ ↑*Plutarch's Morals,* [5 vols. (London, 1718)] Vol. II. p. 454. & Plutarch
from Plato↓

Fuseli said, "Blake is d——d good to steal from."[121]

———

[116] "Conscience of . . . *IT* 9," and "Homer" are in pencil. For the quotation, see
JMN, VIII, 177.
[117] See *JMN,* XIV, 129.
[118] With this phrase, cf. *JMN,* VIII, 370; JMN, XII, 349; "The Scholar," *W,* X,
265; and "Poetry and Imagination," *W,* VIII, 71. For "Shop of power.", see "Inspiration," *W,* VIII, 269.
[119] In pencil.
[120] Samuel Butler, *Hudibras,* part I, canto I, l. 148.
[121] Alexander Gilchrist, *Life of William Blake,* 2 vols. (London, 1863), I, 52; Emerson withdrew both volumes from the Boston Athenaeum December 11–19, 1863.

[111]   *Quotation.*

Père Hardouin [in the Lamotte & Dacier &c controversy of Ancients & moderns, wrote (17⟨4⟩16) his *Apologie d'Homère,* &] said, "Croyez vous donc, que je me serais levé toute ma vie à trois heures du matin pour ne penser que comme les autres?"—which speech I have heard attributed to different Germans of this day. See *Saint Beuve: Mme Dacier*[122]

___

The original of John Barleycorn, see in Hafiz, ⟨Vol 1. p. 429.⟩[123]
↑and of *"When in death I shall calm recline"*↓ [Thomas Moore, "The Legacy," l. 1]

___

We have heard often that ⟨som⟩Mr Sedgwick or somebody divided mankind into Men & Women & Beechers: but Lady Mary Wortley Montague, a hundred years ago, said, "Men & Women and Herveys."[124]

[112]–[113] [blank]
    [114] Elliott Cabot's paper on "Art" has given emphasis to one point among others, that people only see what they are prepared to see.[125] ⟨There are ab⟨b⟩undant examples⟩ Thus who sees birds, except the hunter? or the ornithologist? How difficult it is to me to see certain particulars in the dress of people with whom I sit for hours, and after I had wished to know what sort of waistcoat, or coat, or shirt-collar, or neckcloth they wore.
↑I have ⟨been⟩gone to many dinners & parties with instructions from home & with my own wish to see the dress of the *men,* & can never remember to look for it.↓

___

[122] "Madame Dacier" is in vol. IX of *Causeries du lundi* (1851–1862), which Emerson borrowed from the Boston Athenaeum January 30–March 16, 1864. A vertical line is drawn in ink in the left margin beside " 'Croyez vous . . . autres?' "
    [123] Probably *Der Diwan von Mohammed Schemsed-din Hafis,* trans. Joseph von Hammer, 2 vols. (Stuttgart and Tübingen, 1812–1813); in Emerson's library.
    [124] "and of . . . *recline*' " is added in pencil. For " 'Men & Women and Herveys.' ", see Lady Mary Wortley Montagu, *The Letters and Works,* 3 vols. (London, 1837), I, 67. For "The original . . . Herveys.' ", struck through in ink with a discontinuous vertical use mark, see "Quotation and Originality," *W,* VIII, 186 and 185.
    [125] James Elliot Cabot, "On the Relation of Art to Nature," in the *Atlantic Monthly,* XIII (Feb. 1864), 183–199, and (March 1864), 313–329.

[115] Who teaches manners of majesty, of frankness, of grace, of humility? who but the adoring aunts & cousins that surround a young child? The babe meets such courting & flattery as only kings receive when adult, &, trying experiments every day, & at perfect leisure with these posture masters & flatterers, all day,—he throws himself into all the attitudes that correspond to theirs: are they humble? he is composed; are they eager? he is nonchalant; are they encroaching? he is dignified & inexorable.—And this in humble as well as high houses; that is my point.[126]

[116] Chesterfield says; "I have often said, & do think, that a Frenchman, who, with a fund of virtue, learning, & good sense, has the manners & good breeding of his country, is the perfection of human nature." *Letters.* vol. 1. p. 60[127]

———

↑1863. Paris with a perimeter of 8½ leagues, has 1,700,000 Souls.↓

———

1747, he says; "the Romans counterfeited Attic salt by a composition↑ called Urbanity, which was brought near ⟨to‖ . . . ‖⟩the perfection of the original attic salt." ↑[Chesterfield,] Letters [1845–1853,] I. p. 65↓ Conf. what Roederer says of the word *Urbanité*   FOR 282 [actually 292]

———

Laughter

"↑but↓ I am sure that, since I have had the full use of my reason, nobody has ever heard me laugh." Chesterfield, Letters, Vol 1 p 120[128]

↑Attar begins the four faults of a King

[126] This paragraph, struck through in pencil with a vertical use mark and in ink with a diagonal one, is used in "Social Aims," *W*, VIII, 81–82.

[127] Philip Dormer Stanhope, 4th Earl of Chesterfield, *Letters*, ed. Lord Mahon, 5 vols. (London, 1845–1853). Emerson withdrew volume I from the Boston Athenaeum March 16–26, 1864. The paragraph is struck through in pencil with three vertical use marks.

[128] This quotation, struck through in pencil with a diagonal use mark, is used in "Social Aims," *W*, VIII, 87.

"If he cannnot help laughing in public,
Then has his reverence suffered shipwreck—"↓

[117] ↑*Whitewashing.*↓
A descendant of Lord Chancellor Jeffreys has published lately some correspondence to show that he was a liberal man in his day.

——   Mahomet, too.

Birthday.

"Dii tibi dent annos, de te nam caetera sumes."[129]
                              Ovid to Tiberius. [*Ex Ponto,*]
                              Lib. II. Ep. 1. line 53

Tournure, urbanité, entregent,[130] ⟨—⟩ this is the trinity which makes the creed & the cultus of Society.

⟨1749⟩I do not know why Lord Chesterfield always writes *"min-uties"* for *minutiae.*[131] It looks a vulgarism.

"an harmonious voice" Chesterfield[132] [*Letters,* 1845, I, 119]

Un Anglais arrive bien rarement à une bonne prononciation de notre mot *toujours,* et en général de nos mots terminés en *our. A. Reville* ["Les Ancê-tres des Européens d'après la science moderne,"] Rev[ue]. des deux mondes 1864, Fevr. p 706

[118] *School.*[133] First, see that the expense be for teaching, or that school be kept the greatest number of days & for the greatest number of scholars. Then that the best ⟨building master⟩ teachers & the best apparatus, namely, building, furniture, books, &c be provided.

---

[129] "Gods grant thee years! Thou thyself wilt supply all else." The quotation appears in Lord Chesterfield's *Letters,* 1845, I, 239 and 388.
[130] See *JMN,* VI, 376.
[131] See, for example, Chesterfield, *Letters,* 1845, I, 241 and 335.
[132] This entry is in pencil.
[133] Emerson was elected to the Concord school committee in 1864.

⟨T⟩*School,*—because it is the *cultus* of our time & place, fit for the republic, fit for the times, which no longer can be reached & commanded by the Church. What an education in the public spirit of Massachusetts ha↑s↓ been the war songs, speeches, & readings of the Schools! Every district School has been an antislavery convention for two or three years last past.

This town has ⟨no coal,⟩ ↑no seaport,↓ no cotton, ↑no shoe-trade↓, no water power, no gold, lead, coal, or rock oil, ⟨no seaport⟩ ↑nor marble,↓ nothing but wood & grass ⟨& ice & Mr Tudor⟩[,] not even ice & granite, our New England staples; for the granite is better in ⟨a⟩Acton, Fitchburg, & our ice↑,↓ Mr Tudor said↑,↓ had [119] bubbles in it.[134] We are reduced then to manufacture school⟨masters⟩ ↑teachers↓, which we do, for the southern & western market. I advise the town to stick to that staple, & make it the best in the world. It is your lot in the urn.[135] And it is one of the commanding lots.

Get the best apparatus, the best overseer, and turn out the best possible article. Mr Agassiz says "I mean to make the Harvard Museum such that no European naturalist can afford to stay away from it." Let the Town of Concord say as much for its school. We will make our schools such that no family which has a new home to choose can fail to be attracted hither as ↑to↓ the one town in which the best education can be secured. This is one of those long prospective economies which are sure & remunerative.

see p. 122

[120] ↑*Bons mots.*↓

I am always struck with the speed with which every new interest, party, or way of thinking gets its ⟨n⟩ bon mot & name, & so adds a new word to language." Thus Higginson, & ⟨his⟩ Livermore↑, Hosmer,↓ & the fighting chaplains give necessity & vogue to "muscular Christianity":[136] The language of the ⟨ti‖ . . .‖⟩ day ⟨was⟩ readily suggested to

---

[134] The added commas are in pencil. Frederic Tudor (1783–1864) was known as "the Ice King." See *L,* III, 383, where Emerson notes in 1847 that "Mr Tudor has invaded us . . . & taken 10,000 tons of ice from the Pond [Walden] in the last weeks."

[135] For "It is . . . urn.", see *JMN,* XIII, 269 and 278, where it is attributed to L'Abbé Galiani in Sainte-Beuve, *Causeries du lundi,* 1851–1862, II, 345.

[136] "Muscular Christianity" was a term first applied to the doctrine of the Reverend Charles Kingsley, in a review of his *Two Years Ago,* in the *Saturday Review of Politics,*

some ⟨wit on⟩ theological wit to call hell "a military necessity"; and when some copperhead orator[137] called Slavery a divine institution, a voice from the crowd cried out, "So is Hell." which ⟨is⟩ ↑word became↓ a compendium[n] [121] of ⟨of⟩antislavery argument henceforward.

Old Wesson[138] one day, said, "I thought I was asleep, but I knowed I w'ant."[n]

[12⟨0⟩2] Schools (see p. 119)
We have already ⟨had⟩ seen the effect of our good schools in drawing good families to reside in the place.
Buonaparte said, "the Ecole Polytechnique was the hen that ⟨hatched⟩ ↑laid him↓ the golden eggs."[139]

[123]   ↑Thoreau's Letter.↓
        "Do you read any noble verses? For my part, they have been the only things I remembered, or that which occasioned them, when all things ⟨have⟩else ⟨have⟩ were blurred and defaced. All things ⟨e⟩have put on mourning but they; for the elegy itself is some victorious melody in you escaping from the wreck. It is a relief to read some true books, wherein all are equally dead, equally alive. I think the best parts of Shakspeare would only be enhanced by the most thrilling & affecting events. I have found it so. And so much the more, as they are not intended for consolation."

                    ↑Letter to Mrs Brown from H.D. Thoreau.↓[140]

    [124] Shakspeare   Apr. 23, 1564; died Apr 23, 1616.
Galileo ⟨too⟩ was born February 1⟨6⟩564.

Literature, Science, and Art, III, (Feb. 21, 1857), 176. "Hosmer" may be Emerson's neighbor Edmund; "Livermore" is probably George Livermore (1809–1865), antiquarian, specializing in Biblical works.
    [137] George Francis Train. See Journal VA, p. [239] below.
    [138] Probably Thomas Wesson, of Wesson's Tavern, Concord.
    [139] See p. [94] above.
    [140] The rule above "Letter to . . . Thoreau." is extended around "Letter". For this letter to Emerson's sister-in-law, Mrs. Lucy Jackson Brown, dated January 24, 1843, see Thoreau, *Letters to Various Persons*, ed. Ralph Waldo Emerson (Boston, 1865), p. 13. The quotation, struck through in pencil with a vertical use mark, is used in "Address at the Opening of the Concord Free Public Library," *W*, XI, 500–501.

⟨See o⟩On the subject of his recantation, & the Pope's recantation in 1818, See *WO* p. 32

Dante born ↑1265↓

↑Chaucer   1328 — d 1400↓

Genius is one of the Consolers of our mortal Condition

Cervantes born 9 Oct. 1547, died 23 April, 1616

Like the great wine year   1575 to 1625 was the great age of genius

The little world of the heart is larger, richer, deeper than the spaces of astronomy   *DO* 193

> Born 1564,   1664
>   1764
>   1864[141]

[125] *Old Age.* I told Richard Fuller[142] that he would soon come to a more perfect obedience to his children, than he had ever been able to obtain from them.

———

M. Babinet informs us, that the problem of aerial navigation is on the point of being solved.[143] I am looking, therefore, for an arrival of the remainder of the Prisoners of War ⟨in⟩ ↑from↓ the Libby & Atlanta prisons, by the balloon, descending at some point in Pennsylvania by a night-voyage from the South.[144]

[126] The English journals are flippant & spiteful in their notices of American politics & society, but mean abuse cannot be answered. If the writers were responsible, & could be held to the interrogatory, it would be easy to refresh their short memories with the history of English politics & society. The private memoirs of any age

[141] "1265" and "The little . . . 1864" are in pencil. "Genius is . . . Condition" and "The little . . . astronomy", the latter struck through in pencil with a diagonal use mark, are used in "Shakspeare," *W*, XI, 448. With "Like the . . . genius", cf. *ibid.*, p. 452.

[142] Richard Frederic Fuller, younger brother of Margaret Fuller.

[143] Cf. Jacques Babinet, "Des Tables Tournantes," *Revue des Deux Mondes,* Jan. 15, 1854, p. 418.

[144] Libby was the notorious Confederate prison in Richmond. An agreement to exchange prisoners of war had been reached on July 22, 1862.

of England are full of scandal. Read Lord Hervey [*Memoirs of the Reign of George the second* . . ., 1848] to know how just King, ministers, lords, bishops, & commons were in George I.'s time. Read Wraxall for George III.'s.[145] Were the interiors of the Court & the behaviour of the great lords in any age great [127] & disinterested? Ask Pepys, ask Swift, B⟨a⟩urnet, Bacon. The illusion under which the aristocracy live, ⟨is⟩ amounts to insanity. Lord Bristol plainly believes that it is very good of him to exist, & the Government owes him unceasing thanks. He does nothing for them. Well that is the humor of them all in Lord Hervey's pictures. That immensity of condescension in a fat old lubber does not appear at Washington except in ⟨very old &⟩ ↑men↓ very ↑long↓ distinguished.

It was curious, that, in the first volume of Hervey, the mere mention of Lord Bristol's love for Ickworth, & Walpole's building of his grand seat at Houghton, (?) & Lord Townshend's Raynham, more tickled my fancy, ⟨than all the history⟩ the vision of parks & gardens, than all the history.[146]

[128] 1864 March 26. ⟨Held⟩At the club, where was Agassiz just returned from his lecturing tour, having created a Natural History society in Chicago, where 4500 dollars were subscribed as its foundation by 19 persons.* And to which he recommended the appointment of Mr Kinnicott as the Superintendent.[147]

Dr Holmes had received a demand from Geneva, N.Y. for 51 (?) dol-

*⟨4⟩ 500
         19
    ────
    4500
    500
    ────
$9,500.   When I visited the *"Chicago Nat. History Museum"* in 1865, the fund had become $50,000.

---

[145] Emerson had borrowed the three volumes of Sir Nathaniel William Wraxall, *Posthumous Memoirs of His Own Time*, 3 vols. (London, 1836) from the Boston Athenaeum in 1852 and 1853; he also borrowed volume I of Wraxall, *Historical Memoirs of My Own Time*, 2 vols. (London, 1815) in 1853. For the latter, see *JMN*, XIII, 224–227.

[146] See Hervey, *Memoirs of the Reign of George the Second* . . . , 1848, I, xxx and 113. Emerson borrowed volume I from the Boston Athenaeum March 16–26, 1864.

[147] Robert Kennicott (1835–1866), naturalist and explorer, was appointed curator of the Chicago Academy of Sciences in 1864.

39

lars as costs of preparing for his failed lecture. Governor Andrew was the only guest, Hedge, Hoar, both the Doctors Howe, ⟨Lo⟩Holmes, Lowell, Norton, Woodman, Whipple.

It was agreed that the April Election should be put off till May, and that the next meeting should be on 23 April, instead of 30th, and that we should, on that day, have an [129] open club, allowing gentlemen whom we should designate to join us in honor of Shakspeare's birth-day. The Committee of the Club might invite ↑certain↓ gentlemen ⟨in the name of the⟩also, as the guests of the Club. Emerson, Lowell, & Holmes being the Committee.[148]

[130]   ↑*Diplomatic.*↓

⟨Margaret⟩It was not a bad speech, which, the chambermaid told me, she made in the quarrel in the kitchen: ⟨James or⟩ "Jim called her father 'Old Dimocrat,' whatever that might mean;" and she answered, that "Jim was a 'Buster,' whatever that might mean."

———

Lord Hervey affirms, that, "however incredible, it is literally true, that, when Queen Caroline (of George II) was dying, she advised the King to marry again: whereupon the tears & sobs of the King were renewed, and he exclaimed, 'Non, j'aurai des maitresses': to which the Queen made no other reply, than, 'Ah! mon Dieu! cela n'empêche pas.' "[149]

———

Old Age. The Tribune, April 16, ⟨in its⟩ reports that a New Zealand physician lectured on the ignorance in people of their own complaints, was asked by a lady, "what was the subject of his next lecture?"—"the

———

[148] These members of the Saturday Club, a "party of gentlemen" founded in 1855, include John Albion Andrew (1818–1867), governor of Massachusetts during the Civil War; Frederic Henry Hedge (1805–1890), Unitarian clergyman; Ebenezer Rockwood Hoar (1816–1895), jurist; Dr. Samuel Gridley Howe (1801–1876); Dr. Estes Howe (1814–1887); Charles Eliot Norton (1827–1908), author and educator; Horatio Woodman (1821–1879), Boston lawyer; and Edwin Percy Whipple (1819–1886), critic and essayist.

[149] See Hervey, *Memoirs of the Reign of George the Second . . .* , 1848, II, 513–514. Emerson borrowed volume 2 from the Boston Athenaeum March 26–April 29, 1864.

circulation of the blood,"—replied, "She should certainly attend, for she had been troubled with that complaint for a long time."—[150]

[131] Lowell told me, that, when[n] Mrs Stowe was invited to dine with the Atlantic Club,[151] she refused to drink wine, & it was banished for that day. But Lowell said, "Mrs Stowe, you took wine with the Duke of Argyle, when you visited him?" She acknowledged that she did. And now do you mean to treat us as if we were not as good as he?[n] "No," she said. "Bring some Champagne," cried Lowell, & Mrs Stowe & the company drank. "And how did you know," I asked, "that she did take wine at the Duke's?"—"O, I divined that," he said, "Of course she did."

——

Napoleon told Maximilian, "⟨he⟩You are going to a country which is ⟨a⟩one lump of silver."—What said that French Empress of Brazil?

[13⟨3⟩2][152] Nations have no memories[.]
They are all such unlicked cubs as we see,[n] great mobs of young men, full of conceit & all manner of emptiness. Lord Hervey, Pepys, Clarendon, Ld. Chesterfield, Commines, Wraxall show up the aristocracy;—that it is a gang of rich thieves, instead of a gang of poor thieves[.]
Garrison. Round him legislatures revolve. ↑"Father of his Country more than Washington," said A[lcott].↓

What unexpected revivals we have seen! Maryland & Kentucky are converted. Then Concord may be.

[133] If to the clubhouse people came, if, better, to some town of cheap living, we could call twenty deep men to spend a month, & take our chance of meeting each in turn ↑alone,↓ that were worth

---

[150] This anecdote appears in the New York *Daily Tribune,* April 2, 1864, p. 4.

[151] Started at nearly the same time as the Saturday Club, and with a largely identical membership, the Atlantic Club, though short-lived, led in 1857 to the founding of the *Atlantic Monthly.*

[152] Pages [132] and [133] are in pencil.

while. When a man meets his accurate mate, then ⟨society⟩ life is delicious.

Alcott said of preachers, the "people want some one who has been where they are now"

Yet is Garrison a disagreeable Father of his country.

See Conversation on same topics. *WAR* 276

[13⟨5⟩4] I suppose I must read Renan, *Vie de Jesus,*ⁿ which I fancied was Frenchy. ⟨That⟩ ↑It↓ is a pregnant text, & a key to the moral & intellectual pauses & inactivity of men,—"The creature is subject to Vanity."[153] There is none ⟨w⟩almost who has not this misleading egotism. The efficient men are efficient by means of this Flanders horse. But it destroys them for grandeur of aim, & for highest conversation. ⟨See how t⟩They all gravitate to cities. ⟨See that⟩ God, the inward life, is not enough for them: they must have the million mirrors of other minds, must measure wit with others for mastery, and must have the crowns & rewards of wit [135] that cities give. Yet up & down ⟨in the⟩ ⟨here & there⟩ in every nation, are scattered individual souls with the grace of humility. Geo. Fox, Behmen, Scougal, the Mahometan Saint Rabbia, and the Hindoos, have the art to cheapen the world ↑t↓hereby. So Ossian's "Cathmore dwelled in the wood to avoid the voice of praise."[154] Jesus was ⟨great enough⟩ grand where he stood, and let Rome & London dance after Nazareth. But the thinkers or litterateurs of humility are not humble. Thus Alcott, Thoreau, & I, know the use & superiority of it, but I can't praise our practice.

Every saint as every man comes ⟨at⟩ one day to be superfluous.

[136] Who can doubt the potences of an individual mind, who sees the shock given to torpid races, torpid for ages, by Mahomet, a vibration propagated over Asia & Africa, & not yet exhausted. What ↑then↓ of Menu? What of Buddh?

---

[153] Rom. 8:20. Emerson first borrowed Ernest Renan's *Vie de Jésus* (Paris, 1863), May 9–20, 1864, then *The Life of Jesus,* trans. C. E. Wilbour (New York, 1864), Dec. 27, 1864–March 8, 1865, from the Boston Athenaeum.

[154] See p. [104] above.

[137] The single word *Madame* in French poetry, makes it instantly prose.

Mutiny p 135[155]

[138]   *Scholar*

Montaigne ⟨plainly prefers to⟩ ↑had rather↓ take Europe into his confidence than to tell so much ⟨to⟩ ⟨with⟩ ↑to↓ a French lord; as one may ⟨be⟩ move aukwardly in a parlor, ⟨but⟩ ↑who↓ walks well ↑enough↓ in a crowd.[156] I heard Bandmann read Hamlet's soliloquy, the other day, at Bartol's.[157] In conversation, he was polite & expansive enough, but plainly enjoyed the new expansion that the reading gave him. He stood up, & by musing distanced himself, then silences all the company, & gets out of doors, as it were, by a cheerful [139] cry of a verse or two, & acquires a right to be the hero, & ⟨puts his own sense⟩ abounds in his own sense, & puts it despotically upon us, in look, manner, & elocution. He brought out the broad meaning of the soliloquy truly enough, but, as all actors will, with an *overmuch,* with emphasis & mouthing. They cannot let well alone: but must have the merit of all the refinements & second senses they have found or devised, & so drive it too finely. It is [140] essential to reach this freedom, or gay self-possession, but temperance is essential too.

H. D. T[horeau]. wrote in 1840, "a good book will not be dropped by its author, but thrown up. It will be ⟨as⟩so long a promise that he will not overtake it soon. He will have slipped the leash of a fleet hound."[158]

---

[155] "Mutiny p 135" is in pencil.
[156] "but" is canceled, and "who" added, in pencil.
[157] Cyrus A. Bartol's home at 17 Chestnut Street, Boston, was for many years the meeting place of transcendental thinkers and writers. Daniel E. Bandmann (1840–1905) was a German actor who came to the United States in 1863 and became popular in Shakespearian roles.
[158] See Perry Miller, *Consciousness in Concord* (Boston, 1958), p. 152, where the journal entry is dated August 12, 1840.

address   Dr [Nathaniel L.] Frothingham
             G[ulian]. C[rommelin]. Verplan[c]k
             J[ohn]. G[reenleaf]. Whittier
             Dr Asa Gray
             R[ichard]. H[enry]. Dana[159]

[141][160] Apr. 6.   Wrote to [Edward] Everett, [William Cullen]
               Bryant, [George] Bancroft, [Josiah] Quincy Jr,
               [Samuel Gray] Ward,
        7   [Franklin B.] Sanborn, J[ohn] M[urray] Forbes
                             [George] Ticknor
                             Gov [John Albion] Andrew
                             R[ichard] G[rant] White
Invitation to our   ⟨Ticknor⟩
Centenial celebration   ⟨↑Gov↓ ⟨E⟩Andrew⟩
of Shakspeare's birthday.   [James Elliot] Cabot
                             [Thomas Gold] Appleton
                             ⟨Forbes⟩
                             [James Russell] Lowell
                             [Oliver Wendell] Holmes
                             [Thomas Ridgeway?] Gould
                             Verplank
                             Frothingham
                             Whittier

[142] [Louis] Agassiz	x	Andrew
Appleton	x	Bryant
Cabot	x	Bancroft
[Richard Henry] Dana [Sr.]	x	Verplanck
[John Sullivan] Dwight o		[George William] Curtis
Emerson	x	Frothingham
Forbes	x	Dana
[Nathaniel] Hawthorne ?	x	Whittier

[159] "address . . . R. H. Dana" is in pencil.
[160] Pages [141] and [142] are in pencil. "Invitation to . . . birthday." on p. [141] is circled in pencil.

[Frederick Henry] Hedge o	x	Everett
[Ebenezer Rockwood] Hoar	x	[Francis James] Child
[Samuel Gridley] Howe	x	⟨F⟩Gray
[Estes] Howe[n]	x	White
Holmes		[James Freeman] Clarke
[Henry Wadsworth] Longfellow		[William Morris] Hunt
Lowell	x	[James Thomas] Fields
[[John Lothrop] Motley]	x	[Wendell] Phillips
[Charles Eliot] Norton		[John] Weiss
Pierce? [Benjamin Peirce]		⟨Clarke⟩[Thomas] Hill
[Charles] Sumner?		⟨D⟩[Samuel] Rowse
Ward		[Martin Franklin] Conway
[Edwin Percy] Whipple		Bigelow
[Horatio] Woodman		[George Stillman] Hillard
	x	[Martin] Brimmer
		[Edwin] Booth[161]

[143] The Old President Quincy told me, that, throughout his life, his rule had been, to settle the task of tomorrow morning before he went to bed every night.[162] It were a noble economy for a scholar, & he spoke it in reference to literary work. ——

↑——↓   ————————
↑Bias↓   ↑*Bias.*↓

How grateful to discover in man or woman a new emphasis,[163] which they put on somewhat to which you did not know they attached value; quite out of themselves; & which they never learned of you or of any other! How respectable they become!

[144] [blank]

[145] The world is always equal to itself. The Romance of Arthur, the search for the Sangrail, are original in the 12th Century,

---

[161] The *x*'s which precede several of the names on p. [142] indicate that Emerson had written to them. See *L*, V, 357–373.

[162] "The Old . . . night." is used in "Inspiration," *W*, VIII, 286.

[163] "How grateful . . . emphasis," struck through in pencil with two vertical use marks, is used in "Greatness," *W*, VIII, 310. "Bias" and the short rule above it are added in pencil.

& the whole series of Arthur romances are an offset against the Cid[.]
↑Printed ΦBK Oration↓[164]
Walter Mapes. (1150 to —75,) wrote the Sangrail in Latin.

———

I wrote to Arnold,[165] & should have said; I have heard that the engi-
neers in the locomotives grow nervously vigilant ⟨as they gro⟩ with
every year on the road, until the ⟨w⟩ employment is intolerable to
them; and, I think, writing is more & more a terror to old scribes.

[146] Of Wordsworth Blake writes; "This is all in the highest
degree imaginative, & equal to any poet, but not superior; I cannot
think that real poets have any competition. None are greatest in the
kingdom of heaven. It is so in poetry."[166]

———

Shakspeare the only modern writer who has the honor of a Concordance.[167]

——— ———

the only painter who flatters nature,

———

pulverised into proverbs

———

⟨Mos⟩
all criticism is only a making ↑of↓ rules out of his beauties.[168]

———

"Somnambulic security which makes the poet a poet"
                                        Mommsen   see *VA* 52

[147] great arts now, but no equal poetry celebrates them.
    The Pilgrims came ↑to America↓ before ⟨the⟩ ↑Shakspear's↓

[164] "The world ... Cid" is struck through in ink with a diagonal use mark; cf.
"Progress of Culture," (read before the ΦBK Society at Cambridge, July 18, 1867), *W*,
VIII, 213. For "The World ... itself.", see *JMN*, XIII, 9; "Works and Days," *W*, VII,
174; "The Man of Letters," *W*, X, 247; "Character," *W*, X, 112; "Address at the Dedication of the Soldiers' Monument in Concord, April 19, 1867," *W*, XI, 354; and "Shakspeare," *W*, XI, 452.
    [165] See *L*, V, 361–362 for Arnold's reply (London, June 19, 1864).
    [166] Gilchrist, *Life of William Blake*, 1863, I, 345.
    [167] See *JMN*, XI, 160.
    [168] This sentence is used in "Shakspeare," *W*, XI, 448.

plays were printed, or it would have been dangerous temptation. The
poets would have stayed. ↑at home.↓¹⁶⁹

[148]   "Draw with idle spider's strings
                Most ponderous & substantial things."
                          Measure for Measure [III, ii. 289–290]

"It is too full o' the milk of human kindness."
                          ⟨Hamlet⟩ ↑*Macbeth*↓ [I, v, 18]

———

                "It is twice blessed,
        It blesseth him that gives, & him that takes."
                        Merch[ant]. of Ven[ice]. [IV, i, 186–187]

———

              "in single blessedness."
                        Mids[ummer]. night's Dream [I, i, 78]

——— ————————

              "her hedges even *pleached*
        Like prisoners wildly overgrown with hair
        Put forth disordered twigs."
                        K[ing]. Henry V [V, ii, 42–44]

——— ————————————

              "kecksies" K[ing]. H[enry]. V. [V, ii, 52]
[makeless]¹⁷⁰   seems to come of *Qu'est ce que c'est?*

———

        "But look, the morn in russet mantle clad
        Walks ⟨the⟩ o'er the dew of yon high eastern hill."
                        Hamlet. [I, i, 166–167]

———

        "I will speak daggers to her." *Ham[let].* [III, ii, 414]

———

        "Behaviour, what wert ⟨thou⟩ ↑thou↓
        'Till this man showed thee? & what art thou now?"
                        "Love's Labour's lost" [V, ii, 337–338]

———

¹⁶⁹ "to America" is circled in ink. With "The Pilgrims . . . home.", cf. "Shakspeare," *W*, XI, 453.
¹⁷⁰ "makeless" is written and circled in pencil. See p. [149] below.

[149] The surprise in his choice of words so delights us; "foreign levy." [*Macbeth,* III, ii, 25]—

the trick of making verbs of nouns——

> "Come ⟨f⟩seeling night
> Skarf up the tender eye of pitiful day." *Macbeth.* [III, ii, 46–47]

"he lurched all swords o' the garland." *Coriolanus* [II, ii, 105]

> [*"Shunless destiny"*] ↑*Coriolanus*↓ [II, ii, 116]
> ↑"makeless wife." *Sonnet*↓ [IX, l. 4]
>   "struck
> Corioli like a planet." [*Coriolanus,* II, ii, 117–118]

> "Were I crowned the most imperial monarch,
> Thereof most worthy; were I the fairest youth
> That ever made eye swerve; had force & knowledge
> More than was ever man's; I would not prize them
> Without her love; for her employ them all,
> Commend them, & condemn them, to her service,
> Or to their own perdition."
>   *Winter's Tale* IV. 3 [iv, 383–389]

> "And thou away, the very birds are mute."
>   Sonnet [XCVII, l. 12]

> "Let me not to the marriage of true minds"
>   etc. [Sonnet CXVI, l. 1]

[150] When Sir Nathaniel reads Biron's sonnet addressed to Rosaline, Holofernes comments thus; "You find not the apostrophes, & so miss the accent. Let me supervise the ⟨sonnet⟩canzonet. Here are only numbers ratified; but for the elegancy, facility & golden cadence of poesy, *caret.* Ovidius Naso was the man; and why indeed Naso, but for smelling out the odoriferous flowers of fancy, the jerks of invention? *Imitari* is nothing": &c. &c.

Love's Labor's Lost. [IV, ii, 123–129]

What a set of oracles we might collect! Thus;

> "There is a history in all men's lives,
> Figuring the nature of the times deceased;
> The which observed, a man may prophesy
> With a near aim, of the main chance of things
> As yet not come to life."
>
> 　　　　　　　　　　　[II] *"Henry IV"* [III, i, 80–84]

[151] *Pay as you go* the only safe rule of private affairs.

⟨To a go⟩Punch says, "a man read Hamlet, & said it was all made up of quotations."

I find ⟨it⟩no mention of tobacco in Shakspeare, neither pipes nor snuff, which, one would have said the dates permitted. 'Tis a remarkable case, like Goethe's chronologic relation to steam locomotives.

[152] *History of Liberty*. Un aïeul des deux Gracques parait avoir été un des premiers qui ait enrégimenté des esclaves de bonne volonté, *volones*, en ↑leur↓ promettant la liberté après la victoire.

　　　　　　　　　　　　　Revue des D[eux]. M[ondes].
　　　　　　　　　　　　　　　　↑Sept. 1863↓[171]
"instinct of generosity & liberty in the whole race of Gracchi—"
　　　　　　　　　　　　　　　　　　　⟨See⟩

[153] [blank]
[154]　　　24 April 1864
　　　Yesterday the Saturday Club met to keep the birthnight of Shakspeare, at the end of the third Century. We met at the Revere House, at 4 o'clock P.M. Members of the Club present were

---

[171] Jean-Jacques Ampère, "Les Luttes de la liberté à Rome, Caton et les Gracques," *Revue des Deux Mondes,* Sept. 1, 1863, p. 78, which Emerson withdrew from the Boston Athenaeum April 5–May 30, 1864. "instinct of . . . Gracchi—", below, is Emerson's translation of a phrase in the same essay.

Agassiz,	Norton,	*Guests*
Appleton,	Pierce,	Governor Andrew
Cabot,	Whipple,	Rev. Dr. Frothingham
Dwight,	Woodman,	R. H. Dana, Sen[io]r. Esq.
Emerson,	———	Dr J[ohn]. G[orham]. Palfrey,
Forbes,	17	Rich[ar]d. G. White, Esq.
Hedge,		Rob[er]t. C. Winthrop[172]
Hoar,		Geo. S. Hillard
Holmes,		Geo. W. Curtis
S. Howe,		James F. Clarke
E. Howe,		↑Francis↓ Child
Longfellow,		Dr Asa Gray
Lowell,		James T. Fields
		John Weiss
		Martin Brimmer
		Geo[rge]. T[homas] Davis
		15

[155] We regretted much the absence of Mr Bryant, & J. G. Whittier, Edward Everett, & William Hunt; who had at first accepted our invitations, but were prevented at last;—and of Hawthorne, Dana, Sumner, Motley, & Ward,—of the Club, necessarily absent: also of Charles Sprague, & Wendell Phillips, & T. W Parsons, ⟨wh⟩and George Ticknor, who had declined our invitations.[173] William Hunt graced our hall, by sending us his full-length picture of Hamlet, a noble sketch.[174] It was a quiet & happy [156] evening filled with many good speeches, from Agassiz, who presided, [with Longfellow as *croupier,* but silent,] Dr Frothingham, Winthrop, Palfrey, White, Curtis, Hedge, Lowell, Hillard, Clarke, Governor Andrew, Hoar, Weiss, and a fine poem by Holmes, read so admirably well, that I

---

[172] Robert Charles Winthrop apparently attended without Emerson's approval. See *L,* V, 364, where Emerson wrote to James Russell Lowell, "I shall not vote for Winthrop." A vertical line in ink is drawn to the left of the third column from *"Guests"* downward to "Robt. C. Winthrop".

[173] See "Shakspeare," *W,* XI, 447.

[174] In 1864, William Morris Hunt painted a portrait of the actor Daniel E. Bandmann (see p. [138] above) as Hamlet.

could not tell whether in itself⟨,⟩ it ↑were↓ one of his best or not. The company broke up at 11.30—

[157] One of Agassiz's introductory speeches was; "Many years ago, when I was a young man, I was introduced to a very estimable lady in Paris, who, in the conversation said to me, that she wondered how a man of sense could spend his days in dissecting a fish. I replied, 'Madam, if I could live by a brook which had plenty of gudgeons, I should ask nothing better than to spend all my life there.' But, since I have been in this country, I have become acquainted with a club, in which I meet men of various talents; one man of profound scholarship in the languages; one of elegant literature; or a high mystic poet; or one man of large experience in the conduct of affairs; one who teaches the blind to see, and, I confess, that I have enlarged my views of life; & I think, that, besides a brook full of gudgeons, I should wish to meet once a month such a society of friends."

[158] The only safe topic for an American meeting an Englishman with whom he is una↑c↓quainted, is, France & Frenchmen, whom they can both abuse at pleasure.——
↑and Shakspeare.↓
How to say it, I know not, but I know that the point of praise of Shakspeare, is, the pure poetic power: he is the chosen closet companion,[175] who can, at any moment, ⟨& does,⟩ by incessant surpri⟨t⟩ses, work the miracle of mythologising every fact of the common life; as snow, or moonlight, or the level rays of sunrise,—lend a momentary glory to [159] ⟨a⟩ ↑every↓ pump ⟨or a⟩ ↑&↓ woodpile.

England. When ⟨a man⟩ an inventor ⟨came⟩ brought to Lord Wellington a ball-proof jacket, ⟨the Duke at once proposed that the inventor should test it on ⟨his⟩ ↑the inventor's↓ own person with a file of musketeers on the spot, which proposal was ↑promptly↓[176] declined.⟩ "Excellent," said ⟨the⟩ the Duke, "And you will allow me to test it ⟨at

---

[175] "he is . . . companion," is used in "Shakspeare," *W*, XI, 450.
[176] Added in pencil.

once⟩ on your own person by a file of musketeers on the spot." The proposal was promptly declined.

[160] When I read Shakspeare, as lately, I think the criticism & study of him to be in their infancy. The wonder grows of his long obscurity;—how could you hide the only man that ever wrote, from all men who delight in reading?—then, the courage with which, in each play, he accosts the main issue, the highest problem, never dodging the difficult or impossible, but addressing himself instantly to that,—so conscious of his secret competence; and, at once, like an aeronaut fills his balloon with a whole atmosphere of hydrogen that will carry him over Andes, if Andes be in his path.

[161] The Conservative sends for the doctor, when his child falls sick, though yesterday he ⟨knew⟩ ↑affirmed↓, in the conversation, that the doctors did not know anything. ⟨T⟩In today's exigency he reinforces[n] his faith. So in politics, he votes new subsidies to the king, and, when the Reform agitation rages, he votes la⟨r⟩rger sup⟨li⟩plies to the Government,—going it blind, as boys say. The Reformer believes that there is no evil coming from change, which a deeper thought cannot correct.

[162] We said, that ours was the recuperative age. Pascal is one of its recoveries, not only the Essay on Love, but the pure text of the *Pensées*.

———

See on the point of Renaissance or Recuperation *NY* 78

———

[16⟨2⟩3] Shakspeare puts us all out. No theory will account for him. He neglected his ⟨books⟩ works. ⟨but⟩ Perchance[n] he did not know their value? Aye, but he did; witness the sonnets.
He went into company as a listener, hiding himself, ↑ὸ δ'ᾔιε↓ νυκτι εοικως.[177] Was only remembered by all as a delightful companion. Alcott thinks "he was rhetorician, but did not propound new

[177] " . . . and his coming was like the night." Homer, *Iliad*, I, 47.

thoughts."—a⟨h⟩ye, he was rhetorician, as was never one before, but also had more thoughts than ever any had.

[164] Say first, the greatest master of language, who could say the thing finer, nearer to the purity of thought itself, than any other; and with ⟨a⟩the security of children playing, who talk without knowing it. ↑[and, to this point, what can Carlyle mean by saying what he does of Voltaire's s⟨p⟩uperiority to all men in speech.

        Life of Frederic IV. p. 382]↓[178]

I admire his wealth. I watch him when he begins a play, to see what simple & directest means he uses; never consulting his ease, never, in the way of common [165] artists, putting us off with ceremonies or declamations; but, at once addressing himself to the noblest solution of the problem, having the gods, & the course of human life in view.

The wonder of his obscurity ↑in his life-time↓ is to be explained by the egotism of literary men.[179] To me the obscurity of Alcott is a like wonder.

                    ↑Pub. & Priv. Education↓

Shakspeare should be the[n] study of the University. In Florence [166] Boccacio was appointed to lecture on Dante. But in ↑English↓ Oxford, or in Harvard College, I have never heard of a Shakspeare Professorship. Yet the students should be educated not only in the intelligence ↑of↓ but in the sympathy with the thought of great poets.[180]

The *Sonnets* intimate the old Aristotelian Culture, & a poetic Culture that we do not easily understand whence it came,—[167] smacks of the Middle Ages, & Parliaments of love & poesy, (and I should say, that the string of poems prefixed to Ben Jonson's or Beaumont & Fletcher's plays, by their friends, are more seriously-thought than the pieces which would now in England or America be contributed to ⟨the⟩ ↑any call of↓ liter⟨ature⟩ary ⟨of⟩ friendship.) And yet if

---

[178] *History of Friedrich II of Prussia, Called Frederick the Great,* 6 vols. (London, 1858–1865). Emerson wrote to Carlyle in September 1864, "I had received in July . . . the fourth volume of 'Friedrich,' and it was my best reading in the summer, & for weeks my only reading." See *CEC,* p. 540.

[179] With this sentence, cf. "Shakspeare," *W,* XI, 451, and p. [160] above.

[180] "Shakspeare should . . . poets.", struck through in pencil with single vertical use marks on pp. [165] and [166], is used in "Public and Private Education," in Gohdes, *Uncollected Lectures,* 1932, p. 14. With "Shakspeare should . . . University.", cf. also "Shakspeare," *W,* XI, 451. "Pub. & Priv. Education" is added in pencil.

Whittier, Holmes, Lowell, Channing, Thoreau, Bryant, Sanborn, ↑Wasson,↓[181] Julia Howe, had each made [168] their thoughtful contribution, there might be good reading.

———

I must say that in reading the plays, I am a little shy where I begin; for the interest of the story is sadly in the way of poetry. It is safer therefore to read the play backwards.

To know the beauty of Shakspeare's level tone, one should read a few passages of what passes for good tragedy in ⟨t|| . . . ||⟩other writers, & then try the opening of "Merchant of Venice," Antonio's first speech—

[169] I am inquisitive of all possible knowledge concerning Shakspeare, & of all opinions: yet how few valuable⟨,⟩ criticisms, how few opinions I treasure!—How few besides my own! And each thoughtful reader, doubtless, has the like experience.
Saint Beuve speaks wisely of the *morale* of Homer, in *"Portraits*" Contemporains," Vol. 3, p. 434——[182]

[170] Physiology of Taste were a good subject for a lecture.[183] My epicure should ⟨have⟩sow marjoram in his beds, if it were only to see with eyes the buds: and his windows should look into great gardens.

My physiology, too, would in every point put the real against the showy; as, to live in the country, & not in town; to wear shoddy & ⟨& not broadcloth⟩old shoes; to have⟨;⟩ not a fine horse, but an old Dobbin ⟨that would⟩ ↑with only life enough to↓ drag a Jersey wagon ⟨to the woods⟩ to Conantum, or Estabrook,[184] & there stand ⟨a⟩contented [171] for half a day ⟨in⟩at a tree, whilst I ⟨am⟩ forget him in the woods

[181] David Atwood Wasson (1823–1887), clergyman and author.

[182] Emerson borrowed an unspecified volume or volumes of *Portraits Contemporains,* 3 vols. (Paris, 1852), from the Boston Athenaeum August 3–September 16, 1863; volume 3 was borrowed April 12–May 30, 1864.

[183] See *JMN,* VI, 363, and XIV, 144. Jean Anthelme Brillat-Savarin's *Physiologie du goût; ou Méditations de gastronomie . . .* (Paris, 1853) is in Emerson's library.

[184] Conantum is about two miles south, and Estabrook Farm about two miles north, of Concord center.

& pastures; (as, in England the point is not to make strong beer, but beer weak enough to permit a great deal to be drunk in hot weather; as Mr Flower explained to me at Stratford.)[185]

[172] The intellect is alike old in the father & in his child. We old ⟨boobies⟩ ↑fellows↓ affect a great deal of reticence with the young people, but their wit cannot wait for us. Mrs G⟨reeley⟩ explained to me that her children, (one was 14 years,) did not know what beef was: she had never allowed them to know that sheep & oxen were killed for our food. But my children knew that her children [173] knew as much as they. Plutarch would ⟨make⟩ ↑use↓ great precautions in young people's reading of the poets; & Plato also.[n] But when young & old see "Faust" on the stage, or "Midsummer Night's Dream," or read them in the closet, they come ↑silently↓ to the same conclusions. No age to intellect.[186]

[174] The ⟨War⟩ Cannon will not suffer any other sound to be heard for miles & for years around it. Our chronology has ⟨got⟩ lost all old distinctions in one date,—*Before the War, and Since.*

[175] It is hard to remember in glancing over our sumptuous library-editions & excellent pocket-editions of Chaucer, that for ⟨200⟩ ↑100↓ years these works existed only in manuscripts, accumulating errors & false readings in every individual copy of every new transcriber. 'Tis alarming to reckon the risks, & judge of the damage done.
Chaucer b. 1328   died 1400. Caxton's first book printed in England 1474
Chaucer printed (   )[187]

[176] A ⟨you⟩journalist in London or in New York acquires a facility & élan which throws the slow elaborators for the Edinburgh &

---

[185] Edward Fordham Flower, whom Emerson had visited in July 1848; see *JMN*, X, 427. With "to live . . . weather;", cf. "Resources," in Gohdes, *Uncollected Lectures*, 1932, p. 27.
[186] With this phrase, cf. "Old Age," *W*, VII, 317.
[187] "Chaucer b. . . . printed (   )" is in pencil. "⟨200⟩" is circled in pencil.

the North American into the shade. Thus this lively article "Schopenhauer," in the "N. Y. Commercial Advertiser" of May 13, eclipses
Hedge's learned paper in the "Examiner".[n188]
Schopenhauer said of chaste persons, "they are thorns which produce
roses." He said, "An impersonal God is a word void of sense, invented
by professors of philosophy, to satisfy fools & hackdrivers."—"My
great discovery, is, to show how, at the [177] bottom of all things,
there is only one identical ⟨law⟩force, always equal, & ever the same,
which slumbers in plants, awakens in animals, but finds its consciousness only in man—the Will."—'That is, (continues the journalist,) the
world which we all /⟨see⟩imagine/believe/ we see, is only a phenome-
nal world: above it, but[189] at a tremendous distance, we find the real
world, & this real world is the will. Between these two, he places a
kind of [178] plastic mediator, which he calls *ideas.*'—
    But, it seems, Schopenhauer, ⟨was⟩ in his youth, learned S⟨c⟩an-
scrit, & learned ⟨the⟩ his secret of the Buddhists. "De tribus impos-
toribus" means Fichte, Schelling, & Hegel.[190]

[179] It is, I own, difficult not to be intemperate in speaking of
Shakspeare; ⟨I own that to me he⟩ and most difficult, ⟨to those who are⟩
I should say, to the best readers. ⟨⟨Few and⟩And this, because⟩ Few,[n] ↑I
think none,↓ arrive at any intelligence of his methods. His intellect
does not ⟨j⟩ emit jets of light, ↑at intervals,↓ but is incessant, always
equal to the occasion, [180] & addressing with equal readiness a
comic, an ingenious, or a sublime problem. I find him an exceptional
genius. If the world were on trial, it is the perfect success of this one
man that might justify such expenditure of geology, ⟨fauna⟩ chemistry,
fauna, & flora, as the world was. And, I suppose, if Intellect per-
ceives[n][181] & converses "in climes beyond the solar road,"[191] they
probably call this planet, not Earth, but "⟨the⟩ *Shakspeare*↑.↓ ⟨House.⟩"

[188] Emerson pasted a clipping of this newspaper article, entitled "Buddhism in Europe. Schopenhauer.", in Notebook PH, pp. [228]–[231], and inscribed it "NY Com.
Adv. *Apr* May ↑13↓". For Frederic Henry Hedge's paper, see "Arthur Schopenhauer,"
Christian Examiner, LXXVI (Jan. 1864), 46–80.
[189] "⟨see⟩imagine" and "but" are circled in ink.
[190] "Of three impostors" (Ed.). "Schopenhauer said . . . Hegel." is partly quoted,
partly paraphrased from the New York *Commercial Advertiser* article mentioned above.
[191] Thomas Gray, "The Progress of Poesy," l. 54.

In teleology, they will come to say, that the final cause of the creation of the Earth was Shakspeare,

[182] Alcott said in speaking of children, "I think a son translates the privacy of the family to the public: daughters cannot do it."

Michel Angelo's Third Sonnet.
> The power of a beautiful face lifts me to heaven
> Since else in earth is none that delights me
> And I mount living among the elect souls,
> A grace which seldom falls to a mortal.
>
> So well with its Maker the work consents,
> That I rise to him through divine conceptions
> And here I shape all thoughts & words,
> Burning, loving, through this gentle form:
>
> Whence, if ever from ⟨the⟩ two beautiful eyes
> I know not how to turn my look, I know in them
> The light which shows me the way which guides me to God.
>
> And if, kindled at their light, I burn,
> In my noble flame sweetly shines
> The eternal joy which smiles in heaven.

[183] For a fraction of each class, say, twenty,—(though I think that is too many) in a class of ↑more than↓ a hundred, the whole class is oppressed ⟨with⟩ by a ⟨mathemat⟩ course of mathematics, which is a perpetual fatigue, costing frequently, I am told, 5 or 6 hours for the learning the daily lesson, & that imperfectly, and thus bereaving the student of his necessary outdoor exercise. Add to this, that, at short intervals, occur the mathematical examinations, which are ⟨severe⟩ serious, really testing the knowledge which the student has acquired [184] in the foregoing weeks. The Professor is impartial, & resolved to know the proficiency of each pupil. ⟨A⟩ ↑The↓ few good mathematicians easily ⟨perform⟩ ↑do↓ their ⟨problems⟩ ↑work↓, & leave the room, which remains occupied for five or six hours by the rest, who perform in all that time only a part of the work, & retire exhausted & unhappy.

The young men are not thus worked with impunity. They lose ⟨their⟩ flesh, ⟨th⟩ vigor & spirit. The college, which should be to them a place of delightful [185] labor, where their faculties are invited out to studies useful & agreeable to them, is made ⟨an⟩ odious & unhealthy, and they are tempted to frivolous amusements to rally their jaded spirits. It would be better, ↑no doubt,↓ if they had good teachers. But, in the experience of colleges, it is found, that whilst good mathematicians are rare, good teachers of mathematics are much more rare. It has happened that two or three female teachers in our schools have ⟨shown⟩ had great success [186] & that in the college, ⟨t⟩ *men* ↑geometers & analysts↓ of unquestionable ability ⟨as geometers & analysts⟩, utterly fail in the power to ⟨lead the willing student⟩ impart their methods to the willing student. All the ⟨kn⟩ aid the student gets is from ⟨his classmate⟩ ↑some chum↓ who has a little more knowledge than he, & knows where the ⟨doubt⟩ difficulty he has just surmounted lay. I have just seen four of the↑se skeleton↓ sufferers, to whom all the studies in the University are sufficiently attractive, [187] *excepting the mathematics,* & who find this (which they do not wish to acquire,) thrust into absurd eminence,—absorbing nominally one third of the academic time in the two first years, &, practically, often two thirds, a dead weight on the mind & heart of the pupil, to be utterly renounced & forgotten the moment he is left to the election of his studies, & a painful memory of wasted years & injured constitution, as long as he lives. [188] Languages, Rhetoric, Logic, Ethics, Intellectual Philosophy, Poetry, Natural History, Civil History, Political Economy, Technology, Chemistry, Agriculture, Literary History, as, the genius of Homer, Dante, Shakspeare, & Goethe; Music & Drawing, even,—all these may rightly enter into the curriculum, as well as Mathematics. But it were to hurt the University, if any one of these should absorb a disproportionate share of time. The European Universities gave a like [189] supreme emphasis to the subtleties of logic in the days of Ockham, to Theology, when the priesthood controlled education. ⟨to fit⟩ Until recently, Natural Science was almost excluded, and it is inevitable that a man of genius with a good deal of general power will ⟨at any time⟩ ↑for a long period↓ give a bias ⟨to⟩ in his direction to a University. ⟨But⟩ And that is a public mischief which the guardians of a college are there to watch & counterpoise. [190] In the election of a

58

President, it is not only the students who are to be controlled, but the Professors, each of which ↑in proportion to his talent↓ is^n a ⟨violent⟩ usurper who needs to be resisted.[192]

[19⟨2⟩1] Yesterday, 23 May, we buried Hawthorne in Sleepy Hollow, in a pomp of sunshine & verdure, & gentle winds. James F. Clarke read the service in the Church & at the grave. Longfellow, Lowell, Holmes, Agassiz, Hoar, Dwight, Whipple, Norton, Alcott, Hillard, Fields, Judge Thomas,[193] & I, attended the hearse as pall bearers. Franklin Pierce was with the family. The church was copiously decorated with white flowers delicately arranged.^{n} The corpse was [192] unwillingly shown,—only a few moments to this company of his friends. But it was noble & serene in its aspect,—nothing amiss,—a calm & powerful head. A large company filled the church, & the grounds of the cemetery.   ⟨Everything⟩ ⟨His death is⟩All was^n so bright & quiet, that pain or mourning was hardly suggested, & Holmes said to me, that it looked like a happy meeting.

[193][194] ⟨But⟩Clarke in the church said, that, Hawthorne had done more justice than any other to the shades of life, shown a sympathy with the crime in our nature, &, like Jesus, was the friend of sinners.
I thought there was a tragic element in the event, that might be more fully rendered⟨.⟩↑,—↓in the painful solitude of the man,↑—↓which, I suppose, could not longer be endured, & he died of it.
I have found in his death a ⟨painful⟩ surprise & dis[ap]pointment.^{n}
[194][195] I thought him a greater man than any of his works betray,

[192] Pages [183], [185], [186], and [189] are struck through in pencil with single diagonal use marks, and pp. [184], [187], [188], and [190] with single vertical use marks; "to Theology . . . excluded," on p. [189] is also struck through in pencil with a vertical use mark. For the entire passage, see "Public and Private Education," in Gohdes, *Uncollected Lectures*, 1932, p. 10.

[193] Probably Benjamin Franklin Thomas (1813–1878), judge of the Massachusetts Supreme Court.

[194] On p. [193], the added punctuation is in pencil, and "painful" is canceled in pencil.

[195] On p. [194], "&" and "he would that" are canceled first in ink, then in pencil; "great" and "to me" are canceled in pencil; "frequent &" on p. [195] is canceled in both pencil and ink. On p. [196], "with me" and "to be sure," are canceled in pencil; "most" is canceled in both pencil and ink.

⟨&⟩ that ⟨he would that⟩ there was still a great deal of work in him, & that he might one day show a purer power.

Moreover I have felt sure of him in his neighborhood, & ⟨that the⟩ ↑in his↓ necessities of sympathy & intelligence,—that I could well wait his time,—his unwillingness & caprice,—and might one day conquer a friendship. It would have been a ⟨great⟩ happiness ⟨to me⟩, doubtless to [195]¹⁹⁶ both of us, to have come into habits of ⟨frequent &⟩ unreserved intercourse. It was easy to talk with him,↑—↓there were no barriers;—only, he said so little, that I talked too much, & stopped only because,—as he gave no indications,—⟨I suspected⟩ I ⟨might⟩ ↑feared to↓ exceed. He showed no egotism or self-assertion, rather a humility, &, at one time↑,↓ a fear that he had written himself out.— One day, when I found him on the top of his hill, in the woods, he paced back [196] ⟨with me⟩ the path to his house, & said, *"this path is the only ⟨th⟩remembrance of me that will remain."* Now it appears that I waited too long.

Lately, ⟨to be sure,⟩ he had removed himself the more by the indignation his perverse politics & ⟨most⟩ unfortunate friendship for that paltry Franklin Pierce awaked,—though it rather moved pity [197] for Hawthorne, & the assured belief that he would outlive it, & come right at last.

————

I have forgotten in what year, (↑Sept. 27, 1842,↓), but it was whilst he lived in the Manse, soon after his marriage, that I said to him, "I shall never see you in this hazardous way; we must take a long walk together. Will you go to Harvard & visit the Shakers?" He agreed, & we took a June [198] day, & walked the twelve miles, got our dinner from the Brethren, slept at the Harvard Inn, & returned home ↑by another road↓ the next day. It was a ⟨very⟩ satisfactory tramp⟨,⟩; ⟨&, I remember,⟩ we had good talk on the way, of which I set down some record in my journal.¹⁹⁷

[199] "The Nineteenth Century is an ⟨a⟩Age of progress, & every

———

¹⁹⁶ The added punctuation on p. [195] is in pencil.

¹⁹⁷ "by another road" and the semicolon after "tramp⟨,⟩" are added in pencil; "very" and "&, I remember," are canceled in ink and pencil. For an account of Emerson's walk with Hawthorne, see *JMN*, VIII, 271–275.

one soon will be in his right place." *London "Reader."* 14 May, 1864

———

Reginald ⟨E⟩Taylor, a child of six years, was carried to see his mother's kinsman, President Day.[198] ⟨Th⟩On his return home, he said, "Mother, I think that old man loves God too much. You know I say my prayers when I go to bed: well he talks just so all the time."

———

It is said, that, in the Western courts, ⟨the⟩ it is a rule, that, "a town is a place where they sell whisky."[199]

———

[200] America shall introduce ⟨a⟩ pure religion. Ethics are thought not ⟨not⟩ to satisfy affection. But all the religion we have is the Ethics of one or another holy person. As soon as character appears ↑in the man,↓ be sure love will, & veneration, & anecdotes & fables about ⟨↑the↓⟩ him, & delight of good men & women in him. And, if we think what deeps of grandeur & beauty are known to us in Ethical [201] truth, the divination or insight that belongs to it;—for innocence is a wonderful electuary for purging the eyes to search the natures of those souls th⟨ey⟩at pass before ⟨them⟩ ↑it↓; ⟨the⟩ ↑what↓ armor ⟨that⟩ it is to protect ⟨the good⟩[n] from outward or inward harm, & ⟨the⟩ ↑with what↓ power ⟨with which⟩ it converts evil accidents into benefits to ⟨them⟩ good m⟨an⟩en; the power of its countenance, the power of its presence;—to it alone comes true friendship; to it comes grandeur of situation[n] [202] & poetic perception enriching all it deals with⟨.⟩,—& irresistable moral power⟨.⟩ to suffer & to act.[200]

[203][201] War is the father of all things. [DL 10]
New Chronology of the Cannon. *DL* 174
⟨war appointed its own generals⟩
The war appointed the generals. KL 107

[198] Probably Jeremiah Day (1773–1867), president of Yale University 1817–1846.
[199] See "Table-Talk," in Gohdes, *Uncollected Lectures*, 1932, p. 36.
[200] "America shall . . . deals with⟨.⟩," struck through in pencil with single vertical use marks on pp. [200], [201], and [202], is used in "The Sovereignty of Ethics," *W*, X, 212–213. A vertical line in pencil is drawn in the left margin of p. [200] beside "America shall . . . affection." "the good" on p. [201] is canceled and bracketed in pencil.
[201] Pages [203]–[204] are probably a collection for "Harvard Commemoration Speech, July 21, 1865," *W*, XI, 341–345.

has lifted ⟨more peop⟩ many other people besides Grant & Sherman into their true places
Every nation punishes the general who has not been victorious.

[KL 99]

―――

These dedicated men, who knew on what duty they went, & whose fathers & mothers said, "We gave him up when he enlisted."[202]

―――

Even the prisoner starved to death rendered a service to his country.

KL 165

―――

And sung the mass of cannon from morning until night   [VS 161]

―――

Camps are wandering cities.[203]   WAR 3.

―――

Fama bella stant[204]

―――

Speech to returning company   WAR 174, FOR 65,

―――

They who come today to his funeral, tomorrow will tread in his warpath, & show to his slayers the way to death.   WAR 239

―――

Cards beat the players, & Revolutions beat all the insurgents

WAR 242[205]

[202] "War is . . . things." and "The War . . . enlisted.' ", struck through in ink with single diagonal use marks, are used in "Harvard Commemoration Speech, July 21, 1865," W, XI, 341–342 and 344. "a" is written and a vertical line is drawn in ink in the left margin beside "The war . . . true places"; "The war . . . victorious." and "These dedicated . . . enlisted.' " are also struck through in ink with single vertical use marks.

[203] "And sung . . . cities." is struck through in ink with a vertical use mark. "And sung . . . night" is used in "Harvard Commemoration Speech, July 21, 1865," W, XI, 344. "Camps are . . . cities." is used in "Address at the Dedication of the Soldiers' Monument in Concord, April 19, 1867," W, XI, 355.

[204] "Wars depend upon reputation." Emerson's source is probably Joseph François Michaud et Jean-Joseph-François Poujoulat, Nouvelle Collection des mémoires relatifs à l'histoire de France, 34 vols. (Paris, 1854), I, 526, where it is misquoted from Quintus Curtius in this form.

[205] The passages cited in Journal WAR, p. [174], and FOR, p. [65], and "They who . . . insurgents", struck through in ink with a diagonal use mark, are used in "Harvard Commemoration Speech, July 21, 1865," W, XI, 342–343, 344, and 342. "a" is written and a short vertical line is drawn in ink in the left margin beside "Cards beat . . . insurgents"; for "Cards beat the players," see JMN, IX, 89 and XII, 543.

"War exalts the age, &, when it is over, the dead & the living stand exalted in the world because they had not cared for life."

$Titan.^{206}$

[204] Experience uniform that the gentle soul makes the firm hero after all, &, in fact, the record of the troops on the whole is nobly honorable through the war. *FOR* 65

Principe de guerre, que, lorsqu'on peut se servir de la foudre, il la faut préférer au canon. *Napoleon*

America has a fist that will knock down an empire.

Enthusiasm[207]

The South said "↑We will↓ Rule or Ruin." They ruled & ↑were↓ ruined.

[205] [blank]

[206] In Boston what is the use of calling a ⟨public⟩ meeting in Faneuil Hall to consider Reconstruction, & appointing a sentimentalist like Theophilus Parsons to preside, who calls upon George B. Loring to make a speech?[208]

Benefits of War.   War heals a deeper wound than any it makes. It

[206] Jean Paul Friedrich Richter, *Titan, a Romance*, 2 vols. (Boston, 1862), II, 256 and 206; in Emerson's library. " 'War . . . age," struck through in ink with a diagonal use mark, is used in "Address at the Dedication of the Soldiers' Monument in Concord, April 19, 1867," *W*, XI, 351; cf. also "The Man of Letters," *W*, X, 257. See also Journal WAR, front cover verso; VA, p. [277]; and FOR, p. [50] below.

[207] "Experience uniform . . . Enthusiasm", struck through in ink with two vertical use marks, is used in "Harvard Commemoration Speech, July 21, 1865," *W*, XI, 342–344. "b" is written and single vertical lines are drawn in ink in the left margin beside the French quotation and "Enthusiasm". See also Journal FOR, p. [241] below, for the quotation, which is from Sainte-Beuve's review of "Campagnes d'Egypte et de Syrie, par Napoléon" in volume I of *Causeries du lundi*, 1852–1861.

[208] George Bailey Loring (1817–1891), a Salem physician, agriculturist, and political leader, had lectured in Concord in 1854. Theophilus Parsons (1797–1882) was a Boston jurist and a Swedenborgian.

heals skepticism, unbelief, the frivolous mind which is the spoiled child of a ⟨frivolous philosophy⟩great material prosperity.

&c &c see   Lecture on American Nationality[209]

[207]   *Benefits of* the War.
The disinfectants.   *VA* 118
Power of ideas in the War.   VA 225

We see the dawn of a new era, worth to mankind all the treasure & all the lives it has cost, yes, worth to the world the lives of all this generation of American men, if they had been demanded.[210]

It is commonly said of the War of 1812, that it made the nation honorably known: it enlarged [208] our politics, extinguished narrow sectional parties.

But the States were young & unpeopled. The present war, on a prodigiously enlarged scale, has cost us how many valuable lives; but it has made many lives valuable that were not so before, through the start & expansion it has given. It has fired ⟨ol⟩selfish old men [209] to an incredible liberality, & young men to the last devotion. The journals say, it has demoralized many rebel regiments, but also it has *moralized* many of our regiments, & not only so, but *moralized* cities & states. It added to every house & heart a vast enlargement. In every house & shop, an American map has been unrolled, & daily studied,—& now that peace [210] has come, every citizen finds himself a skilled student of the condition, means, & future, of this continent.[211]

---

[209] "War heals . . . prosperity." is used in the lecture "American Nationality," first delivered on November 12, 1861, at the Music Hall in Boston; see Cabot's abstract of the lecture in *A Memoir of Ralph Waldo Emerson,* 2 vols. (Boston, 1887), II, 783. See also Journal VA, p. [246], and FOR, p. [48] below.

[210] "We see . . . demanded." is used in "Harvard Commemoration Speech, July 21, 1865," *W,* XI, 345.

[211] "The present . . . continent." is used in "Public and Private Education," in Gohdes, *Uncollected Lectures,* 1932, p. 5.

We will not again disparage America, now that we have seen what men it will bear. *Waterville* 184
Nature's Home-Guard[212]

The War is a new glass through which to see things.[213]

[211] Our success sure; its roots in poverty, Calvinism, schools, farms, thrift, snow, & east wind.

———

The war has made the Divine Providence credible to a good many people. ↑They did not believe that Heaven was quite honest.↓[214]

———

I think it a singular & marked result, that it has established a conviction in so many minds that the right will get done; has established a chronic hope for a chronic despair.

———

This victory the most decisive. This will stay put. It will show ⟨y‖ . . . ‖⟩ⁿ ↑your↓ enem⟨y⟩ies ⟨of⟩ that what has now been so well done will be surely better & quicker done, if need be, [212] again.

Elemental men, influences, not made for ballrooms, ⟨with a⟩ ↑men whose↓ⁿ silence more signifies than all your eloquence.

———

— ⟨he says eloquence, but the rogue means loquacity.⟩

———

America. ⟨t⟩The irresistible convictions of men are sometimes as well expressed by braggart lips, or in jeers ⟨a⟩that sound blasphemous,—& that word "manifest destiny," which is profanely used, signifies the

---

[212] This entry is struck through in pencil and ink with single diagonal use marks. "We will . . . bear." is used in "Harvard Commemoration Speech, July 21, 1865," *W*, XI, 345, and in "The Man of Letters," *W*, X, 257; see p. [102] above. The latter essay is part of an address that Emerson gave on August 11, 1863, at Waterville College in Maine.

[213] See p. [103] above.

[214] "The war . . . honest.", struck through in ink with three vertical use marks, is used in "Address at the Dedication of the Soldiers' Monument in Concord, April 19, 1867," *W*, XI, 354.

sense all men have of the prodigious [213] energy & opportunity lying idle here. The poor Prussian or Austrian or Italian escaping hereto, discovers that he has been handcuffed & fettered & fast-⟨bound⟩tied all his lifetime, with monopolies, & duties at every toll-gate on his little cart of corn or wine or straw, or on his cow or ox or donkey, & padlocked lips, padlocked mind, no country, no education, no vote,—↑but↓ passports, police, monks, & foreign soldiers.

[214]   *Loci*   23 July
For Williamstown.[215]

returns the eternal topic the praise of intellect. I gain my point, gain all points, whenever I can reach the young man with any statement which teaches him his own worth. Thus, if I can touch his imagination, I serve him: he will never forget ⟨t⟩it. If I can open to him for a moment the superiority of knowledge to wealth or physical power.[n] Especially works on me at all times any statement of Realism, &, old as my [215] habit is of thrumming on this string, I must continue to try it, till, ⟨I⟩ in a manlier or a divine hour, I can see the truth, & say it. The ⟨sense⟩ ↑sum↓ of it is, ⟨No time⟩ the time is never lost that is devoted to work. If you are well at work on your design, you can well afford not to have customers for the present.[n] (See *supra* p. 19.)[216]
See ⟨E⟩Lecture on "Genius."
    Conduct of Intellect.

I will say to them, that there is no age to Intellect:[217] that, if they read Plato at 20, or at 60 years, the impression is about equal.

[216] ——
If not by genius, then by sympathy.

------

[215] Emerson addressed the Society of the Adelphi at Williams College on July 31, 1865. See p. [218] below.
[216] "I gain . . . worth." on p. [214], struck through in ink with five vertical use marks, and "The ⟨sense⟩ sum . . . present." on p. [215], struck through in ink with four vertical use marks, are used in "Success," *W*, VII, 294.
[217] See p. [173] above. For a summary of Emerson's lecture "Conduct of Intellect," see Cabot, *A Memoir . . .* , 1887–1888, II, 795.

The truth is in the minorities.   ↑Michel Angelo was the conscience
Affirm & affirm.   of Italy. *DL* 236↓

You must be somebody.[218]

The Examiners.

Then the doctrine of the use of low style in the Essay on Criticism.[219]

Imagination,—it is as if one opened the doors of the day, & showed
me new horizons beyond my own.[220]
The primary use of a fact is of petty account: the secondary use as it is
a figure or illustration of my thought, is the real value. First the fact:
second, its impression, or what I think of it.[221]

[217] ⟨Nationality⟩

There has been much instruction lately, I think, in several biographies,
to the point of character *versus* intellect. Thus Goethe, in his correspondence with his Grand duke of Weimar, does not shine. I have not
read the letters, but saw that the Prince had the advantage of the
Olympian genius.ⁿ Certainly it is so in the correspondence between
Voltaire & Friedrich of Prussia. Voltaire is brilliant, nimble, & various,
but Frederick has the superior tone. ↑Byron writes down to Scott:
Scott writes up to him.↓[222]

[⟨278⟩ 218]   Address at Williamstown
Loci   July 31, 1865.
Power of Books   ———————————

---

[218] For "If not . . . minorities." and "Affirm & affirm.", see p. [107] above. For
"You must be somebody.", see *JMN*, XIV, 256.
  [219] See "Art and Criticism," *W*, XII, 283–305.
  [220] A vertical line in pencil is drawn in the left margin beside "Imagination,—it . . .
own."
  [221] "The primary . . . it.", struck through in pencil with a vertical use mark, is used
in "Poetry and Imagination," *W*, VIII, 11.
  [222] "Thus Goethe . . . him.", struck through in pencil with a vertical use mark, is
used in "Greatness," *W*, VIII, 317–318.

To wake the *Imagination*[223]
Reality. Be somebody.[224] Michel Angelo's rule.
⟨Then write on oath⟩Bias of each mind is new, & you shall write only that which you were created to write or say.[225]
Write on oath.
What Inspiration is.

Then the new audience of the Third Estate requires a more catholic speech, and you must use the *low tone.*
All great writers have this.
Then *Compression.*[226]
Then *affirmatives.* Write only affirmatives. Omit the negations.

[219] But there are higher rules & respects. ⟨Character.⟩
Sensibility better than talent.[227] If you have only sympathy, you cannot be spared.
Then, *Character.*
⟨F⟩To find your joy not in ⟨success⟩a popular success, but in excellence of the work.
⟨G⟩Correspondence of Goethe with Grand^n Duke of Weimar.
Marcus Aurelius.

[220] [blank]
[221] It occurred the other day with a force not now retained, that the advocate of the good cause finds a wealth of arguments & illustrations on his way. He stands for truth, & Truth & Nature help him unexpectedly & irresistibly at every step. All the felicities of example, of imagery, of admirable poetry, old religion, new thought, the analogies of Science, ⟨all are his allies,⟩ ↑throng to him↓ & strengthen his position. Nay, when we had to [222] praise John Brown of ⟨|| . . . ||⟩Ossawotomie, I remember ⟨that⟩ what a multitude of fine

---

[223] See "Address at the Opening of the Concord Free Public Library," *W*, XI, 508.
[224] See p. [216] above.
[225] With "you shall . . . say.", cf. *JMN*, IV, 433, a quotation from Augustus and Julius Hare, *Guesses at Truth*, 2 vols. (London, 1827), I, 248.
[226] With "Then the . . . *low tone.*" and "*Compression.*", cf. "Art and Criticism," *W*, XII, 283–284 and 290.
[227] See "Success," *W*, VII, 295, and *JMN*, XIV, 264.

verses of old poetry fitted him exactly, & appeared to have been pro-
phetically written for the occasion.

[223] [blank]
    [224] ⟨The⟩My Bohemian had for his maxim, that he might &
would do as he had a mind to, in Paris, or out of it: 'for,' he said, 'look
at Rousseau & Voltaire, & see, that every kind of ⟨|| . . . ||⟩meanness &
mischief is forgiven to intellect.' ' 'Tis a small game that I play,' he
said, 'but I like it. I have no loss & no disaster that is not consoled, if I
can write a good page.'[228]

[225] Parsons effectively renders Dante's "Euclide geomêtra,"
earth-measuring Euclid, and "l'buono accoglitor del quale Dioscoride"
"Dioscorides
good herbalist that was."[229]

When I ask Ellen if she has made out what "the leopard," what
"the wolf," and what "Lucia," in the *"Inferno,"* [Cantos I and II] signify? she says "No, & I do not wish to: To me they mean leopard,
wolf, & Lucia, & any second [226] & interior meaning would spoil all
for me."[230]

The asteroids are chips of the old star[.][231]

⟨|| . . . ||⟩*Entsagen.*[232]
One drug needs another drug to expel it,—if feasts, then wine; after
wine, coffee; & after coffee, tobacco: if Vanity, then pride; if anger,

---

[228] Emerson turned double quotation marks into single throughout this paragraph by
canceling one of each pair in ink. With "every kind . . . page.' ", cf. "Powers and Laws of
Thought," *W,* XII, 57.
    [229] For *"earth-measuring Euclid,"* and " 'Dioscorides . . . was.' ", see canto IV in
Seventeen Cantos of the Inferno, trans. T. W. Parsons (Boston, 1865), p. 25; in Emerson's
library.
    [230] With this account of Emerson's daughter Ellen, cf. "Poetry and Imagination,"
W, VIII, 12.
    [231] This sentence, struck through in ink with six vertical use marks, is used in
"Progress of Culture," *W,* VIII, 224.
    [232] See *JMN,* IV, 301, and XI, 131.

then war, sword & musket. But Temperance is strength, & [227] Essence is religion. To Be is to live with God.

———

Miss Peabody tells me, that Jones Very, one day, said to her; "To the pre-existent Shakspeare wisdom was offered, but he declined it, & took only genius."

———

I have transcribed the whole passage, however, long ago.

[228] Therienism.[233]

Enfant du peuple. That fair, large, sound, wholesome youth or maid whom we pick out in a whole street full of passengers as a model of native strength, is not to be raised by rule in schools or gymnasia. It is the Vermont or New Hampshire farm, &-a series of farmers laboring on mountain & moor, that produced this rare result. ⟨He brings to the city a constitution⟩ When a good head for ciphering, trade, & affairs is turned out, he drifts to the city counting-room, or perhaps [229] to the law-school, & brings thither a constitution able to supply resources to all the demand made on him, & easily goes ahead of all competitors, has a firm will, cool head, &↑, in the sequel,↓ plants a family which becomes marked through two or three generations for force & beauty, until ⟨ease & wealth⟩ ↑luxury↓ corrupts them, ⟨&⟩as it had destroyed those whom they displaced.

[230][234] "Her turn for poetry was treated as a secret disease" "truth itself was refracted in her mouth."

G.S. of Publishers' Circular.

———

lieux   "Mt. Hymetta's Bee"

"Pas de zèle et beaucoup de diners."
"poisonous malaria, the strange & fatal wind'"[n] began to blow.[235]
Her

———

[233] Alek Therien was the French-Canadian woodchopper described by Thoreau in chapter 6 of *Walden*.

[234] Page [230] is in pencil.

[235] For the five quotations above, see "Our Continental Correspondence," signed "G. S.," in the *American Literary Gazette and Publisher's Circular*, V (Aug. 1, 1865), 138

Buchner. Translation[236]

[231]   1865
Aug[us]t. 13th. A disaster of this year has been the loss of six or seven
valuable pear trees by the pear-blight. I think, in preceding years, single boughs have withered & died, but ⟨mu⟩these have not attracted
much notice; but now I cut off half ⟨a⟩ ↑of each↓ tree with its coppery
leaves & the mournful smell of the sick bark, & shall not save them so.

[23⟨0⟩2] The difference between writers is that one counts
forms, & the other counts powers. ⟨If⟩The gazetteer, in describing
Boston, reckons up the schools, the churches, & the Missionary Societies; but the poet remembers the ↑alcoves of the↓ Athenaeum,
↑⟨⟨the⟩certain books,⟩ or the Bates Library,↓ certain wise & mannered
men, certain fair women, & the ⟨joyful houses⟩ ↑⟨noble⟩ happy homes↓
in which he saw them. The friend,—he is the power that abode with
us: & the book, which made night better than day,—that may be well
counted.[237]

[23⟨1⟩3] Read some sentences yesterday in Macmillan for August (?) (⟨from⟩ ↑in↓ an article on Grote's Book on Plato,) which I
must read again;—a paper by Baine↑,↓ but of no great merit. Looked
thro' a superior article in the Quarterly Review on Carlyle's Friedrich,—a good example of the excellent criticism which in England is
always to be found, whilst poetry is so rare.[238]

Then in the Revue des D[eux]. M[ondes]. [234] found a paper
on the Future Life,[239] which suggested the thought, that one ab-

---

and 139. "Pas de zèle" is used in "Social Aims," *W*, VIII, 85; see also *JMN*, VI, 363, and
Journal FOR, p. [169] below.

[236] See p. [60] above.

[237] Three vertical lines, two in ink and one in pencil, are drawn in the left margin
beside "writers is . . . powers." One vertical line in ink is drawn in the left margin beside
"saw them. . . . counted."

[238] Two articles by Alexander Bain, on George Grote's *Plato, and the Other Companions of Sokrates*, 3 vols. (London, 1865), appear in *Macmillan's Magazine*, XII (July
1865), 193–208 and (Oct. 1865), 457–472. The review, "Carlyle's Frederic the Great,"
appears in the *Quarterly Review*, CXVIII (July 1865), 119–134. The comma after
"Baine" is added in pencil.

[239] Paul Janet, "Un Nouveau Système sur la vie future," *Revue des Deux Mondes*,
May 15, 1863, 422–436.

stains,—I abstain, for example,—from printing a chapter on the Immortality of the Soul, because, when I have come to the end of my statement, the hungry eyes that run through it will close disappointed; *That is not here which we desire:* & I shall be as much wronged by [23⟨6⟩5] their hasty conclusion, as they feel themselves by my /omissions/short-comings/. I mean, that I am a better believer, & all serious souls are better believers in the Immortality, than we give grounds for. The real evidence is too subtle, or is higher, than we can write down in propositions, & therefore Wordsworth's Ode is the best modern Essay on the subject.[240]

[2⟨23⟩36] I fear that what is called religion, but what is perhaps pew-holding, not obeys but conceals the moral sentiment.[241]

———

↑"Michel Angelo fut la conscience de l'Italie." *A. Dumesnil.*↓[242]

It is curious to see how fast old history is the counterpart of our own, as soon as we are intimately let into knowledge of it. Thus I am just now surprised by finding Michel Angelo, Vittoria Colonna, Savonarola, Contarini, Pole, Occhino, [237] & the superior souls near them to be the religious of that day, drawn to each other, & under some cloud with the rest of the world, as the Transcendentalists of 20 years ago in Boston. ⟨It⟩ They were the reformers, the Abolitionists, the radicals of the hour, separated, to be sure, by their intellectual activity & culture, from the masses who followed Luther & Savonarola, yet on their side in sympathy against the corruptions of Rome.[243]

[240] "Then in . . . des D. M." on p. [233] is struck through in ink with a diagonal use mark; pp. [234] and [235] are struck through in ink with single vertical use marks; "that one abstains . . . subject" is used in "Immortality," *W*, VIII, 345–346; "short-comings" on p. [235] is added in pencil.

[241] "I fear . . . pew-holding," is struck through in ink with a vertical use mark; the entire sentence is used in "The Preacher," *W*, X, 228.

[242] Jules Michelet, *Histoire de France,* 17 vols. (Paris, 1835–1867), VII, 391; Emerson borrowed volume 7 of the Paris, 1833–1866, edition from the Boston Athenaeum May 13–June 8 and June 30–September 4, 1865. The quotation is used in "Progress of Culture," *W*, VIII, 216; see also p. [216] above.

[243] A shortened version of "Vittoria Colonna . . . Rome." is used in "Progress of Culture," *W*, VIII, 216–217.

[23⟨4⟩8] People have been burned or stoned for saying things which are commonplaces of conversation today.[244]

↑1865↓ 24 August. Yesterday called on Forceythe Willson[245] at Cambridge, went into the city with him, to the Athenaeum & Union Club.

———

In how many people we feel the tyranny of their talent as the disposer of their activity.

In Wendell Phillips, now the "seul homme d'état in America," I feel [239] that his patriotism or his moral sentiment are not ↑primarily↓ the inspiration of his career, but this matchless talent of debate, of attack, of illustration, of statement,—this talent which was in him, & must be unfolded, that drove him, in happy hours, under most fortunately determining auspices, into the lists, where kings were to be competitors, & nations spectators.

[⟨237⟩ 240] ⟨How then⟩ Our^n best allies, from the beginning of the war until now, are still the Southerners! Our foolish good nature & facility cannot ruin us ⟨because⟩ utterly, before these people will contrive some outrage that will exasperate ↑even↓ us into resolution again. We may well say *not unto us,* and ⟨almost may⟩ ↑yet it would be odd to↓ say, not unto the Lord, but unto the Devil in the Southerner, be the praise!—

[⟨238⟩ 241] The conduct of intellect must respect nothing so much as preserving the sensibility. That mind is best which is most impressionable. There are times when ↑the cawing of crows,↓ a ↑flowering↓ weed, a ⟨raindrop⟩ ↑snowflake,↓ ⟨or⟩ a ↑⟨porter's⟩ boy's willow whistle or a porter's↓ wheelbarrow is more suggestive to the mind than the Yosemite Gorge or the Vatican^n would be in another

[244] This sentence, struck through in ink with a vertical use mark, is used in "Progress of Culture," *W,* VIII, 210–211.

[245] Forceythe Willson (1837–1867), poet, had attracted the attention of Emerson and Lowell with his poem, "The Old Sergeant." Willson lived in Cambridge from 1864 to 1866. A copy of the Cambridge, 1866, edition of *The Old Sergeant,* inscribed to Emerson by the author, and *The Old Sergeant, and Other Poems* (Boston, 1867), are in Emerson's library. See *J,* X, 110–111, and *L,* V, 444 and 489.

hour. In like mood, an old verse, or particular words gleam with ↑rare↓ significance.[246] How to ⟨restore⟩ keep, how^n to recover at will this sensibility?

[⟨239⟩ 242]   *Manners.*

There are things ⟨which are⟩ ↑whose hour is↓ always a little over or not quite come, as, for example, the rule that you shall not go out to dine too well-dressed: which means, that a certain slovenliness ⟨is⟩fits certain persons, but requires perfect aplomb, & clear sensible manners & conversation. Cold scholars cannot afford these liberties.[247]

[24⟨0⟩3] Aretine the first "Bohemian," or literary scamp.[248]

Heine, E. About, later.

—————

newspaper governments

—————

↑*Manners.*↓

Under a commanding thought, all people become as graceful as if they were asleep. That knows how to lay the hands & the feet, as long since it knew how to make them.[249]

[24⟨1⟩4] Chansons de Roland were already ancient under William the Conqueror, 1066, & probably the relatively modern form of the poems dates from 1100.

See *Michelet, Renaissance.* p 31[250]

[24⟨2⟩5] Scotus Erigena, sitting at the table of Charles the Bald, when the King asked him how far a *Scot* was removed from a *Sot,* answered with Irish wit, "By a table's breadth."

—————

[246] "The conduct . . . significance.", struck through in pencil with a vertical use mark, is used in "Powers and Laws of Thought," *W*, XII, 43.

[247] With this paragraph, cf. "Social Aims," *W*, VIII, 88.

[248] For "literary scamp", see *JMN*, XIV, 233.

[249] With "Under a . . . them", cf. "Social Aims," *W*, VIII, 82.

[250] "*Renaissance*" is volume 7 of Jules Michelet, *Histoire de France,* 1835–1867. For "Chansons de Roland . . . 1066," see *ibid.,* VII, 26–27, and *JMN*, XIV, 189, where Emerson cites the Paris, 1833–1866, edition.

The old sharper said, "his conscience was as good as ever it was; he had never used it any."

———

They say in California, that, it takes a gold mine to work a silver mine.

[246] Yesterday at our Cattle show I saw a man sitting in the Town Hall so like to the late President Lincoln, in the whole head, that I called the attention of Rev. Mr Reynolds to him, who at once recognized the fact. It was Elijah Wood of this town: the view was in profile, & he had his hand against his face, covering it a little, & so probably increasing the likeness.[251]

Nature is very rich in patterns, but cunningly, ⟨rep⟩ not so rich as [247] she seems, & so repeats herself. Cousins of fourth & fifth degree have sometimes striking resemblance, & are therefore both repetitions of the common ancestor. Robert Winthrop, when young, strongly resembled the portrait in the Historical Society's Rooms, of Governor Winthrop. Indeed I suppose the Cunning Artist does not quite repeat her type until ↑after↓ four or five generations when all [248] the rememberers are gone, & she can just duplicate every face of the fifth ↑back↓ generation, without risk of confusion or discovery. But I don't think even this interval will be safe now, art having circumvented her with the photograph, which will force her to invent new varieties or lose her reputation for [249] fertility.

5 square feet to each man for ↑hearing↓
7 sq. ft   — .   to dine in
8 d[itt]o —do   to dine best in

The dimensions of the new plan of the Memorial Hall by Ware & ⟨Bru⟩Van Brunt are ↑ft.↓ 120 by 60:

[251] Emerson spoke at the Middlesex Cattle Show on September 21, 1865; see *L*, V, 425–426. Grindall Reynolds succeeded Barzillai Frost as pastor of the First Church in Concord in 1858, and officiated at the wedding of Edith Emerson and William H. Forbes on October 3, 1865. Elijah Wood, Sr. and Jr., are both mentioned in Thoreau's journals; the Wood farm was probably on the Sudbury Road near the Concord River.

of the plan presented to former Committee, 109 by 89.[252]

[250] Mr B. P. Hunt[253] said, that a young man ⟨in⟩of good position in Philadelphia went to the war, & accepted the colonelcy[n] of ⟨of⟩a colored regiment. On his return lately to Phila., all his acquaintances cut him.[n] Judge H[oar]. said to me, that he had long ago made up his mind that the cutting was to be from the other side: that this country belonged to the men of the most liberal persuasion.
This world belongs to the energetical[.][254]

[251]   Sanders in Spain   1846

Now in the time of the Fugitive Slave-law, when the best young men who had ranged themselves around Mr Webster were already all of them in the interest of freedom, & ⟨opposed his⟩ threw themselves at once into opposition, Mr Webster could no longer see one of them in the street; ⟨his⟩ ↑he glared on them but knew them not; his↓ resent-ment↑s↓ ⟨was⟩ ↑were↓ implacable↑.↓ ⟨as they found., ⟨i⟩In short, he cut them.⟩ What did they do? Did they sit down & bewail themselves?[n] No; Sumner & his valiant young contemporaries set themselves to the task of making their views not only clear but prevailing. They [252] proclaimed & defended them & ⟨infected &⟩ ⟨vaccinated⟩ ↑inoculated↓ with them the whole population, & drove Mr Webster out of the world. All his mighty genius, which none had been so[n] forward to ac-knowledge & magnify as they, availed him nothing: for they knew that the spirit of God & of humanity was with them, and he withered & died as by suicide.   Calhoun had already gone, as Webster, by breaking his own head against the nature of things.

[253] *Potentiality.*
    In estimating nations, 'tis well to remember the sovereign nature

---

[252] In May 1865 Emerson had been appointed by Harvard graduates to a committee of nine to consider plans for a memorial for their fellow collegians who had died for the Union. Memorial Hall was completed in 1874; the architects were Henry Van Brunt and William R. Ware.
[253] Benjamin Peter Hunt was once Emerson's pupil and later his valued friend.
[254] This sentence is used in "Resources," *W*, VIII, 138, 144, and 153, and in "Perpetual Forces," *W*, X, 85. See also Journals WAR, p. [29], and VA, p. [1] below.

which often remains when the actual performance is inferior: thus, in England, what destroying criti↑c↓ism we can read or make on its education, its literature, its science, its politics! And yet, the force of that race may still any day turn out a better man than any other.

[254] Theodore will buy a hat, a soft hat, or a beaver, for summer or winter. In his choice, he looks about him⟨,⟩ in the street, or he remembers, that this friend or that reputable citizen wears one of a certain form or color which is becoming. One good instance suffices him, & guides to a certain extent his choice. But he does not consider that it is always character, personal force of some kind in the individual he [255] thinks of, that makes the hat he wears so proper & perfect in its place.

Despair, whining, low spirits, only betray the fact that the man has been living in the low circle of the senses & the understanding. These are exhaustible, & he has exhausted them & now looks backward & bewails them.

[25⟨7⟩6] In Stirling's "Secret of Hegel."

> "The intellectual power from words to things
> Went sounding on a dim & perilous way."[255]

[257] Carlyle is to be defended plainly as a sincere man who is outraged by nothing so much as sentimentalism, or the simulating ↑of↓ reform, & love of nature, & love of truth. Therefore he detests "Progress of Civility," "Enlightenment," "New Ideas," "Diffusion of Knowledge," & all shallow insincerities coming under such names.

[258] ↑November 5, 1865↓
We hoped that in the Peace, after such a war, a great expansion would follow ⟨to⟩in the mind of the country: grand views in every direction,—true freedom in politics, in religion, in social science, in thought. But the energy of the nation seems to have expended itself in

---

[255] Wordsworth, *The Excursion*, III, 700–701, slightly misquoted. See *JMN*, II, 222.

the war, and every interest is found as sectional & ⟨narrow⟩ ↑timorous↓ as before. The Episc⟨a⟩opal church is baser than ever,—perfect Yahoo; the Southerner just the same Gambia negro chief,— ⟨just as much⟩ [259] addicted to crowing, garotting, & stealing, as ever: the Democrat as false & truckling; the Union party as timid & compromising, the scholars pale & expectant, never affirmative;
only ⟨Wilson⟩ Phillips & Frank Bird, only Wilson & Sumner unreconciled, aggressive, & patriotic still.[256]

[260] Apropos to what I wrote (   ) of French Bohemians,[257] I read in my Publishers' Circular's French correspondent (Oct. 16, 1865) "How short-lived is the last generation of literary men & artists here!" The Lamartines, Hugos, Saint Beu⟨e⟩ves, are young as ever, but the↑ir↓ ⟨men⟩ ↑juniors↓ poisoned by nicotine, absinthe, & reckless licentiousness, are all dead.[258]

Nov. 14. Williamstown. I saw tonight in the Observatory, through Alvan Clark's telescope,[259] the Dumb-Bell nebula in the Fox & Goose constellation;
the four double stars in Lyra;
the double stars of Castor;
the 200 stars of the Pleiades;
the nebula in (Perseus?)

[261] Mr Button, Professor Hopkins↑'s↓ assistant, was our starshow⟨er⟩↑man↓ & ⟨Mr⟩J. H. Stanbrough &   Hutton, who have been my Committee of the "Adelphic Union", inviting me here, carried me thither. I have rarely been so much gratified.[260]

---

[256] Francis W. Bird (1809–1894) was an abolitionist and disciple of Theodore Parker; Henry Wilson (1812–1875) joined with Charles Sumner to build the Democratic–Free Soil Coalition.

[257] See pp. [224] and [243] above.

[258] *American Literary Gazette and Publishers' Circular,* V (Oct. 16, 1865), 267.

[259] Alvan Clark (1804–1887) was a lens maker and astronomer.

[260] Theodore E. Button (1844–1905), James Henry Stanbrough (1844–1887), and Alfred John Hutton (1842–1916) were all members of the class of 1866 at Williams College. Albert Hopkins (1807–1872), brother of Mark Hopkins and professor of mathematics and natural philosophy, undertook the establishment of an astronomical observatory in Williamstown, the first ever to be connected with an American college.

⟨T⟩Early in the afternoon Prof. Bascom carried ⟨in⟩me in a gig to the top of the West Mountain, & showed me the admirable view down the Valley in which this town & Adams lie, with Greylock & his attendant ranges towering in front: then we rose to the crest, & looked down into Rensellaer County, New York, & the multitude of low hills that compose it. This was the [262] noted Anti-rent country, & beyond, in the horizon, the mountain range to the West.[261]

Of all tools, an observatory is the most sublime. And these mountains ⟨in⟩give an inestimable worth to Williamstown & Massachusetts. But for the mountains, I don't quite like the proximity of a college & its noisy students. To enjoy the hills as poet, I prefer simple farmers as neighbors.

The dim lanthorn which the astronomer used at first to find his object-glasses, &c. seemed to disturb & hinder him, preventing his seeing his heavens, &, though [263] it was turned down lower & lower, he was still impatient, & could not see until it was put out. When it had long been gone, ↑and↓ ⟨⟨th⟩&⟩ I had ⟨seen⟩ looked through the telescope a few times, ⟨the⟩ the little garret at last grew positively lightsome, & the lamp would have been annoying to all of us. What is so good in a college as an observatory? ⟨You⟩ The sublime attaches to the door & to the first stair you ascend, that this is the road to the stars. Every fixture & instrument ⟨& nail & pin⟩ in the building, ↑every nail & pin↓ has a direct reference to the [264] ⟨m⟩Milky-Way, the fixed stars, & the nebulae. & we leave Massachusetts & the Americas ↑& history↓ ↑outside↓ ↑⟨& history,⟩↓ at the door, when we came in.[n]

Dec. 10, Doctor Jackson shone in the talk on Thanksgiving Day, explaining many things so successfully,—the possibility of the balloon by the aid of gun-cotton (one of whose principal merits, he asserted, was, that it does not foul the barrel or engine as powder does), the Ocean Telegraph, which he thinks far less practicable, & certainly less

---

[261] John Bascom (1827–1911), professor of rhetoric and political science at Williams College, was later president of the University of Wisconsin.

desireable to us, than the Siberian. Then the [265] fact that the patents of the telegraph companies do not really protect the monopoly, for ⟨the⟩what is patented they no longer use, as, the system of "marks on paper", of Morse's patent; for the telegraph is everywhere conducted without paper, being read by the ear. He thinks the ⟨P⟩U.S. Post Office should take possession of the Telegraph as part of the Postal Arrangement, pay a compensation to the Companies, & give its use to the people at a cent a word, & so save the immense transportation of letters, by this imponderable^n [266] correspondence. ⟨T⟩He told the story of the ↑Rumford↓ medal voted to Ericson, by the American Academy, & the ⟨medal⟩money voted to Roper & Co. for valuable improvements on Ericson; from which last he anticipates ⟨a⟩very great practical benefit, ⟨—⟩the Union or double-union engine.^{262}

I. T. Williams told me, the other day, that 97 per cent of caloric was wasted in all attempts to use caloric for force in mechanics. Dr J. says, much is lost, but nothing like so much. He knew Amory's chimney which burns the smoke.^{263} [267] Its advantage is demonstrable, yet it is not used, resembling thus Boyden's turbines, which pretend to save 97 per⟨c⟩ cent of the power of a waterfall, &, being tested, were found to do what they claimed, yet are not used.^{264}

———

It seems to be a fixed rule in the planting & growth of settlements, that the men follow the waters. Thus, on each side of ⟨th⟩a height of land, the people will go to the market that is^n down stream.

^{262} Dr. Charles T. Jackson (1805–1880), scientist and physician, was Lidian Emerson's brother. According to the *Proceedings of the American Academy of Arts and Sciences,* VI (May 1862–May 1865), 26, John B. Ericsson was awarded the Rumford Premium "for his improvements in the management of heat, particularly as shown in his Caloric Engine of 1858." At the meeting of February 9, 1864 (*ibid.,* pp. 238–240), the Rumford Committee reported "three kinds of engines in practical operation; 1st, Mr. Ericsson's . . . 2d, Mr. [Philander] Shaw's; and 3d, Mr. Roper's," and concluded that Mr. Roper's was "the most successful hot-air engine now at work in Boston." (Emerson was elected a Resident Fellow of the Academy at the meeting of January 27, 1864.)

^{263} For "chimney . . . smoke.", used in "Civilization," *W,* VII, 25, see *JMN,* XIV, 52.

^{264} Uriah Atherton Boyden (1804–1879), brother of inventor Seth Boyden, devised an improved turbine water wheel.

[268] I. T. Williams told me that the last time he saw Albert H. Tracy, he told him, that, when he & Cass were in Congress, they became very intimate, & spent their time in conversation on the Immortality of the soul, & other intellectual questions, & cared for little else. When he left Congress, they parted, &, though Mr Cass passed through Buffalo twice, he did not come near him, and he never saw him again until ⟨y⟩25 years after↑ward,↓ they saw each other through open doors at a distance, ⟨at⟩in a great party at the President's House, in Washington. Slowly they advanced towards ↑each↓ other as they could, & at last met, said nothing, but shook hands long & cordially. At [269] last, Cass said, "Any light, Tracy?" "None," answered Tracy, and then said, "Any light, Cass?" "None," replied he. They looked in each others' eyes, gave one shake more each to the hand he held, & thus parted for the last time.[265]

↑Printed in "Immorta⟨t⟩lity."↓

⟨I remember, w⟩When I was a senior in College, I think,—Sam[ue]l Barrett[266] whom I had known in Concord was about to be ordained in the Chamber-street Church and I called upon him in his room in College.—↑I think↓ he must have been a proctor. We^n talked about the vices & [270] ⟨&⟩ calamities of the time,—I don't recall what the grim shadows were, or how we came on them,—but when I rose to go, & asked him what was the relief & cure of ⟨of⟩all this? he replied with cheerful ardor, "Nothing but Unitarianism." From my remembrance of how this answer struck me, I am sure that this antidote must have looked as thin & poor & pale to me then, as now. I was never for a moment the victim of "Enlightenment," or "Progress of the Species," or the "Diffusion-of-Knowledge-Society."

---

[265] Page [268] is struck through in pencil with a vertical use mark; the entire anecdote is used in "Immortality," *W*, VIII, 331–332. Albert H. Tracy (1793–1859), Buffalo jurist, served in Congress from 1819 to 1825. Lewis Cass (1782–1866) was governor of Michigan Territory (1813–1831), U.S. senator (1845–1848, 1849–1857), and Secretary of State (1857–1860).

[266] Samuel Barrett was minister of the Twelfth Congregational Church in Boston from 1825 to 1861. See *L*, I, 159.

[271]   ↑*Carlyle.*↓

I have neglected badly Carlyle, who is so steadily good to me. Like a Catholic in Boston, he has put himself by his violent anti-Americanism in false position, & it is not quite easy to deal with him. But his merits are overpowering, & when I read "Friedrich," I forget all else. His treatment of his subject is ever so masterly, so original, so self-respecting, so defiant⟨,⟩ allowing himself all manner of liberties & confidences with his hero, as if he were his hero's father or benefactor, that ⟨↑while↓⟩ he is proud of him, & yet checks & chides & sometimes puts him [272] in the corner, when he is not a good boy, that, amid ⟨the⟩ all his sneering & contempt for all other historians, & biographers, & princes, & peoples, the reader yet feels ⟨his own mind⟩ ↑himself↓ complimented by the confidences with which he is honored by this ⟨eccentric historian⟩ ↑free-tongued, dangerous companion↓, who discloses to him all his secret opinions, all his variety of moods, & varying estimates of his hero & everybody else. He is as dangerous [273] as a madman. Nobody knows what he will say next,[267] or whom he will strike. Prudent people keep out of his way. If Genius were cheap, we should do without Carlyle; but, in the existing population, he cannot be spared.

The Tribune says of Winter Davis,—"with that power of continuous thought which is essential to every man who has to do with the affairs of the forum or the street."[268]

[274] January 5, 1866. I thought, last night, as so often before, that when one has a task before him in which literary work becomes *business,*—undertaken,[n] that is, for money,—any hearing of poetry or any intellectual suggestion, (as e.g. out of J. H. Stirling's book[269] lately,) ⟨prod⟩brings instant penitence, and the thoughts revert to the Muse, and, under this high invitation, we think we will throw up our undertaking, & attempt [275] once more this purer[,] loftier service. But if

---

[267] See Emerson's letter of January 7, 1866, in *CEC*, pp. 546–547, where "His treatment . . . say next," is used.

[268] See the New York *Daily Tribune*, January 1, 1866, p. 6. Henry Winter Davis, American lawyer and political leader, had died on December 30, 1865.

[269] *The Secret of Hegel;* see pp. [53] and [256] above, and [276] below.

we obey this suggestion, the beaming goddess presently hides her face in clouds again. We have not learned the law of the mind, cannot control & ↑bring at will or↓ domesticate the high states of contemplation & continuous thought. "Neither by sea nor by land canst thou find the way to the Hyperboreans:"—Neither by idle wishing, nor by rule of three⟨.⟩ ↑or of thumb.↓ Yet I find a mitigation or solace of the alternative which I accept (of the paid lectures ⟨I⟩, for instance,) by providing [276] always a good book for my journey, as, Horace, or Martial, or the "Secret of Hegel," ⟨a⟩ ↑some↓ book which lifts quite out of prosaic surroundings, & from which you draw some lasting knowledge.[270]

The Tribune ↑says,↓ "It is time, since the sale of women & children on the auction-block has been banished from our country, that the sale of legislators, whether by the lot or piece, should be banished from our State."[271]

[277] In the "Funeral" of Steele, Sable the undertaker reproaches the too cheerful mute, "Did I not give you ten, then fifteen & twenty shillings a week to be sorrowful? And the more I give you, I think the gladder you are."[272]

[278] 1866
Feb. Philip Hoedemaker, of Kalamazoo, Mich.[273] is now at Utrecht.

Martha Bartlett told me, that a lady said to Miss Andrews, "that the sense of being perfectly drest gave a feeling of peace which religion could never give." ↑I find that this *mot* was one of Fanny Forbes'.↓[274]

---

[270] "We have ... knowledge." is used in "Inspiration," *W*, VIII, 294–295. For " 'Neither by ... Hyperboreans:' ", see *The Odes of Pindar*, trans. Dawson W. Turner (London: Henry G. Bohn, 1852), p. xxii, and *JMN*, XIV, 122.

[271] New York *Daily Tribune*, January 3, 1866, p. 6.

[272] Richard Steele, *The Funeral: or, Grief A-la-Mode*, I, i, 102–104.

[273] See *JMN*, XIV, 353.

[274] " 'that the sense ... give.' " is used in "Social Aims," *W*, VIII, 88. For Martha Bartlett, see *JMN*, XI, 189. Cornelia Frances Forbes was an aunt of Edith Emerson's husband, William H. Forbes. Miss Andrews has not been identified.

Common sense. ⟨P⟩Lord Mansfield or any great lawyer an example of it, though they call it *law*.[275] And ↑Beau↓ Brummel even
⟨was⟩surpassed other fops by having this basis: as, when he was asked,
"what scents he used for his linen?" replied, "Country air & country
washing."

[27⟨7⟩9] *Love.*

⟨To t⟩The maiden only need consider that she passes securely
through ten or a dozen appearances, as in the street, or at an evening
party. The lover will do all the rest; since he is ever working up[,] enriching[,] enhancing her image & attributes, with the smallest aid from
her: so that thus there are two working on her part, & none on his.

[280] The power of manners is a⟨n⟩[n] principal agent in human affairs.
The rich & elegant & the strong-willed not so much talk down as look
down & silence the well-disposed middle class. ⟨The⟩ 'Tis fine that the
scholar or the red republican defies these people, or writes against
them: he cannot get them out of his thoughts. When he meets them
⟨he⟩in the street, he cannot deny them his bow; & when he meets them
[281] in clubs or in drawingrooms, he prizes their attentions, & easily
leaves his own set on any advances from theirs. In England Sir Robert
Peel & Thackeray are only two ⟨examples⟩ out of manifold examples. I
myself always fall an easy prey to superior manners. I remember how
admirable in my youth were to me the southern boys. Andrew Johnson, wont to look up to the planters as a superior race, cannot resist
their condescensions & flatteries [282] &, though he could not be
frightened by them, falls an easy victim to their caresses. Th⟨e⟩is result
was explicitly foretold by M[oncure]. D. Conway & Fred[erick].
Douglas[s].

The remedy of this political mischief should be to train youth in
poverty to a nobler style of manners than any palace can show him, by
Plato & Plutarch, by the Cid, & Sydney, & George Herbert, &
Chaucer.

---

[275] "Common sense. . . . *law.*" is struck through in pencil with one curved and one
vertical use mark; cf. "Eloquence," *W*, VII, 88, and *JMN*, XI, 228.

[283] ⟨Difference of people that⟩ Quick^n people touch & go, whilst heavy people insist on pounding. 'Tis in vain to try to choke them off, & change the conversation to avoid the slaughter-house details. Straightway they begin at the beginning, & thrice they slay the slain. Society shall be distressing, & there's an end of it.

But what a golden lot to draw must be a cool temperament. Here was an imperturbable slut, on whose ear all your explicit directions never so many times repeated made quite no impression, and, when dinner-time came, ⟨was⟩ ↑came↓ no dinner,—but "I forgot all about it," was [284] the unanswerable answer to whatever objurgations. But as the coolness is real, it is a sublime advantage. What contempt must such a nature feel for the tickled & furious little creatures that swarm all around her, always in extremes!

[285] [blank]

[286] "Ce que dit le ruisseau; 'Toujours, toujours, partout, dans tout, pour tout, toujours.' " *George Sand.*^{276}

⟨Ha⟩Have the French no word for *meetings?* for the Revue translates *conciliabula, meetings;* (of women to ⟨res⟩ canvass & resist the Oppian Law). *Réunions,* I suppose, has another color.^{277}

———

Il faut blanchir ↑votre linge sale chez vous.↓^{278}

———

Quand meme, at all hazards.
Tournure, urbanité, entregent.

———

"lots" in the sense of *a great deal* is rendered by *force de.*

———

^{276} "Ce que dit le Ruisseau," *Revue des Deux Mondes,* Sept. 1, 1863, p. 266.

^{277} See J.-J. Ampère, "Les Luttes de la liberté à Rome, Caton et les Gracques," *Revue des Deux Mondes,* Sept. 1, 1863, p. 73, and *JMN,* VI, 376. "⟨Ha⟩" is in pencil.

^{278} "votre linge . . . vous." is in pencil, overwritten in ink.

[287] *Home, comfort, earnest,* & to *stand,* are the four words for which the French language has no equivalent.[279]

[288] [blank]
[289] School Committee
1864
   April 8   Examined Miss E. Skinner
                      Miss L↑aura↓ Dutton
                      Miss   Tidd
                      Miss   E Brown
                      Miss   A Brown
    Elected Miss Eliza Hosmer to the Preparatory School
           Miss Holden to the Intermediate
           Miss E Brown to the H. Barrett School
           Miss Skinner to the N Primary

My charge is Chairman of the High School   &   of the East centre and I am to provide wood for my school   2½ cords oak
                                          ½ cord pine
Next School Committee meeting is first Saturday of May

[290] Aug ⟨Elected⟩ ↑Voted to pay↓ Miss   Rhoades the full
                  price of experienced teachers
    Elected Miss Jeannie Farmer teacher of East Quarter Primary
        District No 2
    Elected Miss Mary Wood teacher of No 6[280]

Schools to begin 28 August

Aug. 31 High School   Beginning of Term
                    Whole number   32
              present today   22

---

[279] For "*Quand meme* [p. [286]] . . . equivalent.", see *JMN,* VI, 376; for "Tournure, urbanité, entregent.", in a smaller hand and possibly added, see also p. [117] above.

[280] Edward Emerson, in *J,* X, 22, supplies the following for pp. [289] and [290]: "Abby" for "Miss A Brown"; "North Quarter School, District No. 7" for "the H. Barrett School"; "East Primary, opposite Mr. Emerson's house" for "East centre"; and "Bateman's Pond School, District No. 6" for "No 6".

Class in Arithmetic   begin Alligation

1.	Latin,	begin Cicero
2.		begin Caesar B.1 Sect 42
3.		begin Viri Romae
		12 in class
	Greek	Xenophon
	French	2 in class

[291]   Geometry — 1 scholar
         Nat. Philosophy— 10 scholars
         Bookkeeping 6

[292]–[295] [blank]
[296] [Index material omitted]
[inside back cover] [Index material omitted]

$\mathcal{GL}$

1861–1862, 1863

Emerson began Journal GL in January 1861 and used it regularly until late January, 1862, but he added at least three later entries, one in August 1862 (p. [341]), and two on January 26, 1863 (pp. [136] and [357]). Two journals immediately follow it: WAR, begun in January 1862, and VA, begun in February 1862.

The covers of the copybook, of marbled brown, red, and blue paper over boards, measure 17.0 × 21.5 cm. The spine strip and protective corners on the front and back covers are of tan leather. "1861" and "GL" are written on the front cover, and a worn "GL" can be made out on the upper right leather corner. Traces remain of two short strips of cloth tape once applied to the front cover near the spine, and two more on the back cover.

There were 296 unlined pages measuring 17.4 × 20.7 cm, but the leaf bearing pages 347–348 has been torn out. The leaves bearing pages 1–2 and 393–394, once loose, are now reattached to the front cover verso and back cover verso respectively with strips of stiff white paper. In his pagination, Emerson repeated 174 and 175; the editors have added subscript numbers to distinguish the two pairs. The verso of page 177 is numbered 278, so that 178–277 are omitted in the numbering. Three other pages were misnumbered and corrected: 33⟨2⟩4, 35⟨5⟩6, and 3⟨58⟩60. The pages are numbered in ink except for pages 88 and 116, numbered in pencil. Eleven pages are unnumbered: 1, 32, 33, 53, 81, 89, 122, 123, 149, 379, and 394. Six pages are blank: 18, 32, 33, 59, 81, and 314.

Laid in inside the front cover are a sheet of white paper, lined in blue and folded once, measuring 19.4 × 24.6 cm and inscribed in ink on both sides (printed as front cover verso$_a$–front cover verso$_b$); a sheet of heavy unlined letter paper torn off along a fold at the left side to measure 11.4 × 17.8 cm, inscribed in ink on one side (printed as front cover verso$_c$); a sheet of white paper faintly lined in blue, folded once, measuring 19.2 × 24.4 cm, partly torn off at the upper and lower left corners, inscribed on one side (printed as front cover verso$_d$); a sheet of white paper lined in blue, torn off along a fold to measure 12.9 × 20.0 cm, inscribed in pencil on both sides with French proverbs, not in Emerson's hand; and a newspaper clipping from the Montreal *Herald* (see Appendix II below). Laid in between pages 140–141 is a newspaper clipping containing Walt Whitman's poem "You and Me Today." Glued to the upper left corner of page 152 is a clipping from the Boston *Daily Traveller* discussing "Mr. Emerson's paper on *Old Age*" (see p. 134, n. 142 below).

[front cover]   1861   GL
                                 GL

[front cover verso] [Index material omitted]
[front cover verso$_a$] Belzoni's Telescope   D 100
All greatness is in degree & there's more above than below.[1]
Good of evil. Give you a public not easily pleased, a pruner of your
orations, an adversary whom you must confute & convince, & not one
to whom you can dictate his opinions & his taste.

_____

Self-respect demanded of us by the most general considerations. *F* 3

_____

We do not have a moment of grandeur in these hurried slipshod lives.

_____

"More than the disciple trust I the sinner." *Orient*[alis]*t.* 226[2]

The persons generally most praised & esteemed are not those whom I
most value, for the world is not receptive or intelligent of Being, but of
Intellect. But heroes are they who value Being. Being cannot be told,
& is left alone not only because little appreciated, but that its influence
is silent & quiet. The world is awed before the great, & is subdued
without knowing why.

[front cover verso$_b$] If we look at the fossil remains of the earliest men
& compare them with the best races of today we shall have a hint that
the like refinement in the types is still proceeding, & that the men of
today cannot be organized in a more advanced age any more than the
saurians in the granite of Mass[achuse]tts[.]
The homage paid to a great man is the expression of our own hope.

_____

Influences

[1] This sentence is used in "Greatness," *W*, VIII, 312–313. See also *JMN*, X, 370.
[2] In Notebook Orientalist, p. [226], Emerson gives the source of this quotation as
"Bostan vol 2 p. 1⟨6⟩7". Emerson borrowed *Moslichedden Sadi's Lustgarten* (*Bostan*),
trans. K. H. Graf, 2 vols. (Jena, 1850), from the Boston Athenaeum October 2,
1863–March 11, 1864.

[front cover verso_c] [Notebook] XO

He who sees the horizon may securely say what he pleases of any tree or twig between him & it. *Orientalist* 217, [actually 207]

Common fame just. NO *70*

───

The man who can make hard things easy is the educator.

[XO 93]

⟨Power⟩ Whatever is dreary & repels is not power but the lack of power[.][3] [XO 93]

───

Eloquence is the art of speaking what you mean & are. [XO 93]

───

Before, all things stand enchanted[,] not tangible. He comes & touches them & henceforth anybody may. *TU* 177, 219, *XO* 173,

[front cover verso _d] ||msm||*ture & Art*
||msm|| Necessity
||msm||ry one admires the beauty of the /*Buccinum harpa*/harp-shell/; but ⟨this beauty was honestly⟩ when we observe that ↑it adds year by year ⟨a new⟩ as it grows, a new lip as the tree↓ every one of these polished ridges that adorn its surface ⌈adds each year a new ⟨liber⟩ ring of liber or bark⌉, like harpstrings, was in turn the outer lip of the shell, we see that the beauty was honestly gained.

"Nothing that is truly beautiful externally, is internally deformed." *Plotinus.*[4]

[1]   *GL*

January, 1861—

We have no guess what we are doing, even then when we do our best; perhaps it will not appear for an age or two yet: then, the dim

───

[3] This sentence is used in "Character," *W*, X, 92. See also *JMN*, XIV, 205.

[4] "||msm||ry one ... *Plotinus.*" is struck through in ink with a vertical use mark. Three short lines in pencil are drawn in the left margin beside "was in ... outer lip". With "ring of liber," cf. p. [104] below. For the quotation, see *Select Works of Plotinus*, trans. Thomas Taylor (London, 1817), p. 116; this volume is in Emerson's library. See also *JMN*, XIII, 296.

outline of the reef & new continent we madrepores were making, will sketch itself to the eyes of the dullest sailer. Luther would cut his hand off sooner than write theses against [2] the Pope, if he suspected that he was bringing on with all his might the pale negations of Boston Unitarianism.

The furious slaveholder does not see that the one thing he is doing, by night & by day, is, to destroy slavery. They who help & they who hinder are all equally diligent in hastening its [3] downfal[l]. Blessed be the inevitabilities.[5]

Another topic is the *reality*[n] as herein; that, the more reason the less government; government is always superseded. In a sensible family nobody ever hears the words *shall* or *shan't:*[n] ⟨all⟩ nobody commands & none obeys: but all conspire & joyfully coöperate: & so in every good club; & command is exceptional, & marks some break [4] in the link of reason, as the electricity goes round the world, without a spark or a sound, until there is a break in the wire or the water chain.[6]

The best thing I heard yesterday was ⟨J⟩Henry James's statement, that, in the spiritual world, the very lowest function was Governing. In heaven, as soon as one wishes to rule, ↑or despises others↓ he is thrust out at the door.[7]

[5] Another fine spiritual statement which he made, was, to the effect, that all which men value themselves for as religious progress,—going alone, renouncing, & self-mortifying, to attain a certain religious superiority,—was the way *from,*[n] not the way *to* what they seek; for, it is only as our existence is shared, not as it is self-hood, that it is divine.[8]

---

[5] "We have no . . . inevitabilities." is struck through in pencil with single vertical use marks on pp. [1], [2], and [3]. "Luther would . . . Unitarianism.", struck through in pencil with a second vertical use mark on p. [1] and another on p. [2], is used in "The Sovereignty of Ethics," *W*, X, 204.

[6] "that, the more . . . chain.", struck through in pencil with single vertical use marks on pp. [3] and [4], is used in "Character," *W*, X, 121.

[7] "In heaven, . . . door." is used in "Character," *W*, X, 121, where it is attributed to Swedenborg.

[8] "Another fine . . . shared," is struck through in pencil with a diagonal use mark, which Emerson extended vertically to the bottom of the page.

[6] Life must have vent, & balance of income & outgo, as described in old lecture on "Expression."[9] & lately in conversation on Health. *CL.* 284

Among the Illusions, is to be remembered that, so frequent among young men, that there are no fit people near them, but elsewhere; no boys of ⟨my⟩John's age, no girls of Almira's.

[7] "But Cathmor dwelt in the wood, to avoid the voice of praise," says Ossian.[10]

Destitution is the Muse of M[ary]. M[oody]. E[merson].'s genius, Destitution & Death. We have said that her epitaph ought to be, "Here lies the Angel of Death." And wonderfully as she varies & ⟨rep⟩poetically repeats that image in every page & day, yet not less fondly & sublimely she returns to the other, the grandeur of [8] humility & privation,[n] as thus; "The chief witness which I have had of a God-like principle of action & feeling is the disinterested joy felt in others' superiority."   "For the love of superior virtue is mine own gift from God."
"To obey God is joy, though no hereafter." "Where were thy own intellect, if greater had not lived."[11]

[9] Popular Errors, e.g. the vulgar ⟨abuse⟩ dispraise of wealth, which disgusts as much as the vulgar idolatry of it.

Benefits of Old Age

Things, & not appearances. Middle life best. To be relieved of the task of making a show.
the humble-conditioned blest above others
Real value of money, culture, languages, art, science, only as keys & passports whereby to communicate.—[12]

---

[9] Cf. "The Poet," *Lectures,* III, 349, and *JMN,* VIII, 106.

[10] See Journal DL, p. [135] above.

[11] "Destitution is . . . lived.", struck through in pencil on p. [7] with two vertical use marks and on p. [8] with one vertical use mark, is used in "Mary Moody Emerson," *W,* X, 404–405.

[12] Two vertical pencil lines are drawn in the left margin beside this sentence.

[10] As soon as one sees that life is one, & God does not create, but communicates his life, all is right. This self-love is much in our way. A wise man, ⟨is as⟩ an open mind, is as much interested in others, as in himself; they are only extensions of himself. They stand on a hilltop, & see exactly what he would see if he were there. He cannot be offended by an honest partiality in others. Alcott said of his company, "I can offend them at any moment.'"n 13

[11] Perfect health is the subjugation of matter to be the servant, the instrument of thought & heart; so that matter is not felt as matter, but only as opulence, & light, & beauty, & joy. As soon ⟨we⟩as we know a particle of matter for itself it is obstruction & defect of health[.]14

[12] It is not my duty to prove the immortality of the Soul. That secret is hidden very cunningly;—perhaps the archangels cannot find the secret of their existence, as the eye cannot see itself,—but, ending or endless, to live while I live.
Yet I find the proofs noble, wholesome, & moral.15

[13] Pay every debt. If you cannot, you may be bankrupt, & content with bankruptcy. Tomorrow try again. 'Tis not your duty to pay the debt, but to try to pay the debt. Do all with a clear & perfect intent. Call in the Universe to witness & sanction, & not skulk into a corner. If it is your part to kill, kill in the face of day, & with the plaudits of the Universe.
Other world! there is no other world. The God goes with you,—is here in Presence. What is here, that is there. & it is by his only strength that you lift your hand.16

13 This entry is struck through in pencil with a diagonal use mark. With "Alcott said . . . moment.' ", cf. *JMN*, X, 156, and "Social Aims," *W*, VIII, 89.
14 A vertical line in pencil is drawn in the left margin beside this paragraph. Cf. *JMN*, XIV, 364.
15 "It is not . . . moral." is struck through in pencil with a vertical use mark and in ink with a wavy diagonal use mark. "It is not . . . live." is used in "Immortality," *W*, VIII, 345.
16 "Other world! . . . hand." is struck through in pencil with three diagonal use marks. For "Other world! . . . world.", see *JMN*, VIII, 183; "The Sovereignty of Ethics," *W*, X, 199; and the lecture "Natural Religion," in Gohdes, *Uncollected Lectures*, 1932, p. 52.

[14] "What matters it by whom good is done?" said Antoninus.[17]

"Of all men," said ⟨|| . . . ||⟩ ↑Grattan,↓ "if I could call up one, it ⟨w⟩should be Scipio Africanus. Hannibal was perhaps a greater ⟨man⟩ captain, but not so great & good a man. Epaminondas did not so much. Themistocles was a rogue."
Grattan said, "The finest passage in Cicero, is his panegyric on Demosthenes."*

↑See this passage in a note to ↑Leland's↓ Demosthenes↓[18]

[15] Classes of Men

He fancied every man he talked with—older than himself.[19]
↑Defoe⟨s⟩ said, "The English↑man↓ of today ⟨are⟩ ↑is↓ the mud of all nations."↓[20]

hommes reglés   good providers, insure themselves, keep a secret, answer letters, know where to find them. canonical, names in the directory, known at the post office.
housekeepers cordially hate anybody who does not dine at family hours. *RO.* 30
Creep into your grave: the Universe has no need of you.

[16] Classes
Talent & insight seem to make no difference in reconciling the

*See Cicero's *Brutus,*   or perhaps his *De Oratore, Dialogi tres.*

[17] See Marcus Aurelius Antoninus, *Meditations,* X, 13. A paraphrase is used in "Greatness," *W,* VIII, 312, and in "Character," *W,* X, 122.
[18] See *The Orations of Demosthenes,* trans. Thomas Leland, 2 vols. (New York, 1831), I, 30 (a quotation from *De Oratore*), and 213–214 (a quotation from *Brutus*). For Grattan's remark, see Henry Grattan the Younger, *Memoirs of the Life and Times of the Rt. Hon. Henry Grattan,* 5 vols. (London, 1839–1846), V, 223.
[19] This sentence is struck through in ink with a vertical and a diagonal use mark. Pages [15]–[17] may be notes for the lecture "Classes of Men," first delivered on November 20, 1860, before the Parker Fraternity at the Music Hall in Boston; see Cabot's abstract in *A Memoir. . . ,* 1887–1888, II, 771–772.
[20] See *JMN,* XIII, 138, and "Race," *W,* V, 51.

JOURNAL GL

disparity between demand & supply in each mental constitution. [HO 64]
Leonardo da Vinci's rule holds here[.]

Contrary Temperament
Wordsworth, Byron, Scott, had no ear for music[.]
To Lord Holland ↑it was↓ ⟨ab⟩ positive p⟨in⟩ain. *HO,* 149.

Story of Bernini & Wren. *IO* 20

Therien & Tuttle. *AZ* 20, 25,

A bag of old copper coins⟨.⟩, what more unpromising? *AZ* 216

[17] I have noticed that people who wash much, have a high mind about it, & talk down to those who wash ⟨little.⟩ less. See RS 65

Culture *CO* 261

Battery & aplomb. *LM* 1[21]

Some people have a talent for m↑i↓sfortune, a talent for missing opportunities. *RO* 89
Englishmen are pasture-oaks,—ours are pine saplings. ↑They are↓ mail-clad men, towers, three stories high &c *GO* 128

[18] [blank]
[19] *Greatness.*
He who has accustomed himself to look at all his circumstance as mutable, to carry his possessions, his ⟨relation⟩ relation to persons, & even his opinions, in his hand, as a bird that flieth, & in ⟨ev⟩all these to pierce to the principle & moral law, & everywhere to find *that,*[n] has put himself out of the reach of ⟨all⟩ skepticism.[22] All its arrows fall short of the eternal towers of his faith.

---

[21] "Culture *CO* 261" and "Battery . . . *LM* 1" are in pencil, as well as the rules above each entry.
[22] "He who . . . skepticism." is used in "The Sovereignty of Ethics," *W,* X, 213–214.

[20] ↑Subjective Life↓[23]

We are partial & only ⟨select⟩ ↑pick↓, like birds, a crumb here & there. Tho' the world is full of food, we can take only the crumbs fit for us. The air rings with sounds, but only a few vibrations can reach our tympanum, de⟨f⟩af to all the thunders around us. Perhaps creatures live with us which we never see, because their motion is too swift for our vision;[24] [21] and 'tis familiar that people pass out of the world unknown, being too good, or too high, or too subtle, for the appreciation of their bystanders. ↑I know three or four men[,]↓ Charles Newcomb, and Alcott, & Channing, ↑who↓ are concealed, as Swedenborg was. These are buried in light, as the stars are by day. ↑I might add Jones Very.↓

↑I have else⟨we⟩where added Samson Reed, & Bailey[.]↓[25]

[22] I know no more irreconcileable persons ever brought to annoy & confound each other in one room than are sometimes actually lodged by nature in one man's skin. Thus I knew a saint of a woman who lived in ecstasies of devotion, "a pensive nun devout & pure,"[26] and who, moved by pity for a poor schoolmistress, undertook one day to give⟨r⟩ her a [23] little vacation which she sorely needed, & took her place in the school: but, when the children whispered, or did not mind their book, she stuck a pin into their arms, & never seemed to suspect the cruelty. I knew a gentle imaginative soul, all poetry & sympathy, who hated every inmate of his house, & drove away his dog, by starving him. Rousseau left his children at the Foundling Hospital. Mrs Ripley at Brook Farm, said the hard selfishness of the socialists ruined the [24] Community. Hawthorne, I believe, ⟨prosecuted⟩ ↑sued↓ the members for their debt to him. Howard ↑the great philanthropist↓ was harsh to his children, & Sterne ↑the sentimentalist↓ had a bad name for hardness to his mother(?)[27]

---

[23] Added in pencil.

[24] "Tho' the . . . vision;" is used in "Powers and Laws of Thought," *W*, XII, 32.

[25] Charles King Newcomb (1820–1894), mystic and one of Emerson's closest friends; Jones Very (1813–1880), mystic poet; and Sampson Reed (1800–1880), Swedenborgian writer.

[26] Milton, *Il Penseroso*, l. 31.

[27] This paragraph is struck through in pencil with single vertical use marks on pp. [22], [23], and [24]. "Read at Music Hall" and "Music Hall" are written vertically in

shortness of life reason for not learning   HO 144
The mind delights in immense time. *NO* 245
Immortality   *LM* 110

———

Willows. *VO* 264[28]

[25]   ↑*Immortality*↓[29]
     All the comfort I have found shall teach me to confide that I shall
not have less in time↑s↓ & place↑s↓ that I do not yet know. I have
known admirable persons, ⟨but⟩ without feeling that they exhaust the
possibilities of virtue or talent. I have seen what glories of climate, of
midnight sky, of summer mornings & evenings.ⁿ The Good Power
can easily provide me millions more as good. I have a good house[,]
[26] a convenient closet which holds all my books & pictures. This is
not ⟨ci⟩ a reason for refusing to die, as if there were no room or skill
elsewhere, that could reproduce for me such conveniences as my like
or enlarging wants may require.
I do not wish to live ⟨only⟩ to wear out my boots.[30]

     [27] The Unity of God is the key to all science. There is a kind
of latent omniscience not only in every man, but in every particle.
This convertibility we so admire in plants & animal structures,
whereby the same ⟨vegetable⟩ bud or leaf becomes bract, sepal, flower,
or seed, or wood, as the need is; by which the repairs & the ulterior
uses are subserved, when [28] one part is wounded, or is deficient, by
another, this selfhelp & self-creation, proceed from the same original
Power which works remotely in feeblest & meanest structures by the
same design; works in a lobster or a mite as a wise man would, if im-

———

pencil in the left margins of p. [22] and p. [23] respectively. John Howard (1726?–1790)
was an English philanthropist and prison reformer.
     [28] "shortness of . . . HO 144" and "Immortality . . . *VO* 264" are in pencil. "The
mind . . . time." is used in "Immortality," *W*, VIII, 334.
     [29] "*Immortality*" is circled in ink.
     [30] "All the comfort . . . boots.", struck through in ink on p. [25] with one vertical
and two diagonal use marks in the shape of an X, and on p. [26] with two diagonal use
marks in the shape of an X, is used in "Immortality," *W*, VIII, 337–338.

prisoned in that poor [29] form,—'tis the effort of God in the extremest frontier of his universe.[31]

We are experimenters. We try out every appetite, passion, & desire that urges us;—make it strong with opinion & crowds &[32]

Guns at Springfield, watches at Waltham, are made—part by part—⟨all⟩ the parts being of one uniform size & structure, so that any screw or ring or wheel missing can be instantly supplied. 'Tis a hint borrowed from nature, as shown in budding & grafting, ⟨only⟩& transfusion of blood, only that, in nature, it is unity in the particles, instead of the parts.

[30] I watched the fair boy & girl[,] one as fair & sweet as the other, both surprised with a new consciousness, which made every hour delicious, each laying little traps for the /admiration/attention/ of the other, & each jumping joyfully into the traps.

[31] Overture of the Quintette Club last evening.
    Tuttle tuttle lira
    tuttle tuttle liro
    tuttle tuttle polywog po
    tuttle tuttle up the stairs
    tuttle tuttle out the window
    tuttle tuttle all the world over
    tuttle tuttle arms akimbo
    tuttle tuttle all ⟨to⟩go smash.

↑Because[n] I have no ear for music,↓ at[n] the concert it looked to me as if the performers were crazy, and all the audience were making-believe crazy, in order to ⟨amuse⟩ ↑soothe↓ the luna⟨c⟩tics, & keep them ⟨quiet.⟩ amused.

[32]–[33] [blank]

---

[31] This paragraph is used in the lecture "Natural Religion"; see Gohdes, *Uncollected Lectures*, 1932, pp. 51–52. "There is . . . universe." is used in "The Sovereignty of Ethics," *W*, X, 183.
[32] "We are . . . crowds &" is in pencil.

[34]   *Fame*

Copernicus has fame by tying his name to the solar system;[n] Newton, by giving name to gravity; Herschel, by ↑finding and↓ naming the planet.

Ben Jonson's verse[33]

"Famâ bella stant." *Q. Curtius*[34]

[...][35]
[35] [...]
[36] ⟨A man⟩
[...]

Edward's gameparty verse

The Kangaroo goes hop, hop, hop,
Until the hunter does her pop,
But when she fears partickler fits,
She ups & pockets all her kits.

[37]   *Brihad Aranyaka Upanishad.*[36]

Death is called *Aditi* because he eats all. This whole Universe is his food. [p. 24]

"the son of a barren woman adorned with a sky flower." p. 13

The passages quoted from the Sruti are remarkable; as,
"One God, he sits at many places: being one, he proceeded to many places."
[p. 80]

---

[33] "Ben Jonson's verse", and the rules above and below, are in pencil.

[34] See Journal DL, p. [203] above.

[35] Pages [34]–[36] bear lines of verse in handwriting other than Emerson's, followed by the inscription, "Ellen's", presumably referring to Emerson's daughter Ellen.

[36] *The Brihad Áranyaka Upanishad, and the Commentary of Śankara Áchárya on Its First Chapter,* translated from the original Sanscrit by Dr. E. Röer (Calcutta, 1856). This is volume 2 of the *Bibliotheca Indica,* probably the volume Emerson withdrew from the Boston Athenaeum February 4–May 2, 1861.

"Thou dost not behold the beholder of the visible."   "How could one know him who knows?" [p. 80]
"Unknown is he who knows." [p. 80]

[38] From the smriti (?) is cited,
"The fire of knowledge burns all actions to ashes." [p. 118]

"Brahma is the truth of truth" [p. 176]
"the organs are ↑the↓ truth, he is the truth of them." p. 176
Yajnavalki said, I will explain to thee the means of obtaining immortality.
Behold, not for the husband's sake the husband is dear, but for the sake of ↑the↓ self is dear the husband.
not for the wife's sake ⟨is d⟩the wife is dear, but for the sake [39] of self is dear the wife.
not for the son⟨'⟩s↑'↓ sake the sons are dear, but for the sake of the self are dear the sons.
not for property's sake ⟨is⟩property is dear, but for the sake of the self is property dear.
not for the Brahma↑'↓s⟨'⟩ sake, the Brahma is dear, but, &c
not for the worlds' sake, the worlds are dear, but &c
not for the gods' sake, the gods are dear, &c
not for the Veda⟨'⟩s↑'↓ sake, the Vedas &c
not for the elements' sake, &c

[40] Behold, not for the sake of the Universe, the universe is dear, but for the sake of ↑the↓ self is dear the Universe.
Behold the self (atma) is verily to be seen, heard, minded, & mediated upon.

The Brahma should disown a person who considers the Brahma caste as something different from (his) self.
The worlds should disown a person, &c
the gods should disown &c

[41] the elements should disown &c
the Universe should disown &c
This self is this Brahma, this Kshattra, these worlds, these gods, these elements, this universe.

As from fire made of damp wood, proceed smoke, sparks, &c. of various kind, thus is the breathing of this great being the Rig Veda, the Yajur Veda, the Sama Veda, the Narratives, the doctrines on Creation (Purana), the Science, the Upanishads,—&c &c; all these are his breathing.

[p]p. [176–]179

[42] The earth is honey for all beings, for the earth are all beings honey.
The waters are honey for all beings; for the waters are all beings honey.
The fire is honey for all beings, &c
The wind is honey, &c
The lightning is honey, &c
Justice is honey &c
Truth is honey &c
Mankind is honey, &c
The soul is honey, &c
    This is that soul, this is immortal, [43] this is Brahma, this is all.
This soul is verily the lord of all beings, the king of all beings. As all spokes are fastened in the nave⟨,⟩ & the circumference of the wheel, thus also all beings, all gods, all worlds, all organs, all souls, are fastened in that soul.

[pp. 181–184]

x   x   x

⟨T⟩He became to every nature of every nature. Therefore, to manifest the nature of him, Indra appears of manifold nature by his *Maias;* for his hundred & ten senses are [44] attached ↑to the body↓ as horses to ⟨the⟩a car; it (the soul) is the senses; it is ten, it is many thousands, nay infinite; it is Brahma, who has not a Before, nor an After, nor a Beside, nor a Without: this is the soul, Brahma, the Perceiver of all.

[p]p. 185[–186]

[45] "Explain to me," said Ushasta, "that Brahma, who is a witness & present, that soul which is within every being."
"It is thy soul which is within every being," replied Yajnavalka.
"Which soul is within every being?"
"Thou," replied Yajnavalka, "couldst not behold the beholder of the beholding; thou couldst not hear the hearer of the hearing; thou couldst not mind the minder of the minding; thou couldst not know the knower of the knowing. [46] This thy soul is within every being. Everything different from it is transient." [p]p. 195[–196].

"He who dwelling in speech is within ⟨the⟩ speech, whom speech does not know, whose body is speech, who from within rules speech, is thy soul, the inner Ruler, immortal.

He who dwelling ⟨within⟩ ↑in↓ the eye is within the eye, whom the eye does not know, [47] whose body is the eye, who from within rules the eye, &c

He who dwelling in the mind is within the mind, &c

He who dwelling in knowledge, is within knowledge, &c

He who dwelling in the seed is within the seed, whom the seed does not know, whose body is the seed, who from within rules the seed,—is thy soul, the inner Ruler, the immortal. Unseen he sees, unheard he hears, unminded he minds, [48] unknown he knows. There is none that sees but he; there is none that hears but he; there is none that minds but he; there is none that knows but he; He is thy soul, the inner ruler, immortal. Whatever is different from him is perishable" [p. 202]

[49] "Brahma is only one-footed, O king of kings. Speech is Brahma. Speech is the place, ⟨the⟩ the ether, the site, the knowledge.
What knowledge, O Yajnavalka!
He said, Verily speech, o king!
By speech a friend is made known. So are made known the Rig Veda, the Sama Veda, the Atharvans, the Narratives, the Upanishads, the memorial verses,
the explanation of tenets, the fruits of sacrifices & of bestowing food, this world, the other world, & all beings. [50] By speech, O King, is Brahma known. Speech is the supreme Brahma. Speech does not desert him who with this knowledge meditates on Brahma.
All beings approach him.
having become a god,
verily he goes to the gods."

"I will give thee a thousand cows big as elephants," said Janaka, King of the Videhas. Yajnavalkya said, "My father admonished me, where one does not instruct, one should [51] not take gifts." [pp. 212–213]

"Death, who is voracity." [p. 12]
"people desire to look upon him who has obtained wealth." [p. 57]

"Whosoever Verily knows the supreme Brahma, becomes Brahma" [p. 92]
"As ⟨a⟩by a foot-print one finds cattle, so a person who thus knows finds fame
& completeness." [pp. 96–97]

———

"Men are like beasts to the gods." [p. 112]

———

[52] "Janaka, king of the Videhas, ⟨asse⟩ having a great desire to
know who among the Brahmins knew best the Vedas, assembled the
Bramins of the Kurus & the Panchálas.
He tied a thousand cows in a stable. The horns of each of them were
surrounded by ten Padahs* of gold. He said to them, 'O venerable
Bramins, whoever among you is the best knower of Brahma, shall
drive [53] home those cows.' The Bramins did not venture to come
forward. Then said Yajnavalkya to his Brahma student, 'O gentle one
drive home those cows.'
'As you command, O knower of the Sama Veda,' replied the disciple,
& drove them home. The Bramins became angry, thinking, 'How
dare he call himself amon[g]st us best knower of Brahma?' Then As-
vala, the Hotar of Janaka, undertook to question him—"
                                                    [p]p. 188[–189]

[54] After the Hotar is silenced, Artabhaga questions him. "When
the speech of the spirit is dissolved into fire, the vital air⟨,⟩ into wind,
the eye into the sun, &c
Where then does this Spirit remain?" Yajnavalkya replied, "Take, O
gentle Artabhaga, my hand, and let us go into a lonely place; there we
shall know the answer of this question. This cannot be decided in a
crowded place." Going there, they deliberated. [55] What they said
there, was work. What they praised there, was work. By holy work,
verily, a person becomes holy; by unholy, unholy."
                                                    [p]p. 193[–194]

———

We are slain by indirections. O 255

———

"The gods like indirect names, & dislike to be named directly." [*The Brihad
Áranyaka Upanishad* . . . , 1856,] p. 217

*a padah is equal to 176 grains Troy

Day

"The sun is the fuel, the day is the flame." [*Ibid.,* p. 264]

Everything in the universe goes by indirection. There are no straight lines.[37] *O* 10

If we could speak the direct solving word, it would solve us too. *Y* 5

[56] In good society, say among the angels in heaven, is not every-thing spoken by indirection, & nothing quite straight as it befel?   from *H* 44

Indirection. *GH* 36, 100,

See story of S⟨et⟩tesichorus & the Locrians. *LO* 59

Conversation not permitted without trope. [GH 36] *IT* 60   ↑It sparkles with tropes↓[38]

[57] We are surrounded by ⟨lab⟩ human thought & labor. Where are the farmer's days gone? ⟨See⟩ They[n] are hid in that stone wall, in that excavated trench, in the rich harvest grown there on what was ⟨wretched⟩ shingle & pine barren. He put his days into the carting from the distant swamp the mountain of muck, which, in more days of shovelling[n] [58] & ⟨f⟩ mi⟨n⟩xing with his barn stuff at home, now makes the cover of fruitful soil.[39]

See also *VA* 147

[37] "Everything in . . . lines.", also in *JMN,* X, 380, is used in "Works and Days," *W,* VII, 181. " 'The sun . . . flame.' " is written in ink over the same in pencil.

[38] For "Conversation . . . with tropes", in pencil, see *JMN,* X, 147–148. "Conversation . . . without trope." is used in "Poetry and Imagination," *W,* VIII, 12.

[39] "We are surrounded . . . soil.", struck through in pencil with single diagonal use marks on pp. [57] and [58], is used in "Perpetual Forces," *W,* X, 75. On p. [57], "wretched" is canceled in both ink and pencil. "*Labor*" is added at the top of p. [58].

[59] [blank]
[60]   *Subjects for April*

———

Doctrine of leasts
    ↑the ⟨co⟩Darwin convertibility of an atom.↓

———

Old Age

———

Imagination

———

An account of some good books.
—— Taylor, Digby,
         Vaughan, H[enry?] More,[40]

———

Boston.   The want of antiquity makes Natural History the refuge
of thoughtful men & poets. ↑VS 284↓[41]
    See of the Zool. lecture *HO* 8

———

———

Perpetual Forces.

———

———

[61] Poetry. Fox's opinion, *PY* [180–185]
           and mine, *CO* [15–]16
    See the force of Imagination by seeing how Imagination makes
all that we call Nature. *CO* 20   *VO* 285

———

Genius

———

The world can't live on old corn or books or men   *VS* 118[42]

———

[40] Except for "Doctrine of leasts" and the period following "books", the material to
this point on p. [60] is in pencil. Emerson began the "Life and Literature" series in Boston in April 1861. For the final list of subjects, see p. [135] below.
[41] "VS 284" is in pencil. A short rule below "Boston." is overwritten by "The want
... poets.", which may have been added.
[42] "The world ... *VS* 118" is in pencil.

105

Art
Civilization

[62] "These are facts that must be caught flying, & by a flying spectator." — *Alcott.*[43]

What magical merit belongs, ⟨to⟩ over all the details of any work, to the grand design! The performance of steam & iron ⟨t⟩locomotive on an iron road, is wonderful anywhere for a few rods or a mile, but is then only a toy; but continued or repeated for many miles, tens or hundreds, [63] & directed on Boston or New York, acquires suddenly an incredible grandeur. ⟨No one⟩ All the details are performed by very narrow ordinary people, but the total effect seems quite out of the reach of any one man, and a godlike gift.

I remember seeing ⟨I⟩in my first visit to Baltimore a pulpit in the Catholic church, which was moveable on the floor from the side to the centre of the church, and as I doubt not was much older than ⟨the⟩ ↑any↓ railroad ⟨which⟩ and should have suggested it.[44]

George Stephenson made the first locomotive in 1814. died 1848⟨,⟩.

[64] The doctrine of the Imagination can only be rightly opened by treating it in connection with the subject of Illusions. And the Hindoos alone have treated this last with sufficient breadth in their legends of the successive Maias of Vishnu. With them, youth, age, property, condition, events, persons, *self,*[n] are only successive Maias, [65] through which Vishnu mocks & instructs the Soul.[45]

---

[43] Cf. Amos Bronson Alcott, *Tablets* (Boston, 1868), p. 174.

[44] This pulpit is described in Emerson's letter to Margaret Fuller from Baltimore, January 7 and 8, 1843. See *L*, III, 116.

[45] "The doctrine . . . Illusions." is struck through in ink with a vertical use mark which has been canceled in ink; *"No, not printed"* is written vertically in the left margin. "subject" is struck through vertically in pencil. With "And the Hindoos . . . Vishnu.", cf. "Works and Days," *W*, VII, 172. "With them, . . . Maias," is struck through in pencil with two diagonal use marks; "With them . . . Soul." is used in "Poetry and Imagination," *W*, VIII, 14–15. A short rule between this and the following paragraph has been extended to a long rule, curved over *"Dream."*, and then extended down the right margin to "chariots".

Dream.[n]

"When he sleeps, then becomes this Purusha unmingled light. No chariots are there, no horses, no roads; then he creates chariots, horses, roads; no pleasures are there, no tanks, no lakes, or rivers; then he creates joys,— tanks, lakes, rivers; for he is the agent." p. 224 *Brihad Aranyaka Upanishad* [1856]

In his dream passing from high to low, he the god displays manifold forms, either playing with women, or laughing, or beholding fearful sights. His pleasure grounds are visible, but he is visible to none. They say, none comprehends the Pervader. [*Ibid.*, p. 225]

[66] I saw at Augusta[46] Mr Wilds, a civil-engineer, whom I had met at Grand Rapids, & who works for the mining companies at Lake Superior. His associate is Edward Emerson of Portland. He told me that at Lake Superior, last year (I think) they came, in their excavations, upon a mass of copper of ↑(3? or 6?)↓ tons standing on end, & on wooden wedges with a wooden bowl or pan near it, & some stone axes or chisels lying around it. [67] Trees had grown above it since it was thus lifted, and they counted on these trees 390 rings.

He told me that his friend Mr Foster who lives at Montreal, when building the Eastern railroad ↑at Kennebunk,↓ had found a nest of bird's eggs ⟨in⟩ten feet below the surface, in the solid rock, and that they turned out a toad in the rock at the same place. He↑Wilds↓ himself was present, & he & the others thought that they saw the toad gas⟨h⟩p on being thrown out. [68] Foster has the eggs now at Montreal[.]

Things are valued in pairs & alone are nought. *CO* 98

Books & manuscripts which are written only for the best. BL 114

Life of Blake—

The patience of Nature. *BL* 181

[46] Emerson lectured in Augusta, Maine, on February 13, 1861.

[69] What will inspire?
Rarey will tame a horse, but I wish that mine should be inspirited.[47]

A. They were alarmed at Havana to hear that L. was coming, fearing
    that he would consume the whole tobacco crop. So greedy a smoker
    should be sated on Virginia.
B Did you like him?
A. I endured him.
B. You are cold. But he pleases ten, where you please one.
[70] A. Of course, since I make a large demand on my companion,
and he none whatever.

[71]   Boston like Florence. *CO* 92
                    her genius *CO* 91
            Town organizations *HO* 191[48] ↑Towns. *BL* 208
All the materialities to be honored *O* 350↓
            Our recent culture. *CO* 49. Its pivotal man, Goethe. *CO* 216

————

        Her theatrical virtue *NO* 76
"Barbarians destroy but create nothing. The delight & glory of the
people of Athens consisted in the exercise of creative power." St John
I p xii[49]
Arrivals in port. *GH* 65
Boston water   *O* 305   Raw material & Feminine American genius.
O 314
            an afflicted land, a people not strong in the knees. *O* 325

————

Letter of Town of Falmouth to Town of Boston. *A* 67
[72] Effect of geology on American mind. *VS* 284

————

Vulgarity   *VS* 35

————

[47] "What will . . . inspirited." is in pencil. With "Rarey will . . . inspirited.", struck
through in pencil with two vertical use marks, cf. *JMN*, XIV, 249, and "Inspiration," *W*,
VIII, 272; for Rarey, see pp. [133]–[134] below.
[48] "Town organizations *HO* 191" is in pencil.
[49] See Journal DL, p. [58] above.

The Boston public, *GL* 80

———

The newspaper says, that who lives one year in Boston ranges through all the climates of the globe.[50] *Mem,* Tallyrand.

———

Influence of great cities   *SO* 78

———

New York & Boston. *DO 123,* 125

———

Americans the underdose. *DO* 137

———

    Boston succumbs. *SO* 204
    Base politics. *VS* 36, 259.
For a hundred years I suppose there has not been wanting a class of really superior men. See what a company they had in 1812[:]
Judge Parsons, Mr Gore, John Adams, J. Q Adams, ⟨Mr⟩ ↑H[arrison].
G[ray].↓ Otis, ⟨Mr⟩ ↑George↓ Cabot, Dr Kirkland. Josiah Quincy, Col. Perkins, Samuel Dexter, Dr Channing, Mr Allston, Judge Davis, ↑Tudor,↓[51]

    [73] Everything yields. The glaciers are *viscous,* or melt & reg-⟨a⟩elate into conformity; & the stiffest patriots falter & compromise; so that will can not be depended on to save us, & if the laws of the Everlasting in nature did not make justice economical & ⟨beneficent⟩lucrative, we should all go to ruin presently. Parties keep the old names, but exhibit a surprising fugacity in creeping out of one snakeskin to form another of equal ignominy & lubricity: and, on Faneuil Hall, the grasshopper of the tower gives a proper hint of the men below.[52]

    [50] This sentence is used in "Boston," *W,* XII, 185.
    [51] Persons not previously or easily identified are: Theophilus Parsons (1750–1813), jurist; Christopher Gore (1758–1829), diplomat and politician; Harrison Gray Otis (1765–1848), statesman; George Cabot (1752–1823), businessman and politician; Thomas Handasyd Perkins (1764–1854), merchant and philanthropist; Samuel Dexter (1761–1816), statesman; John Davis (1761–1847), jurist; and William Tudor (1779–1830), author and editor.
    [52] "Everything . . . Faneuil Hall," is struck through in pencil with a diagonal use mark, which is canceled with two horizontal pencil lines below "ignominy"; "Everything . . . save us," and "Parties keep . . . below." are used in "The Fortune of the Republic," *W,* XI, 520–521. "Read at Music Hall March 1862" is written vertically in pencil in the left margin.

[74] Gurowski asked "Where is this bog?[n] I wish to earn some money: I wish to dig peat."—"O no, indeed, sir, you cannot do this kind of degrading work."—"I cannot be degraded. I am Gurowski."[53]

[75] I am often bewailing the slenderness of the rill of life. Talent & insight seem to make no difference in reconciling the disparity between demand & supply in each mental constitution.—

———— ↑See also Leonardo da Vinci's rule.↓[54]

But the shop of Power, Watt forgot to ⟨name⟩ ↑give us↓ the number of the street.   See *CO* 240, 249, 260.

————

I do not know that the gulf will ever be sho⟨o⟩t, that the supply will ever come up with the demand.

[76] *Good of evil.* Is any one ⟨such a lily-liver⟩ ↑so childish↓ as ⟨to⟩ not to[n] see the use of ⟨⟨all⟩ the⟩ opposition, poverty, & insult⟨, he meets⟩? ⟨Does he not know that ⟨the⟩⟩ Caricatures,[n] ni⟨i⟩cknames, parody, & abuse, ⟨that follow him,⟩[n] ⟨are just as much⟩ ↑are↓ his instructors, ⟨as the⟩ ↑no less than↓ galleries, ⟨the⟩ antiques, and literature.[n] ⟨are? He can no more spare [77] these than those.⟩[55] These echo & confirm his own doubts & suspicions of his short-comings, &, until he surmounts these by ⟨per⟩ new performance & defying superiority, he is only clever, &, as we say, talented, but not yet a master. I often say to young writers & speakers, that their best masters are their faultfinding brothers & sisters at home, who will not [78] spare them, but be sure to pick & cavil, & tell the odious truth. It is smooth mediocrity, ⟨the⟩ weary elegance, ⟨the⟩ surface finish of our ⟨dull⟩ voluminous stock-writers, or respectable artists, which ⟨prosperous inoffensiveness turns⟩ ↑easy times & a dull public call↓ out, without any salient genius, with an [79] indigence of all grand design, of all direct power↑.↓ ⟨on the

————

[53] Count Adam Gurowski (1805–1866), Polish writer, came to the United States in 1849, became a translator for the State Department, and wrote books on slavery and the Civil War. Emerson had borrowed Gurowski's *America and Europe* (New York, 1857) from the Boston Athenaeum February 1–March 11, 1858. The passage is struck through in pencil with a diagonal use mark.

[54] For "Talent & . . . rule.", see p. [16] above.

[55] "Is any . . . to see" is struck through in ink with two vertical and two diagonal use or cancellation marks. "He can . . . spare" is canceled with six vertical lines on p. [76]; the rest of the sentence is struck through horizontally on p. [77].

soul. Prescott, & Irving, & Everett, & Hallam, and⟩ A^n hundred
↑statesmen, ⟨&⟩ historians,↓ painters, & small poets, are thus made:
but Burns, & Carlyle, & Bettine, and Michel Angelo, ↑& Thoreau↓
were pupils in a rougher school.

It is very hard to go beyond your public. If they are satisfied with
your poor performance, you will not easily make better. But [80] if
they know what is good & delight in it, you will aspire, & burn, & toil,
till you achieve it.[56]

Good of Evil.

The chamber of flame in which the martyr passes, is more magnificent than ⟨any⟩ ↑the↓ royal apartment from which majesty looks
out on his sufferings.[57]

> The chamber of flame of the martyr
> Surpasses the palace of kings
> More rich than the royal window
> Looks out

[81] [blank]

[82] Do the duty of the day. Just now, the supreme public duty
of all thinking men is to assert freedom. Go where it is threatened, &
say, 'I am for it, & do not wish to live in the world a moment longer
than it exists.'

Phillips has the supreme merit in this time, that he & he alone stands
in the gap & breach against the assailants. Hold up his hands. He did
me the honor [83] to ask me to come to the meeting at ⟨M⟩ Tremont
Temple, &, esteeming such invitation a command, though sorely
against my inclination & habit, I went, and, though I had nothing to
say, showed myself. If I were dumb, yet I would have gone & mowed
& muttered or made signs. ↑The mob roared whenever I attempted to
speak, and after several ⟨attempts⟩beginnings, I withdrew.↓[58]

---

[56] This paragraph is used in "Progress of Culture," *W*, VIII, 215.

[57] For "The Chamber . . . apartment," see *JMN*, VIII, 370.

[58] According to Edward Emerson, this meeting of the Massachusetts Anti-Slavery
Society was held in the Tremont Temple, Boston, on January 24, 1861. See *J*, VII, 396,
and *JMN*, X, 224.

[84] The speech of the man in the street invariably strong, nor can you mend it. You say, if he could only express himself,—but he does already better than any one can for him.

I said in "Eloquence," that the man who knows most about the matter in hand can always get the ear of an audience, to the exclusion of everybody else.—Well, this is an example in point. That something which each man was created

pass to p. 86—[59]

[85] ↑*Leasts.*↓

All the music, Henry T[horeau]. says, is in the strain; the tune don't signify, 'tis all one vibration of the string. He says, people sing a song, or play a tune, only for one strain that is in it.   I don't understand this, & remind him that collocation makes the force of a word, & that Wren's rule, *"position essential to beauty,"* is universally true, but accept what I know of the doctrine of leasts.[60] ↑Maupertuis is the author of the doctrine that nature uses the minim of power for every change.↓

Leasts. *CO* 77, 85, 147

[86] *from p 84*

to say & do, he only or he best can tell you, & has a right to supreme attention so far. And hence, too, the truth, that all biography is auto-bi↑o↓graphy,[61] or, whatever floats in the world concerning any man was first communicated by himself to his companion; all else is wide of the mark.

[87] "My lord," said the shipbuilder to Lord Dundonald, "we live by repairing ships, as well as by building them, and the worm is our best

---

[59] With "I said . . . else." on p. [84], struck through in ink with two diagonal use marks, cf. "Eloquence," *W*, VII, 85, and *JMN*, IX, 390. "The speech . . . created" and "to say . . . so far." on p. [86] below are used in "Eloquence," *W*, VIII, 125.

[60] With "All the music . . . strain;", cf. "Thoreau," *W*, X, 474. "Wren's rule, . . . *beauty,*' " is used in "Woman," *W*, XI, 410.

[61] For "all biography is auto-biography," see *JMN*, X, 171, and "Theodore Parker," *W*, XI, 285.

friend. Rather than use your preparation, I would cover ships' bottoms with honey to attract worms."

His object was to induce Gov[ernmen]t. to use coal-tar for protecting the bottoms of inferior ships of war, before the days of copper sheathing.[62]

[88] "But Varchi's ↑(tears for liberty")↓ says Grimm, "⟨tears⟩are the tears of a historian; &, well as he speaks of the old ↑free↓ Florence, he has nothing to say ↑in this regard↓ of the new Florence, in which he lives so comfortably." See "Life of M. Angelo" p. 80[63]

[89] I read many friendly & many hostile paragraphs in the journals about my new book,[64] but seldom or never a just criticism. As long as I do not wince, ↑it cannot be that↓ the fault ⟨cannot be⟩ ↑is↓ touched. When ⟨Mrs Rollins⟩ ↑the adept↓ applies ⟨her⟩ ↑this↓ ⟨b⟩galvanic battery now to this part, then to that, on the patient's head, the patient makes no sign, for lungs are sound, & liver, & heart: but, at last, ⟨she⟩ ↑he↓ touches another point, & the patient ⟨cries aloud⟩ screams, for it seems there is bronchitis, or is hip disease.

[90] And when the critics hit ⟨me⟩ ↑you↓, I suppose ⟨I shall⟩ ↑you will↓ know it. I often think I could write a criticism on Emerson, that would hit the white.

The Lyceum should refuse what is written for it. V 22

———

Vulgar people state objections acutely. G 58

[91] 27 Feb., 1861. Long peace makes men routinary & gregarious. They all walk arm in arm. Poverty, the sea, the frost, farming, hunting, ↑the↓ emigrant, the soldier, must ⟨learn⟩teach[n] self reliance, to take the initiative, & never lose their head.

In the South, slavery & hunting & horsemanship & the climate, & pol-

---

[62] See Thomas Cochrane, 10th Earl of Dundonald, *The Autobiography of a Seaman*, 2 vols. (London, 1860), I, 44–45. Emerson withdrew volume 1 from the Boston Athenaeum February 19–28, 1861.

[63] Grimm, *Leben Michelangelo's*, 1860–1863, vol. I.

[64] *The Conduct of Life*, published in December 1860.

itics, give the⟨m⟩ men self-reliance; & the South is well officered, &, with some right, they despise the peaceful north people, leaning on the law, & on each other. In proportion to the number [92] of self-reliant persons, will the power & attitude of the state be.

———

Theodore Parker was our Savonarola.

———

Liberty, like religion, is a short & hasty fruit of rare & happy conditions.[65]

———

[93] French proverbs
"Il n⟨e f⟩'est que le matin en toutes choses."[66]

> Il fait un temps de demoiselle,
> Ni pluie, ni vent, ni soleil.

[94] For really every object in nature is a little window through which the whole universe may be seen. For, every one, say, a cat, or a partridge, or a pickere⟨el⟩l, has relations to all other things, to the state of land & water, to the climate, &, of course, to latitude & longitude, to the atmosphere, to the bulk of the planet, & the system of animals, &, from this single specimen, a Naturalist might gradually make out the *systema Naturae.*

[95] Detachment by illumination is the gift of genius, as I have somewhere written.[67] The poet sees some figure for a moment in an expressive attitude & surroundings, &, without hesitating, because i⟨s⟩t is a mere purposeless fragment, he paints out that figure with what ski⟨n⟩ll & energy he has.

[96] Poetry will never be a simple means, as when history or philosophy is rhymed, or laureate odes on state occasions, are used,

---

[65] This sentence is struck through in ink with a vertical use mark. "Liberty, like . . . fruit" is used in "The Fortune of the Republic," *W,* XI, 539.

[66] See Journal DL, p. [99] above.

[67] Cf. *JMN,* X, 352, and "Powers and Laws of Thought," *W,* XII, 39.

Poetry must be the end to which it is written, or it is nought.[68]

See Spenser's delight in his art for his own skill's sake, in the Muiopotmos *O* 336

[97]   "Oft have I heard, & deem the witness true,
          Whom man delights in, God delights in too."
                              Pons de Capdueil[69] [*O* 1, 162]

———

Is there sufficiency of pounds of power to the area of the man? See *O* ⟨117⟩ ↑115↓

———

    Thine & mine   *O* 132
Alcott & Edward Taylor,—one is the fool of his idea, the other of his fancy.[70] [*O* 136]

———

The noblest Alchemy   *O* 146

———

I go for churches of one. Break no springs. Make no cripples. A fatal disservice does this Swedenborg or other lawyer who offers to do my thinking for me.[71] *O* 152

[98]   ↑Tufts College.↓[72]
Common sense on literary drill. That none but a writer should write, & that he shall not dig. *O* 172

[99]   Life a selection. *O* 270

---

[68] "Poetry will . . . nought.", struck through in pencil with two diagonal use marks in the shape of an X, is used in "Poetry and Imagination," *W*, VIII, 54.

[69] See *JMN*, XIV, 412, where the source is given as *Lays of the Minnesingers or German Troubadours of the Twelfth and Thirteenth Centuries* . . . , ed. Edgar Taylor (London, 1825), p. 220. The lines are used in "Success," *W*, VII, 306, and "Poetry and Imagination," *W*, VIII, 37.

[70] This sentence is marked in the left margin by two pencil lines, one long and one short.

[71] "A fatal . . . me." is used in "The Sovereignty of Ethics," *W*, X, 200.

[72] Emerson gave the lecture "Celebration of the Intellect" at Tufts College on July 10, 1861.

We are mammalia of a higher element, &, as the whale must come to the top of the water for air, we must go to the top of the air, now & then, for thought.

The dance, *O* 294, 306,   *Bacchus, O* 306

———

Life constantly attacks us, &, notwithstanding all our struggles, is eating us up.[73] [O 327]

———

The naturalist witnesses personally the creation of the world. *O* 332

[100] ⟨Life⟩ ↑Welfare↓ consists in or requires one or two companions of intelligence, probity & grace to wear out life with[.][74]

———

We admire our fathers quite too much. It shows that we have no energy in ourselves, when we rate it so prodigiously high.

↑Rather↓ let[n] us shame the fathers by superior virtue in the sons.[75]

[101] ———
I like dry light, & hard clouds, hard expressions, & hard manners.[76]

Persifleurs
    "For Laughter never looked upon his brow."
                Giles Fletcher. ["Christ's Victory and
                    Triumph on Earth," stanza 12][77]

[73] In *JMN,* IX, 449, the sentence is attributed to William Ellery Channing. See "Life is eating us up" in "Montaigne," *W,* IV, 154; "Resources," *W,* VIII, 138; and Emerson's "Visits to Concord" in *Memoirs of Margaret Fuller Ossoli,* 2 vols. (Boston, 1852), I, 210.

[74] This sentence is used in "Social Aims," *W,* VIII, 89.

[75] This sentence, struck through in pencil with a diagonal use mark, is used in "Boston," *W,* XII, 210.

[76] For "dry light," see Journal DL, p. [10] above; for "hard clouds, . . . manners.", see *JMN,* IX, 31.

[77] See *JMN,* XIV, 63.

"because those gentlemen continued to keep the same rank in society when they grew up that they held when ⟨boys⟩they were boys."

Dr A. Carlyle. Autobiography p 28[78]

See below a related passage from Life of Sydney. *GL* 144

[102] Sects are stoves, but fire keeps its old properties through them all. [U 87]

⟨There are⟩ ↑But who knows the↓ periods of fertility & of sterility of souls. Sometimes men descend for the benevolent purpose of leading back apostate souls to right principles.

See U 97

Every man has his Diminisher & his Enlarger in his set. *U* 99[79]

―――

"Manners are stronger than laws."[80]

Dr A. Carlyle [*Autobiography . . .* , 1861, p. 262]

[103] When the thought comes, we stand like Atlas on our legs, & uphold the world. *U* 117[81]

"For the living out of doors, & simple fare, & gymnastic exercises, & the morals of companions, produce the greatest effect in the way of virtue & of vice⟨s⟩."

Plato, [*The Works . . .* , 1848–1854,] Vol. VI. [pp. 165–]166[82]

[104] Only our newest knowledge works as a source of inspiration & thought, as only the outmost layer of liber in the tree.[83]

―――

[78] Alexander Carlyle, *Autobiography of the Rev. Dr. Alexander Carlyle, . . .* (Boston, 1861), pp. 27–28. See *JMN,* XI, 389.

[79] Journal U, p. [99], is torn out, but see *JMN,* XII, 529.

[80] This quotation is used in "Social Aims," *W,* VIII, 81.

[81] Two vertical lines in pencil are drawn in the left margin beside "When the . . . legs,".

[82] The quotation is used in "Country Life," *W,* XII, 142; see also *JMN,* XIV, 165.

[83] This sentence, struck through in pencil with three diagonal use marks, crossed with three more, is used in "Inspiration," *W,* VIII, 295.

Not what you see imports, but with what idea.[84] ⟨Trees are⟩ ↑The most tender, the most radiant, the most sublime landscape is↓ stark as tombstones, except seen by the thoughtful.

What came over me with delight as I sat on the ledge in the warm light of last Sunday, was [105] the memory of young days at College, the delicious sensibility of youth, how the air rings to it! how all light is festal to it! how it at any moment extemporizes a holiday! I remember how boys riding out together on a fine day looked to me! ah there was a romance! How sufficing was mere melody! The thought, the meaning was insignificant[;] the whole ⟨attraction⟩ joy was in the melody. For that I read poetry, & wrote it; and in the light of that memory I ought to understand the [106] doctrine of Musicians, that the words are nothing, the air is all.

What a joy I found, & still can find, in the Aeolian harp! What a youth find I still in Collins's "Ode to Evening," & in Gray's "Eton College"! What delight I owed to Moore's insignificant but melodious poetry! That is the merit of Clough's "Bothie," that the joy of youth is [107] in it. Ah the power of the spring! and, ah the voice of the bluebird! And the witchcraft of the Mount Auburn dell, in those days! I shall be a Squire Slender for a week.[85]

⟨For sources of inspiration,⟩ Greenough said, the Elgin marbles taken together put the horse through all his paces, so that one feels as if he had seen the motion; as in the ph⟨e⟩anakistiscope.[86] So is it with nature, as seen by botanist or zoologist, if poetical.

For sources of inspiration, all poetic men will agree in [108] a respect for fact-books, and more or less skill to turn them to an account ⟨little⟩ ↑least↓ thought-of by those who wrote them:

    Fact books,
    dictionaries,

---

[84] Two vertical lines in pencil are drawn in the left margin beside "Not what . . . idea."

[85] With "What came . . . in it.", cf. "The Harp," *W*, IX, 237–241; with "ah the voice . . . days!", cf. "May-Day," ll. 180–181, *W*, IX, 169. Squire Slender is a half-witted cousin of Shallow in Shakespeare's *Merry Wives of Windsor*.

[86] With this sentence, cf. *JMN*, XIII, 108.

new poetry, by which I mean chiefly, old poetry that is new to me, are the preparatives of the poet for his hour.[87]

See of the indifferency of your subject,[88] *AC* 290

---

[109] Senior Sophister   ↑GO 29, 90   GH 14↓[89]
priority of music to thought   AZ 261

⟨J Q Adams's speech to his class at Cambridge inserted in Σ⟩[90]

---

[110] Clouds & grass are older antiquities than pyramids or Athens.[91]

Nobody can look at a cistus or a brentus(?) without sighing at his ignorance. It is an unknown America. See *A* 39

[111] Mr. Wm Alexander wrote to Dr Blair offering him a thousand pounds if he ⟨c⟩would teach him the art of speaking in public.[92] *Dr A Carlyle's Autobiography*[n] [1861,] p. 363.

One thing strikes me in all good poetry, that the poet goes straight forward to say ⟨the thing in his mind⟩ ↑his thought↓ & the words & images fly to him to express it, whilst colder moods are forced to hint the matter, or insinuate, or perhaps only allude to it [112] being unable to fuse & mould their words & images to fluid obedience[.][93]

---

[87] "little" is canceled, and "least" inserted, in pencil. "new poetry, . . . hour." is struck through in pencil with three diagonal use marks; for "new poetry . . . to me," and for "Fact books," see "Inspiration," *W*, VIII, 294 and 295.

[88] Cf. "Poetry and Imagination," *W*, VIII, 34.

[89] "GO . . . GH 14" is in pencil.

[90] This sentence is in erased pencil. A part of John Quincy Adams's final lecture at Cambridge, delivered July 28, 1809, is used in "Eloquence," *W*, VIII, 123–124.

[91] With this sentence, cf. "Art and Criticism," *W*, XII, 304–305; see also *JMN*, IV, 282.

[92] This quotation, struck through in ink with three diagonal use marks, crossed by a fourth, is used in "Eloquence," *W*, VIII, 117–118. The "w" in "⟨c⟩would" is added in pencil.

[93] This sentence is used in "Poetry and Imagination," *W*, VIII, 30.

[113] The place which I have not sought, but in which my duty puts me, is the right palace. I feel with pleasing awe the immensity of the chain of which I hold the last link in my hand, & am led by it.[94]

A 40

He had the eye to see the navy in the acorn. [A 43]

In him is the source of all the romance, the lustre & dignity which fascinated him. For truth, honor, learning, perseverance, are the Jove & Apollo who bewitched him.[95] *A* 50

[114][96] Concert
flute a toy

audience condescends

The man with a talent is all⟨.⟩↑:↓ story in the journals of a seedy prisoner in the police courts with a flute, who played, &, by common consent, went off without fines.
Whole ponderous machinery of State just to bring out this skill in each[97]

[115] ↑Bards &↓ Trouveurs, *VS* 159   ↑*CL* 167   GL 97↓
                    VO 245   *SO* 114
                    Taliessin   *DO* 106, *LN* 33,
                    AC 294
                    V   *ZO* 141[98]

---

[94] "I feel . . . by it." is used in "Character," *W*, X, 122.
[95] Three vertical pencil lines are drawn in the left margin beside "In him . . . all the".
[96] Page [114] is in pencil.
[97] "The man . . . fines." is struck through in pencil with two vertical use marks, and "The man . . . each" with one. For "story in . . . fines.", see "Perpetual Forces," *W*, X, 80; "The man . . . all⟨.⟩↑:↓" and "Whole ponderous . . . each" are used in "Powers and Laws of Thought," *W*, XII, 48.
[98] "*CL* 167", "GL 97", and "*AC* 294" are in pencil. Journal VS, p.[159], CL, p. [167], DO, p. [106], and ZO, p. [141] are used in the section "Bards and Trouveurs" of "Poetry and Imagination," *W*, VIII, 59, 60, 58–59, and 60. With SO, p. [114], cf. *ibid.*, p. 59.

[116]   ↑*New England*↓
     Southern country officered from New England, preachers, teach-
ers, editors, members of Congress, lawyers, physicians. 'Tis a sort of
Scotland. 'Tis hard to say why: climate is much: then, old accumulation of the means, ⟨colleges⟩ books, schools, colleges, literary society.
As ⟨in⟩ New Bedford, ⟨t⟩is not nearer to the whales, than New London
or Portland, yet they have got all the equipments for a whaler there, &
they hug an oil-cask like a brother. 'Tis hard to say why: [117] I don't
know that Concord ↑or Charles River↓ water is more clarifying to the
brain than the Savannah or ⟨Alabama⟩ ↑Tombigbee↓ ⟨rivers⟩. Yet this
is your lot in the urn.[99] Cherish the school.

     Joy of reading. Alfred   see *VS* 237.
     Frost good for apples & men [cf. H 62]
     manbearing granite [GL 122]
     Advantage of high literary tone, ↑GL↓ 79
          Dr Blair[100] [GL 111]

M[ary] M[oody] E[merson] speaks of her attempts in Malden "to
wake up the soul amid the dreary scenes of monotonous sabbaths,
when nature ⟨app⟩looked like a pulpit."[101]

     [118] Ralph Emerson in Paris, ↑in 1833,↓ said to me that he
possessed a certain advantage there, in business, from the settled belief
of other Americans that there was some magic in speaking French, &
not, like all other arts, mere iteration, a step at a time, like learning a
trade. So is it with public speaking, as Dr Blair might have told Mr
Alexander: and so, I must not doubt, with music & mathematics. The
order of logical learning is one, & the order of wonder [119] or of ex-

     [99] Page [116] is struck through in pencil with a vertical use mark. With "Southern
country . . . physicians.", cf. "Boston," *W*, XII, 196; "Tis a sort . . . ⟨rivers⟩." is used in
ibid., p. 186. "Alabama" and "rivers" are canceled, and "Tombigbee" added, in pencil.
For "this is . . . the urn.", see Journal DL, p. [119] above.
     [100] "Joy of . . . Dr Blair" is in pencil.
     [101] This entry is used in "Mary Moody Emerson," *W*, X, 411. With "when nature
. . . pulpit.' ", struck through in ink with five diagonal use marks, cf. "Character," *W*, X,
107.

hibition, quite another. See what I have written of *Pace,* & of Wilkie's picture.[102]

March 16. I have seldom paid money with so much pleasure as today to Dr Barrett, fifty cents, for taking with a probe a little cinder ⟨f⟩out of my left eye, which had annoyed me for a week.[103]

___

"Time is only truly precious to more highly organized natures."

Goethe[104]

There are men who get a good living by painting the little ornament ⟨of a⟩ or crest on a carriage panel   as, a dragon's head or a bird[.]
So the decorators of crockery ware

[120]   The Calling.
Linnaeus had a specialty
the telescope maker Clark,
Bowditch for the antiquarian in real estate titles
The patent-lawyers as Whiting & Giles
Warren Colburn in mathematics
Charles T Jackson in chemistry
Morphy in chess
Steers in boats[105]
A pug-nosed model in Paris sits for Socrates.

___

M N got a good living by his rare nicety of palate, being employed by the wine merchants as a taster.

___

[102] For the remark of Ralph Emerson, Emerson's second cousin, see *JMN,* IV, 305. For Dr. Blair and Mr. Alexander, see p. [111] above. For *"Pace . . .* picture.", see *JMN,* XIV, 190, 249, 310–311, and 314.
[103] Dr. Henry A. Barrett practiced medicine in Concord from 1845 until his death in 1889.
[104] See *JMN,* IX, 201.
[105] Of those not previously or easily identified, Nathaniel Bowditch (1805–1861), author, was the son of the mathematician and astronomer of the same name; William Whiting (1813–1873), a Concord lawyer; Warren Colburn (1793–1833), American educator; Paul Charles Morphy (1837–1884), world's chess master; and George Steers (1820–1856), naval architect. Giles has not been identified.

Dr Dorr told me of a man in Chicago, who was employed from distant places to make up Insurance Averages.

———

[121] *Concord*
                 The oranges hide under glass
                 The pines laugh out in the snow
                 The pines can wade in snow
                 ⟨Made of the same air that blows outside⟩[106]

But when in May the lilac blooms

———

In 1775, the patriotism in Mass[achuse]tts was so hot, that it melted the snow, & the rye *waved*ʺ on the 19 April[.][107]

                 In ⟨m⟩your garden delicate limes
                 ⟨In my plot no tulips blow⟩
                 ⟨Snow loving pines & oaks instead⟩
                 And weave a carpet for the wood
                 The wintergreen & lycopod
                 Their poverty & hardihood
                           My trees know the way to the sky
                           As well as yours & climb as fast[108]

[122][109] manbearing granite   CO 176[110]

          Where ⟨fr⟩ⁿ ↑off the↓ Gulf the south winds blow
          And where
          The sense with orange & magnolia pleased

[106] "Made of . . . outside", canceled in both ink and pencil, and struck through in ink with three vertical use or cancellation marks, is used in "The Titmouse," l. 78, *W*, IX, 236.

[107] This sentence is struck through in ink with two wavy diagonal use marks.

[108] "My trees . . . fast" is in pencil. "⟨In my plot . . . instead⟩", each line struck through in ink with a vertical use mark, is used in "My Garden," ll. 5–6, *W*, IX, 229.

[109] Page [122] is in pencil.

[110] A curved pencil line separates "CO 176" from "manbearing granite", which also occurs on p. [117] above.

Here half the year
We're
Shrouded in snow
And summer winds are dashed with East
And with Famine checks the feast

Brag not the courage which you lack
Nor take your fathers' names in vain

CL 153

Troubadour   *CL* 167

[123]   The stern old Calvinist
               Doubled religion in his fist

Not for a regiment's parade
Nor evil laws or rulers made
Blue Walden fired its cannonade

These echoes raise
No marsellaise

               ⟨Smilax⟩Where the tough greenbriar in the wilds
               ⟨Green⟩ ↑Its live↓ Arcadian ladders ⟨twines⟩ builds

Wh[111]
               The wind will go down with the sun [E 257]

[124] I told the School Company at the Town Hall, this P. M., that I felt a little like the old gentleman who had dandled ten sons & daughters of his own in succession on his knee, when his grandchild was brought to him, "No," he said, "he had cried kitty-kitty long enough."[112] And yet when I heard now ⟨these⟩ recitations & exercises,[n] I was willing to feel new interest still.

---

[111] "Not for . . . builds" and "Wh" are in pencil. "Not for . . . cannonade" is used in "May-Day," ll. 104–106, *W*, IX, 166.

[112] Emerson was on the Concord school committee, whose members were invited to speak at the end of the winter term; see *J*, IX, 314–315. For "the old gentleman . . . enough.' ", see *JMN*, XI, 262.

[125] I was reminded of Dr Alexander's offer to Dr Blair, of 1000 pounds, if he would teach him to speak with propriety in public;[113] and I thought he might have been instructed for that price in the Concord schools.

I suggested for the ⟨i⟩encouragement or the ⟨a⟩warning of the parents my feeling today, that the new generation was an improved edition of the adult: [126] then I spoke of Faulkner,—who had adorned & honored the town by his sweet & faultless youth[.][114]

In conclusion, I said, that one thing was plain, that the end of the institutions of the town, & the end of the town itself is education.[115]

[127] I intended to say much more to give an account of P[eter] Bulkeley's will   of Eng[lish] ⟨j⟩Judges recommending prisoners to mercy, because they could read & write: of the 16 peers of France who have no other distinction than thought.
↑& the arts of thought, that is writing & speaking↓[116]

[128] Mr Heinzen should know, as materialist, that, every force ⟨is⟩ ↑has↓ worth only so far as it comes to appearance.[117]

"We mark the /aim/animus/, & are untuned," said Goethe.
i.e. ⟨if we read⟩ the book ⟨was⟩ written for the irresistible beauty or force of the story, or of the thought, in the writer's mind, we freely read; but if we detect that Miss Martineau wrote the story to bolster

---

[113] See p. [111] above.
[114] "A boy of charming personality and admirable scholarship from . . . Acton. He had entered college from Mr. Sanborn's school and was killed in crossing the railroad at Cambridge." (J, IX, 316.)
[115] A vertical line in pencil is drawn in the left margin beside this entry.
[116] A vertical pencil line is drawn in the left margin beside this paragraph; "& the arts . . . speaking" is added in pencil. For Peter Bulkeley's will, which includes a list of books that he left to his sons, see J, IX, 316–317. For "the 16 . . . thought.", see JMN, XIII, 337, where the statement is quoted from Francis Lieber, Manual of Political Ethics, 2 vols. (Boston, 1838–1839), II, 125.
[117] Karl Peter Heinzen (1809–1880), German revolutionist, journalist, and author, came to Boston in 1859.

up some dogma of political economy, & thus the book is nothing but a paid opinion, we drop the book.

[129] Theanor & Amphitryon. Z[A] 161

Ridicule ↑is↓ the ⟨a⟩natural offset of terror. A mob can be dispersed by a water-engine, or by a contribution box. How many good expedients I have heard of Beecher & of Phillips which succeeded in stopping the hissing of mobs.

Life affirmative^n V 56.[118]

[130]   ↑*We import our theology.*↓
I remember it was gossiped of —— when he returned from Pari[s], that, though a clergyman, he had accepted all the accommodations of the Palais Royal. So I think we feel that deduction to the merit↓s↓ of Behmen, of Swedenborg, & of other geniuses, that, though great men, they accepted the accommodations of the Hebrew Dynasty, &, of course, cannot take rank with the masters of the world.[119]

[131] Blessed are the unconscious. I wish the man to please himself, then he will please me.

But I cannot make any exceptions. ⟨See the page V ⟨50⟩ 48⟩(See V 50, 48,)[120]

L[idian?]. says "they all do right wrong."
The children wake up in their⟨s⟩ beds at midnight, & say, 'come let's talk about our next New Year's presents.' They will never be young but once.[121]

---

[118] "Life affirmative V 56." is in pencil. Above it "Life affirmative V 56" was also written in pencil and erased, probably earlier than "How many . . . of Beecher", which is written around the erasure. With "Ridicule ↑is↓ . . . mobs.", cf. "Resources," *W*, VIII, 147–148.

[119] With "So I think . . . world.", cf. *JMN*, IX, 107.

[120] "⟨See the . . . 48⟩" is in pencil. For "I wish . . . me.", see *JMN*, IX, 120.

[121] "hef [?]" is written in pencil above the word "beds" but may have been inscribed earlier.

—

Here came Ellen ⟨w⟩ "wishing to be as good as God."

—

The miller ⟨&⟩ ↑bestrode↓ his overloaded horse—& the horse easily drew the waggon & all.

[132] A scholar is a diamond merchant. ↑Montaigne valued sentences↓   ↑See Lect. on *Powers of thought*. p. 11.↓ Maupertuis & his minims, & his epicurism, & his flattening of the poles.[122]

Practical. Idea & Action. see *TO* 27⟨3⟩6

[133] Yesterday I saw Rarey's exhibition in Boston.[123] What a piece of clean good sense was the whole performance, the teaching & the doing! ⟨One⟩ ↑An↓ attack on the customary nonsense of nations in one particular. The horse does not attack you till you attack him. He does not know his own strength, until you teach it him. Just keep yourself then in such position that he always finds you ↑the↓ strongest, & he believes you invincible. Make him not resist you, by always stroking & conciliating him. Hold the drum, or strap up to his nose, let him get acquainted [134] with it, & he will not fear it. When he sh⟨es⟩ies ⟨do not⟩ whip him & he will shy again the more, because [he] has not only the terror of the object, but the terror of the whip, associated.

[135][124]   Six Lectures on
          Life & literature

          Genius and Temperament
          Art

---

[122] "Montaigne valued sentences" is in pencil. For "A scholar . . . merchant.", see Journal DL, p. [108] above. With "Maupertuis & his minims," cf. *JMN*, XIV, 86, and for "his flattening . . . poles.", see *JMN*, XIII, 451.

[123] John Solomon Rarey (1827–1866), an American horse tamer, achieved great success in England and Europe before returning to America in 1860.

[124] Page [135] is in pencil. From April 9 to May 15, 1861, Emerson gave his "Life and Literature" series at the Meionaon in Boston; the six weekly lectures were announced as "Genius and Temperament," "Art," "Civilization at a Pinch," "Good Books," "Poetry and Criticism in England and America," and "Boston." On May 25, he read "Doctrine of Leasts" at Mrs. Parkman's. See *L*, V, 243 and 247.

An account of some good books
Poetry in Eng[lan]d & America
Doctrine of Leasts

Boston

⟨Art⟩

Platonists

[136]   Indianapolis
1863 Jan. 26. *"Titan"* I have read on this journey,[125] and, for its noble
wisdom & insight, forgive, what still annoys me, its excessive efflores-
cence & German superlative. How like to Goethe's Wilhelm Meister,
is its culture, manners, & wisdom! Rome is the best part of it, &
therein it resembles Goethe the more. Now & then, I find a passage
like Charles Newcomb. And how it restores to me the golden thoughts
that once wreathed around Margaret F[uller]. & Caroline [Sturgis
Tappan], & S[amuel]. G[ray]. W[ard]. and Anna [Barker Ward].

[137] March 26, 1861.
      Yesterday wrote to F[rederick]. G[oddard]. Tuckerman to
thank him for his book, & praised Rhotruda.[126] Ellery C[hanning].
finds two or three good lines & metres in the book, thinks it refined
& delicate, but says, the young poets ⟨have⟩ ↑run on↓ a notion that
they must name the flowers, talk about an orchis, & say something
about Indians; but, he says, "I prefer passion & sense & genius to
botany."

Ellery says of Tennyson, "What is best, is, the things he don't say."

[125] For *"Titan"*, see Journal DL, p. [203] above.
[126] *Poems* (Boston, 1860). A copy of the London, 1863, edition is in Emerson's library. The poem "Rhotruda" also appeared in the *Atlantic Monthly*, VIII (July 1861),
72–75, apparently at Emerson's suggestion. For Emerson's letter to Tuckerman, see *The
Complete Poems of Frederick Goddard Tuckerman,* ed. N. Scott Momaday (New York,
1965), pp. xx–xxi, where the date is given as March 28, 1861. The poem is included in
Parnassus, pp. 357–360.

[138] Most men believe that their goodness is made of themselves. Others have the converse opinion. What a probity has W[illiam]. E[merson]. It shines in all his face & demeanor. He has never analysed or inquired into it. But if he thinks at all, he thinks it is a part of him. But, in reality, he exists from that, & all of him, but that, is caducous.

[139] Civilization a mistake. *SO* [88–]89
Self-supporting institutions. *SO* 42
Its words; e.g. analogy, homology. *DO* [1–]2
When will civilization stop?

[140] Qu'est ce qu'un classique?
                    SO 74———82
                    AC 59
          Illusions *LI* 164
          Genius   S[(Salvage) 19, 167, 168]
          Classic in Landscape   S [(Salvage)] 177
          VO 254
          Webster classic, Everett romantic.
"What happened interested them, what is tho't & felt, us." *Goethe*[127]

Antique expresses moral sentiment without cant.

[141] Rareness of genius & poetry. Is it difficult for the gods to appear?
See motto to *W*

χαλεποι δε Θεοι Φαινε(θαι)σθαι εναργεις[128]
                                        Iliad Book 20, 131.

[142] ———
We say he has gained power who has abdicated morals. A good exam-

---

[127] *Winckelmann und sein Jahrhundert*; see *Werke*, 55 vols. (Stuttgart and Tübingen, 1828–1833), XXXVII, 21. For this quotation, and the sentence below, see *JMN*, VI, 398.
[128] "For hard are the gods to look upon when they appear in manifest presence." See *JMN*, IX, 183.

ple of it, is, the bad boys in a school or a college[.]

—— ↑Scholar a diamond merchant:↓

A scholar is a collector of finer coins than the numismatologist, finer shells than the conchologist,[129]

[143] The Crisis.

> "These we must join to wake, for these are of the strain
> That justice dare defend & will the age ⟨m⟩sustain."[130]
>   [Ben Jonson, *The Golden Age Restored,* ll. 130–131]

Majorities, *DO* 169

Aaron Burr's definition of Law   BL 261

Now for the first time we stand among nations for freedom[.]

The wish that never before had legs long enough to wade across the Potomac.[131]

[144]   *Boys* (see above p 101)

Lord Brook, in his Life of Sir Philip Sydney, says,

"Of whose youth I will report no other wonder but this; that though I lived with him, & knew him from a child, yet I never knew him other than a man: with such staidness of mind, lovely & familiar gravity, as carried grace & reverence above greater years: [145][132] His talk ever of knowledge, & his very play tending to enrich his mind." ⟨So as even

---

[129] For "Scholar a . . . merchant:", in pencil, see p. [132] above. For "A scholar . . . conchologist," see Journal DL, p. [87] above.

[130] This couplet is used in "The Fortune of the Republic," *W,* XI, 524; see also *JMN,* XIII, 5.

[131] With "The wish . . . Potomac.", struck through in ink with a vertical use mark, and "Now for . . . freedom", cf. "American Civilization," *W,* XI, 303 and 310.

[132] "greater years:" is followed by a hand sign and "(See next page)". "His talk . . . Cowley, also" is continued on the lower half of p. [145] to the right of the list of names inscribed earlier, boxed in ink; "From last page." is inscribed above it. "So as . . . him to" is finger-wiped.

his teachers found something in him to⟩ &c. [Vol. I] p. 5, Egerton
Brydges' Edition[133]

See of Gray, & of Cowley, also

Yesterday, 30 March, at the Club, which now numbers nineteen.[134]

x	Agassiz	⟨Yes⟩We had present twelve members,
x	Appleton	& guests, Mr Bovee of N.Y.
		Mr Couthouy
x	Cabot	Mr Rowse—[135]
	Dana	
x	Emerson	
	Forbes	
	Hawthorne	
	Hedge	
x	Hoar	
x	Holmes	
x	Howe	
x	Longfellow	
x	Lowell	
	Motley	
x	Norton	
	Pierce	
	↑Sumner↓	
	Ward	
x	Whipple	
x	Woodman	

[133] Sir Fulke Greville, 1st Baron Brooke, *Lord Brook's Life of Sir Philip Sydney. With a Preface, &c. by Sir Egerton Brydges,* 2 vols. (Kent, 1816).

[134] The commas after "Yesterday", "March", and "Club" are in both ink and pencil. In the list below, the x's are in pencil; a wavy vertical pencil line is drawn to the right of the list of names. See Journal DL, pp. [142] and [154] above.

[135] Probably Christian N. Bovee (1820–1904), New York author and lawyer; Joseph P. Couthouy (1808–1864), naturalist, member of the Wilkes exploring expedition of 1838–1842, officer in the Navy during the Civil War; and Samuel Worcester Rowse (see Journal DL, p. [142] above).

[146] I fear, 'tis not for me to recall the perception at night in New Bedford of the potential insight of us all[.][136]

[147] We might call our age the age of ⟨recuperation⟩ ↑Renaissance.↓ We have recovered the Elgin marbles, Nineveh, the pyramid frescoes, Cicero de Republi⟨a⟩ca, the Tischendorf Manuscript, the Champollion inscriptions, Giotto's head of Dante, Milton's Christian Doctrine, reading of papyri

publication of Sanscrit Vedas   2500 years old

the forms & faces of the ⟨bur⟩ people of Pompeii buried in the ashes of Vesuvius

the accurately determined age of men of the stone, bronze, & iron ages, the lacustrine remains
the insight into mythology alike everywhere in its element

recovery of antique statues
reconstruction of the ground plan & elevation of temples which war, earthquake & iconoclasts of all creeds had not been able to utterly disintegrate.[137]

[148][138] Apr. 5. Sent cards to my new course of Lectures to

3	Dr Frothingham
3	C[yrus]. A. Bartol
3	Dr Dewey
3	Mrs Cobb
4	Mr Ward
2	Mr Woodman
2	⟨Mr⟩ ↑E.P.↓ Whipple
2	Capt Couthouy

[136] On the evening of April 2, 1861, Emerson lectured on "Conversation" at New Bedford, Mass.

[137] "earthquake & . . . disintegrate." is run over onto p. [148] to the left of the list of names inscribed earlier.

[138] Except for the "2", written in ink over the "1" before "Mr. Sanbo[r]n", all the numerals on p. [148] are added in pencil.

3 C A Lambard
2 Mr [George Partridge] Bradford
2 Dr Hedge
2 [John] Haven Emerson
3 E[lbridge]. G. Dudley Esq
2 C K Whipple
⟨1⟩2 Mr Sanbo[r]n
2 Miss P[hebe] Ripley
2 Miss Peabody
4 Dr Jackson

[149] 3   Abel Adams
3 Ellen T. E[merson].   ↑Apr. ⟨2⟩17 To be sent
2 Edith E[merson]   W. E. Forster x
3 Mrs. Lowell   H[erman]. Grimm x
                                L[ydia]. M. Child
                                Mrs Marsh↓[139]

[150] When somebody said to ↑Rev.↓ Dr Payson "how much you must enjoy religion, since you live always in administering it," he replied, that nobody enjoyed religion less than ministers, as none enjoyed food so little as cooks.[140]

——

Bishop Clark ↑of Rhode Island↓ told of a dispute in a vestry at Providence between two hot church-members. One said at last, "I should like to know who *you* are."—"Who I am!" cried the other, "Who I am! I am a humble Christian, you damned old heathen, you!"[141]

[151] One capital advantage of old age is the absolute insignificance of a success more or less. I ⟨r⟩went to town & read a lecture yesterday. Thirty years ago it had really been a matter of ⟨much⟩ importance to

[139] Except for the *x*'s in ink, "Apr ⟨2⟩17 . . . Mrs Marsh" is in pencil.
[140] See Asa Cummings, *A Memoir of the Rev. Edward Payson, D.D.* (Boston, 1830), p. 259; in Emerson's library.
[141] Thomas March Clark (1812–1903) was elected Episcopal bishop of Rhode Island in 1854.

me whether it was good & effective. Now it is of none in ⟨that⟩ relation to me. It is long already fixed what I can ⟨&⟩↑& what I↓ cannot do, & the ⟨kno⟩ reputation of the man does not gain or suffer from one or a dozen new performances. If I should in a [152]¹⁴² new performance rise quite beyond my mark, & do somewhat extraordinary & great, that, to be sure, would instantly tell; but I may go below my mark with impunity. 'O, he had a headach, or lost his sleep for two nights,' Great are the benefits of old age!¹⁴³
See Swift's Letter on old age; also,
old age is frowzy.¹⁴⁴

[153] Pliny says, "And luxury ceases not to busy itself in order that as much as possible may be lost whenever a conflagration happens."   Vol. VI, p. 224   Bohn

See what he says of the ⟨p⟩ⁿ wax portraits of the ancestors in every house
"ready to accompany the funeral processions of the family, occasions on which every member of the family that had ever existed was present." vol VI   225¹⁴⁵
How like the adoption ⟨o⟩in the Sradda!

———
Old men are drunk with time.¹⁴⁶

¹⁴² Pasted to the upper right-hand corner of p. [152] is a clipping, reading in part, "Mr. Emerson's paper on *Old Age* is what you expect from the man, but he'll never cause anyone to believe that old age is a desirable thing; and that men pray for length of life is no proof that they love life's lees." "Boston Daily Traveller" is written vertically in the left margin beside it. "Old Age" was delivered November 27, 1861, in Salem, Massachusetts, and published in the *Atlantic Monthly* in January 1862.
¹⁴³ "One capital . . . age!" is struck through in ink with a diagonal use mark on p. [151] and a vertical use mark on p. [152]. "One capital . . . nights,' " is used in "Old Age," *W*, VII, 325–326; with "Great are . . . age!", cf. *ibid.*, p. 323.
¹⁴⁴ With "old age is frowzy.", struck through in ink with a vertical use mark, cf. "Old Age," *W*, VII, 321–322. Swift's letter to John Gay, dated December 2, 1736, appears in *The Works of Alexander Pope, Esq.*, 9 vols. (London, 1760), IX, 289–292; see also *JMN*, VI, 59.
¹⁴⁵ *The Natural History of Pliny*, trans. John Bostock and H. T. Riley, 6 vols. (London, 1855–1857); this volume in Bohn's Classical Library series is in Emerson's library.
¹⁴⁶ With "Old men . . . time.", struck through in ink with four diagonal use marks, cf. "Old Age," *W*, VII, 319. For "the Sradda", see David Urquhart, *The Sraddha, the Keystone of the Brahminical, Buddhistic, and Arian Religions, . . .* (London, 1857); in Emerson's library.

[154] ———

    Mrs L[ydia]. M. Child

———

x   Herman Grimm
              ↑The brook sings on, but sings in vain
        Wanting the echo↓
———   ↑Brook sings on, but there is no song longer
Old Age   in my brain.↓[147]

———

In youth, the day is not long enough. I well remember my feeling (say in 1823, or 4,) that a day of 18 hours would accommodate my plans of study & recreation much better than our poor Copernican astronomy did.

[155] ↑Apr. 18↓
Art. ↑Yesterday I read my lecture on Art. I add;↓
There are as many orders of architecture as ⟨a⟩creatures or tenants or reasons for erecting a building; a ⟨shell⟩seashell, a b⟨e⟩ird's nest, a spider's web, a beaver-dam, a muskrat's house, a gopher's, a rabbit warren, a rock spider's silver counterpane over its eggs; a cocoon; a woodpecker's hole in a tree; a field-mouse's gallery, ↑wasp-paper, a beehive, a lamprey's pyramid↓ are examples. ⟨a⟩So a tree, so the shape of every animal, is the structure, the architecture, which nature builds for a purpose⟨,⟩ which rules the whole building & declares itself at sight.
[156] Some animals have a spare ⟨pair⟩ ↑set↓ of legs as a ⟨b⟩ship carries two suits of sails. Agassiz cut all the legs off of his lizard in succession, & ↑all↓ the ⟨new⟩ legs grew out ↑again↓ as good as new.

[157] I delight to see ⟨the⟩ boys, who have the same liberal ticket of admission to all shops, factories, armories, town meetings, caucuses, mobs, target shootings, as flies have; quite unsuspected, coming in as naturally as the ⟨s⟩ janitor; known to have no money in their pockets; ⟨t⟩& themselves not suspecting the value of their privilege, putting nobody on his guard but seeing the inside of the show, hearing all the asides; there only for fun, & not knowing that they are at [158]

---

[147] This sentence, added to the right of "Old Age" and partially circumscribed in ink, is struck through in ink with two diagonal use or cancellation marks. With "The brook . . . brain.", cf. "Fragments on the Poet and the Poetic Gift," XXVI, *W*, IX, 332.

School as much or more than they were an hour ago in the arith-m⟨e⟩atic class. ⟨I like the↑ir↓ realism ⟨of the boys⟩⟩ⁿ They know truth from counterfeits as quick as chemistry. They detect weakness in your eye & behavior a week before you open your mouth,ⁿ & have given you the benefit of their opinion quick as wink. There are no secrets from them. They know everything[,] ⟨in⟩ⁿ ⟨They know⟩ all that befalls in the fire company, the ⟨real⟩ merits [159] of every engine, & every man at the brakes,— ⟨They learn⟩ how to work it, & all the ⟨terms⟩ ↑names & all the conditions↓ of the ⟨art⟩ practice, & ⟨they⟩ are very swift to try their hand at every part; & so the merits of every engineer, & every engine, ↑&↓ locomotive on the rails. & will coax ⟨a↑n↓ engi-neer⟩ ↑good John↓ to let them ride ⟨in⟩on the engine, & even pull the handles, when ⟨the⟩ it goes into the engine-house. They know every man in the rifle corps & in the artillery, & brag the prowess, & imitate it, of ⟨each⟩ their favorite Samson.[148]

[160] Try them on horses, & see how much they know of racers. Try them on pugilists, on theatres, on ⟨boat⟩ regattas, on jump-ing, climbing, pitching quoits.

They make no mistakes, and have no ⟨s⟩ pedantry yet; but unaffected ⟨op⟩ belief on experience. The elections in the cricket-game, base & football, ↑and the boat,↓ are right, & not l↑i↓able to mistake: they put the round post in the round hole [161] & the square post in the square, & no log-rolling, no managing to put ⟨a man⟩ⁿ ↑an imbecile↓ on the county who can't be elected in his own town, ever happens. Wo wo to the man who never was a boy! They don't pass for swimmers until they can swim, nor for stroke-oar until they can ⟨steer⟩ row: and I desire to be saved from their infinite contempt. If I can pass with them, I can manage well enough with their fathers.[149]

[162]   May 3, 1861
_____

May 1. Wednesday, I read my lecture on Good Books to the Class at the Meionaon.

---

[148] Pages [157], [158], and [159] are struck through in pencil with single vertical use marks. "I delight . . . engine-house." is used in "Education," *W*, X, 138–139.

[149] "They make . . . right," (p. [160]) and "They don't . . . fathers." are used in "Education," *W*, X, 139.

The journals quote Marshal Saxe's saying that for every soldier slain in battle his weight in lead is expended to slay him.[150] Which seems in-side of the truth in the affair of ⟨f⟩Fort Sumpter & of the Baltimore Massacre of Massachusetts troops, in which last only three Mass[achuse]tts soldiers were killed.

An affecting incident of [163] the war ⟨is the⟩occurred on the arrival of the Fifth ⟨Ma⟩Regiment (of Mass[achuse]tts) at Springfield, received ⟨o⟩with such enthusiasm by the people, that a funeral procession, passing by, stopped, & joined in the cheers with which the troops were hailed. [See Boston Journal of Tuesday,⟨]⟩23 April.]
The "National Intelligencer" says of the arrival & performance of the Mass[achuse]tts Eighth Reg[imen]t at Annapolis, that probably no other Regiment in the country could do what this Regiment ⟨a⟩did,— put a locomotive [164] together, lay the rails on the broken railroad, ⟨man⟩ & bend the sails of a man-of-war, (the ↑frigate↓ "Constitution,") which they manned.

Men delight in being well governed. When two men meet, one of them usually offers his vacant helm to the hands of the other.

The country is cheerful & jocund in the belief that it has a government at last. The men in [165] ⟨T⟩search of a party, parties in search of a principle, interests & dispositions that could not fuse for want of some base,—all joyfully unite in this great Northern party, on the basis of Fre⟨d⟩edom. What a healthy tone exists! I suppose when we come to fighting, & many of our people are killed, it will yet be found that the bills of mortality in the country will ⟨be⟩show a better result of [166] this year than the last, on account of the general health; no dyspepsia, no consumption, no fevers, where the↑re↓ is so much electricity, & conquering heart & mind.

So in finance, the rise of wheat paid the cost of the Mexican War; & the check on fraud & jobbing & the new prosperity of the West will pay the new debt.

[150] See "Poetry, Rumors and Incidents," *The Rebellion Record: A Diary of American Events,* ed. Frank Moore (New York, 1861–1868), I, 95, an excerpt from the *New York Commercial,* May 21, 1861. "Marshal Saxe's . . . him." is used in "Courage," *W,* VII, 263.

[167] Sailors touch their hat to the quarter-deck, though there is nobody thereon.

The mate comes to the captain, " 'Tis four bells, sir;"—"Make it so;" replies the captain, & four-bells is struck.

———

"The sea washes out all the ills of man," said the ancient.[151]

———

Dieu parle bien de Dieu

———

Unavailing regrets,
> "those spectres which no exorcism will bind."
> > [Byron, *Childe Harold's Pilgrimage,* IV, xxiv]

Mem. Feb. 9, 1825. I went to Cambridge, & took a chamber in Divinity College.

Feb. 8. my last day in Canterbury.[152]

[168] Southerners do not shrink from the logical conclusion of their premises because it is immoral: neither will they shrink from the practical result, because it is degrading.

> "Short is the date of all immoderate Fame,
> It looks as Heaven our ruin had designed,
> And dared not trust thy fortune & thy mind."[153]
> > *Dryden* [*Absalom and Achitophel,* ll. 847–849]

[169] Our horizon is not far,—say, one generation, or 30 years,—we all see so much. ⟨A few⟩ The older see ⟨2⟩two generations, or 60 years; but what has been running on through three horizons, or 90 years, looks to all the world like a law of nature, & 'tis an impiety to doubt. Thus, 'tis incredible to us if we look into the sermons & religious books of our grand-fathers, ⟨to understand⟩[n] [170] how they held themselves in such a pinfold. But why not? as far as they could

---

[151] See Diogenes Laertius, "Plato," *Lives of Eminent Philosophers,* III, 6.

[152] See *JMN,* II, 332.

[153] Two vertical lines in ink are drawn in the left margin beside this quotation. See *JMN,* II, 336.

see, through two or three horizons, nothing but ministers, ministers, ministers.[154] ↑See M.M.E.'s remark, *GL* 117↓ In other countries or districts, 'tis all soldiering, or ⟨o⟩sheep farms, or shoe-making, or Vermont cattle-driving[.]

[171] 'Tis an inestimable hint that I owe to a few persons of fine manners, & is still as impressive, when I now rarely see them, as of old. They make behavior the very first sign of force, & not performance, or talent, or, much less, wealth. Alike with this was the hint I drew from the foolish story they read me yesterday, that, whilst every body almost has a supplicating eye turned [172] on events & things & other persons, a few natures are central, & forever unfold, and these alone charm us.[155]

[173] *Truth*
Hosmer told me, "when they said, they had treated his ⟨ox⟩ ↑ox↓ well, he asked the ox." When we affect to slight England & Englishmen, I note our immense self-esteem on the subject of Bunker Hill, and Yorktown, & New Orleans. We should not think it much to beat Mexicans or ⟨or⟩ Southerners, but to beat English——
And when the English ↑newspapers↓ disparage America, I note, that the English people ⟨e⟩are emigrating[n] [174₁][156] hither by thousands which expresses their opinion.[157] So the Southerners cannot sufficiently express ↑to Mr Russell↓ their contempt & detestation of the Northerners. Meantime, they are carefully sending their wives & children to the Northern states for protection during the War. As the Wigfalls, the Magruders,[158]

---

[154] "Our horizon . . . ministers.", struck through in ink with single vertical use marks on pp. [169] and [170], is used in "Character," *W*, X, 106.

[155] "'Tis an . . . old." is struck through in ink with two curved use marks. Page [171] is struck through in ink with one vertical use mark, and two diagonal ones in the shape of an X; p. [172] is struck through in ink with one diagonal and two vertical use marks, and two more diagonal use marks in the shape of an X. "'Tis an . . . charm us." is used in "Social Aims," *W*, VIII, 79–80.

[156] Emerson repeated page numbers [174] and [175]; the two sets of pages have been given subscript numbers to differentiate them.

[157] "Hosmer told . . . opinion." is used in "The Celebration of Intellect," *W*, XII, 118. With "Hosmer . . . ox.' ", cf. *JMN*, IX, 64.

[158] Louis Trezevant Wigfall (1816–1874) and John Bankhead Magruder (1807–1871) were both generals in the Confederate Army.

[1751]^{159} C[harles]. K[ing] N[ewcomb]

"Dante picturesque, for he is in an outward world where he feels forms as persons, &, while he feels as a child in a company, he only affirms facts, than meets the idea as Goethe does: he tells h⟨im⟩ow nature has acted toward human persons who are forms, & he sees the Power as lights of them, as we do in life, & describes them as forms & in the places which give us the fact

Milton is picturesque in a grander & less outward   because he gives us character, though [1742] general⟨s⟩ly & outward⟨s⟩ly, so individually (   ) to the forms of Satan & Eve"

[1752]   ⟨A⟩He basked in friendships all the days of spring.

You have power or taste. But taste is power passive or feminine. And every one has some. Take your stereoscope among your acquaintances & see how many find delight in it. Try on the new poem, & see how many it will fit.

[176] ⟨People⟩ ↑Notable persons↓ receive as compliment the freedom of cities. 'Tis a sham gift, like so many of our doings. The personage, 'tis likely, who receives it, is some poet, or ↑some↓ politician. What freedom will it give him? Not of the river,↑—↓for he cannot swim or row⟨,⟩: not of the woods,↑—↓for he is no hunter, & looks on the woods as place to ↑be↓ avoided: not the hills,↑—↓he has not the least inclination to climb barren mountains. I cannot [177] see that the freedom of such a town as ours can be given to any ↑adult↓ who does not possess it already. But they who have the freedom of the town are the *boys,* who use the brook, the pond, the river, the woods, the cliffs, the wild orchards, & huckleberry ⟨b⟩pastures.

Boys, see *AZ* 83, 260,

Realism

The freedom of a town cannot be given to any who does not possess it already. *See above.*

^{159} Pages [1751] and [1742] are in pencil.

[278][160] The misfortune of war is that it makes the country too dependant on the action of a few individuals, as the generals, cabinet officers, &c. who direct the important military movements, whilst, in peace, the course of things is the result of the movement & action of the great masses of citizens.

[279] 1861
July 4. Edward & Edward Bartlett at the boat-race made their mile, ↑in the Vireo,↓ in 12 minutes, ⟨4⟩55 seconds: Higginson & Davidson in 13 minutes, 5 seconds. ⟨in the Vireo.⟩
Tom Hazel, in the footrace with   Clarke, & Madden, made his mile in 5 minutes 20 seconds[.]

Sam Hoar made his mile in single ⟨wherry⟩ in 12 minutes, 25 seconds[.][161]

[280] August 5. The war goes on educating us to a trust in the simplic↑i↓ties, and to see the bankruptcy of all narrow views. The favorite pet policy of a district, the *épicier* party of Boston or N York, is met by ⟨count⟩ conflicting *épicier* party in Philadelphia, another in Cincinnati, others in Chicago & St Louis, so that we are forced still to grope deeper for something catholic & universal, wholesome [281] for all. Thus war for the Union is broader than any State policy, or Tariff, or Mar⟨a⟩itime, or Agricultural, or Mining interest. Each of these neutralizes the other. But, at last, Union Party is not broad enough, because of Slavery, which poisons it; and we must come to "emancipation with co⟨n⟩mpensation to the Loyal States," as the only broad & firm ground. This is a principle.[n] Every thing [282] else is an intrigue.[162]
I wrote to Cabot, that, huge proportions as the war had attained from despicable beginnings, it is felt by all as immensely better than the so-

---

[160] In his pagination, Emerson skips from p. [177] to p. [278].

[161] Those mentioned on p. [279] include Edward Bartlett, son of the Emerson family doctor, Josiah Bartlett; Tom Hazel, playmate of the Emerson children; and Samuel Hoar, nephew of Elizabeth Hoar.

[162] "This is ... intrigue." is used in "American Civilization," *W*, XI, 304. For "Thus war ... intrigue.", see the abstract of the lecture "American Nationality" in Cabot, *A Memoir* . . . , 1887–1888, II, 783.

called Integrity of the Republic, as amputation is better than cancer⟨,⟩:
and we find it out by wondering why we are ⟨f⟩so easy at heart, in spite
of being so beaten & so poor.[163]

[283] A rush of ⟨ideas⟩thoughts is the only conceivable prosperity that can come to me. Fine clothes, equipages, villa, park, & social
consideration cannot cover up real poverty & insignificance from my
own eyes, or from others like mine.[164]

[284] Hodsdon's Life,[165] like this war, this teaching war, is a
good chapter of the Bible which the nations now want. Self-help; trust
against all appearances↑,—↓against all privations↑,↓ in your own
worth, & not in tricks or plotting.[166] Lose the good office, lose the
good marriage, lose the coveted social consideration, that seem [285]
within your reach, if they do not constitutionally belong to you, but
must be won by any shadow of intrigue, any departure from that utterly honest, solid & reverable selfexistency which you are. Honor
shall walk with me, though the footway is too narrow for Friendship or
Success, or what is called Power; and the great sacrifices which [286]
directly become necessary in such a resolution, force us on new &
grander thoughts, open the eyes to the Angels who attend us in pha-
lanxes.

All the pleasure & value of novels is in the exhibition of this poetic
justice, the triumphs of being over appearance.

[287] ⟨Alcott thot the⟩In talking with Alcott of ontology, &c. I
said that few people were entitled to make the catalogue of the powers
& the order of Genesis; that the great primal powers will not sit for
their portraits, and are ever melting into each other,—dodging, one

---

[163] See L, V, 253.

[164] This paragraph, struck through in pencil with three vertical use marks, is used in
"Inspiration," W, VIII, 272.

[165] William Stephen Raikes Hodson, Twelve Years of a Soldier's Life in India . . . ,
ed. G. H. Hodson (London, 1859).

[166] "this teaching . . . plotting." is struck through in pencil with two diagonal use
marks; "trust against . . . plotting." is used in "Education," W, X, 143.

might almost say, behind each other. And it is only a Plato, a Bacon, or a Kant, that may presume to rank them, nor he but delicately & d⟨d⟩iffidently. Alcott said, "Yes he must use a [288] ladder of lightning, & efface all the ⟨she⟩steps as he passed up or down."

————

There is always a larger consideration, just ahead, which the mind can be stimulated to apperceive, & which is the consolation & the energy which in dulness & despair we need.

————

↑If↓ we^n Americans ⟨may⟩ ↑should↓ need presently to remove the capitol to Harrisburg, or to Chicago, there is almost nothing of rich association with Washington City to deter us. [289] More's the pity. But excepting Webster's earlier eloquence, as against Hayne, & John Quincy Adams's sublime behaviour in ⟨H⟩the House of Representatives, & the fine military energy of Jackson in his Presidency, I find little or nothing to remember.

[290] It occurs that I should like to have the statistics of bold experimenting on the husbandry of mental power. In England, men of letters drink wine; in ⟨France⟩Scotland whiskey; in France wine; in Germany beer. In England, everybody rides in the saddle. In France, the theatre & the ball occupy the night. In this country, we have not learned how to repair the exhaustions of our climate. Is the sea necessary in summer? Is amusement, is fishing, is bowling, hunting, [291] jumping, dancing, ⟨a⟩one or all needful? Tristram ↑(?)↓ took care to fight in the hours when his strength increased, for from noon to night his strength abated.[167]

[292]   *Doctrine of Leasts*
Resources. If you want Plinlimmon in your closet, Caerleon, Provence, Ossian, & ⟨mea⟩Cadwallon,—tie a couple of strings across a board, & set it in your window, & you have a windharp that no artist's

————

[167] "It occurs . . . needful?", struck through in pencil on p. [290] with a vertical use mark, is used in "Resources," *W*, VIII, 150. For the reference to Tristram (actually Gawaine), see Sir Thomas Malory, *The Byrth, Lyf, and Actes of Kyng Arthur . . . and . . . Le Morte Darthur*, 1817, I, 114; the anecdote is used in "Inspiration," *W*, VIII, 291.

harp can rival. It has the tristesse of nature, yet, at the changes, a festal richness ringing out all kinds of loftiness.[168]

⟨C⟩Sounds of the animals & of the winds, waters, & forest, are for [293] the most part triste,—whippoorwill, owl, veery, night-hawk, cricket, frog, & toad,—but the thrush, songsparrow, oriole, Bobolink, & others are cheerful.

Stereoscope

[294] Sir Robert Wilson.[169] "I transmit a piece of my new order ribbon. It is not beautiful, but it becomes so when cannon-smoked."
"Bonaparte knows that every Frenchman is a soldier in six weeks,—an advantage not appertaining to any other state"
"Every bullet has its billet."

_____

"but the men must have shoes."

[295] See Sir R. W↑ilson↓ "Private Journal" [*Private Diary . . .*, 1861,] Vol II p. 213 for Bonaparte's speech to the Poles.
Whereof W[ilson]. says, "At all events, this Scene shows Bonaparte to be a man of mettle, &, if he had not murdered the Duc d'Enghien, & Hofer, massacred his prisoners, & poisoned his sick, I should have some respect for him; but now I regard him as a *giant* of *the first class,* whose power of mind, force of character, ambition, & malevolent spirit, are unmatched in modern times" [*Ibid.,* II, 213]

[296] The British nation is like old Josiah Quincy always blundering into some good thing.

"There are limits beyond which France cannot be beat back, & it is the part of a statesman to ascertain those limits, & not to force down public spirit to

[168] "If you . . . loftiness.", struck through in pencil with a vertical use mark, is used in "Inspiration," *W,* VIII, 287.
[169] For the four quotations on p. [294], see Sir Robert Wilson, *Private Diary of Travels, Personal Services, and Public Events, during Mission and Employment with the European Armies in the Campaigns of 1812, 1813, 1814. From the Invasion of Russia to the Capture of Paris,* 2 vols. (London, 1861), II, 147; II, 185; I, 351, and II, 18; and II, 211. Emerson borrowed volume 1 from the Boston Athenaeum August 19–31, 1861, and volume 2 August 31–September 10.

that point where the bounding spring destroys the hand that so unskilfully compressed its elastic power". [*Ibid.,*] Vol. II. p. 150.

↑Sir Robert Wilson↓   see also p. 226

[297] The War is a great teacher, still opening our eyes wider to some larger consideration. It is a great reconciler, too, forgetting our petty quarrels as ridiculous;—

> "On such a shrine,
> What are our petty griefs? let me not number mine."
> [Byron, *Childe Harold's Pilgrimage,* IV, cvi]

But to me the first advantage of the War is the favorable moment it has made for the cutting out of our cancerous Slavery. Better that ⟨defe⟩war & defeats continue, until we have come to that amputation.

[298] ⟨L⟩President Lincoln said, "When we are swimming the river, 'tisn't a good time to swap horses."

I suppose, if the war goes on, it will be impossible to keep the combatants from the extreme ground on either side. In spite of themselves, one army will stand for slavery pure; & the other for freedom pure.
"Famâ bella stant." *Q. Curtius*[170]

[299] The Icelandic Sagas contain noticeable passages showing the belief of the people in foresight or second sight; chiefly in "Burnt Njal."[171]

————

The fortune of Bonaparte turned. There is only one that is strong & unfailing, God, Nature, "General Causes,"—if you wish to veil the Power under ⟨a⟩ neutral names. A nation never falls but by suicide.[172] Bonaparte conquered by using (see p. 325)

[170] For the Latin quotation, see Journal DL, p. [203], and p. [34] above. "I suppose, . . . pure." is struck through in ink with a curved diagonal use mark.

[171] Njála, *The Story of Burnt Njal, or Life in Iceland at the end of the Tenth Century,* trans. G. W. Dasent, 2 vols. (Edinburgh, 1861). Emerson borrowed vol. 1 from the Boston Athenaeum August 19–31, and vol. 2 August 31–September 10, 1861.

[172] This sentence is used in "The Man of Letters," *W,* X, 246; cf. also *JMN,* XIII, 256 and XIV, 78.

[300] I am at a loss to understand why people ⟨rate⟩ ↑hold↓ Miss Austen's novels at so high a rate, which seem to me vulgar in tone, sterile in ⟨artistic⟩ invention, imprisoned in the wretched conventions of English society, without genius, wit, or knowledge of the world. ⟨The⟩ Never was life so pinched & narrow. The one problem in the mind of the writer in both the stories I have read, "Persuasion," and "Pride & [301] Prejudice," is marriageableness. All that interests in any character introduced is still this one, Has he or she money to marry with, & conditions conforming? 'Tis "the nympholepsy of a fond despair,"[173] say rather, of an English boarding-house. Suicide is more respectable. ⟨than so degrading romances⟩

[302] When the troops left at Fort Hatteras wake up the next morning, they look out at their conquest with new eyes. If their commander knows what to do with it, the feeling of victory continues;—but if not, they already are the timorous apprehensive party. A day in Carolina or elsewhere is a splendor of beauty & [303] opportunity to a rational man; to an ox, it is hay, grass, & water; 'Tis heavy to an idle empty man, for it will defeat him. ⟨In⟩The physician, if he apply blister or external inflammation, gives a drop or pill ↑internally↓ for the sake of ⟨inward⟩ reaction⟨.⟩ and a day is an inflammation of nature, which requires an idea or purpose in the man [304] to counteract. In the midst of stupendous difficulties, Napoleon is cheerful & fat, because he sees clearly what to do, & has it to do.[174]

[305] Sept. 9. Last night a pictorial dream fit for Dante. I read a discourse somewhere to an assembly, & rallied ⟨s|| . . . ||⟩ in the course of it to find that I had ⟨qu⟩ nearly or quite fallen asleep. Then presently I went into what seemed a new house, the inside wall of which had many shelves let into the wall, on which great & costly Vases of Etruscan & other richly adorned pottery stood. The wall itself was unfinished, & I presently noticed great clefts, intended [306] to be

[173] Byron, *Childe Harold's Pilgrimage*, IV, cxv.

[174] "When the troops . . . do." is struck through in pencil on pp. [302], [303], and [304] with single diagonal use marks. "Read at Music Hall March *1862*" is written vertically in pencil in the left margin of p. [302], as is "Music Hall" on p. [303]. Emerson gave the lecture "Essential Principles of Religion" on March 16, 1862. The capture of Fort Hatteras, N.C., on August 29, 1861, accomplished by combined naval and land forces, was one of the first Union successes of the war.

filled with mortar or brickwork, but not yet filled, & the wall ⟨threatening to fall⟩ which held all these costly vases, threatening to fall. Then I noticed in the centre shelf or alcove of the wall a man asleep, whom I understood to be the architect of the house. I called to my brother William who was near me, & pointed [307] to this sleeper as the architect, when the man turned, & partly arose, & muttered something about a plot to expose him.

When I fairly woke, & considered the picture, & the connection of the two dreams,—what could I think of the purpose of Jove who sends the dream?

[308] War the searcher, ↑of character,↓ the test of men, has tried already so many reputations, has pricked so many bladders. 'Tis like the financial crises, which, once in ten or twenty years, come to try the men & institutions of trade; using, like them, no ceremony, but plain laws of gravity & force to try tension & resistance. Scott, McDowell, Maclellan, Fremont, [309] Banks, Butler, & I know not how many more, are brought up, each in turn, dragged up irresistibly to the anthropometer, measured & weighed, & the result proclaimed to the universe.[175]
With this ⟨not⟩ dynamometer, & not so much that as *rack* to try the tension of your muscles & bones, standing close at hand, everybody takes the hint, ⟨& grows⟩ [310] drops much of brag & pretension, & shortens his speeches. The fop in the street, the beau at the ball feels the war in the air,—the examiner, the insatiate demand for reality,— & becomes modest & serious. The writer is less florid, the wit is less fantastical. The epicure & the man of pleasure put some [311] check & cover on their amusements. Everybody studies ↑retrenchment &↓ economy.

Every body ⟨rallies⟩ ↑bethinks↓ himself ⟨to know⟩ how he shall behave, if worst ⟨come⟩ should come to worst. It will not always serve,

[175] Besides Winfield Scott, George B. McClellan, and John Charles Frémont, Emerson is referring to Irvin McDowell (1818–1885), major general in command of the Union forces in the second battle of Bull Run; Nathaniel P. Banks (1816–1894), governor of Massachusetts from 1858 to 1861 and major general in the Civil War; and Benjamin Franklin Butler (1818–1893), army officer and politician.

or may not, to stand aloof & contribute ⟨o⟩money. Shall we carry on a war by subscription ↑and politely↓?[n] They will conquer who take up the bayonet, or leave their other business & apply themselves [312] to the business of the war.[176]

The war searches character, & acquits those whom I acquit, whom life acquits, those whose reality & spontaneous honesty & singleness appear. Force it requires. 'Tis not so much that you are moral, as that you are genuine, sincere, frank, & bold. I do not approve those who give money, or give their voices for liberty, from [313] long habit, & the feminine predominance of sentiment; but the rough democrat who hates Garrison, but de⟨s⟩tests these southern traitors. The first class will go in the right way, but they are devoured by sentiments, like premature fruit ripened by the worm.
The "logic of events" has become a household word.[177]

[314] [blank]
        [315] "a plan which Paley pursued with vigor, but of which our Bridgewater Treatises, our Prize Essays, & such School-boy productions, are poor & barren imitations." *Buckle.*[178]

[316] My long sought story which I called "Ivo, Bishop of Chartres" I find in *Joinville, Histoire de Saint Louis.* section 223 ⟨See⟩ ↑See Vol. I↓ p. 264[n][-265] of ↓the↓ *Nouvelle Collection des Memoires relatifs a l'histoire de France.* Par M. M. de Michaud et Poujoulat [34 vols. (Paris, 1854)]

[317] "Whilst the king was at Acre, the Sultan of Damascus sent to him messengers, & complained to him much of the Emirs of Egypt who had slain his cousin the ⟨k⟩Sultan, & promised the king, that, if he ⟨wished to⟩ ⟨to⟩ ↑would↓ aid him, he would deliver to him the

---

[176] Page [310] is struck through in pencil with a diagonal use mark; p. [311] is struck through in pencil with a discontinuous diagonal use mark.

[177] "The war . . . word." is struck through in pencil with single vertical use marks on pp. [312] and [313]. See the abstract of the lecture "American Nationality," in Cabot, *A Memoir . . .*, 1887–1888, II, 784.

[178] See Henry Thomas Buckle, *History of Civilization in England,* 2 vols. (New York, 1862), II, 325.

Kingdom of Jerusalem, which was in his hand. The king decided, that
he would make answer to the Sultan of Damascus by his own messengers. With these messengers went⟨,⟩ ⟨Brother⟩ ↑Friar↓ Ives, the Bre-
ton, of the order of preaching friars, who knew the saracenic. During
[318] their sojourn at Damascus, ↑as they were going from their hotel
to the hotel of the Sultan,↓ Friar Ives saw an old woman who traversed
the street, & carried, in her right hand, a vessel filled with fire, &, in
the left, a vial full of water. Friar Ives asked her, what will you do with
that? She answered him, "that she would, with the fire, burn paradise;
&, with the water, extinguish hell, that it should no longer be;" and he
asked her, "Why do you wish to do thus" "Because," replied she,
⟨that⟩ [319] ↑"I wish that↓ no one henceforth sho⟨ld⟩uld do good ⟨in
order⟩ to have paradise for a recompense, nor ⟨for the⟩ through the fear
of hell, but purely for the love of God, who is so mighty, & can do us
all good, *peut nous faire tout le bien.*"[179]

[320][180] What inspiration in every assertion of the Will! Thus I
find a stimulus in the first proposition of political economy, "Everything in the world is purchased by labor, & our passions are only
causes of labor." Hume.[181]
Adam Smith's first proposition is, "That, all wealth is derived not
from land, but from labor."
Then again ⟨who⟩ how can [321] I read ⟨th⟩without new courage this
sentence? "That security which the laws in Great Britain give to every
man, that he shall enjoy the fruits of his own labor, is alone sufficient
to make any country flourish, notwithstanding these & twenty other
absurd regulations of commerce." *Wealth of N[ations]*.   B. IV. chap.
V.

[322] ↑*1861 October*↓
      Lately I find myself oft recurring to the experience ⟨that⟩ of the
partiality of each mind I know. I so readily ⟨attrib⟩ imputed symmetry

---

[179] For earlier references to this story, see *JMN*, VIII, 174, and IX, 60.
      [180] Pages [320] and [321] are struck through in pencil with single vertical use
marks.
      [181] "Of Commerce," *Essays and Treatises on Several Subjects,* 2 vols. (London, 1772),
I, 271. The quotation is struck through in ink with four diagonal use marks.

to my fine geniuses, on perceiving their excellence in some insight. How could I doubt, that, Thoreau, that Charles K. N[ewcomb]., that Alcott, or that ↑H[enry].↓ James, [323] as I successively met them, was the master-mind, which, in some act he appeared. No, he was only master-mind in that particular act. He could repeat ⟨that⟩ ↑the like↓ stroke a million times, but, in new conditions, he was inexpert; & in new company, he was dumb. ↑See below, p. 329 & 332↓

[324] The vice in manners is disproportion.[182] 'Tis right that the ⟨fire⟩ ↑hearth↓ be swept, & the lamps right, but never interrupt conversation, or so much as pass between the faces of the inmates, to adjust these things. For you lose the end in the means.

[325] (continued from p. 299)
sense against nonsense, direction against indirection, geometry against red tape, nepotism, feudality   but presently he adopted falsehood, red tape, nepotism, & it became a question of numbers, & down he went.

———

Du Guesclin, ↑[b. 1314⟨]⟩ died 1380]↓ sold all his plate, & all his jewels & trinkets of gold & silver which he had brought from Spain, in order to ⟨meet⟩ pay his soldiers.—   Buried at St Denys
[326] He was so ugly & deformed, & his air & manners so ferocious, that he was odious to his family. Armed with a club, which he never let go ↑out of his hand,↓ he was the vexation of his mother, & terror of all young people. They could not teach him to read, nor ever could they find masters from whom he would learn anything; but he wished to strike & cudgel them. [Michaud et Poujoulat, *Nouvelle Collection des Mémoires* . . . , 1854, I, 431]
But willingly all the daughters of France would have spun to pay [327] his ransom[.] [*Ibid.,* I, 432]

———

"Turenne also sold his plate to pay his troops, as Guesclin his lands."
[*Ibid.,* I, 433]

———

[182] With this sentence, cf. "Social Aims," *W,* VIII, 83–84.

H. T[horeau]. forgot himself once[.]

———

Men assume their own existence[.]

———

[328] "Severity is almost always a defect of memory." *Gasparin.*[183]

Originality. How easy it is to quote a sentence from ⟨a⟩ ↑our↓ favorite author, after we have once heard it quoted! how unthought of before! Il n'y a que le premier pas qui coute.[184] 'Tis like our knowledge of a language. We can read currently in German, but if you ask me what is German for horse, or spade, or pump, I cannot tell.

[329] The revolving light resembles the man who oscillates from insignificance to glory, & every day, & all his life long. So does the waxing & waning moon.

See above, p. 322

If you see, what often happens, a dull scholar outstripping his mates, & coming into high stations, you will [330] commonly find, on inquiry, that the successful person possesses some convivial talent;[185] like B. S.

[331] ↑Originality↓
I am not sure that the English religion is not all quoted. Even Jeremy Taylor, Fuller, even George Herbert,—Catholics all,—are only using their fine ⟨talent⟩ fancy to blazon & illuminate their memory. 'Tis Judaea & not England which is the ground. So with the mordant Calvinism of Scotland & America. But the Stoic, M. Antoninus, Zeno, but Pythagoras, but the Hindoo;—these all speak out [332] their own mind, & do not quote. George Fox[,] Jones Very speak originally.[186] See above, p. 130

———

[183] Agénor Etienne Gasparin, *The Uprising of a Great People. The United States in 1861*, trans. Mary L. Booth (New York, 1861), p. 74. Emerson borrowed this work from the Boston Athenaeum November 5–13, 1861.
[184] For the possible source of this phrase, see *JMN*, VI, 41.
[185] See *JMN*, XIV, 310.
[186] This paragraph is used in "Character," *W*, X, 111.

I find conversation so magnetic an affair, that I think two persons are easily deceived as to the genius of each other. Each hears from the other a better wisdom than any other party will ever hear from either.[187] See above, p. 322

[333] M. M. E.
Aunt Mary wished everybody to be a Calvinist except herself.* [188]

Every one has a new scale, & many tones are wanting in each. You shall not tax a man as frivolous, because you find him amusing himself with young people. The question is, through what length of scale does he run, & where does he lay the emphasis.

[33⟨2⟩4] Always let nature & reality ↑& not you↓ be at the expense of entertaining the audience. I felt, in C.'s fine sentences, how fine they must needs be, when he undertook to play all the parts. ↑see p 336↓ The delight of the audience in an image is manifest. When some familiar truth or fact ⟨is⟩ appears suddenly in new suit, mounted on a fine [335] horse, nay, equipped with a grand pair of ballooning wings, we cannot sufficiently testify our surprise & pleasure. It is the new virtue shown us in some unprized old property⟨.⟩, as, when a boy finds that his pocket-knife will attract steel filings & take up a needle. Or the old horse block in the yard is ↑found to be↓ a torso Hercules of the Phidian age.[189]

* Like Dr Johnson's minister in the Hebrides who wished him to believe in Ossian, but did not himself⟨.⟩ ↑believe in him.↓

---

[187] This sentence, struck through in ink with seven vertical use marks, is used in "Social Aims," *W*, VIII, 91–92. *"Printed in Social Aims"* is written in ink vertically in the left margin.
[188] For the source of Emerson's footnote below, see "A Journey to the Western Islands of Scotland," *The Works of Samuel Johnson*, 12 vols. (London, 1806), VIII, 353; in Emerson's library.
[189] "The delight . . . age.", struck through in pencil with single vertical use marks on pp. [334] and [335], is used in "Poetry and Imagination," *W*, VIII, 12–13.

[336]   ⟨s⟩See above p. 334

Martial had said already, "Minus illi ingenio laborandum fuit, in cujus locum materia succes↑s↓erat."[190]

"In what country of the world is not foppery a resource of vanity to conceal natural mediocrity?" Mme de Stael.[191]

[337] 1861 December.
The war begins to turn, & mass to tell against activity.

President Lincoln said well, that the rebels "carried only the ruin of their own country ↑as ground↓ to ⟨f⟩ invoke the aid of foreign nations"[192]

How rare are acts of will. Captain Ingraham became famous by taking away a subject of the United States from the Austrians to whom he was a political offender. General Jackson ⟨"⟩ by "assuming the responsibility"; & now Comr. Wilkes, by taking on his own responsibility Mason & Slidell.[193]

[338] Good writing how rare! Conway writes affectedly or secondarily with all his talent & heat of purpose; so Kingsley, & Hepworth Dixon, & others of Carlyle's imitators.[194] But the old Psalms & Gospels are mighty as ever: ⟨And⟩ showing that what people call reli-

---

[190] "Accordingly I had less occasion for the labour of invention, for which the subject-matter formed a substitute." *Epigrams*, VIII, preface. See *JMN*, VI, 73.

[191] See *JMN*, VI, 78.

[192] Emerson is quoting from Lincoln's annual message to Congress, December 3, 1861.

[193] "How rare . . . will" and "General Jackson . . . responsibility';" are used in "The Fortune of the Republic," *W*, XI, 521. See also Journal WAR, p. 14 below. Duncan N. Ingraham (1802–1891), American naval officer, effected the release of Martin Koszta from Austrian imprisonment in 1853; Charles Wilkes (1798–1877) commanded the ship that halted the British steamer *Trent* on November 8, 1861, and took off by force two Confederate commissioners, James M. Mason (1798–1871) and John Slidell (1793–1871).

[194] Moncure D. Conway (1832–1907), American clergyman, editor, and abolitionist; Charles Kingsley (1819–1875), English clergyman and novelist; William Hepworth Dixon (1821–1879), English historian and editor.

gion is literature; that is to say,—here was one who knew how to put his statement, & it stands forever, & people feel its truth, ↑as he did,↓ & say, *Thus said the Lord,* whil⟨e⟩st it is only that he had the true literary [339] genius, which they fancy they d⟨i⟩espise. In the old grand books, there will be now & then a falsetto, ⟨like⟩ as, in "the Cid," a ⟨man⟩ ↑Moor↓ who makes a malediction on Valencia, before its fall:[195] ⟨but it⟩ ↑which↓ is inflated, ⟨there is⟩ ↑⟨whic⟩has↓ no inspiration. But in Taliessin, the chants of Merlin or T[aliessin]. are good.

A great deal of what is called luck, in literature,—not only in men, but in particular works. Thus [340] ↑Hogg's↓ Kilmeny is a true inspiration wonderful as a chant of Merlin, or sonnets of Shakspeare & how strange that it should have been written by such a muddlepate as James Hogg, who has written nothing else that is not second or third rate. And our Alcott (what a fruit of Connecticut!) has only just missed being a seraph. A little English finish ↑& articulation↓ to his potences, & he would have compared with the greatest.[196]

[341] Under the snow, the ground is covered all winter, with evergreens, though not so-called, as, certain grasses, and the cinque foil, & radical leaves of many plants. ↑clover, whiteweed, buttercup, chickweed,↓

Read lately Sir Robert Wilson
             Max Muller
             Samuel Brown's Lectures
             Count Gasparin
             Buckle   Vol II
             ⟨Samuel Brown's Lectures⟩[197]

[195] See Robert Southey, *Chronicle of the Cid* (Lowell, 1846), pp. 210–212; in Emerson's library.
[196] "Copied" is written vertically in pencil in the left margin beside "A little . . . greatest." The sentence also appears in Notebook Amos Bronson Alcott, p. [20].
[197] For Sir Robert Wilson, Count Gasparin, and Henry Thomas Buckle, see pp. [294], [328], and [315] above. Emerson borrowed Friedrich Max Müller's *A History of Ancient Sanskrit Literature* (London, 1860) from the Boston Athenaeum September 10–November 27, 1861, and Samuel Brown's *Lectures on the Atomic Theory, and Essays Scientific and Literary,* 2 vols. (Edinburgh, 1858), August 27, 1861–May 10, 1862.

Aug. 1⟨1⟩862   I find in Thoreau's "Field Notes" ↑ms.s.↓ ⟨Ja⟩of Jan. 1853. he notes as conspicuous in winter, when the snow is off, ↑green leaves of↓ Buttercup, sorrel, johnswort, & the purplish gnaphaliums, early crowfoot, strawberry, mullein, thistle, hawkweed,[198]

[342] Remember to procure Max Muller's article on Comparative Mythology, in the Oxford Review, 1856. And his late book called Science of Language.[199]

———

How to sleep twenty five hours in twenty four

[343] Intellect egotistical, or, much fine metaphysics is only exultation of seeing farther than the rest.

———

In Taliessin in Mabinogion the man that feeds the fire under the pot ⟨gets⟩is spattered with three drops, & his eyes are opened, and he sees the danger he is in from the witch who set him to watch the pot, & he flees. Suppose the three drops [344] should spatter the crowd in the street, how many would go on to do the errand they are now running after?[200]

———

——— Old Age
Age puts the stone Chapel on you to lift.

———

"Pseudo spiritual." See quotation from Fontenelle. T 46
↑———
Old Age↓
    I ought to have added to my list of benefits the general views of life we get at 60 when we penetrate show & look at facts.

[198] See *The Journal* . . . , 1949, IV, 485.
[199] Friedrich Max Müller, "Comparative Mythology," *Oxford Essays* (London, 1856), pp. 1–87, and *Lectures on the Science of Language* (London, 1861). Emerson borrowed the latter work from the Boston Athenaeum February 26–March 5, 1862.
[200] This entry is struck through in pencil with single vertical use marks on pp. [343] and [344], and "Music Hall" is written vertically in pencil in the left margins of both pages.

[345] ⟨Most⟩ I thought on the worldliness of London life; ↑I↓ most feel the heartlessness, when they talk of heart, "my dear fellow," &c.; and their atheism, when they are religious.

Spallanzani & the bat. The dissector cut out the bat's eyes, & stretched threads across his chamber in various directions. The bat flew about & never touched a thread.[201]

[346] "That effort of identity between the conscious & the unconscious activities that Schelling calls the sole privilege of Genius. 'The infinite (or perfect) presented as the finite is Beauty.' "

Continental Monthly   No. 1 p. 59

[347]–[348] [leaf torn out][202]

[349] What provision stored & storing for the boy that shall be born tomorrow! Here is Plutarch, & Scott, & Milton & Shakspeare, waiting for him: what delicious songs, what heroic tales, what delicate fancies! How they shall fit him, as if made for him only!

[350] Swedenborg, that joyless genius! Never was insight so tedious.
But he is no priest, but a man of real experience fully entitled to speak.

[351] Conscience seems powerless to resist temperament, which makes uncomfortable tyrannical self-seekers of the very sons of light. We ⟨quarrel with⟩ ↑dislike↓ people ⟨for⟩ ↑if↓ their ⟨different⟩ rate of going[n] ↑is different from ours.↓ That indeed is the incompatibility of "crabbed age & youth."[203]

[352]   ↑Realism↓
The knowledge is in the world but the world lives as if it were not: the knowledge is all printed fairly out in books, which are on your shelves, but you are not less astonished & angry when it is spoken in church.

---

[201] See *JMN*, X, 256 and 526.
[202] Page [347] is indexed under "Courage", and p. [348] under "Elizabeth Hoar" and "Manners".
[203] For " 'crabbed age & youth.' ", see Journal DL, p. [91] above.

The knowledge is familiar to you & applied every day by you in your social relations, to your visitors, & to those whom you mean shall not visit you; & you are incredulous of the reality of such [353] potency, when it is proposed to be applied in politics.

[354] *Realism*
Paganism conquers Christianity, just as Greece, Rome. Paganism has only taken the oath of allegiance, taken the Cross, but is paganism still, & outvotes the true men by millions of majority, & ⟨holds⟩ ↑carries↓ the bags, & spends the treasure, & writes the tracts, & elects the minister, & persecutes the true believer.
↑printed in "Character." N[*orth*]. A[*merican*].
Rev⟨e⟩iew.↓ [CII (April 1866), 366][204]

[355] Thought last night ⟨of⟩ how ill agrees this majestical immortality of our popular religion with the population. Will you build magnificently for rats & mice? What could Hanover street do in your Eternal Heaven? Not once in 500 years comes a soul organized for immortal life. "Time is only precious to highly organized natures."[205] What then Eternity?
These we see are raw recruits, 3 months men, not to enlist for the War. Do not sweep the streets to gather members for the Academy, Observatory,

[35⟨5⟩6] The argument refuses to form in the mind. A conclusion, an inference, a grand augury is ever hovering, but attempt to ground it, & the reasons are all vanishing & inadequate. You cannot make a written theory or demonstration of this, as you can an orrery of the Copernican astronomy. [357] 'Tis the Gai Science, & must be sacredly treated.
⟨Only⟩ Speak[n] of the mount only from the mount. Not by literature or theology, but only by rare integrity, by a man permeated & perfumed

[204] This paragraph, struck through in ink with a vertical use mark, is used in "Character," *W*, X, 109–110.
[205] "how ill . . . mice?" is used in "Immortality," *W*, VIII, 348. For " 'Time is . . . natures.' ", see p. [119] above.

with airs of heaven can the vision be clear to an use the most sublime.[206]

1863 Jan. 26.
        I cause from every Nature
        His proper good to flow;
        What his right hand achieveth,
        So much he shall bestow.[207]

[358] Jan. 9, 1862.   *Memory*
We should so gladly find the law of thought unmechanical: but 'tis a linked chain,— ⟨and⟩ drop ⟨out⟩ one link, & there is no recovery. When newly awaked from lively dreams, we are so near them, still agitated by them, still in their sphere; ⟨but⟩—give us one syllable, one feature, one hint, & we should re-possess the whole;—hours of this strange entertainment [359] & conversation would come trooping back to us; but we cannot get our hand on the first link or fibre, and the whole is forever lost. ↑There is a strange wilfulness in the speed with which it disperses, & baffles your ⟨will⟩ ↑grasp.↓↓

[3⟨58⟩60] I ought to have preserved the Medical Journal's notice of R. W. E. in Philadelphia, that, of all the persons on the platform, Mr E. was the least remarkable looking, &c.,—which I could very often match with experiences in hotels, & in private circles, as ↑at↓ the Mayor Elgie's in Worcester, England.
Besides, I am not equal to any interview with able practical men. Nay[,] every boy out-argues, out-states me, insults over me, & leaves me rolling in the dirt. Each thinks that 'tis he who has done it, & I know that every body does or can as much.

[361] J. T. Payne of Charlestown said to me that he had noticed that Englishmen never presume to go behind the workman whom they employ. If they order a coat, or a trunk, or a house, or a ship,

---

[206] This paragraph, struck through in ink on both p. [356] and p. [357] with two diagonal use marks in the shape of an X, is used in "Immortality," *W*, VIII, 346.
    [207] Cf. "Boston Hymn," ll. 57–60, *W*, IX, 203. The quatrain is struck through in ink with two vertical use marks.

they call in the proper person to make it, & they accept what he gives them; whilst an American makes himself a very active party to the whole performance.

[362] Cannot we let people be themselves, & enjoy life in their own way? You are trying to make that man another *you.*ⁿ One's enough.

Go out of doors & get the air. Ah, if you knew what was in the air! See what your robust neighbor, who never feared to live in it, has got from it;—strength, cheerfulness, talent, power to convince, heartiness, & equality to each event.[208]

[363] Sympathy, yes, but not surrender. When I fancy that all the farmers are despairing in the drought, or the frost, I meet Edmund Hosmer, & find him serene, & making very slight account of the circumstance. In the cars, we all read the same fool bulletin, & smile or scowl all as one man, & they who come to ⟨know⟩ ↑ask↓ my opinion, find me only one flat looking-glass more; [364] when I ought to have stayed at home in my mind, & to have afforded them the quite inestimable element of a new native opinion or feeling,—of a new quality.[209]

↑John Quincy Adams engraved on his seal, *Haeret.*↓[210]

[365] The use of "occasional poems" is to give leave to originality. In a game-party or a picnic poem, the writer is released from all the solemn poetic traditions under which he writes at other times, &

---

[208] "Cannot we . . . enough.", struck through in pencil with a curved vertical use mark, is used in "Education," *W*, X, 138. The use mark is extended through "was in the air!", and "Read in Music Hall" is written vertically in pencil in the left margin beside the passage to this point. A vertical line is drawn in pencil in the left margin beside "Go out . . . neighbor, who", extended through "to convince," and another is drawn beside "was in . . . event." One or more of these lines may have been drawn by an editor rather than by Emerson. "Go out . . . event." is used in "Perpetual Forces," *W*, X, 70.

[209] A vertical line in pencil is drawn in the left margin beside "When I . . . circumstance."; and "circumstance. . . . looking-glass more;" is struck through in pencil with a curved vertical use mark. "Read in Music Hall" is written in pencil in the left margin beside "very slight . . . who come". On p. [364], "when I . . . quality." is struck through in pencil with a curved vertical use mark.

[210] "May it stick!" (Ed.).

which suffocate his fancy & spirit, & now amuses himself & indulges his nature, & the result is, that you get often a poem that is in a new style, & hints a new [366] literature. Yet the writer holds it cheap, & could do the like all day. 'Tis like acting in tragedy & comedy. The tragedy is very tedious; for all the players are on stilts, & mouth it like masks. But, in comedy, the same players delight you by their *naturel;* for they ⟨are⟩ understand the part, & play it as in [367] undress.[211]

[368] sources of inspiration.
1, sleep is one, mainly by ⟨the⟩ the sound health it produces; incidentally also, & rarely, by dreams, into whose farrago a divine lesson is sometimes slipped.
2. solitary converse with nature is a second,[n] (or perhaps the first,) and there are ejaculated sweet & dreadful words never uttered in libraries. Ah the spring days, summer dawns, & October woods.
[369] 3. New poetry; what is new to me, whether in recent manuscript or in Caxton ⟨monkish⟩ black letter

—————

4   Conversation ↑(See in this book several passages   as 365,)↓[212]

—————————————————

I know where to find songs new & better than any I have heard.

[370] Proverbs ↑are↓ the poetry, the Solomon, the Socrates of the people. What comfort & strength we have all owed once & again & often to "There are as ⟨many⟩ good fish in the sea as ever came out of it." And, "Well, 'tis as broad as it is long."[213]

[371] How we hate limitation! I like not an eight-day clock, but perpetual motion.

—————————————————

[211] With this entry, cf. "Poetry and Imagination," *W*, VIII, 35–36. On p. [365], "& spirit" is circled in pencil.
[212] "Sleep is . . . slipped.", "solitary converse . . . woods.", "New poetry;", and "Conversation" are used in "Inspiration," *W*, VIII, 280, 287, 294, and 292.
[213] For " 'There are . . . it.' ", see *JMN*, XIII, 399, and VII, 65, 74, 82 and 483. With " 'Well, tis . . . long.' ", cf. *JMN*, VI, 216.

Mr Crump thinks, that, if there is one thing more disagreeable than another, it is getting up in the morning. Especially, (adds Mr C., on second thought,) as people are getting older; for, as long as you lie warm in your bed, one seems to be as good as another; but when you get up, & have to put yourself together, & ⟨ge⟩find your wig, & your [372] teeth, & your spectacles, ↑& cane↓ ⟨&ⁿ your jaundice⟩, you had better been asleep, or not been at all.²¹⁴

[373] Pierpont—"There is a generation. O how lofty are their eyes, & their eyelids are lifted up."
"I have made a covenant with my eyes,"—that they shall not look into any man's face.

[374]   Literary Design
1. *Poetry & Poets:* comprising my discourse *"on Poetry,"* swelled by some passages in an older manuscript, *"The Poet;"* & the chapter on *"Criticism";* & the last year's Lecture on "Poetry & Criticism in England & America."

2. Essay on Originality & Quotation.²¹⁵

———

See a note   *GL* p. 328, 331, 364,

———

[375] To what purpose make more big books of statistics of slavery? There are already mountains of facts, if any one wants them. But people don't want them, they bring their opinions into the world. If they have a paralytic tendency in the brain, they are proslavery while they live: if of a nervous sanguineous temperament, they are abolitionists.

———

²¹⁴ "& your jaundice" is canceled, and "& cane" added, in pencil. For Mr. Crump, see *JMN,* XIV, 317–318, and "Spiritual Laws," *W,* II, 134.
²¹⁵ Passages from "The Poet," *Lectures,* III, 347–365, and the lecture "Poetry and Criticism in England and America," first given in May 1861, are used in "Poetry and Imagination," *W,* VIII, 1–75. The lecture "Poetry and Criticism" was first given in Montreal in March 1860. The essay "Quotation and Originality" (based on the lecture "Originality and Quotation," first given in the spring of 1859 as part of the Freeman Place Chapel lecture series) was first published in the *North American Review,* CVI (Apr. 1868), 543–557.

You wish to convince people that slavery is bad economy. [376] Edinburg Review pounded on that string & made out its case forty years ago, [and Boutwell said to me once,] "If [the Legislature of Kentucky would give me a deed of their state ↑one man owned the state↓ I] would manumit all the slaves & be a gainer by the transaction."216 What then? is this new? No. Every body knows it. As a general economy 'tis certain. But there is no one owner [377] of the state, but a good many particular owners. Mr A owns land & slaves; Mrⁿ B. slaves alone.ⁿ Here is a woman who has no other property, like the lady in Charleston who owned fifteen chimneysweeps, & rode in her carriage. 'Tis clearly a vast inconvenience to each of these to make any change, and they are fretful & talkative, ⟨against it,⟩ & all their friends are, and those less interested are inactive, &, from want of thought, averse to any change. [378] 'Tis like Free Trade, certainly the interest of nations, but by no means the interest of certain towns & districts which tariff feeds as rain the fields. And the eager interest of the few overpowers the apathetic general conviction of the many.

Banknotes rob the public, but are such a daily convenience, that we *go it blind,* as the boys say, for them. So imposts are the cheap & right taxation, but [379] all governments are forced by the dislike of people to pay out a ⟨tax⟩ direct tax, to make life costly to them by ⟨getting⟩ ↑paying↓ twice as much hidden in the price of the↑ir↓ tea & coffee.217

[380] Talent ↑without character↓ is friskiness. ⟨T there⟩The charm of ⟨m⟩Montaigne's egotism & of his anecdotes is that there is a ⟨real⟩stout cavalier, a ⟨well born⟩ seigneur of France at home in his Chateau, responsible for all this chatting, and if it could be shown to be a jeu d'esprit of Scaliger, ⟨it would lose all its⟩ ↑or other scribacious person,↓ written ⟨merely⟩ for the booksellers, & not resting on a real *status* [381] picturesque in the eyes of all men, it would lose all its value. ↑But Montaigne is essentially unpoetic.—↓218

---

216 George Sewall Boutwell (1818–1905) was governor of Massachusetts during the years 1851–1852.

217 "To what . . . & coffee.", struck through in ink with single vertical use marks on pp. [375], [376], [378], and [379], and with two on p. [377], is used in "American Civilization," *W,* XI, 300–302.

218 For "Talent without . . . value.", see *JMN,* VII, 373–374. A vertical line in ink has been drawn in the right margin beside "But Montaigne . . . unpoetic.—"

Jan. 16

It occurred yesterday after my conversation with the chicadee that the Illusions are many & sure, Each has his own, & all are tripped up by one or the other. The men of hard heart & iron will, old merchants & lawyers ⟨are⟩ fall an easy prey to Mother Deb Saco, & Hume, & the rappers. & converse with their dead aunts, like Dr Hare & Mr Shaw & H.[219] Meanwhile the subtlest intellectualist[n] [382] Alcott runs about for books, which he does not understand, & which make a dilettante of him, & making ↑scholars↓ thus his inferiors his superiors, and forfeiting his immense & unique genius, to which all books are trivial.

Then again the question recurs daily, how far to respect the illusion↑s↓? You cannot unmask or snub them with impunity. I know the hollowness & superstition of a dinner. Yet a certain health & good repair of social status comes of the habitude & well informed chat there which have great market value, though none to my solitude.

[383] The War is a new glass to see all our old things through, ⟨& see⟩ how they look. Some of our trades ⟨be⟩ stand the test well. Baking & butchering are good ⟨in⟩ ↑under↓ all skies & times. Farming, haying, & wood chopping don't go out of vogue. Meat & coal & shoes we must have; but[n] coach painting & bronze matchholders ↑we↓ can ⟨wait awhile⟩ ↑postpone↓ for ⟨customers.⟩ a while yet. Yet ⟨a⟩the music was heard with as much appetite as [384₁] ever, and our Quintettes had only to put ⟨in⟩ the "Starspangled Banner" into the Programme, to gain a hurra beside; but the concert could have prospered well without. And so if the Union were beaten, & Jeff Davis ruled Massachusetts, these flutes & fiddles would have piped & scraped all the same, & no questions asked. It only shows that those fellows have hitched on their apple-cart to a star, & so it gets dragged by [385] might celestial. They know that few have thoughts or benefits, but ⟨that⟩ all have ears; that the blood rolls to pulsebeat & tune, that the babe rhymes & the boy whistles, & they throw themselves on a want

---

[219] Emerson's references may be to Daniel Dunglas Home, or Hume (1833–1886), Scottish spiritualist and medium; and Dr. Robert Hare (1781–1858), author of *Experimental Investigation of the Spirit Manifestations* (New York, 1855), whom Emerson met in 1854. See *JMN*, XIII, 127, and Journal KL, p. [34] below.

so universal, and as long as birds sing, ↑ballad singers will, &↓ organ grinders will grind out their bread.[220]

[384₂][221]   Agassiz
              Appleton
              Cabot
              Dana
              Dwight
              Emerson
              Felton
              Forbes
              Hawthorne
              Hoar
              Holmes
              Howe
              Longfellow
              Lowell
              Motley
              Pierce
              Ward
              Whipple
              Woodman
        19

[386]   ↑Jan. 17↓

We will not again disparage America, now that we have seen what men it will bear. What a certificate of good elements in the soil, climate, & institutions is Lowell, whose admirable verses I have just read! Such a creature more accredits ⟨us⟩ ↑the land↓ than all the fops of Carolina discredit it.[222]

---

[220] For "The War ... through," see Journal DL, p. [103] above. For "coach painting" and "Quintettes", see pp. [119] and [31] above. With "hitched on ... star," cf. "Civilization," *W*, VII, 28 and 30.
   [221] The list on this page is inscribed upside down, in pencil. For similar lists of members of the Saturday Club, see p. [145] above, and Journal DL, p. [142] above.
   [222] For "We will ... bear.", see Journal DL, pp. [102] and [210] above. Lowell's "admirable verses" may be "Birdofredum Sawin, Esq., to Mr. Hosea Biglow," *Atlantic Monthly*, IX (Jan. 1862), 126–133; see *J*, IX, 359.

[387] Long ago I wrote of "Gifts," & neglected a capital example. ⟨Frank Browne⟩ ↑John Thoreau, Jr.↓ one day put up a bluebird's box on my barn fifteen years ago, it must be,—and there it is still with every summer a melodious family in it, adorning the place, & singing his praises. There's a gift for you which cost the giver no money, but nothing he could have bought would be so good. I think of another [388] quite inestimable. John Thoreau, Junior, knew how much I should value a head of little Waldo, then five years old. He came to me, & offered to carry him to a daguerrotypist who was then in town, & he, Thoreau, would see it well done. He did it, & brought me the daguerre which I thankfully paid for. In a few months ↑after↓, my boy died, and I have ever since had deeply to thank John Thoreau for that wise & gentle [389] piece of friendship.[223]

⟨There is⟩
To a perfect foot no place is slippery.

⟨As⟩Old Age
As we live longer, it looks as if our company were picked out to die first, & we live on in a lessening minority. In England, ⟨we⟩I have lost ↑John Sterling,↓ Samuel Brown, David Scott, Edward Forbes, Arthur Clough; in Rome, Paul Akers, Mrs Browning, Margaret Fuller; Giles Waldo,
[390] Here dies, last week, the excellent Mary H. Russell; and I am ever threatened ⟨with⟩ by the decays of Henry T[horeau].[224]

---

[223] "Read at Music Hall March 1862" is written vertically in pencil in the left margins of pp. [387] and [388]; "after" is added in pencil on p. [388]. Emerson gave the lecture "Essential Principles of Religion" on March 16, 1862. Frank Browne is probably Emerson's nephew, Francis Charles Browne of Concord. John Thoreau died in January 1842.

[224] John Sterling (1806–1844), British essayist and poet; Samuel Brown (1817–1856), physicist and chemist, and Emerson's host in Edinburgh; David Scott (1806–1849), Scottish painter and engraver; Edward Forbes (1815–1854), naturalist and lecturer; Arthur Hugh Clough (1819–1861); Benjamin Paul Akers (1825–1861), American sculptor; Elizabeth Barrett Browning (1806–1861); Margaret Fuller Ossoli (1810–1850); Giles Waldo, Emerson's enthusiastic disciple whom he met in Washington in 1843; and Mary Howland Russell, a Plymouth friend of Lidian Emerson. Thoreau was to die shortly, on May 6, 1862.

Opinion.

Fluxional quantities. Fluxions, I believe, treat of flowing numbers, as, for example, the path through space of a point on the rim of a cartwheel. Flowing or varying. Most of my values are very variable. My estimate of America which [391] sometimes runs very low, sometimes to ideal prophetic proportions. My estimate of my ↑town↓ mental means & resources is all or nothing,[n] in happy hours, life looking infinitely rich; & sterile at others. My value of my club is as elastic as steam or gunpowder, so great now, so little anon. Literature looks now all-sufficient, but in high & happy conversation, it shrinks away to poor experimenting.

[392] Clough notes, in June 1850, a striking article in the Edin[burgh]. Review, on Goethe, written by Rogers.—[225]

The notice of A H Clough in the Spectator of 23 Nov. [1861] was written by ⟨Dr Stanley⟩ [Thomas] ↑Hughes↓, ⟨(?)⟩ as well as that in the Daily News of 9 January [1862]↑, ⟨says [Charles Eliot] Norton⟩.↓ Mr Palgrave is writing one for Fraser.[226]
In 1851, the whole population of Scotland is short of 3 millions, 2,888,740

[393][227] the dimple in the snow

Poverty reads by th[e] street lamps

---

[225] In a letter to Emerson dated July 22, 1850, Clough attributes the article "Goethe's Festival," *Edinburgh Review* [American edition], XCII (July 1850), 98–115, to Henry Rogers. See *Emerson-Clough Letters,* ed. Howard F. Lowry and Ralph L. Rusk (Cleveland, 1934), letter no. 9.
[226] See Francis T. Palgrave, "Arthur Hugh Clough," *Fraser's Magazine,* LXV (Apr. 1862), 527–536.
[227] Page [393] is torn horizontally just below "Occasional Discourses", about two inches in from the right margin. "the dimple . . . lamps" is in pencil.

Proposed Book of ⟨|| . . . ||⟩Occasional Discourses

———

1. Domestic Life
     ↑Country-Life↓
2. & 3.   Two Antislavery Discourses
4.   1 August Anniversary.
5.   Concord Centennial

———

Speeches on

———

6. Sumner
7. Burns
8. Kansas
9. Cattle-show
10. Parker
11 John Brown

———

Solitude & Society
Old Age
Eloquence
Persian Poetry
Landor
Carlyle
⟨Country Life⟩[228]

---

[228] "Domestic Life", "Country-Life", and "Solitude & Society   Old age" are struck through in ink with single vertical lines. Most of the essays listed were conceived as lectures, and at least fifteen had been published by 1862 as pamphlets or in periodicals and books. Emerson used five of them in *Society and Solitude* in 1870. "Domestic Life" (*W*, VII, 101–133) was first delivered in Boston on November 13, 1859, and published by Moncure Conway in *The Dial*, Cincinnati, I (Oct. 1860), 585–602. The "Cattle-show" address, "The Man With a Hoe" ("Farming," *W*, VII, 135–154), was given in Concord on September 29, 1858, and published in *Transactions of the Middlesex Agricultural Society* (Concord, 1858), pp. 45–52. "Solitude and Society" ("Society and Solitude," *W*, VII, 1–16), "Old Age" (*W*, VII, 313–336), first delivered in Salem on November 27, 1861, and "Eloquence" (*W*, VII, 59–100) as delivered in Boston on February 10, 1847, were printed in the *Atlantic Monthly*, I (Dec. 1857), 225–229; IX (Jan. 1862), 134–140; and II (Sept. 1858), 385–397. "Persian Poetry," also published in the *Atlantic Monthly*, I (Apr. 1858), 724–734, was included in *Letters and Social Aims*, collected with Cabot's aid in 1875. The remaining essays were published after Emerson's death, ten in *Miscellanies*,

[394] [Index material omitted]
[inside back cover] [Index material omitted]

1884, and two in *Natural History of Intellect*, 1893. "Country Life" (*W*, XII, 133–167) was the opening lecture in the Freeman Place Chapel series delivered in Boston on March 3, 1858. The "Two Antislavery Discourses" are probably the address on the Fugitive Slave Law given in Concord on May 3, 1851 (*W*, XI, 177–214), and "The Fugitive Slave Law" (*W*, XI, 215–244) read in New York on March 7, 1854. "1 August Anniversary" refers to the "Address Delivered in Concord on the Anniversary of the Emancipation of the Negroes in the British West Indies, August 1, 1844" (*W*, XI, 97–147), printed in Conway's *Dial*, I (Nov.–Dec. 1860), 649–660, and 716–728. The "Historical Discourse at Concord" (*W*, XI, 27–86), delivered at Concord's second centennial celebration on September 12, 1835, was printed as a pamphlet soon after its delivery, and published in the *American Historical Magazine*, I (Apr., May, June 1836), 125–136, 168–174, and 213–221. "The Assault Upon Mr. Sumner" (*W*, XI, 245–252), a speech delivered in Concord on May 26, 1856, was published in the *National Era*, X (June 19, 1856), 97. The speech on Burns (*W*, XI, 437–443), given January 25, 1859, was printed in *Celebration of the Hundredth Anniversary of the Birth of Robert Burns, by the Boston Burns Club* (Boston, 1859), pp. 35–37. The Kansas speech (*W*, XI, 253–263) was delivered in Cambridge on September 10, 1856. "Theodore Parker" (*W*, XI, 283–293), delivered at a memorial meeting in Boston on June 17, 1860, was published by the Parker Fraternity in *Tributes to Theodore Parker* . . . (Boston, 1860), pp. 14–19. Emerson gave one speech on John Brown at a meeting in Boston on November 18, 1859 (*W*, XI, 265–273), published in *The John Brown Invasion. An Authentic History of the Harper's Ferry Tragedy* (Boston, 1860), pp. 103–105; another in Concord on the day of Brown's execution, December 2, 1859; and a third in Salem on January 6, 1860 (*W*, XI, 275–281), printed in James Redpath, *Echoes of Harper's Ferry* (Boston, 1860), pp. 119–122. "Walter Savage Landor" (*W*, XII, 337–349) appeared in *The Dial*, II (Oct. 1841), 262–271. "Carlyle" may refer to a manuscript written immediately after Emerson visited Carlyle in 1848 (ms. in Houghton Library), the review of *Past and Present* in *The Dial*, IV (July 1843), 96–102 (*W*, XII, 379–391), or other material from journals and letters, some of which may survive in "Carlyle," *W*, X, 487–498.

$\mathcal{W}\!\mathcal{AR}$

1862–1864

Emerson began Journal WAR in January 1862 (p. [1]), for the purpose of keeping notes on the Civil War, as the title indicates. He probably continued to use it until late March, 1864, shortly after he dated p. [276] March 13.

The covers of the copybook, of marbled tan, blue, and red paper over boards, measure 17 × 21.5 cm. The spine and protective corners on front and back covers are of tan leather. "1862" and "WAR" are inscribed in ink on the front cover. The spine is mended with four strips of tape.

Including the flyleaves (1–2, 285–286), there were 292 pages measuring 17.6 × 21 cm, but three leaves were cut out between pages 78–79 before numbering, and the two leaves bearing pages 65–68 have been torn out. Page 26⟨3⟩4 was misnumbered and corrected in ink. Two pages were numbered 267; the second was corrected to 267½, and the verso of page 268 numbered 270 to correct the sequence. Most of the pages are numbered in ink, but twenty-four pages are numbered in pencil: 36, 37, 152, 153, 198, 208, 210–215, 240, 241, 245, 246, 248, 252, 254, 258, 262, 270, 280, and 284. Pages 243, 250, 256, and 260 are numbered in both pencil and ink. Twenty-two pages are unnumbered: 1, 38, 39, 41–43, 83, 93, 113, 149, 161, 176, 180, 181, 191, 201, 209, 216, 217, 224, 231, and 286. Fourteen pages are blank: 52, 78, 158, 166, 168, 179–181, 185, 187, 208, 221, 253, and 255.

Pasted to the left margin of page 64 is a newspaper clipping reprinting an 1860 letter from Franklin Pierce to Jefferson Davis, and on page 187, a clipping giving the text of President Lincoln's message to Congress on March 6, 1862. Laid in after page 285 are two folded sheets headed "West Point notes", printed as pages 285$_a$–285$_g$ below. The first, a sheet of white paper measuring 20.2 × 24.6 cm, folded once to make four pages, embossed after folding with a stationer's mark resembling a death's-head, is inscribed in ink and pencil on all four sides. The second is a sheet of light blue paper lined in darker blue on one side, measuring 20 × 25.4 cm, and folded once to make four pages, three of which are inscribed in ink. A printed booklet, "OFFICIAL REGISTER OF THE OFFICERS AND CADETS OF THE U.S. MILITARY ACADEMY," for June 1863, and two more clippings, one from the *Herald* dated February 15, giving "JEFFERSON DAVIS' PROCLAMATION TO THE REBEL ARMIES," the second another report of Lincoln's March 6, 1862, message to Congress, are laid inside the back cover.

[front cover]   1862
                                   WAR

[front cover verso] "Vesuvius stands in this pastoral poem of Nature,
& exalts everything, as War does the Age." [Johann Paul Friedrich Richter,]
"Titan" [1862, II, 255–256]

For Intellect see p 254
                    284
                    74

                        ———

        "Not hate but glory made these chiefs contend,
        And each brave foe was in his soul a friend."
                Hector to Ajax, *Iliad,* Book VII. [ll. 364–365][1]

                        ———

[1]   January 1862
                        War
                        &
                     Politics
                      ↑&
                Washington City.↓
                    1861–2

"War is the father of all things," *Heraclitus*[2]

    ———

We sung the mass of lances from morn until the night.[3]

    ———

"Faults lay on either side the Trojan towers." *Elphinston*[4]

    [1] Homer, *The Iliad,* trans. Alexander Pope (Boston, 1806); this edition is in Emer-
son's library.
    [2] See Journal DL, p. [10] above.
    [3] Augustin Thierry, *History of the Conquest of England by the Normans* . . . , trans.
Charles C. Hamilton (London, 1841), p. 21. The paraphrase, written in pencil, is used in
"Harvard Commemoration Speech, July 21, 1865," *W,* XI, 344. See *JMN,* XIII, 172
and Journal DL, p. [203] above.
    [4] This entry is James Elphinston's translation of Horace, *Epistles,* I, ii, 16, which
Samuel Johnson used as the epigraph to *The Rambler,* no. 119. See Johnson's *Works,* 12
vols. (London, 1806), V, 306; in Emerson's library. See also *JMN,* VI, 24.

[2] The Reform-bill took in new partners, & Chartism again takes in more.[5]

"Omnia sunt misera in bellis civilibus, quae majores nostri ne semel quidem, nostra aetas saepe jam sensit: sed miserius ni⟨l⟩hil quam ipsa victoria: qua etiamsi ad meliores venit, tamen eos ipsos ferociores, impotentioresque reddit: ut, etiamsi naturâ tales non sint, necessitate esse cogantur. Multa enim victori, eorum arbitrio per quos vicit, etiam invito facienda sunt." *Cicero.* M. Marcello Epist 8.1.4[6]

[3] Every principle is a war-note.[7]

_____

War civilizes; for it forces individuals & tribes to combine, & act with larger views, & under the best heads, & keeps the population together, ⟨as if cities⟩ producing the effect of cities; for camps are wandering cities.[8]

_____

Εις οιωνος αριστος, περι πατριδος μαχεσθαι. *Homer*[9]

_____

[4] The Southern people, like all people of very limited education & ↑social↓ intercourse, are narrow & conceited, and as arrogant as the negroes in the Gambia river.   ↑or the European kings,↓ (See *FOR* 88.)[10]

---

[5] See *JMN*, X, 316.

[6] "All is misery in civil wars; our ancestors never even once had that experience; our generation has already had it several times; but nothing is more miserable than victory itself; for though it falls to the better men, it nevertheless makes those very men more arrogant and less self-controlled, so that even if they are not so by nature, they are compelled to be so by necessity. For there are many things a victor is obliged to do even against his will at the caprice of those who helped him to victory." *Epistulae ad Familiares,* IV, ix, 3.

[7] This sentence is used in "Perpetual Forces," *W*, X, 87, and "Address at the Dedication of the Soldiers' Monument in Concord, April 19, 1867," *W*, XI, 353. See *JMN*, V, 193; XII, 78, 214, 215; and XIV, 239, 335.

[8] See Journal DL, p. [203] above.

[9] "One omen is best, to fight for one's country." *Iliad*, XII, 243. The translation is used in "Poetry and Imagination," *W*, VIII, 33, and "Demonology," *W*, X, 13. See *JMN*, VI, 47, and XII, 287.

[10] "The Southern . . . river.", struck through in ink with one diagonal and one vertical use mark, is used in "Address at the Dedication of the Soldiers' Monument in Concord, April 19, 1867," *W*, XI, 355. Cf. *JMN*, IX, 114.

Though practically nothing is so improbable or perhaps impossible a contingency for me, ⟨I⟩yet I do not wish to abdicate so extreme a privilege as the use of the sword or the bullet. For the peace of the man who has forsworn the use of the bullet seems to me not quite peace.

[5] "Whilst a citizen of Massachusetts can traverse the whole extent of the British Empire, &, whatever his color, creed, or condition, at home, his natural rights shall be as firmly protected as those of the Queen on her throne; the moment he crosses the line which divides the slave from the non-slave states, he is subject to indignities & [6] lawless outrage unsurpassed by the selfish cruelty of the most wild & inhospitable barbarians." G.W. Bassett. [*A Northern Plea for the Right of Secession* (Ottawa, Ill., 1861), p. 1]

"Sovereignty ceases with the transgression of natural justice. *Then* the sovereign, whether a monarch, or a tyrannical majority, becomes himself the culprit, & justly subject to any righteous power that may restrain him—"
Ibidem [p. 5]

[7] See to it, not that the republic receives no detriment, but that liberty receives no detriment. [*Ibid.*, p. 16]

Lord Bacon says, "it was held in England, that a good war, especially at sea, pays its own charges, &, on land, by creating markets for industry at home."[11]

drubbed by fatalism they concede like Curtis

[8] An article in the Constitution of the Provisional Govt. of the South Confederacy.
"The Govt. hereby instituted shall take immediate steps for the settlement of all matters between the States forming it & their late confederates of the U.S. in relation to the public property & ⟨& debt⟩ public debt at [9] the time of their withdrawal from them; these States hereby declaring it to be their ⟨earnest⟩ wish & earnest desire to adjust everything pertaining to the common property, common liabilities & common obligations of that Union upon principles of right, justice, equality, & good faith." [G. W. Bassett, *A Northern Plea* . . . , 1861, p. 17]

[11] See *JMN,* XIII, 215.

[10] And "one of the first acts of S. Carolina, after her secession, was to appoint three commissioners to the ↑U. S.↓ general Govt., to negociate in reference to the possession of the forts, & all other matters of conflicting interest between the two powers." G. W. Bassett [*Ibid.*, p. 19]

[11] ——
Happily we are under better guidance than of statesmen. We are drifting in currents, and the currents know the way. It is, as I said, a war of ⟨i⟩Instincts.

———

Then I think the difference between our present & our past state, is ↑in our favor;↓ it was war then & is war now, but war declared is better than undeclared war.[12]

———

   [12] ↑The war begins to turn, and↓ Mass begins to tell ⟨m⟩against activity.[13]

"Every bullet has its billet."

———

But the men must have shoes.

———

"Buonaparte knows that every Frenchman becomes a soldier in six weeks;—an advantage not appertaining to any other state." *Sir R[obert]. Wilson*[14]

⟨Shall⟩ We[n] raise an army of ablebodied men, & employ them to catch flies!

[13] "There are limits beyond which France cannot be beat back, & it is the part of a statesman to ascertain those limits, & not to force down public spirit to that point where the bounding spring destroys the hand that so unskilfully compressed its elastic power." Sir R. Wilson's Journal, Vol. II. p 150[15]

———

[12] This and the preceding entry are struck through in pencil with a diagonal use mark; with "Happily we . . . the way.", cf. "The Fortune of the Republic," *W*, XI, 543.
   [13] See Journal GL, p. [337] above.
   [14] For this and the two preceding entries, see Journal GL, p. [294] above.
   [15] See Journal GL, p. [296] above.

[14] How rare are acts of will! Every such act makes a man famous, ↑J. Q. Adams,↓ ⟨Ingraham⟩ & Jackson & ⟨Wilkes⟩ Ingraham, and Wilkes.[16]

Famâ bella stant. *Q. Curtius.*[17]

The southerners complained of "the electing of Lincoln by insulting majorities,"

[15] Misfortune of war that it makes the country too dependent on the action of a few individuals ↑&c   GL 278↓[18]

"To slay a soldier costs his weight in lead," said Marshal Saxe.[19]

"The wounds inflicted by iron are to be healed by iron, & not by words."[20]

Custom makes the soldier.[21]

[16] "It was a great instruction that the best & highest courages are but beams of the Almighty." *Mrs Hutchinson.*[22]

English nationality is very babyish, and most exhibitions of nationality are babyish.[23]

[17] Every principle is a war-note.[24]

---

[16] "How rare . . . famous," is struck through in pencil with three diagonal use marks. See Journal GL, p. [337] above.

[17] See Journal DL, p. [203], and GL, pp. [34] and [298] above.

[18] The insertion is in pencil.

[19] See Journal GL, p. [162] above.

[20] Johannes von Müller, *An Universal History,* 4 vols. (Boston, 1831–1832), III, 14; in Emerson's library. The quotation is struck through in pencil with a diagonal use mark. See *JMN,* XII, 222.

[21] Cf. "Courage," *W,* VII, 263.

[22] Lucy Hutchinson, *Memoirs of the Life of Colonel Hutchinson . . . ,* 4th ed., 2 vols. (London, 1822), I, 312; in Emerson's library. The quotation, struck through in ink with a vertical use mark, is used in "Courage," *W,* VII, 273, and "Civilization," *W,* VII, 30. See also *JMN,* XIII, 427.

[23] Cf. *JMN,* XI, 399.

[24] See p. [3] above.

_____

Gibraltar may be strong ↑& Sebastopol stronger,↓ but ideas are impregn⟨i⟩able.²⁵

_____

And I summon you to regard with due honor those men who born in each evil age, as soon as they are born take a beeline to the rack of the inquisitor, the axe of the tyrant, like Jordano B↑r↓uno, Vanini, Huss, Paul, Jesus, & Socrates.²⁶

The very glaciers are viscous, & men are; but the compensations hold & the laws work. *GL* 73²⁷

[18] Our commerce has somewhat grand in its power: the telegraph enterprize was grand in design, & is already of immense benefit. But our politics are petty & expectant. The government ⟨are⟩ ↑is↓ paralyzed, the army paralyzed. And we are waiters on Providence. Better for us, perhaps, that we should be ruled by slow heads [19] than by bold ones, whilst insight is withheld.²⁸
Yet one conceives of a head capable of taking in all the elements of this problem, the blockade, the storefleet, the naval landings, insurrection, English ill will, French questionability, Texas[.]

[20] Governments are mercantile, interested, & not heroic. Governments of nations of shopkeepers must keep shop also. There is very little in ⟨all⟩ our history that rises above commonplace. In the Greek revolution, Clay & Webster persuaded the ⟨go⟩ Congress into some qualified declaration of sympathy. ⟨In⟩ Once we ⟨gave⟩ ↑tendered↓ Lafayetteⁿ a national ship, [21] gave him an ovation and a tract of public land (200 000 acres?). We attempted some ⟨national⟩ testimony of national sympathy to Kossuth & Hungary. We subscribed & sent out corn & money to the Irish famine. ⟨We made⟩ ↑These were↓ spas-

²⁵ This sentence, struck through in ink with a vertical use mark, is used in "Civilization," *W*, VII, 30.
²⁶ "men who . . . Socrates." is used in "Courage," *W*, VII, 274. See *JMN*, XIV, 95.
²⁷ This sentence is struck through in pencil with a vertical use mark.
²⁸ Single vertical lines are drawn in pencil in the left margin on p. [18] and in the right margin on p. [19] beside "And we . . . withheld."

modic demonstrations. They were ⟨cens⟩ridiculed as sentimentalism, they were sentimentalism,[n] for it was not our natural attitude. We were not [22] habitually & at home philanthropists. No, but timorous sharp shopmen, and each excuses himself if he ⟨mingles in the conversation about⟩ ↑talks↓ politics, for leaving his proper province, & we really care for our shop & family, & not for Hungary & Greece, except as an opera, private theatricals, or [23] public theatricals.[n] And so of slavery. We have only half a right to be so good; for Temperament cracks the whip in every Northern kitchen[.]

Interests were never persuaded. Can you convince the shoe interest or the iron interest by reading Milton & Montesquieu?[29]

———

Govt. has no regard for men until they become[n] property; then, it has the tenderest.

[24] The ⟨st⟩thinking class are looked at inquisitively in these times by the actors, as if some counsel were expected from them. But the thinker seldom speaks to the actor in his time, but ever to actors in the next age. ↑See *VA* 282.↓ Milton & Algernon Sidney were not [25] listened to in their own time, but now are consulted with profit, & have just authority. The philosopher ⟨looks⟩ ↑speaks↓ over the heads of the contemporary audience to that advancing assembly he sees beyond; as Dr [John] Reed of ⟨Brid|| . . . ||⟩Bridgewater, after he was blind, preaching one day in his church, saw the congregation, nor did it occur to him that it was strange that he [26] should see them until he left the Church[;] then he asked his son if he had said or done anything unusual today. His son said ⟨no⟩ he had observed nothing more than that he spoke with unusual animation. But the Doctor bethought him that he had seen the Congregation, yet that [27] the persons composing it were strange to him, & not his old acquaintances of the town;—↑and asked himself if it were perhaps↓ an audience of persons in the spiritual world?

[29] This entry, struck through in ink with a vertical use mark and marked with a vertical line in ink in the left margin, is used in "American Civilization," *W*, XI, 300–301. See *JMN*, XIV, 405.

[28] ↑In lack of affirmatives, negatives.↓³⁰ ⟨The⟩ One of the best of our defences is this bad one, that such is the levity & impatience of the mind, that tyranny & any falsehood becomes a bore at last, as well as Aristides; & nations get weary of hearing ⟨of popery &⟩ of the divine origin of popery & of Slavery. ↑There came a day when↓ Union-saving [29] became ridiculous. It is much as we used to comfort ourselves when Douglas threatened to be President, that his habits were bad, & that he was killing himself with whiskey, or the ⟨consoling⟩ assurances of Louis Napoleon's failing health with which the English journals ↑periodically↓ console⟨d⟩ their readers, or as when we meet a prosperity, because our enemy has made a blunder.
We shall never be saved so. This world belongs to the energetical[.]³¹

[30] England has no higher worship than Fate. She lives in the low plane of the winds & waves, watches like a wolf a chance for plunder; values herself as she becomes wind & wave in the low circle of natural hunger & greed: never a lofty sentiment, never a [31] ⟨d⟩Duty to civilization, never a generosity, a moral self-restraint. In sight of a commodity, her religion, her morals are forgotten⟨, blown sky-high⟩. Why need we be religious? Have I not bishops & clergy at home punctually praying, & sanctimonious from head to foot? Have they not been paid their last year's salary?

[32] The Government has no regard for men, until they become property; then it has the tenderest.³²

War
"You should start too formidable to be attacked"³³
                              See *SO* 27
"The wounds inflicted by iron are to be healed by iron, & not by words."³⁴ *B* 120

---

³⁰ Cf. "Resources," *W*, VIII, 138.
³¹ "We shall . . . energetical" is in pencil. See Journal DL, p. [250] above.
³² This sentence is struck through in ink with a vertical use mark. See p. [23] above.
³³ *The Confidential Correspondence of Napoleon Bonaparte with His Brother Joseph, Sometime King of Spain,* 2 vols. (New York, 1856), I, 170.
³⁴ See p. [15] above.

[33]   Washington
         arboricu↑l↓tural centre. See Patent Office Report[35]
"The position of Washington is particularly favorable for [arboriculture] sit-
uated as it is near the boundaries of two Regions,—the Carolina⟨s⟩ & the Al-
leghany,—while about ten of the most southern trees have their northern
limits along the coast near ⟨the⟩Chesapeake Bay, & full fifteen far Northern
species reach the same latitude along the higher Alleghanies. Every tree, not
only of our country, but of all temperate [34] climes, may be cultivated
⟨profitably here⟩at this natural ↑botanical↓ (as it is the political) centre of the
Union." *"Agricultural Report"* in "Patent Office Report, 1860." p 445

———

"That cannot profit the bee, which is hurtful to the swarm"[36]

[35] For Parnassus
     "Man is the nobler growth" &c

Wherever snow falls, man is free. Where the orange blooms, man is
the foe of man.[37]
President Lincoln said well that, "the rebels carried only the ruin of
their own country as ground to invoke the aid of foreign nations."[38]

[36] Certainly it were happier, if energy, if genius, should appear in
the government, to enact & transcend the desires of the people. But
that is too much to hope for, as it[n] is more than we deserve. For, how
can the people censure the govt as dilatory & cold,—⟨whi⟩ the people
which has been so cold & slow itself at home? I say it were happier,
[37] if genius should appear in the govt.,[n] but if it do not, we have got
the first essential element, namely, honesty. And let us hold that gift
dear.[39]

---

[35] "Washington . . . Report" is in pencil.
[36] Cf. Marcus Aurelius, *The Meditations . . . with the Manual of Epictetus, and a
Summary of Christian Morality,* trans. Henry M'Cormac (London, 1844), p. 43; in Emerson's library.
[37] "Wherever snow . . . man.", struck through in pencil with a vertical use mark, is
used in "Civilization," *W,* VII, 25–26; cf. "Voluntaries," ll. 35–42 (*W,* IX, 206), and
Journal VA, p. [45] below.
[38] See Journal GL, p. [337] above.
[39] This paragraph is in pencil.

Our only safe rule in politics heretofore, was, always to believe that the worst would be done⟨,⟩. Then we were not deceived.

[38]⁴⁰ I conceive the strength of the North to lie in
↑1.   Its moral rectitude on this matter.↓
↑2.↓ Its genius, manners, habits, tenure of land, & climate,ⁿ ↑all↓ which indispose it to slavery

[39] Its weakness to lie in
Its timorous literalism
It does not use genius which must always act in difficult crises, but sticks by usage & letter when these are ridiculously inapt

[40]   Revolution
See account of ↑English opinions of↓ French Revolution of 1848, in *LM* 18
In 1848 a surprising discovery was, that Paris was the Capital of Europe. Both government & people, throughout Germany, took no primary step, but waited for Paris, & made that their model.

―――――
"C'était une génération révolutionnaire que la revolution moissonnait, car il est vrai de dire, selon le mot célèbre, que dans tous les temps comme dans tous les pays elle dévore ses enfans." *Gaston Boissier.* ["Caelius et la Jeunesse Romaine au Temps de César,"] *Revue des Deux Mondes,* Vol. 39. [actually 49, Jan. 1, 1864,] p. 74

[41] The govt is not to be blamed. The govt with all its merits is to be thanked & praised for its angelic virtue compared with anything we have known for long. But the times will not allow us to say more ↑in compliment↓. I wish I saw ↑in the people↓ that inspiration, that, if the govt could not obey the same, it would leave the government far behind, & create on the moment [42] the means & heroes it wanted. Better the war should more deeply threaten us, threaten fracture in what is still whole, punish us with burned capitals & slaughtered ⟨thousands⟩ ↑armies↓, & so exasperate us to energy & exasperate our sec-

――――
⁴⁰ Pages [38] and [39] are in pencil.

tionalism, esprit du corps, nationality. There are scriptures written in-
visibly in me⟨s⟩n's hearts ⟨that do [43] not the⟩ ↑whose↓ letters do not
come out until they are enraged. They can be read by the light of war
fires by eyes in peril[.][41]

Hollow Image[42]

[44] What a benefit would the government render to every city,
village, & hamlet in the states, if it would tax whiskey to the point of
prohibition. Was it Bonaparte who said that he found vices very useful
to him? He got five millions from the love of brandy, & he should be
glad to know which of the virtues [45] would pay him as much. Tobacco & opium have broad backs & will very cheerfully ⟨pay high⟩
carry the load of armies for the joy they give & the mischief they do.[43]

———

trop de cordes a son arc—[44]

———

[46] In every house from Canada to the Gulf, the children ask
the serious father, what is the news of the war today? And when will it
be better times? The girls must go without new bonnets, the boys have
no gifts, no journeys. All the little hopes that made the ↑last↓ year
pleasant, are deferred↑.↓[45]

[47] What of America?
The certificate of value is not measures of wheat, or cotton, or iron,
but the kind of man the country turns out.[46] Goethe saves Germany,

[41] This paragraph, in pencil, is struck through in pencil with single vertical use marks
on pp. [41], [42], and [43]; "with all its merits", "thanked &", and "far" on p. [41],
and "exasperate us to energy &" and "sectionalism, esprit du corps," on p. [42] are circled in pencil for revision or cancellation. The paragraph is used in "American Civilization," *W*, XI, 302–303.
    [42] In pencil.
    [43] This paragraph, struck through in ink with single vertical use marks on pp. [44]
and [45], is used in "Civilization," *W*, VII, 31.
    [44] "trop de . . . arc—" is in pencil.
    [45] This paragraph, struck through in ink with a vertical use mark, is used in
"American Civilization," *W*, XI, 298; "last" and the added period are in pencil.
    [46] "What of . . . turns out.", struck through in ink with two vertical use marks, is
used in "Civilization," *W*, VII, 31. Cf. Journal GL, p. [386] above.

as Pindar ⟨t⟩Thebes; & England will run a great while crops on crops
of ⟨n⟩dulness, on the strength of one Shakspeare. Well we have had
Lowell lately, & can be a reputable place to be born in for a year certainly.

[48] But ⟨when⟩ though these patrial values are ⟨very⟩ ↑as↓ fluxional as
broker's quotations, subject to every burst of sunshine or shade, and
depend on a recent ⟨election of a rogue⟩ⁿ ↑malignant mob↓, or the
manifestation of a hero, ⟨yet⟩ that raise or break our confidence in popular intelligence, [49] yet when we look over this ⟨c⟩ constellation of
cities which animate & illustrate the land, & see how little the government has to do with their daily life, how selfhelped & selfdirected all
families are, knots of men in purely natural Societies,—societies of
trade, of kindred blood, of habitual hospitality, house & house, ⟨a⟩ man
acting on man by weight of opinion, of longer [50] or better directed
industry, the refinement & the refining influence of women, the invitation which experience & permanent causes open to youth ⟨& pov-
erty⟩& labor. When I see how much each virtuous & gifted person
whom all men consider lives with & stands affectionately related to
scores of excellent people who are not known far from home, [51] &
perhaps with great reason reckons all these people ⟨much⟩ his superiors
in virtue & in the symmetry & force of their qualities, just as the link-
boy or the lighthouse makes more figure at night than thousands of
men or ⟨cities⟩ ↑a city↓ of houses;—I see what cubic values America
has. And she offers a better certificate of civilization than great cities
or enormous wealth.[47]

[52] [blank]
[53] America growing, towns on towns, states on states, and the
cities; and wealth, ⟨which is always interesting, ⟨()for from wealth
power cannot be divorced) is piled in architectural mountains. California quartz mountains dumped down in N.Y., to be repiled archi-
tecturally along shore from Canada to Cuba, & thence westward to

---

[47] "yet when . . . qualities," and "I see . . . wealth.", struck through in ink with single vertical use marks on pp. [49], [50], and [51], are used in "Civilization," *W*, VII,
32.

California again. [54] John Bull interests you; come see the Jonathan-ization of John.[48]

[55] It is impossible to /disengage/extricate/ oneself from the questions ⟨of the⟩ ↑in which your↓ age ↑is involved↓. You can no more keep out of politics than you can keep out of ↑the↓ frost[.]⁴⁹

[56] Shall it be said of America, as of Russia, "it was a fine fruit spoiled before it had ripened"?

[57] The peace of the world is kept by striking a new note, when classes are exasperated against each other. Instantly, the units part, and form in a new order, and those who were opposed, are now side by side.⁵⁰   ↑Printed in Φ.B.K. Addr[es]s↓

[58] For slavery, extirpation is the only cure.⁵¹

———

"If you pass this law," said Mirabeau to the assembly, "I swear to dis-obey it."⁵²

———

    "None any work can frame
    Unless himself become the same."⁵³

⁴⁸ Page [53] is struck through in ink with a vertical use mark; "towns on . . . again." is used in "Civilization," *W*, VII, 31. "California quartz . . . John.", struck through in pencil with single vertical use marks on pp. [53] and [54], is from a letter to Carlyle dated March 11, 1854 (*CEC*, p. 499); "towns on . . . piled in" and "John Bull . . . John." are used in "Boston," *W*, XII, 200.
⁴⁹ See Journal DL, p. [101] above.
⁵⁰ This paragraph, struck through in ink with three vertical use marks, is used in "Progress of Culture," *W*, VIII, 210.
⁵¹ "extirpation . . . cure." is used in "Speech on Affairs in Kansas," *W*, XI, 261. See *JMN*, XIV, 384.
⁵² This quotation is struck through in ink with a vertical use mark. See *JMN*, XIV, 404.
⁵³ The couplet, used in "Poetry and Imagination," *W*, VIII, 43, is attributed to Dante in a translation from Pico della Mirandola in Thomas Stanley, *The History of Philos-ophy* . . . (London, 1701), p. 197 [misprinted 179]. See also *JMN*, XIV, 413.

[59] "Time drinketh up the essence of every great & noble action which ought to be performed & which is delayed in the execution." *Vishnu Sarma.*[54]

It was Pericles's policy to avoid a battle.
See also the opinion of Paulus Aemilius, given to Scipio, in *Plutarch* 3 vol. p. 51[55]

[60] Don't underestimate the wish to make out a presentable cause before foreign nations. We wish to come into court with clean hands; and, looking at our affair through the eyes of France (or England) or Germany, through the eyes of liberal foreigners, wonderfully helps our commonsense to rally. Now the world is full of maxims to this purport, "There can be no true valor in a bad cause."[56]

[61] "One omen is good, to fight for one's country."[57]
"Ye shall not count dead but living, those who are slain in the way of God."[58]

"Be sure you are right, then go ahead."[59]

It is of immense force that you go for a public & universal end, & not for your pot & pantry. Then not only England & Austria but the

---

[54] *The Hĕĕtŏpădes of Vĕĕshnŏŏ-Sărma, in a Series of Connected Fables, Interspersed with Moral, Prudential, and Political Maxims . . .* , trans. Charles Wilkins (Bath, 1787), p. 149. Printed in "Veeshnoo Sarma," *The Dial*, III (July 1842), 84. See *JMN*, VIII, 485. The quotation, struck through in ink with a vertical use mark, is used in "American Civilization," *W*, XI, 309.

[55] See *JMN*, VI, 31.

[56] The quotation is paraphrased in "The Celebration of Intellect," *W*, XII, 118. See *JMN*, IV, 24 and 34, and VI, 319, where it is attributed to an "ancient gleeman".

[57] See the quotation from Homer on p. [3] above.

[58] Quoted from Mahomet in *Practical Philosophy of the Muhammadan People, Exhibited in Its Professed Connexion with the European, So As to Render Either an Introduction to the Other; Being a Translation of The Akhlāk-I-Jalāly, the Most Esteemed Ethical Work of Middle Asia, from the Persian of Fakīr Jāny Muhammad Asäad,* trans. W. F. Thompson (London, 1839), pp. 94–95. See *JMN*, IX, 200. The quotation is used in "Immortality," *W*, VIII, 343.

[59] See *A Narrative of the Life of David Crockett, of the State of Tennessee, Written by Himself* (Philadelphia and Boston, 1834), epigraph to title page.

youth everywhere are with you; Woman is⟨,⟩ with you; Genius is; Religion is.

[62] Otherwise, you work against the grain. You have seen a carpenter on a ladder with a broadaxe chopping upward chips & slivers from a beam:—how aukward! ⟨how impotent!⟩ ⟨w⟩At what disadvantage he works! Now see him on the ground, chopping his timber under him. The weight of ⟨the planet⟩ ↑gravity↓ brings down the ax at every stroke. That is to [63] say, the planet itself ⟨works⟩ splits his stick.

⟨All our arts aim to⟩ So we put our sawmill on the edge of a waterfall & the river never tires of turning my wheel. The river is good natured & never hints an objection. I who had so much ill temper & laziness & shirking to endure from my hand sawyers.

We had letters to send, couriers couldn't go fast enough nor far enough; broke their wagons, foundered their horses, [64]⁶⁰ dreadful roads in spring; in winter snow drifts; in summer heats, could not get their horses out of a walk. Well, we found out that the air & earth were full of electricity, & it was always going our way, just the way I wanted to send. Would he take a message? just as lief as not: had nothing e‖lse‖ⁿ to do, & [65]–[68] [2 leaves torn out]

[69] to hitch ⟨a star on⟩ his wagon ⟨on⟩ to a star, & see his ⟨household errand⟩ ↑chore↓ done by the gods themselves.
That is the way we are strong,—by borrowing the might of the elements; and the force of steam, gravity, galvanism, light, magnets, wind, fire, serve us, & cost us nothing.⁶¹

[70] We have not yet found a kerosene lamp to supersede the sun[.]

⁶⁰ A newspaper clipping, pasted to the left margin, contains the text of a letter of January 6, 1860, from Franklin Pierce to Jefferson Davis, urging Davis to consider running for President in the 1860 election and attacking radical abolitionism in the North.
⁶¹ "It is of immense . . . nothing.", struck through in ink with single vertical use marks on pp. [61], [62], [63], [64], and [69], and in pencil with an additional vertical use mark on p. [64], is used in "Civilization," W, VII, 27–29 and 30. The use marks in ink on pp. [64] and [69] were evidently made after pp. [65]–[68] were torn out, and the journal closed while the ink was still wet. With "hitch his . . . star," (p. [69]), cf. p. [70] below, and Journal GL, pp. [384]–[385] above.

Hitch your wagon to a star. Do the like in your choice of tasks. Let us not fag in paltry selfish tasks which aim at ⟨petty⟩ private benefit alone. No god will help. We shall find all the teams going the other way[,—] Charles's Wain, the Great [71] Bear, Orion, Leo, Hercules, every^n god will leave us. Let us work rather for those interests which the gods honor & promote, justice, love, utility, freedom, knowledge[.]

The evil spirits also serve a wise & just govt. It taxes the vices. see above, p. 44^{62}

↑"We are ⟨me⟩ citizens of two ⟨noble⟩fair cities," said the Genoese nobleman to the Florentine artist, "and, if I were not Genoese, I should wish to be Florentine": "And I," replied the artist, "if I were not Florentine,"—"You would wish to be Genoese," said the other. "No," replied the artist, "I ⟨w⟩should wish to be Florentine."↓^{63}

[72] "The integrity of moral principles is of more consequence than the interest of nations." *De Stael.*^{64}

For Morals see *"Nat. Religion"* p 27
          See also Lect called *"Moral Forces"*
          also Lect. called *"Cause & Effect⟨s⟩"*^{n} pp. that follow p. 90
          Immoral Law Ib[id]. p 79
See also for Morals, *WAR* 277^{65}

[73] As soon as a man is seen ⟨facing⟩ ↑turning up↓ West ↑street↓, is he necessarily bound for California?

---

^{62} "Hitch your . . . p. 44" is struck through in ink with single wavy vertical use marks on pp. [70] and [71]. "Hitch your . . . knowledge" is used in "Civilization," *W*, VII, 30. Cf. p. [69] and Journal GL, pp. [384]–[385] above. With "The evil . . . vices.", cf. "Civilization," *W*, VII, 31.
^{63} This quotation, struck through in pencil with a vertical use mark, is used as an epigraph to "Boston," *W*, XII, 181.
^{64} See *Germany*, 3 vols. (London, 1813), III, 188, and *JMN*, VI, 36. The New York, 1814 edition is in Emerson's library.
^{65} "For Morals . . . *WAR* 277" is in pencil. "Natural Religion" was delivered February 3, 1861; "Moral Forces" April 13, 1862; "Cause & Effect" January 6, 1861.

[74] Ideas impregnable.[66] Numbers are nothing. Who knows what was the population of Jerusalem? 'Tis of no importance whatever. We know that the saint & a handful of people held their great thoughts to the death;

and that the mob rejected & killed him; [75] and, at the hour, ⟨the mob thought⟩ ↑fancied↓ they were up, & he was down; when, at that very moment, the fact was the reverse. The principles triumphed & had begun to penetrate the world.

And 'tis never of any account how many or how rich people resist a thought.[67]

[76]   ↑Culture.↓

The world is full of pot & pan policy. Every nation is degraded by the hobgoblins it worships instead of the eternal gods. Thus ↑popery, thus↓ Calvinism, thus tariff, thus mesmerism, thus custom, thus luxury, thus slavery;—and civility as it advances to the light ⟨sheds them⟩ casts away these crusts for simple⟨r⟩ good sense [77] ⟨for catholic &⟩ ↑and↓ universal modes.[68]

"Never was there a jar or discord between genuine sentiment and sound policy." *Burke*[69]

[78] [blank]
[3 leaves cut out]
[79][70]   Visit to Washington.

31 January, 1862.

At Washington, 31 January, 1 Feb, 2d, & 3d, saw Sumner, who on the 2d, carried me to Mr Chase, Mr Bates, Mr Sta⟨u⟩nton, Mr Welles,

---

[66] "Ideas impregnable." is struck through in pencil with two diagonal use marks. See p. [17] above.

[67] A vertical line is drawn in pencil in the left margin beside "And tis . . . thought."

[68] With "⟨for catholic . . . modes.", cf. p. [61] above.

[69] *Letters on a Regicide Peace*, letter III, in *The Works of the Right Honorable Edmund Burke*, 7 vols. (Boston, 1826–1827), IV, 431; in Emerson's library. See *JMN*, VI, 24.

[70] The word "disappear" was inscribed at the top of p. [79] earlier than the present entry and subsequently canceled.

Mr Seward, Lord Lyons, and President Lincoln.[71] ⟨Mr⟩The President impressed me more favorably than I had hoped. A frank, sincere, well-meaning man, with a lawyer's habit of mind, good clear statement of his fact, correct enough, not vulgar, as described; but with a sort of boyish cheerfulness, or that kind [80] of sincerity & jolly good meaning that our class meetings on Commencement ⟨d⟩Days show, in telling our old stories over. When he has made his remark, he looks up at you with great satisfaction, & shows all his white teeth, & laughs. He argued to Sumner the whole case of Gordon, the slave-trader, [81] point by point, and added that he was not quite satisfied yet, & meant to refresh his memory by looking again at the evidence.[72]

⟨He⟩ All this showed ⟨great⟩a fidelity & conscientiousness very honorable to him.

When I was introduced to him, he said, "O Mr Emerson, I once heard you say in a lecture, that a Kentuckian seems to say by his air & manners, *"Here am I; if you don't like me, the worse for you."*

[82] In the Treasury Building I saw in an upper room a number of people, say, 20 to 30 ↑seated at long tables↓ all at work upon Treasury Notes, ↑some↓ cutting & some filling up, &c, but the quantity under their multitudinous operation looked like paper-hangings, & when I saw Mr Chase, I told him I thought the public credit required the closing of that door on the promenaders of the gallery. Mr Hooper [83] told me that in ↑the manufacture of↓ a million notes (I think,)— $66. disappeared. Mr Staunton, who resembles Charles R. Train, though a heavier & better head & eye, made a good impression, as of an able determined man, very impatient of his instruments, &, though

[71] Charles Sumner (1811–1874), senator from Massachusetts, was chairman of the Committee on Foreign Affairs; Salmon P. Chase (1808–1873) was Secretary of the Treasury; Edward Bates (1793–1869) was Attorney General; Edwin M. Stanton (1814–1869) had been Attorney General in 1861, but became Secretary of War in 1862; Gideon Welles (1802–1878) was Secretary of the Navy; William H. Seward (1801–1872) was Secretary of State; Richard Bickerton Pemmell, First Earl Lyons (1817–1887), was the British minister at Washington.

[72] Lincoln later decided to sustain the conviction and sentence of Nathaniel P. Gordon, of Portland, Maine, who was hanged in New York on February 21, 1862, for slave-trading, the first person to be executed for this offense in the United States.

he named nobody, I thought he had Maclellan in mind.[73] When somewhat was said of England, he said England is to be met in Virginia.—
" 'Mud'! O yes, but [84] there has been mud before. Ah the difficulty
is n't outside,— ⟨it's⟩'tis^n inside." He had heard that Gov. Andrew had
come to the city to see him about the Butler-Andrew difficulty.[74]
Well, why doesn't he come here? If I could meet Gov. Andrew under
an umbrella at the corner of the street, we could settle that matter in
five minutes, if he is the man I take him for. [85] But I hear he is
⟨waiti⟩ sitting on his dignity, & waiting for me to send for him. And, at
that rate, for I learn there are 70 letters, I don't know that anything
can be done. Both Sumner & I assured him that Gov. Andrew was
precisely the man to meet him cordially & sensibly without parade &
offhand.

[86] Mr Seward received us in his dingy State Department. We spoke
as we entered the anteroom, or rather in the corridor, with Gov. Andrew & Mr. [John Murray] Forbes, who were waiting. Sumner led me
along, & upstairs, ⟨in⟩& into the Secretary's presence. He began, "Yes
I know Mr E[merson]. The President said ↑yesterday↓, when ⟨I^n told
him⟩ ⟨I said⟩ I was going to tell him a story, 'Well, Seward, don't let it
be smutty.' And I remember when a ⟨man⟩ ↑witness↓ was asked in
court, 'Do you know [87] this man?' 'Yes, I know him.'—'How do
you know him?' 'Why I know him. I can't say I have carnal knowledge of him, &c———' "

———

Well, with this extraordinary exordium, he proceeded to talk a little
more, when Sumner said, "I met Gov. Andrew waiting outside. Shan't
I call him in?" "O yes," said Seward⟨,⟩. ⟨So⟩ Sumner went out &
brought in him & Mr Forbes. Mr Seward took from the shelf a large
[88] half smoked cigar, lighted & pulled at it. Sumner went into a corner with Andrew, & Mr F. seized the moment to say to the secretary,

[73] Samuel Hooper (1808–1875), Republican congressman from Boston, supported
national banking laws establishing a uniform currency. Charles R. Train (1817–1885) was
a Boston lawyer, politician, and a member of Congress from 1859 to 1863.
[74] The dispute between Andrew and General Benjamin Franklin Butler
(1818–1893), whom Andrew had appointed, was probably over Butler's offer of his
troops to help the governor of Maryland suppress any possible slave uprising in the spring
of 1861.

that he ⟨hoped⟩ saw there was an effort making to get Gordon the slavetrader pardoned. He hoped the Govt. would show to foreign nations that there was a change, & a new spirit in it, which would not deal with [89] this crime as heretofore. Seward looked very cross & ugly at this; twisted his cigar about, &, I thought, twisted his nose also, & said coarsely, "Well, perhaps you would be willing to stand in his place," or something like that, & rather surprised & disconcerted Mr Forbes, but, ↑Mr Forbes↓ seeing that, though we had risen to go, Sumner still talked with Andrew, he went up to him, put his hands about him, & said, [90] "don't you see you are obstructing the public business?",ⁿ or somewhat to that effect, & so we made our adieus. Mr S↑eward↓. came up to me, & said, "will you come & go to church with me tomorrow, at $10\frac{(3)1}{4}$, & we will go home afterwards, & get some lunch or dinner." I accepted. &

[91] Sumner then carried me into some of the chambers of the Department, into the office of Mr Hunter, who has been chief clerk, I believe, he said for 14 or 15 years, into the Library, where Mr Derby presided, & where I found [Adam] Gurowski at his desk, growling;[75] into the chamber where the Treaties with foreign nations, some of them most sumptuously engrossed & bound, & inclosed, were shown [92] us, as the Belgian treaty,—and a treaty with the French Republic, signed by Buonaparte, countersigned by Talleyrand;—and, far richer than all, the Siamese Treaty, & presents,—Siamese,—I think,—not Japanese treaty, tied up with rich ↑red↓ silken ropes & tassels, & the sublime of tea-caddy style, written a⟨n⟩s on moonlight.

[93] Then, in another chamber, the Washington Papers, bought of Judge Washington by Congress for $20 000, were shown us. We opened several volumes to see the perfect method & clerical thoroughness with which Washington did all his work. I turned to the page on which the opinion of Marquis de Lafayette w⟨h⟩as given in an⟨l⟩swer to a requisition of the General, before [94] ↑the↓ battle of Yorktown, &c &c[.]

[75] William Hunter (1805–1886) was chief clerk of the State Department and later Second Assistant Secretary of State. Mr. Derby has not been identified. For Gurowski, see Journal GL, p. [74] above.

All these /inestimable books/vols. of original letters, &c., of Wash-
ington/ preserved in plain wooden cabinets ↑there↓ on the ground
floor, not defended from fire; and any eager autograph-hunter might
scale the windows, & carry them off.

[95] We then went to Lord Lyons, & had a pleasant interview↑.↓
⟨with him.⟩ He told us that the Queen had sent him the order of the
Bath, &c. on which Sumner congratulated him.

Sumner insisted in carrying me to Baron Ger⟨oult⟩olt; the dean of the
Diplomatic Corps, as the oldest resident, saying, that nothing could be
more charming than he & his family[,] [96] his daughters looking like
pastel pictures, & he told me very pleasing anecdotes of his intercourse
with the Baron.[76] President L↑incoln↓ had said to Sumner, "If I could
see Lord Lyons, I could show him in ⟨a moment⟩ ↑five minutes↓ that I
am heartily for peace." S[umner]. had thought nothing could be more
desireable, but it would not do to come between Seward & the [97]
President, nor to tell Seward, who would embroil them, nor to tell
Lord Lyons, whom it would embarrass: So he had gone to Baron
Geroult, to state to him the President's remark, & ask his counsel.
The Baron was enchanted with the expression of the President, but
agreed with Sumner, it was impossible to put them (Pres[iden]t &
Lord L[yons].) face to face, without grave impropriety & mischief.
[98] And Seward & Lyons, it seems, are strangers, & do not understand each other; whilst Lyons & Sumner are ⟨i⟩on the most confidential footing. Well, now that the prisoners are surrendered,[77] Sumner
went to Lyons, & told him what had passed, & he too was very much
gratified with it, & thanked Sumner for not telling him before, as it
would only [99] have distressed him. ⟨But,⟩ Meantime,[n] I did not see
the Baron, who was ill in bed, nor the pastel daughters.

We called on the Russian Minister, but he was not at home.

⟨After this,⟩ ⟨a⟩As ⟨Mr⟩ ↑Judge↓ Chase had invited us to dine with him

[76] Baron Gerolt, the Prussian Minister to the United States, had been in Washington
since 1854.

[77] On November 8, 1861, Captain Charles Wilkes of the United States Navy
stopped and boarded the British mail steamer *Trent* en route from Havana to St. Thomas
and arrested, in international waters, former Senators James M. Mason of Virginia and
John Slidell of Louisiana. The boarding and arrest and subsequent detention of passengers
on a British ship caused a serious diplomatic crisis between Great Britain and the United
States.

at 5 o'clock, we went thither, & saw his pretty daughter Kate, who alone with [100] her father did the honors of the house. Mr C. said, "slavery was not to be destroyed by a stroke, but in detail. I have twelve thousand boys ↑(slaves)↓ at Port Royal, whom I am organizing, & paying wages for their work, & teaching them to read, & to maintain themselves. I have no objection to put muskets in their hands by & by. [101] I have two men, Mr Re⟨n⟩ynolds & Edward L. Pierce, who are taking the care.[78] And I ⟨am going to⟩ ↑want↓ Congress to ⟨get⟩ give me a little box of government, about as big as that écritoire, (two or three officers, a superintendant, &c) & I think we shall get on very well." He & Sumner appeared to agree entirely in their counsels. They both held, that, as soon as a state seceded, it ⟨only⟩ [102] gave up its state organization, but did not thereby touch the national Government. The moment Arkansas or Mississippi seceded, they would have said, 'Certainly, if you do not like your state Govt., surrender it, and you lapse instantly into U.S. territory, again:' And they would have sent immediately a [103] territorial governor to the first foot of that land which they could reach, & ↑have↓ established U.S. power in the old form.

[104] From Mr Chase we went to General Fremont, but unhappily he had stepped out, & Mrs Fremont detained us, "because he would surely step in again, in a few minutes." She was excellent company, a musical indignation, a piece of good sense & good humor, but incessantly accusing the government of the [105] vast wrong that had been done to the General. Mr Senator Wade had read all their documents, (Wade, the Chairman of the Joint Committee of ⟨i⟩Inquiry of the two Houses,) & had expressed himself, in terms more terse than elegant, to her on the outrage done to Fremont, & she sat wondering when the Report of the Committee was to burst like a shell on the government.[79]

---

[78] Chase, a leader of anti-slavery forces in the Cabinet, was in charge of an experiment in educating and organizing a group of slaves captured at Port Royal, North Carolina. Pierce, an associate of Chase, had studied law under him. Reynolds has not been identified.

[79] John C. Frémont had been dismissed as commander of Union forces in the West on October 24, 1861. Senator Benjamin Franklin Wade of Ohio (1800–1878) was chairman of the Joint Congressional Committee on the Conduct of the War. Mrs. Frémont (1824–1902) was the daughter of Senator Thomas Hart Benton of Missouri.

[106] She introduced me to Major Zagyoni[,] the captain of Fremont's Body Guard, the hero of Springfield, Mo., a soldierly figure, who said, that "he was as well as his inactive life permitted."[80]

She showed me two letters of her son who had once been designed for our ↑Concord↓ school, but when she came to find how much his reading, spelling, & writing [107] had been neglected in his camp education,—for he could ride, & perform the sword exercise, but was a shocking bad writer,—she[n] was afraid to send him among cultivated boys, & had sent him into Connecticut, where he had made already great progress. She showed me two of his letters in proof, one written at his first ⟨as⟩ coming to school, very rude, ⟨indeed,⟩ & [108] one later, ⟨&⟩showing great improvement.

The next morning, at $10\frac{1}{4}$, I visited Mr Seward, in his library, who was writing, surrounded by his secretary & some stock brokers.——

After they were gone, I said, "you never come to Massachusetts." "No," he said, "I have neither had the power nor the [109] inclination." His father died early, & left him the care, not only of his own family, but of his cousins' property, three fiduciary trusts, and he had much on his hands. Then he early saw, that, whatever money he earned was slipping away from him, & he must put it in brick & stone, if he would keep it, & he had, later, obtained a tract of [110] land in Chatauque (?) County, which, by care & attention, had become valuable, & all this had occupied him, until he came into public life, & for the last 15 (?) years, he had been confined in Washington.

⟨He ha⟩ Besides, Massachusetts was under a cotton aristocracy, [111] & Mr Webster worked for them: he did not like them, & had as much as he could do to fight the cotton aristocracy in his own state: so he had never gone thither. On general politics, he said; "I am a peacemaker. I never work in another method. Men are so constituted that the possession of force makes the demonstration[n] [112] of force quite unnecessary. If I am six feet high & well proportioned, & my adversary is four feet high & well proportioned I need not strike him,—he will do as I say. ⟨When⟩ On the day when the political power passed over to the free states, the fate of slavery was sealed. I saw it was only a question of time, and I have remained [113] in that belief. I was not

[80] Major Charles Zagonyi, a Hungarian, led a successful cavalry charge of the "Frémont Bodyguard" against Confederate forces at Springfield, Missouri, on October 25, 1861.

wise enough to foresee all that ha⟨p⟩s happened since. But it is not important, all was then settled, & is turning out as ⟨w⟩I expected. All the
incidents must follow, both at home & abroad. England & France are
only incidents. There is no resisting this. The Supreme Court follows
too. Grier & Wayne ⟨& all the⟩ ↑at this moment↓ are just as loyal as
any judges."[81]
[114] But he spoke as if "all was done & to be done *by him*, by the
executive, & with little or no help from Congress. They do nothing.
Why, there are twelve points which I gave them, at the beginning of
the session, on which I wished the action of the government legiti-
mated, and they have not yet touched one of them. And I am liable for
every one of all these parties whom I have [115] touched in acting for
the government. And ⟨if I⟩ the moment I go out of office, I shall put
my property into the hands of my heirs, or it might all be taken from
me by these people."
He said, "⟨I⟩A soldier in the Wisconsin (?) regiment mutinied, ⟨&
would go home⟩ his time was out, & he would go home. I ⟨arreste⟩ ordered him to be arrested. I was presently summoned to appear before
[116] Judge Wayne, of the Supreme Court, ⟨to⟩ by the *habeas corpus.*
I said, Go instantly to Judge Wayne, & ask him whether he will give a
⟨verdict⟩ decision for the Government; if he will, he may have the soldier; if he will not, the summons must be disobeyed. ⟨G⟩Judge Wayne
⟨said⟩ answered, he would decide for the government; & so I suffered
the soldier to be sent to him.
[117] Well, this was against all law, but it was necessary. If ⟨the⟩ we
had done otherwise, all the regiments would have disbanded, & Washington ↑been↓ left without protection."
We went to Church. I told him "I hoped he would not demoralize me;
I was not much accustomed to churches, but trus↑t↓ed he would carry
me to a safe place." He [118] said, he attended Rev. Dr Pyne's
Church⟨,⟩. On the way, ⟨I⟩we met Gov. Fish, who was also to go with
him.[82] Miss Seward, to whom I had been presented, accompanied us.

---

[81] Robert C. Grier (1794–1870) and James M. Wayne (c. 1790–1867), associate
justices of the Supreme Court, had voted with the majority to return Dred Scott to his
owner.
[82] The Rev. Smith Pyne (1803–1875) was pastor of St. John's Episcopal Church in
Washington. Hamilton Fish (1808–1893), Whig and later Republican political leader in
New York State, had served as congressman, governor, and senator.

I was a little aukward in finding my place in the Common-Prayer Book, & Mr S[eward]. was obliging in guiding me, from time to time⟨;⟩. [119] But I had the old wonder come over me at the Egyptian stationariness of the English church. The hopeless blind antiquity of life & thought,—indicated alike by prayers & creed & sermon,—was wonderful to see, &⟨, in⟩ amid worshippers & in ⟨a⟩ time↑s↓ like th⟨is⟩ese. There was something exceptional too in the Doctor's sermon. His church was all made up of secessionists; he had remained [120] loyal, they had all left him, & abused him in the papers: And in the sermon he represented his griefs, & preached Jacobitish passive obedience to powers that be, as his defence. In going out, Mr S. praised the sermon. I said that the Doctor ⟨I f⟩ did not seem to have ⟨acc⟩read the Gospel according to San Francisco, or the [121] Epistle to the Californians; ↑he↓ had not got quite down into these noisy times.

Mr S. said, "Will you go & call on the President? I usually call on him at this hour." Of course, I was glad to go.

We found in the President's chamber his two little sons,—boys of 7 & 8 years perhaps,—whom the barber was dressing & "whiskeying their hair," as he said, not much to [122] the apparent contentment of the boys, ↑when↓ the cologne got into their eyes. The eldest boy immediately told Mr Seward, "he could not guess what they had got." ⟨he⟩ ↑Mr Seward↓ "bet a quarter of a dollar that he could.—Was it a rabbit? was it a bird? was it a pig?" he guessed always wrong, & *paid his quarter* to the youngest, before the [123] eldest declared it was a rabbit. But he sent away the mulatto to find the President, & the boys disappeared. The President came, and Mr Seward said, "You have not been to Church today." "No," he said, "and, if he ↑must↓ make a frank confession, he had been reading for the first time Mr Sumner's speech (on the Trent affair)."[83] [124] Something was said of newspapers, & of the story that appeared ⟨of⟩ in the journals, of some one who selected all the articles which Marcy should read, &c, &c,[84]

The President incidentally remarked, that for the N.Y. Herald, he certainly ought to be much obliged to it for the part it had taken for

[83] For the Trent affair, see p. [98] above.
[84] Probably Randolph Barnes Marcy (1812–1887), who had become a brigadier general and chief of staff to McClellan in 1861.

the Govt. in the Mason & Slidell business. [125] Then Seward said somewhat to explain the apparent steady malignity of the "London Times." It was all an affair of the great interests of markets. The great capitalists had got this or that stock: as soon as anything happens that affects their value, this value must be made real, and the ⟨J⟩ "Times" must say just what is required to sell those values. &c. &c. The Government had little or no voice in the matter. [126] "But what news today?" "Mr Fox has sent none. Send for Mr Fox." The servant could not find Mr Fox.[85]

The President said, he had the most satisfactory communication from Lord Lyons;

also had been notified by him, that he had received the order of the Bath, & he, ↑the President,↓ had received two communications from the French minister. [127] France, on the moment of hearing the surrender of the prisoners, had ordered a message of gratification to be sent, without waiting to read the grounds: then, when the dispatches had been read, had hastened to send a fresh message of thanks & gratulation. Spain also had sent a message of the same kind. He was glad of this that Spain had done. For he knew, that, though Cuba sympathized [128] with secession, Spain's interest lay the other way. Spain knew that the Secessionists wished to conquer Cuba.

Mr Seward told the President somewhat of Dr Pyne's sermon, & the President said, he intended to show his respect for him some time by going to hear him.

[129] We left the President, & returned to Mr Seward's house. At dinner his two sons, Frederic, his private secretary, & William (I think) with Miss Seward, were present. ⟨S⟩Mr S. told the whole story of the conversation with the Duke of Newcastle. On seeing the absurd story in the English papers, he wrote to Thurlow Weed, to go to the Duke, & ask an explanation.[86] Mr Weed called on the Duke, who said, that he was exceedingly [130] grieved that he had given public-

[85] Gustavus V. Fox (1821–1883) was Assistant Secretary of the Navy.

[86] At a reception in Albany Seward had said, perhaps jokingly, to the Duke, who was accompanying the Prince of Wales on his tour of North America in 1860, "that he was soon to be in a position where it would be his duty to insult Great Britain, and he should proceed to do so" (Frederic Bancroft, *The Life of William H. Seward*, 2 vols. [New York, 1900], II, 225). As Colonial Secretary, the Duke repeated Seward's remark to other members of the British Cabinet as if it were serious. Thurlow Weed (1797–1882), editor

ity to the circumstance, but that the facts w⟨o⟩ere substantially as they had been stated in the ⟨papers⟩"Times."

"Now," said Seward, "I will tell you the whole affair as it happened. When those people came here, I gave them a precise programme for their whole journey,[n] which they [131] exactly kept. If they went to the prairie, it was because I had so set it down; if they went to New York or to Boston, I had so directed; if they were received at the White House, instead of being sent to a hotel in Washington, I had so directed. I did not go to meet them at Philadelphia, or N. Y. or Boston, but kept away. But when, at last when they were ready to leave the country, I went to [132] Albany, to dine with them at Gov. Morgan's⟨,⟩. ⟨An⟩ There were 24 or 25 at table, & there never were people more happy than they were. They were ⟨very⟩entirely gratified & thankful for ⟨al⟩ all that had been done for them, & al[l] the course of the tour. The conversation lapsed at table, as it will, into tete à têtes, & I ⟨s⟩occasionally spoke across the table [133] to the Duke, & said to him, that 'I had not joined them at Boston, or at N. York: ⟨th⟩ indeed, that, as there was always a certain jealousy of England, in the dominant democratic party, and I wished to serve them, & keep up the most friendly feeling in the country toward them, I had avoided going too much ⟨wi⟩to them.' Well, they all understood[n] [134] it, & we parted, both the prince & the Duke expressed ⟨themselves⟩ ⟨to⟩their gratitude & good feeling to me in language which I cannot repeat, it was so complimentary."

[135] Mr Seward said, that his most intimate friend had been, for very many years, Mr Thurlow Weed, of Albany. ⟨h⟩He was in habit of fullest correspondence with him on all subjects, and every year on the first of January, "Mr Weed's daughter has ⟨the⟩ ↑⟨his⟩ my↓ last year's ⟨correspondence⟩ ↑letters↓ bound up into a volume. And there they all lie, twelve volumes of ⟨his⟩ ↑my↓ letters on her centre table, open [136] to all to read them who will." In all this talk, Mr S.'s manner & face were so intelligent & amicable, that I, who had thought him so ugly, the day before, now thought him positively handsome.

---

of the Albany *Evening Journal*, New York Republican leader, and confidant of Seward, had been sent to Great Britain to lobby for the Union cause.

↑See Mr Moseley's remark to me concerning Seward↓

Mr Moseley told me, at Buffalo, in   that there was a time when he
thought Mr Seward was in danger of being only a moral demagogue,
& (I think) was only saved ⟨by⟩from it by Mr Weed's influence.[87]

[137] At 6 o'clock, I obeyed Mrs Hooper's invitation, & went to
dine (for the second time that day). I found Mr [Samuel] Hooper &
his son & daughters, Governor & Mrs Andrew, & Mrs Schuyler.
Governor Andrew had much to say of Mr Seward. He thought he
surpassed all men in the bold attempt at gas-ing other people, & pull-
ing ⟨the⟩ wool over their eyes. He thought it very offensive. He might
be a donkey,—a good many men are,— [138] but he didn't like to
have a man by this practice show that he thought him one. I told him
that I had much better impressions of Mr S. but I did not relate to him
any conversations. Mrs Schuyler, I found, had very friendly feelings
towards Mr Seward, & I found he had told her the same story about
the Prince & Newcastle. She told me how ⟨intim⟩ much attached Talleyrand, when [139] in this country, had been to her grandfather,
General Hamilton; that, after his death, he had borrowed a miniature
portrait of him of Mrs Hamilton; that Mrs Hamilton had begged him
to bring it back to her, but he had refused, & ↑had↓ carried it with him
to France; that when Colonel Burr was in Paris, he had ⟨called on Tal-
leyr⟩ written a note to Talleyrand, expressing his wish to call on him,
& asking him to appoint an hour. Talleyrand did not wish to see [140]
him, but did not know how to decline it. So he wrote him a note, saying, that he was ready to see him when he should call, but he thought
it proper to say, that the picture of Col. Hamilton always hung in his
cabinet. Burr never called.

[141] I ought ⟨to⟩not to omit, that, when Sumner introduced me
to Mr Welles, Secretary of the Navy, & asked him if there were anything new? Mr Welles said, "No, nothing of importance," & then remarked, that "he observed the journals censured him for sending ves-

[87] "See Mr ... Seward" is added in pencil. "Mr. Moseley ... influence.", in ink,
may have been added later.

sels drawing too much water, in the Burnside expedition.[88] Now, he said, This was not the fault of [142] his department. We (the Navy) only send 17 (I think) vessels in all the hundred sail; the war department sent all the rest: he had nothing to do with them, and the overdrawing vessels were all ⟨of⟩ storeships & transports, &c. of the War Department's sending."

[143] I breakfasted at Mr Robbins's, with Mr Sherman of the Senate, & Colfax of the House.[89] In talking with the last, he said, That, Congress had not yet ⟨g⟩come up to the point of confiscating slaves of rebel masters, no, but only such as were engaged in military service.

I said, "How is it possible Congress can be so slow?"

He replied, "It is owing to the great social power here in Washington of the Border [144] States. They step into the place of the Southerners here, & wield the same power."

When I told Sumner what Seward had said to me about England, & Duke of Newcastle, he replied, "He has not been frank with you. I have heard him utter the most hostile sentiments to England. On the 27th May (I believe) he said to me talking of England, 'God damn 'em, I'll give 'em [145] hell,' kicking out his foot with violence."

Sumner showed me ⟨l⟩several English letters of much interest which he had just received from Bright, from the Duke of Argyll, & from the Duchess of A[rgyll]., all relating to our politics, & pressing emancipation.[90] Bright⟨s⟩ writes that thus far the English have not suffered from the war, but rather been benefitted by stopping manufacturing & clearing [146] out their old stocks & bringing their trade into a more

[88] The military expedition to the coast of North Carolina during January 1862 under the command of Brigadier General Ambrose E. Burnside sailed without the low-draft vessels and landing craft necessary for efficient unloading and transport on that coast. The expedition reported logistical difficulties in late January.

[89] John Sherman (1823–1900) was a senator from Ohio; Schuyler Colfax (1823–1885), later Vice-President, was a representative from Indiana.

[90] John Bright (1811–1888), radical English politican, George Campbell (1823–1900), eighth Duke of Argyll and Lord Privy Seal in the British Cabinet, and his wife Elizabeth were strong supporters of the Northern cause.

healthy state. But, after a few months, they will be importunate for cotton.

The Duchess of A. sent S[umner]. some fine lines of Tennyson ["Helen's Tower"] written at the request of Lord Dufferin for the tomb of his Mother[.]

[147] The Architect of the Capitol is Mr Walter of Boston[.][91]

I spent Sunday Evening at the house of Charles Eames, late Minister to Venezuela, whom I knew many years since at the Carlton House, New York. At his house I found many new & some old acquaintances[:] Governor Fish, Gov Andrew, N[athaniel]. P. Willis, Gurowski, Mr Nicolay the President's private secretary, and another young gentleman who shares I believe [148] the same office & is also I was told a contributor to the "Atlantic Monthly", ↑(Hay, probably,)↓ but whose name I have forgotten.[92] Young Robert Lincoln, the president's son, was also there, and Leutze, the painter, who invited me to see his picture which he is painting for a panel in the Capitol, "The Emigration to the West."[93] No military people I think were present. And when I went [149] home at a late hour I was vexed to have ⟨missed⟩ forgotten that Mr Secretary Staunton had invited me to call on him at his house this evening.

I was delighted with the senate chamber in the Capitol, & its approaches. I did not remember in France or in England that their legislative bodies were [150] nobly housed. The staircases & surrounding chambers are sumptuous & beautiful. The structure is so large, that I needed a guide, and could not find my way out, after I lost Spofford.[94]

---

[91] The Capitol architect at this time was Thomas Ustick Walter (1805–1887) of Philadelphia.

[92] For Emerson's acquaintance with Eames (1812–1867), see *JMN*, VIII, 202. Others not previously identified are Willis (1806–1867), popular author and journalist; John G. Nicolay (1832–1901), Lincoln's private secretary and later a diplomat and historian; and John Hay (1838–1905), Nicolay's assistant and later Secretary of State.

[93] Emanuel Leutze (1816–1868) painted "Westward the Course of Empire Takes Its Way" on the wall of the west staircase in the House of Representatives.

[94] Ainsworth Rand Spofford (1825–1908), Chief Assistant to the Librarian of Congress, later became Librarian of Congress.

It is the fault of the building that the ↑new↓ wings are built in a larger style, so that the columns of the centre look small.

[151] And the Capitol fronts the wrong way, its back being towards the present city of Washington. It was designed that the city should occupy the other slope, & face the Capitol. But the owners of the land held prices so high, that people bought the other side of the Capitol, & now the city is grown there.

[152] In the Congressional Library I found Spofford Assistant Librarian. He told me, that, for the last twelve (?) years, it had been under Southern domination, & as under dead men. Thus the Medical department was very large, and the Theological very large, whilst of modern literature very imperfect.

[153] There was no copy of the "Atlantic Monthly," or of the "Knickerbocker," none of the "Tribune," or "Times," or any N.Y. Journal. There was no copy of the "London Saturday Review" taken, or any other live journal, but the "London Court Journal," in a hundred volumes, duly bound.

Nor was it possible now to mend matters, because no money could they get from Congress, though an appropriation[n] [154] had been voted.

[155] 1864 March. Captain O[liver]. W[endell]. Holmes tells me, that the Army of the Potomac is acquiring a professional feeling, & that they have neither panics nor excitements, but more selfreliance.
———
Power of trifles. In Paris, they said, "It rains, there will be no revolution today."[95] So the politics of Europe always feel the effect of a good wine-crop. Build a good cupola on the top of your house, and one of your boys will soon know all the stars.   ↑Pentelican marble quarries make sculptors & the Persians were not naval people for want of forest timber.↓[96]

---

[95] For "In Paris . . . today.' ", see *JMN,* XII, 126.

[96] For "the Persians . . . timber.", see Conrad Malte-Brun, *Universal Geography, or a Description of All the Parts of the World, on a New Plan, According to the Great Natural Divisions of the Globe* . . . , 8 vols. in 17 (Boston, 1824), II, 300; in Emerson's library.

[156]   "Quand on boit trop on s'assoupit,
         Et l'on tombe en délire;
         Buvons pour avoir de l'esprit,
         Et non pour le detruire."
                                      Panard.

———

Lord Chancellor Jeffreys is being white washed before the ⟨r⟩Royal
Soc[iet]y of Literature by the production by Mr Walcott of an autograph letter of his showing more freedom in his politics than his
neighbors had[.]

———

And Mahomet
and Richelieu—see Saint Beuve
and the "Saturday Review," see [Matthew] Arnold[, "The Literary
Influences of Academies,"] in Cornhill Magazine[, Vol. X, No. 56,]
Aug. 1864. [pp. 154–172]

[157] *Plenty of Men.* No lack of men in the rail-cars; in the hotels;
going to see Cubas, or Booth; caravans of men going to Idaho mines,
to Pike's Peak, to Lake Superior.

[158] [blank]
        [159] There is an incurable frivolity of character which in action
has all the effect of wilful treason[.][97]

        [160] In my old "Fugitive Law Speech" in Concord, (and Cam-
bridge) I find the following paragraph in relation to some speech I had
read in a newspaper of Edward Everett. But I remember, that, when I
consulted files of papers, I could not find any report of such a speech
⟨.⟩by him.

                        ———

                      Extract.

———

        Mr Everett, misled by the same superficial view as Mr Webster,
talks of a bloody line of castles along [161] the blackened frontier between Maryland & Pennsylvania, between Ohio & Virginia! Does he

[97] Cf. *JMN,* XIV, 384.

know ⟨that⟩ that the people are kindly neighbors, of the same families, father & son, cousins, partners in trade. The only castles they know are Depots; the only dragoon is the Expressman; & instead of a bloody line of castles, there is an interminable [162] whitish line of flour-barrels, a bastion of boxes of shoes, a barricade of kegs & water-pails. Mr Everett has been reading in the history of the Middle Ages, or in his *"Amadis of Gaul,"* & not in the faces & manners & hearts of his countrymen.

———

↑Whether Everett or my imagination invented the picture, it is matter of fact today. 1862.↓

———

[163] "A strong army in a good fleet which neither foot nor horse is able to follow cannot be denied to land where it list: for ships without putting themselves out of breath will easily outrun the soldiers that coast them." "A fleet may sail in one night from point to point what an army could not span in six days."   Sir W[alter]. Raleigh

[164] Custom makes the soldier.[98]

"It more avails to have been accustomed unto the like than only to have rude strength." *Vegetius*

[165] The war is an eye-opener; and a reconciler, forgetting our petty quarrels as ridiculous.

"On such a shrine,
What are our petty griefs? let me not number mine."[99]
[Byron, *Childe Harold's Pilgrimage*, IV, cvi]

[166] [blank]
[167] Majorities, the argument of fools[,] the strength of the weak. One should recall what ⟨l⟩Laertius records of Socrates's Opinion of the common people, that, "it was as if a man should ⟨except⟩ ↑ob-

———

[98] See p. [15] above.
[99] See Journal GL, p. [297] above.

ject↓ against a piece⟨e⟩ of bad money, & accept a great sum of the
same."
For Leasts see also ⟨"Ethical⟩ ↑"Essential↓ Principles of Relig." p 1
     and "Health."[100]

[168] [blank]
[169]   History of Liberty

———

He is free who owns himself.

———

The State is older than any particular states.

———

[170]   *History of Liberty.*

———

See the admirable citation from King Alfred's will in *EA* p. 80

———

Free press. See the story of Dr Jacoby's book, *FOR* 82,

———

Story of Professor Stenzel displaced for being of the Burschenschaft
10 years before. *DL* 94, *FOR* 89

———

King Alfred's speech

———

"Pope Calixtus III., in 1456, issued a bull against a comet"
          (See Essay of *R. M.* ["A Modern Bull against Comets"] in
          the "Friend of Progress" Vol. 1. No. 5. [(Mar. 1865), p.
          146])

[171]   History of Liberty.

———

The Sicyonians, who buried nobody within their walls, sent to Delphi
to inquire, where they should bury Aratus; and had this answer:

---

[100] "For Leasts . . . Health.' " is in pencil. Emerson delivered the lecture "Essential
Principles of Religion" on March 16, 1862, and "Health" on December 14, 1862, before
the Parker Fraternity in Boston.

> "What holy rites for liberty restored
> Sicyon shall pay to her departed lord,
> She asks; Who grudges him a resting place
> Of earth, ⟨& seas⟩of skies,ⁿ & seas, is the disgrace."[101]

[172] He who does his own work frees a slave, He who does not his own work, is a slave-holder. See *V* 67

———

History of Liberty. See Δ, paragraphs on *Man.* p. 94

Varnhagen von Ense says, that, after all wars in Germany, the aristocracy grow strong:—in the "Thirty Years War," in the "Seven Years," & in the "Emancipation War". Frederic the Great weeded out every officer not noble from his army. Dr Erhard told of a fellow who reeled drunk out of a gin shop, &, hearing [173] the cannonade on account of the capture of Paris, ⟨instantly⟩ cried out, "There, ↑do you↓ hear↑?↓ ⟨you,⟩ the War is over,—the nobility have conquered." Erhard thought this chap had shown the deepest ↑political↓ insight.
[*Tägebucher*, 1861–1870, I, 28]

———

"When the government fears, that is already a step forward" (for the people) said Gans. *Varnhagen* [*Ibid.,*] I. p. 97
"Wenn die Regierung sich furchtet, so ist das schon ein Fortschritt."

For example. There comes a time when books, once printed with impunity, now make too much impression, & are suppressed.

[174] You men who come back have not lost your time. Certain truths have been imprinted on you. ⟨the⟩ You have ⟨studied⟩ seen the world. You have learned somewhat of your country. Without dishonor you have seen Virginia & Carolina. It has been true though people have tried to disguise it for years that a man of the free states could not travel on his necessary [175] business in that country without seeing or hearing something on which it was necessary he should shut his

———

[101] For "The Sicyonians . . . disgrace.' ", see *JMN*, VIII, 83. The anecdote is taken from Plutarch's life of Aratus, but Emerson's edition has not been ascertained.

eyes & his ears. If he said what he thought, he was ⟨in⟩ certain of ↑in-jury or↓ insult; if he did not speak, he lost his own respect. You have been able to see & hear much ⟨that⟩ ↑disagreeable↓ truth, without loss of your own honor. No one will hereafter be able to persuade you that [176] no state of society is ⟨so⟩ sweet & happy & enlightened, unless it is founded on stealing. You ⟨have⟩ can teach us. And I know that your votes, your charities, your plans of life & courses of action will draw incessantly on this painful experience of the last year. [177] You have earned the freedom of this town & this state. We welcome you home to the houses & lands that are dear to you, to your old companions & to new friends.[102] We shall never see you without respect & gratitude. These are they who bore our sins on their shoulders, & by their suffer-ings we are at peace.

[178] Sweet are the uses of adversity,[103] and, I am sure, that many a time in these weary weeks by night & by day our ⟨plain⟩ quiet land-scape, ⟨& plain houses⟩ the silent river & the inland ponds, & the plain houses thereby have loomed up in your fancy; ⟨as⟩ ↑and Fairhaven, &↓ Walden Pond, & Nine Acre Corner, & the East Quarter schoolhouse you would have given a month's wages to look upon[.][104]

[179]–[181] [blank]
[182]   Public duty

Those who stay away from the election think that one vote will do no good. 'Tis but one ⟨m⟩step more to think one vote will do no harm. But if they should come to be ⟨un⟩interested in themselves,—in their career,—they would no more stay from the elections, than from honesty or from affection[.][105]

↑See IO 28↓[106]

---

[102] "freedom of . . . dear to you," is struck through in pencil with a faint curved ver-tical line, possibly a use mark.

[103] Shakespeare, *As You Like It*, II, i, 12.

[104] Five Concord soldiers taken prisoner at Bull Run on July 21, 1861, were ex-changed and returned home on June 12 and 13, 1862. This paragraph, pp. [174]–[178], is probably a draft of welcoming remarks to them. See *J*, IX, 432, and *L*, V, 279.

[105] This paragraph, struck through in pencil with a vertical use mark, is used in "The Fortune of the Republic," *W*, XI, 523. See *JMN*, XIII, 304.

[106] In pencil.

[183] "Le Premier Consul n'a eu besoin que de ministres qui l'entendissent, jamais de ministres qui le suppléassent." *Roederer*[107]

[184] "A republican govt., so far from proving that all men are free & equal, owes its merit to the very reverse, that it does away with artificial distinctions, by wh. natural inferiority is disguised, & superiority is kept under." J. C. Thompson[108]

[185] [blank]
[186] *Whiggery.*   ↑Its doctrine is,↓
Better endure tyranny according to law a thousand years than irregular & unconstitutional happiness for a day. Of course, he had rather die in the hands of a physician than be cured by a quack.[109]

[187] [blank][110]
[188] Strange that our government, so stupid as it is, should never blunder into a good measure. In U⟨a⟩tah, the leading issues are not those of our national parties; yet the Government invariably adopts the bad side.

We have no character. In the European crisis, we should be of great weight, if we had character. But Austria, [189] France, & Russia, can say, "look at America! 'Tis worse than we." &c. &c. AC 274 [actually 273]

I grieve to see that the Government is governed by the hurrahs of the soldiers or the citizens. It does not lead opinion, but follows it.

[190] August 30, 1862.
⟨L⟩Several urgent motives point to the Emancipation.

---

[107] Sainte-Beuve, *Causeries du lundi,* 1851–1862, VIII, 297. Emerson borrowed volume 8 from the Boston Athenaeum November 23–December 7, 1854, and January 30–March 16, 1864. See *JMN,* XIII, 312.

[108] See *JMN,* XIV, 252.

[109] For "Of course, . . . quack.", see *JMN,* XIV, 230.

[110] Attached to p. [187] is a clipping giving the text of President Lincoln's message to Congress on March 6, 1862, proposing compensation for any state adopting a gradual abolishment of slavery.

1. The eternal right of it.

2. The military necessity of creating an army in the rear of the Enemy, &⟨,⟩ throughout his country, & in every plantation, compelling him to disband his army, & rush home to protect his family & estate.

3. The danger of the adoption by the South of [191] the policy of Emancipation. France & England may peaceably recognize the Southern Confederacy, on the condition of Emancipation. Instantly, we are thrown into falsest position. All Europe will back France & England in the act, because the cause of the South will then be the cause of Freedom, the cause of the North will be that of Slavery.

See the effect of recognition. It breaks at once the blockade. [192] The South at once ⟨ac⟩will acquire a navy, buying ships of France & England, & buying sailors & officers too, if needed, of them, and will face us on the sea, &, at least, protect themselves. Then our war is fruitless. Our enormous debt ⟨is real⟩ remains real. The Border states sympathize with the South, &, not wishing to pay this debt, join⟨s⟩ the South. Neither will California, Wisconsin, Minnesota, care to pay the debt, but will secede. Utah combines with California,[n] [193] being always hostile to the States. The Mississippi Valley ↑north & south↓ combines to save the river.[n] ⟨combines north & south⟩And an eastern tier of States is left to bear the load, and the load is too great, & the debt is repudiated.

Emancipation makes all this impossible. European govts. dare not interfere for Slavery, as soon as the Union is pronounced for Liberty.

[194]   ↑*1862*↓
France says I know very well the avoirdupois of the North, but it will not succeed, because it will not take this step (of emanicpation) to make its weight tell.

↑*1863*, 1 January, *1864*, February 15. Now it has been fully taken[.]↓

Strange that some strong-minded president of the Womans' Rights Convention should not offer to lead the Army of the Potomac. She could not do worse than General Maclellan.

It becomes our government[n] [195] to ⟨make⟩ ↑provide↓ a double supply of arms & ammunition, for we furnish both sides with these articles.

Realism
   "No general is satisfied unless he has an army. Answer him (St Cyr) that a general always has troops enough, if he knows how to employ them, & if, instead of sleeping in town, he bivouacs with his men."   *Bonaparte.*[111]
                                                                see *SO* 30

[196] With the South the war is primary; with the North it is secondary; secondary of course to their trade, then also to their pleasure. The theatres & concerts are filled as usual.
   I don't know that the government can carry on a war; and it has ever been in the minds of our people who know ↑how↓ public action drags, & how efficient is private [197] enterprise, to turn it over to private hands, & let Adams's Express undertake by contract the capture of Richmond, of Charleston, of the pirate Alabama, & any other designated parts of the war. But if England & France should really ⟨attack us s⟩ move to dismember the Union, there might then be energy instantly roused to concentrate our force on the storming of Richmond, Charleston, Savannah,[n] [198] & Mobile, so as to make the Govt. master of all the ports; then we should say to Europe, "⟨Surely⟩ the ports are all open, we are happy to see your trade here," and, if ⟨further⟩ hostility were to follow with Europe, it would probably soon be made the hoop to hold us staunch.

[199] Feeble patriotism in America
See Lord Dundonald's ship carpenter *GL* 87[112]

   Insanity of the south. I acquit the South on that plea;
"But never more be officer of mine."[113]

---

[111] Napoleon, *The Confidential Correspondence* . . . , 1856, I, 151. The quotation is struck through in pencil with a vertical use mark; "a general . . . men.' " is used in "Works and Days," *W*, VII, 176.
   [112] "Feeble patriotism . . . *GL* 87" is in pencil.
   [113] Shakespeare, *Othello*, II, iii, 249. See *JMN*, XIV, 298.

[200] I wrote C[harles]. G. Loring, Esq., who sent me his "Correspondence with Edwin Field, Esq"   1862[114]

The aspects of our problem are too complex than that a foreigner can be expected to do justice to them all. Mr Field declines to look longer. An Englishman is too preoccupied. One thing is plain to me, that our constitutionality can only appear to ourselves. Foreigners cannot give the requisite attention to see ⟨the⟩them. Broad [201] grounds, as, if one party fights for freedom, or for slavery, they can appreciate. But our constitutionality, on which we so pique ourselves, of ↑one party↓ fighting at the same time ⟨in⟩*for* slavery in the loyal states, &, in the rebel states, *against* it, is too technical for distant observers, & only supplies them with the reproach that our cause is immoral. And if the war will alter our *status* on this point, & alter it soon, it will be worth all our calamities.

[202]   Army
Mutiny. "When the extinguisher takes fire, 'tis an aukward business."[115]

[203] Bonaparte said to Bubna, the Austrian diplomat↑ist↓, in 1809. Speaking of the campaign of 1809, "My great advantage is in being constantly on the offensive with you, not only at large (en grand), but also in detail, & in every particular moment. I am not on the defensive except when I do not see you, for instance, in the night: but, as soon as I see you, I resume the offensive, I form my plan, & I force you to fly ⟨from⟩ ↑before↓ my movements."
↑Gentz's Diary p 205↓[116]

[204]   *Bonaparte*
Bubna relates of Bonaparte; Il lui a juré qu'il ne faisait jamais de plan d'avance, pas même la veille d'une bataille, mais toujours dans le moment ou il voit la position et les desseins probables de son ennemi.

---

[114] *Correspondence on the Present Relations between Great Britain and the United States of America* (Boston, 1862).

[115] Thomas Moore, *Memoirs, Journal, and Correspondence* . . . , ed. Lord John Russell, 8 vols. (London, 1853–1856), III, 167. See *JMN*, XIV, 416.

[116] *Tagebücher von Friedrich von Gentz* (Leipzig, 1861); in Emerson's library.

"Votre armée serait tout aussi bonne que la mienne, si je la comman-
dais; toute autre armée qui se mesurera avec vous, russe, prussienne,
etc. sera sûre d'être battue." [205] "Pourquoi se lamenter sur la perte
de quelques lambeaux de terrain qui vous reviendront pourtant un
jour? Tout cela peut durer tant que j'existe. La France ne peut pas
faire la guerre au-dela du Rhin. Bonaparte l'a pu; mais avec moi tout
est fini."

Diary of Gentz. p. 205–6

[206] Gentz's Diary inevitably translates itself into American
war, as I read. *Mutato nomine de te.*[117] The hopeless state of Austrian
affairs in 1806, 7, 8, 9, the ⟨l⟩ ⟨want⟩ ↑incapacity↓ of generals, the conceit, weakness, & infatuation of the grand dukes, the infatuation of the
Emperor, & the total disorganization of the government

[207] "This beast, called the 'State' thrusts itself everywhere
before our steps, showing its teeth, & lets us not pass on. He only is
safe who springs on its back, & feeds himself on it as vermin."
said Varnhagen von Ense in Berlin, in 1836
Varnhagen [von Ense], [*Tagebücher,* 1861,] I. 25.

"Humboldt is grim & indignant over our affairs here. When in the
stagnation anything happens, 'tis sure to be pitiable. Professor
Stenzler in Breslau, the Sanscrit scholar, is displaced since it has been
discovered that, ten years ago, he belonged to the Burschenschaft,"
&c.   [*Ibid.,*] I. 34

[208] [blank]
[209][118]   Negro Soldiers
If the war means liberty to you you should enlist. It does mean liberty
to you in the opinion of /Jeff Davis/the South/ for ⟨they s⟩ ↑the↓
South[n] says, we fight ⟨for⟩ to plant slavery as our foundation. And of

---

[117] "The name having been borrowed from you" (Ed.).
[118] Pages [209]–[219] are in pencil. On March 6, 1863, Thomas Russell asked
Emerson to speak at a meeting to raise funds for Robert Gould Shaw's Negro regiment.
This may be a draft for that speech, given March 20. See *L,* V, 318 and 320.

course we who resist the South, are forced to make liberty of the
negro our foundation. I speak for the forces above us those issues
which are made for us over our heads, under our feet, paramount to
our wills.[119] If you will not fight for your liberty who will[?] [210] If
you will not, why then take men as they are and the Universe of men
will say you are not worth fighting for. Go & be slaves forever & you
shall have our aid to make you such. You had rather be slave than
freemen. Go to your own place[.]

Plainly ⟨if⟩ we must have a worthy cause for such ⟨men⟩ soldiers
as we send to battle or they shall not go. Do you think such ⟨soldiers⟩
↑lives↓ as this city [&] state have [211] yielded up already, the children of this famed city, the children of our public schools, the children
of Harvard College, the best blood of our educated counties, objects of
the most romantic hope & love, poets & romancers themselves[—]I
attended the funeral of one of them & heard ⟨the⟩[n] with hearty assent
the voice that said that the whole state of S Carolina was not worth
th⟨e⟩at one life[—] [212] that these precious young men ↑Lander,
Lowell, Putnam, Dwight, Willard,↓ ↑the voice will choke to name
them↓ are given up to bring back into the Capitol of Washington the
reckless politicians who h⟨d⟩ad reeled out of it with threats to destroy
it, or come back into it to rule again?[n] Never.[120] Better ⟨blow⟩ put gunpowder under its foundations & plough up the ground where its
streets stand ↑than↓ they die for the disgraceful ⟨to⟩dynasty which had
brought our freedom to be a lie & our civilization ⟨& trade⟩[n] & wealth
[213] to dishonor as a partnership of thieves[.]
No[,] they died for the largest & noblest sentiment[,] the largest interpretation that could be put on the meaning & action of the North[,]
died ⟨w⟩for what an American ↑might die for↓ not to

[119] A vertical line is drawn in pencil in the left margin beside "I speak ... wills".
[120] Major General Frederick West Lander, a civil engineer from Massachusetts, died
in Virginia on March 2, 1862. Lieutenants James Jackson Lowell and his cousin William
Lowell Putnam, classmates at Harvard, joined the 20th Massachusetts Volunteers together; Putnam was killed at the battle of Ball's Bluff on October 21, 1861, and Lowell on
July 4, 1862, near Richmond. Lieutenant Colonel Wilder Dwight, a Harvard graduate
who read law in E. R. Hoar's office, helped raise the Second Massachusetts Regiment, was
wounded at Antietam while leading it, and died September 19, 1862. Major Sidney Willard, also a Harvard graduate and a promising young lawyer, died at Fredericksburg on
December 14, 1862.

[When such men march & die it is not for a technical Union[,] one so called but really][121]

And the Governor of this Commonwealth nobly ⟨said⟩ spoke the sense of his people when he said we will enlist if you send us out for freedom & [214] not if you send us out to return slaves. ⟨I know⟩ Whatever mean carpers & the owls & jackals ⟨of⟩[n] who squeak & gibber to the contrary will say, he spoke the voice of patriot fathers & mothers ↑who offered their sons↓ & of the patriot youths who offered up themselves, when he said, see that the cause is clear & great, & you shall have them & us; but we go not to restore those falsehearted usurpers of the power of Union ⟨to t⟩ or the like of them to their places. God in his mercy forbid [215] but to restore the spirit of the American constitution & not its forced & falsely construed letter[,] not to restore those men but to exclude & brand them forever & put upright sound men in their places

not to maintain slavery but to maintain freedom & to limit ↑& end↓ slavery as wa

⟨limit & end slavery as soon as it could⟩ limits[n] & a speedy dissolution to slavery

limits & a purpose to end slavery at the earliest day   as it was in the beginning is now & ever shall be[122]

[216] My opinion may not interest you & I will not bore you with it,[n] but such as it is it is myself & if you wish my aid it must be in conformity with my opinion. You ask me to fight, to send soldiers, to go myself. With all my heart, if your objects are mine. I will fight for freedom. I will ⟨fight⟩ not ⟨to⟩fight to secure any more power to slaveholders. They had already, as our history shows, far too much. I will not fight to force them to remain in the Union. I had rather they [217] would go out[.]

          Negroes good soldiers
they love music, dress, order, parade,

---

[121] "When such . . . really" is bracketed and struck through in pencil with a diagonal use or cancellation mark.

[122] From the *Gloria Patri,* or "Lesser Doxology." Emerson quotes the English version of the *Book of Common Prayer.*

they have a couth temperament & *abandon*,   & Gen H.'s opinion
      of their desperate courage.

Fitness of the hour. At this moment the Negro an object of kindness
to all nations.
      cowed
Periodicity of errors & periodicity of races & civilities.
Negro nearer to geology than others.
Exhausted perhaps in his first era

[218]   I am not black in my mind
          ↑But↓ born to make black fair:
                 ↑⟨In⟩On the battlefield my master find,—
                    His white corpse taints the air.↓[123]

Perhaps only his period is larger, & his return to light requires a better
medium than our immoral civilization allows[.]

Slavery has kept his race down[.]
Civilization sanctioning marriage is always selecting the flower of each
sex for marriage & dropping any disqualification[.]
But in the license under which this race has suffered, this selection ⟨ha⟩
was not

[219]   "So long as the Judge protects us
             By heart & genius cheered,
             And free in council sits he
             Who free gives his judgment

             So long in lieu of all weapons
             A song is our shield;
             Feeling of right & honor
             Is constitution enough."
                      See Varnhagen [von Ense, *Tagebücher*, 1861,]
                         vol 1. p. [246]

[123] The first two lines of verse are enclosed on the left by a half circle in pencil partly
overwritten by the added lines.

Voltaire Rousseau were Xns [Christians] & did not know it[124]
Dumas
Renan

[220] In every crisis people look for the master of the situation, who is usually slow to appear. We have found none in America. But in England, which our politics immensely concern, they have found none. The one ↑foreign↓ interest of England is to ⟨provide⟩ assure herself in all times of the alliance of America, as bound by blood, language, trade, power, and equal civilization.

[221] [blank]
    [222] ⟨O⟩*The Commentaries of Messire Blaize de Lasseran Massencome de Montluc, Mareschal de France. Translated by Charles Cotton. 1674, Lond.*[125]

"Nothing can more spite a man of courage than to be left at home to burn his shins by the fire, whilst other men are employed abroad in honorable action."
                                                                                    p. 12
"↑M de Bourbon↓ gave us a company of men for safe conduct but the devil a penny of money or a bit of bread." p. 14[126]

[223] He writes of Andrew Doria (Andrea d'Aurea,) 1528, "It seemed as if the sea stood in awe of this man." p. 18.[127]
"Genoa"

    The days of peace were years to me. [p. 30]

"When a man is once possessed ⟨of⟩with fear, & that he loses his judgment, as all men in a fright do, he knows not what he does, and it is the principal thing you are to beg at the hands of Almighty God, to preserve your understanding entire, for, what danger soever there may be, there is still one way or other to get off, &, perhaps, to [224] your honor. But when fear has once

---

[124] With "Voltaire Rousseau . . . it", cf. "Character," *W*, X, 110.
[125] Emerson borrowed this volume from the Boston Athenaeum May 25–June 9, 1863.
[126] " 'M de Bourbon . . . p. 14" is in pencil.
[127] This quotation is used in "Greatness," *W*, VIII, 308.

possessed your judgment, God ye good even! You think you are flying towards the poop, when you are running towards the prow, &, for one enemy, think you have ten before your eyes,—as drunkards do, who see a thousand candles at once" p. 80[128]

I erected a gallows [& indeed I had, & have ever had, a little scur⟨y⟩vy character of being liberal of the rope]" p. 97[129]

[225][130] West Point Academy makes a very agreeable impression on me. The innocence of the cadets, the air of probity, of veracity, & of loyalty to each other struck me, & the anecdotes told us confirmed this impression. I think it excellent that such tender youths should be ⟨so⟩ made so manly & masterly in rough exercises of horse & gun & cannon & mortar[,] [226] so accurate ↑in French,↓ in Mathematics, geology, and engineering, should learn to draw, to dance, & to swim.
I think the⟨re⟩ir ambition should be concentrated on the↑ir↓ superiority in Science,—being taught, that, whoever knows the most must command *of right,* & must command *in fact,* if just to himself. Let them have no fears, then, ⟨about⟩ ↑of↓ prejudices against West Point. [227] "West Point a hot bed of aristocracy," is a word of some political hack, which seems to rankle in their memories. ↑Rather↓ let[n] them ↑accept it, and↓ make West Point a true aristocracy, or "the power of the Best," ⟨s|| . . . ||⟩best scholars, best soldiers, best engineers, best commanders, best men,—and[n] they will be indispensable to their government & their country; will[n] be, as they [228] ought, the nucleus of the army, though it be three fourths or nine tenths volunteers;—they will be the shop of power, the source of instruction, the organization of Victory. Watt said, "he sold power in his shop." Ah! that is what all men wish to buy, if they can only have the pure article. Something finer, I think, than Watt meant, or had. [229] Or if he had it, he forgot to tell us the number of the shop. In regard to the points to which

[128] "your honor. . . . eyes,—" is struck through in pencil with a vertical use mark. The entire quotation is used in "Resources," *W*, VIII, 147.

[129] " 'I erected . . . p. 97" is in pencil.

[130] The entries on pp. [225]–[235] are a record of Emerson's visit to the United States Military Academy at West Point in June 1863, when he was appointed a member of a committee of visitation. See also Journal DL, p. [99] above.

the attention of the Board was called, ⟨I think⟩ the "Administration" appeared ↑to me↓ judicious, & more mild in fact than the printed rules led us to look for. Thus, on inquiry for the "dark prison," we found there was none, the room once used for this, having been for some years appropriated to other uses.

[230] One fact appeared plainly, that this Academy was free of the ⟨perpetual obstacle in⟩ ↑bête noir of↓ colleges, namely, criminal justice.

Here they are once & forever freed from every question by means of ⟨military organization⟩ martial law. Every cadet is instantly responsible ⟨for his behaviour⟩ to his superior officer, for his behavior, & is sent to [231] the guard-house, or has ⟨a⟩one or two hours' patrol-duty added to his day's work, or, ⟨if the offence⟩ ⟨loses⟩ ↑is put down↓ a long row of steps on his ladder of merit, or, ↑if the offence is grave,↓ is discharged from the Academy.

I think that the point of competitive examinations should be urged on the Congress, and that a severer preliminary test should be required for admission. The Academy [232] should be relieved of the task of teaching to ⟨parse⟩ spell & parse English. Thus the course of study might be less superficial, or the application of science might ↑be↓ carried into detail in other schools.

The discipline is yet so strict, that these military monks, in years, never ⟨go⟩ pass the limits of the post, & know nothing of the country immediately around [233] them. It is pleasant to see the excellence ⟨of⟩& beauty of their fences, which cost nothing & need no repairs, namely, the Hudson River on one or two sides, & the mountains on the other sides. There is nothing beyond ⟨no⟩the post, no village, no shops, no bad company. It is two miles to Cozzens' new Hotel, but over a desert road, & there ⟨th⟩ any cadet would be under dangerous observation.

[234]   *Books for West Point*
_____

Life of Hodson

Life of Lord Herbert of Cherbury

Tom Brown　　at Rugby

d[itt]o　　　at Oxford

Correspondence between Napoleon & Joseph Buonaparte

Lives of the French Savans. By Arago.

George Herbert's Poems.

Life of Maj. General, Sir Wm Napier[131]

[235] At West Point, I entered some of the ⟨rooms⟩ chambers of the cadets in the barracks, & found two cadets in each, standing as if on guard. Each chamber was perfectly clean, & every article orderly disposed. ⟨Wh⟩The mattrass on the camp iron bed was rolled up into a scroll.ⁿ "Who makes your bed?" "I do." "Who brings your water?" "I do." "Who blacks your shoes?" "I do."[132] In the ⟨fl⟩ battery drill, I saw each handsome dainty boy whom I had noticed in the Examination, flying over the field ⟨or⟩in the caissons, or loading or working the gun, all begrimed with powder. In the mortar practice, in the siege

---

[131] This list includes Hodson's *Twelve Years of a Soldier's Life in India* . . . , 1859 (see Journal GL, p. [284] above); *Life of Edward, Lord Herbert of Cherbury, Written by Himself* (London, 1826), which Emerson borrowed from the Boston Athenaeum May 25–June 9, 1863; Thomas Hughes, *School Days at Rugby* (an 1872 edition with his daughter Ellen's name in it is in Emerson's library) and *Tom Brown at Oxford,* 2 vols. (New York, 1860–1861), in Emerson's library, also Ellen's (see *JMN,* XIV, 482); Napoleon's *Confidential Correspondence with His Brother Joseph,* 2 vols. (New York, 1856), which Emerson had read in 1856 (see *JMN,* XIV, 47–49); probably François Arago, *Biographies of Distinguished Scientific Men,* trans. W. H. Smyth, Baden Powell, and Robert Grant (London, 1857), which Emerson withdrew from the Boston Athenaeum October 31, 1857–January 14, 1858 (see *JMN,* XIV, 156); and Henry Austin Bruce, ed., *Life of General Sir William Napier,* 2 vols. (London, 1864), which Emerson withdrew from the Boston Athenaeum August 18–September 2, 1864.

[132] The paragraph to this point is used in "The Man of Letters," *W,* X, 251. See Journal DL, p. [99] above.

battery drill, each was promptly performing his part in the perfect exercise.

[236] ↑Lincoln↓ We must accept the results of universal suffrage, & not try to make it appear that we can elect ⟨great⟩ ↑fine↓ gentlemen. ⟨No,⟩ We^n shall have ⟨popular⟩ coarse men, with a fair chance of worth & of manly ability, but not polite men, not men to please ↑the↓ English⟨men⟩ or French.[133]

[237] You cannot ⟨g⟩ refine Mr Lincoln's taste, or /clear his judgment/extend his horizon/;[134] he will not walk dignifiedly through the traditional part of the President of America, but will pop out his head at each railroad station & make a little speech, & get into an argument with Squire A. & Judge B.[;] he will write letters to Horace Greeley, and^n [238] any Editor or Reporter ⟨that writes a letter to him⟩ or saucy Party committee that writes to him, & cheapen himself. But this we must be ready for, and let the clown appear, & hug ourselves that we are well off, if we have got good nature, honest meaning, & fidelity to /popular/public/ interest, with bad manners, instead of an elegant roué & malignant selfseeker.

[239] If our brothers or children are killed in the battle, we owe to them the same courage & selfrenunciation in bearing well their death, which they showed us in sacrificing themselves.

They who come today to his funeral, tomorrow will tread in his warpath, & show to his slayers the way to death.[135]

────

[240] ↑on the morals of parties↓
But how came he on that side?
See *Westminster Rev[iew]*. on London Times *NO* 83

[133] Emerson circled "polite men" in ink, perhaps to cancel it, then fingerwiped part of the circle and extended it to enclose "not polite men".

[134] Emerson circled "clear his judgment" for revision or cancellation, and inserted "extend his horizon" above "or clear his".

[135] This sentence, struck through in ink with a vertical use mark, is used in "Harvard Commemoration Speech, July 21, 1865," *W*, XI, 344. See Journal DL, p. [203] above.

"For the eye altering alters all." *Blake*[136]

In seeing M. M. O. ↑Otis↓ the other day, I did not like it that she appeared rather to endure her beauty than to animate or create it.

"L'amour est l'oeil, aimer c'est voir." *Aimé De Loy.*

[241] You are the pickets[.]
The ⟨eternal⟩ difference between you & your enemies is eternal; it is the difference of motive. Your action is to build, & their action is to destroy: yours to protect and to establish the rights of men; and theirs to crush them.

Machiavel himself said, " 'Tis not the violence which repairs, but the violence which destroys, that is to be blamed"

↑*Friendship*↓
Chacun a son gout. Froissart says of his youth, "I loved all those who loved dogs & birds."
homme amoureux was, in that age, equivalent to *homme comme il faut.*

[242] We say, the cards beat all the players, were they never so skilful; that revolutions beat all the insurgents, be they never so determined & politic; and Providence continues the race of great kings, (though a⟨s⟩ driveller should sit on the throne,) by the intervention of a great minister, as the policy of Henry IV. of France was carried forward by Richelieu, in the insignificance of Louis XIII.[137]

[243] Le comte de Crillon disait un jour (1781?) a M. d'Allonville, "Si l'univers et moi professons une opinion↑,↓ et que M. Necker en émît une contraire, je serais aussitôt convaincu que l'univers et moi nous nous trom-

---

[136] "The Mental Traveller," l. 62; in Alexander Gilchrist, *Life of William Blake,* 1863, II, 101. Emerson borrowed this volume from the Boston Athenaeum December 11–19, 1863, and April 29–May 6, 1864. The line is used in "Greatness," *W,* VIII, 319.
[137] A pencil line is drawn vertically in the left margin from "all the players," down to "by Richelieu,". "We say . . . insurgents," is used in "Harvard Commemoration Speech, July 21, 1865," *W,* XI, 342; "revolutions beat . . . politic;" is used in "The Fortune of the Republic," *W,* XI, 530. See Journal DL, p. [203] above.

p⟨io⟩ons".[138] *St Beuve Causeries* [*du lundi,* 1851–1862,] Vol. 7. [p. 273]
↑The power of quoting could no farther go.↓

Classes

It makes a great difference whether a man lives with his face or his back to the window.
one boy's clothes are always neat; ⟨an⟩ his brother's, always torn.
Leasts
Trifles is a very convertible word. Your trifles are my gods. The child's soap bubbles are Newton's problems[.]

[244] Conclusion of "Success" to be found at the end of Lect. called "Moral Sense" as read at Music Hall

Of Wordsworth's poem "To H. C. six years old," William Blake writes; "This is all in the highest degree imaginative, & equal to any poet, but not superior. I cannot think that real poets have any competition. None are greatest in the kingdom of heaven. It is so in poetry." "Natural objects always did & now do weaken, deaden, & obliterate [245] imagination in me. Wordsworth must know that what he writes valuable is *not* to be found in Nature."ⁿ *Wm Blake.* See [Alexander Gilchrist,] *Life* [*of William Blake,* 1863,] Vol 1 p 345[139]

He adds to this last remark—"Read Michael Angelo's sonnet, Vol 2, p. 179. of this Edition." [*Ibid.,* p. 345]

Blake spoke of the Spirits, & had talked with Voltaire. "I asked," says Crabbe Robinson, "in what language Voltaire spoke: he answered, 'To my sensations it was English. It was like the touch of a musical key: he touched it probably French, but to my ear it became English.' " [*Ibid.,* p. 348]

[138] "Le comte . . . tromp⟨io⟩ons.' " is struck through in ink with three vertical use marks; a translation is used in "Quotation and Originality," *W*, VIII, 190. A vertical line is drawn in ink in the left margin beside the quotation from Crillon. The comma after "opinion" is added in pencil.

[139] For " 'This is all . . . poetry.' ", see Journal DL, p. [146] above. " 'Natural objects . . . in me." is used in "Inspiration," *W*, VIII, 290.

[246] Blake said, "I have never known a bad man who had not something very good about him." [*Ibid.*, p. 354][140]

It was Fuseli, who said, "Nature puts me out." [*Ibid.*, p. 370]

[247] We do not clearly see what shall be, or how religion & enthusiasm are to come to us Americans which we sorely need. For the imported religions are used up↑,↓ & we want power to drive the ponderous state. Incredulity verges on despair↑.↓ We think we can defy any crisis↑,↓ any teacher↑,↓ any Providence↑,↓ to reproduce[n] [248] for us the enthusiasm of Greece after the Persian invasion,—the enthusiasm for Beauty: or that of Europe in Early Christianity; &, later, in the Crusades; and in the ages when plainly mankind expected that the world was shortly coming to an [249] end: or the fire of Arabia in Islamism; or the power & terror of France in 1789.[141]

We can see that the Constitution & law in America must be written on ethical principles, so that the entire power of the spiritual world can be enlisted to hold the loyalty of the [250] citizen, & to repel the enemy as by force of Nature. The laws of old empires stood on the religious convictions. Now that those religions are outgrown, the empires lacked strength. But Christianity is no longer what it was a thousand or even a hundred years ago. [251] ⟨It is R⟩ Romanism in Europe does not represent the real opinion of enlightened men. The Lutheran Church does not represent in Germany the opinions of the↑ir↓ Universities. In England, the gentlemen, the journals, & now, at last, the churchmen & bishops, have fallen away from the Anglican Church. [252] And in America, where are no legal ties to churches, the looseness appears dangerous.[142]

[140] "Blake said . . . good" is used in "Greatness," *W*, VIII, 317.
[141] "We do not . . . shall be," is struck through in ink with a vertical use mark; the paragraph is struck through in ink with single vertical use marks on pp. [247], [248], and [249]; "we want . . . state." is used in "Character," *W*, X, 111–112. The added punctuation is in pencil.
[142] This paragraph, struck through in ink with single vertical use marks on pp. [249], [250], [251], and [252], is used in "Character," *W*, X, 112; "We can . . . Nature." is used in "The Fortune of the Republic," *W*, XI, 540.

[253] [blank]

[254] See how the Greeks wrote their metaphysics,—in the names & attributes of their gods,—Apollo for Genius, Themis for E⟨h⟩thics, Mercury for Eloquence, Muses for Poetry, Daedalus for Art; Parcae for Fate; Mnemosyne for Memory; Metis for Counse⟨s⟩l; Prometheus Forethought; Epimetheus after-thought; Jove for supreme Reason; Comus, & Momus, & Silenus, & Graces, for Laughter & Wit.

[255] [blank]

[256] My humorous friend told me, that old age was cheap: ⟨& economical: he did not go to the dentist, for⟩ Time drew out his teeth gratis, and a ↑suction-↓plate would last him as long as he lived: he ⟨did not⟩ ↑does not↓ go ⟨longer⟩ to the hairdresser, for Time cut off his hair; and he had lived so long, & bought so many clothes, that he should not need ↑to↓ b⟨y⟩uy any more[.]

↑N. said in the car to a chance companion—"Yes, but I am an old man & can't do so or so." Instead of the indignant denial he expected, the stranger replied, "Yes, You are an old man & that makes [257] a difference."↓

↑Vain was his use of the dodge of old men—giving themselves for ten years older than they are: the companion quietly accepted it as true.

Boston & N.Y. see supra p. 71, also, *FOR* 267↓[143]

New York, 22 Dec.

The muskrat on our rivers has two doors, one to the water, & one to the land. Our Boston merchants have already a ↑sea-↓door, ⟨to the sea,⟩ but they are rather pinched by the Hoosac Mountain on the land side, & they want a land-door; so they have made an extension of their

---

[143] "a difference.' " is run over onto the bottom of p. [257]. "Vain was . . . *FOR* 267" is fitted around it at the bottom of the page and set off from it by a curved line in ink; the long rule above the insertion separates it from "New York . . . railroad.", inscribed earlier.

gallery to N. York, & ⟨the⟩ build their land-door here, ↑in N.Y.,↓ fac-
ing St Louis & Chicago & the Pacific railroad.[144]

[258]   *Art.*
     I must remember Leonardo Da Vinci as a *mannered* artist, when
I recall that *one face* which, in all ⟨the⟩ ↑his↓ St Johns or Madonnas ⟨of
his that I saw,⟩ looked out on me, ⟨as if⟩ as I once heard of ⟨Leslie⟩
↑Newton↓ that some Sally Sullivan ↑(?)↓ was in all his pictures, ↑& of
Greenough* that he carved himself into his sculptures.↓ Dr Johnson,
Carlyle, & John Wilson, in "Moss Side" &c, are victims of their own
manner.[145]

———
↑Parmegiano is mannered. His figures attitudinize as in second class
society, at watering places. Martin is mannered. You can tell his pictures at a look.↓

     [259] Flagg (of Little & Brown) tells me that the reason of the
delay of the remaining volumes of the "Biographie Générale" (whose
last Tome ends with   ) is the difficu↑l⟨t⟩↓ty of writing the article of
"Napoleon III.," which the next Tome should contain.

———
Frederic the Great said to M. de Suhm, "Sir, if you wrote & spoke
only in Chinese, I should learn Chinese at once to converse with you."
     See *S. Beuve Causeries* [*du Lundi*], [1851–1862,] 7. p. 365

———
     As a pendant to this, see the anecdote of Madame de Tessé &
Mme de Stael.   *FOR* 169[146]

[260] In reply to the vulgar opinion of English & other Savans, that
we must accumulate facts, & distrust theory,—I like well these sen-

     * I saw in his Medora his own face, & in his Achilles, I think, his
form[.]

———
[144] Emerson delivered the lecture "Fortune of the Republic" at the Mercantile Library in Brooklyn on December 21, 1863.
     [145] "Moss Side" is one of the tales in *Lights and Shadows of Scottish Life* by John
Wilson (1785–1854), whom Emerson had met in Edinburgh in 1848 (see *JMN*, X, 220).
     [146] "Frederic the Great . . . you.' " is struck through in pencil with a diagonal use
mark, and "As a pendant . . . de Stael." is struck through in pencil with a vertical use
mark.

tences of Saint Beuve; "Je ne sais plus qui a dit; On commence toujours par parler des choses, on finit ⟨|| . . . ||⟩quelquefois par les apprendre. Le fait est que les mieux doués commencent par deviner ce qu'ils finissent ensuite par bien savoir."

[Sainte-Beuve,] *Portraits Contemp[orains]*. [1852,] II 444[147]

[261]   George E. Tufts.
          Care of Dr S. F. Dickinson
          98 Lawrence street
          Brooklyn, N. Y.[148]

———

Classes of Men. see Saint Beuve's remark on great political men.

HO 242

———

"C'est une bête: il n'a que du genie."

———

[262] Renan writes *"Vie de Jesus."* Many of his contemporaries have no doubt projected the ⟨like⟩ same theme. ⟨I did w⟩When I wrote "Representative Men," I felt that Jesus was the ↑"Rep.↓ Man" whom I ought to sketch: but the task required great gifts,—steadiest insight & perfect temper; else, the consciousness of want of sympathy in the audience would make one petulant or sore, in spite of himself. ⟨M⟩Theodore Parker, [26⟨4⟩3] of course, wished to write this book; so did Maria Child in her Book of Religions, and Miss Cobb, and Alcott, and I know not how many more.[149]

[264] ↑"It is difficult for the gods to appear."↓

———

[147] Emerson borrowed an unspecified volume or volumes of *Portraits Contemporains* August 3–September 16, 1863; he borrowed volume 2 from the Boston Athenaeum December 2–11, 1863.

[148] While in New York in late December, 1863, Emerson tried to locate Tufts, who had written him a letter in November he had found interesting. See Journal FOR, p. [235] below, and *L*, V, 341–342.

[149] Emerson is probably referring to Lydia Maria Child's *Progress of Religious Ideas through Successive Ages*, 3 vols. (New York and London, 1855), in his library; and Frances Power Cobbe (1822–1904), a prolific writer on religion.

In 300 years of Arabian & Persian culture, only seven great poets.
↑quot vates, tot rebar deos.↓[150] See Goethe, [*Werke,* 1828–1833,] VI. p. 136

———

See in D'Herbelot the account of the Arabian Fariabi[,] an oriental Crichton.[151]

———

In town, a stout soldier, an Irishman, walked before me, large, & with all too much motion. ⟨a⟩A little boy stopped him, "Please give me a cent." Soldier stooped to find out what he said, & then, with unfeigned astonishment said, "A cent! Great God! I give you a cent?" & rushed indignantly forward.

[265] ↑1864↓ Feb 8.
At the dinner given the other night, Feb. 4, at the Union Club to Gen. Burnside, after much talk of the accounts of our several battles given by the reporters of the press, in which accounts the general plainly had no confidence, & so of the ignorance ⟨of⟩ on the part of all subaltern officers, who could not know any more than they saw:—In despair Mr Charles Storey looked up, & said, "Well, General, do you then think we have true history in Caesar's Commentaries?" There was a sudden laugh which [266] went round the whole table, gradually increasing in volume & cheer.

———

How hardly we forgive any mispronunciation, as *I*⟨t⟩-talian for Italian; Brunelles-*she,* for Brunelleschi; Lȳ-ceum, for Ly cē um.

Drummond reports, that Ben Jonson said to him, that, "Donne, for not keeping of accent, deserved hanging"[152]
Would he hang Whittier for pronouncing *rōmance* and āl-lies?

[150] "As many as are poets, so many will I think gods" (Ed.).
[151] Barthélemy D'Herbelot, *Bibliothèque Orientale, ou dictionnaire universal contenant tout ce que sont connoître les peuples de l'Orient* . . . (Paris, 1697), p. 337.
[152] William Drummond of Hawthornden, *Notes of Ben Jonson's Conversations with William Drummond (January, 1619),* Shakespeare Society Publication no. 8 (London, 1842), p. 3. The quotation is used in "Poetry and Imagination," *W,* VIII, 53.

[267] Nesselrode said, "Il faut avoir le diable au corps pour etre bon diplomate"

Feb. 19. Last night heard Chapin lecture, for the first time.[153] He has a powerful, popular voice which agreeably stimulates the house, and, rarely, he drops the orotund, which is like a↑n↓ infantry company firing one at a time, & uses a quieter tone which penetrates all ears, & deepens the silence[.]

But I thought it is not a question whether we shall be a nation, or [267↑½↓] only a multitude of people. No, but whether we shall be the New Nation, the leading Guides & Lawgivers of the world, as having clearly chosen & firmly held the simplest & best rule of political society.[154]

What a town was Florence with Dante, Ghiberti, Giotto, Brunelleschi, Da Vinci, Michel Angelo, Raffaelle, Cellini, Guicciardini, Machiavelli, Savonarola, Alfieri, Galileo!

[268] The obstacle which the philanthropic movements meet, is, in the invincible depravity of ⟨s⟩the virtuous classes. The Excellent women who have made an asylum for young offenders, ↑boys of 10 to years,↓ and who wish, after putting them through their school, to put them out to board in good farmers' or mechanics' families, find the boys do well enough, but the farmer & the farmer's wife, & the mechanic's wife, behave brutally. What then? One thinks of Luttrel's [270] speech about the soldiers fraternizing with the mob; "Egad, ⟨when⟩ it's aukward when the extinguisher catches fire."[155] And I remember that Charles Barnard had not made up his mind, whether Dr Tuckerman, his chief, relieved or made ↑more↓ pauperism.[156]

---

[153] The reference is probably to Edwin Hubbell Chapin (1814–1880), Universalist minister and popular lecturer.

[154] This entry is used in "The Fortune of the Republic," *W*, XI, 538.

[155] See p. [202] above.

[156] Joseph Tuckerman (1778–1840) was a Unitarian "minister at large" among the Boston poor. Charles F. Barnard was ordained in 1834 as a "minister at large" in Boston and founded the Warren Street Chapel the following year. See *JMN*, V, 59n, and X, 21n.

[271] Dr Charles T. Jackson will have nothing to do with the survey of gold mines; because he has no confidence that they can be profitably worked by any stock-company: the workmen in such mines will carry off all the gold. In California & Oregon, Every miner for himself: & on such terms only can they be wrought.

[272] 28 Feb. 1864, Yesterday at the Club with Cabot, Ward, Holmes, Lowell, Judge Hoar, Appleton, Howe, Woodman, Forbes, Whipple, with Gen. Barlow & Mr Howe of Nova Scotia, for guests. But cramped for time by late dinner & early hour of the return train,—a cramp which spoils a club. For you shall not, if you wish good fortune, even take pains to secure your right & left hand men. ⟨A⟩The least design instantly makes an obligation to make their time agreeable, which I can never assume.
Holmes was gay with his Preadamite mentioned in the Scriptures, Chap First. And Appleton "with that invariable love of hypocrisy which delights the Saxon race," &c.

[273] The "Spectator" says of the three obituary notices of Thackeray by Dickens, Trollope, & Kingsley, only Dickens's is equal to the subject: the others strain to write up, & fail. It was said lately of Goethe's Correspondence with the Duke of Weimar, that the Duke's letters are the best. The experience is familiar, day by day, that of two persons, one of character & one of intellect, Character will rule, & intellect must bow.[157] It is interesting in Goethe's case because of his patronizing [274] tone to all the world.

[275] France, in 1789, improvised war, &, in 1803, improvised civilization. *See in Ste Beuve. article Biot. Nouveaux Lundis.* [12 vols. (Paris, 1863–1870),] Vol. II. p. 81[158]

——— ↑Superlative in Nature.↓
It is such a drought that there is dust ⟨i⟩on the rivers.

[157] With "It was said . . . bow.", cf. "Greatness," *W*, VIII, 317, and Journal DL, p. [217] above.
[158] Emerson borrowed this volume from the Boston Athenaeum February 27–March 11 and December 17–19, 1864. The article is a review of M. Biot's *Essai sur l'histoire générale des sciences pendant la révolution française.*

River Mançanares at Madrid.

Berthollet's report on the poisoned brandy to the Committee of Public Safety. He put the brandy through a filter, & then drank it. ⟨Saltpetre too.⟩[159]—"How dare you drink it?" said Robespierre. "I did a bolder thing," replied Berthollet, "when I put my name to that ⟨r⟩Report," ⟨answ⟩— as having resisted the panic of suspicion which made the tyranny of [276] the Committee of Public Safety.—[*Nouveaux Lundis,* 1863-1870, II, 81]

March 13.[160] Last night talked with Alcott who returns much lately to the comparison between English & American genius. I gratified him by saying, that our ⟨performance⟩ intellectual performance, taken with our sentiment, is perhaps ⟨worth⟩ better worth than their performance ↑taken↓ with their limitation or ⟨&⟩ downward tendency. For certainly we cannot count or weigh living writers with theirs.

But how to meet the demand [277] for a religion. A few clergymen here, like Hedge & Clarke, retain the traditions, but they never mention them to me, and, if they travelled in France, England, or Italy, would leave them ↑locked up↓ in the same closet with their sermons at home, &, if they did not return, would never think to send for them. Beecher, Manning, Bushnell,[161] hold a little firmer, & more easily to theirs, as Calvinism has a more tenacious vitality;—but that is doomed ↑also,↓ & will only die last: ⟨How then is the⟩ ↑for Calvinism rushes to be Unitarianism as Unitarianism rushes to be Naturalism.↓ [278] ↑How then is the↓ new generation to be edified? How should it not? The life of these ⟨traditions⟩ once omnipotent traditions was really not in the ⟨fable⟩ legend, but in the moral sentiment & the metaphysical fact which the legends enclosed;—and these survive. A new Socrates, or Zeno, or Swedenborg, or Pascal, or a new crop of geniuses, like those of the Elizabethan age, may be born in this age, &, with happy

---

[159] "Saltpetre too.", circled in ink, is written below "then drank it." and "—'How dare . . . Robespierre." is fitted around it.

[160] See Journal DL, p. [133] above.

[161] Probably Rev. Jacob Merrill Manning (1824-1882) of Boston, and Horace Bushnell (1802-1876) of Hartford, Connecticut, an inspired liberal Congregational preacher and writer.

heat & a bias for theism, bring asceticism & duty & magnanimity into vogue again.[162]

[279] In the most vulgar times, in the bronze as in the oaken age, ⟨m⟩ a certain number of men of organic virtue are born—   men & women of native integrity, and indifferently in high & low families. But there will always be a class of imaginative men, whom poetry, whom the love of Beauty leads to the adoration of the moral sentiment. And these will provide it with new histories, forms, & songs. Perhaps the Churches will become Hospitals, Ragged Schools, Offices to find Employment [280] for the Poor, & Guardians for foundlings & orphans. Perhaps the mania or frenzy that made the Crusades, or the Colonization of New England, or Millerism, or the modern Revivals, will run into philanthropies & education of the sailor & street-boy, and the Reform of convicts & harlots:—as now into the /Port Royal/Hilton Head/ mission⟨aries,⟩s, and Nurses at Washington. At any time, it only needs the ↑contemporaneous↓ appearance of a few ⟨noble &⟩ superior & attractive men, to give a new & noble turn to the public mind.[163]

[281] I said to A[lcott]. that we old fellows occupy ourselves with the history or literature of the Sentiment, and not as once with the essence itself. I remember in my life happy weeks, when I said to myself, I will no longer respect Success↑,↓ or the finishing & exhibition of my work↑;↓⟨:⟩[n] but every ⟨step of⟩ stroke on the work, every step taken in the dark toward it, every defeat, even, shall be sacred & luminous also.[164] Am I not always in the Great Presence? I will not postpone my existence, but be always great & serene with that inspiration.

[282] Alcott thought, that successful men were liable to such

---

[162] "But how . . . Naturalism." is struck through in ink with a diagonal use mark on p. [276] and a vertical use mark on p. [277]. "A few clergymen . . . Naturalism." is used in "Character," W, X, 116–117. "How then is . . . again." is used in "The Sovereignty of Ethics," W, X, 208.

[163] "But there . . . mind." is struck through in ink with two vertical use marks on p. [279] and one on p. [280]. "histories, forms, . . . Employment" is struck through in pencil with an additional vertical mark. "In the most . . . Washington." is used in "Character," W, X, 117–118.

[164] The added punctuation is in pencil.

fall, but that unsuccessful men had nothing else⟨,⟩ but the sentiment to return to. And that is just, and the sentiment may by such habitude come to steep & meliorate the man,—come to be character instead of a rhetoric.

The resources, I say, remain or renew, day by day: The Old Eternal Ghost, the Jove, refuses to be known, but refuses to depart: then, the sporadic probity I spoke of, capriciously scattered, is yet always present to keep society sweet. Then Enthusiasm,—from [283] pure Vision, down to its most clouded form of Fanaticism,—is the miraculous ⟨motor or spring⟩ ↑leaping lightning↓ not to be measured by the horsepower of the Understanding.[165]

And the unanimous approbation of Society & of Governments is secured, as a rule, to godliness, because of its usefulness.

[284] Words used in a new sense & figuratively, dart a diamond lustre that delights; & *every*ⁿ word admits a new use, & heaven beyond heaven.[166] Almost it is not even friends, but this power of words that is best.

Barriers of man impassable. ↑They who should be friends cannot pass into each other.↓ Friends are fictions founded on some single momentary experience.

———

Thoughts let us into realities. Nothing of religious tradition, not the immortality of the soul is incredible, after we have experienced an insight, a thought. But what we want is [285] consecutiveness. 'Tis with us a flash of light, & then a long darkness, & then a flash again. This separation of our days by a sleep almost destroys identity. Ah! ⟨if⟩ could we turn these fugitive sparkles into an astronomy of Copernican ⟨g⟩worlds!

Scarcely a link of memory holds yesterday & today together, with

[165] "Then Enthusiasm,—" is struck through in pencil with two short vertical marks; "miraculous" is circled for revision or cancellation, and "motor or spring" is circled and canceled. "Enthusiasm,— . . .Understanding." is used in "Progress of Culture," *W*, VIII, 229.

[166] "Words used . . . use," struck through in pencil with a vertical use mark, is used in "Inspiration," *W*, VIII, 294.

most men; I mean, in their minds. Their house & trade & families serve them as ropes to give a coarse continuity. But they have forgotten the thoughts of yesterday, and they say today what occurs to them, & something else tomorrow.[167]

[285ₐ][168] *West Point notes*
        Short cycles or periods.
        rapid rallies, as by a good night's sleep.[169]
⟨Im⟩ sublime point is the value of a sufficient man: ⟨then multiply or⟩ cube this value by the meeting of two or of more who perfectly understand & support each other, you have then organi⟨s⟩zed victory.[170]
⟨Two are on trial⟩ Wherever one is tried, two are on trial. The examiner is instructed whenever the pupil is examined.[171]
Civil[izatio]n built on powder
Is Civilization built on ⟨power⟩ powder?
[285ᵦ] ↑built on buttons.↓ ↑Is there only cotton or 200 000 plants↓[172]
        One of the most agreeable points was the apparent probity of the Students, and the honorable anecdotes told of their veracity and esprit du corps.

"Republic has no need of chemists," was said of the death of Lavoisier.

Bonaparte called the "Ecole Polytechnique" "the hen that laid ⟨all the⟩ ↑him↓ golden eggs."[173]

[167] "Thoughts let . . . tomorrow." is used in "Inspiration," *W*, VIII, 272–273. "But what . . . worlds!" is also used in "Powers and Laws of Thought," *W*, XII, 52–53.

[168] Laid in after p. [285] are two folded sheets headed *"West Point notes"*. The first, folded once to make four pages (designated [285ₐ]–[285ᵈ] by the editors), is inscribed on all four sides. The second is folded to make four pages, three of which (designated [285ₑ]–[285g] by the editors) are inscribed. See p. 169 above for a bibliographical description. They must have been notes for an informal address to the Cadets; see *J*, IX, 515.

[169] "Short cycles . . . sleep." is used in "Inspiration," *W*, VIII, 280.

[170] See Journal DL, p. [94] above.

[171] See Journal DL, p. [93] above.

[172] "Civiln built on powder" is in pencil; "⟨power⟩" is circled in ink. See Journal DL, p. [104] above.

[173] See Journal DL, pp. [94] and [122] above.

[285$_c$] innocence & protection
Military monks. in years rarely ⟨go cross⟩ pass the limits of the post.[174]

pure power
difference between a soldier & his cannon.
leaning to pure science of the schools.
humanity of kings is justice[175]
Gen. Scott's maxims
Bible of soldier. Montluc↑,↓[176]
Lord Herbert, The happy warrior
the humble monk↑,↓
   uniforms are masks↑,↓
pure power.↑,↓   Plutarch

Montluc, Lord Herbert, Happy warrior, Constancy, ↑Major Hodson↓
Loyalty of soldiers to each other

   [285$_d$] Courage   God prefers Atheism to fear

Power is what they want & if only they know the shop where it is to be
bought be sure they will come fast enough & ⟨bring⟩ sell all that they
may buy. Only have the ⟨article⟩ pure article[.][177]
Aristocracy,—the more the better
   Dio
   ⟨Curtus⟩, *Metius Curtius*
   Codrus

[174] See pp. [232]–[233] above.
[175] Cf. *JMN,* XIV, 47, from Napoleon, *The Confidential Correspondence . . . ,* 1856,
I, 181; used in "Abraham Lincoln," *W,* XI, 337.
[176] This entry is used in "Address at the Dedication of the Soldiers' Monument in
Concord, April 19, 1867," *W,* XI, 361. See *JMN,* XIV, 351, where Emerson cites his
source as *Southey's Common-Place Book.* Southey's source is the introductory editorial notice to *Collection universelle des mémoires particuliers relatifs à l'histoire de France,* ed. Antoine Perrin, 64 vols. (London and Paris, 1785–1791), XXII, xv. The added commas are
in pencil.
[177] Courage   God . . . pure article" is in pencil. With "Courage   God . . .
fear", cf. Journal DL, p. [103] above. With "Power is . . . article", cf. *JMN,* XI, 437,
used in "Inspiration," *W,* VIII, 269; see also pp. [228]–[229] above, and Journal DL, p.
[108] above.

Your ways inspire ⟨th⟩lively curiosity. I thought 2 days suff[icien]t. I could willingly spend ⟨ten times⟩ twenty, & know the power & hope^n & caree⟨e⟩r of each youth[.]

[285$_e$] At this hour when ⟨the im⟩ magnitude of the stake is of the existence of liberty in this country, & the preservation of the liberty of mankind, when the value of a vote is a value to the whole world of sober men[,] I cannot affect to speak politely of the idle party who ⟨can⟩^{n} professing to   [285$_f$] ⟨love liberty⟩ hate slavery can divide the vote of Mass. on this question. It is casting firebrands and am I not in sport. It is a dastardly treachery. ⟨v⟩They strew sugar on this bottled spider; and↑,↓ as if it were a small thing[,] as if it were indifferent who governed[,] they peril the safety of mankind. I can understand it of the old ↑men good in their time but↓ who have ceased to think [285$_g$] or to be responsible now ⟨these⟩ in their ↑easy-↑chair↓s,↓ ⟨days,⟩ but for the men in their manhood ⟨it⟩to join with these for some petty griefs or personalities or for good following & because they have eaten too much pound cake—it argues an incurable frivolity of character which has all the effect of a wilful ⟨treachery⟩ treason.[178]

[286] [Index material omitted]
[inside back cover] [Index material omitted]

[178] With "it argues . . . treason.", cf. p. [159] above.

$\mathcal{VA}$

1862–1863

Emerson began Journal VA in February 1862 (page [3]), and used it concurrently with DL and WAR until March 1863 (page [286]), the same month he began FOR.

The covers of the copybook, of marbled tan, blue, and red paper over boards, measure 17.0 × 21.4 cm. The spine strip and protective corners on the front and back covers are of tan leather. "1862" and "$\mathcal{VA}$" are inscribed in ink on the front cover.

Including flyleaves (1–2, 295–296), there are 296 unlined pages measuring 17.4 × 20.6 cm. The flyleaves, once loose, have been reattached with strips of stiff white paper. Emerson numbered two leaves 132–133, then corrected them to read 132, $132\frac{1}{2}$, $132\frac{2}{3}$, and 133; he skipped 138 and 139 in the numbering. Six other pages were misnumbered and corrected: $\langle 65 \rangle 66$, $6\langle 6 \rangle 7$, $6\langle 7 \rangle 8$, $10\langle 0 \rangle 2$, $1\langle 6 \rangle 35$, and $2\langle 2 \rangle 30$. Most of the pages are numbered in ink, but four are numbered in pencil: 16, 28, 124, and 197. Seventeen pages are unnumbered: 1, 17, 29, 49, 83, 99, 176, 177, 196, 215, 226, 245, 252, 253, 257, 287, and 296. Eleven pages are blank: 2, 30, 49, 50, 77, 97, 175–178, and 196.

Laid in inside the front cover are: a sheet of white paper torn evenly at the right and cut unevenly at the bottom to measure 12.6 × 20.3 cm, inscribed in ink on both sides (printed as front cover verso$_a$–front cover verso$_b$); a sheet of letter paper torn off at the left and cut unevenly at the bottom to measure 12.6 × 20.0 cm, inscribed in pencil and ink on the recto, and in ink on the verso (printed as front cover verso$_c$–front cover verso$_d$); and a newspaper clipping headlined "THE NEW OVERLAND ROUTE," giving changes in the mail route through Colorado and Utah, and over the Rocky Mountains, caused by the "savages." A newspaper clipping headlined "THE ATLANTIC." is pasted to the lower left corner of page $6\langle 6 \rangle 7$. Pasted to the right margin of page 136 is a sheet of white paper torn off from a larger sheet to measure 17.0 × 19.5 cm, lined on one side, and inscribed in ink on both sides (printed as pages 136$_a$–136$_b$).

[front cover]   1862
                                       VA

[front cover verso] [Index material omitted]
For "Classes of Men," see
    "Poetry & Crit[icis]m in Eng & America"[1]
    a page on sympathy

Estabrook a tract nearly two miles square, making four square miles. p
172

[front cover verso_a] I hear with some surprise the uneasiness felt
by ⟨off⟩ army men at the temporary neglect of the interests of the
Army by the Government & of the popular preference of the volunteer force. It is unavoidable that there should be a stress laid on the
volunteer ⟨A⟩army, ⟨when⟩ in a moment when a million of men were to
be taken from their business, their families, & thrown [front cover
verso_b] into the dreadful risks of war, vastly more dreadful to them
from their total unacquaintance ⟨of⟩[n] ↑with↓ the science, that teaches
to ↑prevent &↓ elude ⟨&⟩[n] ↑as well as to↓ resist. But of course the
numbers of the army & officers were totally incompetent to fulfil this
duty, & it needed every inducement of honor, of reward, of public en-
couragement & thence conciliation of goodwill of the people to enrol
& ⟨arm⟩ equip this ⟨immense⟩ army.

[front cover verso_c] It is believed that it is easier in this community to
build a suitable Hall than to ensure a fit monument. There are several
competent architects but few sculptors who have a skill that commands assent[.]
    The beautiful is never plentiful & on an occasion like this we hes-
itate to run the risk of a new monster[.]

---

[1] "Classes of Men," first delivered on November 20, 1860, before the Parker Fraternity, was also read four times during Emerson's 1863 lecture tour: on January 5 in Toronto (where it was followed the next day by a lecture on "Criticism"), January 8 in Rochester, New York, February 5 in Pittsburgh, and February 24 in Montreal. "Poetry and
Criticism in England and America" was delivered first on May 8, 1861, in Boston. See
Cabot, *A Memoir* . . . , 1887–1888, II, 771–772 and 776–777 for abstracts of the lectures.

We have good architects for civil & domestic architecture, and 13 years ago ⟨that⟩ⁿ Horatio Greenough on his return from [front cover verso_d] Italy told me he thought that ⟨the⟩ ↑domestic architecture,↓ ⟨art of building private houses⟩ had never been carried to greater perfection↑.↓ ⟨than here;⟩
No people lived in better houses than were in Mass[achuse]tts[.]

[1]   *VA.*
                                  1862

This world belongs to the energetic. De Tocqueville.[2]

        Use will in man new grace reveal
        The gleam which Labor adds to steel.[3]
        ————————————

[Index material omitted]

[2] [blank]
[3] Feb. 1862
Correctness very rare. It is difficult to get ⟨the pattern⟩ a new shirt made on the measures of the pattern. The value of a carpenter is that he is trained to measure exactly. But ↑Captain Rich told me↓ it is ⟨said to be⟩ impossible to duplicate the model of a ship. And 'tis said the Emperor of Austria, though he sent an architect to Rome to get the [4] dimensions of the Sistine Chapel, & sent Mozart to write by ear the ⟨music⟩ ↑score↓ of the *Miserere,* failed at last to reproduce the perfect musical effect in Vienna.
No proofreader believes that the author can correct his own proof; and I am sure no author believes that any [5] reader of his verses will copy them accurately. An engraver like Raffaelle Morghen is as rare as a painter like Raffaelle Sanzio. The Swedenborgians say with despair that there seems a fatality to hang over Swedenborg's text, that,

_____

[2] The quotation is used without attribution in "Resources," *W,* VIII, 138, 144, and 153, and "Perpetual Forces," *W,* X, 85. See p. [162] below, Journal DL, p. [250], and WAR, p. [29] above.
[3] The verse is written in ink over the same in pencil.

↑though↓ with honest purpose, he cannot be correctly quoted by one out of their church.[4]

↑Hence the inestimable value of photography↓

[6] ——
    the Mche|| . . . ||von furnace.

———

The Englishman in China, seeing a doubtful dish set before him, inquired, *"quack-quack?"* The Chinese replied, *"bow-wow."*

Mrs L↑ivermore↓[5] told us of a ⟨man noted in the West for his⟩ stuttering wit, in the West who was much offended with ⟨a⟩the rowdy manners of the son of a friend with whom he was talking. The father agreed he was very bad, but what could he do with him? "Why, if he was my son, I'd app-p-point his f-f-funeral at 4 o'clock tomorrow, P.M., & I'd be sure to have him ready."

[7] Every thing good is the result of antagonisms, and the height of civilization is ⟨the most⟩ absolute self-help, combined with most generous social relation. A man must have his root in nature, draw his power directly from it, as a farmer, a miller, a smith, a shepherd, a sailor does; as Bonaparte, or Archimedes, or a railroad Engineer, or Thoreau, or Agassiz does. He must [8] be such, that, set him down where you will, he shall find himself at home, shall see how he can weave his ⟨lines⟩ useful lines here as there, & make himself necessary to society by the method in his brain. This is selfhelp, & this is common; but the opposite element that makes him, while ↑he draws↓ all values to him, feel an equal necessity to [9] radiate or communicate all, & combine the largest accumulation with bounteous imparting, raises the useful to the heroic. ⟨With the improvement of⟩ As men refine, they require manners indicating the highest style of man, and, as soon as they have seen this ⟨nobility of⟩ magnanimity, they exalt the

————

[4] A hand sign following "church." at the bottom of p. [5] points to "Hence the . . . photography", inscribed at the bottom of p. [4], and separated from the matter above it by a two-page rule.

[5] "ivermore" is added in pencil, possibly by someone other than Emerson.

saint, as Saint Louis, or Carlo Borromeo, or the Cid, or Sir Philip Sidney, or Bayard, over all [10] the degrees in the Golden Book; & the Church with its martyrs & selfsacrificers becomes adorable in their eyes. ⟨It⟩ Just in proportion as this healthy light comes upon the mind, it condemns the selfishness which accumulates & does not impart, & the ruder and grosser drone who does ↑not↓ even ⟨not⟩ accumulate, ⟨at all,⟩ but robs those who do.[6]

[11] This is the gorilla who makes slaves of poor men.

H D T[horeau]

Broadest philosophy narrower than the worst poetry. *Y* 36

Criticism on him in 18⟨3⟩51. *CO* 125

Perhaps his fancy for Walt Whitman grew out ↑of↓ his taste for wild nature, for an otter, ↑a↓ wood-chuck, or a loon.

⟨——⟩⟨h⟩He loved sufficiency, hated a sum that would not prove: loved Walt & hated Alcott.

"It were well if the false preacher of Xy[Christianity] were always ⟨&⟩met & balked by a superior more living & elastic faith in his audience just as some missionaries [12] in India are balked by the easiness with which the Hindoos ⟨incline⟩ believe every word of miracle & prophecy ⟨being⟩ only surprised that they are much less wonderful than those of their own scriptures which also they implicitly bele↑i↓ve" *H. D. T.*[7]

[13] The vital refinements are the moral & intellectual steps. The appearance of the Seven Wise Masters, of the Stoic Zeno, of the acute & loyal Socrates, of Anacharsis, of ⟨the Ess⟩ Moses, the Essenes, of Jesus, of Buddh, and, in modern Christendom, of the realists, Savonarola,

---

[6] "be such . . . who do." is struck through in pencil with single diagonal use marks on pp. [8], [9], and [10]. "Read at Music Hall" is written in pencil vertically in the left margin on p. [8], and "Music Hall" in the left margins of pp. [9] and [10]. On March 16, 1862, Emerson delivered the lecture "Essential Principles of Religion" before Theodore Parker's congregation at the Music Hall.

[7] " 'It were . . . H.D.T." is in pencil. See *The Journal . . .*, 1949, IV, 250.

Huss, & Luther, are the causal facts which carry forward nations, & the [14] race to new self examination & conviction, & raise the universal standard,[8] compelling all to mend or affect to mend their behavior.

This morale civilization we[n] neglect, and ⟨think⟩ measure our advance by percussion-caps, lucifer-matches, rubber-shoes, gas-light & steam-power; but it is security & [15] freedom & exhilaration,[n] depending on a heal⟨h⟩thy morale in the Society, that leaves the mind alert, self-helping, & inventive.[9]

Therien came to see Thoreau on business, but Thoreau at once perceived that he had been drinking; and advised him to ↑go home &↓ cut his throat, and that speedily. Therien did not well know what to make of it, but went away↑,↓ &↑⟨,⟩↓ Thoreau said↑,↓[10] he learned that he had been repeating it about town, which he was glad [16] to hear, & hoped that by this time he had begun to understand what it meant.

The old school of Boston citizens whom I remember in my childhood had great vigor, great noisy bodies or I think certain sternutatory vigor, ⟨that⟩ ↑the like whereof↓ I have not heard ⟨the like⟩ again. When Major B, or old Mr T. H. took out their pocket handkerchiefs[n] [17] at ⟨meeting⟩ ↑church↓, it was plain they meant business; they would snort & roar through their noses, like the lowing of an ox, & make all ring again. Ah, it takes a Northender to do that!

[18] It is curious how negligent ⟨w⟩the public is of the essential qualifications of its representatives. They ask if a man is a republican? Yes. Is he a man of talent? Yes. And is he honest, & not looking for an office or a bribe? Yes, he is honest. Well then choose him by acclamation, & they go home & tell their wives with great satisfaction [19] what a good thing they have done. But they forgot to ask the fourth

---

[8] Page [13] is struck through in ink with a discontinuous vertical use mark; "The vital . . . standard," is used in "Civilization," *W*, VII, 32–33.

[9] This paragraph is struck through in ink with single vertical use marks on pp. [14] and [15]; "percussion-caps, . . . Society," is used in "Civilization," *W*, VII, 33.

[10] The commas after "away" and "said" are added, and the comma after "&" added and canceled, in pencil.

question, not less important than either of the others, & without which the others do not avail;—*Has he a will?*[11] Can he carry his points against opposition? Probably he has not. When he finds himself at Washington with men of fixed ideas, with polite men from the Southern & Middle States, with hard [20] bronzed politicians from the Border States who have no question about their view of the matter,[12] and assume that any difference of opinion on your part is a momentary ignorance of the necessities of the position, your wise, honest republican, after making a few courteous attempts at arguing the point, [21] & finding how weak his voice is compared with theirs, settles i⟨n⟩t in his mind that 'tis of no use to talk with such people; that he can still vote against them. But those strong well-persuaded men have just the same power in the debate as in the hotel-parlour, & give the worthy representative the same mortifying sense of incapacity there, & more mortifying, because ⟨the⟩ⁿ [22] his humiliation is exhibited on ⟨an open⟩ ↑a public↓ stage. Now there is no real force in the reasons of these men. If he had presence of mind & diligence to analyse their argument, he could expose its weakness, but they have a habitual self-reliance, & a way of putting their personality over you, which he has not. This evil would be diminished if [23] he had been long used to them↑,↓ had come to know how much better is their onset than their real grounds & means warrant↑,↓ how ignorant & vulnerable they are. But he finds them full grown, in possession of the field, & talking down to him↑,↓ & he overestimates their force. The Southerners keep their representatives in ⟨office↑,↓⟩ ↑Congress for many years,↓ & we commit the fault [24] of sending new men every session.[13]

---

[11] "Has he a will?" is underlined in pencil.

[12] Underlying "and assume that any" are two lines in partially erased pencil:
   "Of warning how the erring dish
   ⟨Ran away⟩ ↑Eloped↓ with the young spoon"

[13] This paragraph is struck through in pencil with single diagonal use marks on pp. [18], [19], [20], [21], [22], and [23]. Written in the left margins of these pages are "Read at Music Hall March" (p. [18]), "Read at Music Hall" (p. [19]), "Music Hall, March" (p. [20]), "Read at Music Hall, March" (pp. [21] and [22]), and "Music Hall" (p. [23]). On March 16, 1862, Emerson delivered the lecture "Essential Principles of Religion" before Theodore Parker's congregation at the Music Hall. "It is curious . . . has not." (pp. [18]–[19]) is used in "Aristocracy," *W*, X, 50. The added punctuation on p. [23] is in pencil; the commas after "warrant" and "him" are overwritten in ink.

Holmes came out late in life with a strong sustained growth for two or three years, like old pear trees which have done nothing for ten years, & at last begin & grow great. ⟨L⟩The Lowells come forward slowly. & H. T[horeau]. remarks, that men may have two growths like pears.

[25] March 3, 1862. The snow still lies even with the tops of the walls across the Walden road, and, this afternoon, I waded through the woods to my grove.[14] A chicadee came out to greet me, flew about ⟨me⟩ within reach of my hands, perched on the nearest bough, flew down into the snow, ⟨&⟩ rested there two seconds, then up again, just over my head, & busied himself on the dead bark. I whistled to him through my teeth, and, (I think, in response,) he began at once to whistle. [26] I promised him crumbs, & must not go again to these woods without them. I suppose the best food to carry would be the meat of shagbarks or castille nuts. Thoreau tells me that they are very sociable with wood-choppers, & will take crumbs from their hands.[15]

———

Voices have their various manners also. I remember when Greenwood began to preach, though he indulged a playful fancy that had perhaps [27][16] caught its trick from [Edward] Everett, yet the effect of that fine bass voice was, as if he were a rocky cliff, & these pretty descriptions only flowers & colors thereon. He could well afford them—they might bloom or fade—he remained fast.[17] Other Speakers have nothing left, but put themselves entirely into their speech, as [Wendell] Phillips.

Some voices are warnings: some voices are like the bark of a dog.[18]

"les caresses de sa parole."

[14] Cf. "May-Day," ll. 35–40, *W*, IX, 164.

[15] See p. [174] below, and "The Titmouse," *W*, IX, 233–236.

[16] The lines of verse printed below were inscribed first on the page, in pencil, and overwritten in ink by "caught its . . . sa parole.' "

[17] Francis W. P. Greenwood (1797–1843) was a prominent Boston clergyman at the time Emerson was pastor of the Second Church.

[18] With "Some voices . . . dog.", struck through in ink with a diagonal use mark, cf. "Social Aims," *W*, VIII, 83.

Come little Pequot
He has a friendly heart
And greets
And leaves his fastness
The wanderer
     stranger passing his retreat

⟨The feet that⟩ ↑Hastes wh||e||n you↓ pass his sylvan fort
↑⟨Hastes⟩ to do the honors of his court↓
Comes near
Flies near your shoulder & your hand
     ↑Friendly as owner of the land↓
With frank courage

Like a pet asking to be fed
Yes if the world has any bread
⟨Nor shall I hither come⟩
↑Taught by thy heart↓ I go my pet
With glad remembrance of my debt

[28]   ⟨Nor long ere⟩ ↑And soon again thy client comes↓
     ⟨Nor shall I hither come⟩
⟨Without a⟩ ↑Loaded with↓ store of seeds & crumbs
⟨For whilst the world has⟩ ↑Thou first whilst earth yields↓
     any bread
In sign of honor shalt be fed

perched on the bough then darts below
And wrote his mark upon the snow
Whistled his notes
Played his fine feats
     ↑Ran thro his fine gymnastic play↓
Clung
Head downward cl⟨u⟩ing↑ing↓ to the spray
Showed ⟨off⟩ his gymnastic play

[29]   The little hermit though he live apart
Hath a hospitable heart

Hastes when you pass his sylvan fort
To do the honors of his court

↑As fits the owner of the land↓
Flies ⟨near⟩ round you grazes your hand
⟨F⟩Taught by thy heart I go my pet
With glad remembrance of my debt
And soon again thy comrade comes
Loaded with store of seeds & crumbs
Thou first whilst teeming earth yields bread
In sign of honor shalt be fed[19]

[30] [blank]

[31] "The Cordelier said that he had found, that, among believers or misbelievers, never kingdom ruined itself, or changed its master, except by defect of justice. Now let the king of France take care to do true & prompt justice to his people, for it is thereby that our Lord will let him hold his kingdom in peace as long as he lives." *Joinville* [*Histoire de Saint Louis*, in Michaud et Poujoulat, *Nouvelle Collection des Mémoires* . . . , 1854, I] p. 184, Section ⟨2⟩30

[32]   *Pudency of goodness.*

The illusion that strikes me ⟨most⟩ as the masterpiece of Maia, is, the timidity with which we assert our moral sentiment. We are made of it, the world is built by it, Things endure as they share it, all beauty, all health, all intelligence exist by it; yet 'tis the last thing we dare utter, [33] we shrink to speak it, or to range ourselves on its side. We presume strength of him or them who deny it. Cities go against it, the college goes against it. We presume the State will go against it. Every new assertor of the right surprises us, & we hardly dare believe he is in earnest.[20]   ↑See *VA* 121↓

---

[19] The verse on pp. [27], [28], and [29], in pencil, is a draft of "The Titmouse," ll. 33–42 and 79–84, *W*, IX, 234 and 236; see pp. [25]–[26] above. The version published in the *Atlantic Monthly*, IX (May, 1862), 585–587, lacks ll. 83–88. The first four lines on p. [28] are struck through in pencil with a diagonal use or cancellation mark. "perched on . . . play", struck through in pencil with three diagonal use marks on p. [28], may have been intended for insertion at an arrow in the left margin of p. [29], following "Flies ⟨near⟩ . . . hand". The first three lines on p. [29] are struck through in pencil with a vertical use mark, and "Hastes when . . . & crumbs" with another; "Taught by . . . & crumbs" is struck through in pencil with a diagonal use mark.

[20] This paragraph, struck through in pencil with single diagonal use marks on pp. [32] and [33], is used in "Perpetual Forces," *W*, X, 87–88. See also *JMN*, XII, 239.

[34] Dr [Charles T.] Jackson said, that, at Jalapa in Mexico, the "army fuse" was first used ↑by us,↓ or first observed by the Mexicans;— ⟨that⟩ two cannons, having been left in the public square, a great crowd of Mexicans ran up to capture them. When they were all r⟨is⟩ushing up in a mass, the cannons went off without any visible ⟨canonee⟩cannoneers, [35] & discharged grapnel (is it, or shrapnel?) directly into the heart of the crowd. If the cannons had begun to sing ⟨"The Starspangled banner",⟩ ↑"O say do you see by the dawn's early light,"↓ they would not have been more astonished, & were quite ready to believe that ⟨no⟩"bayonets think", & cannons also.

[36]   ↑La Nature aime les croisemens.↓[21]

[Montgomery] Blair rightly thinks, that, [Salmon P.] Chase, because he was always a Whig, will not have nerve. ⟨t⟩The Unitarians, born unitarians, have a pale shallow religion; but the Calvinist born & reared under his rigorous, ascetic, scowling creed, & then ripened into a Unitarian, becomes powerful, as Dr Channing, Dewey, Horace Mann, Wasson, Garrison, & others. [37] So is it in politics. A man must have had the broad audacious Democratic party for his nursing-mother, and be ripened into a Free soiler, to be efficient; as [Andrew] Jackson, as Benton, as Potter, [Benjamin Franklin] Wade, Blair, Hickman, [Andrew] Johnson, & [George Sewall] Boutwell, were.[22]

———

Captain Jarvis wishes to sell Francis Rodman his farm ↑(70 acres in all,)↓ comprising 43 acres of excellent land near the buildings, an orchard which two years ago yielded 200 barrels of apples; and 27 acres of meadow & swamp land containing wood; for $7000.00[.][23]

[21] The quotation, attributed to Fourier in *JMN*, IX, 50, is used in "Inspiration," *W*, VIII, 289. See also *JMN*, X, 44.

[22] Those not previously or easily identified include Thomas Hart Benton (1782–1858), a U.S. senator for thirty years; either Robert Brown Potter (1829–1887), a New York lawyer and a Union general during the Civil War, or his brother Clarkson Nott Potter (1825–1882), also a lawyer and later a Democratic congressman; Francis Preston Blair, Jr. (1821–1875), a lawyer, soldier, once a Free-Soil Democrat and now a Republican congressman, and the brother of Lincoln's Postmaster General; and probably John Hickman (1810–1875), another Free-Soil Democrat turned Republican, at this time a congressman from Pennsylvania.

[23] Capt. Jarvis was the brother of Emerson's friend Dr. Edward Jarvis, and a son of Francis Jarvis, whose land lay over the Concord bridge near the start of the Old Carlisle Road.

[38] Arabians say, 'the horse was created a day or two before Adam.'
"He fled on a ⟨horse⟩ mare which would catch a falling tear."
Read *"Les Chevaux du Sahara"*[24]

"These are not courses for your horses," said Si Ben Zyan in conclusion, "for your horses, you Christians, who go from Algiers to Blidah, 13 leagues, as far as from my nose to my ear, & yet believe you have made something of a journey." [*Ibid.,*] p. 58

[39] These ⟨were⟩ rightly seen were but superficial effects, but the credence of men it is that moulds them, & creates one or another surface. And ⟨as soon as⟩ the mind, as it opens, transfers very fast its choice from the circumstance to the cause, from the false to the true, ⟨from the work to the maker⟩ from courtesy to love, from inventions to Science, from ↑law or public opinion in↓ ⟨London or [40] or^n Boston law or⟩ ↑Washington ↑or London,↓↓ ⟨public opinion,⟩ to the tyrannical ↑⟨selfrevealing⟩↓ idea that slowly reveals itself; from ⟨the⟩ ⟨all⟩ ↑all↓ that talent executes & vaunts, to the ⟨appearing⟩^{n} ⟨cen⟩sentiment that fills the heart & dictates the future of nations.[25]
A new & purer moral sentiment ⟨is the⟩ civilizes civilization; casts backward all that was sacred into ↑profane↓^{n} [41] ⟨barbarism⟩, as ⟨an oil lamp cast⟩ the flame of oil ⟨is a shadow⟩ casts a shadow when shined upon by the flame of the Bude light.[26]

I know these powers are not ⟨in nature⟩^{n} often entrusted to the same hand. The ⟨power⟩ ↑hands↓ to complete are not often given to the seeing soul. The prophet is filled with vision, & careless of its slow fulfilment [42] in events. Enough to him to behold it, & announce that which must be; careless even of its distinct declaration; too happy in seeing its centrality & invincibility. What to him is its ⟨clumsy⟩ administration in the clumsy hands of ⟨stupid⟩ ↑dull↓ men,[27] whom it con-

---

[24] Melchior Joseph Eugène Daumas, *Les Chevaux du Sahara, et les moeurs du désert* (Paris, 1858), pp. 61 and 60.
[25] "the credence . . . of nations." is used in "The Sovereignty of Ethics," *W*, X, 211–212.
[26] "A new . . . light.", struck through in ink with single vertical use marks on pp. [40] and [41], is used in "Civilization," *W*, VII, 33.
[27] "stupid" is canceled, and "dull" inserted, in pencil.

founds? the fire burns their hands, confounds their understandings. The [43] Higher Law is a jibe↑.↓[28] ⟨to⟩ Apes[n] & baboons ⟨&⟩ chuckle & gibber over it, whilst it suffocates their laughter & decomposes them.[n] What is a generation of able statesmen? What a Democratic Party, or a Whig party, or a strong Cabinet, or ⟨a⟩ the largest political combination, the Four Great Powers, or the Five? ⟨↑They are↓ A wretched ↑⟨gang⟩↓ mess of rogues & thieves in⟩In this august presence⟨.⟩, ↑they are thieves.↓ [44] Well assured is he that what he beholds is not powerful, but *power;* that it measures time, & ⟨distributes &⟩ fashions ↑its↓ instruments.

[45] It is not the target's fault, if I cannot hit it.

———

Freedom does not love the hot zone. The snow-flakes are the right stars of our flag, & the Northern streamers the stripes.[29]

———

Latimer's story, that his father taught him not to shoot with his arms, but to lay his body to the bow, should be remembered by writers. The labial speech instead of the stomachic, afflicts me in all the poetry I read, even though ⟨of⟩ ↑on↓ a gay or trifling subject. Why has never the poorest country college offered me a professorship of rhetoric? I think I could have taught an orator, though I am none.[30]

[46] ↑24 March↓
S[amuel]. Staples yesterday had been to see Henry Thoreau.[31] Never spent an hour with more satisfaction. Never saw a man dying with so much pleasure & peace. Thinks that very few men in Concord know Mr Thoreau; finds him serene & happy.

[28] With "The Higher . . . jibe", cf. *JMN*, XI, 248, and "Worship," *W*, VI, 209.
[29] This paragraph is struck through in ink with two diagonal use marks. With the first sentence, cf. Journal WAR, p. [35] above, and "Civilization," *W*, VII, 25–26. With "The snow-flakes . . . stripes.", cf. p. [56] below, and "Voluntaries," ll. 41–42, *W*, IX, 206.
[30] "Latimer's . . . shoot with" is marked in the left margin with two short vertical lines in ink; cf. "Poetry and Imagination," *W*, VIII, 31, and *JMN*, XIV, 304. "See p. 44" is written following "afflicts me" at the bottom of p. [45], and "in all . . . none." is continued on the lower half of p. [44], separated from the earlier transcription by a long rule, and headed "continued from p 45".
[31] Samuel F. Staples was the Concord town jailer.

Henry praised to me lately the manners of an old, established, calm, well-behav↑e↓d river, as perfectly distinguished from those of a new river. A new river is a torrent; an old one slow & steadily supplied. What happens in any part of the old river relates to what befals in every other part of it. 'Tis full of compensations, resources, & reserved funds.[32]

[47] ⟨in⟩When we have a success, I wrote, it is because our adversary has made a fault. I hate that we should be saved only as Providence takes care of idiots & drunkards, or, as we say, Fortune favors fools.

———

  I find the following in old journal.

———

  No man but is so much a skeptic as ↑not↓ to feel a grateful surprise now & then at finding himself safe & sound, and things as he thought them. ⟨P⟩U 65

[48] Music Hall Materials

For the passage on "Pace," see ⟨I⟩in my MSS of *"Intellect"* the division marked "Conduct of Intellect"
For the passage on N. England haste in character, see "Varieties" in the MSS of "Intellect."

———

Kilmeny.

———

See in this book *VA*
Selftruth p. 100; wholes p. 82[33]

———

Resources

———

[49]–[50] [blank]

---

[32] A hand sign at the bottom of p. [46] points to "'Tis full . . . funds.", run over onto the bottom of p. [47] and separated from the matter above it by a long rule.
[33] "See in . . . p. 82" is in pencil.

[51] ↑All nationality soon becomes babyish,[34] even in Carlyle.↓

The⟨re⟩ question between egotisms can never be settled. England makes Greenwich the first meridian; France, Paris; America, Washington. Who shall decide on the world's part against these private interests?

↑*Morals.*↓

Saint Pierre says of the animals, that "a moral sentiment seems to have determined their physical organization."

Studies of Nature. Vol 1 p 23[35]

⌈Identity⌉

"The Universe," said Newton, "was produced at a single cast."[36]

ap *St Pierre* [*Ibid.,* I, 99]

[52] Elliot Cabot quotes to me from "Mommsen, who is full of good sayings," "die schlafwandle⟨s⟩rische Sicherheit die den Dichter zum Dichter macht."[37] ↑the somnambulic security which makes the poet a poet.↓

C[harles]. G[odfrey]. Leland writes me that the name of the author of the "Old Cove" is Henry Howard Brownell of East Hartford, Connecticut.[38]

————

W. tied up tight in temperament—

E. E.

————

[34] See Journal WAR, p. [16] above.

[35] Jacques Henri Bernardin de Saint-Pierre, *Studies of Nature,* trans. Henry Hunter, 5 vols. (London, 1796); in Emerson's library. "Saint Pierre . . . organization." is used in "The Sovereignty of Ethics," *W,* X, 184.

[36] " 'The Universe . . . cast.' " is used in "Progress of Culture," *W,* VIII, 224, and the lecture "Natural Religion." See Gohdes, *Uncollected Lectures,* 1932, p. 50.

[37] See Theodor Mommsen, *Römische Geschichte,* 3 vols. (Berlin, 1856–1857), II, 431. See Journal DL, p. [146] above. Two vertical lines in ink are drawn in the left margin beside the German quotation.

[38] Leland (1824–1903), a Philadelphia journalist and humorist, became the editor of the *Continental Monthly* in Boston in 1862. Brownell (1820–1872), a Connecticut lawyer, was publishing poetry in newspapers in 1862; he later became Farragut's secretary and a popular war poet. The "Old Cove" appears in "Let Us Alone" in Brownell's *Lyrics of a Day: or Newspaper-Poetry* (New York, 1864), pp. 16–17; in Emerson's library. Emerson printed the poem as "The Old Cove" in *Parnassus,* 1875, p. 502.

[53] April 2, 1862. Yesterday I walked across Walden Pond. Today I walked across it again. I fancied it was late in the season to do thus; but Mr Thoreau told me, this afternoon, that he has known the ice hold to the 18th April.

April 9. The cold days have again arrested the melting of the ice, & yesterday I walked again across the middle of Walden, from one side to the other[.]

April 10. Today, I crossed it again on foot.

————

I believe it broke up on the 19th 20th[.]
↑see VA 60↓[39]

[54] The valuable part of "Cottle's Reminiscences" is the Account of John Henderson the wonderful scholar, ↑(born at Limerick, Ireland,)↓ who died at Oxford, in 1788, in the 32d year of his age.[40] We should have an adequate sketch of Cotes, of Chatterton, of Faryabi,

[55] The exclusions of fine society are all in the interest of the invitations, not out of any ill will, but only resolute measures for affirming & securing the delight of the best conversation. And when I find myself excluded, I take part with the exclusives, & not with the malcontents.[41]

[56] Spring. Why complain of the cold slow spring? the bluebirds don't complain, the blackbirds make the maples ring with social cheer & jubilee[,] the robins know ⟨they⟩ the snow must go & sparrows with prophetic eye that ↑t↓hese bare ⟨twigs⟩ ↑osiers yet↓ will hide their future nests in the pride of their foliage. And you ↑alone↓ with all your six feet of experience are the fool ⟨by⟩ of the cold of the present mo-

---

[39] "see VA 60" is in pencil.
[40] Joseph Cottle, *Reminiscences of Samuel Taylor Coleridge and Robert Southey* (New York, 1847), pp. 361–368.
[41] "when I . . . malcontents." is marked with a vertical line in pencil in the left margin. With this paragraph, cf. "Social Aims," *W,* VIII, 90–91.

ment, & cannot see the southing of the sun. Beside↑s↓ the snowflake is freedom's star.[42]

[57] I make it a rule, & keep it when I can, ⟨t⟩not to go to my debtor to ask for money excepting when I have already money. If you go when your need is great, he ↑penetrates to that fact &↓ treats you as a beggar; in the other case, ↑you go en grand seigneur↓ *en seigneur.*[43] I⟨ts⟩n like manner, in society where you are not intimate, 'tis better not to go except when you are full of facts, [58] full of thoughts, with an agreeable piece of information to give, &c.; ⟨I⟩that is, it is better for me & such as I am, who depend on their head, & ⟨not on⟩ ↑have no↓ animal spirits. ↑"It is not one of Mr. Coffin's good looking days."↓[44]

⟨It⟩See a poetical description of a calm at sea in Dyer's Poems.

[59] ↑Criticism↓
'Tis objected to Florian, that there is no wolf in the story.
Marie Antoinette said, "she felt as if eating milkporridge."[45]

[60] April 16. Heard the purple finch this morning, for the first time ↑this season↓.[46] Henry Thoreau told me he found the Blue Snowbird, (*Fringilla hiemalis,*) on Monadnoc, where it breeds. It is never seen here in summer. Redwinged black⟨w⟩bird sings *gurgalee,* & the grackle talks with it hoarsely.
Edward tells me he found the eggs of the *Fringilla hiemalis* on Monadnoc.
18 April. The ice not broken up [61] on the pond this very warm day, though I could not get on ⟨to the ice⟩ ↑it↓ from Wyman's cottage landing. Mr Channing was on the ice yesterday.

---

[42] Page [56] is struck through in ink with a vertical use mark. "twigs" is canceled, and "osiers yet" added, in pencil. "Why complain . . . sun" is used in "May-Day," ll. 164-176, *W,* IX, 169. With "Besides the . . . star.", cf. "Voluntaries," l. 41, *W,* IX, 206, p. [45] above, and Journal WAR, p. [35] above.
[43] With "I make . . . *en seigneur.*", struck through in ink with two diagonal use marks in the shape of an X, cf. "Social Aims," *W,* VIII, 85. See also *JMN,* XIV, 327. "you go . . . seigneur" is added in pencil.
[44] A short rule following "animal spirits." is overwritten by the insertion.
[45] See *JMN,* XIII, 122, where these two remarks are quoted from Arsene Houssaye, *Men and Women of the Eighteenth Century,* 2 vols. (New York, 1852), I, 163 and 172.
[46] Added in pencil.

Addison Fay tells me that the expenditure of gunpowder in war does
↑not↓ compare in amount with that of peace[.]⁴⁷

[62] Resources
In *GL* pp 292, 175 I have indicated some of my pastimes instead of
whist & hunting. The chapter of these however is much longer, &
should be most select. The first care of a man settling in the country
should be to open the face of the earth to himself by a little knowledge
of nature, or a great deal of knowledge, if he can, of birds, plants, &
astronomy, in short, the [63] art of taking a walk. This will ⟨take⟩
↑draw↓ the sting out of frost, ⟨the⟩ dreariness out of November &
March, & ⟨the⟩ drowsiness out of August. To know the trees is, as
Spenser says of the ash, "for nothing ill." S⟨p⟩hells, too, how hungry I
found myself the other day at Agassiz's Museum, for their names.

But the uses of the woods are many, & some of them for the
scholar high & peremptory. When his task requires the wiping out
from memory "all [64] trivial fond records that youth & observation
copied there,"⁴⁸ requires self-communion & insights: he must leave
the ⟨streets⟩ house, the streets, & the club, & go to wooded uplands, to
the clearing, & the brook. Well for him if he can say with the old
Minstrel, 'I know where ↑to find↓ a new song.'⁴⁹

[65] 12 May 1862⁵⁰
Edward will require for his ↑rail-↓ticket to St Josephs   42.25
Expense at Albany 1.50, at Chicago 2.
    elsewhere 1.00 per day, say   7.
From St Josephs to Omaha, say, 3   3.
    horse   50.

⁴⁷ Addison G. Fay, a Concord resident, had been active in the Concord Lyceum for
many years, frequently as secretary or curator.
    ⁴⁸ Shakespeare, *Hamlet,* I, v, 98–99 and 101.
    ⁴⁹ *"Resources"* is inserted as a heading at the top of p. [64]; "pastimes . . . longer,"
and "The first care . . . new song.' ", on pp. [62]–[64], are used in "Resources," *W,*
VIII, 150 and 151–152. "Minstrel, . . . song.' " is marked in the left margin with a vertical pencil line. See p. [195] below, and Journal FOR, pp. [96] and [97] below.
    ⁵⁰ For a more detailed itinerary of Edward Emerson's transcontinental trip, see p.
[75] below.

251

By Andersen's Estimate his expense then should be   82.
Expenses at St Francisco   30.
        contingences   25.
                                                          _____
                                                          239

14 May. I think ⟨a⟩he had about $218. in cash after buying his ticket to
St Josephs for 42.25

↑Mem↓[51]
Oct. 20 On Edward's return it appears that the whole cost of his out-
fit, trip, & return, is about $550.

[⟨65⟩66] May, 1862.
    Of the most romantic fact the memory is more romantic.[52]

_____

See Cowper's Ice palace of Moscow.[53]

[6⟨6⟩7][54] dead-sweet

[6⟨7⟩8][55]   Books bequeathed to me
                              by Henry D. Thoreau.[56]

_____

    [51] Added in pencil.
    [52] This sentence is used in "Memory," *W*, XII, 104.
    [53] *The Task*, bk. V, "The Winter Morning Walk," ll. 127–168. Emerson printed
these lines as "The Ice Palace" in *Parnassus*, 1875, pp. 288–289.
    [54] Pasted to the bottom of this page is a newspaper clipping, headlined "THE AT-
LANTIC" and beginning "This standard monthly opens its October number with an ap-
propriate article by the late Mr. Thoreau, entitled 'Autumnal Tints'—a subject which he
was singularly qualified to treat. . . . Mr. Hawthorne contributes a batch of entertaining
gossip about 'Leamington Spa,' another of his series of European reminiscences." Two
passages, "A friend [of] the late author of 'Charles Auchester,' gives some touching personal reminiscences of 'Elizabeth Sara Sheppard.' " and "three original poems, one 'An
Arab Welcome' by T. B. Aldrich," are marked in both the right and left margins of the
clipping by single vertical ink lines; the first is also marked by two vertical pencil lines on
the page to the right of the clipping, and one to the left.
    [55] The *x*'s on pp. [68]–[71] are added in pencil.
    [56] With the exception of volume 1 of the *Rig Veda Sanhitá*, these books, from the
collection given to Henry Thoreau by Thomas Cholmondeley in 1855, are still in Emerson's library.

↑x↓ Rig Veda Sanhita [*A Collection of Ancient Hindu Hymns*]
    First Ashtaka,   Vol I. 1850
    Second Ashtaka.   Vol II. 1854
2   translated by H H Wilson [London]

_____

↑x↓ [Isvara Krishna, *The*] Sank⟨j⟩hya Karika[, *or Memorial Verses in
    the Sánkhya Philosophy*]
        translated by H. T. Colebrooke
    and the B⟨as⟩hashya or commentary of Gaurapada
1   translated by H. ⟨W⟩H. Wilson
                            Oxford, 1837

_____

↑x↓ [Saddharmapundarika, *Le*] *Lotus de la bonne loi*
    Traduit du Sanscrit,
            par ⟨N⟩M. E. Burnouf.
1   4to   Paris. 1852.

_____

[69] ——
↑x↓ Le Bhagavata Purana[; *ou Histoire Poétique de Krichna*]
        Traduit par M E Burnouf
3)   3 vols. ⟨q⟩4to
                            Paris 1840–8

_____

↑x↓ Institutes of [*Hindu Law; or the Ordinances of*] Menu
1)   Translated by Sir Wm Jones. 1 vol 4to
                    London 1825

_____

↑x↓ [*Two*] Treatises on the Hindu Law of Inheritance.
    Translated by
1)   H. T. Colebrooke. 1 vol 4to
                    Calcutta, 1810

_____

↑x↓ Select Specimens of the Theatre of the Hindus. Translated from
    the Sanscrit by H. H. Wilson
2)   in two volumes, 8.vo Lond. 1835

_____

253

↑x↓ Vol. XV. of the Bibliotheca Indica. [*The Taittiríya, Áitaréya, Śvétáśvatara, Kéna, Íśá, Katha, Praśna, Mundaka, and Ma'ndukya Upanishads*]

Translated by E. Roer.

1) Upanishad   Calcutta 1853

[70] ↑x↓ [*The*] Aphorisms of the Nyaya [*Philosophy*]

By Gautama.

Eng. translation.

1)   1 Vol. 12mo   Allahabad. 1860 [actually 1850–1854]

———

↑x↓ Colebrooke's Miscellaneous Essays. [2 vols. (London, 1837)]

⟨1⟩2)   Vol. 1 & 2

↑x↓ [*The*] Vishnu Purana[, *a System of Hindu Mythology and Tradition*]

Translated from the Sanscrit

1)   By H H Wilson

London 1840

1 Vol. 4to

———

↑x↓ [*Mahābhārata,*] Nala & Damayanti[; *and Other Poems*]

Translated by

1)   Rev H. H. Milman

1 Vol. 8vo   [Oxford,] 1835

[71] ———

↑x↓ [*The*] Aphorisms of the Mimansa [*Philosophy*]. [*With Extracts from the Commentaries . . .*]

By Jaimini.

San⟨e⟩scrit & English.

1) 1 pamphlet— [Allahabad,] 185⟨7⟩1

———

↑x↓ [Sadānanda Yogīndra, *A*] Lecture on the Vedanta[, *Embracing the Text of the Vedánta-Sára*].

1)   1 pamphlet. [Allahabad,] 1860 [actually 1850]

———

↑x↓ [Visvanath Panchanana Bhattacharya, *The*] Bhasha Parichchheda [*and its Commentary The Siddhanta Muktavali, an Exposition of the Nyaya Philosophy*].

1)   1 pamphlet— [Calcutta,] 1851

---

[72]   Romance.

May 25. Harriet Prescott has the courage of genius, as Elizabeth Sheppard had, whom she celebrates.[57]

It is an easy list to count off, our romantic writers.

Bettine von Arnhim

George Borrow

Elizabeth Sheppard

[73]   ↑Romance↓

There is too much vulgarity in D'Israeli ↑than↓ that I should willingly add his name, for all the golden thread that he has woven into his diaper⟨s⟩. Goethe only vitiates his claim to romance, by his largeness, & by having valued himself more on his other & conventional merits. But the effect & the test of my romanticists is that they move me [74] precisely as true poets do; as Merlin, Taliessin, or those few golden sentences that have come to me from the Bards.

↑See a map of Utah in Pacific R.R. Exploration vol. XI.↓[58]

John L. Lathrop Hannibal Mo.

George ⟨FR⟩CR Tappan, Denver, K[ansa]s[59]

---

[57] Harriet Elizabeth Prescott Spofford (1835–1921) was a Massachusetts writer, the protegée of T. W. Higginson and the author of *Sir Rohan's Ghost, A Romance* (Boston, 1860). Elizabeth Sara Sheppard (1830–1862), English novelist, was the author of *Charles Auchester, A Memorial* (New York, 1853), in Emerson's library; see p. [67] above.

[58] U.S. Department of War, *Reports of Explorations and Surveys, to Ascertain the Most Practicable and Economical Route for a Railroad from the Mississippi River to the Pacific Ocean,* 12 vols. in 13 pts. (Washington, 1855–1860). Vols. 1–3, 5–7, and 10 are in Emerson's library, but see Emerson's letter of thanks to Charles Sumner on May 26, 1862, *L*, V, 275, in which he writes, "I believe my set of the 'Pacific Railroad Exploration' is complete to the XII volume."

[59] "John L. . . . Ks" is in pencil. See *L*, V, 273, for Tappan, who agreed to travel with Edward Emerson and Cabot Russell for part of their trip to California.

255

[75] 1862

Edward left ⟨h⟩Concord 12 May

        arrived at Omaha, Nebraska, Monday. 19th

        arrived at Fort Kearney, June

        arrived at Fort Laramie   July 10

        Arrived at Fort Bridges   Aug 4

        Arrived at Salt Lake City   ⟨S⟩Aug 9th

↑By stage from Deep Creek ↑173 miles from Salt Lake↓ to↓

                          Carson   Aug 29

↑By stage to Placerville & Folsom, ↑then↓ by rail↓

                        Sacramento   Aug 31

                        San Francisco   Sept 5

        Sailed for Panama   Sept 11

        Arrived at Panama   Sept 25

        Arrived at Aspenwall by rail 3½ hours   Sept 25

        Sailed for New York   Sept 25

        Arrived at New York   Oct. 3

        Arrived at Concord   Oct 6

[76] "It was as if Jove had offered me a continent, and I had used it⟨,⟩ to hunt for truffles," I told Alcott, in reply to his question touching

[77] [blank]

[78]   ↑*Compensation.*↓

Much mischief from the negro race. We pretended to christianize them⟨. They are unaltered, but we are heathenized by them.⟩ ↑but they heathenized us.↓[60]

The Supreme Court under Southern dictation pronounced, that, "the negro had no rights which the white man was bound to respect." Today, by the rebellion, the same rule holds & is worked against the Southerner; "The rebel has no rights which negro or white man is bound to respect." The world is upside down [79] when this dictum

---

[60] A vertical pencil line is drawn in the left margin beside this entry.

comes from the Chief Justice of the Supreme Court of the United
States of America.[61]

Resources or feats. I like people who can do things. When Edward &
I struggled in vain to drag our big calf into the barn, the Irish girl put
her finger into the calf's mouth, & led her in directly. When you find
your boat full of water at the shore of the pond & strive to drag it ⟨up⟩
ashore ⟨&⟩to empty it, Tom puts a round stick underneath, & 'tis on
wheels directly.[62]

[80]   ↑Romance↓
June 6, 1862. ⟨I wish I⟩ ↑If we↓ could tell accurately the evanescing
effects of an imaginative ⟨work⟩ ↑book↓ on ⟨me⟩ ↑us↓ as ⟨I⟩ ↑we↓
read⟨.⟩! Thus Milman's Translation of "Nala & Damayanti" is nearer
to my business & bosom than is the news in today's "Boston Journal."
And I am admonished & comforted, as I read. It all very nearly concerns me. We are elevated by beauty. I walk in marble galleries & talk
with kings the while.[63]

[81] To my chapter on the celebration of Intellect belongs the
incident of Nala's exchange of his skill in horses for Rituparna's skill in
dice or in mathematics.[64]

[82] *Wholes*
The correspondence or balance everywhere. ⟨Ther⟩ If the host

[61] "when this . . . America." is run over onto the bottom of p. [79], and separated
from "Resources or . . . wheels directly.", inscribed earlier, by a long rule. For the first
sentence, "The Supreme . . . respect.' ", see *JMN*, XIV, 253. Emerson is quoting from
Chief Justice Roger Taney's opinion in the Dred Scott decision in 1857.
[62] This entry is struck through in pencil with a diagonal use mark. "I like . . .
things." is used in "Powers and Laws of Thought" and "Celebration of Intellect," *W*,
XII, 47 and 119. See also *JMN*, IX, 367, and XII, 593. "When Edward . . . in directly."
is used in the lecture "Resources"; see Gohdes, *Uncollected Lectures*, 1932, p. 25. See also
Journal FOR, p. [96] below, and *W*, VIII, 392. "When you . . . wheels directly." is used
in "Resources," *W*, VIII, 145.
[63] "I wish I" and "I" are canceled in both pencil and ink, "me" is canceled in pencil,
and "If we", "us", "we", and the exclamation point after "read" are inserted in pencil
overwritten in ink. For the translation, see p. [70] above.
[64] See Journal DL, p. [88] above.

has duties, so has the guest. If I receive good news every day, & give none of myself, I am in false position, a⟨s⟩m a consumer & not a producer. What right has any one to read in the journal accounts of Victories, if he has not bought them by his own valor, treasure, or personal [83] sacrifice, or by service as good in his own department?[65] Beware that national victories are not private defeats to you & me.

[84] How dismal this tragedy of common society. A grain of good meaning drenched & buried in pounds & tons of bad temperament;—the good meaning coming to light on call now & then, but instantly overwhelmed by the dreary habitude & hebetude of folly & egoism.[66]

[85] A clear eye will find keeping & tie in all the circumstance, & its origin in self: will feel itself complimented equally by invitation & neglect: it ⟨is itself that⟩ is served by privacy as by crowds, ⟨&⟩ itself ⟨that⟩ tinges the sky with cherries & roses, or with ink.

Poet walking on the clouds with the security of a grenadier.

[86] In the garden, put pansies that make mouths at you, every one droller & more elfish than the last, mumps & measles, as if you had Punch done in flowers.

Our tawny Massachusetts

    Nec deus intersit nisi dignus vindice nodus
    Inciderit[67]

[87] I told Alcott, who read me his paper "on the Garden," that it was written in the ⟨style⟩ unnecessary vagabond style of Burton's

---

[65] "If the host . . . every day," and "right has . . . department?" are struck through in ink with single vertical use marks on pp. [82] and [83].
[66] "Read at Music Hall June 1862" is written vertically in the left margin in pencil. The paragraph is struck through with a vertical use mark in pencil.
[67] "And let no god intervene, unless a knot come worthy of such a deliverer" (Horace, *Ars Poetica*, l. 191). See *JMN*, V, 356, and XIII, 240. The quotation is in pencil.

"Anatomy ⟨m⟩of Melancholy," stringing together all unchosen possible things that might, could or would be said, and therefore requires
leisure & lassitude of the desart in order to be read. Nobody in busy
trading political, much more in scientific [88] literary ⟨ca⟩eras, could
find days or hours to read it in. Such must be intercalated by idle gods
for idle men in monasteries or English Colleges. ⟨But H⟩ 'Tis ⟨e⟩inex-
cusable in a man who has messages to men, who has truths to impart,
to scribble these ↑flourishes↓. He should write that which cannot [89]
be omitted,[n] every sentence a cube, standing on its bottom like a die,
essential & immortal. When cities are sacked & libraries burned, this
book will be saved,—prophetic, sacred, a book of life,
For, truly considered, the work of writers is like that of capitalists.
Suppose in London, Amsterdam, or New York, ⟨the⟩ ↑a company of↓
proprietors should agree to found a bank or treasury for[68] [90] lend-
ing money at fixed rates, and, each having subscribed what amount he
would contribute to the stock, they should begin bringing in their
strongboxes; one brings his keg of ten thousand doubloons; one, his
box of Spanish dollars; one, his bag of gold Napoleons; one, his un-
coined box of nuggets; & so on: ⟨a⟩At last one gentleman brings in
some sheets of beautifully engraved bank notes with very handsome
vignettes of Liberty, & Commerce, & Agriculture, each note "promising to pay a thousand dollars," but all counterfeit. ↑What will the
other partners say?↓

[91] Carlyle's III vol. of Friedrich ↑a↓ masterpiece. Now sovereignly
written, above all literature, dictating to the world below[,] to citizens,
statesmen, scholars & kings, what they shall think & accept as fatal &
final for their salvation. It is mankind's Bill of Rights, the *Magna
Charta,* or Declaration of Independence, or right royal Proclamation
of the Intellect ascending the throne, announcing its good pleasure

---

[68] "it was written . . . treasury for" is struck through in pencil with a diagonal use
mark on p. [87], a vertical use mark on p. [88], and a diagonal use mark on p. [89]. See
pp. [154] and [158] below. Two discontinuous pencil lines are drawn vertically in the left
margin on p. [89], the first from "be omitted." to "a book of life," the second from "a
cube," to "burned,". Cf. the report of the lecture "Books" in Gohdes, *Uncollected Lectures,* 1932, pp. 39-40.

that [92] hereafter, *as heretofore,* & now once for all, the world shall be governed by common sense & law of morals, or shall go to ruin.

But the manner in which the story is told, ↑the author sitting like↓ the supreme Demiurgus, & trotting out his heroes & heroines like puppets, coaxing & bantering them, amused with their good [93] performance, ↑patting them on the back,↓ talking down to them as ↑naughty↓ dolls when they misbehave, communicating his information always in measure, just as much as the young reader can understand, hinting the future when it would be use⟨l⟩ful, recalling ⟨the⟩ ↑now & then↓ some ↑illustrative↓[n] antecedents of the actor, ⟨when⟩and impressing the reader with the conviction [94] that ⟨his⟩ ↑he is in↓ possession of the entire history centrally seen, that his diligence & investigation have been exhaustive, & that he has descended on the petty plot of Prussia from higher & cosmical surveys.

Then the soundness & breadth of his sense & the absolute independence of the tone is one to put kings in fear. And as [95] every reader of this book ⟨m⟩shares, according to his intelligence, the haughty tone of this genius, & shares it with delight, we recommend to all governors,—English, French, Austrian & other, to double their guards, & look carefully to the censorship of the press, during the next twenty years.[69]

[96] the disinfecting process[n]
the untuning
Who counts these in his economy of day & life? Yet not to count these, is to estimate by shows for substances.

> "Bourgeon de Mars, Enfans de Paris,
> Si un éschappe bien vaut dix."
> > French proverb[70]

───────

The man Maclellan ebbed like a sea.[71]

---

[69] Emerson received volume 3 of Carlyle's *History of Frederick the Great* early in June, 1862; see *L,* V, 279. He used pp. [91]–[95] in a letter to Carlyle on December 8; see *CEC,* pp. 535–536.

[70] See *JMN,* VI, 29, where this proverb is quoted from Bacon's *Advancement of Learning.*

[71] This sentence and the rule above it are in pencil.

[97] [blank]
    [98] ↑Art.↓

——————

[Two things in picture;
1. representation of nature, which a photograph gives better than any pencil, and a *camera obscura* better than a photograph, and which is a miracle of delight to every eye.
2. an ideal representation, which, by selection & much omission, & by adding something not in nature, but profoundly related to the [99] subject, & so suggesting the heart of the thing, gives a higher delight, & shows an artist, a creator.][72]
    ↑[I have copied the above into *ART* p. 80]↓

[100]   ↑Self-Respect↓
    If a man only stands by himself, society permits him to be prodigal or hoarding; straitlaced or ⟨luxurious⟩ licentious; pedantic or illiterate; kind or unkind to his next relations; & so through all the rights & wrongs; only let him entirely believe in himself, & act after his belief, all else does not signify much, or people[n] learn very fast to treat him respectfully & conform themselves; so essential [101] is *a* standard, any standard or fixed point. Da Vinci's maxim was, that, the proportions of a body to itself were of first importance.

    I read a good sentence of General Scott's in the newspaper, that "resentment is a bad basis for a campaign."

    [10⟨0⟩2] Henry T[horeau]. remains erect, calm, self-subsistent, before me, and I read him not only truly in his ⟨j⟩Journal, but he is not long out of mind when I walk, and, as today, row upon the pond. He chose wisely no doubt for himself to be the bachelor of thought & nature that he was,—how near to the old monks in their ascetic religion! He had no talent [103] for wealth, & knew how to be poor without the least hint of squalor or inelegance.
Perhaps he fell, all of us do, into his way of living, without forecasting

——————

[72] The square brackets around "Two things . . . creator." are in pencil, possibly by someone other than Emerson.

it much, but approved & confirmed it with later wisdom.[73] And I find myself much approving lately the farmer's scale of living, over the villager's. Plain plenty without luxury or show. This draws no wasteful company, & escapes an army of cares. What a ludicrous figure is a village gentleman defending his few rods of clover from the street boys who lose their ⟨d⟩ ball in it once a day!

[104] I am so sensible to cold, that one of the abatements of the displeasure of dying is the pleasure of escaping the east winds & north winds of Massachusetts.

That marble scamp in the corner[74]

Style in Manners.

I ought to have preserved that sketch of Bonaparte travelling from Paris to the Army, with his coach full of books & journals, which he rushed through, one after the other, throwing each out of the window as fast as it was read.[75]

[105] ↑June 1862↓

I know a lady who has that sovereign sweetness of temper, that she receives the simplest details of any statement of any business from woman or child with such happy anticipating intelligence, that it acquires at once importance, breadth & better intent, from her welcome. Mrs Ripley used to say in Waltham, "I bless God every day for Mary Ripley's existence." So think I of my Ben⟨e⟩venuta.[76]

---

[73] "He chose . . . thought & nature" is struck through on p. [102] with a vertical use mark in ink, which is then extended to the bottom of the page; "He chose . . . no talent" is struck through with a second vertical use mark in pencil; "for wealth . . . inelegance.", on p. [103], is struck through in ink with one diagonal and two vertical use marks; one vertical and the diagonal are extended through "later wisdom." "He chose . . . & nature" and "He had . . . later wisdom." are used in "Thoreau," *W*, X, 454. This essay was first published in the *Atlantic Monthly*, X (Aug. 1862), 239–249, and was used again as the "Biographical Sketch" in Thoreau's *Excursions* (Boston, 1863).

[74] "That marble . . . corner" is in pencil.

[75] This anecdote, struck through in pencil with two vertical use marks, is used in "Address at the Opening of the Concord Free Public Library," *W*, XI, 504.

[76] This page is indexed "Ellen" in Index Major, p. [139]. Mary Ripley, later Mrs. George F. Simmons, was the daughter of Sarah Alden Ripley, wife of Emerson's half-uncle, Samuel Ripley.

[106] 'Tis the powerful good temperament,—once out of humor acres of roses will not avail more than one buttercup to console you[.][77]

Prudence will put a literary man in a bachelor's chamber with fewest duties or dependences↑.↓ He[n] will probably be driven to a hotel at last, though it seems to me safest to be a boarder in a good family [107] with (other people's) children about his knees, since he can have none of his own.

Freckles are beautiful—in lilies[.]

[108] Henry Thoreau writes, "Journal of ↑July↓ 1852"
"The youth gets ⟨ready⟩together his materials to build a bridge to the moon, or, perchance, a palace or temple on the earth, &, at length, the middle aged man concludes to build a woodshed with them."[78]

"There is sport in the boy's water-mill, which grinds no corn, & saws no logs, & yields no money,—but not in the man's."
                                        H. D. T[horeau]. *Journal*[n] 1852[79]
_____
He loved the sweet fragrance of Melilot.
_____
The bass at Conantum   16 July.[80]

[109] Peter Robbins assured Henry, that yesterday's rain had not reached the potatoes after all. "Exorbitant potatoes!" ⟨he⟩ ↑H.↓ adds, "it tak⟨s⟩es very serious preaching to ⟨rea⟩ convert them"

He is very sensible of the odor of waterlilies
    "no one has ever put into words what the odor of the waterlily ex-

[77] This entry is in pencil.
[78] See *The Journal* . . . , 1949, IV, 227. The quotation, struck through in ink with a vertical use mark, is used in "Thoreau," *W*, X, 482.
[79] See *ibid.*, p. 228.
[80] See *ibid.*, pp. 219 and 228. "He loved . . . Melilot.", struck through in ink with a vertical use mark, and "The bass . . . July." are used in "Thoreau," *W*, X, 481.

presses. A sweet & innocent purity. The perfect purity of the flower is not to be surpassed"

———

"Every poet has trembled on the verge of science"

———

Thinks at Becky Stow's swamp of the Revue des deux Mondes.

———

↑1852 Aug[us]t. 6.↓ "Hearing that one with whom I was acquainted had committed suicide, I said, I did not know when I planted the seed of that fact, that I should hear of it." ——— ↑*Thoreau*↓[81]

[110] ↑If↓ ⟨T⟩there is a little strut in the style, ⟨but⟩ it is only from a vigor in excess of the size of his body. His determination on natural history is organic: he sometimes felt like a hound or a panther &, if born among Indians, would have been a fell hunter: restrained[,] modified by his Massachusetts culture ↑he↓ played out the game in this mild form of botany & ichthyology.[82]

[111] ↑H D T.'s *Journal 1852* p. 23↓
He examined "the heaps of small stones ⟨in⟩about the size of a walnut, more or less, which line the river shallows,—one every rod or two. The recent ones frequently rising by more than half their height above the water at present, i.e. a foot or 1½ feet & sharply conical, the older flattened by the elements & greened over with the thread-like ↑stem of↓ *Ranunculus filiformis.*
Some of these heaps contain two cartloads of stones, & as, probably, the creature that raised them took up one at a time, it must have been a stupendous labor."[83]

[112] I see many generals without a command, ⟨like⟩ ↑besides↓ Henry.

[81] For the entries on p. [109], see *The Journal* . . . , 1949, IV, 232, 235, 239, 236, and 280. With " 'no one . . . surpassed' ", cf. "Thoreau," *W*, X, 481.
[82] "His determination . . . ichthyology.", struck through in ink with a vertical use mark, is used in "Thoreau," *W*, X, 471–472.
[83] See *The Journal* . . . , 1949, IV, 221. With this paragraph, cf. "Thoreau," *W*, X, 466, and p. [132⅔] below.

↑Great men not alone.↓

There is somewhere ⟨aⁿ piece of a mountain⟩ a pillar of rock, called "Adam's Peak," but that is not the usual style of nature, not ⟨pillars⟩ a column, not ⟨a pole of rock⟩ ↑granite bean-pole or flag-staff↓, but a mountain with due support; the nucleus may be a rocky shaft⟨.⟩, but, [113] unsupported, it would soon fall, as a bean pole at the ⟨winter⟩ ↑first↓ storm. So is it with eminent men. A fine genius always ⟨supposes⟩ implies some society of its mates, ⟨though less⟩ if unequal.

——

A chemist is rich in a formula expressing one new combination⟨.⟩; itⁿ makes his fortune & his fame. A poet, in a new image, or only in a new resemblance he has found, as of the parrot's neck to the stem of the Arum.

[114] What a new face courage puts on everything![84] 'Tis the difference of midday from midnight.

Mr Burke said, ⟨that the name⟩ of Lord Chatham, ⟨kept the name of England respectable.⟩ "His name keeps the name of this country respectable in every other."[85]

N. stays at home, not to rub the polish from his shoes.

[115] Ah! the inconvertibility of the sentimental↑ist↓, the soul that is lost by mimicking soul. Cure the drunkard, heal the insane, sweeten the morose, mollify the homicide, civilize the Pawnee. But what lessons for the debauchee of sentiment? Was ever one converted? A deep aping or mimicry that has adhered like a parasite, until it sucks the ↑vital↓ juices, & makes the malformations as of false flowers on shrubs, which are found to be stingings of insects, or the warts on the plum tree[.][86]

---

[84] This sentence is used in "Resources," *W*, VIII, 146.

[85] Paraphrased from "Mr. Burke's Speech on American Taxation. 1774." See *The Works*, 1826–1827, I, 477; in Emerson's library.

[86] This paragraph is struck through in pencil with two diagonal use marks in the shape of an X; "the inconvertibility . . . converted?" is used in "Social Aims," *W*, VIII, 105–106. "Music Hall" is written in pencil vertically in the left margin.

[116] The innocence & ignorance of the patient is the first difficulty. A rough realist or a neighborhood of realists would be prescribed, but that is like proposing to mend your bad road with diamonds. Then poverty, war, imprisonment, famine, ⟨arctic cold⟩ Labrador with mercury at Zero, would lop the garrulity & check the grimacing. In a world where a remedy exists for every mischief if it were only an ⟨Indian⟩ ↑boy's↓ cracker⟨s⟩ to silence [117] cats under dormitory windows.[87]

———

The way to have large occasional views, as in a political or social crisis, is to have large habitual views. When men consult you, it is not ↑that↓ they wish you to stand on your toes & pump your brains, but to apply your wisdom to the present question[.][88]

I defend myself against failure in my main design by making every ⟨moment⟩ [118] ↑inch of the road to it pleasant.↓[89]

The points that glowed a little in yesterday's conversation, were, that the North must succeed. That is sure, was sure for 30 or 60 years back, was in the education, culture, & climate of ⟨the⟩ our people;— they are bound to put through their undertakings. The exasperations of our people by the treacheries & savage↑ness↓ of the Southern warfare are most wholesome disinfectants from the potent influence of [119] Southern manners on our imagination.[90] It was ⟨sure⟩ ↑certain↓

[87] "Music Hall   June '62" is written in pencil in the left margin of p. [116]. "The innocence . . . famine," struck through in pencil with a vertical use mark, is used in "Social Aims," *W*, VIII, 106. "The innocence . . . mischief if " is struck through in pencil with a second vertical use mark, which is canceled by three short pencil strokes from "In a world" down, and "The innocence . . . with mercury" with a third; "mischief . . . windows." is marked with single vertical ink lines in the left margin of p. [116] and the right margin of p. [117]; see p. [183] below. In the last sentence, "Indian" is canceled, and "boy's" added, in pencil.

[88] "The way . . . question", struck through in pencil with a diagonal use mark, is used in "Social Aims," *W*, VIII, 99. "The way . . . to have" is marked in the left margin with two vertical pencil lines. "Music Hall" is written vertically in the left margin in pencil.

[89] "I defend . . . every" is struck through in pencil with a diagonal use mark, and marked in the left margin with two vertical pencil lines.

[90] Two faint vertical pencil lines are drawn in the left margin beside "of our people . . . disinfectants from"; "wholesome disinfectants from" is marked with two additional heavy vertical pencil lines.

also that the Southerner would misbehave;[n] that he will not keep his word; that he will be overbearing, rapacious. Slavery corrupts & denaturalizes people, as it has done Anna B⟨r⟩arnard. There is no more probity in a slaveholder than truth in a drunken Irishman. Our success is sure. Its roots are in our poverty, our Calvinism, our schools, our thrifty habitual [120] industry, in our snow, & east wind, & farm-life, & sea-life.[91] ↑These able & generous merchants are the sons & grandsons of farmers, & mechanics & sailors.↓

Logic of Events. Yes. President Lincoln, S. thought, must fail as inevitably as President Davis.

We insulted the abolitionist, but he instructed us.

There is who can afford to wait.[92]

Party heats are so much whiskey, & simply intoxicate[.]

[121] In the caprice & credulity of people, all these rumours & opinions ↑take their↓ ⟨a⟩rise, to which Whigs & statesmen & cities attach great w⟨ait⟩eight, shaking their heads, & looking grave. "But Kentucky, but Baltimore, but Wall street, ⟨S⟩& State street,"—"Ay, be sure we had not thought of that,"

The rumor⟨ed⟩s[n][,] the opinions are allowed to have importance, & therefore we must wait, & Congress is justified & the President is right in caution, & in suspending his purpose. But by listening thus in here, & out there, [122] to each new report, one is left in a chronic puzzle, & incapacity to move. By & by, a strong wind of a battle or of one energetic mind appears↑,↓[93] & the whole drift & scud with all its forms of bears, mountains, & dragons, vanishes out of sight, and the plain way of reason & right reappears once & forever. Why did we not obey it? This, only this, persists to be, & is forever wisdom & power.

[123]   *Reading.*

I wish only to read that which it would be a serious disaster to have missed. Now how many foreign or domestic opinions on ou↑r↓ war shall I suffer for not knowing? I do not know that Lord Palmer-

---

[91] "Our success . . . sea-life." is marked with double vertical pencil lines in the left margins of pp. [119] and [120].

[92] Two short vertical pencil lines are drawn in the left margin beside this sentence.

[93] Comma added in pencil.

ston or Lord Russell's opinion or existence is of the least importance. Not that fly of less.[94]

[124] The human mind ⟨is⟩ cannot be burned, nor bayonetted, nor wounded, nor missing.

Henry Thoreau fell in Tuckerman's Ravine, at Mount Washington, and[n] sprained his foot. As he was ↑in the act of↓ getting up from his fall, he saw for the first time the leaves of *Arnica Mollis!* ↑the exact balm for his wound.↓[95]

[125] ↑*Thoreau*↓
"Every poet has trembled on the verge of Science."

"If you would obtain insight, avoid anatomy."

"It requires so much closer attention to the habits of the birds, that, if for that reason only, I am willing to ⟨m⟩omit the gun."[96]

[126]   ↑*Thoreau*↓
By what direction did Henry entirely escape any influence of Swedenborg? I do not remember ever hearing him name Swedenborg.
    If we should ever print Henry's journals, ⟨it⟩ you may look for a plentiful crop of naturalists. Young men of sensibility must fall an easy prey to the charming of ⟨his⟩ ↑Pan's↓ pipe.[97]

[127] "The river is my own highway, the only wild & unfenced part of the world hereabouts." H.D.T.
"How much of the world is widow's thirds, with a hired man to take negligent care of it!"   H.D.T↑horeau↓[98]

---

[94] This paragraph is struck through in pencil with two diagonal use marks.
[95] "Henry Thoreau . . . *Mollis!*", struck through in ink with a diagonal use mark, is used in "Thoreau," *W*, X, 464.
[96] For this and the two preceding quotations, see *The Journal* . . . , 1949, IV, 239, 9, and 11. " 'Every poet . . . Science.' " also occurs on p. [109] above.
[97] With the last sentence, cf. "Thoreau," *W*, X, 465. The paragraph is marked with a vertical pencil line in the left margin.
[98] For this and the preceding quotation, see *The Journal* . . . , 1949, IV, 77.

"The constant inquiry which Nature puts, is, 'Are you virtuous? then you can behold me.' Beauty, fragrance, music, sweetness, & joy of all kinds are for the virtuous. That I thought when I heard the telegraph harp today."[99]

H.D.T. June 5, 18⟨3⟩⟨1⟩52

[128] See H. D. T. of Evelyn, in his Journal 1852 (June 9) p. 97. and, of sound, p. 97

"as the philosopher in Seneca desired only bread & herbs to dispute felicity with Jupiter,"— *Evelyn*[100]

"The perception of beauty is a moral test."

─────

"Unquestionable truth is sweet, though it were the announcement of our dissolution."[101]

[129] ↑H. D. T.↓
"What were the firefly's light if it were not for darkness?"

↑─────

Thoreau.↓
"You may not suspect that the milk of the cocoa nut, which is imported from the other side of the world, is mixed. So pure do some truths come to us, I trust."

↑─────

Thoreau↓
        "How watchful we must be to keep the crystal well ↑that↓ we were made, clear,—that it ⟨may⟩be not turbid by our contact with the world, so that it will not reflect objects. What other liberty is there worth having, if we have not freedom & peace in our minds, if our inmost & most private man is but a sour & turbid pool."
        —"If within the old man, there is not a young man,—within the

[99] See *ibid.*, p. 80. With this sentence, cf. "Thoreau," *W*, X, 474, and p. [131] below.
    [100] For this quotation and the citations above it, see *The Journal* . . . , 1949, IV, 84, 85, and 88. The quotation is struck through in pencil with a diagonal use mark.
    [101] For this and the preceding quotation, see *ibid.*, pp. 126 and 129.

sophisticated one, an unsophisticated, then he is but one of the Devil's Angels."

Oct. 1853 p. 185[102]

[130] H. D. T↑horeau.↓   *Few Mornings.*

"I came near awaking this morning. I am older than last year. The mornings are further between. The days are fewer. Any excess,—to have drunk too much water, even, the day before, is fatal to the morning's clarity. But in health the sound of a cow-bell is celestial music." &c

Ms. Journal, July 1852. p. 230

―――

"How much—how perhaps all that is best in our experience in middle life may be resolved into the memory of our youth! I remember how I expanded. If the Genius visits me now, I am not quite taken off my feet, but I remember how this experience is like, but less than [131] that I had long since." *Field Notes Jan 1853*[103]

Rev E L Magoon   66 Philip St
Aug. 22   Albany, N. Y.

―――

John Smith says of the Bermudas, "No place known hath better walls or a broader ditch."[104]

―――

Jan. 9, 1853. "The Telegraph harp again. Always the same ⟨r⟩unrememberable revelation it is to me. It is something as enduring as the worm that never dies. Before /the/me)qu?/ it was, & will be after. I never hear it without thinking of Greece. How the Greeks harped upon the words immortal, ambrosial. They are what it says," &c. p. 4.[105]

[132]   *Thoreau*

"I look back ⟨not into the night⟩ for the era of this creation, not into the night, but to a dawn for which no man ever rose early enough."

"Field Notes." Jan. 1853 p 38

―――

[102] For the four quotations on p. [129], see *ibid.,* IV, 146, and V, 453 and 454.

[103] For this and the preceding quotation, see *ibid.,* IV, 198 and 460. "Rev E L . . . Albany, N. Y." is inscribed in pencil at the top of p. [131], followed by a long rule and "that I . . . *Jan 1853*" in ink. "H D T" is inserted in ink above the pencil inscription.

[104] See Thoreau's *Journal . . . ,* 1949, V, 21.

[105] See *ibid.,* IV, 458. For the telegraph harp, see also p. [127] above, and "Thoreau," *W,* X, 474. "me)qu?" is circled in ink.

"We cannot well afford not to see the geese go over a single spring, & so commence the year regularly." *Ib.* p 103

"If you make the least correct observation of nature this year, you will have occasion to repeat it with illustrations the next, & the season, & life itself is prolonged." *Ib.* 124[106]

[13⟨3⟩2½] H. D. T.↑horeau↓
" 'Trench says, a wild man is a willed man.' Well, then, a man of will, who does what he wills or wishes,—a man of hope, & of the future tense,—for not only the obstinate is willed, but far more the constant & per⟨ceiving⟩severing. The obstinate man, properly speaking, is one who will not. The perseverance of the saints is ⟨a⟩ positive willedness, not a mere passive willingness. The fates are wild, for they will, and the Almighty is wild above all—as fate is."
↑*Field Notes,* Jan. 1853. p. 46↓[107]

[132⅔] "A large fresh stone-heap 8 or 10 inches above water, just below there, quite sharp, like Teneriffe."
H.D.T. June, 1854, p. 307

"Men may talk about measures till all is blue & smells of brimstone, & then go home, & sit down, & expect their measures to do their duty for them. The only measure is integrity & manhood."
1854. June 19, p. 309.

"I am not so much reminded of former years as of existence prior to years," 1854 p 376[108]

[133] See his account of snapping-turtles, in *"Field Notes."* August, 1854, p. 430, 453,
"They thus not only continue to live after they are dead, but begin to live before they are alive." Sept. 2, 1854.[109]

---

[106] For the three quotations on p. [132], see *The Journal* . . . , 1949, IV, 478, and V, 86 and 100. Emerson marked "If you . . . correct" with two short vertical ink lines in the left margin, then extended one the length of the quotation.
[107] See *ibid.,* IV, 482.
[108] For the three quotations on p. [132⅔], see *ibid.,* VI, 369, 371, and 427. For the first, see also p. [111] above.
[109] See *ibid.,* VI, 473–474, and VII, 4 and 6.

"The day is short,—it seems to be composed of two twilights merely."

Dec. 1854, p. 92[110]

––––––

"Ah how I have thriven on solitude & poverty,—I cannot overstate this advantage." Jan. 1855   p. 48[111]

––––––

"I buy but few things, & those not till long after I begin to want them, so that when I do get them, I am prepared to make a perfect use of [134] them & extract their whole sweet."

(this of buying a spy-glass) Apr. 10, 1854(?)

"If I would preserve my relation to Nature, I must make my life more moral, more pure, ⟨more⟩and innocent. The problem is as precise & simple as a mathematical one. I must not live loosely, but more & more continently."

Nov. 23, 1853 ↑p 279↓

"The air over these fields is a foundry full of moulds for casting bluebirds' warbles." 1857. Feb. 18[112]

[1⟨6⟩35] "How can we expect a harvest of thought who have not had a seed time of character. Already some of my small thoughts,—fruit of my spring life,—are ripe, like the berries which feed the first broods of birds, & other game are prematurely ripe & bright, like the lower leaves of herbs which have felt the summer's drought."

–––––––––––––––––––––––––––––––––– 1854 Aug. 7[113]

(*Of the seasons, & Winter.*)

"It is solid beauty. It has been subjected to the vicissitudes of millions of years of the gods, & not a single superfluous ornament remains. The serverest & coldest of the immortal critics shot [136] their arrows at & pruned it, till it cannot be amended." 1856 Dec. 7

"Again & again I congratulate myself on my so-called poverty." Feb. 1857 "When I have only a rustling oak-leaf, or the faint metallic cheep of a tree-sparrow for variety in my winter walk, my life becomes continent & sweet as the kernel of a nut."   Mss. 1857. Feb. 8

[110] See *ibid.*, VII, 82.

[111] See *ibid.*, VII, 46, actually dated September 19, 1854.

[112] For this and the two preceding quotations, see *ibid.*, VI, 192, V, 517, and IX, 270.

[113] See *ibid.*, VI, 426. " 'How can . . . character." is used in "Thoreau," *W*, X, 483.

"The woodfrog had 4 or 5 dusky bars whic||h|| matched exactly when the legs were folded, showing that the painter applied his brush to the animal when in that position." 1857, Sept. 12[114]

Thoreau

[136$_a$][115] I remember that in London a distinguished member of the English Parliament ⌈Now Lord⌉ told me gayly enough, but without concealing his contempt, that in h⟨s⟩is travels he had happened to meet successively three of our foreign ministers ⟨not o⟩neither of whom could speak any other language but his own. [136$_b$] This happened in 1848, but I fear ⟨if he had know the e⟩ ⟨this great disadvantage of our^n ⟨foreign representatives⟩ country in foreign courts has not been amended. continued⟩ we have continued to suffer this great disadvantage in foreign courts.   ↑R.W.E.↓

[137] "A broad leech on a turtle's sternum,—apparently going to winter with it." 1857 Dec. 2.

"There's as great an interval between the thrasher & the woodthrush, as between 'Thomson's Seasons' & Homer." 1853. June 14. p 333

"At this season (10 May) the traveller passes thro' a golden gate on causeways where these willows are planted, as if he were approaching the entrance of Fairy Land. & there will surely be found the yellowbird,—and already from a distance is heard his note, *a tche tche tche—tcha tchar tcha.* Ah willow willow, ah, could not *he* truly arrange for us the difficult family of ↑the↓ willows better than Boner or Barrett of Middletown!" 1853. p. 169[116]

[140][117] July, 1862. I suppose the war does not recommend slavery to any body. If it cost ten years of war, & ten to recover the general pros-

---

[114] For this and the three preceding quotations, see *The Journal* . . . , 1949, IX, 168, 245, and 246, and X, 31.

[115] Pasted to the right margin of p. [136] is a sheet of white paper torn off from a larger sheet to measure 17.0 × 19.5 cm, lined on one side, and inscribed in ink on both sides; it has been numbered [136$_a$]–[136$_b$] by the editors.

[116] For the three quotations on p. [137], see Thoreau, *The Journal* . . . , 1949, X, 218–219, and V, 255 and 134.

[117] The verso of p. [137] is numbered "140".

perity, the destruction of slavery is worth so much. But it does not cost so much time to get well again. How many times France has been a war-field! Every one of her towns has been sacked; ⟨every⟩ the harvest has been a hundred times trampled [141] down by armies: And yet, when you suppose, as after the first Napoleon's time, that the country must be desolate ⟨a new harvest a new⟩ ↑a↓ year's labor, a new harvest, almost ⟨one⟩ ↑the hours of one perfect↓ summer day create⟨s⟩ prodigious wealth, & repair⟨s⟩ the damage of ten years of war. What was it Goethe said of Nature's tilth? "This field has been reaped for a thousand years, but lo! a little sun & rain and all is green again."[118]

[142] I read with entire complacency that part of the history of art when the new spiritualism set the painters on painting the saints as ugly & inferior men, to hint the indifference of all circumstance to the divine exuberance. And ↑I↓ remember this with great satisfaction at the photographist's shop.

[143] Goethe said, that we are in hell: and I find this Civil War abominabl⟨e⟩y in my way, and, if peace comes again, I can still find blackbears enough in ⟨my⟩bad neighbors, ⟨l⟩failing resources, & ↑ah & alas!↓ the pathos of the house.

Young Athenians sat whole days drawing the figure of Sicily in the dust[.]
↑Broke all the statues of Mercury↓
Suppose ⟨one⟩ in Boston ⟨th⟩all the orthodox churches should be burnt in one night[.][119]

[144] Matthew Arnold ⟨tells⟩writes well of "the grand style,"[120] but the secret of that is a finer moral sentiment. 'Tis very easy for Al-

---

[118] "a year's labor . . . of war." is struck through in ink with three vertical use marks; with "a year's . . . green again.' ", cf. "The Man of Letters," *W*, X, 248. With "the hours . . . of war.", cf. "The Emancipation Proclamation," *W*, XI, 319.
[119] "Young Athenians . . . night" is in pencil. "Broke all . . . night" is used in "Character," *W*, X, 105.
[120] See *On Translating Homer: Last Words* (London, 1862), in Emerson's library, a gift from Arnold in July 1862 (see *L*, V, 279), and *On Translating Homer: Three Lectures Given at Oxford* (London, 1861), which Emerson borrowed from the Boston Athenaeum July 14–August 27, 1862, and withdrew again December 9, 1862.

cott to talk grandly, he will make no mistake. 'Tis certain that the poetic temperament of W[illiam]. E[llery]. C[hanning]. will utter lines & passages inimitable by any talent.

'Tis woodthrush & cat-bird.

"Cette splendeur d'expression qui emporte avec elle la preuve des grandes pensées." *Vauvenargues.*[121]

Collins and Gray are examples in English verse⟨.⟩↑, & M[ary]. M[oody]. E[merson]. in prose.↓ [145] & Plotinus & Proclus in prose.

[146] Fact-books, if the facts be well & thoroughly told, are much more nearly allied to poetry than many books are that are written in rhyme.[122]

[147] Labor hides itself in every mode & form. It is massed & blocked away in that stone-wall for a hundred years; it is twisted & screwed into that fragrant hay which fills the barn; it ⟨smiles⟩ ↑thanks me↓ in the perfect ⟨cond⟩ form & condition of these ⟨fruit⟩ trees now clean of caterpillars & borers, ↑rightly↓ pruned, ⟨into perfect shape,⟩ & loaded with fruit. [148] It^n is under the house in my well, it is over the house in the slating & copper; it grows in my corn; it delights me in ⟨my flowers⟩ ↑the flower-bed↓; it keeps the rain out of my library; it keeps the cow out of my garden; miasma out the town;[123]
↑See *GL* 57↓

It was like a ⟨pi⟩ stick of Stewart's refined candy with the sugar omitted[.][124]

------

[121] Quoted in Sainte-Beuve, *Causeries du lundi*, 1851–1862, III, 109; see *JMN*, XIII, 491.

[122] This sentence, struck through in ink with a diagonal use mark, is used in "Inspiration," *W*, VIII, 295.

[123] This paragraph, struck through in pencil with one vertical and one diagonal use mark on both pp. [147] and [148], is used in "Perpetual Forces," *W*, X, 75.

[124] This sentence is in pencil. For Stewart (Stuart), see *JMN*, VIII, 365.

[149] *Kleinstadtisch.* "An earthquake in Persia attributed to burying a Scotchman there." *Aitzema* 1669–79

one of W. E. C[hanning].'s Extracts[125]

[150] Why are people so ⟨n⟩sensitive about the reputation of General Maclellan? There is always something rotten about a sensitive reputation. Besides, is not General Maclellan an American citizen? And is it not the first attribute & distinction of an American to be abused & slandered a↑s↓ long as he is heard of?

[151] What a transmuter is Nature! here are these boughs loaded with pears which in March were heavy with icicles.[126]

———

The religion of ⟨our⟩ one ⟨day⟩ ↑age↓ is the literary entertainment of the next.[127] ↑printed in *"Character"*↓

———

Le terrible don de la familiarité[128] remains important. A man's connections must be looked after. If he surpasses everybody in moth-erwit, yet [152] is scholar like the rest, be sure he has got a mother or father or aunt or cousin who has the uncorrupted slang of the street, the pure mud, & which is inestimable to him as spice & alterative, and which delights you in his rhetoric, like the devil's tunes when put to slow time in church-music.

[153] All ⟨his⟩M[ary]. M[oody]. E[merson].'s language was happy but inimitable as if caught ⟨in⟩from some dream.[129]

I read with great satisfaction of the epoch in Art when ugly people were painted ⟨|| . . . ||⟩for Saints.[130] ↑see above p. 142↓

---

[125] *"Kleinstadtisch.* . . . Extracts" is struck through in pencil with a diagonal use mark. For "Kleinstadtisch", see Journal FOR, p. [68] below.

[126] This entry is in pencil.

[127] This sentence, struck through in ink with a vertical use mark, is used in "Charac-ter," *W*, X, 105.

[128] This phrase is used in translation in "Art and Criticism," *W*, XII, 286.

[129] This sentence, struck through in pencil with two diagonal use marks, is used in "Mary Moody Emerson," *W*, X, 403–404.

[130] "I read . . . satisfaction" is struck through in pencil with a short diagonal use mark.

[154] The art of the writer is to speak his fact & have done. Let the reader find that he cannot afford to omit any line of your writing, because you have omitted every ⟨v⟩word that he can spare. You are annoyed—are you?—that your fine friends do not read you: they are better friends than you knew, & have done you the rarest service. Now write so that they must. When [155] it is a disgrace to them that they do not know what you have said, you will hear the echo.[131]

——————   ——————————

↑Benefit of Conceit↓

When you next write on conceit, have the good nature to see it as it is, a balsam, a sugar on the lip of the cup to sweeten the sad potation to all mortals. ↑See below, p. 168↓

——————

'Where there is no difficulty there is no praise.'

——————

[156] ↑Aug. 13↓

W. E. C[hanning]. remarked today, that, as the rebels burned their cotton & their towns, it would not be strange if they should Emancipate their slaves.

August 13. 1862. This day took up the bridge which crosses the brook in my pasture, in order to put a stop to the travel of the neighborhood through my yard.

November 7, 1862. This day had the bridge replaced again by Francis Buttrick.

[157] ——

On the bottom of the shell of the ↑wood↓ tortoise ⟨Testudo⟩ Emys insculpta is painted an oak leaf.

[131] This paragraph is struck through in pencil with two diagonal use marks on p. [154] and three on p. [155]; "they are . . . service." is also struck through in ink with five diagonal use marks on p. [154]. Cf. pp. [88]–[89] above, and pp. [158]–[159] below.

↑——
The stem of the arum has the colors of the parrot's neck.[132]
——↓

⟨T⟩Elizabeth Hoar found a tortoise eating a yellow toadstool, a few days since.

———

W. E. C[hanning]. finds the *podalyria tinctoria* to be the favorite flower of the humblebee.

———

Abel Adams observed the robin run⟨ing⟩ning a few steps, then listening, then running again & listening: he hears the worm,—drags it out of its hole, kills it by strokes of his beak in different places, then doubles it all up, & carries it off to his young.[133]

[158] Alcott brings me his Essay on the Garden. It has the old faults,[n] false taste, sentimentalism, ambition of ⟨r⟩fine writing, ever[n] so many ventures, in the hope that each may turn out a good one. I tell him that he is not to write anything but necessary words. He is not to write anyth⟨n⟩ing that I can afford not to ⟨see⟩ ↑read↓, can omit & never miss it. ⟨But⟩ He had better never write a [159] line to the end of the world than write thus. But he is incorrigible. ↑You shall write↓ what[n] must be said, not what ⟨mt⟩may be said.

When you write, you are to have the same resistless momentum that any good workman has in his work. Something is to be done which is worth doing, & it must be done now. You must not lose your presence of mind. Despair is no muse, he who finds himself hurried & gives up carrying his point now, writes in vain. Goethe had *urkraftige behagen,* stout comfortableness, stomach for the fight.[134]

[160] He that made the world lets that speak, & does not also employ a town-crier. See R 44[135]

———

[132] See p. [113] above.

[133] Abel Adams was Emerson's old friend and financial adviser.

[134] Pages [158] and [159] are struck through in pencil with single diagonal use marks. See p. [87] above. With "Something . . . done now.", cf. "The Man of Letters," *W*, X, 255. For "You must . . . the fight.", see *JMN*, XIV, 235. "Despair is no muse" is used in "Considerations by the Way," *W*, VI, 265.

[135] Journal R, p. [44], is blank.

[161]   ↑26 Aug., 1862↓.

Little Waldo, when I carried him to the circus, & showed him the clown & his antics, said, "It makes me want to go ⟨to⟩ home,"[136] and I am forced to quote my boy's speech often & often since. I can do so few things, I can see so few companies, that do not remind me of it! Of course, if I had the faculty to meet the occasion, I should enjoy it. Not having it, & noting how many occasions I cannot meet, life loses value every month, & I shall be quite ready to give place to whoso waits for my chair.

[162]   28 Aug[us]t, 1862.

Yesterday in town talked with George Sennott, Esq. who hoped the rumor true that Sigel had shot [Irvin] McDowell, for he liked that any man should shoot any other, as that showed character, whilst most men would do nothing either good or bad, but only compromise & neutralize. He railed at Sumner, & thought the war had only brought out two New England men, [Benjamin F.] Butler & [Nathaniel P.] Banks. Banks had learned much from Rantoul, who was far his superior.[137] He invited me to attend a democratic primary meeting at Young's Hotel 5 Sept. at 12 o'clock[.]

"This world belongs to the energetic"[138]

[163] The incisive style of all English writers from ↑A.D.↓ 1600 to 1700 seems no longer attainable. It resembles the force of the words of children. These old garden-books like Evelyn &   have it. 'Tis a kind of baby-talk, which we can no longer use.

---

[136] See *JMN,* VII, 358.

[137] George Sennott was a Massachusetts lawyer who offered his services in the defense of John Brown. Franz Sigel (1824–1902), who emigrated to the United States in 1852, was a Union general, as was McDowell. This rumor may have arisen from the second battle of Bull Run on August 29–30, 1862; Sigel's troops were among the first into action, while McDowell delayed; in the investigation that followed, McDowell was relieved of his command. For McDowell, Butler, and Banks, see Journal GL, pp. [308] and [309] above. Robert Rantoul, Jr. (1805–1852) was a political reformer and Free-Soiler who was appointed to the Senate in 1851 to fill Webster's unexpired term; see *JMN,* XI, 251.

[138] See p. [1] above.

When I compare my experience with that of my own family & coevals, I think, that, in spite of the checks, I have had a triumphant health.

[164] The aphorism of the lawyers ⟨Lex⟩ *non curat de minimis* ↑*praetor,*↓ like most of their wisdom is to be reversed; for the truth is, *in minimis existit natura.*[139] ↑In Nature, nothing is insignificant because it is small.↓ The bee is essential to the marriage of the plants.

———

[165] I believe in the perseverance of the saints. I believe in effectual calling. I believe in life Everlasting.

———

As people grow old, they find a personal meaning in the word, "To the froward thou shalt show thyself froward."

———

Nature is always victor, & reckons surely on our sympathy.

———

What commandments the Master of the Universe wishes to proclaim, he impresses on the constitutions of men.[140]

[166] *"Classes of Men."* Add the class of "Influences," as described in Lecture on *"Morals."* p. 47 ↑and Lecture on "Genius," at the conclusion.↓[141]

As people rise in the social scale they think more of each other's opinion than of their own. And 'tis hard to find one who does not measure his business & daily performance from their supposed estimate. And yet, his own is the only standard. Down in the pits of hunger & want,

———

[139] *"non curat . . . praetor"* may be translated as "the magistrate is not concerned with leasts" (Ed.). Emerson translated *"in minimus . . . natura"* as "nature works in leasts"; see *JMN,* XIII, 21, and XI, 17, where it is attributed to Malpighi; see also Journal DL, p. [11] above; and cf. "Works and Days," *W,* VII, 176.

[140] A pencil line is drawn vertically in the left margin beside "Nature . . . sympathy." "What commandments . . . men." is struck through in ink with a vertical use mark.

[141] For "Classes of Men," see the front cover verso above. Emerson delivered the lecture "Morals" on April 26, 1859, as the last of six lectures at the Freeman Place Chapel. "Genius and Temperament" was given in Boston on April 9, 1861, the first of six lectures in the "Life and Literature" series.

life has a new dignity, from this doing the best, instead of the [167] seemly. The sailor on the topmast in a storm, the hunter amidst the snow drifts, the woodman in the depth of the forest, cannot stop to think how ⟨he⟩ ↑they↓ look⟨s⟩, or what London or Paris would say, & therefore his garb & behavior have a certain dignity, like the works of Nature around him: he would as soon ask what the crows & muskrats think of him.—[142] ↑And this habit of selfreliance forms ⟨his⟩the manners you admire in Kit Carson or Captain Holdrege↓[.]

[168] How kind this keeping the eyes shut! the little rhymester is just as much pleased with his *vers de société* as the poet with his images;[n] ↑that electrify us.↓ On the whole, is happier; for he thinks they are good, and the poet is always wretched at his short-comings.

[169] How shallow seemed to me yesterday in the woods the speech one often hears from tired citizens who have spent their ⟨f⟩brief enthusiasm for the country, that nature is tedious, & they have had enough of green leaves. Nature & the green leaves are a million fathoms deep, & ↑it is↓ these eyes ⟨it is⟩ that are superficial. Homer, Orpheus, ⟨C⟩Kalidasa have not exhausted nature so that Shakspeare, Burns, & Wordsworth find no ⟨room⟩ ↑more to say↓. Pliny had come to the end of Natural History, but there was room left ↑for↓ [170] Linnaeus, Newton, ⟨Cuvier⟩ Goethe, Cuvier, & Agassiz. To the heroic I will show myself heroic, says Nature.[143]

Henry said, "I wish so to live as to derive my satisfactions & inspirations from the commonest events, so that what my senses hourly perceive, my daily walk, the conversation of my neighbors may inspire me, & I may dream of no heaven but that which lies about me."

⟨The⟩ Nature, like every language, yields ⟨you on⟩ each only his own.

[142] With "The sailor . . . forest," cf. "Resources," *W*, VIII, 144. "he" and "s" are canceled, and "they" added, in pencil.
[143] "nature is tedious, . . . left for" is struck through in pencil with two diagonal use marks, and "Nature & . . . left for" with two more. With "Nature & . . . exhausted nature", cf. "Resources," *W*, VIII, 137 and 139. Two short vertical pencil lines are drawn in the left margin beside "To the . . . Nature."

The scold & the felon draw [171] all the baseness of English, the saint all the purity & rapture, the poet & artist, ⟨draw⟩ music & grandeur.

"Our stock in life, our real estate is that amount of thought which we have had, which we have thought out. The ground we have thus created is forever pasturage for our thoughts."   H.D.T.

1857. May 3[144]

"We find only that we look for." *H D T*

[172] "Sometimes in our prosaic moods, life appears to us but a certain number more of days like those which we have lived. And so it would be, if it were not for the faculty of imagination."   H.D.T.

Feb. 1859

"We *condescend* to climb the crags of earth." H.D.T. May 23, 1854[145]

———

Estabrook Farm, ↑Concord.↓ "There is a tract of pasture, woodland, orchard, & swamp, in the north part of this town, through which the old Carlisle road runs,—which is nearly two miles square, [173] without a single house, & scarcely any cultivated land in it.—4 square miles."   H. D. Thoreau

1853 June. p. 292

Beech-trees. "They impress you as full of health & vigor, so that the bark can hardly contain their spirits, but lies in folds or wrinkles about their ankles, like a sock, with the embonpoint wrinkle of fat infancy."   H D T

↑Nov.↓ 1853 p 221[146]

[144] See Thoreau's *Journal . . .* , 1949, IX, 350, where it is dated May 1, 1857. This entry, struck through in pencil with a diagonal use mark, is used in "Perpetual Forces," *W*, X, 77.

[145] For this and the preceding quotation, see *The Journal . . .* , 1949, XI, 445, and VI, 294.

[146] For this and the preceding entry, see *ibid.,* V, 225 and 474. For Estabrook Farm, see also Notebook HT, p. [9] below.

↑——

Estabrook Farm, a tract nearly 2 miles square, making four square
miles

——↓

[174] In Journal 1853–4, p. 403, Henry ↑Thoreau↓ records some
facts from an old "Waste Book" he had found in ⟨a⟩ Deacon Brown's
garret, of 1742, of Ep⟨r⟩hraim Jones, sales from a country store, & remarks,
"There is no more authentic history of those days than this waste book contains."

See a lively account of the Titmouse playing with Therien in
↑H.D.T.'s↓ Journal 1853–4, p. 444[147]

[175]–[178] [blank]
      [179] Learn to adorn every day with sacrifices. Good manners
are made up of petty sacrifices. Temperance, courage, Love, are made
up of the same jewels.
"Dès que le sacrifice devient un devoir et un besoin pour l'homme, je ne vois
plus de limite à l'horizon qui s'ouvre devant moi."[148] *Ernest Renan* [*Essais de
Morale*, 1860, p. iv]
"L'homme de genie n'a droit qu' à une seule chose, c'est qu'on ne lui rend
pas la vie impossible ou insupportable." E. Renan
                                          [*Essais de*] Morale. [1860,] p 368

      ⟨See⟩ ↑Mem.↓ too his reference to *le beau memoire de M. Naudet
dans les Memoires de l'Academie des inscriptions et Belles Lettres. T.
XIII. nouvelle série*   for slaves of Crassus [*Ibid.*, p 367]

[180] If we were truly to take account of stock before the Last Court
of Appeals,—that were an inventory. What are my resources? A few
moral maxims, confirmed by much experience, would stand high on

---

[147] For the entries on p. [174], see *ibid.*, VI, 77–79 and 110. See pp. [25]–[29]
above for Emerson's similar experience with a chickadee and his use of it in an early draft
of "The Titmouse."
      [148] "Learn to . . . jewels." and Emerson's translation of the quotation are used in
"Social Aims," *W*, VIII, 106.

the list, constituting a supreme prudence. Then the knowledge, unutterable, of my strength, of where it lies, of its accesses, & facilitations, & of its obstructions; my conviction of principles,—that is great part of my possession. Having them, 'tis easy to devise [181] or use ⟨wi⟩ means of illustrating them,—I need not take thought for that. Certain thoughts, certain observations, long familiar to me in night-watches & daylights, would be my capital, if I remove to Spain, or China, or, by stranger translation, to the planet Jupiter or Mars, or to new spiritual societies.

To work by your strength,—never to speak, or act, or behave, except on the broad basis of your [*Naturel*,—] constitution,[149]

[182]   ↑Resources↓

The riches of the memory would be much for entertainment & for guidance; the great perceptions of principles that must apply to future as to past, to one world as to another world, would be more.[150]

_____

Feats & Resources
See of dealing with a mob, *GL* 139

[183]   ↑Resources↓

If Cabot, if Lowell, if Agassiz, if Alcott come to me to be messmates in same ship, or partners in the same colony, what they chiefly bring, all they bring, is, their thoughts their ways of seeing & classifying[n] things.[151] And how a sweet temper can cheer, how a fool can dishearten the days!

_____

Thoreau in a rainstorm on the river ↑with Channing,↓ lands his boat, draws it ⟨up⟩ ashore, turns it over in a twinkling against a clump of alders with cat-br⟨ar⟩iars which keep up the lee side, crawls under it, & lies there for an hour on the ground, delighted with his stout roof[.][152]

Nov. 1853. p 247

[149] Page [180] is struck through in pencil with one diagonal and one vertical use mark, and p. [181] with a diagonal use mark. "If we . . . societies." is used in "Perpetual Forces," *W*, X, 76–77. With "To work . . . strength," cf. Journal DL, p. [107] above. With *"Naturel,"* cf. "Education," *W*, X, 144.

[150] This sentence is struck through in pencil with a diagonal use mark.

[151] "what they . . . things." is used in "Perpetual Forces," *W*, X, 77.

[152] See *The Journal* . . . , 1949, V, 493. "Thoreau in . . . roof", struck through in pencil with a diagonal use mark, is used in "Resources," *W*, VIII, 145.

Dr ↑C. T.↓ Jackson silences cats under his window at night by throwing out a lighted Indian cracker.[153]

[184] How remarkable the principle of iteration in rhetoric! We are delighted with it in rhyme, in poetic prose, in song, above all, allowing a line to be not only a burden to the whole song, but, as in Negro melodies, to be steadily repeated 3 or 4 times in immediate succession. Well, what shall we say of a liturgy? what of a litany? What of a Lord's Prayer, ↑the burial service↓ which is echoed & reechoed from one end of man's life to the other?[154]
In optics no number of reflections of the same object displeases; and, in acoustics, no number of echoes displeases, rather in both the more the better.
Wren said, a /portico/colonnade/ may be continued ad infinitum.[155]
↑Irish woman, as soon as she has told her fact, tells it again; & Wm Prescott, Esq repeated his argument once for every juror.↓

[185] Concentration expresses control of thoughts, holding ⟨as⟩them as lanthorns to light each other & the main fact.

J↑ohn↓. E↑verett↓.'s phrase that so took the youth, was, "when the harp of victory is ringing in the morning wind." But I hear the wind-harp sounding funeral marches of faery kings & knights fallen in battle.[156]

↑——
Punch & Judy in Nature.
——↓

There is satire too in Nature, as when she goes over the ground of her nobler works again ⟨i⟩on a low & even base series, & makes the phallus which grew in the yard yesterday[.]

---

[153] See pp. [116]–[117] above.
[154] With this paragraph, cf. "Poetry and Imagination," *W*, VIII, 47–48 and 53–54. Cf. also *JMN*, VII, 210–211.
[155] A vertical ink line is drawn in the left margin beside "In optics . . . infinitum."
[156] John Everett (1801–1826) was Edward Everett's brother and a Harvard classmate of William Emerson. Emerson's youthful enthusiasm for his oratory (see *L*, I, 66) was tempered by time (see *JMN*, XI, 266).

[186] In speculating on the future in politics, we deal with what a fluxional protean incalculable element. These rebels, those Whigs, some miscreants get the power. Well, what then? Their sons will be men not like themselves, but like you. Every element of power & humanity slips into their ↑new↓ kingdom in the children of some of their subjects, and Wendell Phillips will be under a new name their next President. If I were to choose the fathers of the red republic, I would [187] as readily enlist the ↑betrayers of their country,↓ Curtises, Hallets, & Fernando Woods, & others as low in the scale of intellect & character, as better men. For these men have an energy which is a certificate of health, and, as they have now got nearly as low in morals as the laws of nature permit, they will presently pause before Furies which they dare not face. They have an instinct which warns them not to rouse the antagonisms which [188] will crush them, as the fiercest rat in the ship will not gnaw through to the water, and, having exhausted their resources of spite, the novelty so attractive to the young will be for them on the side of every virtue.[157]

From Varnhagen Von Ense's Diary

"Time will come when we shall treat the jokes & sallies against the myths & church-rituals of Christianity, as, for instance, in the way Voltaire, Frederick the Great & D'Alembert have done,—goodnaturedly & without offence. Yea, a godlier [189] Christ will divert himself thereon with approbation, as already now on the naïve, rough, often irreverent treatment which those objects are evermore encountering from the people & popular poets & popular preachers. Since, at bottom, those men mean honorably, their polemics proceed out of a religious striving, and what Christ meant & willed is in essence more with them than with their opponents, who only ⟨carry⟩ ↑wear↓ & misrepresent the *name* of Christ"[158]

See infra, *VA* 208

[157] "as readily . . . on the side" is struck through in pencil with single diagonal use marks on pp. [187] and [188]. George Ticknor Curtis (1812–1894), United States Commissioner in Boston, ordered the return of fugitive slave Thomas Sims in April 1850. Benjamin Franklin Hallett (1797–1862) was editor of the Boston *Daily Advocate* and leader of radical antimasonry; for Emerson's low opinion of him, see *JMN,* XIV, 405. Fernando Wood (1812–1881) was a Tammany Hall politician; in 1862 he was mayor of New York.
[158] " 'Time will . . . offence.", struck through in ink on p. [188] with one vertical use mark and in pencil with another, and "Since, at . . . *name* of Christ", struck through in

When I bought my farm, I did not know what a bargain I had in the bluebirds, bobolinks, & thrushes. ⌈as little did I know what sublime mornings & sunsets I was buying.⌋[159]

[190] Singular delusion. A lawyer says without ⟨t⟩shame, I am not an abolitionist. I am a lawyer[,] my life devoted to the study & ⟨practice⟩ ⌈⟨defence⟩⌋ ⌈maintenance⌋ of rights of persons & property, and I go for the last outrages ⟨of⟩ on both. I have no objection to a strong white man by the judicious use of handcuffs & ⟨whip⟩ cartwhip forcing any number of black men & women to do his work. ⟨H⟩ ⟨As if he should say⟩ I am a lawyer, but have no objection [191] to counterfeiting. ⟨I am no enemy to robbers.⟩[n] God forbid I should resist a poisoner or practitioner of the garotte. I am a teacher of youth, & by taste a religionist, but I defy you to put your hand on any act ⟨of mine⟩ or word of mine ⟨to resist⟩ in behalf of what was unpopular. So far has Slavery poisoned the air of America, that ⟨the⟩ ⟨it is⟩ an assertion of freedom ⟨is⟩ marks vulgarity.[160] Who can brand me with having ever spoken the truth [192] if there was a whimper against it? I call Heaven to witness that I will never do anything disagreeable to the respectable classes.

A singer cares little for the words of the song, he will make any words glorious. I think the like rule holds of the good reader. I call him only a good reader who can read sense [193] & poetry into any hymn in the hymn-book[.][161]

Such egotists, & by nature, it seems as if Nature would by & by ⌈pass a new Homestead bill &⌋ provide each of us with a world ⟨p⟩apiece.[162]

---

ink on p. [189] with a vertical use mark, are used in "Character," *W*, X, 110. "When I . . . buying.", printed below, was inscribed first at the top of p. [189], circumscribed in ink, and this paragraph continued below it.

[159] "When I . . . buying." is used in "Concord Walks," *W*, XII, 171.

[160] "word of . . . vulgarity." is struck through in pencil with a diagonal use mark.

[161] This paragraph is used in "Eloquence," *W*, VIII, 120–121.

[162] The insertion is in pencil. A caret has been added and canceled in pencil before "by & by" and another inserted in pencil after it.

Was it Judge Warren who said "that when he borrowed any-body's remark in conversation he always made little quotation marks with his fingers in the air"?

[194] We are not sure that the heavens are quite honest.[163]

———

Sensibility is all.[164] The poorest place has all the real wealth of the richest as soon as genius arrives. How magical the poor pond under C.'s eyes; and I remember Cabot's thoughts on Art.

———

[195] ↓*Subjects.*↓[165]
Perpetual Forces.
Resources, *VA* 62, *GL* 175, 292, 79, 116, 170, 180, *GL* 175, 292, *VA* 171,[166]
Feats.
Pace and Scale. *VA* 103, 48, ⟨190⟩170,
Labor. *VA* 147   *GL* 57
Common Joys. *FOR* 81, *VA* 189,

———

↑Cheap↓

———

Influence. See *VA* 166, *KL*

———

[196] [blank]
[197] ⟨Resour⟩ Perpetual Forces

Gravity, Electricity, Heat,
Love
Duty

———

[163] Two short vertical pencil lines are drawn in the left margin beside this sentence.
[164] This sentence is used in "Perpetual Forces," *W*, X, 82. See Journal FOR, p. [14] below.
[165] For a related list of lecture subjects, see p. [48] above.
[166] "175," "79," "116," "170," "180," "175," and "292," are struck through in pencil with short diagonal use or cancellation marks.

Labor
Influences
Intellect
Imagination
Memory
Will

Temperament & the snapping Turtle
    The locomotive.
    Clouds, winds, & Fire, in the Veda
    persuade the gunpowder to explode slowly.
    power of seeds to show the virtues in the ground.[167]

[198] Art has for its aim to suggest these forces, & best from the fewest & simplest materials. And Beauty does.[168]

"Il n'y a que le matin en toutes choses."[169]

One happy thought is the parent of every genial work. ↑So is it classic.↓[170]

Eloquence. See Discourse at Music Hall on Cause & Effect.

Circulation   Wash of the sea   Wash of the air $\langle r \rangle^n$ Affinity & repulsion secures the same circulation in chemic atoms. Vegetation the same[171]
Eloquence
Music

------

[167] Page [197] is in pencil. See *JMN*, XII, 237–239, for similar notes drawing on Journal VA for "Perpetual Forces," *W*, X, 67–88. See also Journal FOR, pp. [8], [32], and [33] below. With "Temperament . . . Turtle", cf. the abstract of the lecture "Classes of Men," in Cabot, *A Memoir* . . . , 1887–1888, II, 771–772, and Appendix II.

[168] Two pencil lines are drawn vertically in the left margin beside "Art has . . . materials."

[169] For this French proverb, used in "Inspiration," *W*, VIII, 286, see Journals DL, p. [99], and GL, p. [93] above, and KL, p. [13] below.

[170] Two pencil lines are drawn vertically in the left margin beside this entry.

[171] "Circulation   Wash . . . same" is in pencil.

[199] We know little of the higher laws of health[,] ⟨r⟩how to use our resources in order to secure the grand result of perception & will. We remain long in neutral states vegetating half alive waiting for the resurrection of our powers[;] we hold ourselves cheap & insult ourselves by skepticism. But we pass, we know not how, into such company, or into such solitude, that suddenly we begin to see [200] dimly among the same facts or opinions we idly held, a certain order & force: their sequences appear. O happy! for these facts that we now discern are not accidental or factitious, but the real truth of things, of which some God vouchsafes us the perception. They will not change, & now seem important, & then absurd, but will always be as they show themselves today. When they are told, [201] men will own them as true. But when a man of talent sets himself to invent something,—though it costs him a week or a year, it is a toy, it is a knickknack, it amuses for a time, but it has no root, no man has any interest to keep it on earth, & it perishes utterly.[172]

[202] Excellence is a perfect excuse. Do it well, & it matters little what. Classic poetry is very cold, but the omnipotence of the muse is in Lycidas. How partial, like mutilated eunuchs, the musical artists appear to me in society! Politics, Bankruptcy, Frost, famine, war,— nothing concerns them but a scraping on a catgut, or ⟨blowing⟩ ↑tooting↓ on a ⟨bass⟩ French horn. The crickets in the ⟨field⟩ ↑grass↓ chirp their [203] national song at all hours, quite heedless who conquers, Federals or rebels, in the war, and so do these, & yet (see above, p. 100)

"If there is a spring, there will be a stream." *Swedenborg.*

From our boat in Walden Pond we saw the bottom at great depth, the stones all lying covered with moss or lichen as they looked of a greenish gray color. Ellery said, There is antiquity. How long they have lain there unchanged!

---

[172] This paragraph is struck through in pencil with single diagonal use marks on pp. [199], [200], and [201].

[204] The country seems to be ruined not so much by the malignity as by the levity of people. A vast force of voters allow themselves by mere compliments & solicitations of a few well-dressed intriguers to promise their support to a party whose wish is to drag back slavery into the Government of the Union.

[205] Great is the ⟨merit⟩ ↑virtue↓ of the Proclamation.[173] It works when men are sleeping, when the Army goes into winter quarters, when generals are treacherous or imbecile.

Wm B. Brinley
  Tyngsboro
   Mass[achuse]tts
28 Oct., 1862

[206]   ↑En France, tout arrive.↓
Mrs S↑edgwich↓[174] said, that it was well enough to go to N York or to London, but she did not think it needful. She had found that by sitting still in Lenox, year after year, all the people she had heard of & wished to see came by, sooner or later. I do not know but one might apply this to books. Reading depends on the reader. ⟨In⟩ A^n ⟨highly⟩ susceptible reader finds hints & [207] oracles in a newspaper. All the sentences that make the best fruit of Milton's, Shakspeare's, Plato's genius, come to the attentive listener, though he have never ransacked libraries for them[.]

Two are the causes of all things,—mind, indeed of such things as by some reason are produced,—and Necessity, of such as exist by some force. According to powers & faculties^n of bodies.

Of these things it is

[173] The preliminary emancipation proclamation was issued September 22, 1862.
[174] Probably Elizabeth Dwight Sedgwick, whose school Emerson's daughter Ellen had attended in 1853 and 1854.

There is besides in this univ of[175]

[208] Nature somewhat ↑Exemplar↓ whic[h] may last & be intelli—[176]

_____

"Voltaire was an apostle of Christian (gesinnungen) ideas, only ⟨they⟩ were these names hostile to him, & he never knew it otherwise."[177]

Varnhagen Von E⟨nse⟩'s Diary [Tagebücher,
1861–1870,] ↑Vol.↓ I, 80.

See above *VA* 188

In this connexion, later, V. v. E. ⟨says⟩ repeats the text, one son said No, and went; the other said Yes, & went not.[178]

_____

Ernest Renan says of the materialists of 18th century & their continuators in the 19th, "Ils prêchaient le vrai spiritualisme, l'humanité, la pitié, l'équ⟨te⟩ité sociale, et ils trouvaient bon de se dire matérialistes, de nier dans les termes l'idée dont ils fondaient la réalité."

Essais de Morale. [1860,] p. 62   ↑See FOR 68↓

[209]   ↑*People's Party.*↓

The Proclamation has defined every man's position. In reading every ⟨o⟩speech, or any sentence of any speech, but a few words show at once the *animus* of the men, shows them friends of Slavery; shows us that the battleground is fast changing from Richmond to Boston. They unmask themselves, &, though we tried to think them freemen, they are not. Look where they rage, at Sumner. They find not Lincoln, for they do not think him really [210] antislavery, but the abolitionist they can find is Sumner, and him they hate. If Sumner were

_____

[175] "Two are . . . bodies." is written in ink over an earlier draft of the same in erased pencil, only partially recovered; in the pencil version, "such" is inserted over an unrecovered cancellation. "Of these . . . univ of '', probably an unerased part of the earlier inscription, is in pencil.

[176] This entry is scrawled in pencil.

[177] The translation, struck through in ink with one straight and one curved vertical use mark, is used in "Character," *W,* X, 110. See Journal WAR, p. [219] above.

[178] Matthew 21:28–30. "one son . . . went not." is used in "Character," *W,* X, 110–111.

pro-slavery, there would be ↑no↓ chemical analysis ⟨& solar micro-scope⟩ & magnifying glass needed to exhibit his foibles.

It seems to promise an extension of the war. For there can be no durable peace, no [211] sound Constitution, until we have fought this battle, & the rights of man are vindicated. It were to patch a peace to ⟨m⟩cry peace whilst this vital difference exists.

[212] And you are fond of music. How delightful! my brother is a musician, & we can send for him to entertain you at any time. ⟨An⟩And what instrument does he play on? On the bass drum.

---

1 November. Yesterday, 31 October, I found the foliage more richly colored, I think, in the woods, than on any day of this season. Earlier at the time when we usually find the richest color, some warm misty weather [213] seemed to rob it prematurely, &, when the sun came out again, the landscape was rusty. Yesterday & today the mildest[,] most poetic of days, and, as usual, ⟨it seems⟩ this equilibrium of the elements seems to be the normal state, and the northeast wind the exception.

[214] A flock of fine large sparrows (?) flew in such perfect time as if the globed flock were one ball, forward, forward, swift & steadily,— that I thought no drill of ⟨troop⟩ cavalry could ever reach that perfection of manoeuvre.

Health.

The flame of life sometimes fli⟨i⟩ckers high above the wick, as if ⟨it⟩ ↑it could↓ [215] easily detach itself, & leave your old body in the lurch. I call it health only when the flame jets equally & robustly from every part & particle. Powers of a fine temper how signal. Prosperity begins with that presence. 'Tis the perpetual difference of fine weather & storms[.]

[216] The bankers believe that the moment peace shall allow a return of trade we shall have better times than were ever known.

↑The rotten firms broken up[,]↓ the^n markets ⟨are⟩ all cleaned out, the old stocks got rid of, all is hungry for supply.^{n} ⟨& the ⟨bro⟩ rotten firms & companies all broken up.⟩ Well, I think also it will be a better time in Church & State. This detestable slavery being killed out, the lips of the church↑m↓an will no longer be padlocked on that & other public sins. [217] It will be easy to stretch moral rules to the↑ir↓ universal extent. We shall be able to say "moral" in th[e] widest sense, & supp↑l↓y the names of saints b⟨ut⟩y the diviner Conscience, Antoninus, & Zeno, & Pascal, & A Kempis.

[218] In this Country, it is looked upon as unmanly not to vote.

We cannot spare any advantages, and, ⟨I find it moral to enumerate⟩ though King David had no good from making his census out of vain glory, yet I find it moral & invigorating to men in this gloom of the public to enumerate the potences that wait on man, to count the arrows^{179} [219] in his quiver, ⟨of⟩ the sticks in his fagot of forces[.]

In art, they have got that far, the rage for Saints & crucifixions & pietàs is past, and landscape & portrait, & history, & *genres* have come in.^{180} It is significant enough of the like advance in religion.

[220] I suppose, if we could go into houses & family circles⟨,⟩ we should find that each ⟨one⟩ of the independent electors & each ⟨one⟩ of the high candidates, too, is not original in his vote, or his platform, but is under personal influences. He is ⟨very⟩ free & unembarrassed in his discourse with you, a man of the people, making up his mind [221] on general grounds of public good. But, at last, he disappoints you, &, still talking plausibly, votes and acts with the enemy. It is that he has a tyrant in his acquaintance who takes care to visit him at proper moments, has acquired an influence by manners, & belonging to a more accomplished circle, flatters his ambition, & poisons his ear against ⟨all⟩ his natural allies & plain duties, & controls his vote. [222] ↑This is ⟨a

---

^{179} For "We cannot . . . advantages," see *JMN,* X, 54. "We cannot . . . arrows", struck through in pencil with a diagonal use mark, is used in "Perpetual Forces," *W,* X, 69–70; cf. also "Men are made up of potencies." in "Resources," *W,* VIII, 137.
^{180} *"genres"* is underlined in pencil.

thing⟩ ↑an affair↓ of degrees.↓ That ⟨nisc⟩mischievous person who poisons his ear is ⟨also⟩ himself reached ⟨& controlled⟩ & used by ⟨others⟩
another, or by others. Everything is in series. But the whole inter-
weaving of the social canvas betrays an absence of original perception
& will, in any quarter, as if God had left himself out of the world.

[223] Wendell Phillips gives no intimation of his perfect eloquence in casual intercourse. How easily he wears his power, ⟨wholly⟩
↑quite↓ free & disengaged, ⟨no hint   it does not   he is⟩ nowise absorbed in ⟨th⟩any care or thought of the thunderbolt he carries concealed. I think he has more culture than his own, is debtor to generations ↑of↓ gentlemen behind him. Conway says, that, when Phillips
speaks, Garrison observes delighted the effect on the audience &
seems to see & hear everything [224] except Phillips, is the only one
in the audience who does not hear & understand Phillips.
↑But I think Phillips is entirely resolved into his talent. There is not an
immense residuum left as in Webster[.]↓

——————

The Rappers revealed the worthlessness of testimony; that no
man was competent to testify on facts falling under his eyes. And an
election discloses this poverty of character, that we have no gentlemen.

[225] Every man is at the mercy of his own son. No matter how
brave, talented, or dogmatic, he must have such breadth ⟨of⟩ in his
opinions, that his son cannot outsee him, or he will have to surrender
them. Ergo, the Christian religion will triumph & slavery will go to
the wall.

I look on the Southern victories as I look at those of the Mussulman
over Christendom   due to fanaticism[,] to the petulance & valor of
a people who had nothing else & must make a brilliant onset & raid
here & there. But ideas & their slow massive might are irresistible at
last. The few [226] lessons which the first had to teach are learned by
the last in one or two campaigns, ⟨it⟩but the last vegetates eter-
nally.

The other reaches its short ⟨day⟩ ↑acme↓ & decomposes ⟨a⟩in a day; violence & cunning are no match for wisdom[.]
⟨You must⟩ For^n they must find dogmas that are not ridiculous, that none can travestie,   but that still return immortal like the sky, how long soever ⟨they⟩ ↑you↓ have hid yourself in cellars.

[227] Such is the saturation of things with the moral law, that you cannot escape from it. You may kill the preachers of it, but innumerable preachers of it survive: the violets & roses ⟨preach it⟩ & grass preach it, ⟨the⟩ rain & snow & wind & frost, moons & tides, every change & every cause in nature is nothing but a disguised missionary.[181]

———

Mem.

———

Wednesday, 12 Nov. gave Mr Barrett the house-key.[182]

[228] ⟨Some natures⟩ Most men ⟨in⟩ have so little hold on the sources of strength, that the common accidents of ⟨the⟩ ↑every↓ day prove defeats, & are solemnly treated as such, & they are in the dumps over every day's bulletin, just as a boy's fort is blown down or undermined by the first wind or shower. As Aunt Mary said of Talleyrand, "he is not constituted for a future state." Others, like Alcott, never destroy, but [229] are always busy in reconstructing; look⟨s⟩ beyond the passing cloud to a clear horizon, know that serene weather, an equilibrium of elements, is the normal state.[183]
Of Alcott, the whim of writing is a false instinct, like Goethe's for sculpture, over which both of them lost much good time.
It is said Mr Lincoln has a policy & adheres to it. He thinks emanci-

---

[181] Pages [225], [226], and [227] to this point are in pencil. "Every man . . . son.", marked with two vertical pencil lines in the left margin of p. [225], is cited in notes for the lecture "Perpetual Forces" in *JMN*, XII, 237; "the petulance . . . in a day;" on pp. [225]–[226] is used or paraphrased in "Perpetual Forces," *W*, X, 88. "Such is . . . missionary.", struck through in pencil on p. [227] with a vertical use mark, is used in *ibid.*, p. 86. "the saturation . . . the moral" is struck through in pencil with a second short vertical use mark.
[182] Probably Jonathan Fay Barrett, who, according to Emerson's letter of July 17, 1862, wished to rent the house of Mrs. Brown (Lidian's sister). See *L*, V, 283.
[183] See p. [213] above.

pation [2⟨2⟩30] almost morally wrong, & resorts to it only as a desperate measure, & means never to put radicals into power. When he puts one into office, as Fremont, or Phelps, or Lane,   he takes care to neutralize him by a democrat or a Kentuckian who will thwart him.[184] And prudent people say, "quite right, for these hotheads have no administrative talent." [231] Perhaps not; but they can not have less than the ruling party, which has shown none ⟨at all⟩ ↑whatever↓. Perhaps, also, they have a great deal. They respect principles, which it may still be believed, have a certain force, if not in the Whig Club, yet in the Universe of men.

Besides, those defeats are incidents & not crises [232] to a well principled man, not affecting the general result, (which he contemplates as a foregone conclusion,) any more than headwinds or calms to a good sailor, who uses them also to make his port.

M⟨ro⟩oral tendency is the regnant West wind, resulting from the astronomic motion of the planet,

[233] I must think that the immense advantage of power of resistance on a foot of solid land outweighs all advantages of motion in the attack ⟨of⟩ by ships. After Ericson has built his ironclad, if the problem is, how to resist it & destroy it from a battery in N.Y. or Boston harbor, I think Ericson, if you offer him the ↑sea-↓attack or the ↑land↓ defence, I must think Ericson or any other man in his senses would choose the last as the [234] most feasible. For it is a choice between an anvil afloat & an anvil on ⟨the continent.⟩ ↑shore.↓ There is a speedy limit to the weight of metal a ship can carry, & then to the explosive force its decks & timber↑s↓ can resist; but there is no limit to the resistance of the planet; ⟨if⟩ it is used to earthquakes & volcanoes & lightning, & minds them no more than peas. Why not [235] then to a gun which throws 400 or 800 pounds of iron ball?[n]

Varnhagen von E[nse]. says, "No nut without a shell. Without the earthly & common, no existence. The heavenly must dive into the im-

[184] John Wolcott Phelps (1813–1885), a West Point graduate, was a brigadier general in 1862 when he organized the first Negro troops for the federal army, but resigned when they were disavowed and disbanded. James Henry Lane (1814–1866) was both a senator from Kansas (1861–1866) and a Union general.

pure, purify & raise it, whilst itself suffers thereby.—Who can have nothing to do with the unclean, must yet permit others to do so for him. How much that was necessary to the promulgation of Christianity, could not Jesus do, but Paul did it for him. Schleiermacher said once, in Halle, with frolic boldness (lustige Keckheit), 'Without Paul, the thing would not have got on far.' "

Varnhagen [von Ense]'s Diary, [Tagebücher,
1861–1870,] Vol I. p. 74

[236] Well, yes, all our political disasters grow as logically out of our attempts in the past to do without justice, as thistles & nettles out of their seeds. One thing is plain; a^n certain personal virtue is essential to freedom, & it begins to be doubtful whether our corruption in this country has not gone a little over the mark of safety, and now, when canvassed, we shall [237] be found to be made up of Fernando Woods, Joel Parkers, & Mayor Wightmans, the divine knowledge has ebbed out of us, & we do not know enough to be free.[185]

There never was a nation great except through trial. A religious revolution cuts sharpest, & tests the faith & endurance. A civil war sweeps away all the false issues on which it begun, & arrives presently at real & lasting questions[.][186]

[238] A movement in an aristocratic state does not argue a deep cause. A dozen good fellows may have had a supper & warmed each other's blood to some act of spite or arrogance, which they talk up & carry out the next month, or one man, Calhoun, or Rhett, [239] may have grown bili⟨ious⟩ous, & his grumble & fury are making themselves felt at the Legislature. But, in a Democracy, every movement has a deepseated cause[.]

---

[185] Joel Parker was the governor of New Jersey. Joseph Milner Wightman (1812–1885), a prosperous Boston instrument maker and politician, was elected mayor of Boston in 1860, for two years.

[186] Pages [236] and [237] are struck through in pencil with single diagonal use marks. "Well, yes . . . free." is used in "Perpetual Forces," W, X, 86.

G[eorge] F Train said in a public speech in New York, "Slavery is a divine institution." "So is hell," exclaimed an old man in the crowd.[187]

---

[240] A boy who knows that a bully lives round the corner which he must pass on his way to school takes sinister views of streets & of school; and a sensitive politician ⟨a⟩suffers his ideas of ↑the part↓ New York & Pennsylvania are to play in the reconstruction of the Union to be fashioned by the election of Fernando Wood & his [241] fellows. He thinks New York peopled with ruffians & that we must do without her. I am not going to gratify Wood & Brooks & Bennett, so much. As well leave Boston out, because it has a worthless Mayor.[188]

[242][189] In poetry, the ⟨essential⟩ charm is of course in the power of the thought which enforces beautiful expression. But the common experience is, fine language to clothe commonplace thoughts, if I may say thoughts. And the effect is, dwarfs on stilts.
'Tis a fine expression of Arnold's "the lyrical cry," though the examples he gives are not well⟨-⟩chosen.

[243] When we build, ⟨we⟩ our first care is to find good foundation. If the surface be loose, or sandy, or springy, we clear it away, & dig down to the hard pan, or, better, to the living rock, & bed our courses in that. So will we do with the state. The War is serving many good purposes. It is no respecte⟨s⟩r of respectable persons or of ⟨faded⟩ worn out party platforms[.][190] [244] ⟨It⟩ War is a realist, shatters everything flimsy & ⟨decayed⟩ ↑shifty,↓ ⟨breaks through all⟩ sets aside all false issues, & breaks through all that is not real as itself, comes to organi[z]e opinions & parties, resting on the necessities of man,[n] like its own cannonade comes crushing in through party walls that have stood fifty or sixty years as if they [245] ↑were↓ solid. The screaming

---

[187] A vertical line is drawn in ink in the left margin beside this entry. See Journal DL, p. [120] above, and *JMN,* XIV, 310.
[188] This paragraph, struck through in pencil with two vertical use marks on p. [240] and a diagonal use mark on p. [241], is used in "Perpetual Forces," *W,* X, 86–87. The "worthless Mayor" may be Joseph M. Wightman (see p. [237] above) or Frederic W. Lincoln, Jr., who succeeded him in 1862.
[189] Page [242] is struck through in pencil with a wavy diagonal use mark.
[190] Page [243] is struck through in pencil with a diagonal use mark. With "dig down ... pan," cf. the lecture "American Nationality," abstracted in Cabot, *A Memoir,* 1887, II, 783.

of leaders, the ⟨unanimous⟩ votes ↑by acclamation↓ of^n conventions, are all idle wind. They cry for mercy but they cry to one who never knew the word. He is the Arm of the Fates and as has been said "nothing prevails against God but God." ↑Everything must perish except that which must live.↓^191

[246] Well, this is the task before us, to accept the benefit of the War: it has not created our false relations, they have created it. It simply demonstrate⟨d⟩s the rottenness it found. We watch its course as we did the cholera, which goes where ⟨malaria⟩ ↑predisposition↓ already existed, took only the susceptible, set its seal on every putrid spot, [247] & on none other, followed the limestone, & left the granite. So the War. Anxious Statesmen try to rule it, to slacken it here & let it rage there, to not exasperate, to keep ⟨out⟩ the black man out of it; to keep it ⟨from⟩ well in hand, nor let it ride over old party lines, nor much molest trade, and ⟨the⟩ ↑to↓ confine it to the ⟨seat of war⟩ ↑frontier of the 2 sections.↓ Why need [248] Cape Cod, why^n need Casco Bay, why need ⟨th⟩ Lake Superior, know any thing of it? But the Indians ↑have been bought, & they↓ come down on Lake Superior; ⟨and⟩ Boston & Portland are threatened by the pirate; ⟨and,⟩ more than that, ↑Secession unexpectedly shows teeth in Boston↓ our parties have just shown you that the war is already in Massachusetts, ⟨and⟩ as in Richmond[.]^192

[249] Let it search, let it grind, let it overturn, &, like the fire when it finds no more fuel, it burns out. The war will show, as all wars do, what ⟨is⟩ wrong is intolerable, what wrong makes & breeds all this bad blood. I suppose that it shows two incompatible states of society, ⟨a⟩freedom & slavery. If a part of this country is civilized up to a clear insight of freedom, & of its necessity⟨.⟩, [250] and another part is not so far civilized, then I suppose that the same difficulties will continue;

---

191 "War is . . . God.' " is struck through in pencil with single diagonal use marks on pp. [244] and [245]; the use mark on p. [245] was later extended through "Everything . . . live." With " 'nothing prevails . . . God,' ", cf. a passage from Goethe, *Dichtung und Wahrheit*, cited in *JMN*, V, 147, and used in "Demonology," *W*, X, 18.

192 This paragraph is struck through in pencil with single diagonal use marks on pp. [246], [247], and [248]. For other passages on "benefit[s] of the War", see Journal DL, pp. [206] and [207].

the war will not be extinguished; no treaties, no peace, no Constitutions ⟨can smother the feud.⟩ ↑can paper over the lips of that red crater.↓

Only when, at last, so many parts of the country as can combine on an equal & moral contract,—not to protect each other [251] in polygamy, or in ⟨eating men⟩ kidnapping, or in eating men,—but in humane & just activities,↑—↓only so many can combine firmly & durably.[193]

I speak the speech of an idealist. I say let the rule be right. If the theory is right, it is not so much matter about the facts. If the plan of your fort is right it is [252] not so much matter that you have got a rotten beam or a cracked gun somewhere, they can by & by be replaced by better without ⟨alteration of your design,⟩ ↑tearing your fort to pieces.↓ But if the plan is wrong, then all is rotten, & ⟨th⟩ⁿ every step adds to the ruin. ⟨My belief is⟩Then every screw is loose, and all the machine crazy. The question ⟨is⟩ stands thus, [253] ⟨then⟩ reconstruction is no longer matter of doubt. All our action now is new & unconstitutional, & necessarily so. To bargain or treat ⟨with⟩ at all with the rebels, to make arrangements with them about exchange of prisoners ⟨is unconstitutional,⟩ or hospitals, or truces to bury the dead, all unconstitutional & ⟨mu⟩ enough to drive a strict constructionist out of his wits. [254] Much more ⟨any the⟩ in our future action touching peace, any & every arrangement short of forcible subjugation of the rebel country, will be flat disloyalty, on our part.

Then how to reconstruct. I say, this time, go to work right. Go down to the pan, see that your works ⟨this time⟩ turn on a jewel. Do not make an impossible mixture[.]

[255] Do not ⟨build⟩ lay your cornerstone on a shaking morass that will let down the superstructure into ⟨the⟩ ↑a↓ bottomless pit again[.]

Leave slavery out. Since (unfortunately as some may think,) God is God, & nothing satisfies all men but justice, ⟨L⟩let us have that, & let us stifle our prejudices against commonsense & humanity, & agree that every man shall have what he honestly earns, and, if he is a sane

---

[193] Page [249] and p. [251] to this point are struck through in pencil with diagonal use marks.

[256] & innocent man, have ⟨a fair⟩ an equal vote in the state, and a fair chance in society.

And I[,] speaking in the interest of no man & no party, but simply as a geometer of his forces, say that the smallest beginning, so that it is just, is better ↑& stronger ↓ than the largest that is not quite just.

[257] This time, no compromises, no concealments, no crimes ⟨tucked⟩ that cannot be called by name, ↑shall be↓ tucked in under another name, like, "persons held to labor," meaning persons stolen, & "held", meaning held by hand-cuffs, when they are not under whips.

Now the smallest state so formed will & must be strong, the interest & the af⟨tion⟩fection of every man will [258] make it strong by his entire strength, and it will mightily persuade every other man, & every neighboring territory to make it larger, and it will not reach its limits until it comes to people who think that they are a little cunninger than the maker of this world & of the consciences of men.[194]

[259] Carlyle at least is not deceived by the hypocrisies of his age. He knows what London religion & patriotism are worth, & the bellowing of their professions he does not mind. But he seems to have made a covenant with his eyes not to see the foibles of his Cromwells & Fredericks.

[260] Of Plutarch the surprising merit is ↑the↓ facility with which he deals with subjects which other men strain themselves to reach to. He gossips of heroes & philosophers ⟨& s||a||ges⟩& poets, of virtues & genius, of love & empires. It costs him nothing to recite ↑⟨recall⟩↓ all that is best in history; he prattles history.[195]

[261] Nov. 29. ↑1862↓ Great harvest this year of apples & pears. I suppose I have sold a hundred barrels of apples, when I add the August & September sales to the winter apples.—Beurre Diels have been

---

[194] "I speak . . . it is" is struck through in pencil on p. [251] with a diagonal use mark extended from the use mark above it. Pages [252], [253], [254], [255], [256], [257], and [258] are struck through in pencil with single diagonal use marks.

[195] This paragraph, struck through in pencil with a vertical use mark, is used in "Plutarch," *W*, X, 301.

our excellent fruit for the last month, & were still perfect at Thanksgiving. Passe Colmans perfect also on that day. We had a profusion of Seckels & of Louise Bonnes. We had 2 to 3 barrels of Bonne↑s↓ Louise↑s↓, & not less than ⟨5⟩4 barrels of Glout Morceaux ↑(which proved excellent from 22 Dec. to 6 January)↓ ↑; and now to 6 February↓[196]

[262] What a convivial talent is that of Wendell Holmes! He is still at his Club, when he travels in search of his wounded son;[197] has the same delight in his perceptions, in his wit, in its effect, which he watches as a belle the effect of her beauty; would still hold each companion fast by his spritely, sparkling, ⟨f t⟩ widely-allusive talk, as at the Club-table: tastes all his own talent, calculates every stroke, [263] and yet the fountain is unfailing, the wit excellent, the *savoir vivre* & *savoir parler* admirable.

[264] Isaac Hecker, the Catholic priest, came to see me, & desired to read lectures on the Catholic Church, in Concord. I told him that nobody would come to hear him, such was the aversation of people, at present, to theological questions; & not only so, but the drifting of the human mind was now quite in another direction than to any churches. Nor could I possibly affect the smallest interest in [265] anything that regarded his church. We are used to this whim of a man's ⟨w⟩choosing to put on & wear a painted ⟨church⟩petticoat, as we are to whim↑s↓ of artists who wear a mediaeval cap or beard, & attach importance to it; but, of course, they must say nothing about it to us, & we will never notice it to them, but will carry on general conversation, with utter reticence as to each other's whimsies: [266] but if once they speak of it, they are not the men we took them for, & we do not talk with them twice. But I doubt if any impression can be made on Father Isaac. He converted Mrs Ward, &, like the lion that has eaten a man, he wants to be at it again, & convert somebody.[198]

---

[196] "(which . . . January" and "; and . . . February" are added in pencil.

[197] Emerson had ridden from Boston to Springfield with Holmes at the start of his western tour, probably on January 3 or 4, 1863. Holmes's son had been wounded at Antietam in September and was in Philadelphia, ill. See *L*, V, 305.

[198] Anna Barker Ward was the wife of Emerson's old friend Samuel Gray Ward. Emerson mentions her sudden conversion in a letter to Clough, May 17, 1858. See also *JMN*, XIV, 330 and 331.

[267] "A bank of England note is worth its nominal value on the Exchange, for the very reason that it is not worth a farthing in Westminster Hall." *Burke.*[199]

[268] I write laboriously after a law, which I see, & then lose, & then see again. And, I doubt not, though I see around me many men of superior talent, that my reader will do me the justice to feel that I am not contriving something to surprise or to tickle him, but am seriously striving to say that which is.

[269] We used, forty years ago, religious rites in every house, which have disappeared. There is no longer, in the houses of my acquaintances, morning or evening family prayer, or grace said at table, or any exact observance of the Sunday, except in the houses of clergymen.
I have long ceased to regret this disuse. It is quite impossible to put the dial-hand back. The religion is now where it should be. Persons are discriminated as honest, as veracious, as [270] generous & helpful, as ⟨having⟩ conscientious, or having public & universal regards; are discriminated according to their aims, & not by these ⟨formal observances.⟩ ↑ritualities.↓[200]

[271] Poverty, sickness, a lawsuit, even bad ↑dark↓ weather, & politics (such as now), spoil a great many days in the scholar's year⟨s⟩, hinder him of the frolic freedom /necessary/friendly/ to spontaneous flow of thought.[201] And that makes the use of clubs: in the large, discursive, happy talk, truths detach themselves as thoughts, spars flake off from the eternal wall, and not only the company enjoy them, but the scholar most of all; he takes possession of them, & uses them

---

[199] Paraphrased from *Reflections on the Revolution in France* (see *The Works,* 1826–1827, III, 259). See *JMN,* VI, 39.

[200] "We used . . . disappeared." is struck through in ink on p. [269] with a discontinuous vertical use mark. "The religion . . . ritualities." is struck through in ink with a diagonal use mark on p. [269] and a vertical one on p. [270]. "printed 'Character' " is added in a fine pen at the bottom of p. [269], and two additional vertical use marks are added in the same pen, one through "The religion . . . should be.", the second through "The religion . . . honest,". This entry is used in "Character," *W,* X, 107 and 108. Cf. *JMN,* XI, 137.

[201] "friendly" is added in pencil.

[272] henceforward as powers. Bad politics, the public disasters, instruct us heavily, sober us, cure us of bragging, but they are bad subjects for the muse: they drag us down usually into corners & party
views. If I read a book on whatever subject,↑—↓no matter how remote or ⟨obscure the to⟩ now deeply buried the events & actors be,—if
the author write deeply, & with a stroke of genius, he is instantly
[273] modern, though it be Egypt & affairs of mummies, and I see
that one fact is as good as another fact, a ⟨little⟩ ↑petty↓ example as a
near & great example, to show the omnipresent law of life & rational
beings.

This in answer to the ⟨question⟩ ↑query,↓ Is any person master of
the American question at this moment? No, none can accost such
question with advantage, unless he is born for it. That a man is wise or
deep [274] does not make his opinion important; for men are locally
or topically wise & deep.[202] Burke had a genius for his politics, & was
a prophet in Parliament, but none "on the Sublime & Beautiful." Alcott would be just the reverse.

—————

To the Artist. Always leave some play for the Imagination. Do not
explain all to the eye.

—————

Dec. 22. Glout Morceaux in great favor for the last fortnight. ↑⟨J⟩7
January↑, 7 Feb[ruar]y,↓[203] the same.↓

[275] "⟨W⟩Spring, when the minute crimson-starred female flowers of the
hazel are peeping forth on the hillsides." Thoreau[204]

—————

Under "Resources," one should write, "No great painter is nice
in pencils."[205]

I should have noted whilst they were fresh in mind the consternation
& religious excitement caused in my good grandfather & his compan-

—————

[202] Two short vertical pencil lines are drawn in the left margin from "important;"
down to "deep."
[203] ", 7 Feby," is in pencil.
[204] See The Journal . . . , 1949, V, 457.
[205] See JMN, V, 142, and VI, 126.

ions by the death of one soldier at Bunker Hill. Let us believe it was the first [276] or it would discredit the history of the carnage. Similar was the impression made by a death in their neighborhood on the family of Samuel Moody, as appeared in a letter which Ellen read to me. One would think that nobody ever died before, or, that our great grandfathers were the longliving patriarchs of Shem & Seth & Enoch's time.

[277] A Lyceum needs three things, a ⟨crowd, and⟩ ↑great deal of↓ light, ⟨&⟩ of heat, ↑& of people↓. At Pittsburgh we wanted all three,[206] and usually we lack one or the other.

——————

[Richter,] *Titan.* [1862,] Vol. II. p 204, 205, 206, 208, 210, 212, 256.[207]

[278] The "Spiritualists' " experiences as related by themselves read like a caricature of the poet's experience in writing[.]

[279] After the annexation of Nice & Savoy, a frenchman at A.——House, said, "je vais prendre quelque chose,"
"You are quite right," was the reply, "it is the custom of your country."[208]

[280]   Diary of Friedrich von Gentz
Gentz says of Metternich, "Il a des moyens; il a du savoir faire; il paye beaucoup de sa personne."[209] [*Tagebücher von Friedrich von Gentz,* 1861, p. 257]

[281] Diary of Varnhagen von Ense [*Tagebücher,* 1861–1870,] Vol 1 p 84

---

[206] Emerson lectured in Pittsburgh on February 3 and 5, 1863. See *L,* V, 311, n. 49.
[207] See Journal DL, p. [203], and WAR, front cover verso above, and FOR, p. [50] below.
[208] Page [279] is in pencil.
[209] Two short vertical lines are drawn in ink in the left margin beside "de sa personne."

"I defended the essence of Wilhelm Meister, but I say so only after Goethe & Rahel, that, pure loveliness, & right goodwill, are the highest manly prerogatives, before which all energetic heroism (thatkraftige Heldenthum) with its lustre & fame must recede."[210]

At Seydelmann's playing of Goethe's Faust, were present Bettine, the Savignys, Mendelsohn, Gans, Werder, &c—"I must laugh," says V. "that they asked my judgment; a judgment is a landing, & I was sailing on the high sea." [*Ibid.,*] I, 93

[282] ↑George Borrow; "Wild Wales."↓
"After all, what a beautiful thing it is, not to be, but to have been a genius." [says George Borrow, at the birthplace of Huw Morris, the Welsh poet, who died 1708.][211]
↑And ⟨therefore⟩ ↑because↓ the thinker seldom speaks to the actor in his time, but ever to actors in the next age. [See *WAR* 24]↓

———

A Welsh bard Robert Lleiaf, 240 years ago, sang thus;
        I will go to the land of Mona, notwithstanding the water of the Menai, across the sand, without waiting for the ebb."

On this verse, the people were expecting for 200 years to see a bridge across the Menai, which, at last, the genius of Telford accomplished. [Borrow, *Wild Wales,* 1862, I, 338–339]

[283] Almost as old as Lleiaf's is another verse in the Welsh "Greal" which is thus translated;
        "I got up in Mona, as soon as t'was light,
        At nine, in old Chester my breakfast I took,
        In Ireland I dined, & in Mona, ere night,
        By the turf fire I sat in my own ingle nook."

[210] "but I say . . . recede.' ", struck through in pencil with one vertical use mark and in ink with three, is used in "Character," *W*, X, 121.
[211] George Borrow, *Wild Wales,* 1862, I, 234 and 218; Emerson borrowed volume I from the Boston Athenaeum February 28–March 6, 1863.

Borrow thinks this a prophecy of the power of steam, as the feat described it would be quite easy to accomplish in these days. [*Ibid.,* I, 341–343]

[284] I am a bard least of bards.

I cannot, like them, make lofty arguments in stately continuous ⟨numbers⟩ ↑verse↓, ⟨teaching or⟩ constraining the rocks, trees, animals, & the periodic stars to say my thoughts,—for that is the gift of great poets; but I am a bard, because I stand near them, & apprehend all they utter, & with pure joy hear that which I also would say, &, moreover, I speak interruptedly [285] words & half stanzas which have the like scope & aim.

> Befalls again what once befel[212]

> What I cannot declare
> Yet cannot all withhold[213]

[286]   ↑March, 1863↓
———

The Englishman is well-packed
———

See in [Borrow,] *"Wild Wales,"* [1863,] Vol III. p. 20, the eulogy of the umbrella.
———

Reading Varnhagen Von Ense's Diary [*Tagebücher,* 1861–1870]
———

See his account of power of language [*Ibid.,*] Vol 1. page 59–60
———

Of French language as one of the weapons of culture. [*Ibid.,*] Vol. 1 p. 141
———

——— ↑Christianity ⟨out of⟩driven out of its native language. [*Ibid.,*] I. 68↓
———

[212] "May-Day," l. 178, *W,* IX, 169.
[213] "My Garden," ll. 51–52, *W,* IX, 231.

Before Hegel, Heraclitus said, "Nothing is, everything becomes." see article "Hegel" in ⟨Encyclopedie⟩ ↑Biographie↓ Generale²¹⁴

———

A good paragraph from Varnhagen on Philosophy of History, I have translated in *T* 81

———

[287] "The ⟨V⟩Aristocratic (Vornehme) which all hunt after, to which every one sacrific⟨s⟩es, is really nowhere, it is a hollow air picture; no one has it, and every one acts only so, als gehöre es ihm mit an." [Varnhagen von Ense, *Tagebücher,* 1861–1870, I, 118]

———

"Read in the English Bible & considered the Gospels only under the head of Free-Thought, ↑Novelty,↓ boldness, and ↑/enlightening/aufklarung/.↓   The Gospels belong to the most spirited & boldest (innovation) ↑aggressive↓ writings. No leaf thereof could attain the liberty of being printed, obtain the license of the censorship of Press today. There stick Mirabeaus, Rousseaus, [288] Diderots, and Fichtes, & Heines, & Borne's, & many another therein."²¹⁵ Varnhagen [*Ibid.,*] I. p 170

———

"I saw history the form of all traditions, & I thought it not worth while ↑to clutch out↓ the truth therein, ⟨to ↑heraus↑zu↓klauben↓⟩ & quite lost pains ↑to crush↓ the false↑.↓⟨therein⟩ ⟨to ↑eindrangen.↓⟩²¹⁶
    The main thing is the Being (Sein), which alone ⟨stands⟩ ↑subsists↓ & avails. I think   this ⟨in a visible reality (wirklichkeit) as the genuinest self⟩ somehow represented in a visible reality, as the genuine self, whereon our images, our appearances, pass over as clouds. [289] What helps it to deck myself out for posterity, to clothe myself in honor & fame? Do I in the least thereby change my essence, or is that counterfeit picture me? I said yesterday, 'the great phantasies

———

²¹⁴ *Nouvelle Biographie Générale,* 46 vols. (Paris, 1852–1866), XXIII, 739–753; in Emerson's library.
²¹⁵ "The Gospels . . . today." is struck through in ink on p. [287] with four diagonal and two vertical use marks. "Diderots, . . . therein.'" is struck through in pencil on p. [288] with one vertical use mark. "The Gospels . . . therein.'" is used in "Character," *W,* X, 105.
²¹⁶ "herauszuklauben" and "eindrangen", not canceled, are inserted in pencil.

which they call religions.' Also. 'He is an artist who makes (fasst) thoughts as pictures.' "

Varnhagen [*Ibid.,*] vol 1 p 247

The Germans have our phrase "out of our midst," "aus unsrer Mitte." see Varnhagen [*Ibid.,*] 1. p 336

[290] pd Edith for E[dith] D[avidson][217] 5.00
$$\frac{7.00}{12.}$$

In politics there was no voice against this edict,—no constitution, no States General, no resistance, except only the *Nature of things.*

See Varnhagen, [*Ibid.,*] I. 347

The King not supported as far as he wished by the orthodox. This slowness checks him, as to supply it, is against his maxim. "He will recognize what is, not make what is not." [*Ibid.,*] p 349

————

in the position of the Pope to Copernicus[218]

————

Schelling in a public lecture ↑at Berlin↓ charged Boehmen with borrowing largely from Spinosa;— ⟨an⟩ ↑a fatal↓ anachronism ⟨of years.⟩ ↑see Varnhagen [*Ibid.,*] I [383]↓ since Boehme died 8 years before Spinoza was born.

Bohme born 1575; died, 1624.
Spinosa born 1632; died, 1677.

[291] Harmann said↑, "↓Every book is to me a bible↑,↓ & every business ↑(Geschaft)↓ a prayer↑."↓[219]

————

[217] Emerson's account book for 1863 records receipt of money for Edith Davidson's use in February and for her board in October, several payments in February and December to Ellen Emerson for her young protegée's use, and one such payment on April 8 to Edith Emerson while Ellen was in New York. See *Life,* p. 415, and *L,* V, 437.

[218] "pd Edith . . . Copernicus" is in pencil.

[219] "(Geschaft)" and the added punctuation are in pencil.

Guizot was great under pressure.

The Supreme court feels outside pressure, and who does not?

Mem. Write to *Mrs Agnes Franz*
                    Drawer No. 10
                    Albany, N. Y.

"What is religion?" said Tholuck, at his lecture in the Berlin University. After a pause he answered, "Religion is unconditional subjection to Jesus Christ." Next day was written on the hall door, "What is Tholuck? *Answer.* Unconditional subjection to Eichhorn"
                    Varnhagen [von Ense, *Tagebücher,* 1861–1870,] II 309

[292] Will you tell the hungry weavers to eat hay?

When the Sile⟨a⟩sian weavers were starving for work, Bettine wrote to the King, that "he should build the Dom of Cologne into a thousand ⟨h⟩cottages."

Great thoughts & a pure heart should we ask of God, said Goethe once. Then again, Man may also grant to himself some⟨thing⟩ good.
                    Varnhagen [*Ibid.,*] I. 7[-8].

Personality, &c. what alone endures. Varnhagen [*Ibid.,*] I. 17
          "*Our* part is—what we uphold" [*Ibid.,* I, 17]

[293] "How we learn ⟨we⟩ anew to prize ⟨the⟩ ↑what is↓ distinguished, ⟨the⟩ ↑&↓ genuine among men,—to revere & love the↑se↓, to give them their due, when we have for a time been forced to ⟨have to do⟩ ↑deal↓ with the vulgar, & to study them! Not only ⟨to⟩ ↑in↓ a Goethe, a Rousseau, we ⟨do live[?]⟩ ↑justify it,↓ but also ⟨to⟩ ↑in↓ every patrician (Vornehmen), that he repelled these vulgar from him, and, ⟨if⟩ ↑though↓ he also ⟨is⟩ ↑were↓ blockhead, he served the other blockheads right, that he despised them. On Nobility & Aristocracy is my latest perception this— ⟨Are⟩ the accomplishments (Vorzuge), which

[294] the highest class should possess ↑are↓ decayed out of them (aus ihnen gewichen) yet are ⟨they⟩ ↑these↓ not to be found in the lower. With us, now, are the higher class servile, *blasé,* tasteless, gossiping (prahlerisch); but the Middle class (Burgerlichen) who ⟨n⟩ press nearest on them, are ⟨such⟩ ↑all this↓ in greater degree. Against the first, we feel indignation; against the last, only disgust. And so ⟨presses still⟩ ↑crowds again↓ the aristocracy, of Culture on that of rank."

Varnhagen [*Ibid.,*] I. [41–]42

[295] "Und so drängt sogar noch die Aristokratie der Bildung wieder zu der des Standes hin!" [*Ibid.,* I, 42]

See also Varnhagen, on religions,—↑copied↓ in *FOR* 41

"He is an artist who gives thoughts as pictures."
Ein Kunstler ist, wer Gedanken als Bilder fasst. [*Ibid.,* I, 247]

"The great phantasies which they call Religions."[220]

[*Ibid.,*] Vol. 1. 247

[296] [Index material omitted]

Humblebee's flower?
named in this book[221]

[inside back cover] [Index material omitted]

---

[220] See p. [289] above.
[221] "Humblebee's flower?", in pencil, is circled in pencil; "named in this book", in pencil, is half circled in pencil to connect it with the circled question.

FOR

1863–1864

Emerson probably began Journal FOR in March 1863, after concluding Journal VA in that month; its first dated entry is April 15 (p. [79]). Its last dated entry is January 13, 1864 (p. [242]); he must have written in it for several weeks after that, ending in February or March.

The covers of the copy book are of tan marbled paper over boards measuring 17 × 21.4 cm. The spine strip and protective corners of the front and back covers are of tan leather. "1863" and "FOR" are written near the top of the front cover.

There are 300 unlined pages measuring 17.5 × 20 cm; pages 1 and 300 are mended by pasting. Most are numbered in ink, but forty-eight are numbered in pencil: 22, 26–34, 36, 37, 40, 41, 50, 51, 60, 66, 68, 74, 80, 82, 86, 88–91, 110, 120, 130, 140, 150, 152, 153, 170, 187, 193, 228, 232, 234, 244, 246, and 291. Eight pages are numbered in ink over pencil: 70, 72, 83–85, 87, 100, 233. Twelve pages are unnumbered: 1, 35, 49, 55, 95, 181, 245, 296, 297, 298, 299, and 300. Two pages are misnumbered: 20, numbered as 19 ([19₂] in the text), and 21, numbered as 20. Emerson corrected misnumberings on twenty-seven pages. Twenty, misnumbered in ink, are corrected in ink: 20⟨4⟩3, 2⟨0⟩11, ⟨265⟩271, 2⟨6⟩72, 2⟨6⟩73, 2⟨6⟩74, 2⟨6⟩76, 2⟨6⟩77, 2⟨6⟩78, 2⟨6⟩79, ⟨270⟩280, ⟨271⟩281, ⟨272⟩282, ⟨273⟩283, ⟨274⟩284, 2⟨7⟩85, 2⟨7⟩86, 2⟨7⟩89, 2⟨8⟩94, and 2⟨8⟩95. Two pages misnumbered in pencil are written over in ink: ⟨200⟩210 and ⟨278⟩2⟨7⟩88 (on this page Emerson repeated the mistake in ink before correcting it). On two pages misnumbered in pencil, Emerson corrected in ink only the mistaken digit: 2⟨5⟩60 and 2⟨6⟩70 Three pencil misnumberings are corrected in pencil: 2⟨8⟩90, 2⟨8⟩92, and 2⟨8⟩93. Nine pages are blank: 22, 39, 49, 268, 289–291, 296, and 297.

[front cover] 1863
FOR

[front cover verso] ———
Forces & Forms.
———

[Index material omitted]

"An arch never sleeps."[1]

[Index material omitted]

[1]   ↑1863.↓   R. W Emerson
                                Force

                    "If this great world of joy & pain
                    Revolve in one sure track;
                    If Freedom, set, will rise again,
                    And virtue, flown, come back;
                    ⟨Wo to the⟩ ↑Peace, peace, ⟨y⟩O↓ purblind crew, who fill
                    The heart with each day's care;
                    Nor gain, from past or future, skill
                    To bear, & to forbear!"

                                                          Wordsworth.[2]
                    [For right, to toil and dare.]

[2] "The steam-engine of Watt blotted the word 'distance' out of the dictionary." *Kossuth.*

[3] "If there is a spring, there will be a stream." Swedenborg.

"The animal being must elect & borrow↑s↓ the grounds ↑elements↓ & constituents of its blood from the whole ↑(↓circumambient↑)↓ world."   Swed[enborg][3]

"Nature makes almost as much demand upon our faith as miracles themselves."[4] *Swedenborg.* ↑And M[atthew]. Arnold said, that, Nature would be a terror, were it not so full of beauty.↓

---

[1] The quotation is used in "Memory," *W*, XII, 101.

[2] *Yarrow Revisited, and Other Poems* (Boston, 1835), p. 182; in Emerson's library. The insertion in line 5 and the bracketed line are Emerson's wording. See *L*, V, 315.

[3] Cf. *The Economy of the Animal Kingdom* . . . , trans. Augustus Clissold, 2 vols. (London and Boston, 1845–1846), II, 227; in Emerson's library. "must", "elect &", "grounds", and "& constituents" are circled in pencil for revision or cancellation. The "s" inserted after "borrow", "elements", and the parentheses around "circumambient" are added in pencil. " 'If there . . . spring.' " also occurs in Journal VA, p. [203] above.

[4] Cf. *ibid.*, I, 188. The quotation is used in "Demonology," *W*, X, 12. See *JMN*, XI, 117.

[4]   *Beauty.*
"Forms are perfect in proportion to the simplicity of the ideas that they commence from." Swed.[5]

"Nothing stands in Nature's way.↑—↓Nothing is difficult to her, as she goes by insensible degrees, proportionally & harmonically from one extreme to another."   Swed.[6] ↑(copied in Naturalist)↓

"Unless the sun flowed in unceasingly, all things formed out of nature would perish, & nature herself would return to her source." *Swedenborg* [*The Economy of the Animal Kingdom* . . . , 1845–1846, II, 240]

[5] "There are some living creatures that can out of their own natures raise up a light in the dark when they are inflamed with desire." *Swed.*
                                                        [*Ibid.,* II, 245]
⟨——⟩
↑I suppose the reference is to fireflies & glowworms.↓
————
But how shall weakness write of force?

[6] ⟨W⟩ (I like to see our young Irish people, who arrived here in their shabby old country rags, after a few months labor drest so well & gaily.) When a young Irishman after a summer's labor puts on for the first time his new coat, he puts on much much more. His good ⟨cloth⟩ & becoming clothes set him on thinking that he must behave like people who are so drest. And silently & steadily his behavior mends.[7]

[7] "It is the experience of every man who has either combated difficulties himself, or attempted to guide others through them, that the controlling law shall be systematic action." *Dr Kane*[8]

[5] Cf. *ibid.,* II, 230. A vertical line is drawn in pencil in the left margin beside this sentence.
    [6] Cf. *ibid.,* I, 164.
    [7] "I like . . . gaily." is struck through in ink with a diagonal use mark curved to underline "well & gaily." "When a . . . mends.", struck through in ink with a diagonal use mark and in pencil with a wavy vertical use mark, is used in "Social Aims," *W,* VIII, 87.
    [8] Elisha Kent Kane, *Arctic Explorations: The Second Grinnell Expedition in Search of Sir John Franklin, 1853, '54, '55,* 2 vols. (Philadelphia, 1856), I, 353.

It is never quite so dismal weather out of doors as it appears from the house window. Neither is the hardship of campaigning so dreary as it seems to us who see not the reaction. Neither is the battlefield so horrible, nor wounds, nor death, as we imagine.

[8] Take up a spade full of loam. Who can guess what it holds: ⟨but⟩ ↑now↓ put a ⟨peachstone or a walnut or an orange seed⟩ ↑few seeds or nuts↓ into it, & let it ⟨⟨i⟩lie⟩lie in the sun & rain, & by & by you find that cheap dirt was all full of peaches, walnuts, & oranges.[9]

↑Poet↓ knows[n] the way to his nectar as well as toper to his tavern, or farmer to Brighton.[10]

[9] Arnold's sentence, that Nature would be a terror, were it not so full of beauty. (?)[11]

> What ⟨f⟩central flowing forces, say,
> Make up thy splendor, matchless Day!

⟨The⟩ ↑What↓ forces ⟨that⟩ go to make the brilliant phenomenon of a day.[12]

The perpetual change: look at that cloud-rack that overspreads us in the morning: tomorrow it will be a lake or a ⟨v⟩river flowing calmly [10] in an old bed ⟨betw⟩ ⟨overhung by⟩ b⟨u⟩ounded by firm shores, overhung by beautiful forests, & itself passing down to the sea, there tossing in tempests against the rocky coast.
Look at these trees loaded with icicles, come again, and they will bend to the ground in the autumn sun with perfumed golden pears.[13]

---

[9] "Take up . . . oranges.", struck through in pencil with a vertical use mark, is used in "Perpetual Forces," *W*, X, 71.

[10] With this sentence, cf. "Inspiration," *W*, VIII, 272, and *JMN*, XIV, 240.

[11] "Arnold's sentence, . . . beauty." is struck through in ink with a diagonal use mark. See p. [3] above.

[12] The couplet, in pencil, is used as the epigraph to "Perpetual Forces," *W*, X, 67, and in "Fragments on Nature," XI, *W*, IX, 340. In the sentence, "The" and "that" are canceled and "What" inserted in pencil.

[13] "The perpetual . . . coast." is struck through in pencil with a diagonal use mark on p. [9], and on p. [10] with three diagonal use marks, one of which extends through "the autumn", but is canceled below "rocky coast." with two short horizontal lines.

[11] We affirm & affirm, but neither you nor I know the value of what we say. Every Jersey wagon that goes by my gate moves from a motive & to an end as little contemplated by the rider as by his horse.[14]

If any of us knew what we are doing, or whither we are going, ↑R 138↓ then when we think we know best!
Locomotive. S[15]

[12] And what number of Southern majors & colonels, & of Yankee lawyers & state Secretaries thanking God in the Boston tone, will suffice to persuade the dreadful secrecy of moral nature to forego its appetency, & cause to decline its chase of effect?

[13] ———
The floor holds us up by a fight with agencies that go to pull us down. The whole world is a series of balanced antagonisms.[16]

———

↑Circumstance also must be right.↓
"The want of building timber—↑xxxx↓ seems to have prevented the Persians from establishing a navy in the ports they possess on the Persian Gulf" Malte Brun [*Universal Geography* . . . , 1824–1831, II, 300]

↑See infra p 47 Power of Circumstance.
The Pentelican Marble ↑its ⟨security⟩ obedience & security under the chisel,↓ made the sculptor.
The sea makes the sailor.↓[17]

[14] This entry is struck through in pencil with a curved diagonal use mark, and a vertical pencil line is drawn in the left margin beside it. For "We affirm . . . say.", see *JMN*, XIII, 319.
  [15] "If any . . . best!" is written in ink over erased pencil reading "If any . . . going! ↑then . . . best↓"; "R 138", added after "going!", and "Locomotive. S" are in pencil. For "Locomotive.", see Journal VA, p. [197] above.
  [16] This sentence is used in "Powers and Laws of Thought," *W*, XII, 53. See *JMN*, XI, 371–372 and 374.
  [17] "its ⟨security⟩ . . . chisel," is crowded to the right of "The sea . . . sailor.", partly circumscribed in ink, and its intended position indicated by an inverted caret. See Journal WAR, p. [155] above.

[14] The sensibility is all.

Every one knows what are the ordinary effects of music, of putting people in gay or mournful or martial mood. But these are its effects on dull subjects, & only the hint of its power on a keener sensibility. The story of Orpheus, of Arion, of the Arabian minstrel, are not fables but /experiments of/the record of/ the same iron at white heat.[18] Thoreau's Telegraph wire [15] is an example & Wordsworth's poem on "Sound." See ["Stanzas on the Power of Sound,"] "Yarrow Revisited," &c [Boston, 1835,] p. 213.

To prize sensibility, see the subjects of the poet; they were insignificant, until he raised them.[19]

⟨And⟩

↑*printed in Concord Address,* 1873↓

When I sprained my foot, I fancied that Nature had sprained hers. ↑How much more the blind, the deaf, & the ideot must bewail the indigence of ⟨n⟩Nature!↓[20]

[16] The human mind cannot be burned, nor bayonetted, nor wounded, nor missing.[21]

One man's voice will instantly lead a crowd to cheer the passing regiment; but another voice tries the cheer without effect.[22]

As dwelt in memory a trace
Of the old home of Adam's race

----

[18] "The sensibility . . . heat." is struck through in pencil with one vertical use mark and "Every one . . . heat." with a second; the passage is used in "Perpetual Forces," *W*, X, 82. "the record of" is in pencil.

[19] Two pencil lines are drawn vertically in the left margin beside "To prize . . . insignificant,".

[20] "When I . . . hers." is struck through in ink with a diagonal use mark; "When I . . . Nature!" is used in "Address at the Opening of the Concord Free Public Library," *W*, XI, 502 and 503. See *JMN*, XIV, 311 and 312.

[21] See Journal VA, p. [124] above.

[22] This sentence is used in "Social Aims," *W*, VIII, 83.

As if in humankind abode
Of Eden paths which Adam ⟨T⟩trode
And the old ⟨passion⟩ love ⟨since⟩ ↑through↓ ages glowed²³

[17] After the storm, come perfect days, neither hot nor cold, when it is a joy to live:
and the equilibrium of the elements is then felt by all to be the normal state, & the hurricane the exception.

[18] The delight in the first days of spring, the "wish to journeys make," seems to be a reminiscence of Adam's Paradise, & the longing to return thither.
↑'Tis that which sets all ⟨men⟩ ↑mortals↓ a roving
in the month of May.↓²⁴

——— ———

Who would live in the stone age, or in the bronze or the iron age, or in the lacustrine? I prefer the cotton, the calico, the paper, & the steam of today.²⁵

[19₁]²⁶ "It must not be imagined that any force or fraction of ⟨o⟩a force can be ever annihilated. All that which is not to be found in the useful effect produced by the motive power, nor in the amount of force which it retains after having acted, must have gone towards the shaking & destroying of the machine."²⁷ *Arago.* [*Biographies of Distinguished Scientific Men,* 1857,] *Life of Carnot.* p [p. 303–] 304
↑See extract also from Faraday, in *VO* 139↓

²³ The verse, in pencil, is struck through in pencil with a vertical use mark. "since" is canceled and "through" added in ink. Cf. "May-Day," ll. 92–93, *W,* IX, 166, and the prose version on p. [18] below.
²⁴ "The delight . . . thither." is struck through in ink with a diagonal use mark. "men" is canceled and "mortals" added in pencil. "'Tis that . . . May." is added in two lines to the right of "thither." "The delight . . . May." is developed in "May-Day," ll. 83–103, *W,* IX, 166.
²⁵ This paragraph, struck through in ink with a vertical use mark, is used in "Progress of Culture," *W,* VIII, 208.
²⁶ Emerson repeated page number [19]; the editors have supplied subscript numbers to identify the pages.
²⁷ See *JMN,* XIV, 160.

[19₂] ↑*Marriage.*↓

⟨A m⟩He who marries into a well-known & considered family, marries ↑perhaps↓ a little from his memory;[28] but he who marries marked personal traits in a new & unknown race, as Louis Napoleon his Eugenie, has a right to rely on forces fresh from the mint of ⟨n⟩Nature, wherein labor, courage, commonsense, & health may have stored great resources.

[20]   ↑Printed in "Self Reliance"↓
Power is in Nature the essential measure of Right.[29]

"Power is never far from necessity." *Pythagoras*[30]

Power is as often in one head, as in a nation; for power is after reality, & not after appearance; after quality, & not after quantity.[31] (See *infra,* p 145)

[22][32] [blank]
[23]   ↑Perpet[ual]. Forces↓
How we love to be magnetized! Ah ye strong iron currents, take me in also! We are so apologetic, such waifs & straws, ducking & imitating, and then the mighty thought comes sailing on a silent wind⟨ow⟩, and fills us with its virtue, and we stand like Atlas on our legs & ↑can↓ uphold the world.[33]

[24]   Fate
          Periodicity,   ↑in Moral sense↓
          Recuperative force
          Power of Leasts   ↑See Lect. on Art 1861[34]

---

[28] "perhaps" is added in pencil.
[29] This sentence is struck through in ink with a vertical use mark; two pencil lines are drawn vertically next to it in the left margin. "Printed in 'Self Reliance' ", inserted above it, is connected to the sentence with a wavy stroke in ink; see "Self-Reliance," *W,* II, 70.
[30] See *JMN,* VI, 24.
[31] This sentence is used in "Progress of Culture," *W,* VIII, 220.
[32] The verso of p. [20] is numbered "22".
[33] "Perpet. Forces" is added in pencil. "We are . . . the world." is struck through in pencil with a diagonal use mark. See *JMN,* IX, 66–67.
[34] "in Moral sense" and "See . . . 1861" are added in pencil.

Examples of Intellectual Force
Power of Thought ↑(see↓ (Tufts College Discourse.)
Temperament
Possession of truth or Knowledge
Love
Want

———

Great day of the first feat of the Ocean Telegraph
                                    "Cause & Effect"
Persistency, in the Naturalist
                    see Yarmouth Dis[course].[35]

[25][36] The earth's towers have no vertigo
        See Lecture on "Art" 1861

———

Fontenelle's sentence on the simplicity in Lecture on "Nat[ural]. Religion"[37]

———

Beneficent inevitabilities. *"Nat. Relig"*

———

Ox's horn is made up of hairs
branch of a tree is nothing but a leaf whose serratures have become twigs[38]

———

The Musician in "Genius"[39]
The Genius using no choice
waiting & obeying its infusions
Talent is masterless

[35] "Examples of . . . Yarmouth Disc." is in pencil. For the "Tufts College Discourse.", delivered July 10, 1861, see "The Celebration of Intellect," *W*, XII, 111–132. The "Yarmouth Disc.", "Education," was delivered September 27, 1861; cf. "Education," *W*, X, 155–156.

[36] Pages [25]–[27] are in pencil.

[37] Probably the quotation in *JMN*, VI, 336, used in "The Naturalist," *Lectures*, I, 74, and "Character," *W*, X, 109.

[38] "branch of . . . twigs" is used in "Historic Notes of Life and Letters in New England," *W*, X, 338, where it is attributed to Goethe. Cf. *JMN*, IV, 285, and "Goethe," *W*, IV, 275.

[39] This line is struck through in pencil with a diagonal use mark.

possession   the soul of God poured [26] thro' the thoughts of men
Nothing good without fanaticism
What is the source of power[40]
The two powers are Genius & Fortune

___

Mystery of triangulation, of the Trinity in theology, & in philosophy, runs thro' nature. The father, mother, & child are a single example.

[27] You cannot coax powder to explode slowly;[41]
swearing will not help
praying will not help
chemistry alone can

Gravitation inexorable
Chemistry also
lightning
& heat[42]

As if it were some memory dim
Of Eden[43]

[28] The animal borrows the elements of its blood from the whole world.[44]
We breathe by all the air
We drink from rivers
We ↑stand &↓ walk by the aid of the gravity of the planet ⟨& succor ourselves⟩ we are warmed by the sun, & succor ourselves
daily from universal forces,   ↑Our roots are in nature & draw out all her strengths, pump up the Atlantic Ocean, if we need; all the atmosphere, all the electricity of the world.↓[45]

[40] "the soul . . . of men" and "What is . . . power" are used in "Perpetual Forces," *W*, X, 88.
[41] See notes for "Perpetual Forces" in *JMN*, XII, 237.
[42] See "Perpetual Forces" in the *North American Review*, CXXV (Sept. 1877), 271–272, a paragraph omitted in *W*, X, and cf. "Perpetual Forces," *W*, X, 70–71.
[43] See pp. [16] and [18] above.
[44] See p. [3] above.
[45] "We breathe . . . world." is in pencil. Cf. "Perpetual Forces," *W*, X, 76.

[29]⁴⁶ "Cause is an arrow which will go through a cart of sand to effect"
The Persians in their litanies praise that Divine Necessity "not subject
to novelties, and the great is small; the tall, short; the broad, narrow;
& the deep is as a ford to Him"

[30]⁴⁷ Family likeness in the Greek Gods. Socrates says, "the Laws
below are sisters of the laws above."⁴⁸ So really are the material elements ⟨not the ⟨s⟩cousins or sisters of⟩ ↑of close affinity to↓ the moral
elements. But they are not their cousins, but they are themselves.
They ⟨appear to be⟩ ↑are↓ the same laws acting on superior & inferior
planes. On the lower plane, it is called Heat; on the higher, Love.
↑Whenever you enunciate a physical law, I hear in it a moral rule.↓

[31] Swedenborg's genius is the perception of the doctrine of inspiration, that "the Lord flows into the spirits" of angels & men.⁴⁹
παντα ρει⁵⁰

[32]⁵¹   *Commonplaces* for Forces
Temperament   & snappingturtle
Persistency of Naturalist. *Yarmouth*
Adirondac   Ocean Telegraph. *Moral Forces* p 87

———

Fate, *FO[R]* 29, 11,

———

Nothing good without fanaticism
None any work can frame
Unless himself become the same⁵²

———

Eloquence a power, Sketch of Thoreau, in *Cause & Effect.*

---

⁴⁶ Page [29] is in pencil. "to Him" is circled in pencil.
⁴⁷ Pages [30]–[31] are in pencil.
⁴⁸ The quotation is used in "Progress of Culture," *W,* VIII, 223; see *JMN,* VI, 32.
⁴⁹ This sentence, in pencil, is used in "Inspiration," *W,* VIII, 277.
⁵⁰ See *JMN,* XIV, 145, and "Quotation and Originality," *W,* VIII, 200, where
Emerson translates the Greek: "all things are in flux."
⁵¹ Page [32] is in pencil.
⁵² See Journal WAR, p. [58] above.

Reason↑'s↓ not lodged in us, ↑we might say↓ but we in that.

See *Lecture on Education* at Music Hall

Moral force, Higher Law &c   *VA* 43

Napoleon, See *"Disc. on Essential Principles of Religion"*

[33] The sun has lost no beams,
The earth ⟨has lost⟩ no virtues,
↑Gravity is as adhesive↓
Electricity ⟨is⟩ as swift, heat as expansive, ⟨gravity as adhesive,⟩ light as
joyful, air as virtuous, water as medicinal, as in the beginning. And the
magazine of thought & the heart of morals are as rich & omnipotent
as at the first day.[53]

[34] *Ideal Politics*
   ↑——
         A good cause, a universal interest.↓
I like to have men or governments ride on these strong horses↑.↓ ⟨on a
good cause on an universal interest⟩ ⟨It⟩ Thus a righteous edict of the
govt. works when we sleep, when the army goes into winter quarters,
when generals are treacherous or imbecile; works at home among the
citizens, among the women, among the troops;[n] works [35] down
south among the planters, in the negro cabins; works oversea among
candid virtuous people ⟨talking⟩ discussing America in their sitting-
rooms; comes thence in a tone ever growing firmer up into cabinets, &
compels ⟨c⟩parliaments & privy councils to hear⟨.⟩& obey it.[54]

elasticity of a man. A grain of air will expand & clothe the planet &
sixty atmospheres be condensed as one, if you have only force; cork,
india rubber, [36] ⟨r⟩ steel-spring, hydrogen, gunpowder,—what are
these to this airy agent,—Man, who ↑now↓ is fed on a few grains of

---

[53] "The sun . . . day.", in pencil, is struck through in pencil with a diagonal use mark
and used in "Perpetual Forces," *W*, X, 71.
[54] "*Ideal Politics* . . . it." is in pencil; single vertical lines are drawn in pencil in the left
margins of pp. [34] and [35] beside "Thus a . . . obey it."

corn, & finds his duties less & less till he comes to suicide, & now takes up the powers of other men, the reserved force of kingdoms, the accumulations of old ages, all the elements of Nature, rules them, & wants Nature to pass a new Homestead Bill & ⟨give us⟩ ↑provide us with↓ a world apiece.[55]

[37] Byron's power is not to create scenes or characters, but to name the nameless, to give permanence by expression to feelings too evanescent to be held by less apprehensive genius.[56]

↑copied in [Notebook] *CR* 76,↓

Forces.

My point is, that the movement of the whole machine, the motive force of life, & of every particular life, is moral. The world stands on our thoughts, & not on iron or cotton; and the iron of iron, the fire of fire, the ether & [38] source of all the elements, is moral forces.[57]

Force of *Naturel* or Bias, *infra* p. 2⟨6⟩00

[39] [blank]
[40]   *Uses of the War.* ↑(continued *infra* p. 48.)↓
1. diffusion of a t⟨h⟩aste for hardy habits.

Appeal to the roots of strength: *infra* p. 122,

The moral gravitations. see *infra* p. 126.[58]

Besides, war is not the greatest calamity. 'The saloons are worse than war to their customers.' see *infra* p. 131

---

[55] "elasticity of . . . apiece." is in pencil.
[56] "Byron's power . . . genius." is struck through in ink with two diagonal use marks in the shape of a V.
[57] "particular life . . . forces.", struck through in pencil with three diagonal use marks on p. [37] and two in the shape of an X on p. [38], is used in "Perpetual Forces," *W*, X, 88.
[58] This entry is struck through in ink with a vertical use mark.

War organizes. see p. 131[59]

see p. 204 *infra*

What munificence. p 229[60]

We are coming, thanks to the war, to a nationality.

It has created patriotism. We regarded our country as we do the world. It had no enemy & we should as soon have thought of vaunting the atmosphere or the sea, ↑but let the comet or the moon or Mercury or Mars come down on us[,] we should get out our buffers & electricities & stand for the Earth with fury against all comers[.]↓↓[61]

[41]   ↑*Varnhagen.*↓
    "I thought today much on the Religions. They are the strongest helps of Man and each takes to himself what fits him,—the Jew, Jehovah; the Catholic, the Virgin Mary; the Protestant Jesus.   ⟨the Saviour.⟩ To have religion, to have a creed, means to give up yourself unconditionally to an image, to a thought,⟨—⟩& who can or must do that,—to whom that thing succeeds,—has incontestably a great hold & consolation. ↑(trost)↓[62]   Whoever ⟨on⟩ ↑is directed on↓ steady free thinking, ⟨is turned,⟩ⁿ whose piety fastens not on fixed images,— seems in many respects [42][63] to have a harder lot, & ⟨a⟩ to represent a more difficult side of humanity. And the Divinity, who sees the different strivings which belong to it, ⟨sees⟩ looks ↑surely↓ with greater approbation on those who ↑have↓ the most difficult approach to him, as a General reckons those troops the best, on whom he lays the most duties, to whom he gives the least rest or indulgence. I may say, ⟨to⟩ ↑for↓ the alert outposts of the Lord, ⟨is⟩ it is impossible [43] to expect

---

[59] With "War organizes.", cf. "The Man of Letters," *W*, X, 248; cf. also Journal WAR, p. [3] above.
    [60] "see p. 204 . . . p 229" and the rule above it are in pencil.
    [61] "but let . . . comers" is added in pencil; Emerson turned the journal sideways and continued "moon or . . . comers" in the left margin.
    [62] "(trost)" is added in pencil.
    [63] *"Varnhagen"* is added in ink at the top of pp. [42], [43], [44], [45], and [46].

a quiet watch. The proud line-troops, & ↑"the old↓ Guard↑"↓ will ever think themselves better than the light chasseurs & ⟨garrison⟩ sharpshooters (Schu↑t↓zen)."

Varnhagen [von Ense, *Tagebücher*, 1861–1870,]
Vol. I. p[p.] 45[–46][64]

Of ⟨h⟩History.

"⟨With the greater ⟨lapse of time⟩ course of ages⟩[n] ↑In great periods of time,↓ must the manifold↑est forms↓ /already/hitherto(?)/ not determinable, assume a quite different ⟨form⟩ ↑shape↓. Whole peoples & their literatures will be crowded into a fort of Bibles. The tradition remains in incessant movement, will be ever new sifted. Every age has another sieve, & will sift it out again. Something [44] is continually lost by this treatment, which ⟨the successor⟩ ↑posterity↓ cannot ⟨again⟩ recover."[65]   Varnhagen, [*Ibid.,*] I. 55

"How few men are on the height where a free oversight over the world-uproar (weltwirrwarr) is possible. The best people with whom we have to do,—how limited! how must they be reconsidered, to do them right. ⟨To ⟨the⟩ inward m⟨a⟩en is most wanting⟩ ↑Introverted men lack↓ the outer world— ⟨they are⟩ unacquainted with it, or unwonted to it, ↑they↓ misunderstand all, misinterpret, know not [45] the issue of things. I had not before thought that perception & experience ⟨s⟩ were so rare, & ⟨also⟩ so ⟨weighty⟩ important. Satisfactory intercourse can only ↑exist↓ under great pre-arrangements, ⟨exist,⟩ that of like insight of the world (ähnlichen welt anschau⟨ng⟩ung)[n] is one of the first,—not the point of view, (which may be unlike)—but the object itself, the ⟨stuff⟩   . At least a nimble talent is helpful, which steadily & easily supplies the want of experience. Th⟨is⟩ese ⟨privilege↑s↓⟩ ↑advantages↓ of the [46] higher class will still ⟨lang⟩ long exist; the power of Means is quite on this side, the influence on the whole immense, and, in detaii, ⟨very⟩ ↑constantly↓ perceptible. The

----

[64] Emerson borrowed this volume from the Boston Athenaeum March 5–April 6, 1863.

[65] "hitherto(?)" is in pencil. "in incessant . . . again." is struck through in ink with two vertical use marks. In the last line, "again" is circled and canceled in pencil. "The tradition" and "Every age . . . recover.' " are used in "Character," *W*, X, 112.

knowledge of the French language, for example, is one of these means: ⟨no⟩ one who has it not, appears like a ⟨wingless one⟩ ↑beast↓ among the ⟨winged⟩ ↑birds↓,—⟨every⟩ ↑at any↓ moment, he ⟨remains⟩ ↑is left↓ alone,—must ever wait until the others sink again to him,— [47] must wait with all his accomplishments & other powers."[66]

Varnhagen's Diary [*Ibid.*,] I. 141

Force of Circumstances.

A steamengine is nothing but a teakettle ⟨with⟩[;] put a little ⟨paper⟩ ↑card-↓wheel at the nose, and it turns it: Make the kettle larger, and ⟨the⟩ ↑↑instead of the↓ card,—↓ ⟨wheel larger⟩ ↑a wheel↓ of wood or of iron, & it turns it as well. But ⟨this⟩ if the tea-kettle is cold, or ⟨there⟩ you have no water, the thing cannot be done. The enemy has surprised a town ten miles off. You load the cannon & ammunition & ⟨ar⟩troops ⟨into⟩ on the cars, but all the army cannot drag or move[n] them. But if you can only get up the fire, & ⟨the⟩ get the wheel to the nose of the teakettle, it goes off like a bird.

[48]   *Benefits of the War.*
                    Continued from p. 40
Benefits the war will have brought to the Church & society. *VA* 216

⟨O⟩ Sharpens the eyes, opens the mind of the people, so that truths we were once forbidden to speak, I hear shouted by mobs, saluted by cannon, redacted into laws.

Emancipation of Maryland, of Tennesee, of Missouri, of Louisiana.

In quiet times, the wilful man has his way; in war, the truthful man.

⟨Southerners⟩ ↑The rebels↓ our best friends. *DL* 240

---

[66] A single vertical line in pencil is drawn in the left margin beside "The knowledge . . . him,—" on p. [46], and in the right margin beside "must wait . . . powers.' " on p. [47].

Made the Divine Providence credible to many who did not believe Heaven quite honest. *DL* 211, 206,

———

Danger of dinner tables, since the peace. *KL* 170,

———

Even the starved martyrs of Andersonville served their country, as the seed of the church. *KL* 165

———

See KL 148

———

[49] [blank]
[50]   *Culture*
Titan[67]
"Vesuvius," said Albano, "stands there in this pastoral poem of Nature, and exalts everything, as a war does the age." [p]p. [255–]256   II

—"And when it is over, the dead & the living stand exalted in the world, because they had not cared for life." p. 206   II

   [51] "There is really an earthquake coming," said Agata, "I actually feel it. Good night!"
"God grant one," said Albano.
"O why?" said Linda eagerly, but in a low tone.
"All that the infinite mother wills & sends is to me today childishly dear, even death;—are not we too part & parcel of her immortality?" said he.
"Yes," replied Linda, "man may feel & believe ⟨in⟩this in joy: only in sorrow let him not speak of immortality; in such impotency of soul [52] he is not worthy of it." [II, 257–258]

Albano's spirit rose up from its princely seat to greet its lofty kinswoman, & said, "Immortal one! and though no one else were so!"   II. 258.

"If a man has only a will once for all, which goes through life, not alternating from minute to minute, from being to being, that is the main thing."
                                    II 268[–269]

   [67] The quotations on pp. [50]–[53] are from Richter, *Titan, A Romance*, 1862; see Journal VA, p. [277] above.

[53] "he had, what was so rare, a *whole* will." II. 296

In the beauty of the boy, I detect somewhat passagère, that is, that will not stay with *me.*

Cyril the young lover found the image of Gertrude so vivid in his solitude, that he believed he had found some night-telescope which penetrated not only darkness but walls, & rendered her form to his eyes. He drew from it an assurance to his passion.

[54] A Catalogue of *Forces* should include,
↑On↓ Eloquence; see ⟨my⟩ description of H[enry]. D. T[horeau].'s speech in my Lecture on *"Cause & Effect."*

———

See a page on "Moral Forces" in my Lecture of that title, p. 81.

———

Imagination a motive power: see same Lecture, p. 85

———

For Moral forces, see *"Cause & Effect,"* the inserted pages that follow p. 90.

———

Force of money, see p. 210 *infra*

[55][68]
    [56] "In the stable you↑'d↓ take him for a slouch, but lead him to the door, & when he lifts up his eyes, & looks abroad, by thunder! you'd think the sky was all horse."

⟨W⟩H[oratio] Woodman's horse that would eat farther into a haymow in one night, than he would turn round & run out again the next morning.
    The man at Providence said "he felt so cross ⟨before⟩ ⟨in the morning⟩ ↑before breakfast↓, but he got out of the door, & ran round the state two or three times, & then he felt better."

———

[68] The page is blank except for the autograph, "———F. A. W. Davis   Indianapolis Indiana", not in Emerson's hand, at the top of the page.

"And then Eng[lan]d was ⟨so⟩such a little place, that he didn't like to go out at night, for [57] fear he should get pushed off into the sea."[69]

When we quarrel, how we wish we had been blameless! ↑G 86↓[70]

No man but is so much a skeptic as to feel a warm surprise now & then at finding himself safe & sound, & things where he left them.[71]

———

Nature would be a terror but for her beauty, said Arnold[.][72]

[58]   ↑*Affirmative & Negative*↓

    "You tell me a great deal of what the devil does, & what power he has: when did you hear from Christ last?" asked Father Taylor of some Calvinistic friends.

———

When Thoreau heard a cricket or a blue bird, he felt he was not far from home after all. He found confirmation of all his human hopes in the smell of a water lily.—But the froth or spittle on the ⟨n⟩alders & andromedas in June made the ⟨bushes⟩ walk disagreeable to him.

                             See Journal 1854, p. 282[73]

[59] ↑*Oddity and Concert.*↓

    There must be concert, there must be compromise, if you call it so. Suppose each rail-road company preferred a guage of its own; a ↑car↓ wheel of its own, that would fit no other road. Suppose the scholar preferred to use, instead of English letters, characters of his own, & printed his book in them; and rules of conduct, & of manners, which he had invented, against the accepted & universal rules of morals & behavior.

[69] " 'In the stable . . . sea.' " is in pencil. "fear he . . . sea.' " runs over onto the bottom of p. [57], and is separated from "Nature would . . . Arnold" above it by a rule in pencil.
[70] "G 86" is in pencil.
[71] See Journal VA, p. [47] above.
[72] See pp. [3] and [9] above.
[73] See *The Journal* . . . , 1949, VI, 347, 352, and 350.

[60] Machinery is ⟨very⟩ good, but motherwit is better.[74] Telegraph, steam & balloon & newspapers are like spectacles on the nose of age, but we will give them all gladly to have back again our young eyes.

———

The sisters all went to the ball. When Gertrude arrived, she brought the ball with her, which now begun with new illumination.

———

Captain Bobadil received a wound in his foot.[75] In spite of the hurt, he jumped for joy on the other. Now said he, my fortune is made. Trust me if I am not a veteran & a hero from this time forth.

[61] Pitch your tone low. A prudent man accepts the lowest name with which his enemies seek to disgrace him, as Tully takes *Cicero,* as political parties "Know nothings," "Copperheads," "Locofocos," & the like; so he will be Grubstreet, parson, atheist, or worse, if worse be, and by native force makes the nickname illustrious. ↑'Tis the way to disarm malignity.↓

The Superlative, so dreary in dull people, in the hands of wit gives a fillip or shock most agreeable to the drowsy attention, & hints at poetic power. ⟨Mrs Bell⟩[76]

[62]   *Montesquieu.*

⟨1⟩*250* years nothing in aristocracy.

"Quoique mon nom," says Montesquieu, "ne soit ni bon ni mauvais, *n'ayant guère que deux cent cinquante ⟨d⟩ans de noblese prouvée,* cependant j'y suis attaché." [Sainte-Beuve, "Montesquieu," *Causeries du lundi,* 1851–1862, VII, 34][77]

"Un homme qui écrit bien n'écrit pas comme on écrit, mais comme il écrit; et c'est souvent en parlant mal, qu'il parle bien." *Montesquieu* [*Ibid.,* p. 44]

---

[74] "very" is canceled in both ink and pencil.

[75] The name Bobadil, but not the anecdote, is taken from the farcical soldier in Ben Jonson's *Every Man in His Humour.*

[76] Canceled in pencil.

[77] Emerson borrowed volume 7 from the Boston Athenaeum December 2, 1863–January 6, 1864; this volume is also in Emerson's library.

"Il a bati Chalcedoine ayant le rivage de Byzance devant les yeux."
Montesquieu[n] [*Ibid.,* p. 44]

"L'étude a été pour moi le souverain remède contre les dégouts de la vie,
n'ayant jamais eu de chagrin qu'une heure de lecture n'ait dissipé."[78] *Ibidem*
[p. 42]

"L'esprit que j'ai est un moule, on n'en tire jamais que les mêmes portraits." ↑*Montesquieu*↓[n] *St Beuve, Causeries.* vol. 7 [p. 39]

↑"L'amour de l'étude est presque en nous la seule passion éternelle;
toutes les autres nous quittent a mésure que cette misérable machine qui nous
[63] les donne s'approche ⟨a⟩de sa r⟨a⟩uine." ↑Montesquieu.↓ *Causeries* Vol
vii p 47↓[79]

Speech I should have made Nov. 22

Country wants men. No want of men in the railroad cars, in
Brighton market; in the city, in Washington street, men to see Booth,
to see Cubas, to see the great organ, to fill Faneuil Hall.[80] ⟨I⟩Every
where, hosts of men. ⟨Indeed i⟩In the swarming population, the drain
of the Army, and all the loss by war, is a drop of the bucket. But the
country wants them, wants every body. To be sure, there are many
that should not go,—those exempted by age, by infirmity, ↑so ⟨en-
gaged⟩ held↓ by peremptory engagements to their civil ⟨socie⟩ domestic or ⟨pecuniary⟩ ↑professional↓ affairs, as that the loss of them out of
these would be the greatest disaster. But for the multitude of young
able men, there is not this necessity to stay. Let them go. "One omen
is good, to ⟨die⟩fight for one's country."[81] Every kind of man is

---

[78] This quotation is struck through in pencil with a diagonal use mark, and a vertical
line is drawn in ink in the left margin beside it. A translation is used in "Address at the
Opening of the Concord Free Public Library," *W,* XI, 505.

[79] "L'amour . . . qui nous" is struck through in pencil on p. [62] with four diagonal
use marks, and a vertical line is drawn in ink beside it in the left margin. "les donne . . . p
47" runs over onto the bottom of p. [63]. A translation is used in "Immortality," *W,*
VIII, 341, and in "Address at the Opening of the Concord Free Public Library," *W,* XI,
504–505.

[80] Cf. Journal WAR, p. [157] above.

[81] See Journal WAR, pp. [3] and [61] above.

wanted, every talent, every [64] virtue; the artillerist, the horseman, ⟨the⟩ sharpshooter, ⟨the⟩ engineer, secret-service man, ⟨the⟩ carpenter, ⟨the⟩ teamster, ⟨the⟩ clerk; the Good, to be the soul & religion of the camp; the bad, because to fight & die for one's country ⟨covers⟩ not covers, but atones for a multitude of sins. And what? will you send them to die with Winthrop, Lowell, Dwight, Shaw, Bowditch? Yes, when I consider what they have sealed & saved, freedom for the world⟨,⟩; yes a thousand times yes." ↑Young they were old; had only crowded 4 score into 30.↓ It was well worth the inestimable sacrifice↑, or to blot out one generation were well.↓ The War an exceptional struggle, in which the ⟨ver⟩first combatants are met,—the highest principles against the worst. What a teacher! what a field! what re-sults!

⟨h⟩Now I well know how grave & searching this ordeal is, [65] how it has taught courage! Anxiety of the youth, sensible, tender, from school, college, counting-room, with no experience beyond football game, or school-yard quarrel, now to ⟨throw himself⟩ ↑leap↓ on a bat-tery, or a file of bayonets. He says, I know not how it will be with me; one thing is certain, I ⟨cannot afford⟩can well die,—O yes,—but I can-not afford to mis-behave. Dearest friends will know tomorrow, as the whole earth will know, whether I have kept faith with them. But the experience is uniform, that the gentle soul makes the firm hero after all.[82] Case of C. D. And ⟨then the encouragement⟩ in fact the record of the troops on the whole is nobly honorable thro' the war.

Lastly, the Encouragements from the prodigious results already se-cured[.]

[66] Ernest Renan finds that ⟨we have met⟩ Europe has twice as-sembled for Exhibitions of industry, & not a poem graced the occa-sion; & nobody ⟨made a⟩ remarked the defect. The prophet of our age, Fourier, predicted, that, one day, instead of by battles & oecumenical councils, the rival portions of humanity would dispute to each other the excellence in the manufacture of little cakes. ↑[*Essais de*] Morale

[82] "I ⟨cannot . . . mis-behave." and "But the experience . . . after all." are used in "Harvard Commemoration Speech, July 21, 1865," *W*, XI, 343 and 342. See Journal DL, p. [203] above.

[1860,] p[p. 356–]357↓ —See what Coleridge says of the improved husbandry & breeds in the highlands.[83]

[67] Aplomb rules.—He whose word or deed you cannot predict, who answers you without any supplication in his eye, who draws his determination from within, & draws it instantly,—that man rules.[84] There ⟨onl⟩are only two such known to me just now, the French Emperor & General ⟨|| . . . ||⟩.

↑Culture↓
Most people are not finished men, but sketches merely.
↑and this for not finding their native bias?↓

[68] See an extract from Ernest Renan in *VA* ↑188↓ 208   on the materialists of the 18th & 19th centuries[.]

I ought thereto to have added the sentence which follows—
"Ils prêchaient le Dieu véritable, celui qu'on sert par la justice et la droiture, et ils se disaient athées."[85]   [Renan,] *Essais de Morale.* [1860,] p. 62

"Kleinstadtisch," provincial, village politics[86]

[69] Of Augustin Thierry, Ernest Renan says, "Durant sa période de complète activité il ne prit part à la poli↑ti↓que militante que par un carbonarisme inoffensif." Ernest Renan [*Ibid.,*] p 124

↑Inspiration↓
"Quand ses yeux affaiblis ne lui permirent plus de lire les monuments écrits, ce don singulier d'intuition se porta sur l'architecture. Parcourant avec M Fauriel le midi de la France, et n'ayant tout juste de vue que ce qu'il fallait pour se *conduire,*ⁿ il retrouvait en présence des ruines, toute son facilité de lecture."[87] *Ib*   p 115

---

83 "Ernest Renan . . . highlands.", struck through in pencil with a vertical use mark, is used in "The Man of Letters," *W*, X, 245–246. Emerson borrowed Renan's *Essais de Morale* from the Boston Athenaeum February 16–April 6, 1863. See Journal DL, p. [89] above.
    84 "He whose . . . rules." is used in "Social Aims," *W*, VIII, 80.
    85 A translation of this quotation is used in "Character," *W*, X, 111.
    86 See *JMN*, XI, 399.
    87 Two vertical lines in ink are drawn in the left margin beside "vue que . . . lecture."

[70] Men have intelligence to read opinions, but not intelligence to see direct facts: as ⟨one⟩we see objects in nature by reflected light.

———

↑The mo⟨n⟩rning ⟨cob⟩webs /mocked/forbade/ the storm↓[88]
The robin listened for the worm

———

"No great discovery was ever made without a great guess."
———   *Sir Isaac Newton*
Old Age. An indignation meeting proposed

[71] ⟨In⟩President Lincoln should remember that humanity in a rul-e⟨d⟩r does not consist in running hither & thither in a cab to stop the execution of a deserter, but, as Napoleon said, "justice is the humanity of Kings."[89] Gustavus was charged with ⟨mistaking⟩ ↑confounding↓ the duty of a carbine & of a general.

↑———
Art↓

———

Pugin distinguishes "ornamented construction from constructive or-nament."

[72]   Michel Angelo
In 1540, Francesco d'Ollanda[,] miniature painter in service of King of Portugal, visited Rome, & saw⟨e⟩ there Michel Angelo, as well as Vittoria Colonna. His MS. Journal was discovered by Count Rac-zynsky, in Lisbon. Grimm uses a French translation of this.[90]

[73] April, 1863—
This running into the Catholic Church is disgusting, just when one is looking amiably round at the culture & performance of the young people, & fancying that the new generation is an advance on the last. Sam. Ward says, ⟨our⟩the misfortune is tha⟨s⟩t when the young people have this desire, there is nothing on the other side to offer them [74]

———

[88] "cob" is canceled and "forbade" added in pencil.
[89] With the quotation, marked in the left margin with a vertical line in ink, cf. Journal WAR, p. [285c] above.
[90] See Journal DL, p. [7] above.

instead.[91] And it is true that stoicism, always attractive to the intellectual & cultivated, has now no temples, no Academy, no commanding
Zeno or Antoninus. It accuses us that it has none,—that pure Ethics is
not now formulated & concreted into a *cultus*, a fraternity with assem-
blings & holy days, with song & book, with brick & stone.

[75] Why have not those who believe in it, & love it, left all for
this, & dedicated themselves to write out its scientific scripture to become its Vulgate for millions? I answer for one, that the inspirations
we catch of this law are not continuous & technical, but joyful sparkles
& flashes, and are recorded for their beauty,—for the delight they
give,—not for the↑ir↓ obligation; and that is their priceless good to
men that [76] they charm & uplift, not that they are imposed.[92]
These words out of heaven are imparted to happy uncontrollable Pindars,
Hafizes, Shakspeares, & not to Westminster Assemblies of divines.

And yet ⟨tis⟩ it must be confessed that the new world lies in chaos
& expectation until now; that this mad war has made [77][93] us all mad,
that there was no minority to stand fast for eternal truth, & say, cannons
& bayonets for such as already knew nothing stronger: but we are here
for immortal resistance to wrong: we resist it by disobedience to every
evil command, and by incessant furtherance of every right cause[.]
↑ˣBut in regard to Ward's remark, cited above p. 73, ⟨the⟩ it must be
said, that *there is the eternal offset of the moral sentiment.* The Catholic
religion stands on morals & is only the effete state of formalism↑;↓ &
morals are ever creating new channels & forms.↓[94]

[78] ↑Morals↓
It has not yet its first hymn. But, that every line & word may be
coals of true fire, ↑perhaps↓ ages must roll ere these casual wide-falling
cinders can be gat⟨t⟩hered into a broad & steady ⟨flame on the⟩ altar-
flame.[95]

[91] With "This running . . . instead.", cf. *JMN*, XIV, 129.
[92] "And it . . . imposed." (pp. [74]–[76]) is used in "The Sovereignty of Ethics,"
W, X, 209. *"Morals"* is added at the top of p. [76].
[93] *"Morals"* is added at the top of p. [77].
[94] A vertical line is drawn in ink in the left margin beside "But in . . . *sentiment."* The
semicolon after "formalism" is added in pencil.
[95] This paragraph is used in "The Sovereignty of Ethics," *W*, X, 209.

[79] ↑"The mills of God grind slow but grind fine."↓[96]
"Don't cry, Miss Lizzie, the Lord is *tadious,*—but he is sure."

↑1863↓[97] April 15.[n] I find Walden entirely open, and I have failed to know on what day; probably on Saturday 11 & Sunday 12th.

↑*Pseudo-spiritual.*↓
At Portland,[98] I found that the poor spirits who had afforded much information & exhibition of nimbleness, & jugglery, to the Woodman family, & were rising to much importance in [80] the gossip of the city, were suddenly silenced, dis⟨t⟩heartened, & quite extinguished, by ⟨being⟩ Mrs Woodman's finding that the Aristocracy resisted the ⟨whole⟩ movement; instantly she withdrew her patronage, drove all the mediums[n] & sympathizers from her house, & the poor spirits, being effectually snubbed, [81] have not ⟨whimpered⟩ tapped or whimpered since.

The "saloons" in the village are worse than war to their customers[.]

Edmund Hosmer, talking of English lords, says, Christ was right, that, few are saved.

The bird in the rain is well off, he is made of ⟨the⟩ rain, ⟨yet⟩ but man is at many removes[.]

States secretary Antonio Perez said, if God should be weary of monarchies—

Subject, Common joys—The best in the world is the universal.—
    ↑See VA 189↓[99]

---

[96] Cf. "Retribution," Longfellow's translation from the *Sinngedichte* of Friedrich von Logau.
    [97] In pencil.
    [98] Emerson lectured in Portland, Maine, on April 12, 1863.
    [99] "The 'saloons' . . . See VA 189" is in pencil. For "The 'saloons' . . . customers", see p. [40] above. For "States secretary . . . monarchies—", see *Letters of Alexander von Humboldt to Varnhagen von Ense,* trans. Friedrich Kapp (New York, 1860), p. 193, and *JMN,* XIV, 356. Cf. "Boston Hymn," ll. 5–6, *W,* IX, 201.

[82] How can you stop the freedom of the press? In 1845 when the censorship was tyrannical in Prussia "Dr Jacoby ⟨in⟩ of Koningsberg printed a book which contained nothing else than Royal Orders in Cabinet, Addresses, Letters, &c. of the present King, & by the mere arrangement of these made the bitterest satire, so scandalous did the contradictions & obscurities appear. The Police sharply hunted out the book, & huddled it aside. That again was a satire."
[83] see Varnhagen [von Ense], [*Tagebücher*, 1861–1870,] III. p. 240[100]

———

France. Rahel said, that, "you find Germany in Paris, but not Paris in Germany." [*Ibid.,* III, 326]

———

April 17. Alcott defended his thesis of personality, last night; but it is not a quite satisfactory use of words. We speak daily of a government, of power⟨,⟩ used to personal ends. And I see profound need of distinguishing the First Cause as ⟨p⟩superpersonal. It deluges us with power[;] [84] we are filled with It, but there are skies of immensity between us & it.[101] But Alcott's true strength is in the emphasis he gives to partnership of power against the doctrine of Fate. There is no passive reception: the receiver to receive must play the God also. God gives, but, it is God, or, it takes God, also, to receive. ⟨G⟩He finds or fancies Goethe [85] priest of Fate, &, writing Faust he never liberates, because he is prisoner himself.

———

Of me, Alcott said, "some of the organs were free, some fated; the voice was entirely liberated; And my poems or ⟨e⟩Essays were not rightly published, until I read them!"

———

The French have good reason for their word *aplomb*, ⟨N⟩ every one of them has it.
See Surette in the Town Hall.[102]

[100] Emerson borrowed this volume from the Boston Athenaeum April 6–May 15, 1863.
[101] Single vertical lines are drawn in pencil in the left margins of pp. [83] and [84] beside "We speak . . . & it."
[102] Louis A. Surette was a Concord resident, and president of the Concord Lyceum from 1861 to 1867.

[86] 20 April, 1863.

Abraham Jackson, Esq. was here yesterday, & speaks of his old experience of the College at Cambridge. He owed more to Jones Very, who was Greek Tutor, than to almost any or all others in the faculty. Any enthusiasm, any literary ambition or attempt was sure to be snubbed by teachers, as well as by the public opinion of the classes. Only expense, only money, [87] was respectable. He remembers Dr Walker with respect, ⟨but not Felton⟩ and Doctor Beck⟨.⟩, ↑but not Felton.↓ In the Law School, he had better experience, from Judge Story, Mr Greenleaf, & Charles Sumner. And now, when the question arises—how shall money be bestowed ⟨r⟩for the benefit of learning?—his recollection of the University does not appear edifying.

[88] ↑The insufferable insolence of these upstarts, like that of the ne-groes on the Gambia River↓[103]

Kings.

"The king (of Prussia) has said to the Graf von Munch Belling-hausen, in Konigswarth, that he uses quite no people with ideas; ideas he has enough himself,—he uses only servants to execute them."

Varnhagen's Diary, 29 Sept. 1846
[Varnhagen von Ense, *Tagebücher,* 1862,] III. p. 446

"Joseph Bonaparte had in possession the letters of the ↑last↓ King of Prussia to Napoleon: they passed into the hands of his adju-tants, & were bought of [89] these, by our present king, ↑(1846,)↓ for 26 000 thalers. It is said their tone was profoundly ↑/de-muthig/servile/↓, & highly disgraceful to the writer.[104]
The Czar Nicholas has paid for similar letters of his brother Alexander, 30 000 Thalers." *Varnhagen [Ibid.,]* III. 448

Insert the story of Professor Stenzel of Breslau, the Sanscrit scholar, displaced from his chair ↑in 1836↓ because it was discovered that, ten years before, he had belonged to the Burschenschaft.[105]

Varnhagen [Ibid., I, 34]

---

[103] Cf. Journal WAR, p. [4] above, and *JMN,* IX, 114.
[104] Emerson left a blank space after "profoundly", in which he inserted "demuthig" and "servile" in pencil.
[105] For this story, see Journal DL, p. [94], and WAR, pp. [170] and [207] above.

Emperor of Austria's opinion ⟨of Knowledge⟩↑, that knowing too
much only gives people the head-ache.↓[106]

[90][107]   Was it a squirrel's pettish bark
                              or hark
                       Where yon wedged line the Nestor leads
                       ↑Steering north↓ with^n raucous ⟨voice⟩ ↑cry↓
                       Thro' tracts & provinces of sky
                       ⟨Northward steering⟩
                       Each night descending
                       To a new lan⟨s⟩dscape of romance
                       ⟨To⟩ ↑By↓ lonely lakes ↑to men↓ unknown[108]
                       ⟨Thro⟩By purple peaks & rosy palaces
                       In deep abysses of imperial sky

                       the sifted harvest came[109]

[91]↑29 March↓ The hazel shows his crimson ⟨crest⟩ ↑head↓
                       T⟨h⟩o grace the roadside in the glen,
                       The maple bark is turned to red,
                       Whitest lakes are green again.

                       By brookside grows the hellebore
                       Where grows the strongleaved hellebore
                       Ere yet the April cowslip opes
↑28 Apr.↓   By brawling brooks
                       The maple rosy in the sun[110]

---

[106] "that knowing . . . head-ache." is struck through in pencil with two diagonal use
marks. See *JMN*, XIV, 283.
     [107] Pages [90] and [91] are in pencil.
     [108] "Was it . . . unknown" is used in "May-Day," ll. 21-27 and 29, *W*, IX,
163-164.
     [109] This line is apparently an alternate for "The harvest brought today" on p. [91]
opposite it.
     [110] A vertical line is drawn in pencil to the left of "By brookside . . . sun".

Selfsown my stately garden grows
The winds & windblown seed
⟨The⟩ ↑Cold↓ April rain & ⟨earlier⟩ ↑colder↓ snows
My hedges plant & feed
From mountains far & valleys near
The harvest brought today
Shall t⟨ri⟩hrive in all weathers without fear
Wild planters plant away![111]

[92] Apr. 21, 1863.

↑W[illiam]. E[merson]. 109. 22d Street↓[112]

The ⟨"Journal" 's⟩ ↑"Herald's"↓ correspondence ↑from Washington, N.C. (Gen Foster)↓ speaks of the negroes ↑⟨pickets⟩↓ ⟨frequently⟩ seen with a musket in one hand, & a spelling book in the other.

"Some of them lie behind the breast-works, with a spelling book in one hand, & a musket in the other."[113]

Voltaire wrote in his 83d year to D'Argental, "Il faut combattre jusqu'au dernier moment la nature et la fortune, et ne jamais désespérer de rien jusqu'à ce qu'on soit bien mort."[114]

[93] Beranger to those who asked about the *de* before his name,—

Je mis vilain
vilain, vilain;
Je honore une race commune,
Car sensible, quoique malin,
Je n'ai flatté que l'infortune.[115]

I have never recorded a fact which perhaps ought to have gone into my sketch of "Thoreau," that, on the 1 August, 184[4], when I

[111] "Selfsown my . . . away!" is used in "Walden," ll. 9–16, *W,* IX, 371.

[112] The insertion is in pencil.

[113] For this quotation, struck through in pencil with a diagonal use mark, see "Books" in Gohdes, *Uncollected Lectures,* 1932, p. 42.

[114] See Voltaire's *Oeuvres Complètes,* 52 vols. (Paris, 1877–1885), L, 263.

[115] P. J. Béranger, "Le Vilain," *Oeuvres Complètes* . . . (Paris, 1844), pp. 157–159. See *JMN,* XI, 384.

read my Discourse on Emancipation,[116] in the Town Hall, in Concord, and the selectmen would not direct the sexton to ring the
⟨church⟩meeting-house bell, Henry went himself, & rung the bell at
the appointed hour.

[94] It were worth while to notice the jokes of Nature, she so
rarely ⟨ma⟩ departs from her serious mood. The "punch" faces in the
English violets is one; the parrot is one; the monkey; the lapwing's
limping, & ⟨other⟩ the like petty stratagems of other birds.

Saladin ⟨carried⟩ caused ⟨a⟩his shroud to be made & carried it to
battle as his standard. Aunt Mary has done the like all her life, making
up her [95] shroud, & then thinking it pity to ⟨have⟩ let it lie idle, ⟨&⟩
wears it as night-gown or day-gown until it is worn out; (for death,
when asked, will not come;) then she has another made up, &, I believe, has worn out a great many. And now that her release seems to
be really at hand, the event of her death has really something ↑so↓
comic in the eyes of everybody [96] ⟨&⟩ ↑that↓ her friends ⟨will⟩ fear
they shall laugh at the funeral.
    ↑Hannah Parsons relates, that, for years ⟨she⟩ ↑M[ary] M[oody]
E[merson]↓ had her bed made in the form of a coffin; and delighted in
the figure of a coffin made daily on her wall by the shadow of a
church.↓[117]

The blot for symmetry   *LO*   ↑Resources *VA* 62, 79, 113, 180
⟨——⟩Thoreau's boat in rain. *VA* 183   *GL* 175, 292,↓[118]
The calf. *VA* 79
___

The potato to stir up the molten glass
___

Whortleberry twigs to catch the threads of the silkworm's cocoon

---

[116] "Address Delivered in Concord on the Anniversary of the Emancipation of the
Negroes in the British West Indies, August 1, 1844," *W*, XI, 97–147.
    [117] "Saladin . . . worn out;" is struck through in pencil with single vertical use marks
on pp. [94] and [95]. "Saladin . . . church." is used in "Mary Moody Emerson," *W*, X,
428–429 and 432.
    [118] "Resources . . . 292," was added first in pencil, then overwritten with almost the
same in ink; the pencil version reads "Resources VA 79, 62 . . . 2⟨6⟩92,".

The hat-tree made by beheading the shrubs.

[97] *Resources.* is a good subject for an extended chapter, though it may turn out that the list is not very long.
Natural History is⟨,⟩ in the country, a principal one. see *VA* 62
Conversation & all personal ⟨&⟩ preparation & advantage for it, & all external helps to it, as Clubs, &c.

Poetry is a main one;
                Try the might the Muse affords,
            And the balm of thoughtful words.[119]
Astronomy too, as, in Plato.

[98] *Resources*
windharp
Stereoscope[120]

Man of leisure in the country comes to be ⟨q⟩a quiddle in his fences, in his ⟨h⟩firewood, in his pears, & fruitroom. great comfort in it wine, p. 191[121]

Knowledge of French language, *See supra* p. 46

[99] We can easily tell of Whittier or Longfellow or Patmore, what suggestion they had, what styles of contemporaries have affected their own. We know all their possible feeders. But of Donne, of Daniel, of Butler, we do not, & read them as selfeducated & originals, imputing to them the credit of now forgotten ⟨co⟩ poets. Still more is this true of Saadi [&] Cervantes[.]
                ↑Copied in [Notebook] *CR* 65↓[122]

---

[119] "Fragments on the Poet and the Poetic Gift," X, ll. 1–2, *W*, IX, 329.
[120] Cf. "Resources," *W*, VIII, 148.
[121] "Man of . . . p. 191" is in pencil.
[122] Page [99] is in pencil. "We can . . . Cervantes" is struck through in pencil with a diagonal use mark.

[100] Schleiermacher (or another) said of Rahel von Ense; "We see well, that Rahel, as by her race, so by her genius, was from those regions whence the Bible comes to us."[123]

"The human soul is by nature a Christian,"[124]

"⟨Where come from⟩ ↑Whence we come,↓ & /where/whither/ we ⟨hinströmen⟩ ↑flow to,—↓that is as good a member of us as those which we ⟨use⟩have in daily use." (or) in the uses of time.)   im Zeitigen Gebrauch.[125]

Varnhagen [von Ense], *Denkwurdigkeiten* [1843–1859,] VIII. 729

[101] The mothers are wont to say "They can never be children but once—surely let them go to the ball." But I find the Germans say, *"You never can live but once;* 'tis cruel to deny them going to Italy or to Athens."

———

"Occasional Poems" good, because every body ⟨p⟩ has more presence of mind, more wit & fancy, more play of thought on the incidents that occur at his table, or about his house, than in the politics of Poland or India[.]

[102] 4 May, 1863. On Friday morning 1 May, at 3 o'clock, died Mary Moody Emerson, at Williamsburg, New York, aged 88 years, 8 months. Hannah Haskins Parsons, her niece, who has, since her childhood, been in some sort dedicated to the care & nursing of her Aunt, has for the last four years taken entire charge of her, & ⟨now⟩, having with incredible patience & tenderness attended her throughout her long decline, [103] & closed her eyes, now attended the remains to Concord, & arrived here on Saturday Night. This afternoon (Monday) the body was taken from the Receiving Tomb ⟨&

---

[123] Karl Augustus Varnhagen von Ense, *Denkwürdigkeiten und vermischte Schriften,* 9 vols. (Leipzig, 1843–1859), VIII, 714. Emerson borrowed this volume from the Boston Athenaeum April 13–May 15, 1863.

[124] *Ibid.,* p. 722. Two vertical lines are drawn in ink in the left margin beside this translation.

[125] Two vertical lines in pencil are drawn in the left margin beside " '⟨Where come . . . use.' " "Where come from" is canceled, and "Whence we come," and "whither" are added, in pencil.

c⟩to the grave in my lot in S⟨h⟩leepy Hollow, & deposited in a vault therein, in the presence of Elizabeth Hoar, Elizabeth Ripley, Mary Emerson Simmons, Lidian Emerson, Ellen Tucker Emerson, Edith Emerson⟨,⟩ and myself. The day was cloudy & warm↑,↓ with [104] mist resting over the South, & the rain waited until an hour after she was laid in the ground.[126]

↑I said, we have never a right to do wrong.↓

⟨I said⟩ It is our business to write the ⟨statute morally into⟩ moral statute into the Constitution, & give the written only a moral interpretation. Beecher said, ⟨this is in action⟩ 'Tis very well for you & me to say this in lectures, but, when it comes to practice, we can only go to the Constitution. We might have bought our land with a different line, or ought to have bought more, or less; but all this is foreign to the subject, we have only to refer to the deeds. I answer: Any right of land from ↑written↓ deeds is an imperfect right,—a right only of agreement & convenience; [105] but the right to freedom is a perfect right, and any invasion of it noxious to human nature, & invalid therefore.

[106] "When the Queen of Sheba saw the ascent by which Solomon went up to the temple of the Lord, there was no more spirit in her."[127] [1 Kings 10:5, 2 Chronicles 9:4]

Mercifully blind—

A guiding star to the ⟨u⟩arrangement & use of facts is in your leading thought.[128]

The bird in the rain is well off,—he is made of the rain, but man is at many removes.[129]

---

[126] The comma after "warm" is added in pencil. See *L*, V, 325–326 for another account of Mary Moody Emerson's burial.
[127] A pencil line is drawn vertically in the left margin beside this quotation.
[128] "Mercifully blind . . . thought." and the three adjacent rules are in pencil. See Journal DL, p. [89] above.
[129] See p. [81] above.

[107] The argument for Christianity in the dogmatic & mythologic extension seems to ⟨be⟩ rest on a certain low esteem of human nature, & so finds proof of inspiration & divine interference wherever there is believed to exist any foresight or any fineness of adaptation. Hence men of large mental & moral ⟨activity⟩ perception, having anticipated the revelation, do not need it, & the argument has no force for them.

[108] "The coldest weather" (writes M[ary] M[oody] E[merson] in her journal, ⟨Vale⟩Concord 1821) "ever known. Life truly resembles a river, /always/ever/ the same, never the same. And perhaps ⟨the greatest⟩ ↑a greater↓ variety of internal emotions would be felt by remaining with books in one place, than pursuing the waves which are ever the same. Is the melancholy bird of night↑,↓ covered with the dark foliage of the willow & cypress↑,↓ less gratified than the gay lark amid flowers & suns↑?↓"¹³⁰
↑See also [Notebook] *M M E. 4.* 168↓

"It is mortifying to fluctuate in our opinions respecting anything which is not novel, especially one's self. Yet as to mind & heart, I alter very much. Yet how stationary that [109] little self! How many stars have set & risen, suns perhaps expired, & angels lost their glory, since I have droned in this place!"

———

Ennui
"The pursuit of planting a garden or raising a nation occupies the mind, but, at bottom of the heart remains a void which we do not like to feel or complain of. The same ennui may be felt when the pursuits are intellectual or religious, but not in measure. One bustles, & is illuded by the hope of doing good, & stifles ↑this gnawing↓ discontent for higher objects in [110] the spiritual world. How much happier to be employed with those very objects which are already above!" Jan. 31.

June 1863

¹³⁰ A vertical line is drawn in pencil in the left margin beside " 'The coldest . . . ever the same.", a second beside "same, never . . . ever the same.", and another beside "Is the . . . suns?' ". "the greatest" is canceled and "a greater" inserted in pencil; commas after "night" and "cypress" and the final question mark are added in pencil. "Life truly . . . suns?' " is used in "Address at the Opening of the Concord Free Public Library," *W*, XI, 499.

↑*Resources*↓

Life is in short cycles or periods. We have rapid rallies. After utter prostration & despondency, a good night's sleep restores us to full power.[131]

↑*One Man & two Men.*↓

The sublime point in experience is the value [111] of a sufficient man. Cube this value by the meeting of two or more such who understand & support each other, you have then organized victory.[132] Wherever one is tried, two are on trial,—the judge as well as the prisoner. The examiner is instructed whenever the pupil is examined. ↑Always something unexpected leaps from the controversy. Thus the churchmen's attacks upon Bishop Colenso have ↑more↓ damaged them than he did, through the bad morals they have shown.↓[133]

[112] /At West Point, I saw/Who goes to the army, or to West Point, sees/ a civilization built ↑shall I say?↓ on buttons,—no, built on powder. It is not quite creditable ↑to our invention↓ that all the instruction in engineering, infantry, cavalry, artillery, rigidly rests on this one accident of our chemistry, ↑gun↓ powder. A new inv↑e↓ntion tomorrow would change all the art of war, just as our commerce & civ[ilizatio]n are so built on cotton [113] as to have deceived the South States & many other States into neglect of ⟨of⟩all other possibility ↑and of morality↓. But cotton is only one of 200 000 plants known to our Botany;—
And powder is but one of million combinations that are to be tried in turn.[134]

---

[131] For "Life is . . . sleep", see Journal WAR, p. [285$_a$] above.

[132] See Journal DL, p. [94], and WAR, p. [285$_a$] above.

[133] "Wherever one . . . examined." is struck through in pencil with a diagonal use mark; a pencil line is drawn vertically in the left margin beside "Wherever one . . . shown." See Journal DL, p. [93], and WAR, p. [285$_a$] above. John William Colenso (1814–1883), English bishop of Natal, was deposed and excommunicated in 1863 for not requiring polygamous Zulu converts to divorce their wives, and for declaring the Pentateuch a forgery.

[134] "At West . . . saw" and "built . . . buttons,—no," are circled in ink for revision or cancellation. With "At West . . . on cotton", struck through in pencil on p. [112] with

"The Republic has no need of chemists," was said of the death of Lavoisier. Buonaparte called the "Ecole polytechnique" "the hen that
⟨he⟩laid him golden eggs."¹³⁵

[114] S[amuel]. G[ray]. W[ard]. thought the new generation
better than the last. We have had peace & its disablings. You will have
the excitement & training of war. The mischief is such that I hear
sometimes the sentiment expressed that to remove this Mountain of
Calamity from ⟨thes⟩our institutions were worth the expenditure of an
entire generation. Who is he that will not be one? I believe if ⟨they⟩
↑men↓ saw surely this issue in the sacrifice, that many [115] are ready
to be offered. It sweetens the cup of grief of mothers, that the loss of
their youthful hero has served to ⟨g⟩close up this crater of death in the
forum. We do not often have a moment of grandeur in these hurried,
slipshod, aimless lives.¹³⁶

I attempted to comfort E in the profligacy of the infant by recit-
ing my experience of children who were profound scoundrels and
grew up to be "ornaments of society."

[116] I find in "Life of Lord Herbert" a romantic state of society, in which courage & the readiness for extreme events give a wonderful superiority ⟨to our own⟩ over any experience of our own. I wish
⟨to see⟩ society to play Kings, to be kings; we are not, & these men
are.¹³⁷   .

Take egotism out, and you would castrate the benefactors.
Luther, Mirabeau, Napoleon, John Adams, [117] Andrew Jackson, &

---

a diagonal use mark, and "But cotton . . . in turn.", struck through in pencil with a vertical use mark, cf. "The Fortune of the Republic," *W*, XI, 512–513. See also Journal DL,
p. [104], and WAR, pp. [225] and [285ₐ]–[285ᵦ] above, for Emerson's visit to West
Point in June 1863 as a member of the Board of Visitors to the United States Military
Academy.

¹³⁵ See Journal DL, pp. [94] and [122], and WAR, p. [285ᵦ] above.

¹³⁶ For "the new generation . . . disablings.", and "We do not . . . lives.", see Journal DL, pp. [104] and [102] above.

¹³⁷ Emerson borrowed the *Life of Edward, Lord Herbert of Cherbury, Written by
Himself* (London, 1826) from the Boston Athenaeum May 25–June 9, 1863. See Journal
WAR, pp. [234] and [285ᵧ] above.

our nearer eminent public servants—Greeley, Theodore Parker, Ward Beecher, Horace Mann, Garrison, would lose their vigor.

"In heaven," said Swedenborg, "no attention is paid to person, nor the things of person, but to things abstracted from person."

See Henry James ↑*"Substance & Shadow"*↓ [1863,] p. 35

———

↑Nature's Education↓

Nature wishes to grow, & to grow unobserved; so she allures the child out of doors, & puts a hoop & a ball in his hands, then he forgets himself, & rushes [118] into the conditions of growth, & comes in to his supper hungry, & off, then, to solid sleep, & grows every minute of the day & night, like a cornfield.

[119] Whenever we have true philosophy, it will surely be spoken in right tone. If Kant & Sir W[illiam]. Hamilton are too arid, Henry James is quite too petulant & scolding. Socrates is humane, & his irony only covers a profound delight & piety. Swedenborg deserves James's praise of sincere dealing, but this witty & elegant Billingsgate which diverts ⟨him⟩ ↑James↓ so hugely, ought to warn the reader whom first it scares, that it is not quite to be trusted, that there must be some deduction from pure truth to generate all this wrath.

[120] The Southerner says with double meaning, "Cotton is King," ⟨mean⟩—intimating that the art of command is the talent of their country. We reply, 'Very likely, but we prefer a republic.'

"Great rogues soon show themselves," and a great army whose whereabouts is not known, as at this moment Lee's, is like the hiding of fire.[138] If there is volcano, if there is ocean, if there [121] is eclipse in our neighborhood, we soon find it[.]

At Washington, in 1862, I met Governor Andrew, who had Mr Forbes, Mr Ward, & Mr Amory, with him⟨; because,⟩: he said, he had particularly solicited them to go along with him, since a single man at

———

[138] This was probably written shortly before the battle of Gettysburg (July 1–3, 1863) when Lee was moving the Army of Northern Virginia into Pennsylvania. For the quotation, see *JMN*, VIII, 122.

Washington was nobody, & was thrust aside. I had not expected to
find a Governor of Massachusetts playing the part of unprotected female. And he too one of the most [122] industrious & devoted patri-
ots the war has brought out.

A benefit of War is, that the appeal not being longer to letter & form,
but now to the roots of strength in the people, the moral aspect becomes important, & is urgently presented & debated. Whilst, in preceding quiet times, custom is able to stifle [123] this discussion as
sentimental, & bring in the brazen devil ↑himself.↓[139]

Certain it is that never before since I read newspapers, has the morale
played so large a part in them as now.

An arborvitae native in Natick
      Water Lily June 5
——
Whitehall Pond in Hopkinton the source of Musketaquid River.
                  See Thoreau Ms Journal. June 1854. p. 274[140]

[124] "Menander had finished the comedy all but the verses.—"[141]
That marks the distinction between the classic & romantic schools.
↓Classik das Gesunde, Romantisch das Kranke. *Goethe* See also
Spruche p. 248↓[142]

24 June. Agassiz declares that he is going to demand of the Community that provision should be made for the study of Natural Science on
the ↑same↓ scale as that for the support of religion.

[125] Agassiz says, at Heidelberg, Tiedemann was his teacher of
Anatomy; of whom he learned dissection. Afterwards, at Munich,

---

[139] "himself." is in pencil.
[140] See *The Journal* . . . , 1949, VI, 342.
[141] See *JMN*, XIV, 63.
[142] The insertion is crowded in after "schools.", from which it is set off by a wavy
vertical line. For Goethe's saying, which is used in "Art and Criticism," *W*, XII, 304, see
JMN, XIV, 61. Goethe's *Sprüche in Reim und Prosa* (n.p., n.d.) is in Emerson's library.

Dollinger was his teacher, and, one day, he asked D. "why he was not enlarged by so much as Tiedemann had taught him, whilst he ↑was↓ sensibl⟨y⟩e of his progress since he had been with D.?" Dollinger answered, "Tiedemann ⟨was⟩is a prosector. I am a professor."

At ⟨Arceuil⟩ ↑Arcueil↓, near Paris, Laplace, Cuvier, Decandolle, Gay Lussac, Biot, Humboldt, Ber↑thollet,↓ met once every week to prepare business for the Institute; and there are four volumes [126] published of Memoires or Transactions at Arceuil, which are the essence of all that was done in that time.

As I have elsewhere written, When [the Master of the Universe ⟨wishes⟩directs events,] ↑Jove has points to carry,↓ he impresses his will on the structure of minds.[143] Every one stands stupefied at the course of the War. None so wise as to have predicted anything that has occurred. Every one reads the ballot of the people on each [127] new question with ↑⟨glad⟩↓ surprise, and[n] the ⟨liber⟩ pious & once hopeless lover of freedom with trembling joy. And this surprise shows that nobody did it, or thought it, but the Lord alone.

You must not go to the sermons in the churches for the true theology, but talk with artists, naturalists, & other thoughtful men who are interested in verities↑,↓ & note how the idea of God lies in their minds. Not the less how the sentiment of duty & [128] impulse of virtue lies in the heart of the "bobbin-woman," of any unspoiled daughter or matron in the farm-house;—these are the crucial experiments, these the wells where the coy truth lies hid.[144]

↑*Truth*. The devil is the Eternal Liar.↓

In reading Henry Thoreau's Journal, I am very sensible of the vigor of his constitution. That ⟨same⟩ oaken strength which I noted whenever he walked or worked or surveyed wood lots, [129] the same unhesitating hand with which a field-laborer accosts a piece of work which I should shun as a waste of strength, Henry shows in his literary ⟨la-

---

[143] "When the Master . . . minds." is used, minus the insertion, in "Character," *W*, X, 99.

[144] Single vertical lines are drawn in pencil in the left margins of pp. [127] and [128] beside "You must . . . hid." The comma after "verities" is added in pencil.

bor⟩ ↑task↓. He has ⟨intellectual⟩ⁿ muscle, & ventures on & performs feats which I am forced to decline. In reading him, I find the same thought⟨s⟩[,] the same spirit that is in me, but he takes a step beyond, & illustrates by excellent images that which [130] I should have ⟨said⟩ ↑conveyed↓ in a sleepy generality. 'Tis ⟨just⟩ as if I went into a gymnasium, & saw youths leap ⟨&⟩, climb, & swing with a force unapproachable⟨.⟩↑,—though their feats are only continuations of my initial grapplings & ⟨& j⟩jumps.↓

It was a favorite anecdote at Divinity College in 1826, the Unitarian Committee man in N. Carolina who ⟨demanded his pay for preaching⟩ snubbed the poor preacher when he demanded his pay. "Who sent you"? "The Lord sent you! I don't think he knows there is any such man!"¹⁴⁵

[131] I see in the street ↑about the "saloons"↓ plenty of boys & men who are nuisances, but who only want a master to make them useful to themselves & to society. Slave-holding has then its good side. ↑"The saloons," said E[dmund]. Hosmer, "are worse than war to their customers."↓¹⁴⁶

All decomposition is recomposition. What we call consumption is energetic growth of the fungus or whatever new order. War disorganizes, but it also organizes[;] it forces individuals & [132] ⟨individuals⟩ ↑states↓ to combine & act with larger views, & under the best heads, & keeps the population together, producing the effect of cities; for camps are wandering cities.¹⁴⁷

June 29: 'Tis a rule of manners that we keep cool, & avoid tension. A lady loses her charm, as soon as she admires too easily & too much. In man or woman, the face & the person lose all power, when they are [133] on the strain to express approbation.¹⁴⁸

---

¹⁴⁵ This paragraph is in pencil. See *JMN*, XIII, 57.
¹⁴⁶ See pp. [40] and [81] above.
¹⁴⁷ "All decomposition is recomposition." and "War disorganizes ... organizes" are used in "The Man of Letters," *W*, X, 248. With the first, cf. also "Quotation and Originality," *W*, VIII, 204. For "it forces ... cities.", see Journal DL, p. [203] and WAR, p. [3] above. See also *JMN*, XIII, 291, p. [40] above and Journal KL, p. [53] below.
¹⁴⁸ "'Tis a rule ... approbation." is used in "Social Aims," *W*, VIII, 85 and 86.

The logic of Socrates reaches through all actions, all pleasures[.]

Selden C. Willey, Campton Village. 6 miles from Plymouth, N.H.

Selden J. Finney, at Lowell, during July, recommended by Catharine F. Stebbins. of Rochester N.Y.

Miss Caroline Gray, Buena Vista, Roxbury.

[134] My feeling about Henry James's book [*Substance and Shadow*] is that he is a certain Saul among the prophets. The logical basis of his book a certain pure & absolute theism:—there is but one Actor in the Universe,—there is no self but devil;—all must be surrendered to ecstasy of the present Deity. But the tone in which all this is taught is in perpetual [135] contemptuous chiding & satire.

The Arabs measure distance by horizons, and scholars must.[149]

'Twas odd that I woke at midnight, & mused on the indifference of all subjects to genius. Not dainty & fastid⟨us⟩ious is he, but accosts the nearest fact, high or humble. Like General Lee, "he carries his base with him," & shows you that God & his eternities are equally near to every point of humanity.

[136] Dr Rimmer's theory of sculpture.

Saadi, in the Bostan, makes the keeper of the horses say, "It is required as a talent of rulers, that every inferior person should be ↑well↓ known to him." So old is our rule. [*Moslicheddin Sadi's Lustgarten*] Bostan, [1850, I,] p. 42

[137]   ↑Inspiration alternated↓
Sometimes the electrical machine will not work; no spark will pass; then, ↑presently,↓ the world is all a cat's back, all sparkle & shock. Sometimes there is no sea-fire; and again the sea is all aglow. Some-

---

[149] See Journal DL, p. [104] above.

times the Aeolian harp is dumb all day in the window; & again it is
garrulous, & tells all the secrets of the world. In June, the mornings
are noisy with birds; &, in July, already they are getting old & silent.
↑Il n'y a que le matin↓
    ↑Napoleon's 1806 & 1807↓[150]

[138] Channing thinks Carlyle does not recognize the people, in
"Life of Friedrich"[.]
July 16 ⟨W⟩Rode this p.m. with Channing in wagon to White Pond.
'Tis perhaps ten years ago since I was there with him before, and in
the reflections of the larger grown trees in the lake noticed the same
peculiarities. The trees were all done in minute squares, as in the cro-
chet work of girls; the colors of the foliage, russet & ruddy, added to
the beauty. Pines on the distant shore, of which we saw only the short
stem veiled above by [139] the branches,—in the water showed the
stem of the tree to the top! We were on the farther side of the pond at
the "Cove," & talked with a party, ⟨of⟩—a young man & three young
women from Sudbury 3½ miles distant. They left the shore in a boat.
⟨W⟩ C[hanning]. & I agreed that a picnic is like a "revival," it changes
a man in an instant, & he forgets his home & habits, & thinks he will
come & live with Nature. But he returns to his village to put up his
horse, ⟨gets his [140] letters⟩ ↑stops↓ at the Post Office, takes tea with
his family, and does not for ten years get a glance at the Paradise
again. ↑After a bath in the Pond↓ came^n home by the beautiful road
through Nine-Acre-Corner, where ⟨all⟩ the farms were in richest array.
An old hemlock tree in one field should teach every body to plant ⟨a
he⟩and guard a hemlock, that it may some day be old.

↑words affords cords swords hordes boards lords↓[151]

[141] ↑Doctrine of Leasts.↓
    I should write on the power of minorities. Every book is written
with a constant secret reference to the few intelligent persons whom

---

[150] "Sometimes the . . . 1807" is struck through in pencil with a diagonal use mark.
For "Napoleon's . . . 1807", in pencil, see p. [275] below, and cf. *JMN*, XIV, 48.
"Sometimes the . . . silent." and "Il n'y a . . . matin" (see Journal VA, p. [198]) are used
in "Inspiration," *W*, VIII, 273–274 and 286.
    [151] "words affords . . . lords" is in pencil.

the writer knows or believes to exist in the million. Hosmer said,
"Christ was right, that few are saved." The artist has always the masters in his eye, though he affect to flout them. ⟨R⟩Michel Angelo is
thinking of Da Vinci, & Raffaelle is thinking of Michel Angelo. And
so in all the arts. McKay the shipbuilder thinks of Steers,—and Steers,
of Pook. Agassiz ⟨of⟩& Owen are addressing ostentatiously [142] the
American & English people, but really writing to each other. Everett
dreams of Webster. Tennyson would give all his popularity for ⟨the⟩ a
verdi⟨t⟩ct in his favor from Wordsworth.[152] Every generous youth capable of thought & action, with however bold a front & stoic demeanor, dwells in a little heaven within, with the images of a few men
& a few women, perhaps with two or one.

The names of the masters at the head of each department[n] [143] of
science, art, or quality are ⟨often⟩ little known to the world, but are always known to the adepts. As Robert Brown in Botany, Gauss in
Mathematics,
And I remember the good story Brisbane told me of his ⟨own⟩ search
in Paris after a master in the Science of Music. Invisible to all the rest,
this hierophant is resplendent to him. Indeed all his own work & culture forms the eye to see him.[153]

[144] The doctrine of culture of knowledge is that it comes from
the gods into one head, or a few heads, then down to the nearest re-
ceivers, & slowly thence to the multitude.[154]
It is quite the same with religious ⟨teacher⟩ souls, with Behmen, with
Fox, with Christ, with Buddh.
It is always one story, the introduction[n] of ↑Plotinus[,] Ammonius↓[.]

---

[152] "Every book . . . million." and "The artist . . . ostentatiously" are struck through
in ink with single vertical use marks on p. [141] and "the American . . . Wordsworth."
with two on p. [142]. With the exception of "Hosmer said . . . saved.' ", the paragraph is
used in "Progress of Culture," *W*, VIII, 219. For Hosmer's remark, see p. [81] above.

[153] "The names . . . Mathematics," struck through in ink with three diagonal use
marks on p. [142] and one vertical use mark on p. [143], and "Invisible to . . . him." are
used in "Progress of Culture," *W*, VIII, 219–220.

[154] With "The doctrine . . . multitude.", cf. pp. [189] and [227] below; *JMN*, X,
314; and "The Man of Letters," *W*, X, 249.

[145] ("That eternal Mr Graeter") *IT* 89

See influence of Ruskin
                    Darwin
                    Goethe
Intellectuality works down LM 57[155]

(In art, Winckelmann)

See in politics the importance of minorities of one, as of Socrates, of
Phocion, Cato, Lafayette, Carnot, Arago. Silent minorities of one also.
Thoreau, Very, Newcomb, Alcott,
For the power is after reality, & not after appearance; after quality, &
not after quantity:[156]

[146] ⟨T⟩Christianity existed in one ⟨man⟩ ↑child↓. But if the child had
been killed by Herod, would the element have been lost? God sends his
message, if not by one, then quite as well by another or could have
made every heart preach his commandment. When the Master of the
Universe has ⟨purposes⟩ ↑⟨ends⟩ends↓ to fulfill, he impresses his ⟨pur-
pose⟩ ↑will↓ on the structure of minds.[157]

[147]   ⟨Edmund Vincent
       Ann Arbor   Milwaukee, Wis.⟩

———

↑Ellery↓ Channing always speaks of the landscape as of a painting.

———

When Le Nòtre had completed the Gardens of the Tuileries, Colbert
wished to close them on the public. Charles Perrault resisted the inter-
diction, & obtained that this promenade should remain open to the citizens of Paris & to children. " 'Je suis persuadé,' disait il à Colbert, au

[155] "Plotinus Ammonius" (p. [144]) and "See influence . . . LM 57" are in pencil.
[156] "See in . . . Arago." and "For the . . . quantity:", struck through in ink with single vertical use marks, are used in "Progress of Culture," *W*, VIII, 220. For "For the
power . . . quantity:", see also p. [20] above.
[157] This paragraph, struck through in ink with a vertical use mark, is used in "Character," *W*, X, 98–99. For the last sentence, see p. [126] above.

milieu de la grande allée, 'que les jardins des Rois ne sont si grands et si spacieux, qu'afin que tous leurs enfans puissent s'y promene⟨s⟩r.' Le sourcilleux ministre ne [148] put s'empêcher de sourire." *Saint Beuve.* [*Nouveaux lundis,* 1863–1870, I, 300–301][158]

I went to Dartmouth College,[159] and found the same old Granny system which I met there 25 years ago. ⟨Dr Lord the⟩ President ⟨h⟩Lord has an aversion to emulation, as injurious to the character of the pupils. He therefore forbids the election of members into the t⟨h⟩wo literary societies by merit, but arranges that the first scholar alphabetically on the list shall be assigned to the [149] ↑Adelphi↓ ⟨Society⟩, & the second to the ↑Mathesians↓, the third to the ↑Adelphi↓, & the fourth to the ↑Mathesians↓; and so on,ⁿ every ⟨one⟩ ↑student↓ belonging to the one or the other.—"Well, but there is a first scholar in the class, is there not, & he has the first oration at Commencement?" "O no, the parts are assigned by lot."—The amiable student who explained it, added, that it tended to remove disagreeable excitement from the societies. I answered, Certainly and it would remove more [150] if there were no ⟨societies⟩ ↑college↓ at all. I recommended morphine in liberal dose⟨s⟩, at the College Commons. I learn, since my return, that the President has resigned;—the first good trait I have heard of in the man.

———

The accusation of being a heretic, hitherto in every country formidable[,] is ⟨no lon⟩ not so here today.

———

[151] Beranger told Rouget de Lisle, "À quarante deux ans, je n'avais pas de feu dans mon taudis même au plus fort de l'hiver. J étais résigné, et il m'est arrivé quelques rayons de soleil."
                    Saint Beuve. Nouveaux Lundis[, 1863–1870,] I, 183.

[158] Emerson borrowed this volume from the Boston Athenaeum July 24–August 1 and October 5–14, 1863.
    [159] Emerson delivered an address on the Scholar at Dartmouth on July 22, 1863; see "The Man of Letters," *W,* X, 239–258.

"Presque tous les bons ou↑v↓riers vivent longtemps: c'est qu'ils accomplis-
sent une loi de la Providence."[160] *Beranger* [*Ibid.*, I, 192]

[152] Temper ⟨th⟩the mortar. Do not write polemics, but
morals. It must be that you are the victim of talent, *noyé dans talent* as
they said of

"Les Francais commencent tout, et n'achèvent jamais rien."[161]

————   ————

Subjects.   Shakspeare in 1864

————

               California

————

[153] Resources

————

       Alternation of employment. See how Newton "refreshed"
       himself

————

       Life of Newton, p. 235[162]

————

Subjects   *Resources.* See *supra* p 81, 97,
           Greatness,   see *SO* 93
           Curiosities of Literature,   ↑*infra* 269↓

————

       Criticism on Bryant, Byron,

————

       Common joys. see *supra* p. 81

————

       Society.

[160] Emerson used a translation of "Presque tous . . . longtemps:" in "Old Age," *W*,
VII, 321.
   [161] This and the preceding entry are in pencil. For *"noyé dans talent"*, from Etienne
Dumont, *Recollections of Mirabeau* . . . , see *JMN*, IX, 137, and "The Scholar," *W*, X,
279.
   [162] "Resources . . . p. 235" is in pencil. With "Alternation . . . himself ", cf. *JMN*,
XIII, 428, and "Resources," *W*, VIII, 149 and 150. Sir David Brewster, *The Life of Sir
Isaac Newton* (New York, 1831) is in Emerson's library.

———

Influences of a great city. *see* ↑*FOR* 83, 106,↓ p. 257 *infra*

———

Massachusetts. see *infra* p. 265

———

Tennyson

———

Carlyle[163]
Doctrine of Leasts, 141

———

The good of bad people; good in everybody. see p. 201

———

[154] Catherine the Great, after talking with Diderot & Grimm, said, on rising to go to a council of state, "Maintenant, il faut songer au ga-⟨ne⟩gnepain." [Sainte-Beuve, *Nouveaux lundis,* 1863–1870, I, 340.]

The more ambitious a state is, the more vulnerable. England, France, have ships, towns, colonies, treasure, & can very ill afford to give every Yankee skipper a chance to hack at these. A mob has nothing to lose, & can afford to steal. But England & France [155] not.

All⟨l⟩ degrees in the republic of letters, as in every other state; men of useful & popular talent for daily use, wh⟨i⟩ose efficiency is exactly limited, & not embarrassed by ideal expansions. They can, as lawyers & statesmen, furnish you with just the amount of information or explanation this quarter of an hour requires, just as a marketman [156] measures out to you a peck or a half of a half peck of peas.
And there are those who cannot do this, but are not less wanted, are

---

[163] *"Resources."* and *"Greatness,"* are struck through in ink with single diagonal use marks. "Curiosities of Literature," and "Common joys." are each struck through in ink with two diagonal use marks. "*FOR* 83, 106," is in pencil. "Tennyson" and "Carlyle" and the rule between are in pencil. "Resources" was the opening lecture in the "American Life" series, delivered in Boston on November 27, 1864. The sixth lecture, "Character," contained a section on *"Greatness"*; see "Character," *W*, X, 102. Emerson developed "Influences of a great city" and "Massachusetts" in the fourth lecture, "Table-Talk"; see Gohdes, *Uncollected Lectures,* 1932, pp. 36 and 38. He discussed English and American writers in the fifth lecture, "Books"; see *ibid.,* pp. 40 and 41.

much more wanted,—who know the foundations of law & politics, and
are to the lawyer as the botanist is to the market man. Mediocre people wish to utilize you, to make of Newton a bank-clerk, and in all
ways act to pull you down from [157] a high career. ↑(See infra, *FOR*
158)↓
Hawthorne unlucky in having for a friend a man who cannot be be-
friended; whose miserable administration ⟨can⟩ admits but of one excuse, imbecility. ⟨H⟩Pierce was either the worst, or he was ⟨what Conway calls him,⟩ the weakest of all our Presidents.

[158] I was to write that our people have false delight in talent, in a
showy speech, a lawyer who can carry his point, in Webster, Choate,
Butler, Banks, in Macaulay, & in innumerable Goughs & Dunlaps
without considering their soundness or truth. But the measure in art &
in intellect is one; To what end? Is it yours to do? Are you bound by
character & conviction to that part you take? The very definition
[159] of Art is, the inspiration of a just design working through all the
details.[164] But the ⟨being dazzled by the⟩ ↑forsaking the design to produce effect by showy↓ details, is the ⟨shipwreck⟩ ↑ruin↓ of any work.
Then begins shallowness of effect; ↑intellectual↓ bankruptcy of the
artist. All goes wrong. Artist & public corrupt each other. Now the
public are always children. The majority are young [160] & ignorant,
⟨&⟩ unable to distinguish tinsel from gold, ornament from beauty. But
⟨it ⟨infinitely⟩ concerns⟩ the scholar ⟨to⟩ ↑must↓ keep faith with himself.[165] His sheet-anchor is sincerity; and, when he loses this, he loses
really the talent of his talent[.]

Mem. Aug. 25. Coombs worked ⅔ of a day on the apple trees grub-
bing out borers, & declared it was the best time in the year for it.

[161]   Taháwus
    Thrust on ⟨my eye⟩ ↑/our eyes/the eye/↓ its unexpected form.[166]

---

[164] A vertical line is drawn in pencil in the left margin beside "of Art . . . details."
[165] "&", "it", and "concerns" are canceled in pencil; "must" is added in pencil.
[166] "my eye" is canceled in pencil; "the eye" and "our eyes" are added in pencil.
Tahawus—"he who splits the sky"—is the poetic Indian word that Charles Fenno Hoff-
man proposed as an alternative name for Mount Marcy (elevation 5,344 ft.), the highest
of the Adirondack peaks. Cf. "The Adirondacs," l. 10, *W,* IX, 182.

In the war, the American government stands for the ideal or semi-ideal side[.][167]

The regiment—it is the colonel & the captains.

Is Wordsworth a bell with a wooden tongue?[168]

[162]   Miscellanies. Vol. II[169]

Discourse at Concord on First of August 1844
Address to the Citizens of Concord on the Fugitive-Slave-Law. 3 May, 1851
Lecture in the Tabernacle, N.Y.
    Seventh of March, 1854.
Lecture in Boston 1855
American Civilization
    Substance of Lecture at Washington Jan. 1862
Emancipation ⟨1 Jan⟩ ↑Sept.,↓ 186⟨3⟩2

[167] Cf. the lecture "Fortune of the Republic," in *W*, XI, 644 and 645.

[168] The image is from a consolatory remark made to one of Confucius' disciples: "The empire has been long without the principles of truth and right; Heaven is going to use your master as a bell with its wooden tongue." See James Legge, *The Chinese Classics . . .*, 5 vols. (Hong Kong and London, 1861–1872), I, "Prolegomena," p. 77. Volume I contains "Confucian Analects, The Great Learning, and The Doctrine of the Mean." See *L*, V, 338, dated October 16, 1863.

[169] The first volume of "Miscellanies" was undoubtedly *Nature; Addresses and Lectures,* published by James Munroe & Co., Boston, in 1849, and reprinted as *Miscellanies; Embracing Nature, Addresses, and Lectures* by Phillips, Sampson & Co., Boston, in 1856. Fifteen of the lectures and articles listed below appear in an 1862 list for a "Proposed Book of Occasional Discourses" in Journal GL, p. [393] above. Of those which appear only in this 1863 list, two were used in *Society and Solitude* in 1870: "Books" (*W*, VII, 187–221), published in the *Atlantic Monthly,* I (Jan. 1858), 343–353; and the first half of "American Civilization" ("Civilization," *W*, VII, 17–34) as given in Washington, D.C. on January 31, 1862, and published in the *Atlantic Monthly,* IX (Apr. 1862), 502–511. Part of the speech given at Sleepy Hollow Cemetery on September 29, 1855, was used in "Immortality" (*W*, VIII, 321–352), published in *Letters and Social Aims* in 1875. The remainder, including the second part of "American Civilization" (*W*, XI, 295–311), and the rest of the "Address to the Inhabitants of Concord at the Consecration of Sleepy Hollow" (*W*, XI, 427–436), were published after Emerson's death in *Miscellanies,* 1884. The "Lecture in Boston 1855" may have been either the lecture on slavery given January 25 (ms. in Houghton Library), or "Woman" (*W*, XI, 403–426), given September 20 before the Woman's Rights Convention. "The Emancipation Proclamation" (*W*, XI, 313–326),

[163] Address to Kossuth; May, 1852
Speech at Sleepy Hollow Cemetery. 1855
Speech on the Sumner Outrage. May, 185⟨8⟩6,
Speech at Cambridge on Kansas Affairs. Sept., 1856.
Speech at Burns Festival, 25 Jan., 1859.
Speech on John Brown, Dec., 1859.
Speech on Theodore Parker⟨s⟩, 1860.

> Domestic Life (Conway's "Dial")
> Books   (Atlantic)
> Eloquence   (Atlantic)
> Carlyle   (Dial)
> Landor   (Dial)
> Peace   (Aesthetic Papers)

[164] Persian Poets   (Atlantic)
> Society & Solitude.   (Atlantic)
> Old Age.   (Atlantic)
> ⟨American Civilization⟩

[165] Carlyle has sacrificed to force of statement. One would say, none has ever equalled his ⟨power⟩ executive power in the use of English. He makes an irresistible statement, which stands, & which every body remembers & repeats. It is like the new Parrot↑t↓ guns.[170] There were always guns & powder. But here today are latest experiments & ⟨b⟩a success which exceeds all [166] previous performance in throwing far, & in crushing effect. Much is sacrificed for this, but this is done. So with Carlyle's projectile style.

———

probably the same lecture as that delivered October 12, 1862, before the Parker Fraternity in Boston, was printed as "The President's Proclamation" in the *Atlantic Monthly*, X (Nov, 1862), 638–642. The "Address to Kossuth at Concord, May 11, 1852" (*W*, XI, 395–401) was published in *Kossuth in New England: A Full Account of the Hungarian Governor's Visit to Massachusetts;* . . . (Boston, 1852), pp. 222–224. The lecture on "Peace" ("War," *W*, XI, 149–176), delivered March 12, 1838, before the American Peace Society in Boston, was published as "War" in *Aesthetic Papers,* ed. E. P. Peabody (Boston, 1849), pp. 36–50.

[170] The "t" is added in pencil. The new gun, invented by Robert P. Parrott, had a wrought-iron hoop welded into the breech to prevent it from bursting.

Sennott quotes, from Calhoun (?) the phrase, "the fatal exercise of domineering talk."

———

I can almost pardon scorn in a person who walks well.

———

War to the knife, war to the eye.

———

incandescent souls—
famished curiosity.

[167] Taine generalizes rashly, & writes; "La race façonne l'individu, le pays façonne la race. Un degré de chaleur dans l'air et d'inclinaison dans le sol est la cause première de nos facultés et de nos passions." &c. Saint Beuve remarks on this; "Entre un fait aussi général et aussi commun à tous que le sol et le climat, et un résultat aussi compliqué et aussi divers que la variété des espèces et des individus qui y vivent, il y a place pour quantité de causes et de forces plus particulières, plus immediates, et tant qu'on [168] ne les a pas saisies, on n'a rien expliqué."   *"Causeries du Lundi."* [1851–1862] Vol. 13, p. 213–214.

See also a just censure in the like spirit on Taine's proposed formula of each mind, as of Livy.
        ——— ibid. p. 222–3

↑homesickness↓
"Mal de la capitale." *Mme de Stael.*[171]

"O le ruisseau de la rue du Bac!" cried Mme. de Stael, when they showed ↑her↓ the mirror of Lake Leman. She said to M. Molé, "Si ce n'était le respect humain, je n'ouvrirais pas ma fenêtre pour voir la baie de Naples pour la première fois, tandis que je ferais cinq cents [169] lieues pour aller causer avec un homme d'esprit que je ne connais pas."[172]   St Beuve Portraits de Femmes [1852,] p 139

---

[171] Charles Augustin Sainte-Beuve, *Portraits de femmes* (Paris, 1852), p. 136. Emerson borrowed this book from the Boston Athenaeum October 5, 1863–January 27, 1864 and December 17–19, 1864. The 1856 edition is in his library. "homesickness" is in pencil. A vertical line is drawn in pencil in the left margin beside the quotation.

[172] A translation of this quotation is used in "Social Aims," *W*, VIII, 94, and "Table-Talk," in Gohdes, *Uncollected Lectures*, 1932, p. 33.

———

She said, "Mes opinions politiques sont des noms propres."[173] [*Ibid.*,
p. 129]

———

Chapitre "De l'amour," dans "L'influence des Passions."[174]

———

"N'ayez pas de zèle." *Talleyrand* [*Ibid.*, p. 128]

———

Mme. de Tessé said, "Si j'étais reine, j'ordonnerais à Mme de Staël de
me parler toujours."[175]

           Saint Beuve—Portraits de femmes [1852,] p. 140
See the contrast of Coppet & Ferney   *ibid* p[p. 140–]141

[170] ↑1863↓ Oct. 7 ↑When he passed the woods on the way to the
city,ⁿ how they reproached him!↓
Scholar joined every club & society, accepted every invitation to soi-
rees, but, when the hour came, declined one & the other, in favor of
the book or meditation at the moment occupying him, & which
derived a new zest from the offered invitation: And at last it appeared
that this caprice was calculated.

———

     Tentasse decorum est.[176]

———

     [171] depascitur vultu.[177]
"tangles of Naeera's hair" [Milton, *Lycidas*, l. 69]

happy expression of Dan[ie]l. Webster that "Long Island Sound
ought to be lighted up like a ballroom."

———

[173] "She said, . . . propres.' " is struck through in pencil with a diagonal use mark.
[174] Madame de Staël's *De l'influence des passions sur bonheur des individus et des na-*
tions (Lausanne, 1796) is mentioned by Sainte-Beuve in *Portraits de femmes*, 1852, pp. 102
and 134.
[175] " 'N'ayez pas . . . toujours.' " is struck through in pencil with a diagonal use
mark. " 'N'ayez pas de zèle.' " is used in "Social Aims," *W*, VIII, 85. See also *JMN*, VI,
363, Journal DL, p. [230] above, and p. [171] below. "Mme. de Tessé . . . toujours.' " is
used in translation in "Social Aims," *W*, VIII, 95. See also Journal WAR, p. [259]
above.
[176] "It is fitting to be tried" (Ed.).
[177] "He is wasted in face" (Ed.).

In manners, how a man makes his inferiors his superiors, by a little heat⟨.⟩! ↑Ayez pas de Zêle↓[178]

In manners, how impossible to overcome an unlucky temperament, unless by living with the well-bred⟨,⟩ from the start!
↑——
Of Temperament, see *Orientalist*, p 225↓
——

Intellectual men pass for vulgar, & are timid & heavy with the elegant: but exhibit the best style [172] if the elegant are intellectual.[179] But the dancer⟨'⟩s' violin, or Beethoven's music even, degrades them instantly in manners, if they are not also musical.
Laws of society, a forever engaging topic. At Sir Wm Molesworth's house, I asked Milnes to get me safely out: he behaved very well.[180] ⟨A great fortune is⟩An impassive temperament⟨.⟩ ↑is a great fortune↓: Que de chos⟨s⟩es ↑dont↓ je peux me ⟨do⟩ passer![181] even dancing & music, if I had that. F. B. the lawyer, told me that a couple of glasses of wine might be taken with advantage, when he was to address a jury. And [173] the evening society is no doubt ⟨better⟩ ↑easi⟨er⟩lier↓ faced for the preceding dinner.

Young men think that ⟨vigor requires⟩ the manly Character requires that they should go to California, or India, or to war. When they have learned that the parlor demands as much courage as the sea, or the camp, they will be willing to consult their own strength & education in their choice of place.[182]

[174]   ↑*Aplomb.*↓
State your opinion affirmatively, & ⟨not⟩ without apology. Why need you who are not a gossip, talk as a gossip, and ⟨as⟩tell eagerly what

---

[178] This entry, struck through in pencil with a diagonal use mark, is used in "Social Aims," *W*, VIII, 86 and 85. For the insertion, see p. [169] above.

[179] "In manners, how impossible . . . style" is struck through in pencil with a diagonal use mark. "In manners . . . start!" and "Intellectual men . . . intellectual." are used in "Social Aims," *W*, VIII, 79 and 82.

[180] See *JMN*, X, 532.

[181] The French sentence is from Renan, *Essais de morale*, 1860, p. 374.

[182] "Young men . . . place." is used in "Greatness," *W*, VIII, 304.

↑the Journals, or↓ Mr Sumner, or Mr Stanton, say. The attitude is the main thing. John Bradshaw was all his life a consul sitting in judgment on kings.[183] Carlyle has best of all men in England kept the manly attitude in ⟨this⟩his time. His errors of opinion are as nothing in comparison with this merit, in my opinion. And, if I look for a counterpart in my neighborhood, Thoreau & Alcott are the best, & in majesty Alcott exceeds. This aplomb cannot be mimicked. It is the speaking to the heart of the thing.[184] And [175] a person of a feeble spirit, if intellectual, is instantly reinforced ⟨if his⟩ ↑by being put into intellectual↓ company↑,↓[n] ⟨is intellectual,⟩ &, to the surprise of everybody, becomes a lawgiver.   See *infra*, p. 199[185]

⟨To keep a⟩ School↑-keeping↓[n] is a dreary task, only relieved by the pleasure the teacher takes in two or three ⟨or four⟩ bright & beautiful pupils. The majority of the children will be ⟨brutal, or,—to use a milder word,—⟩[n] infidels⟨,⟩↑,—↓and the consoler is—the appearance of genius ↑& noble nature↓ in one or another.[186]

[176] *Confucius* ↑Born B.C.[n] 551.↓ says, "Now ↑all↓ over the empire carriages have ⟨all⟩ wheels of the same size;⟨"⟩ all writing is with the same characters; & for conduct there are the same rules." [Legge,] Doctrine of the Mean. [*The Chinese Classics* . . . , 1861–1872, I, 288]

———

See a passage in the Notes of *Legge*. [*Ibid.*,] Vol. 1. p. 294
"Of their seeing & hearing, their thinking & revolving, their moving & acting, men all say, It is from *Me*. Every one thus brings out his self, & his smallness becomes known. But let the body be taken away, & all would be

---

[183] The reference to John Bradshaw, one of the regicide judges, is from John Milton, *The Second Defense of the People of England,* in *Prose Works,* ed. James Augustus St. John, 5 vols. (London, 1848–1853), I, 268, in Emerson's library. The sentence is used in "Character," *W*, III, 109–110, and "Samuel Hoar," *W*, X, 441. See also *JMN*, VI, 347.

[184] "Why need . . . main thing." is struck through in pencil with a diagonal use mark. "State your . . . main thing." is used in "Social Aims," *W*, VIII, 86. "Carlyle has . . . opinion." and "This aplomb . . . thing." are used in "Carlyle," *W*, X, 497.

[185] "a person . . . p. 199" runs over onto the bottom of p. [175] and is set off from the other entry on the page by a long rule.

[186] "To keep a" is canceled and "-keeping" added in pencil. "or four" is canceled in both pencil and ink. "brutal, . . . word,—" is canceled in pencil. "& noble nature" is added in pencil.

Heaven. How can the body be taken away? Simply by subduing & removing that self-having of the ego. This is the taking it away. That [177][187] being done, so wide & great as Heaven is, my mind is as wide & great, & production & transformation cannot be separated from me. Hence it is said,—how vast is ⟨this⟩his Heaven!"   Note. p. 294

The text is, "Call him man in his ideal, how earnest is he! Call him an abyss, how deep is he! Call him Heaven, how vast is he!" [*Ibid.*, p. 294]
I am reading a better Pascal.

"It is said in the *Book of Poetry*, 'Over her embroidered robe she puts a plain single garment.' ⟨Just⟩ so it is the way of the superior man to prefer the concealment of his virtue, while [178][188] it daily becomes more illustrious, and the way of the mean man to seek notoriety, while he daily goes more & more to ruin. It is characteristic of the superior man, appearing insipid, yet never to produce satiety; while showing a simple negligence, yet to have his accomplishments recognized; while seemingly plain, yet to be discriminating. He knows how what is distant lies in what is near.
—— when↑ce↓ the wind proceeds from, how what is minute becomes manifested," Vol 1. Legge [*Ibid.*, p]p. [294-]295

[179] "↑tho'↓ The fish sinks & lies at the bottom, it is clearly seen." [*Ibid.*, p. 295]

"In hewing an axe handle, the pattern is not far off." We grasp one axe-handle to hew ⟨an⟩the other. [*Ibid.*, p. 257]

"In all things, success depends on previous preparation, & without such preparation, there is sure to be failure. If what is spoken be previously determined, there will be no stumbling." [*Ibid.*, pp. 275-276]

he proceeds;
"If a⟨l⟩ffairs be previously determined, there will be no difficulty with them. If one's actions be ⟨&c⟩ ↑previously determined,↓ there will be no sorrow in

---

[187] "Question. What is a sea-horizon? 12 miles, or 24? Boulevard & avenue" was inscribed in ink at the top of p. [177] earlier, a long rule added, and "being done . . . p. 294" continued below it.
[188] "Confucius" is added at the top of p. [178].

connection with them. If principles of conduct ⟨&c⟩ ↑be↓, the practice of them will be inexhaustible" *Legge* [*Ibid.*, p.] 276[189]

[180]   Confucius
"It is characteristic of ⟨the most⟩ entire sincerity to be able to foreknow."
                                                                    Ib p 281

"The individual possessed of complete sincerity is like a spirit."[190]
                                                                    [*Ibid.*, p. 282]

"The way of heaven & Earth may be declared in a sentence:—They are without any doubleness, & so they produce things in a manner that is unfathomable." [*Ibid.*, p. 284]

Heaven is a shining spot, yet sun, mo⟨n⟩on, stars, constellations are suspended in it; the earth is a handful of soil, but sustains mountains like Hwa & Yoh without feeling their weight, & contains rivers & seas without leaking away: ↑the↓ water we behold is but a ladleful, yet [181] iguana, iguanodon, turtle & dragon & whale [*Ibid.*, pp. 284–285]

To the colleges, "Learning without Thought is labor lost: thought without ⟨labor⟩ learning is perilous." [*Ibid.*, p. 14]

"The accomplished scholar is not a utensil." [*Ibid.*, p. 14]

——————

Here is an acute observation that belongs to "Classes of Men."[191]

——————

"The Master said, The faults of men are characteristic of the class to which they belong. By observing a man's faults, it may be known that he is virtuous."   *Legge* [*Ibid.*,] *1.* p. 31

——————

[189] " 'In all . . . stumbling.' " and "he proceeds; . . . *Legge* 276" are struck through in pencil with single diagonal use marks.
    [190] " 'It is . . . foreknow.' " and " 'The individual . . . spirit.' " are struck through in pencil with single diagonal use marks.
    [191] The lecture "Classes of Men" was first given in Boston before the Parker Fraternity on November 20, 1860.

"The superior man thinks of virtue, the small man thinks of comfort."[192]

[*Ibid.,*] p. 32

[182]   ↑*Culture*↓
"It is from music that the finish is received." Confucius [*Ibid.,* p. 75]

"The subjects on which the Master did not talk, were—extraordinary things, feats of strength, disorder, & Spiritual beings." [*Ibid.,*] p. 65

"If the search for riches were sure to be successful, tho' I should become a groom with whip in hand to get them, I will do so. As the search may not be successful, I will follow after that which I love."[193] [*Ibid.,*] p 62

"Is virtue a thing remote? I wish to be virtuous, & lo! virtue is at hand."
[*Ibid.,*] p 68

[183]   ↑Confucius↓
"The master said, I have not seen one who loves virtue as he loves beauty."
[*Ibid.,*] p. 86

———

"Confucius said to Ke Kang, 'Sir, in carrying on your govt. why should you use killing at all? Let your evinced desires be for what is good, & the people will be good: the relation between superiors & inferiors is like that between the wind & the grass. The grass must bend when the wind blows across it.' Ke Kang, distressed about the number of thieves in the state, inquired of Confucius ⟨about⟩ how to do [184][194] away with them? Confucius said, If you, sir, were not covetous, although you should reward them to do it, they would not steal."[195] [*Ibid.,*] Vol 1 p[p]. 122[–123]

"Your good careful people of the villages are the thieves of Virtue."
[*Ibid.,*] p. 188

---

[192] This quotation is struck through in pencil with a diagonal use mark.

[193] This quotation, struck through in pencil with a diagonal use mark, is used in "Social Aims," *W,* VIII, 100.

[194] "Confucius" is added at the top of p. [184].

[195] " 'Confucius said . . . & the grass." is struck through in ink on p. [183] with a vertical use mark, which Emerson extended through "The grass must . . . across it.' "; "Ke Kang, . . . steal.' " is struck through in ink with a vertical use mark on p. [183], and three diagonal use marks on p. [184]. The entire quotation is used in "Character," *W,* X, 120; "Confucius said, 'If you . . . steal.' " is used in "Speech at Banquet in Honor of the Chinese Embassy, Boston, 1868," *W,* XI, 473.

"Tze Kung asked, Is there one word which may serve as a rule of practice for all one's life? The Master said, Is not Reciprocity such a word? What you do not want done to yourself, do not to others."[196] [*Ibid.*, p. 165]

[185]　　↑Confucius↓
"The superior m⟨en⟩an is correctly firm, & not firm merely."

[*Ibid.*, p. 169]

"The superior man cannot be known in little matters; but he may be intrusted with great concerns. The small man may not be intrusted with great concerns, but he may be known in little matters."[197] [*Ibid.*, p. 168]

Confucius (was with his disciples under the shade of a large tree)[198]

[*Ibid.*, "Prolegomena," p. 79]

A Ching man said, there was a man at the east gate having the disconsolate appearance of a stray dog, (meaning Confucius)[.][199] Life Legge [*Ibid.*, "Prolegomena," p. 79]

[186] The founder of the Tsin Dynasty burned all the Histories & classic books in the Empire, & "books of the Hundred Schools" (excepting those in the hands of the govt.). The next year (2⟨07⟩11 B.C.)[,] it being discovered that 460 scholars had violated the prohibitions↑,↓ they were all buried alive in pits. The Emperor's eldest son, Foo Soo, remonstrated with him↑,↓ but was sent off from court to be with the general who was building the great wall.[200]

See Legge. [*Ibid.*,] *Prolegomena* [pp. 6–9]

Confucius born 551 B.C.

---

[196] With this quotation, cf. "Speech at Banquet in Honor of the Chinese Embassy, Boston, 1868," *W*, XI, 473. See p. [187] below.

[197] A vertical line is drawn in pencil in the left margin beside this quotation.

[198] "(was with . . . tree)" is struck through in ink with two curved use or cancellation marks.

[199] Two vertical lines are drawn in pencil in the left margin beside "A Ching . . . Confucius)".

[200] The inserted commas are in pencil.

Some strong examples again of oriental punishments in Malte Brun; Article *Persia*. [*Universal Geography . . .*, 1824–1831, II, 292–294]

———

[187] "After the death of ↑King↓ Wan, was not the cause of truth lodged ⟨with me⟩ here in me↑?↓[201] If Heaven had wished to let this cause of truth perish, then I, a future mortal, should not have got such a relation to th⟨e⟩at cause? While heaven does not let the cause of truth perish, what can the people of Kwang do to me?" [Legge, *The Chinese Classics*, 1864, I,] Prolegomena p. 96

He anticipated the speech of Socrates, & the *Do as be done by,* of Jesus.[202]

"The bird chooses its tree, the tree does not chase the bird," he replied to ⟨King Wan⟩ ↑Kan Wang↓.[203] [*Ibid.,* "Prolegomena," p. 84]

[188] 'Tis strange, ⟨he said,⟩ that it is not in vogue to commit hari-kari as the Japanese do at 60. Nature is *so* insulting in her hints & notices, does not pull you by the sleeve, but pulls out your teeth, tears off your hair ↑in patches↓, ⟨puts out⟩ ↑steals↓ your eyesight, ⟨makes a bad mask of your face, puts,⟩ ↑twists your face into an ugly mask,↓ in short, ↑puts↓ all contumelies upon you, without in the least abating your ⟨vanity or⟩ zeal to make a good appearance, and all this at the same time that she is moulding the ↑new↓ figures around you into wonderful beauty ↑which, of course is only making your plight worse↓. ↑See *infra*, p. 292↓[204]

[189] A day is a magnificent work, but a day ⟨of⟩ ↑is one thing to↓ Shakspeare & ⟨a day of King James are unlike⟩ ↑another to↓ John A Coomb↓.[205]

———

[201] The question mark is added in pencil.

[202] With this entry, cf. "Speech at Banquet in Honor of the Chinese Embassy, Boston, 1868," *W,* XI, 472. See p. [184] above.

[203] "Kan Wang" is added in pencil.

[204] "he said," is canceled in pencil and ink; "puts out" is canceled and "steals" added in pencil; "new" and "See *infra*, p. 292" are added in pencil.

[205] "of" is canceled and "is one thing to" added in pencil; "a day . . . unlike" is canceled and "another to . . . Coomb" added in pencil.

———

The knowledge of Europe leaks out into Persia, & India, & to the very Caffres. Every joke of ⟨Sheridan⟩ Rabelais, Sheridan, & Tom Appleton, travels across the ⟨line⟩Line, & you will find it at Capetown.
↑printed I think in *"Originality & Quotation"*↓[206]

———

You can take better care of your secret, than another can.[207]

The scholar died leaving nothing but his desk & pens. [Chardin, *Voyages . . . en Perse, . . . ,* 1811, V, 14]

"Three things are known only in three places; Valor, which knows itself only in war; Wisdom, w⟨———⟩hich   only in anger; and friendship which ——— only in need." *Persian sayings* ⌊Chardin⌋ [*Ibid.,* p. 16]
"Either death, or a friend."[208] [*Ibid.,* p. 16]
"Three things lengthen life,—fine clothes, fine house, and a beautiful woman." [*Ibid.,* p. 21]

[190] ↑Franklin said, "Travel lengthens life."↓[209]
What Arabian Rochefoucauld said?
"The reason why grandfathers love their grandchildren so much, is because they are the enemies of their enemies, inasmuch as they wish the death of those who wish theirs."   *Ap. Chardin* V. Vol. 21.

The king's servant is king himself. [*Ibid.,* p. 22]

"Who does not teach his child a profession, brings him up to steal."
[*Ibid.,* p. 22]

[206] "The knowledge . . . Capetown.", struck through in ink with two diagonal use marks and marked in the right margin with a vertical line in pencil, is used in "Speech at the Second Annual Meeting of the Free Religious Association, at Tremont Temple, Friday, May 28, 1869," *W,* XI, 487. See p. [227] below. The insertion is set off from the sentence below with a curved line.
[207] Sir John Chardin, *Voyages du Chevalier Chardin, en Perse, et Autres Lieux de l'Orient . . . ,* ed. L. Langlès, 10 vols. (Paris, 1811), V, 11. Emerson borrowed this volume from the Boston Athenaeum October 16–31, 1863.
[208] Two vertical lines are drawn in ink in the left margin beside this translation, which is used in "Social Aims," *W,* VIII, 89.
[209] "Franklin said . . . life.' " is added in pencil.

"Pensez au voisin, avant que de penser à la maison." [*Ibid.*, p. 23]

"Who cultivates one garden at a time will eat birds:
Who cultivates many gardens at once, the ⟨wi⟩birds will eat ↑up↓
him." [*Ibid.*, p. 24] ↑Well, our farmers cultivate many gardens—in
their too many acres.↓²¹⁰

————

Un peu de beauté vaut mieux que beaucoup de richesses. [*Ibid.*, p. 30]

————

[191] "My heart is on my son, the heart of my son is on a stone."
                                                          [*Ibid.*, p. 25]

"Who wishes pearls must cast himself into the sea; & who wishes
greatness, must wake allⁿ ↑⟨every⟩↓ night."   [*Ibid.*, p. 26]

"⟨If you⟩ use wine ill, you will become a wretch; ⟨if you⟩ use it well, you
will become an illustrious man."²¹¹ [*Ibid.*, p. 26]

"⟨You must⟩ eat at your table, as you would eat at the table of a
king."²¹² [*Ibid.*, p. 27]

If you don't throw the hook, you won't catch the fish. [*Ibid.*, p. 28]

You must go by night in order to arrive by day at the moment. [*Ibid.*,
p. 28]

[192] When the wolf has found ⟨the⟩ flesh, he never ⟨troubles himself⟩
↑asks↓ whether it is the camel of Abraham or the ass of Antichrist.
[*Ibid.*, p. 30]

Humility. ↑*ap.* Chardin↓ "Faites vous terre, si vous voulez porter du
fruit, c'est à dire, qu'il faut être humble pour faire de bonnes actions."
[*Ibid.*, p. 32]

————

²¹⁰ "Well, our . . . acres." is added in pencil; the short rule below is overwritten by
"farmers".
²¹¹ "If you" and "if you" are canceled in pencil.
²¹² This translation, struck through in pencil with a diagonal use mark, is used in
"Social Aims," *W*, VIII, 85, where Emerson attributes it to Confucius.

Sensibility.

The world is an echo which returns to us what we say.[213]

[*Ibid.*, p. 33]

Les bons mo⟨s⟩ts des rois sont les rois des bons mots.[214] [*Ibid.*, p. 92]

The Sultan /Casbin/Casvin/ said, "I have not so much fear of the swords of men, as of the needles of women." [*Ibid.*, p. 113]

[193] Dzoul-Noun of Gr⟨eat⟩and Cairo said to the King, "I have learned that one ↑to↓ whom you have ⟨sent with⟩ ↑given↓ power in⟨to⟩ the country treats the subjects with severity, & ⟨suffers⟩ ↑permits↓ daily violences & wrongs to take place." The king replied, "There will come a day when I will severely punish him."↑—↓"Yes, you will wait until he has taken all the ⟨goods⟩ ↑property↓ of the subjects, & then, ⟨by great strokes you will⟩ ↑you will bestir yourself, &↓ snatch them from him, & will fill your treasury. But what good will that do to ⟨yu⟩your po⟨r⟩or & miserable people?" The king was ashamed, & ordered ⟨his⟩ ↑the↓ instant punishment of the offender[.][215]
Chardin, 5th Vol p[p. 103–]104

[194] ⟨The time to eat⟩ Do not eat until the appetite is voracious, *nor speak until the necessity is extreme,* nor ⟨sleep⟩lie down until you sleep standing,[216] [*Ibid.*, p. 113]

The miller is an idle man & makes the ⟨stream⟩brook ↑or the wind↓ do his work. The poet is an idler man, hates the trouble of ↑consecutive↓ thinking, but ⟨has had the wit to fasten pens on the end of⟩ ↑observing that↓ these tempestuous passions of his ⟨which⟩ search

---

[213] This translation is used in "Greatness," *W*, VIII, 319. See p. [236] below.

[214] This sentence, struck through in ink with three diagonal use marks, is used in translation in "Saadi," *The Atlantic Monthly*, XIV (July 1864), 33–37, and Emerson's preface to Saadi, *The Gulistan or Rose Garden*, trans. Francis Gladwin (Boston, 1865), p. xiii.

[215] This paragraph, struck through in ink with two diagonal use marks, is used in Emerson's preface to Saadi, *The Gulistan . . .* , 1865, pp. xiii–xiv.

[216] *"nor speak . . . extreme,"* is underlined in pencil. The sentence in Chardin goes on: "et s'approcher d'une femme, quand la passion d'amour est au suprême degré."

all his knowledge, all his thought, all his sentiment, in their fury;—he fastens pens on ↑the end↓ [of] these, & they write songs, ⟨&⟩ prophecies, ⟨&⟩ tragedies & lampoons, that last till the morning of the Resurrection.

↑The daily problem is how to get force.

Borrowed the hint of the selfregistering thermometer.↓[217]

[195] Chardin has a Persian saying in reference to the works of a poet whose name I cannot find in Von Hammer;

"Si les vers élégans de ⟨Dhouair⟩Dhoair Faryaby te tombent sous la main, ne manque pas de les dérober, fut-ce meme dans ⟨t⟩le temple sacré de la Mekke."[218] [Chardin, *Voyages . . . en Perse, . . . ,* 1811, V, 131]

———

I love a book, as Montaigne, Bayle, or Heyne did, not quite as Gam. Bradford.

———

[196] People do not read much. ⟨If th you wish to ⟨can have the⟩ keep the secret of a⟩The beautiful ⟨passage⟩ ↑sentence↓ ⟨a hundred pages⟩ ↑was↓ on the ⟨th|| . . . ||⟩102 page of the printed volume⟨,⟩.[n] ⟨a⟩ ↑I know that the↓ hundred pages will protect it↑,↓ ⟨for you⟩ as well as ⟨all the keys of your cabinet.⟩ ↑if it were locked in my safe.↓

↑He tears into a book for a sentence as a woodpecker grubs into a tree for a worm[.]↓[219]

———

In Rhode Island, they say, a "transient person," meaning a foot-traveller.

———

Illusion.[n]

The youth longs for a friend: when he forms a friendship, he fills up the unknown parts of his friend's character with all virtues of man. [197] The lover idealizes the maid, in like manner. The virtues & graces which they thus attribute, but fail to find in their chosen com-

———

[217] "The miller . . . Resurrection." is struck through in pencil with a diagonal use mark, which is extended through "The daily . . . thermometer."

[218] The quotation is struck through in ink with a vertical use mark and in pencil with a diagonal one; a vertical line is drawn in ink in the left margin beside it. Emerson used a translation of it in his preface to Saadi, *The Gulistan . . . ,* 1865, p. vi.

[219] "He tears . . . worm" is written in pencil in two lines to the right of "cabinet.⟩".

panions, belong to man & woman, & are therefore legitimately required, but are only really ⟨unfolded⟩ ripened, here one, & there the
other, ⟨in⟩ distributed in scattered individuals in a wide population.
Fourier meant this, when he said, "it took 1728 men to make a human
phalanx, or one man,"[220]
[198] But this illusion is constant,—a siren song in the ears of every
susceptible youth. Saadi says in his Kasside.

> "Let no land, no friend, be to thy mind an end;
> For sea & land are wide, & there are many men.
> Not *one rose* blooms, not *one green tree,*—
> The trees are all green; full of roses is space;
> Art thou ⟨condemned⟩ ↑confined↓ to one ⟨fool⟩ ↑door↓, as
>   the hen to one corn grain[221]
> Why ⟨soarest thou⟩ not ↑soar up↓ to heaven ⟨as⟩ ↑like↓ the
>   doves?
> ↑Fly↓ from[n] tree to tree, like the bul-bul, ⟨fly,⟩
> And run not ⟨as⟩ ↑like↓ the foolish grouse into a net."

[*Von Hammer,* p. 208][222]

See also, [in Von Hammer, p. 210] the excellent Kassaid ⟨which⟩on
Old Age, which follows this.

[199] *Aplomb.* Another text of aplomb, besides that cited above (p.
174. ↑p 85,↓), is, the senate of Egyptian Kings sitting silent in the
Hall of the Dead from age to age, & when a new King arrives among
them, they rise whilst he takes his seat among them. See also a trait
quoted from Confucius, *supra* p. 178

God tied the tongue to the Understanding, but C.'s has got untied.[223]

   Arabian hospitality
"Bring in the guest, said Hatem⟨,⟩ ↑Tai.↓ ⟨since⟩ I never eat alone."[224]

----

[220] The quotation is used in "Historic Notes of Life and Letters in New England,"
W, X, 350. See *JMN*, VIII, 209, and XIII, 240.
   [221] "fool" is canceled, and "door" added, in pencil.
   [222] Joseph Von Hammer-Purgstall, *Geschichte der schönen Redekünste Persiens, mit
einer Blüthenlese aus Zweyhundert Persischen Dichtern* (Vienna, 1818); in Emerson's library.
   [223] This sentence is in pencil.
   [224] "Tai." is added, and "since" canceled, in pencil.

Hatem the type of hospitality, Nushirvan of kingship, Lokman of wisdom, Iamschid ↑Hatem Tai who roasted his wonderful horse to entertain the messengers of the Sultan who had come to ask for the horse in the name of the Sultan↓[225]

[200] ↑*Bias*↓ tremendous force of the spring which we call ⟨the⟩ native bias of character.

It needs this & that incessant nudge of necessity or of passion to drive us from idleness & bring the day about, but what prodigious force must that spring have, whose impulsion reaches through all the days, through all the years, & keeps the old man constant to the same pursuits as in youth!
———↑'Tis like the diurnal, annual, & centennial variations of the magnet.↓
For Alcott, I have always the feeling, that the visiter will not rightly see him; for he is like a piece of Labrador spar, which is a dull stone enough until you chance to turn it to the particular angle whe⟨n⟩re its colors appear, & it ⟨is⟩becomes a jewel.[226]

Men that are great only to one or two men.

[201] ↑Railroad.↓
The railroad justifies its monopoly of a strip of land ↑100 miles long↓ suddenly & ⟨violently⟩ ↑inconveniently↓ taken from every man's cornfield or house lawn, or between his house & barn, or through his bedchamber, with the greatest violence to his private comfort,↑—↓ ⟨by⟩ ↑through↓ its constant occupation of it ⟨by⟩ all day[,] all night by successive loaded trains.[227]

---

[225] This anecdote of Hatem Tai is in pencil. Emerson may have found it in volume 1 of *Moslicheddin Sadi's Lustgarten* (*Bostan*), 1850. " 'Bring in . . . Sultan" is used in Emerson's preface to Saadi, *The Gulistan* . . . , 1865, pp. xii–xiii.
[226] See *JMN*, IX, 23, and "Experience," *W*, III, 57.
[227] "by" is canceled and the dash and "through" added in pencil.

↑Good out of evil.↓

One must thank the genius of Brigham Young for the creation of Salt Lake City,—an inestimable hospitality to the Overland Emigrants, and an efficient example to ↑⟨the⟩all men in↓ the vast desart, teaching how to subdue [202] & turn it to a habitable garden. And one must thank Walt Whitman for service to American literature in the Apalachian enlargement of his outline & treatment.

———

Nobody wishes to be ridiculous, but it is some consolation to know that every body is ridiculous ↑when↓ in false position, & ⟨he⟩you no more than others.

———

Attitude. Nature the best posture-master. The attitudes of children are gentle, persuasive, royal, in their games & talk in the house, & in the street, before they have learned to cringe [20⟨2⟩3] or to trade & to be obsequious. 'Tis impossible but thought disposes the limbs, & walks, & is masterly or secondary. No art can contravene it, or conceal it.[228] So also will the thought control the sentence and the style, strive against it as you may. The subject↑,—↓⟨is⟩I must so often say,—is indifferent: any word, every word in the language, every circumstance, becomes poetic, when in the hands of a higher thought. ↑'Tis a problem that Genius can very well solve—to illuminate every low or trite word you can offer it. Give your rubbish to Shakspeare, he will give it all back to you in gold & stars.↓[229]

[204] My interest in ⟨the⟩ ↑my↓ Country is not primary, but professional⟨,⟩. ⟨so to speak,⟩ I wish that war as peace shall bring out the genius of the men. In every company, in every town, I seek intellect & character; & so in every circumstance. War, I know, is ↑not an u⟨mit⟩nmitigated evil: it is↓ a potent alterative, tonic, magnetiser, reinforces manly power a hundred & a thousand times. I see it come as

———

[228] "Attitude. . . . conceal it.", struck through in pencil with single diagonal use marks on pp. [202] and [203], is used in "Social Aims," *W*, VIII, 82.

[229] A vertical line is drawn in pencil in the right margin beside "The subject . . . thought.", which is used in "Poetry and Imagination," *W*, VIII, 34. "'Tis a problem . . . stars." is written in ink over almost the same in pencil; the pencil version has "give them all", and the comma is lacking after "Shakspeare".

↑a⟨n⟩ ↑frosty↓↓ October, which shall restore intellectual & moral power to these languid & dissipated ⟨minds⟩populations.[230]

[205] On the whole, I know that the cosmic results will be the same↑,↓ whatever the daily events may be. The Union may win or lose battles, win or lose in the first treaties & settlement: ↑Sutlers & pedlers may thrive on some abuse,↓ but Northwest trade, & Northeastern production, & Pennsylvania coalmines, and New York shipping, and white labor, though not idealists, gravitate in the ideal direction. Nothing less large than justice to them all can keep them in good temper.[231]

[206] because in matters of such compass as the interests of a nation every partial action hurts   offends some party[232]

[207] The difficulty with the young men is not their opinion & its consequences, not that they are copperheads, but that they lack idealism. A man for success must not be pure idealist,—then he will practically fail; but he must have ideas, he must obey ideas, or he is a ⟨hog, his head is punk.⟩ ↑brute.↓ A man does not want to be dazzled with a blaze of sunlight,—he will be sunblind; but every man ⟨wants⟩ ↑must have↓ ⟨⟨sun⟩light⟩ ↑glimmer↓ enough to keep him from knocking his head against the walls & posts. [208] And it is in the interest of civilization, & good society, & friendship, that I hate to hear of wellborn & gifted & amiable men↑,↓ that they have this low tendency, this despair. Their death is no loss to their country. ↑skeptical as felons.↓[233]

↑Oct. 23.↓
Anecdote for [Notebook] Σ would be Sam Dexter's defence of Self-

[230] A vertical line is drawn in pencil in the left margin beside this paragraph.

[231] "On the whole . . . may be." and "Pennsylvania coalmines . . . temper." are used in "The Fortune of the Republic," *W*, XI, 542–543. The comma after "same" is added in pencil.

[232] "because in . . . party" is in pencil.

[233] With this entry, cf. "The Fortune of the Republic," *W*, XI, 536. "sun" is canceled in ink and "light" in pencil; "glimmer", the comma after "men", and "skeptical as felons." are added in pencil.

ridge: and also Daniel Webster's speech at Salem, "If this be law, let the foundations of this house be turned up with the plough."²³⁴

What a taunt ⟨is this⟩ [209] in an English paper is this comment on Lord Brougham's speech at Edinburgh, "He has lived too long."

The reward which his puritan conscience brought to Samuel Hoar to indemnify him for all it had cost him, was, that his appearance in court for any party in a suit at once conciliated court, jury, & by-standers, to that side which the incorruptible man defended.

[⟨200⟩210] power of money, that it will buy the ⟨blooming⟩ ↑miraculous flowering↓ of the Nightblooming Cereus or the Victoria Regia in your ⟨evening⟩ ↑parlor↓ to add the splendor of secret nature to the lustres of your soirée;   and, ⟨that,⟩ if your cause be really honest, that you can buy with money the immense weight of Mr Hoar's s⟨ixty⟩eventy years of virtue to ⟨*dazzle* the *jury*⟩ shine on your claim, & dazzle the jury ⟨in⟩to your benefit.²³⁵ I justified to Wiley yesterday Confucius's speech about making money↑,↓ (see *supra* p. 182) lest he should rashly resign his position at Chicago↑,↓ [⟨201⟩211] and cited David Hume's autobiography in confirmation.²³⁶ I might have cited Dr Johnson's ⟨saying⟩ ↑story↓ ⟨to Boswell,⟩²³⁷ of the man who wanted to go somewhere in Egypt: it was unsafe, so he hired a troop of dragoons. There is always something which the stingiest wishes to buy. A man who never gives will give an acre of land for a seat in a window where he can see a certain ⟨passenger⟩ ↑President, or General, or Walter Scott,↓ ⟨s⟩go by once,—to make the poor devil a happy poet for one moment.

²³⁴ Samuel Dexter (1761–1816), noted Boston lawyer, defended T. O. Selfridge from a murder with the statement: "And as for me, may my right arm drop powerless when it fails to defend my honor." See *J*, IX, 542. Webster's sentence, in "The Murder of Captain John White," *The Works*, 6 vols. (Boston, 1851), VI, 76, is used in "Speech on Affairs in Kansas," *W*, XI, 261. See *JMN*, XIV, 387, and Journal WAR, p. [212] above.

²³⁵ With "The reward . . . defended.", p. [209], and "if your cause . . . benefit.", cf. "Samuel Hoar," *W*, X, 442.

²³⁶ Benjamin B. Wiley, a Chicago banker, friend of Emerson, and enthusiast of Thoreau's writings. The commas after "money" and "Chicago" are in pencil.

²³⁷ "to Boswell," is canceled in pencil.

[212] *Attitude,* yes that is all; that is what the orator brings, or he may leave his oration at home. How to make a poor, despised, seedy-looking cause & ↑their seedy-looking↓ assembly, each person in which ↑assembly↓ seems to come in half-ashamed of the company, & only to stay, through an odious sense of duty,—how to make these ↑warm,↓ bright, firm, honorable, proud, ↑populous, jubilant,↓ &⟨,⟩ in short, the only great cause & assembly in the world,—that is, in each case, the orator's problem.

[213] ——

We can let the year go round, if we know that October brings thoughts, & Ma⟨y⟩rch lustres, & May love, and the tenth year honor for the insults & ribaldry of the ↑nine↓ foregoing winters.[238]

Concord Library
——————

⟨W⟩Correspondence of Napoleon with Joseph of Spain
 See a notice of this, in *"Causeries du Lundi"* [1851–1862,]
  ⟨v⟩   vol. XII. 3⟨1⟩09
Pascal. "L'Amour."
Saadi. "Bostan"
Saint Beuve, Oeuvres
Hittell's Resources of California
Burton's Hand Book of the Prairie
Bayle[239]

[214] *Books.*
"Les lettres, c'est une espèce de paisible et magnifique Hotel des Invalides pour les passions: Elles n'y sont plus qu'à l'état de gouts innocents, comme dans les Champs Elysées du poëte." *Sa*↑*i*↓*nt Beuve,* following out a hint of Frederic le Grand↑.↓[240] *Causeries* [*du lundi*], [1851–1862,] Vol. 12, p. 314

[238] "nine" is added in pencil.
[239] "Saint Beuve, Oeuvres" and "Bayle" are in pencil. The list includes John Shertzer Hittell's *The Resources of California* (San Francisco and New York, 1863); "Burton's Hand Book of the Prairie" has not been identified.
[240] The period is added in pencil.

——

"Peculiar" children.

M said, "no, couldn't stay from home a single night, for B was so constituted that he could not be left alone." E. added the testimony↑,↓
that he would tell this & that lie barefacedly, *with perfect unconscious-
ness.*"[241]

——

Shall we go to war with England on account of Punch's pictures? or
Lord Brougham's drivel, for which I am sorry, for he needed all his
merits to keep him from his follies.

[215]   "Who⟨so⟩ loves his friend with ⟨all⟩ his heart ↑of hearts↓
         Bends not his head ⟨on the day when it rains arrows."⟩
             ↑⟨when⟩ ↑though↓ the sky rain⟨s⟩ darts,↓   ⟨Saadi⟩
         O ⟨friend⟩, our lifetime wastes to ⟨nothing⟩ ↑⟨no⟩ ↑no lofty↓
             end↓
         ⟨If ⟨friend⟩ ↑the soul↓ is not united⟩ ↑Till the hero is
             matched↓ with ↑an equal↓ friend.
         Poison ⟨is⟩ ↑⟨were⟩↓ ⟨⟨antidote⟩balsam⟩ ↑from↓ the hand of
             ⟨the sweetheart,⟩ ↑my love were food,↓
         The sweet & the bane do the heart good.
         Knowst thou why Saadi sits ↑ever↓ alone?
         Because he cannot ⟨sever himself⟩ ↑part↓ from the ⟨beloved.⟩
             ↑darling one.↓"
                     *Saadi   Von Hammer [Geschichte der schönen
                     Redekünste Persiens . . . , 1818,]* p 213

         Had I the world ⟨to⟩ ↑for↓ my enemy
         ⟨Through⟩ ↑Yet kept↓ the treasure of a true friend,[242]
         Never should I ask whether ⟨there⟩ ↑things↓ were
         Or were not, in this world.
         A ship on the high seas
         Doth the ⟨th⟩state of a lover resemble.
         Overboard cast they the cargo
         If so they can save their lives.
                     Saadi Ib. 213

[241] The comma after "testimony" is added in pencil. "E." is probably Elizabeth
Palmer Peabody; see Journal KL, p. [49] below.
     [242] "to" and "Through" are canceled, and "for" and "Yet kept" added, in pencil.

The eye is good, yet when it sleeps—it is better.

[*Ibid.,* p. 212]

[216]   *Salveⁿ senescentem.*[243]

Saadi's poem on Old Age.

Now is the time when weakness comes,↑—↓& strength
    goes
The ⟨enchant⟨ment⟩ers power⟩ ↑magic↓ of sweet words—
    ⟨goes hence⟩ ↑I lose↓
The harvest wind ⟨comes,⟩ ↑cuts keen:↓ ⟨& this sheen—&
    this light⟩ ↑the tender sheen & shade↓
⟨Which thou on ↑the↓ fragrant garland sawst,—departs.⟩
↑And ⟨light⟩ pink & purple light upon thy garland fade↓
To my foot fails the power—of ⟨longer⟩ ↑manly↓ stride ↑in
    streets↓;
Happy ⟨is⟩ he who ↑soonest↓ to his ↑orchard↓ hut—⟨hence
    goeth⟩ ↑retreats↓.
Saadi's whole power lies—in sweet words
⟨Let this remain,—so care I not—what goeth. ↑to beasts &
    birds↓⟩ⁿ
↑Keep this   all the rest ⟨I give to⟩ may go to beast &
    birds↓[244]

[*Ibid.,* p. 215]

———   ———

Saadi

———

Love's smart is /more worth/better fate/
Than the body's /well-being/best estate./[245] [*Ibid.,* p. 212]

———

Saadi   No soul has he   who no friend has
———   Little joy has he   who no garden has

---

[243] "Hail, old age" (Ed.).

[244] The cancellations and insertions in ll. 2, 3, and 5 are in pencil; "cuts keen" is
traced over in ink. In l. 4, "And light" and "fade" are added in pencil; "light" is canceled
and "fade" traced over in ink. In l. 6, "hence goeth" is canceled and "retreats" added in
pencil. In l. 8, canceled in ink, "goeth" is also canceled in pencil, and "to beasts & birds"
is added in pencil. With "Saadis whole . . . beast & birds", cf. Emerson's preface to Saadi,
The Gulistan . . . , 1865, p. ix. See p. [246] below.

[245] "more worth" and "well-being" are circled in pencil, and "better fate" and "best
estate" added in pencil.

Who with a moon face	Can refresh his heart
Enjoys a luck	Which has no bounds
A dungeon is that house	Which solitude fills
If ⟨like Saadi⟩ they have not,	Like Saadi, a rose bed

[*Ibid.*, p. 212]

[217] *Eyes.* The evil eye, ⟨wh⟩against which the Persians guard themselves by han⟨ing⟩ging an ⟨a⟩ox-head at the gate.

The French claim, that, *l'art de conter sans* ↑*art*↓ ⟨i⟩belongs to Lafontaine alone, *c'est là tout son secret, aucun de ses concurrens ne l'a deviné.*

"When the robbers are in earnest, they throw themselves on a troop of soldiers as on women," say↑s↓ ⟨the Persians⟩ ↑Saadi.↓ [*Moslicheddin Sadi's Lustgarten*] Bostan. [1850, I,] p 22,   meaning, that,
When the robbers are greathearted, it shows that the army is women.

[218] It was an excellent custom of the Quakers, (if only for a school of manners) the silent prayer before meals. When ⟨all hav⟩ the table is ready, & ⟨all have sat down,⟩ ↑the family have taken their places,↓ they ⟨all⟩ compose themselves, & sit for the space of a minute quite still, then open their napkins, & begin to eat. It has the effect to stop ⟨the⟩ ↑mirth &↓ idle talking, & introduce a moment of reflection[.] ⟨from which⟩ ↑After this pause,↓ ⟨each⟩ ↑all↓ begin⟨s⟩ again their usual intercourse from a vantage-ground. It would rebuke those violent manners which ⟨so⟩ many [219] people bring to the table, of wrath, & whining, & heat in trifles.[246]

"Thus much weight of ⟨pro⟩food will carry thee: if thou take more, thou must carry it;" says Saadi's Physician.[247]

⟨S⟩Cats have a coat, & I have none. Saadi

---

[246] This paragraph is struck through in pencil with a vertical use mark on p. [218] and a diagonal use mark on p. [219]. "It was . . . meals." and "It has . . . trifles." are used in "Social Aims," *W*, VIII, 86.

[247] *The Gulistan, or Flower-Garden, of Shaikh Sadī of Shiraz* . . . , trans. James Ross (London, 1823), p. 257. See *JMN*, IX, 38.

The poet or thinker must always be in a rude nation the chief authority on religion. All questions on its truth & obligation will surely come ↑home↓ to him for their answer. As he thinks & speaks, will the intelligent men believe. A certain deference must therefore be shown to him by the priests.[248]

[220]   ↑No song so tuneful, said the fox,
             As the ⟨near⟩ ↑rich↓ crowing of the cocks.↓[249]

The fox admires no song so much as the crowing of a cock. There is something peculiar in his taste in music. ↑He cannot get too near to him.↓

↑*Transubstantiation.*↓

Every one would be poet, if his intellectual digestion were perfect;[250] if the ⟨material fact⟩ ↑grass & ⟨turneps⟩ carrots↓ passed well through all the four stomachs, & became pure milk. But in Crumplehorn's cream, there is sometimes a tang of turnep; and, in the gay pictures of the orator, a reminder, now & then, of autobiography,—staring eyes of duns, or schoolmasters, or cousins, or critics, who have tormented him, far on this side of heaven. I could guess his [221] ⟨biography⟩ griefs better from his poetry than from the ⟨decorous⟩ ↑polite↓ biography which introduces the book. Uncle Greenough's story of Dr Chauncy will not out of my memory.[251]

And it is a first point in all sprightly writing, good health. The boy who comes in from hunting tells his story well, interlarding it with lucky allusions to Homer & Virgil, to the college songs, and Walter Scott: ⟨but⟩ ↑whilst↓ the sedentary scholar is not served by animal spirits, & has no plumes for his bare fact.[252]

---

[248] "The poet . . . priests.", struck through in pencil with a vertical use mark, is used in Emerson's preface to Saadi, *The Gulistan* . . . , 1865, p. ix.

[249] The verse is in pencil; "tune" is mended in darker pencil.

[250] "Every one . . . perfect;" is used in "Poetry and Imagination," *W*, VIII, 35.

[251] For the "story of Dr Chauncy", see *JMN*, XIV, 348, and "Eloquence," *W*, VIII, 127.

[252] "And it . . . fact." is struck through in pencil with a diagonal use mark. "but" is canceled and "whilst" added in pencil. With "And it . . . health.", cf. "Poetry and Imagination," *W*, VIII, 40, and *JMN*, IX, 406. "The boy . . . Walter Scott:" is used in "Education," *W*, X, 140.

[222] ↑1863, 2 November.↓

'Tis incident to great place that it has no privacy. The world must know how the King eats, & washes, & shaves, & cleans his teeth. Nations must know that the Empress Eugenie has lost some hairs from the top of her head, and, in every village in America, the girls are wearing a knot of flowers in that place, in consequence of the Empress's thin hair.

————

Those who come ↑today↓ to mourn the hero, ↑tomorrow,↓ will tread in his warpa↑t↓h, & show his ⟨vic⟨or⟩tors.⟩ ↑slayers↓ the way to death,[253]

————

I cannot read of Madame Recamier without thinking of Anna Ward.

[223] ↑*Recamier*↓

"la liaison avec Canova, le marbre de celui-ci, qui, cette fois, pour être idéal, n'eut qu'à copier le modèle." *Saint Beuve. Mme. Recamier.* [*Causeries du lundi,* 1851-1862, I,] p. 123

"Du jour ou j'ai vu que les petits Savoyards dans la rue ne se retournaient ⟨pas⟩ ↑plus,↓ j'ai compris que tout était fini."   [*Ibid.,*] p. 123

I remember Haydon's measure of the beauty of a picture in the shop windows, was, the regard of the poor Italians in the street.

Three Montmorencys, "Matthieu de M., qui fut depuis un saint; Adri⟨a⟩en, depuis duc de Laval; bien plus tard le fils d'Adrien, qui se trouvait ainsi le rival de son père, tous l'(Recamier) aimaient de passion." [*Ibid.,*] p. 121

See *infra* p. 284

[224]   ↑*Individuality.*↓

There are people whose strong individuality traverses, like the Arethusa fountain, the bitter waters of the sea, & arrives pure. We

---

[253] This sentence, struck through in ink with a vertical use mark, is used in "Harvard Commemoration Speech, July 21, 1865," *W,* XI, 344. "today" is added in pencil; "vic⟨or⟩tors." is canceled and "slayers" added in pencil. See Journal DL, p. [203], and WAR, p. [239] above.

magnify our national customs↑,↓ & fancy the barriers of ⟨a⟩the age & the nationality invincible; but, at any time, a new man will reestablish France, or feudal England, or ancient Greece, in whatever is ⟨e⟩most exceptional in its genius & practice, through all his relations, in Puritan Boston. It is in vain to murmur at Bonaparte or Goethe or Carlyle. They conquer for themselves an absolute allowance↑,↓ which↑,↓ however↑,↓ does [225] not extend beyond themselves or become hereditary, though elsewhere it may be or has been the custom of a country.[254]

⟨We⟩ It is with difficulty that we wont ourselves in the language of the Eastern poets in the melodramatic life as if one should go down to Lewis's Wharf & find an ivory boat and a pink sea. He thinks he is at the opera.[255]
↑as e.g. in the Chinese "Two Cousins."↓

[226] ↑*Courage*↓[256]
    A political gentleman wheeled a barrel of apples ↑in a wheelbarrow↓ from Newburyport to Boston, & through the city to the Tremont House, in obedience to a bet ↑on the election↓ he had made with a boarder of that hotel. It cost courage to undertake & perform it, but the less on account of the éclat; & the last miles were done with attendance of drum & trumpet. Thoreau thought none of his acquaintances dare walk with a patch on the knee of his trowsers to the Concord Post Office. ⟨or⟩ What[n] ↑young↓ lady in Boston would go into Washington street with a tin pail?↑—Yes ↑but↓ every sensible woman would carry a pail to the fire; & every man would stick on a patch if wounded or freezing.↓

[227][257] Republican Manners
Greatness
You must have a source higher than your tap. Wedgewood bravely took Flaxman to counsel, & drew on Etruria in England; sent vases &

---

[254] The added commas in this paragraph are in pencil.
[255] This paragraph is in pencil.
[256] In pencil.
[257] Except for "Republican Manners", pp. [227], [228], and [229] are in pencil.

pitchers ⟨to⟩ in boxes to every court in Europe, & formed the taste of the world. Renaissance on the breakfast table.

Boutwell had the like sagacity[,] knew that the permanent power & so the popular respect must rest on a principle.

Talleyrand said or Metternich ↑(see *Supra* p 144, 189)↓ Revolutions begin in the best heads & run steadily down to the populace. The law of water & all fluids is true of wit.

[228] You must be idealists; as ⟨Romans⟩ Greeks were, & still give you the law; as Judea was; as Egypt was; as ⟨Gr⟩Romans were. Life is ideal; Death is to break up our styles.

This the use of War to shatter your porcelain dolls; to break up in a nation Chinese conservatism, death in life.[258] Benefits of War Richter. Prayer of Achilles.

Translated in Scott's verse

Imperfect intellectual digestion.[259] A thought makes solitude in a crowd. ⟨l⟩Lover goes not into the street, where the silver ⟨fa↑e↓t⟩ ↑feet↓ are, but into the forest.

[229] How the war teaches our youth of the *haute volée.*

The felon is the extreme of the *haute volée* school.

Hectic benefits the complexion.

War breaks up St Germaine.

Saadi says, the subjects are of the opinion of their master in ↑matters of↓ religion[.]

What munificence has the war disclosed! How ⟨it c⟩ a sentiment could unclasp the grip of avarice, & the painfullest economy![260]

Do I not know how to play billiards & whist? ⟨yet I⟩ Do^n I not know the violin & flute? yet I will throw myself on those bayonets[.]

---

[258] "You must have . . . life." is struck through in pencil with single vertical use marks on pp. [227] and [228]. "You must . . . breakfast table.", "Boutwell had . . . on a principle.", and "Talleyrand said . . . of wit." are used in "The Fortune of the Republic," *W*, XI, 511–512 and 514. Metternich's saying is also used in "The Man of Letters," *W*, X, 249. See *JMN*, X, 314, and XIV, 421. For "Death is . . . styles.", see *JMN*, VIII, 271.

[259] With this phrase, cf. p. [220] above.

[260] See p. [40] above.

[230] We are coming (thanks to the war) to a nationality. Put down your foot & say to England, I know your merits and have paid them in the past the homage of ignoring your faults. I see them still. But it is time to say the whole truth,—that you have failed in an Olympian hour, that when the occasion of magnanimity arrived, you had it not⟨:⟩—that you have lost character.

Besides; your insularity, your inches are conspicuous, ↑and they are to↓ count against ⟨cubits & furlongs.⟩ ↑miles.↓ ⟨In a question⟩ When it comes to divide an estate, the politest men quarrel. Justice is above your aim. You are self condemned.[261]

[231][262] When the merchant reads the ⟨Pro⟩Broker's stock list, ⟨he⟩ if his own shares are depreciated, he does not less read with pleasure the firmness of the ↑other↓ quotations, as ⟨learning⟩ ↑indicating↓ the soundness & integrity of the community, which give value to all property, & his with all.

———

Ideal politics. *supra* p. 34

———

Renan's speech, *supra* p 66

———

↑Young↓ Copperheads[263] p 208

In America the govt is acquainted with the opinions of all classes[,] with the leading men in middle & even the leaders of the low. The President comes near enough to these. If he does not, the Caucus does, & ⟨it⟩ what is important will reach him. Not so far enough from this is Eng[lan]d, France, Austria,ⁿ ⌐and indeed America in the late ⟨Go⟩Administrations.⌐[264]

———

[261] This paragraph, in pencil, is struck through in pencil with a vertical use mark. See p. [40] above.

[262] Page [231] is in pencil.

[263] "Copperheads" is struck through in pencil with a vertical use mark. The passage cited is used in "The Fortune of the Republic," *W*, XI, 536.

[264] "In America . . . Austria, and" is struck through in pencil with a vertical use mark; the rest of the passage is written vertically in the left margin. "the govt is . . . him." is used in "The Fortune of the Republic," *W*, XI, 529.

[232]²⁶⁵ When our young officers come back from the Army, on a forty days' furlough, they find ⟨thei⟩ apathy & opposition in the ⟨count⟩ cities.²⁶⁶

Washington & Cromwell,—one using a moral, the other a revolutionary policy. The Govt. of Algiers & of Turkey is, tho' it last for ages, revolutionary. If we continued ⟨to thr⟩ in Boston to throw tea into the bay at pleasure, that were revolutionary. B⟨on⟩ut our *revolution* was in the interest of the moral or anti-revolutionary.²⁶⁷ Slavery is Algiers or perpetual [233]²⁶⁸ revolution. Society upside down, head over heels, & man eating his breakfast with pistols by his plate. It is man degraded to cat & dog. & Society has come to an end, and all gentlemen die out.

Thus a violent conservatism is more revolutionary than abolition or freedom of speech & of press.
'Tis like shutting your window when you have lighted a pan of coals in the unchimneyed apartment.

[234] ⟨A man⟩ There are degrees & limits: a man may make a capital speech in Exeter Hall, & yet not dictate to the English throne.²⁶⁹

————

Every body likes a pronounced character. A man who makes a speech & does not wish to hurt anybody, can be unheard without loss. In England, which is a better organized *public* than any other, they have a rapid ticketing of each man, & a rapid toleration of him when so ticketed. Holyoake & Urquhart & O'connell and Smith O'brien. But nobody there or here likes a whiffler or a trimmer.

[235] November 5. Letter from George E. Tufts, Rawson, New York, postmarked Cuba, N.Y.

²⁶⁵ Pages [232]–[234] are in pencil.
²⁶⁶ This entry is struck through in pencil with a vertical use mark.
²⁶⁷ "moral or" is circled in pencil for revision or cancellation.
²⁶⁸ "Want of idealists in our Repub.   *Supra* 156, 161," was inscribed earlier at the top of p. [233], and the paragraph begun on p. [232] continued after a long rule below it.
²⁶⁹ See p. [270] below.

"Life is a flame whose splendor hides its base."
"Throwing out the fashionable travellers, there may be among the rest many with whom travel is the instinctive half-conscious groping of the heart-antennae, the sad, hungering, listening search for some answer to the soul's demands, the holy pilgrimage to the shrine of its ideal, that flits just beyond the reach of external vision." This from Tuft's letter.[270]

↑*Education.*↓
"Who does not teach his child a trade or profession brings him up to steal," say the Persians.[271]

[236]   Character
"Difficile à acquérir, mais plus difficile a perdre," says Adrienne Le Couvreur of the friendship of Fontenelle.[272]

"Ferdousi n'a pas besoin d'avoir lu Horace ni Ovide pour dire les mêmes choses qu'eux." St Beuve. *Causeries* vol 1[273]

↑Eloquence↓
Abbé Galiani said, Beware of a freedom of the press established by edict. "Savez vous ma définition du *sublime oratoire?* C'est l'art de tout dire sans être mis à la Bastille, dans un pays ou il est defendu⟨e⟩ de rien dire"[274]

The world, it is an echo.[275]

↑Eloquence↓
"On a toujours la voix de son esprit."

[270] For Tufts' letter (November 1, 1863) and Emerson's reaction, see *L*, V, 341–342 and Notebook OP Gulistan, p. [109]. See also Journal WAR, p. [261] above.
[271] See p. [190] above.
[272] A vertical line is drawn in ink in the left margin beside this sentence. See Sainte-Beuve, "Adrienne Le Couvreur," *Causeries du lundi*, 15 vols. (Paris, 1883), I, 212.
[273] See "Le Livre des rois par le poëte persan Firdousi," *ibid.*, I, 339.
[274] The quotation is struck through in pencil with two diagonal use marks. See *ibid.*, I, 47. A translation was used in the lecture "Table-Talk"; see Gohdes, *Uncollected Lectures*, 1932, p. 32.
[275] See p. [192] above.

[237] In speaking of England, I lay out of question the truly cultivated class. They ⟨ar⟩exist in England, as in France, in Germany, in America, in Italy, and they are like Christians, or like poets, or chemists, existing for each other ⟨&⟩ across all possible nationalities, strangers to their people & brothers to you. I lay them out of question. They are ⟨not⟩ sane men as far removed as we from the bluster & mendacity of the London Times, & the shop-tone of Liverpool. They, like us, wish to be exactly informed, & to speak & act for the public good & not for party.

Shall we go to war with Eng[lan]d for Punch's pictures? or for the opinions of the drunken lord S, or the soft   Continued p 238[276]

[238] Originality
A ⟨g⟩well-read man ⟨n⟩can always find the opinion & thesis of a new writer, be he who he will, & however original,—⟨in⟩ already printed in an old book. Thus Madame du Deffand had Carlyle's horror at eloquence. Every new writer is only ⟨an old vo th⟩ a new crater of an old volcano.

Having penetrated the people & known their unworthiness, ⟨I⟩ we can well cease to respect their opinion, even their contempt, & not go to war at our disadvantage for the avoiding of this. Who are they that they should despise?——these people who cringe before Gort-⟨achoff⟩chakoff & Napoleon. Let us remember the wise remark of General Scott, "Resentment is a bad basis for a campaign."   I am not sure of the wisdom of Burke's saying, "Contempt is not a thing to be despised."[277]

[239] *Eloquence*
"La plume est le premier, on l'a dit, le plus sûr des maîtres pour façonner la parole." ↑*Saint Beuve.*↓ "Stylus optimus et praestantissimus effector et magister." ↑*Cicero*↓[278]

[276] Page [237] is struck through in pencil with a vertical use mark. "Shall we . . . p 238" is in pencil. See p. [214] above.
[277] "Having penetrated . . . despised.' ", in pencil, is struck through in pencil with a vertical use mark. For Scott's saying, see Journal VA, p. [101] above. For Burke's saying, from *Letters on a Regicide Peace*, letter III, see *JMN*, VI, 25.
[278] "The pen is the best and most eminent author and teacher [of eloquence]." Cicero, *De Oratore*, I, 33, 150.

What are the fine verses of Solon, to the effect, that, the orator has not
the harmony of thought & speech until from 42 to 5⟨9⟩6 years of
age?[279]

see *Saint Beuve Causeries [du lundi,* 1851–1862,] Vol 1. p. 85.

A wit is helped by his past, as ⟨much⟩ ↑well↓ as a hero. We begin to
laugh as soon as he begins to speak, ⟨and⟩ ↑—↓as soon as he comes in.

"J'ai pour idée que l'on est toujours de son temps, et ceux-là mêmes qui en
ont le moins l'air." *St. Beuve*[280]

[240] The virtues speak to virtues, vices to vices, each to their
own kind, in the people with whom we deal. If you are suspicious &
drily on your guard, so is he or she. If you risk frankness & generosity,
they will respect it now or later.[281]
The other law is, that the action ⟨of the⟩carries all the qualities of the
actor, as the egg of the bird. I am revealed in my face, form, constitution, gait, manners, speaking, writing, expenditure, dress, & dealing.

[241] "C'est un principe de guerre," said Napoleon, "que, lorsqu'on peut se
servir de la foudre, il la faut préférer au canon."[282]

"Quand un de ses rêves favoris lui échappait, il avait l⟨e⟩a faculté ⟨comme il
disait⟩ de prendre son esprit, comme il disait, et de le porter ailleurs." *St.
Beuve [Causeries du lundi,* 1851–1862,] I. p. 183

↑The baker's boy, Gen.↓ Drouot, studied by the light of his father's
oven in the early mornings[.][283]

---

[279] Two vertical lines are drawn in pencil in the left margin beside "not the harmony
. . . age?".
[280] See *Causeries du lundi,* 1883, I, 119.
[281] This paragraph is struck through in pencil with a diagonal use mark.
[282] A translation of this quotation is used in "Inspiration," *W,* VIII, 279 and "Harvard Commemoration Speech, July 21, 1865," *W,* XI, 343; see also Journal DL, p. [204]
above.
[283] "The baker's . . . mornings" and the rules above and below it are in pencil. See
Sainte-Beuve, *Causeries du lundi,* 1883, I, 237.

Fiske of Waltham wrote his Greek grammar in bed to save fire & clothes.

[242] 1863
In October, Sumner was elected to the Saturdayrians[.]

———

In that country, a peculiarity, that. a⟨s⟩fter ⟨‖ . . . ‖⟩60 years, a certain mist or dimness, a sort of autumnal haze, settled on the figure, veiling especially all decays. ⟨Very⟩ Gradually," year by year, the outline ⟨faded⟩ became indistinct, and the halo gayer & brighter. At last, there was only left a sense of presence, & the virtue of personality, as if Gyges never turned his ring again. It was an immense social convenience.
↑———
Valca 22 Oct[obe]r↓[284]

Beecher at breakfast illustrated the difference between the impulsive mob in N.Y. Cooper Institute & the organized mob in L⟨ondon⟩iverpool meeting. "In one, you go by a corner where the wind sucks in, & blows your hat off, but, when you get by it, you go along comfortably to the next corner. In the other, you are on the prairie, with no escape from the irresistible northwester." Jan. 13. 1864

[243] ↑Leasts.↓
Rochefoucauld said "Tout arrive en France." Not less, everything ha⟨s⟩ppens at Hull.
↑Mrs Sedgwick told me that every body passed thro' Lenox first or last.↓[285]

They said of Guizot, "that what he knew this morning, he has the air of having known from all eternity."[286] 'Tis the rapid digestion of the journalist. Presence of mind.

[284] The rule and "Valca 22 Octr" are in pencil.
[285] Two vertical lines are drawn in ink in the left margin beside "Rochefoucauld said . . . last." See p. [257] below.
[286] See Sainte-Beuve, *Causeries du lundi*, 1883, I, 322, and VIII, 508. The translation is used in "Eloquence," *W*, VIII, 128.

↑Copied in *CR* 37↓

In poetry, Nature bears the whole expense. In prose, there must be concatenation, a mass of facts, and a method. 'Tis very costly; only a capitalist can take hold of it; but, in poetry, the mere enumeration of natural objects suffices. Nay[,] Tennyson is a poet, because[n] he has said, "the stammering thunder," or, "the wrinkled sea beneath him crawls" & Longfellow "the plunging wave"[.][287]

[244] Don't vindicate providence, don't take ⟨care⟩ ↑charge↓ of the weather, & apologize for the climate. Have you not cares & frets enough of your own? The equator will take care of itself[.]

———

Natural check on fashions. As soon as you refine your mantilla or bonnet a ribbon too far, some surly goodsense extinguishes it with a↑n↓ aquascutum, which is the rage in a fortnight,[288]

———

⟨"*Clubs*↑.↓"⟩[289] ↑"Criticism", or "Third Estate in Literature"↓ Among the examples of white-washed reputations, is eminently that of Richelieu, as presented by *Saint Beuve*. See "*Causeries* [*du lundi,*]" [1851–1862,] Vol. 7[, 176–208][290]

[245] But the trait which most characterises Saadi↑,↓ & has almost ⟨become⟩ made his name a synon⟨i⟩↑y↓m for the quality, is cheerfulness. His name means *Fortunate,* and ⟨as⟩ the quality betrays ↑⟨to⟩↓ a well constituted or healthy man. All the anecdotes intimate a happy soul to which victory is habitual, easily shedding mishaps & with ⟨more⟩ sensibility to pleasure, ⟨than to pain⟩ & power ⟨to⟩ of resources against pain.[291]

---

[287] This paragraph is struck through in pencil with a diagonal use mark. "Copied in *CR* 37" is in pencil. "Nature bears . . . expense." is used in "Social Aims," *W*, VIII, 96, and the lecture "Table-Talk"; see the report of the lecture in Gohdes, *Uncollected Lectures,* 1932, p. 35. With " 'the stammering thunder' ", cf. "Merlin and Vivien," l. 940; see *JMN*, XIV, 289. " 'the wrinkled . . . crawls' " is from "The Eagle," l. 4.

[288] "Dont vindicate . . . fortnight," is in pencil.

[289] The added period, in pencil, is overwritten by a caret in ink.

[290] Emerson borrowed this volume from the Boston Athenaeum December 2, 1863–January 6, 1864; it is also in Emerson's library.

[291] This paragraph, struck through in pencil with a diagonal use mark, is used in Emerson's preface to Saadi, *The Gulistan* . . . , 1865, pp. vii–viii. The comma after "Saadi" is added in pencil; the cancellation and revision in "synonym" are in pencil; "to" (added after "betrays") is canceled in pencil.

[246] Time is short but always long enough for the finest trait of courtesy[.]

Cheerfulness flowing from the vision of the laws that control the world & from the wise bounty of his own heart. Then again this his genius, this his poet's robe & garland. Beauty in the world & an answering beauty in his own artistic ↑skill,↓ the beauty that he sees he can create. "Saadi's whole power lies in sweet words, Let this remain—I care not what is taken" See *supra*, p 216

[247] The human race is interested in Saadi whilst the cynical tone of Byron which helps nobody ⟨would⟩ only owes to his genuine talent for melodious expression its lingering longevity[.]

Saadi is the poet of ↑friendship,↓ love, ⟨of beauty⟩ of heroism, self devotion, of joy, ⟨of friendship⟩ bounty, serenity, and of the divine Providence[.][292]

Climate where the sunbeams are perpendicular.[293]
     Africa is the stove of Greece, which can therefore afford to have its windows open to the north.

[248] I remember reading a gay paper of N. P. Willis, seriously advising the New York youth not to follow anxiously the fashion in hats, but to see to it what kind of hat became him, & to buy that, for that every becoming hat was in fashion. That was good sense. I should say of dress in general, that some people need it, & others need it not. Thus ⟨the⟩ ↑a↓ king ↑or ⟨the⟩a general↓ does not need a fine coat. And a commanding person may save himself all solicitude on that point. Longworth at Cincinnati received me to dine in the muddiest boots & trowsers, all his family [249] being in gala. And Montaigne says, in his ⟨castle⟩ ↑chateau↓, his servants & equipages can answer for him.

---

[292] Page [246] and p. [247] to this point are in pencil. "Time is . . . courtesy" is partially circumscribed in pencil to set it off from the entry below it. "Cheerfulness flowing . . . world" and " 'Saadis whole . . . taken' " on p. [246], and "The human . . . Providence", struck through in pencil with a vertical use mark on p. [247], are used in Emerson's preface to Saadi, *The Gulistan* . . . , 1865, pp. vi–ix.
[293] "Climate where . . . perpendicular." is used in "Boston," *W*, XII, 183.

⟨But⟩ ⟨And t⟩This also is the rule in society. Some persons do not need this care. There are always slovens in state street who are not less considered. But some persons do. If a man have ⟨manners, aplomb, & talent,—⟩ manners & talent,—he may dress roughly & carelessly. If however a man has not aplomb, has sensibility,—as certain youths whom I know,—it is a grand economy to go to a good tailor at the beginning [250] of ⟨each⟩ ↑the↓ season, & dress himself irreproachably. He can then dismiss all care from his mind, & may easily find that slight confidence a fortification, ⟨to his mind⟩ that turns the scale in social encounters, & ⟨suf⟩ allows him to go gaily & without second thought into ⟨th⟩ conversations where ⟨othe⟩ else he had been dry & embarrassed. It has the effect of that double glass of wine which my lawyer said he took with advantage when he was about to address the jury.[294]

[251] Louis XI, Commines tells us, none so humble in words & dress.

———

Admirable word applied to Louis XI., "le don de manier les esprits par son accent, et par *les caresses de sa parole.*"[295]

———

↑*Originality.*↓
Montesquieu it seems is only the continuator of Commines. See *Saint Beuve. Causeries* [*du lundi,* 1851–1862,] I. p. 240

"Notre Seigneur," says Commines, "ne veut point qu'un royaume se moque de l'autre."

[252] How we turn our passions to account! It is not Arnoult, it is not Spiers, it is French novels that teach us French, & German that

---

[294] "I should say . . . jury." is struck through in pencil with single vertical use marks on pp. [248] and [250], and a diagonal one on p. [249]. "I should say . . . point." and "there are . . . embarrassed." are used in "Social Aims," *W*, VIII, 87–88. Nicholas Longworth (1782–1863) was a lawyer, landowner, and horticulturalist whom Emerson met in 1852; see *JMN*, XI, 521, and *L*, IV, 328 and 330. At the beginning of p. [250], "each" is canceled and "the" added in pencil.
[295] Two vertical lines are drawn in pencil in the left margin beside *"les caresses de sa parole."* A translation of "le don de . . . *parole.*" is used in "Eloquence," *W*, VIII, 122, where it is attributed to Commines. See Sainte-Beuve, *Causeries du lundi,* 1883, I, 250.

teach us German. The passions ⟨teach u⟩ rush through the resistance of grammar & ⟨new⟩strange vocabulary, ↑&,↓ facility being once obtained, the feebler appetite of taste & love of knowledge suffice to habituate us in the new land.[296]

———

↑*Words.*↓
⟨Our⟩ Words[n] sink to their worst applications; as, *financier*⟨s⟩ to sharpers on change; *politican*⟨s⟩ to demagogues, ⟨&⟩ wirepullers, & lobby-men; *professor*⟨s⟩ to conjurors; *artist* to cooks & milliners;

[253] ⟨How⟩ What an element in our social fabric is ⟨the⟩ money & the currency, war shows us fast enough. You have bought long mort-⟨a⟩gages o⟨n⟩f perfect security, you have bought City of Boston's, or Massachusetts' fives or sixes, or annuities for sixty years. But specie currency stops, and you are paid in paper. How fares it ⟨now⟩ ↑at this moment↓ with annuitants in Richmond? But you have been wiser than your whole generation, & have stipulated to be paid in gold. But gold it seems through the immense yield of the mines [254] is depreciated in value one half. (So I read in Galbraith.) The only currency that is always sterling is personal values,—courage, self command, manners, wit, learning, & geometry.

The Poet is always awaited by the people. He has only the overdose of that quality whereof they have the underdose. We did not know them until they show their taste by their enthusiastic welcome of his genius. A foreign criticism might easily affect to make little account of him, unless their applauses showed [255] the high historic importance of his powers. In these songs & ⟨cassides⟩ elegies, ⟨we⟩ breaks into light the national mind of the Persians & Arabians. These monotonies which we accuse, accuse our own. A new landscape, new costume, new religion, new manners & customs, under which ⟨the old⟩ humanity nestles very ⟨well⟩ ↑comfortably↓ at Shiraz & Mecca, with ⟨equal⟩ ↑good↓ appetite, & with moral & intellectual results that cor-

———

[296] This paragraph is struck through in pencil with a diagonal use mark. "How we ... vocabulary," was used in the lecture "Table-Talk"; see the abstract in Cabot, *A Memoir . . .* , 1887, II, 790. Émile Arnoult gave Emerson French lessons in 1847; see *L*, III, 409.

respond point for point with ours at London & New York. It needs in every sense a free translation, just as they attribute [256] to the east wind, what we say of the west.[297]

Every age has its true religion, and its mythology. In every company in which a poem is read, you may be sure, a part hear the exoteric, and a part the es⟨e⟩oteric sense.

[257] I believe I have never expanded a topic touched in my *"New England"* lectures on the City into which a great fortune falls every day, as of some exile who has ⟨made a great fortune⟩ ↑acquired wealth↓ at New Orleans or Rio, & comes in ↑early↓ old age to Paris or to New York to spend it. But every ⟨day⟩ ↑week↓ also a ship comes in to the port of Boston, ↑with ↑gold or↓[n] opium, oil, or guano,↓ which adds to somebody's pile a hundred thousand dollars, &, of course, enhances by so much the real estate of the county in which this new competitor proceeds to buy⟨.⟩ ↑land.↓[298]

Every city has its rival city, its ridiculous suburb, its old times, & its joke. Boston has Hull,* & its banter with New York journalism.[299]

[258] Boutwell said to me, the other day, "⟨i⟩It makes no difference whether we gain or lose a battle, except the loss of valuable lives: we gain the ⟨cau⟩advantage from month to month." There has been no example like ours of the march of a good cause as by gravitation, or rather, by specific levity, against particular defeats. It is like the progress of health in sleep. You have removed the causes of disease, (& one of them is your restless doing,) & all mends of itself. It is like the replacement of the dislocated bone, [259] as soon as you have re-

* "All are but parts of one Majestic Hull".

---

[297] "The Poet . . . attribute" is struck through in ink with single vertical use marks on pp. [254] and [255]. "He has only . . . west." is used in Emerson's preface to Saadi, *The Gulistan . . .* , 1865, pp. vi–vii.

[298] "falls every day . . . land." is struck through in pencil with a diagonal use mark; "gold or" and "land." are added in pencil. With "the City . . . spend it.", cf. *JMN*, XIV, 61–62, and "Boston," *W*, XII, 187.

[299] For Hull, see p. [243] above. With " 'All are . . . Hull'.", Emerson's note below, cf. Alexander Pope, *Essay on Man*, I, 267.

moved the obstruction. The vanity of no man is gratified: the Abolitionist would so willingly put in his claim. The sublime God puts him
back into the same category of egotism with the Copperhead.[300]

I remember when I feared—what one still newly escaped shud-
ders to think of,—that a little more success, a wiser choice of candidate
by the Southern party,—say, of Jefferson Davis, instead of Pierce or
Buchanan,—had enabled them by a coup d'état [2⟨5⟩60] to have
strained the whole organism of the government to the be⟨n⟩hoof of
Slavery,—to have insisted, by all the ↑courts,↓ marshals, & army &
navy of the Union, on carrying into effect a right of transit with Slaves
from state to state. It ⟨th⟩had then only been necessary ⟨to⟩for rich
democrats in N Y, Pennsylvania & Connecticut to buy slaves, & it is
not easy to see how ⟨they⟩ the ardent abolitionists—always a minority
hated by the rich class,—could have successfully resisted. [261] The
effect however would have been to put the *onus* of resistance on the
North, and, at last, the North would have seceded. We had been the
rebels, & would have had the like difficulty to put our states into secession as the Southerners had.[301]

[262] "These are matters of arrangement, ⟨more⟩ not of ↑legal↓
value," said the broker[.][302]

↑1⟨1⟩5 Novr. At the town meeting, one is impressed with the accumu-
lated virility of the four or five men* who speak so well to the point, &
so easily handle the affairs of the town: only four last night,* and all so
good, that they would have satisfied me, had it been in Boston, or in
Washington.[303] The speech of Judge Hoar was perfect, and to that
handful of people who heartily applauded [263] it. When a good man
rises in the cold & malicious assembly, you think, "well, it would be

* Heywood, Fay, Brooks, Hoar.

[300] This paragraph is struck through in pencil with single vertical use marks on pp.
[258] and [259].
[301] "organism of . . . how ⟨they⟩ the" and "The effect . . . states" are struck through
in pencil with single vertical use marks on pp. [260] and [261].
[302] "legal" is added in pencil.
[303] "At the town . . . Washington.", struck through in pencil with a diagonal use
mark, is used in "Social Aims," *W*, VIII, 102.

more prudent to be silent. Why not rest on a good past? Nobody doubts your talent & power: And, for the present business, we know all about it, and are tired of being pushed into patriotism by people who stay at home." But he, taking no counsel of past things, but only of the inspiration of his today's feeling, surprises them with his [264] tidings, his better knowledge, his larger view, his steady gaze at the new & future event, whereof they had not thought, and they are interested like so many children, & carried off out of all recollection of their malignant nonsense, and he gains his victory by prophecy, where they expected repetition. He knew beforehand that they were looking behind, & that he was looking ahead, & [265] therefore it was wise to speak. What a godsend are these people to a town! and the Judge, what a faculty! he is put together like a ↑Waltham↓ watch, or like a locomotive just finished from the Tredegar ⟨w⟩Works.[304]

Why has a judge two ears? That he may keep one ↑open↓ for the accused.

―― ↑*Boston.*↓

The Boston of ↑↑Franklin,↓ Adams, Otis, Quincy, Warren,↓ Horatio Greenough, of Wendell Phillips, of Jonathan Phillips, of Edward Everett, of Allston, of Brook Farm, of Edward Taylor, of Daniel Webster, of Samuel Dexter, of Buckminster, Channing, Greenwood, of Charles Sprague, of Starr King, of Billings the architect, [266] of ⟨s⟩Mrs Julia Howe, Margaret Fuller, of a class of forgotten but wonderful young men, burning too fast to live long, but who marked not less the powers of the air & soil, John Everett   Clark Harris the Orientalist, Edward Lowell, Edward & Charles Emerson,   Fisk, who wrote his Greek grammar in his bed; not having clothes enough: the Boston of Beecher, of[n] ↑Horace Mann, Parker,↓ Sumner, Lowell, Holmes, Agassiz, Longfellow, Pierce, Dana, Ward, ↑Hoar,↓ Hunt, Henry James, Peter Hunt, ↑Newcomb,↓[305] the Boston which animates other souls born of it, or adopted spiritually into it, &, ⟨drawing⟩ in all quarters of their dispersion, drawing inspiration

------

[304] "When a good [p. [263]] . . . ⟨w⟩Works." is used in "Eloquence," *W,* VIII, 116–117.
[305] "Newcomb" is added below the line in pencil. For "Fisk," see p. [241] above.

from it;—Furness, Beecher, Channing, [267] Fremont, even, Bryant, Greeley

Nay[,] the influences are so wide, & the names crowd on me so fast, that I must take the Boston Directory or the National Census to exhaust them. The neighborhood of Thanksgiving Day makes me look at our cousins of New York with a kinder eye, and I remember that the Germans say, that, Vienna is the first ⟨g⟩German city, Berlin the second, & New York the third: and I shall say, that New York is the second city of Bostonians; and, whenever we shall so far have inoculated that centre of nations, ⟨that⟩ by our crowding immigration from New England, that they shall give a republican vote, I will concede, that it is the first.

[268] [blank]
[269] Make the government accurately *representative.*[n]

You must live in great cities, as Bayle writes, "J'ai fait comme toutes les grandes armées qui sont sur pied pour ou contre la France, elles décampent de partout où elles ne trouvent point de fourrages ni de vivres."[306]

↑Nationality.↓
    Come, for once get out of sight of the steeples of your town.
____
Middle class country, middle class President.[307]

[2⟨6⟩70] Beecher at Exeter Hall is superb:—his consciousness of power shown in his jocular good humor & entire presence of mind; the instant surrender of the English audience, as soon as they have found a master; he steers the Behemoth,—sits astride his very snout, ↑strokes his fur,↓ tickles his ear, & rules him; secures the English by the

---

[306] Emerson's source may have been Sainte-Beuve, "Du génie critique et de Bayle" in volume I of *Portraits littéraires,* 1852, which he borrowed from the Boston Athenaeum October 31–December 2, 1863.
    [307] This entry, struck through in ink with one vertical and four diagonal use marks, is used in "Abraham Lincoln," *W,* XI, 334. Cf. also the lecture "Table-Talk," in Gohdes, *Uncollected Lectures,* 1932, p. 38.

method & circumstantiality of statement which they love, by figures, and then by downright homely illustration of important statements. His compliment to Wendell Phillips as the first orator of the world,— did he not say so?— [⟨265⟩ 271] recalls Byron's line

> "And Jura answers from h⟨er⟩is misty shroud
> Back to the joyous Alps that call to h⟨er⟩im aloud."[308]
>
> [*Childe Harold's Pilgrimage,* III, xcii, 867–868]

↑They write better, but we read more out of their books than they do. They have better blowpipe, ⌈we have not yet narrowed our heat to a focus[.] A continent full of coal.⌉↓[309] England possesses drastic skill[,] always better artists than we: Carlyle a better writer, Gladstone or Bright a better debater, I suppose, than any of ours. Tennyson a better poet; but is the scope as high? is the material of Tennyson better, or does not our dumb muse see stars & horizons they do not? In England, in France, in Germany, is the popular sentiment as illuminated as here? As I wrote the other day,—our native politics are ideal.[310] These women, old wives sitting by the chimney side here, shrill [2⟨6⟩72] their exclamations of impatience & indignation, shame on Mr Seward, shame on the Senate, &c, for their want of humanity, of mere morality;—they stand on the ground of simple morality, & not on the class feeling ⟨of⟩ which narrows the perceptions of English, French, German people, at home. We are affirmative. They live under obstructions & negations. England's six points of Chartism are still postponed. ⟨We have⟩ They have all been granted here to begin with. England has taken in more partners, ⟨th⟩& stands better on its legs, than once, but still has huge load to carry. [2⟨6⟩73] See how this moderates the ferocity incident elsewhere to political changes. We, in the midst of a great Revolution, still enacting the sentiment of the Puritans, and the dreams of young people 30 years ago; we, passing out of the old remainders of barbarism into pure Christianity & humanity, into freedom of thought, of religion, of

----

[308] "Beecher at . . . his ear," is struck through in pencil with a vertical use mark. "Beecher at . . . aloud.' " was used in the lecture "The Fortune of the Republic"; see *W*, XI, 646–647.

[309] "we have not . . . coal." is written down the right margin of the page.

[310] See p. [161] above, and the lecture "Fortune of the Republic," *W*, XI, 644 and 645.

speech, of the press, & of trade, & of suffrage, or politic↑a↓l right; & working through this tremendous ordeal which elsewhere went by be-headings, & massacre, & reigns of terror,— [2⟨6⟩74] passing through all this & through states & territories, like a sleep, & drinking our tea the while. 'Tis like a brick house moved ⟨through our streets⟩ from its old foundations & place, & passing through our streets, whilst all the family are pursuing their domestic work inside.[311]

I hate to have the egotism thrust in with such effrontery. This revolution is the work of no man, but the ⟨eternal⟩ effervescence of na-ture. ⟨Before Abraham was, I am. [John 8:58]⟩ It never did not work.[312] But nothing that has occurred ⟨t⟩but has been a surprise, & as much to the leaders [275] as to the hindmost. And not an abolitionist, not an idealist, can say without effrontery, I did it. It is the fly in the coach, again. Go boost the globe, ⟨to⟩or ⟨block⟩ ↑Scotch↓ the globe, to accelerate or retard it in its orb. It is elemental, it is the old eternal gravitations: beware of the swing, & of the recoil! ⟨If y⟩ Who knows, or has computed, the periods? A little earlier, & you would have been burned or crazed; a little later, you are unnecessary. If I had attempted in 1806, what I performed in 1807, said Napoleon, I had been lost. Fremont was [2⟨6⟩76] ⟨broken⟩ ↑superseded↓ in 1861, for what his ⟨breakers⟩ ↑superseders↓ are achieving in 1863. And many the like examples.[313] The Republicans of this year were the Whigs & demo-crats of 1856. Mazzini & Kossuth ⟨e⟩'tis fine for them to sit in ⟨Lon-don⟩ committee in London, & hope to direct revolution in Italy, Hun-gary, & Poland. Committees don't manage revolutions. A revolution is a volcano, and ↑from↓ under every body's feet flings its ⟨vast confla-gration⟩ ↑sheet of fire↓ into the sky. More than that, let not the old thinker flatter himself↑.↓ ⟨any more.⟩ 'You may have your hour [2⟨6⟩77] at 30,' says Jove, '& ⟨perhaps⟩ lay for a moment your hand on the helm, but not at 60. I ⟨rec⟩ draft only between the ages of 20 &

---

[311] "As I wrote . . . inside." is struck through in pencil with single vertical use marks on pp. [271], [272], [273], and [274].

[312] "This revolution . . . work." is used in "The Fortune of the Republic," *W*, XI, 530.

[313] Pages [275] and [276] to this point are struck through in pencil with single ver-tical use marks. With "If I . . . lost.", cf. p. [137] above, and *JMN*, XIV, 48.

45⟨,⟩. Only Quincy Adams in a whole generation of men do I allow to lay an iron hand on the helm at 75.'

⟨The Earth,⟩ Our[n] civilization and these ideas are reducing ↑the earth↓ to a brain. See how by telegraph & ⟨rai⟩ steam,—those two straps of more than Merlin's art,—the earth is anthropized,[n] has an occiput, and a fist that will knock down an empire. What a chemistry in her magazine.

[2⟨6⟩78] How all magnifies N↑e↓w England & Massachusetts! A. said, her ice burns more than others' fire.[314]

——

I will tell you why I value Boston, because, when I go to enumerate its excellent names, I do not take ⟨up⟩down the Boston Directory, but the National ⟨Census, or⟩ History to find them.

[2⟨6⟩79] Curiosities of Literature.
Ana, Bayle, Arnold,

What sort of muse is *la haine des sots livres?* St Beuve says of Boileau, "Pour verve unique il avait la haine des sots livres"[.]³¹⁵

My collection of Stories in Σ ⟨is⟩ ↑should be↓ a new *Gesta Romanorum,* or Gulistan, or Bostan, ⟨to⟩the value of which is a new Vatican or Louvre containing masterpieces of Sculpture or picture.
The anecdote of Montesquieu & the boatman should be repeated, in spite of triteness. [Sainte-Beuve, *Causeries du lundi,* 1851–1862, VII, 42–43]

[⟨270⟩ 280] The rebels in the effrontery with which, in their failing fortunes, they adhere to their audacious terms of peace, have well instructed us⟨.⟩; and I rejoice to see we are likely to plant ourselves with rigor on the condition of absolute emancipation as the first point with which each rebel state must comply. Their women, too, have taught our women, who have excellently learned the lesson.

---

³¹⁴ With "her ice ... fire.", cf. "May-Day," ll. 142–143, *W,* IX, 168.
³¹⁵ See "Boileau" in volume 1 of Sainte-Beuve, *Portraits littéraires.*

[⟨271⟩ 281] It will go hard but we shall better the instruction.

———

Remarkable letter of J. M. Botts to the Richmond Examiner (?) in the journals, saying, that every man in the Confederacy⟨,⟩ regrets ↑at↓ this moment the Rebellion, &, if ⟨it⟩ ↑the work↓ were to do again, would not do it.———[316]

———

⟨Dec⟩Nov. 27, 1863

Philip Randolph[317] writes me, "If I could only feel as secure as some appear to be, that the rigorous conditions of national success would be complied with, there is no degree of power & honor among nations which I [⟨272⟩ 282] would not hope for. I do not feel despondent, but I have this uncertainty, this sense that we are still at the mercy of events, ⟨&,⟩ instead of holding our fate in our own hands as we might do⟨,⟩. I cannot help feeling that even the tried friends of freedom, even those whose moral vision has heretofore been keenest, do not recognize the full magnitude of the work that is to be performed, & are too secure."

———

The clergyman declared that he believed in Hell, as a military necessity.[318]

———

[⟨273⟩ 283] Friendship a better base for treating of the soul than Immortality. Then it affirms it inclusively. See *below.*
—— ↑————————————————————————↓

↑Conversation.↓
Montesquieu est con⟨u⟩venu luimeme, qu'en causant, s'il sentait qu'il etait écouté, il lui semblait dès lors que toute la question s'évanouissait devant lui.[319] *Saint Beuve* [*Causeries du lundi,* 1851–1862,] Vol VII p 60

[316] "it" is canceled, and "the work" added, in pencil.
[317] Philip Physick Randolph, grandson of the surgeon Philip Syng Physick, had been a correspondent of Emerson's since he wrote to arrange a visit to Concord in July 1851; they probably met in Philadelphia in January 1854.
[318] See Journal DL, p. [120] above.
[319] The quotation is struck through in pencil with a diagonal use mark. The heading "Conversation" and the added rule above it are in pencil. A translation is used in "Clubs," *W,* VII, 241–242.

———

Franklin ↑Said,↓ ↑"This↓ Life is rather a state of embryo, a preparation for life. A man is not completely born, until he has passed through death."[320] [*Ibid.*, VII, 145]

———

Franklin, nous dit Mallet du Pan, répéta plus d'une fois à ses élèves de Paris, que celui qui transporterait dans l'état politique les principes du Christianisme primitif, changerait la face de la société. [*Ibid.*, VII, 137]

[⟨274⟩ 284] Ducis said of Chateaubriand, "il a le secret des mots puissants" [*Ibid.*, VII, 170]

———

Mere "Natural objects always did & do weaken, deaden & obliterate imagination in me," said W[illiam]. Blake.

———

"One thought fills immensity." *Blake*

———

"The tigers of wrath are wiser than the horses of instruction." Blake[321]

———

Humility "Autant ils sembleront s'approcher de Dieu ⟨s approcher⟩par intelligence, autant ils s'en éloigneront par leur orgeuil." *ap. Saint Beuve.*

Of William Blake, see *WAR* p. 244

[2⟨7⟩85] Because a man is a good jeweller, & carves his gem in a year, will you make him a street paver?

————

> *Henry James's "Substance & Sh[ad]ow"*
> Heart, head, hand, p. 243
> Angel & devil, 248
> Angels no politicians 251
> Transcendentalist 253
> Gentleman 254

[320] This translation is used in "Immortality," *W*, VIII, 339.

[321] For this and the two preceding quotations, see Alexander Gilchrist, *Life of William Blake*, 1863, I, 345 and 81. Emerson borrowed this volume from the Boston Athenaeum December 11–19, 1863. The first quotation is used in "Inspiration," *W*, VIII, 290. See Journal WAR, pp. [244]–[245] above.

> Swedenborg's service 280
> Kant insulted 3⟨6⟩51
> Clergy, 16, 24, 238,
> Swedenborg 35[322]

[2⟨7⟩86]   Language.
"Pages" a luck↑y↓ name

———

A good translation of *suaviter in modo, fortiter in re,* is, "an iron hand in a velvet glove."[323]

———

Muth und mass = spur & rein.

———

Humboldt's extraordinary talent in imaginative or descriptive names as "volcanic paps," "geologic horizon"

———

and Lesley's

———

Old fogy, highfalutin, quaker-gun, deaconing the barrels of apples,

———

[287] Men's names have become common nouns; as
> Gorgias,
> Martinet, lieutenant colonel du regiment du Roi, mort marechal
>   de camp
>   *S. Beuve "Nouv. Lundis."* [1863–1870, I,] p. 323

*ferret*ing a secret

[⟨278⟩288]   German Language.[324]
 ↑See *SO* 104↓
Der Mensch denkt, Gott lenkt.
  ↑proposes↓ ↑disposes↓[325]

---

[322] For the quotations from *Substance and Shadow,* 1865, pp. 243, 248, 238, and 35, see Journal DL, pp. [91], [92], and [95], and FOR, p. [117] above.

[323] The translation is used in "Poetry and Imagination," *W,* VIII, 14.

[324] "German Language." is written in ink over the same in pencil.

[325] "proposes" and "disposes" are added in pencil. "Man proposes, but God disposes" is used in "The Preacher," *W,* X, 232.

―――――

"Und wer weiss was noch alles!" as we literally say in English, "and who knows what all?"

―――――

Have we English for Schadenfreude?
          ↑⟨spoil the fun⟩ ↑kill-joy↓↓
          ↑wet-blanket↓[326]

―――――

"Muth und Mass in schönen Verein."
spur and rein.

―――――

wohlauf

―――――

Lebemann (Goethe [*Werke,* 1828–1833,] VI. 73.)

―――――

Form, stoff, *Gehalt.*[n]
Geist.

―――――

[2⟨7⟩89]–[291] [blank]
[2⟨8⟩92]   French Language.
                    ―――――――――――

"Que de choses dont je peux me passer!" [Renan, *Essais de Morale . . .* , 1860, p. 374][327]

―――――

"Ils n'y tiendront pas." says Renan of the names of ↑*hommes*↓ *industriels* inscribed on the front of the Crystal Palace beside ⟨*certain*⟩ ↑certain↓ *noms immortels dans la science.* [*Ibid.,* p. 368]

―――――

Balzac, in a letter to the Marchioness of Rambouillet, first hazarded the word *l'urbanité. Roederer* [*Mémoire pour servir à l'histoire de la société polie en France* (Paris, 1835),] p 184[328]

―――――

Je sais bien ce que je veux dire, mais le mot me manque.
                              v. *Roederer,* [*Ibid.,*] p. 186

―――――

[326] "spoil the fun" and "wet-blanket" are in pencil.
[327] See p. [172] above.
[328] This volume is in Emerson's library.

	↑Biot,↓
Pronounce	Un chien comme on en a peu, relief, peser, O ciel, tyrannie, innocence, jolie, monsieur, ses sept sages, queue, comme il faut, mot, sens, sang, tous, noeud, oeuf,

Translate [this town which is so much smaller than New York]
     [bribe]

[2⟨8⟩93] "Il falloit savoir prodigieusement pour prêcher si mal."
                                              La Bruyère.

s'orienter. dépayser. désorienter.

"Non que je veuille dire que l artiste nous dépayse." *Saint Beuve*

"il ne se gêne pas."

"Le tout compose un Perrault comme il n'y en eut jamais jusqu'ici, et comme
il ne s'en verra plus."   *Saint Beuve*

—↑"les sciences↓ pas même la curiosité de se tenir au courant de leurs résul-
tats généraux." *Saint Beuve*[329]

C'etait encore de son vivant (whilst he was living)
               Saint Beuve

montre, *show,* is their name for a *watch.*

Chardin says the English call *la jaunisse, "yallow yander"*
               [*Voyages . . . en Perse . . . ,* 1811, V, 183]
Translate *Esprit de corps* into English.
    ↑clannish; public spirit of a guild, an association.↓[330]

---

[329] This and the three preceding quotations are from Sainte-Beuve, *Nouveaux lundis,*
1863–1870, I, 295, 296, and 298; Emerson borrowed volume I from the Boston Athenaeum July 24–August 1 and October 5–14, 1863.
   [330] "Translate . . . association." is in pencil; "Translate . . . English." is overwritten
in ink.

Le Prince Henri v⟨enoit⟩int en France, du vivant de Frédéric

Louis XVI avait de l'éloignement pour Frédéric,
Le Prince Henri avait du penchant pour Louis XVI.[331]

[2⟨8⟩94] L'article que vous désirez (on the duties & conduct of kings who wish well, but want knowledge,) j'en ai commis le soin à Prométhée; il est le seul qui puisse le fournir: mes facultés ne s'étendent pas aussi loin. Frédéric. *Saint Beuve Causeries [du lundi, 1851–1862,]* Vol. XII. p 326

La Margrave de Bareith says of the French, "J'ai un *chien de tendre* pour eux, qui m'empêche de leur vouloir du mal." [*Ibid.*, p. 331]—We say, "*a sneaking kindness.*"

"mal de la capitale." *De Stael*[332]

————

"Il y a des natures qui naissent pures, et qui ont reçu *quand même* le don d'innocence." *Saint Beuve*

————

↑*Recamier.*↓
"des hommes venus de bien des côtés differents étaient réunis; Montmorency, Moreau, Fox, Erksine, & beaucoup d'autres! On était en presence, on s'observait; c'etait a qui ne commencerait pas." *Saint Beuve. Recamier.*[333]

à part, apart	l'arrière pensée, second thought
gène, constraint	l'apropos,
gener, to bore	se tenir debout, stand
mal de la capitale;	mince
banal	heurté
morgue	
Esprit du corps	

[2⟨8⟩95] Qu'en savez vous? What do you know about it all?[334]

————

[331] For this and the two preceding lines, see Sainte-Beuve, *Causeries du lundi,* 1851–1862, XII, 323 and 325.

[332] " 'mal de . . . *De Stael"* is in pencil. See p. [168] above.

[333] For this and the preceding quotation, see "Madame Récamier," *Causeries du lundi,* 1883, I, 126 and 134.

[334] "Qu'en savez . . . all?" is in pencil.

"Rien ne manque à sa gloire: il manquait à la nôtre." *Saurin*

_____

Qu'en dira-t-on?

_____

"La conversation comme talent n'existe qu'en France."[335]

_____

"J'ai envie d'aller dormir à la belle étoile." Geo Sand[336]

_____

Rien en relief, was Mme de Geoffrin's motto.
     Voila qui est bien.[337]
               [Sainte-Beuve, *Causeries du lundi,* 1851–1862, II, 247]

_____

"Ne ferais je pas mieux, Madame, de m'asseoir sous la table, afin de pouvoir vous passer la serviette plus rapidement?" said Comte d'Orsay to ⟨the Duchess of⟩ ↑Lady↓ Holland[.]

_____

many senses for one sound
sang, sans, sens, sent, sain, cent, [T 152]

[296]–[297] [blank]
[298]–[300] [Index material omitted]
[inside back cover] [Index material omitted]

---

[335] A translation of this quotation is used in "Social Aims," *W,* VIII, 94.
[336] Cf. *JMN,* VI, 376.
[337] See *JMN,* XIII, 277.

KL

1864–1865

The earliest dated entry in Journal KL is that of September 21, 1864 (p. [87]), but Emerson probably began it in late spring or summer, 1864, and used it, concurrently with Journal DL, through June, 1865. One late entry dated Feb. 1869 occurs on p. [164].

Journal KL is a double-ender, the other part of which, poetry notebook KL[A], runs upside down and backward with respect to KL from pages 278 to 223. The covers of the copybook, of marbled brown, blue, red, and black paper over boards, measure 17.1 × 21.0 cm. The spine strip and protective corners on the front and back covers are of tan leather, badly worn. Traces remain on the spine of "KL" inscribed in ink. "1864–5" is inscribed in ink on the front cover, and "KL" on the upper right leather corner.

Including flyleaves (1–2, 279–280), there were 280 unlined pages, but the leaves bearing pages 25–26 and 41–42 have been torn out. The pages are numbered in ink except for nine pages numbered in pencil: 14, 24, 196–201, and 223. Eleven pages are unnumbered: 1, 2, 6, 10, 12, 73, 184, 185, 215, 226, and 280. Two pages are numbered 233, followed by 235. Eighteen pages are blank: 2, 27, 62, 82, 140, 204, 215, 222, 225, 227, 229, 231, 233, 235, 249, 257, 277, and 279. Fifty-seven pages are blank in this sequence but are used for Notebook KL[A]: 223, 224, 226, 228, 230, 232, 234, 236–248, 250–256, 258–276, and 278. Pages 1–51 in the KL[A] sequence are numbered sequentially in pencil.

Laid in between pages 279 and 280 are the following, labeled "Notes on Charles Sumner March '74" by Edward Emerson: a sheet of heavy white unlined paper torn off from a larger sheet to measure 12.8 × 20.0 cm, inscribed in pencil on both sides (printed as 279$_a$–279$_b$); a sheet of unlined letter paper torn off to measure 11.4 × 17.7 cm, with a stationer's mark reading "DELARUE & Co. LONDON" pressed into the upper left corner, inscribed in ink on both sides (279$_c$–279$_d$); a sheet of the same paper as pages 279$_a$–279$_b$ above, torn off to measure 12.8 × 20.2 cm, inscribed in pencil on the recto (279$_e$) and in ink on the verso (279$_f$); a sheet of thin, unlined letter paper measuring 12.5 × 20.4 cm, inscribed on both sides in ink (279$_g$–279$_h$); a sheet of white paper faintly lined in blue on one side, stamped with a stationer's mark (a classic woman's head in left profile), measuring 19.4 × 24.5 cm, folded once to form four pages, three of which are inscribed in ink (279$_i$–279$_k$); a sheet of pale blue paper torn off at the top and right side to measure 12.5 × 20.0 cm, inscribed in ink on both sides (279$_l$–279$_m$); a newspaper clipping giving correspondence between Henry

Ward Beecher and Charles Sumner, January 13 and 14, 1873; and a printed card ("AUTOGRAPH. Presented to the FRENCH FAIR . . . Boston, April, 1871.") inscribed on the recto in ink and pencil with notes probably unrelated to Sumner (279ₙ).

[front cover]   1864–5   KL

[front cover verso] ↑Examined '77↓[1]

To the front!

Τεχνη τυχην εστερξε και τυχη⟨ν⟩ τεχν⟨ν⟩ην. *Agatho Bohn's Aristotle*, Rhetoric p. 38[2]

"Logic the fist, & rhetoric the hand." *Zeno*

[1]   R. W. Emerson—
                        KL.
                        1864

[2] [blank]
[3][3] ⟨the⟩The genius of a race or family is a stream always equal to it-self and if the present tenant fishes it too much, the next tenant, his son, will find the stream poor, & must ⟨forbear⟩ ↑withhold↓ his nets & seines. Hence we say, a great man has not a great son. But this prov-erb has marked exceptions: &, it is also observed, that intellect runs in races.

[4] I too am fighting my campaign[.]

So many things require the top of health[,] the flower of the mind↑,↓ ⟨and⟩ the engraver must not lay stone walls, nor the ↑king's↓ lapidary pave streets. 'Tis fine health that ⟨makes⟩ helps itself with lucky ex-

---

[1] Added in pencil.
[2] "Chance is beloved of Art, and Art of Chance." *Aristotle's Treatise on Rhetoric* . . . , trans. Theodore Buckley (London, 1850), p. 38, n. 9, quoted from *Nichomachean Ethics*, VI, iv, 5.
[3] Page [3] is in pencil.

pressions & fit images:—All things offer themselves to be words & convey its meaning. But lassitude [5] has nothing but prose.[4]

What omniscience has music! ↑So absolutely impersonal, & yet↓ every^n sufferer feels his secret sorrow ⟨reached.⟩ ↑soothed.↓
⟨The wilde⟩
Within, I do not find wrinkles & used ⟨face,⟩ ↑heart,↓ but unspent youth.

Value of an opposition. Only the heat of party can hatch the egg—can formulate the truth which your party overlooks, & which is & will hereafter be admitted to be the ↑needed↓ check on your statement.[5]

[6] inspired orator, inspired poet, &, (in the light of my last reading I should add) inspired critic.[6]

'Tis bad when believers & unbelievers live in the same manner. I distrust the religion.

La carrière ouverte aux talens

A good stand. I notice that the spider finds ↑it↓ a good stand wherever he falls: he takes the first corner, and the flies make haste to come.[7]

[7] ↑*Inspiration*↓
I have found my advantage in going to a hotel with a task which could not prosper at home. I secured so a more absolute solitude,^{n} for it is almost impossible for a housekeeper who↑,↓ ⟨is also⟩ in the coun-

---

[4] "I too . . . prose." is in pencil. For "the flower of the mind", see *JMN*, VI, 179 and "The Method of Nature," *W*, I, 213–214, where the phrase is attributed to Zoroaster.

[5] "What omniscience . . . statement." is written in ink over almost the same in pencil. "So absolutely . . . yet", "heart," and "needed" are added, and "reached." and "face," canceled, only in the ink inscription. The pencil draft reads "I do not . . . face within but . . . youth." in the second sentence, and "which ⟨makes⟩ ↑is↓ & will" in the last.

[6] "inspired orator, . . . critic." is in pencil.

[7] "La carrière . . . come." is written in ink over almost the same in pencil; "it" is added only in the ink inscription, and the pencil version, which is run over onto the bottom of p. [7], reads "& the flies come."

try, ↑is also↓ a small farmer, & who has guests ⟨⟨to⟩also⟩ in the house, to exclude interruptions & even necessary orders, though I bar out by system all I can, & resolutely omit to my constant loss all that can be omitted. In the hotel, I have no [8] hours to keep, no visits, & can command a↑n↓ astronomic leisure. At home the day is cut up into short strips. In the hotel, I ⟨have no sympathy with⟩ ↑forget↓ rain, ⟨or⟩ wind, ⟨or⟩& cold, ⟨or⟩ heat. At home, I remember ↑in my library↓ the wants of the farm, & have all too much sympathy. I ⟨revere⟩ ↑envy↓ the abstraction [9] of some scholars I have known, who ⟨can⟩ ↑might↓ sit ⟨down⟩ on a curb-stone in state street & solve their problem. I have more womanly eyes. All the conditions must be right for my success, slight as that is. ⟨And⟩ What^n untunes is as bad as what cripples or stuns me. Therefore I extol the prudence of Carlyle, who, for years, projected a library [10] at the top of his house, ↑high↓ above the ⟨⟨reach⟩range of⟩ orbit of all housemaids, and ⟨above the⟩ ↑out of↓ ear-shot of doorbells. Could that be once secured,—a whole floor,—room for books, & a good bolt,—he could hope for six years of history. ↑And he kept it in view till it was done.↓ And I remember that Henry Thoreau, with his cynic will, [11] yet found certain trifles disturbing the delicacy of that health which composition ⟨required⟩ exact-ed,—namely, the slightest ⟨chill, ↑t↓he⟩ ↑irregularity↓ or the drink-ing too much water on the preceding day. And ⟨M⟩George Sand's love of heat agrees with mine. Even the ⟨pen⟩ steel pen is a nuisance.[8]

[12] A capital prudence, too, I learned from old President Quincy, who told me that he never goes to bed at night, until he has ⟨ap-pointed⟩ laid out the studies for the next morning.[9]

---

[8] "I have found . . . nuisance." is struck through in ink with two diagonal use marks in the shape of an X, one short diagonal use mark, and two vertical use marks on p. [7]; one vertical and two diagonal use marks in the shape of an X on pp. [8], [9], and [10]; and four diagonal use marks in the shape of two X's on p. [11]. "Printed in Inspiration" is written at the bottom of p. [7] and circled in ink. "Inspiration" is inserted at the top of p. [9], and *"Inspiration"* at the top of p. [11]. "I have found . . . stuns me." and "And I remember . . . nuisance." are used in "Inspiration," *W*, VIII, 288–289 and 290. See also Notebook HT, p. [20] below.

[9] "A capital . . . morning.", struck through in ink with one vertical and two diagonal use marks in the shape of an X, is used in "Inspiration," *W*, VIII, 286. See Journal DL, p. [143] above.

The capital rule must not be forgotten of "une demiheure par jour de lecture suivie et sérieuse,"   or, as Van Helmont says, "study of Eternity."[10]

———

For Trouveurs, see *CL* 167

[13] ↑Inspiration↓
And the first rule for me would be to defend the morning↑.↓ ⟨from⟩ Keep all its dews on. *Il n'y a que le matin en toutes choses.*

Goethe thanks the flies that waked him at dawn as the Musagetes.[11]

———

And where shall I find ↑the record of↓ my brag of places, favorite spots in the woods & on the river, whither I once went with security for a poetic mood?

[14] Memory. I have several times forgotten the name of Flamsteed; never that of Newton. I can easily drop several poets out of the Elizabethan chronology, but not Shakspeare. And here, as in all else, I see, we may safely put the *onus* of ↑being↓ remembered on the *object.*[12]

⟨Londons Crystal Palace⟩
Paris "Exposition" in 1855.[13]
Manchester   1857

[15] In my paper on "Civilization,"[14] I omitted an important trait, namely, the increased ⟨value⟩ respect for human life. The difference between the oriental nations, ↑on one side,↓ & Europe &

———

[10] Jean Baptiste van Helmont, *Oriatrike or, Physick refined. The Common Errors therein Refuted, and the Whole Art Reformed & Rectified . . .* , trans. J[ohn]. C[handler]. (London, 1662), p. 12; see *JMN*, XIV, 57, and "The Celebration of Intellect," *W*, XII, 131.
    [11] "And the first . . . *choses.*", struck through in ink with three diagonal use marks and with two more in the shape of an X, is used in "Inspiration," *W*, VIII, 286. "Goethe . . . Musagetes." is struck through in ink with three diagonal use marks, two of them extended to meet the marks above, and crossed with a fourth; lines from Goethe's poem "Musagetes" are quoted *ibid.,* pp. 284–286.
    [12] "Memory. . . . *object.*", in pencil, is used in "Memory," *W*, XII, 108 and 107.
    [13] "Londons Crystal Palace" is in erased pencil. "Paris . . . 1855." is in pencil.
    [14] Probably "American Civilization" (see *W*, XI, 295–311), published in the *Atlantic Monthly* in April 1862.

America, on the other, lies mainly herein. The Japanese in ⟨London⟩ France are astonished, 'tis said, at the vast apparatus & expense of a ↑capital↓ trial: and see some examples of Eastern slaughter in F⟨o⟩OR 186. Remember General Scott's maxim, too, [16] about the sacrifice of one life more than necessity requires.

↑The↓ French say, that "the special characteristic of English art is the absence of genius." *ap.* M. Chesneau

———

↑Inspiration↓
    M[ary]. M[oody]. E[merson]. writes, "How sad, that atmospheric influences should bring to dust the communions of soul with the Infinite!"—meaning, ↑how sad↓ that the atmosphere should be an excitant. But no, she should be glad that the atmosphere & the dull rock itself should be deluged with deity,—should be theists, ⟨unitar⟩Christian, Unitarian, poetic.[15] See [Notebook] *M M E.* Vol. II, p. 190

[17] ↑Inspiration↓
Shall I add to my list of electrics, after Sleep, Conversation, New Poetry, Fact-books, ↑&c.,↓ certain ⟨places,⟩ ↑localities,↓ as, mountaintops, the shores of large bodies of water, or of rapid brooks, as excitants of the muse? And yet the experience of some good artists would prefer the smallest & plainest chamber with one chair & one table to these picturesque liberties.[16]

[18] You shall not read politic⟨s⟩↑al debates,↓ nor history, nor any French book, nor Montaigne. You may read Plutarch; you may read Plato; you[n] may read Ossian, Chaucer, & the Trouveurs, and Hafiz. ↑& the Hindoo mythology & Ethics:*↓[17]

---

[15] This paragraph is used in "Inspiration," *W,* VIII, 284.

[16] This paragraph is struck through in ink with one vertical use mark and with two diagonal use marks in the shape of an X, and in pencil with a diagonal use mark; "shores of . . . liberties." is struck through in pencil with a vertical use mark; "certain . . . liberties." is used in "Inspiration," *W,* VIII, 290. "Sleep, Conversation, New Poetry, Fact-books," refer to sections of the same essay, pp. 280, 292, 294, and 295.

[17] "You shall . . . Chaucer, &" is struck through in ink with two diagonal use marks, crossed with a third; the first sentence is struck through in ink with a vertical use mark, then extended diagonally parallel to the third. "You shall . . . Ethics:*", struck through in pencil with a diagonal use mark, is used in "Inspiration," *W,* VIII, 295. The asterisk calls attention to the continuation of the passage at the bottom of the page.

Good & bad days is the question. Most are ⟨improv⟩unprofitable. Allston never left his studio two days in succession. One was sufficient rest; the second was thrown away.[18]

---

*And images from whatever quarter⟨.⟩, and the [19] ⟨& the⟩ costly words which the mind comes to use⟨.⟩! namely, the whole inventory of the elements & of events.

For the Romaic Poem of "Charon" see *Goethe, Nachgelassene Werke* Vol. 4. p. 78.[19]

I think Hans Andersen's story of the cobweb cloth woven so fine that it was invisible,—woven for the King's garment,—must mean Manners, which do really clothe a princely nature. [20] ⟨And he who has them not⟩ Such can well go naked. In the gymnasium, or ⟨i⟩on the sea-beach, his superiority does not leave him. But he who has not this fine garment of behavior, is very studious of dress, cannot appear with any calmness until [21] he is carefully drest in what clothes he thinks most becoming, in which he hopes to lie *perdu*n & not be exposed.[20]

⟨Mr⟩ ↑Dr↓ S. Hawtrey, Master of Eton, says, "I refer to another feature which an Eton education calls into existence,—I mean a kind of serenity & repose of character; this will be at once recognized as a well-known characteristic of freeminded [22] English gentlemen, & I think Eton has its full share in perpetuating this characteristic in an age in which there is much vieing with, much outrunning & outwitting one another." This is not irony in ⟨Mr⟩Dr Hawtrey,[21] though it reads so⟨.⟩ ↑⟨th⟩on this side the water.↓

---

[18] "Allston never . . . away.", struck through in ink with five diagonal use marks and in pencil with one, is used in "Inspiration," *W*, VIII, 291.

[19] The fifteen volumes of the *Nachgelassene Werke* are volumes 41–55 of *Werke*, 55 vols. (Stuttgart and Tübingen, 1828–1833), in Emerson's library.

[20] This paragraph, used in "Social Aims," *W*, VIII, 80–81, is struck through in pencil with single diagonal use marks on pp. [19] and [20], and two diagonal use marks on p. [21]. It is struck through in ink on p. [19] with two diagonal use marks, crossed with a third; on p. [20] with one vertical use mark, a diagonal use mark across that, and two short diagonal use marks from "not⟩ Such" to "who has not"; and on p. [21] with three diagonal use marks, crossed with a fourth.

[21] Probably Edward Craven Hawtrey (1789–1862), provost of Eton from 1852 to 1862. The paragraph to this point, struck through in pencil with single diagonal use

↑In 1863, Paris Population 1,696,151. souls.↓[22]

—— ↑*Hazing.*↓
The Freshmen, it is said, go enthusiastically into the "⟨e⟩Early closing movement." What is so pathetic as the poor ↑Freshman↓ boy behind his shutters?

[23] "La maitrise ↑/freedom/dignity/↓[23] de l'esprit francais, au moins depuis Louis XIV., est bien plus dans la forme, que dans le fond des choses." *Renan* ["L'Instruction supériure en France, son histoire et son avenir,"] *Rev*[*ue*]. *des D*[*eux*]. *M*[*ondes*]. May [1]. 1864. [p. 84]

Of Paris, he writes, after saying that the provincial Academies of France have no original studies,——
Cette brillante Alexandrie sans *succursales* ↑church, chapel of ease,↓ ⟨en⟩↑m'↓inquiète et m'effraie. Aucun atelier de travail intellectuel ne peut être comparé a Paris: on dirait une ville faite exprès pour l'usage des gens d'esprit: mais qu'il faut se défier de ces oasis au milieu d'un desert. Des dangers perpetuels les assiègent. Un coup de vent, une source tarie, quelques palmiers coupés, et le désert reprend ses droits.[24] [*Ibid.,* p. 88]

[24] When ⟨I read⟩ Renan speaks of France, or any Englishman ↑Macaulay↓ of England, or any American of America, I feel how babyish they are[.][25]
I suppose hardly Newton, or Swedenborg, or Cervantes, or Menu, can be trusted to speak of his nationality[.][26]

Nationality babyish.
kleinstadtisch[27]

---

marks on pp. [21] and [22], is used in the lecture "Public and Private Education"; see Gohdes, *Uncollected Lectures,* 1932, p. 13.

[22] "In 1863, . . . souls." is in pencil.

[23] These two words are inserted in pencil.

[24] In the first sentence of the quotation, "*succursales*" is underlined, and "church, chapel of ease," added, in pencil. "Cette brillante . . . droits." is struck through in pencil with a diagonal use mark.

[25] "When ⟨I . . . are", in pencil, is struck through in pencil with a diagonal use mark. This page is indexed "Esprit du corps".

[26] This sentence is written in ink over the same in pencil.

[27] For "Nationality babyish.", in ink, and "kleinstadtisch", in pencil, see Journal VA, pp. [51] and [149] above.

[25]–[26] [leaf torn out]²⁸
[27] [blank]

[28] Wilkinson's Tract on smallpox at once explains the success & the happy temper of the man. For, with this genius for his profession, Medicine ⟨at⟩becomes a heroic art. Every discovery that he makes he has presently↑ a signal occasion to apply & verify↑,↓ ⟨it⟩ to the delight of the patient, & of a host of ⟨deeply⟩ trembling friends who cannot enough reward & praise him. [29] No place is obscure, no country dreary or ungrateful to such a talent. Wherever is pain, wherever life is valuable, he is greeted as a demigod↑—

See the spider's good stand.
supra, p 6↓²⁹

———

I invited lately four of these skeletons to supper—

[30] ⟨⟨———⟩The⟩ It is a trait of the English, that they are more Englishmen, than they are men.³⁰

———

The grief of old age is, that, now, only in rare moments, & by happiest combinations or consent of the elements can we attain those enlargements & that intellectual *élan,* which were once a daily gift.

——— ———

↑*France.*↓
The French version of Terence's line, is, "Je suis femme, et Parisienne, et rien de ce qui est étranger ne me parait tout à fait humain."³¹   Lagardie   Causeries Parisiennes

²⁸ Page [25] is indexed under "English," "Egoism," "French Lang.," and "Towns," and p. [26] under "Conversation."
²⁹ "Wilkinson's Tract . . . demigod" is struck through in pencil with single diagonal use marks on pp. [28] and [29]. The dash after "demigod" and "See the . . . *supra,* p 6" are added in pencil. "Medicine . . . art." and "No place . . . demigod" are used in the lecture "Resources"; see Gohdes, *Uncollected Lectures,* 1932, p. 25. James John Garth Wilkinson (1812–1899), an English physician and a prolific writer on Blake, Swedenborg, and medicine, was a strong opponent of vaccination.
³⁰ This sentence is struck through in pencil with a diagonal use mark.
³¹ Terence's original line, from *The Self-Tormentor,* I, i, 25, is "Homo sum: humani nil a me alienum puto." ("I am a man. I hold that what affects another man affects me.") See *JMN,* XI, 303. "The French . . . Parisiennes", struck through in pencil with a diagonal use mark, is used in an English translation in the lecture "Table-Talk"; see Gohdes, *Uncollected Lectures,* 1932, p. 37.

[31] "As ⟨many⟩ good fish in the sea as ever came out of it⟨.⟩;"
" 'Twill be all the same a hundred years hence."—

Great comfort to the popular ear in these two proverbs.

———

Add, There is always a way.
And "The world is always equal to itself."[32]

"Hortense, ↑ci-devant↓ Queen of Holland entreated Mme de Stael &
Madame Recamier to meet Prince Auguste of Prussia at Saint Leu, &,
from her chateau took them out on a drive. Mme. de Stael, at a fine
point of view, was reminded of Italy. Hortense, now Duchesse de
Saint Leu, said, 'Avez vous ⟨été⟩donc été en Italie?' ⟨All the⟩ [32]
↑⟨rest⟩↓ All^n cried out with one voice, 'Et Corinne, Corinne⟨,⟩!' The
Duchess blushed, & the conversation took a new turn." *Memoires de
Recamier*[33]

———

To Nat[ural]. Hist[ory] of Int[ellect]. belongs the analogy of
spatial distance & qualitative difference.

———

Mme de Stael preferred conversation[.][34]

———

our New Chronology of the cannon   DL 174[35]

American literature, like our politics, is like the raft again, as compared with the ship. Destroy a few men, & English or French literature is gone; but [33] our people are all educated to read & write.

Paris population 1,696,151.
Solitude of morning. *AC* 243 [actually 24⟨3⟩6][36]

[32] "And 'The . . . itself.' " may have been added. See *JMN*, XIII, 9, for many uses
of this sentence (and for "As ⟨many⟩ . . . of it"); see also p. [53] below, Journal DL, p.
[145] above, and "Character," *W*, X, 112.
[33] "All the" is canceled, and "rest" added and canceled, in pencil. See *Souvenirs et
correspondance tirés des papiers de Mme. Récamier* . . . , 2 vols. (Paris, 1859), I, 270–272.
[34] Cf. "Social Aims," *W*, VIII, 94.
[35] "our new. . . DL 174" is in pencil.
[36] "Paris population . . . *AC* 243" is in pencil.

One man by his manners pins me to the wall; ⟨&⟩ ↑with↓ another, I walk among the stars.[37]

"Mothers hid their sons, wives their husbands, companions their friends," lest they should be led by St Bernard's eloquence to join the monastery. Morison's Life of St B. p. 17[38]

[34] Men are good where they have experience, but not off their beat. Hence Dr Robert Hare & Mr R. G. Shaw, & many other men reckoned of excellent sense, tumble helplessly into mesmeric spiritism, & prove its most credulous dupes, because ⟨th⟩here they have ↑no↓ guide.[39] It is in government, as it is in War. It was said, many officers can manoeuvre a regiment[n] [35] or a division, who could not get a hundred thousand men in or out of Hyde Park, without confusion. So in government. There is plenty of administrative skill in trade & civil affairs, management of railroads & factories, which is at once at a loss & unequal to the disposition of the affairs of an Empire.

[36] A good text was that medical observation suggested by the distemper of the cattle at Chenery's & elsewhere,—namely that ⟨we⟩ men carry the seeds of diseases in their constitutions latent, & which remain latent, during much, perhaps during the whole of their life. But if it happen that the patient loses, from any cause, his normal strength, instantly these seeds begin to ripen, & the disease, so long latent, [37] becomes acute, & conquers him.

———

I have more enjoyed, in the last hours of finishing a chapter, the insight which has come to me of how the truths really stand, than I suffered from seeing in what confusion I had left them in my statement.

June, 1865

[37] This sentence, struck through with four diagonal use marks in ink and one in pencil, is used in "Social Aims," *W*, VIII, 83.

[38] James Cotter Morison, *The Life and Times of Saint Bernard, Abbot of Clairvaux. A.D. 1091–1153* (London, 1863); in Emerson's library. " 'Mothers hid . . . p. 17" is struck through in pencil with a diagonal use mark extended from the pencil use mark above; the anecdote is used in "Eloquence," *W*, VIII, 122.

[39] See Journal GL, p. [381] above.

[38] St ⟨fr⟩Francis rode all day along the border of the Lake of Geneva, &, at night, hearing his companions speak of the lake, inquired What lake?

Morison's Life of   p. 75[40]

'Tis like Alcott's inquiry about pond lilies.

[39] Power of ridicule. In Paris, after the hearth of Mme. de Poplinière was found to turn on a pivot of steel, which Marechal de Richelieu who lived in the adjacent house, caused to be made,—the toy-shops were full of little turning hearths for presents.

It is a tie between men to have read the same book, and it is a disadvantage not to have read the book or books your mates have read, [40] or not to have read it at the right time, so it may take the place in your culture it does in theirs, & you shall understand their allusions to it, & not give it more or less emphasis than they do. Yet, ⟨if⟩ the strong character does[41] [41]–[42] [leaf torn out][42]

[43] Great men are the universal men, men of the common sense. ↑not provincial, Raffaelle not a mannerist↓ Every body would paint like Raffaelle, if every body could paint at all. see *TU* 269

Yonder meadow is full of milk, but it needs a cow to extract it.— ↑and a bee the honey.[43] See *infra*, p. 153↓

I find in *Y* 229,— [Shakspeare's fault that the world appears so empty. He has educated you with his painted world, & this real one seems a huckster's shop.]

[40] This anecdote, actually of St. Bernard, is in Morison, *The Life and Times of Saint Bernard* . . . , 1863, p. 75.

[41] "It is a tie . . . does", struck through in pencil with single diagonal use marks on pp. [39] and [40], is used in "Address at the Opening of the Concord Free Public Library," *W*, XI, 507. It was also used in the lecture "Books," which Emerson delivered on December 25, 1864; see Gohdes, *Uncollected Lectures*, 1932, p. 39.

[42] Page [41] is indexed under "Imagination," and p. [42] under "Coombs," "Subjects," "E.W.E.," "Influence," "Nature," and "Realism." See Notebook HT, p. [19] below.

[43] "Yonder meadow . . . honey." is struck through in ink with a vertical use mark, fingerwiped below "extract it.—".

[44] "We can never compete with English in manufactures, because of the low price of labor in Europe,"—say the merchants, day by day. Yet, this season, half or two thirds of our laborers are gone to the war, and we have reaped all the hay ⟨& wheat⟩ by the use of the horse-mower & the horse-rake; the wheat, by MacCormick's reaper; &, when the shoemakers went, then, by the use of the new pegging machine & scrap-machine, we [45] make ⟨300⟩ ↑600↓ pairs of shoes every day at Feltonville, & can let Weymouth send away 100 shoe-makers to the war in the regiment that has just departed. We make horseshoes by machine as well at Pittsburg. We ⟨do⟩ can spare ↑all the↓ ⟨sailors⟩whalemen to the navy, for we draw oil out of the rocks in Pennsylvania; we can spare the Cuba sugar, for we made 7 000 000 ⟨tons⟩gallons of sorghum molasses ⟨last year:⟩ ↑⟨in 1860⟩↓ in 1860, though the article was not known here in 1850.[44]

Parlor democrats

[46]   Massachusetts has 7000 square miles;
                a shore line (sea & river) of 764 miles.

1860.   population 1,230,000.
                rate of mortality in Mass[achuse]tts. 1 in 92

        Value of property per^n head, $235.

1860.   Value of all property real & personal $815,000,000

1860. In this year, the machinery of Mass[achuse]tts was returned as capable of doing the work of more than a hundred million of men. ↑p. 36 of David Wells's "Our Burden and our Strength."↓[45]

[44] This entry is struck through in pencil with single diagonal use marks on pp. [44] and [45]. Cf. the report of the lecture "Resources" in Gohdes, *Uncollected Lectures*, 1932, p. 24.
[45] Emerson quoted this statement from Wells's pamphlet, published in New York by the Loyal Publications Society in 1864, in the lecture "Resources"; see Gohdes, *Uncollected Lectures*, 1932, p. 24.

[47] In that theme of ⟨i⟩*Inspiration*,[n] 'tis to be noted, that we use ourselves, & use each other: some perceptions,—I think the best,— are granted to the single soul:—they come from the depth, & go to the depth, & are the permanent & controlling ones.—Others it takes two to find. We must be warmed by the fire of sympathy to be brought into the right conditions & angles of vision.[46]

[48]   Kings
"Quand la bonne foi serait bannie de la terre, elle devrait se retrouver dans le coeur des rois." said the French King John, who was taken prisoner at Poitiers.

[49] *On rit avec toi, et tu te fâches.*

Sir George Lewis said, "life was very tolerable, if it were not for the pleasures."
      There is always a way.
Why saltpetre in old houses?
Robert Brown's Writings
T threw his cigar into the grass, & persuaded Matilda Jane it was a glowworm.[47]
"failed beautifully"

———

      The French say the English are so decorous that they put pantaloons on the legs of the pianos.

———

      Miss Peabody, who knows none but phoenixes, describes her newest child as "having an immense thirst for society."
↑Her last was a boy who was a scamp, & was described as "so constituted that he could not be left alone."↓[48]

[50] *Manners.* Their vast convenience I must always admire. The perfect defence & isolation which they effect makes ⟨that⟩ an insuper-

---

[46] "we use . . . vision.", struck through in pencil with a diagonal use mark, is used in "Inspiration," *W,* VIII, 292–293.
   [47] "Why saltpetre . . . glowworm." is in pencil.
   [48] The insertion is at the bottom of p. [48], set off by a wavy line above it.

able protection. Though he wrestle with you, or swim with you, ⟨live⟩lodge in the same chamber, sleep in the same bed, he is yet a thousand miles off, & can at any moment finish with you. Manners seem to say, 'You are you, & I am I.'[49]

[51]   ↑The following page should have been printed in *Solitude & Society*, in the Chapter called '*Old Age.*'↓[50]

Old age brings along with it↑s↓ uglinesses the comfort that you will soon be out of it,—which ought to be a substantial relief to such discontented pendulums as we are. To be out ⟨de⟩of the war, out of debt, out of the drouth, out of the blues, out of the dentist's hands, out of the second thoughts, mortifications & remorses that inflict such twinges & shooting pains,—out of the next winter, & the high prices, & company below your ambition,—surely [52] these are soothing hints. And, ↑harbinger of this,↓ what ⟨an⟩a↑n↓ ⟨daily⟩ alleviator is sleep, which muzzles all these dogs for me every day! Old Age. 'Tis proposed to call an indignation meeting.

———————

I never met anything so manifestly created to be seen, and it would have been idiocy not to look.

[53] ↑*Man*↓
The ⟨animal⟩ ↑body↓ borrows the elements of its blood from the whole world. & the mind its belief.[51]

The tradition is never left at peace, but must be winnowed again by the newcomers. "Every age has another sieve, & will sift it out again." See *FOR* 43

World always equal to itself, & keeps itself equal. All decomposition is recomposition. See *FOR* 31 [actually 131][52]

———————

[49] This paragraph, struck through in pencil with a vertical use mark, is used in "Social Aims," *W*, VIII, 81.

[50] "The following . . . *Age.*' " is added in pencil.

[51] A vertical pencil line is drawn in the left margin beside this entry.

[52] With this and the preceding entry, cf. "Character," *W*, X, 112. See also p. [31] above.

Our Democratic party shows itself very badly in these days, simply destructive, and would tear down God from Heaven if they could.

[54] Talk with Alcott last night

Men have no scale. Talents warp them. They don't see when their tendency is wrong, don't discriminate ⟨instantly⟩ be↑t↓ween the rank of this & that perception.[53]

A gossiping rambling talk, & yet kept the line of American tendencies. The English & French are still 30 or 40 years back in theology. What questions do bishops & universities discuss! We have silently passed ⟨by⟩ beyond all such Debateable Lands.

[55] Want of scale appears in this; each[n] of the masters has some puerility, as Carlyle his proslavery whim; Tennyson, English class feeling; University men, churchmen,   not humanity, heroism, truth. Our faculties are of different ages. The Memory is mature, sometimes the imagination adult, & yet the Moral sense still swaddled & sheathed. Yet on the credit of their talent, these masters are allowed to parade this baby faculty, all fits & folly, [56] in the midst of grown company.

We have freedom, ↑are↓ ready for truth, but have not the executive culture of Germany. They have good metaphysics,—have made surveys, sounding every rod of way, set their foot on every rock, and where they felt the rock they planted a buoy & recorded ⟨the⟩it. Kant, Hegel, Schelling, are architects. Scope is not sufficient. We have scope, but we [57] want the Copernicus of our inward heaven. Let us be very mum at present about American literature. One of these ages, we too will set our feet on Andes' tops.

We ⟨have gre⟩lack ⟨of rich⟩ repose. As soon as we stop working, or active thinking, we mope: there is no self-respect, no grand sense of sharing the Divine presence. We are restless, run out & back, talk fast, & overdo.[54]

[58] Nothing in the universe so solid as a thought.

[53] "Talk with . . . perception." is in pencil.
[54] With this paragraph, cf. "The Fortune of the Republic," *W*, XI, 531–532.

[59]⁵⁵ An Indian came to the white man's door & asked for rum.
"O no, ↑said the farmer↓ I don't give rum to Indians, they steal my pigs & chickens."
"O me ↑⟨not⟩ ↑no↓ steal; me↓ good Indian↑.↓ ⟨not steal.⟩"
↑—↓"But good Indians don't ask for rum," replied the farmer.
"Me no good Indian, me dam rascal."

[60] Use of towns I considered in an old Journal in many points. But we are far from having the best aesthetics out of them. The French & Italians have made a nearer approach to it. A town ↑in Europe↓ is a place where you can go into a café⟨e⟩ at ⟨any⟩ a certain hour of every day, buy *eau sucrée,* or a cup of coffee, for six sous, &, at that price, have the company of the wits, scholars & gentlemen fond of conversation. [61] That is a cheap & excellent club, which finds & leaves all parties ⟨in⟩on a good mutual footing. ⟨We⟩ That is the fame of the "Café Procope," the "Cafe Grec" of Rome, the "Cafe de Trinità" of Florence, & the principle of it exists in every town in France & Italy. But we do not man⟨g⟩age it so well in America. Our clubbing is much more costly & cumbersome.⁵⁶
⟨One might say that⟩ Theⁿ test of civilization is the power of drawing the most benefit out of cities.

[62] [blank]

[63] The young men in America take little thought of what men in England are thinking or doing. That is the point which decides the welfare of a people,—*which way does it look?* If to any other people, it is not well with them. If occupied in its own affairs & thoughts & men, with a force which excludes almost the notice of any other [64] people, as the Jews, as the Greeks, as the Persians, as the Romans, as the Arabians, as the French, as the English, at the best times in their history have done,—they are sublime, & we know that, in this abstraction, they are executing excellent work.⁵⁷

---

⁵⁵ Page [59] is in pencil.
⁵⁶ "A town . . . conversation." and "Our clubbing . . . cumbersome." are used in the lecture "Table-Talk"; see Cabot's abstract in *A Memoir* . . . , 1887–1888, II, 789, and Gohdes, *Uncollected Lectures,* 1932, p. 36.
⁵⁷ "The young . . . work.", struck through in pencil with single vertical use marks on pp. [63] and [64], is used in "Social Aims," *W,* VIII, 103–104, and in the lecture "The Fortune of the Republic"; see *W,* XI, 647.

It may be safely affirmed that when the highest ⟨idea⟩ ↑conception,↓ the lessons of religion, are imported, the nation is [65] not culminating, has not genius, but is servile. The less America looks abroad, as now, the grander its promise.

A true nation loves its vernacular tongue. ↑A completed nation does not import its religion. Duty grows everywhere, like children, like grass, and we need not go to Asia to learn it.↓[58]

[66] 'Tis a good word of Niebuhr in speaking of the respect which somehow the "oracles" obtained in the ancient world,—"Did man, in those early periods, stand nearer to Nature⟨.⟩?" See Lieber's Reminiscences—*p. 188*[59]

Suetonius said of Caesar, *"Jure necatus est:"*[60] but the similar sentence of Niebuhr is perhaps more authoritative.

See Ibid. p 166

In Italy a nobleman said to Niebuhr, "I understand the present Pope is not even a man of family." "O," replied N., "I have been told that Christ himself[n] [67] was not a man of family; and St Peter, if I recollect well, was but of a vulgar origin. Here in Rome we don't mind these things." [*Ibid.,*] p 167[61]

↑"Nearly↓ all[n] (the statues) we see & admire in Rome has been dug out of the ground, & is but the gleaning. Everything above the surface of the ⟨ground⟩ earth had been burnt for lime."* Niebuhr⟨s⟩. [*Ibid.,*] p[p. 166,] 165

* Compare what is said of Nineveh, *VO* 243.

[58] "It may . . . nation is" is struck through in pencil on p. [64] with a vertical use mark; "when the . . . servile." and "A true . . . learn it." are used in "Character," *W*, X, 111. See also *JMN*, X, 94.
[59] Francis Lieber, *Reminiscences of an Intercourse with Mr. Niebuhr the Historian, During a Residence with Him in Rome, in the Years 1822 and 1823* (Philadelphia, 1835), which Emerson borrowed from the Boston Athenaeum September 10–October 29, 1864.
[60] Cf. "et iure caesus existimetur" ("and was justly slain"), Suetonius, *The Lives of the Caesars,* I ("The Deified Julius"), LXXVI.
[61] "In Italy . . . p 167" is struck through in pencil with single diagonal use marks on pp. [66] and [67].

"When Frederic II. sought to induce the Turks to make war against Russia, they answered, "Canst thou make twenty five years of twenty?" An armistice had ⟨a⟩five years to run.

Niebuhr. [Ibid., p. 160]

[68]   ↑*Germany*↓
"As it always has been in Germany, no plan-maker was to be found."

Niebuhr. [Ibid.,] p 161[62]

"Michel Angelo was the man to be the first King of Italy."[63] [*Ibid.,* p. 79]

"I ⟨have⟩ never forget anything I once have seen, read or heard." *Niebuhr* [*Ibid.,*] p. 84

and I should say of Michel, that the power of his pictures & works is not so much correct art, as it is great humanity. I accept easily all the criticism I hear on his style: It does not lessen him.

[69] *The naïveté with which English accuse Americans of love of money, is beautiful. Niebuhr, with equal simplicity, accuses the French; and every nation every other nation;—as if it could be otherwise, men being such, & money being such.[64]

See [*ibid.,*] p. 86—*Lieber's Niebuhr*

Popes do not believe in miracles more than other people. [*Ibid.,* p. 87]

[70] It was a good speech of [Edwin Percy] Whipple's, ⟨i⟩amid some talk, long years ago, against the Southerners who "would dissolve the

* But I believe it is sometimes profligate, & the ⟨mere⟩ coarse artifice of the rogue who cries, Stop thief!

---

[62] See *JMN*, VI, 373.

[63] A line ending in an arrow connects " 'Michel Angelo" with "and I should say" below.

[64] "The naïveté . . . such.", struck through in pencil with two diagonal use marks, is used in the lecture "Table-Talk"; see Gohdes, *Uncollected Lectures*, 1932, p. 37.

Union,"—"that he could↑n't take a man's arm in Washington st, &↓ walk down to state street↑,↓ ⟨with ⟨hardly any man⟩ ↑him↓⟩ without wishing to dissolve the Union with him."[65]

"People had formerly much more time than we have. Consider all the time eaten up by morning calls & evening parties."

[Lieber, *Reminiscences of . . .*] *Niebuhr* [1835, p. 96]

———

Various powers: Power of getting work out of others, which Napoleon had. [*Ibid.,* p. 111]

[71] When I go to talk with Alcott it is not so much to get his thoughts as to watch myself under his influence. He excites me, & I think freely. But he mistakes me, & thinks, if J. is right, that I come to feed on him.[66]

[72] It is mortifying ⟨to see⟩that all events must be seen by wise men even, through the ⟨micrifying⟩ ↑⟨l⟩↓ diminishing lens of ⟨their⟩ ↑a petty↓ interest. Could we have beli[e]ved that England should have disappointed us thus? that ⟨when⟩ no man in all that civil, reading, brave, cosmopolitan country, should have looked at our revolution as a student [73] of history, as philanth[r]opist, eager to see what new possibilities for humanity were to begin,—what the inspirations were; what new move on the board the Genius of the world was preparing. ⟨b⟩No, but every one squinted; Lords, Ladies, statesmen, scholars, poets, all squinted,—like Borrow's gipsies⟨,⟩ when he read St. John's Gospel.[67] [74] Edinburg, Quarterly, Saturday Review, Gladstone, Russell, Palmerston, Brougham, nay Tennyson; Carlyle, I blush to say it; Arnold. Every one forgot his history, his poetry, his religion, & looked only at his shoptill, whether his salary, whether his ⟨earnings t⟩ small investment in the funds, would not be less: whether the stability of English order [75] might not be in some degree endangered. No Milton, no Bacon, no Berkeley, no Montesquieu, no Adam Smith was

———

[65] See *JMN*, XIV, 86.
[66] Cf. "Inspiration," *W*, VIII, 292.
[67] See *JMN*, XIII, 158, and "Religion," *W*, V, 229–230.

there to hail a new dawn of hope & culture for men, to see the opportunity for riddance of this filthy pest which dishonored human Nature; to cry over to us, "Up & God ⟨go⟩ with you! ↑And for this slavery, —↓ Off with its head! [76] We see & applaud; the world is with you; such occasion does not come twice. Strike for the Universe of Men!"

No; but, on the other hand, every poet, every scholar, every great man, as well as ↑the rich,↓ thought only of his pocket book, & to our astonishment cried, *Slavery forever! Down with the North!* ↑*Why does not England join with France to protect the slaveholder?*↓ [77] I thought they would have seized the occasion to ⟨entreat⟩ ↑forgive↓ the Northerner every old grudge; to forget their dislike of his rivalry, of his social short-comings; forget, in such a moment, all petty disgusts & ⟨seen⟩ ↑would see↓ in him the honored instrument of Heaven to destroy this rooted poisontree of ↑five↓ thousand years.

[78] We shall prosper, we shall destroy slavery, but by no help of theirs. They assailed us with mean cavils, they sneered at our manners, at our failures, at our shifts, at the poverty of our treasury, at our struggles & ↑legal & municipal↓ irregularities, in the presence of mortal dangers. They cherished our enemies, they [79] exulted at the factions which crippled us at home; whenever the allies of the rebels obstructed the great will & action of the Government, they danced ⟨with⟩ ↑for↓ joy.

They ought to have remembered that great actions have mean beginnings; poor matters point to rich ends, that[68]   (See p. 95 *infra*)

[80] Alas for ⟨them⟩ England, she did not know her friends. 'Tis a bad omen for England, that, in these years, her ↑foreign↓ policy is ignominious, that she plays a sneaking part with Denmark, with France, with Russia, with China, with America.

[81] ↑*The War.*↓
     The War has cost us many valuable lives; but perhaps it has compensated us, by making many lives valuable that were not so before,—through the start & expansion it has given them. It has de-

---

[68] Shakespeare, *The Tempest*, III, i, 3–4; see *JMN*, VI, 26.

moralized many rebel regiments; but I hold that it has *moralized* many of ours.[69]

Gov. Andrew says; the fact that young men leave the farms to go into the cities to ⟨d⟩trade, is perhaps balanced by the disposition of the fathers to return from trade to their native farms.—[70]

[82] [blank]
[83] ↑Farming: Manure:↓
N. C. Mecker, Dongola, Illinois, at the Am. Institute Farmers Club, N. Y. says;
"What every farmer wants, & is unwise if he do not have it, is a piece of ground which he can depend upon, ⟨w⟩let the season be what it may. He wants ground where the seeds will come up quickly; where plants will grow from the first, right along, night & day; where drought only will check the growth; where rain will produce wonderful changes; where insects cannot destroy the young leaves as fast as they grow; where the crop matures, even though frosts come earlier than ever before known. [84] They want ground that shall be sure every time. Land simply rich, naturally rich, like our prairies, will not be enough. An acre of manured land on the naturally richest farm in Illinois will yield astonishingly more than any other acre, particularly if it (the season?) is unfavorable, for then it will beat it out of sight."

N. Y. Tribune, Sept. 17. 1864

———

Remember Madden's rule to Dr Johnson, about having fruit enough in an orchard,—"enough to eat, enough to lay up, enough to be stolen, & enough to rot on the ground."[71]

[85] Among resources, too, might be set down that rule of my travelling friend, "When I estimated the costs of my tour in Europe, I added a couple of hundreds to the amount, to be cheated of, & then gave myself no more uneasiness when I was overcharged here or there."

[69] "The War . . . ours.", struck through in pencil with a diagonal use mark, is used in the lecture "Public and Private Education," given in Boston on November 27, 1864; see Gohdes, *Uncollected Lectures,* 1932, p. 5.
[70] "Gov. Andrew . . . farms.—" is in a smaller hand and may have been added.
[71] James Boswell, *The Life of Samuel Johnson* (London, 1827), p. 493; in Emerson's library.

So Thoreau's practice to put a hundred seeds into every melon hill, instead of 8 or 10;

Affirmative.
John Newton said, "the best way to prevent a bushel being filled with chaff, is to fill it with wheat."[72]

Trench "on the Study of Words."
——"Past & Present of the Eng. Language."[73]

[86] When a man writes descriptions of the sun as seen through telescope, he is only writing autobiography, or an account of the habit & defects of his own eyes.

Henry Thoreau found the height of the cliff over the river to be ↑ft.↓ 231.09[.]

---

[87] ↑1864↓
Sept. 21. Hon. Lyulf Stanley, Wendell Phillips, & Agassiz, Channing, & Alcott, here↑.↓ ⟨together⟩Agassiz is really a man of great ability, breadth & resources, a rare & rich *Nature,*[n] and always maintains himself,—in all companies, & on all occasions. I carried him to Mrs Mann's. And, afterwards, to Bull's, &, in each house, he gave the fittest counsel in the best way. At the Town Hall, he made an excellent speech to the farmers, ⟨entirely⟩ extemporaneous, of course, but with method [88] & mastery, on the question of the location of the Agricultural College, urging th⟨a⟩e claims of Cambridge. Judge French ⟨n⟩followed him with a very good statement of the history of the affair from the beginning until now.[74]

---

[72] Cf. "One proposes to fill a bushel with tares; now if I can fill it first with wheat, I shall defy his attempts" in *The Works of the Rev. John Newton . . . to Which are Prefixed, Memoirs of His Life, &c. by the Rev. Richard Cecil, A.M.,* 2 vols. (New York, 1851), I, 60.

[73] Richard Chenevix Trench, *On the Study of Words* (New York, 1854), and *English Past and Present* (New York, 1855).

[74] When Carlyle's young friend Edward Lyulf Stanley (1839–1925) came to Concord, Emerson, pleased to find him "on *our* side in politics," invited Phillips, Agassiz, El-

Agassiz thinks, that, if he could get a calf elephant, and young enough, that is, before birth, he should find the form of the [89] Mastodon: that, if he could get a ta⟨b⟩pir calf ⟨f⟩before birth, he should find the form of the Megatherion. But, at present, these are practical impossibilities, as the↑y↓ require hundreds of dissections; hundreds, that is, of live subjects.

↑Resources.↓
I learned from [Ephraim] Bull, that a perfect protection of the grapes from frost is a smoke or smudge[.]
'Tis like Linnaeus, & his ↑immersion of timber↓ to destroy the cynips.

[90]   ↑*Three considerations.*↓
On the Agric. College question much is to be said for Harvard.
1. If Amherst College has ⟨c⟩mineral, & chemical, & literary collections to offer, Cambridge more. Cambridge selects its teachers from the Continent,—has the first choice. If, in any college, a first rate man is found, Cambridge takes him away. Amherst & the country colleges have only the second ⟨&⟩or third choice.
2. Then for the charge that the tone of Cambridge is aristocratic & indolent, that will no more apply to the [91] ⟨young⟩ students of the Agricultural College, than to the shoemakers or merchants that plant themselves there.
3. When you have Niagara River to cross, your canoe does not help you; nor, if the country ⟨c⟩around should collect a hundred canoes, ⟨neither⟩ will that help you: you want a steamboat. And for a high & perfect education, as your country academy, called a college, cannot give it, so neither is it any better that you make twenty colleges. No, you want a University.

[92] "Whoever can learn to write can learn to draw."
"Whoever can speak can sing."[75]

---

lery Channing, and Alcott to meet him. See *L,* V, 382, and *CEC,* p. 540. Mary Peabody Mann, widow of Horace Mann, had bought a house in Concord in 1860. Ephraim Bull, who developed the Concord grape, was another Concord neighbor. Henry Flagg French, father of sculptor Daniel Chester French, was president of the Massachusetts Agricultural College at Amherst in 1865–1866. See *L,* V, 430.
[75] For this sentence, see *JMN,* VIII, 138, and "Eloquence," *W,* VII, 61.

At Goose Pond, great herons, ducks,

———

The Romans were essentially farmers. [Lieber, *Reminiscences of . . .*] *Niebuhr.* [1835, p. 95]

Dec. 1   Yesterday, in the fine afternoon, I counted about fifty wild geese on Walden Pond.

[93]   ↑1864↓
24 September. Yesterday with Ellery walked through "Becky Stow's Hole," dry-shod, hitherto a feat for a muskrat alone.[76]
The sky & air & autumn woods in their early best. This year, the river meadows all dry & permeable to the wa↑l↓ker. But why should nature always be on the gallop? Look now & instantly, or you shall never see it: Not ten minutes' repose allowed. Incessant whirl. And 'tis the same with my companion's genius. You must carry a stenographic press in your pocket to save his commentaries on things & men, or they are irrecoverable. I [94] tormented my memory just now in vain to restore a witty criticism of his, yesterday, on a book.

———

Room! room! breathing space! play ground! horizon! Ah! in him were chambers in ⟨his⟩ ↑the↓ brain, halls, palaces, champaigns heaven-wide.

> Though Love recoil, & ⟨R⟩reason cha⟨s⟩fe,
> There came a voice without reply,
> ' 'Tis man's perdition to be safe,
> When for the Truth he ought to die.'[77]

[95] The American Nationality is now within the Republican Party. Hence its security. In like manner, ⟨the cause⟩[n] ↑in view of all the nationa⟨t⟩lities of the world, the battle↓ of humanity is now in the American Union, & hence the weakness of English & European opposition.[78]

[76] "Becky Stow's Hole" was a swamp between the Bedford Road and the Lexington Road, about a mile from Emerson's house.
[77] "Sacrifice," *W*, IX, 296. The quatrain is struck through in ink with a vertical use mark.
[78] This paragraph is used in Emerson's letter of September 26, 1864, to Carlyle, *CEC*, p. 541.

Napoleon's word, that, in 25 years, the United States would dictate the poli⟨cy⟩tics of the world, was a little early; but the sense was just, with a Jewish interpre[ta]tion^n [96] of the ↑"forty days" &↓ "seventy weeks." It is true, that, if we escape bravely from the present war, America will be the controlling power.

[97] 'Tis a defect ⟨that⟩ in our manners that they have not yet reached the prescribing a term to visits. That every well-dressed lady or gentleman should be at liberty to exceed ten minutes in his or her call on serious people, shows a ⟨rude⟩ civilization still rude. ↑I was made sensible of this at Washington, if not already.↓ A ⟨strict⟩ universal etiquette should fix an iron term, after which a ⟨new⟩ moment should not be allowed without explicit leave given on request of either the giver or receiver of the visit. There is inconvenience in such strictness, but vast [98] inconvenience in the want of it. To ↑trespass on↓ a public man is trespass ⟨is⟩ on a nation's time. Yet Presidents of the United States are afflicted by rude Western & Southern gossips, until the gossip's immeasurable legs are tired of sitting. ↑Printed in *Social Aims*↓^{79}
What prudence again does an impressionable ⟨sen⟩ susceptible scholar need in the security of his chair & table! They must be remote from the work ↑of the house↓ & the knowledge of the feet that come & go in the house. Mr Allston had two or three rooms in different parts of Boston, [99] that he could not be found. For ⟨these⟩ ↑the↓ delicate muses ⟨are ⟨stunned⟩scared⟩ ↑lose their head↓ if their attention or intention is once diverted.^{80}

↑Printed in *"Inspiration."*↓

A party or politics without any *cheerful* prospect!

---

^{79} Pages [97] and [98] are struck through in pencil with single diagonal use marks; "Tis a defect . . . sitting.", struck through in ink with one vertical use mark and two diagonal use marks in the shape of an X on p. [97] and three diagonal use marks on p. [98], is used, minus the insertion, in "Social Aims," *W*, VIII, 91. "Printed in *Social Aims*" is circumscribed in ink.
^{80} "What prudence . . . table!" is struck through in ink with three diagonal use marks, one of which was extended to the bottom of the page; "What prudence . . . diverted.", struck through in ink with two more diagonal use marks on p. [98], and three diagonal use marks in ink and one in pencil on p. [99], is used in "Inspiration," *W*, VIII, 291.

↑*Success.*↓[n]

War. Every nation, [like the Venetians,] punishes the general who has not been victorious.[81]

What a pity that Beauty is not the rule, since every body might have been handsome as well as not. Or, if the moral laws must have their revenge, like Indians, for every violation, what pity that every body is [100] not promoted on the battle field, as our generals are; that is, instantly embellished by a good action. My servant squints & steals: I persuade her to better behavior: she restores the long lost /embroidered purse/trinkets/, &, at the same time, the *strabismus* ⟨is⟩ ↑should be↓ healed.[82]

[101] ↑*Manners.*↓

Moore wrote, (& 'tis his best verse,) ↑of Campbell,↓
    "True bard, & simple, as the race
    Of ⟨tr‖u‖e⟩heaven born poets always are,
    When leaning from their starry place
    They're children near, but gods afar."[83]

What a harness of buckram, wealth & city life puts ⟨into⟩ ↑on↓ our poets & literary men, even when men of great parts. Alcott complained to me of want of simplicity in Lowell, Holmes, Ward, & Longfellow: & Alcott is the right touchstone to test them⟨.⟩; ⟨He is⟩ true ⟨vegetable⟩ litmus to detect the acid.

Agassiz is perfectly accessible, [102] has a brave manliness which can meet a peasant, a mechanic, or a fine gentleman with equal fulness. Henry James is not spoiled; Bryant is perfect; ⟨the⟩ New York has not hurt him.[84] Whittier is unsoiled. Wasson is good company for prince

---

[81] See Journal DL, p. [203] above.

[82] "embroidered purse" is circled in ink, for revision or cancellation.

[83] Thomas Moore, "Verses to the Poet Crabbe's Inkstand," ll. 29–32, misquoted. See *JMN*, IV, 8, and XIV, 173.

[84] "not spoiled; . . . hurt him." is struck through in pencil with a faint vertical line, perhaps accidental, but cf. Emerson's remarks at the Bryant Festival on November 5, 1864, printed in *The Bryant Festival at "The Century"* (New York, 1865), pp. 16–19, reprinted in Ralph Waldo Emerson, *Uncollected Writings* (New York, 1912), pp. 20–22.

or plowman. Rowse also. I should be glad if James Lowell were as simply noble as his cousin Frank Lowell, who, my wife once said, "appeared like a king." [103] Caroline Tappan has perfect manners. Charles Newcome & Channing are saved by genius. Thoreau was with difficulty sweet. Anna Ward has never lost her broad humanity, and suggests so much that is told of Madame Récamier.

But in all the living circle of American wits & scholars is no enthusiasm. Alcott alone has it.

"Enthusiasm a delight, but may not always be a virtue." M[ary]. M[oody]. E[merson].
The Enthusiast will not be irritated, sour, & sarcastic.

[104] Wealth of Nature the only good. 'Tis vain to accuse scholars of solitude, & merchants of miserliness: they are really so poor that they cannot help it. Poverty is universal. "Ah blessed Ocean, 'tis good to find enough of one thing."[85] Genius delights because of its opulence. We scorn the poor littérateurs,[n] who hide their want by patchwork of quotations & borrowings; & the poor artist, who, ⟨for⟩ ↑instead of↓ the rapid drawing ⟨of⟩on a single conception, laboriously etches after his model with innumerable stipplings,

[105] What a saving grace is in poverty & solitude, that the obscure youth learns the practice instead of the literature of his Virtues![86] One or two or three ideas are the gods of his Temple, & suffice him for intellect & heart for years. They condescend to his shoe-shop, or his hoe & scythe & threshing-floor.

The solitary worshipper knows the ⟨inside⟩ ↑essence↓ of the thought: the scholar in society sees only its fair face.[87] Very, Taylor of Amesbury,[88]

---

[85] With " 'Ah blessed . . . thing.' ", cf. *JMN*, XIV, 363, and "Resources," *W*, VIII, 138–139.
[86] This sentence is used in "Education," *W*, X, 141.
[87] This sentence is used in "Education," *W*, X, 142.
[88] See pp. [137]–[138] below.

M[ary]. M[oody]. E[merson]. writes; "After all, some of the old
Christians were more delivered [106] from external things than the
(modern) Speculative, who are anxious for society, books, ideas,—&
become sensitive to all that affects the organs of thought. A few single
grand ideas, which become objects, pursuits, & all in all!" See [Note-
book] *M. M. E.* Vol. II, 8

M. M. E. & her contemporaries spoke continually of Angels & Archangels, with a good faith, as they would have spoken of their parents,
or their late minister. Now the word palls,—all the credence gone.[89]

[107] The War at last appoints the Generals, in spite of parties &
Presidents. Every one of us had his pet, at the start, but none of us
appointed Grant, Sherman, Sheridan, & Farragut,—none but themselves.[90] ↑Yet these are only shining examples. The fruit of small
powers and virtues is as fixed. The harvest of potatoes is not more sure
than the harvest of every talent.↓

––––––

Great difference in life of two consecutive days. Now it has grip, tastes
the hours, fills the horizon, & presently it recedes, ⟨an⟩ has little possession, is somnambulic.

––––––

We read often with as much talent as we write. ↑The retrospective↓
    [108] The retrospective value of a new thought is immense. 'Tis
like a torch applied to a long train of powder.[91]

[109] A page of [Notebook] M[ary]. M[oody]. E[merson]. (vol II.
212) gives much to think of the felicity of greatness on a low ground
of condition, as we have so often thought a rich Englishman has a better lot than a king. "No fair object but affords me gratification, and
with common interests." And, (on p 201) she writes, "they knew by
hearsay of Apes of men, vampire despots, crawling sycophants—"

––––––

[89] This entry, struck through in pencil with a vertical use mark, is used in "Character," *W*, X, 106.
    [90] A short rule below "none but themselves." is overwritten by the insertion. "The
war . . . Sherman," is used in "Harvard Commemoration Speech, July 21, 1865," *W*, XI,
341. See Journal DL, p. [203] above.
    [91] "The retrospective . . . powder.", struck through in pencil with a diagonal use
mark, is used in "Powers and Laws of Thought," *W*, XII, 21.

See, however, what she writes of middle class virtue (Vol II p. 219–220)!

[110] Criticism. I read with delight a casual notice of Wordsworth in the "London Reader," in which, with perfect aplomb, his highest merits were affirmed, & his unquestionable superiority to all English poets since Milton, & thought how long I travelled & talked in England, & found no person, or none but one, ↑& that one, Clough,↓ sympathetic with him, & admiring him aright in face of Tennyson's culminating talent & genius in melodious verse. What struck me ⟨i⟩now was the certainty with which the best opinion comes to be the established opinion. This rugged rough countryman walks & sits alone, assured of his sanity & ⟨of⟩ his inspiration, & writes to no public,—sneered [111] at by ⟨t⟩Jeffrey & Brougham, branded by Byron, blackened by the gossip of Barry Cornwall & DeQuincey, ⟨&⟩ down to Bowring,—for they all had disparaging tales of him, yet ↑himself↓ no more doubting the fine oracles that visited him than if Apollo had brought them visibly in his hand:
and here & there a solitary reader in country places had felt & owned them, & now, so few years after, it is lawful in that obese material England, whose vast strata of population are nowise converted or altered, yet [112] to affirm unblamed, unresisted, that this is the genuine, & the rest the impure metal. For, in their sane hours, each of the fine minds in the country has found it, & imparted his conviction, so that every reader has somewhere heard it on the highest authority:
    "And thus the world is brought
    To sympathy with hopes & fears it heeded not."[92]

[113] English genius is more truly shown in the drawings in Punch, than in all their watercolor & Royal Academy exhibitions; just as their actors are dreary in tragedy, & admirable in low comedy.

---

[92] "Criticism. I . . . heeded not.' ", struck through in pencil with one vertical use mark on p. [110], two on p. [111], and one on p. [112], is used in the lecture "Books," which Emerson delivered on December 25, 1864, at the Music Hall in Boston; see Cabot, *A Memoir* . . . , 1887–1888, II, 790. For the couplet from Shelley's "To a Skylark," ll. 39–40, misquoted, see *JMN*, V, 293.

Leasts.

⟨⟨T⟩In dwarfs,—⟩[93] The^n greatness of a dwarf consists in being little; ⟨therefore, ⟨if⟩ you can⟩ get a smaller dwarf than Major Stratton or General Tom Thumb, & he is greatest of all.

[114]   ↑*Criticism.*↓

Dr Holmes, one day, said to me, that he disliked scientific matter introduced into ↑(literary)↓ lectures, "it was meretricious."

⟨Oceanic Wealth⟩ ↑Prodigality↓ of Nature. She can afford millions of lives of men to make the movement of the earth round the sun so much as "suspected." Millions of lives to add only sentiments & ↑single↓ poetic aperçus, which at last ripen & combine in a poet.[94] What ↑power↓ does not a prudent man learn of the thrift of living long in the same place, & under [115] a dry roof! Art, conversation, manners, music, become possible,—impossible before. Wealth also. What ↑power↓ then does not Nature owe to her duration, of amassing infinitesimals into cosmical forces![95] How much time a man's poetic experiences cost him. He abandons business & wealth for them. How much time Love costs him!

> "the time I lost pursuing
> The light which lies
> In woman's eyes
> Has been my heart's undoing."
>   [Thomas Moore, "The Time I've Lost in Wooing,"
>   ll. 1–5, misquoted]

Ah yes, but ↑if ⟨l⟩his love was well directed,↓ it has been his mind's upbuilding.[96]

[116] How often I have to say, that every man has material enough in his experience to exhaust the sagacity of Newton in working it out. We have more than we use. We know vastly more than we digest.

---

[93] "⟨⟨T⟩In dwarfs,—⟩" is circled in ink, for revision or cancellation.
[94] "She can . . . 'suspected.' " is used in "Poetry and Imagination," *W*, VIII, 24. "Nature. . . . poet." is used in "Resources," *W*, VIII, 139–140. A short rule below "& combine in a poet." is overwritten by "What power does".
[95] This sentence is used in "Resources," *W*, VIII, 140.
[96] "if ⟨l⟩his . . . directed," is inserted and circled in pencil.

⟨We⟩ ↑I↓ never read poetry, or he⟨r⟩ar a good speech at ↑a↓ caucus, or ↑a↓ cattle-show, but it adds less stock to my knowledge, than it apprises me of admirable uses to which what I knew can be turned. [117] I write this now on remembrance of some *structural*ⁿ experience of last night,—a painful waking out of dream as by violence, & a rapid succession of ⟨a⟩ quasi-optical shows following like a pyro-⟨chnic⟩technic exhibition of architectural or grotesque flourishes, which indicate magazines of talent & inve⟨s⟩ntion in our structure,⁹⁷ which I shall not arrive at ↑the control of,↓ in my time, but perhaps my great grandson [118] will mature & bring to day.

9 Oct. Yesterday at Mr Geo L. Stearns's at Medford, to meet Wendell Phillips, & Mr Fowler of Tennesee.⁹⁸ The conversation political altogether, & though no very salient points, yet useful to me as clearing the air, & bringing to view the simplicity of the practical problem before us. Right-minded men would very easily bring order out of our American [119] chaos, if working with courage, & without by-ends. These Tennesee slaveholders in the land of Midian are far in advance of our New-England politicians. They see ↑&↓ front the real questions. The two points would seem to be absolute Emancipation, ⟨&⟩ —establishing the fact that the United States henceforward knows no color, no race, in its law*, but legislates for all alike,—one law for all men: [120] —*that* first; and, secondly, make the confiscation of rebel property final, as you did with the tories in the Revolution.

Thereby you ⟨instantly⟩ ↑at once↓ open the whole South to the enterprise & genius of new men of all nations, & extend New England from ⟨the⟩ Canada to the Gulf, & to the Pacific. You redeem your wicked [121] Indian policy, & leave no murderous complications ⟨requi⟩ to sow the sure seed of future wars. It was good in Fowler,

* See St Beuve's [actually Renan's] claim for France, *T* 108,

⁹⁷ "How often . . . structure," is struck through in pencil with single vertical use marks on pp. [116] and [117].
⁹⁸ George Luther Stearns (1809–1867), a merchant-manufacturer, long an ardent Free-Soiler, tried repeatedly to draw Emerson into his antislavery activites. Joseph Smith Fowler (1820–1902), an educator until the war, sympathetic with the South but opposed to slavery, was at this time state comptroller in the military government of Tennessee.

⟨a⟩his marked ⟨but⟩ ↑though↓ obscure recognition of the higher element that works in affairs. We seem to do it,—⟨but⟩ it gets done; but ↑for our will in it,↓ it is much as if I claimed to have manufactured the beautiful skin & flavor of my pears.

[122] Certain memorable ⟨ex⟩words[,] expressions that flew out incidentally in late history, as, for example, ↑in↓ Lincoln's letter, "To ⟨w⟩all whom it may concern," are caught up by men,—go to England, go to France,—reecho thence with thunderous report to us, & they are no longer the ⟨chance⟩ ↑unconsidered↓ words they ⟨are⟩ ↑were↓, but we must hold the government to them: [123] they are powers, and are not to be set aside by reckless speeches of Seward, putting all afloat again.

———

Oct. ⟨11⟩12. Returned from Naushon, whither I went on Saturday, 8th, with Professor ⟨Goldwin Smith⟩, of Oxford University, Mr ⟨C. B. Sedgwick⟩, ⟨John Weiss⟩, & ⟨George Ward⟩.[99] Mr [John Murray] Forbes ↑at Naushon↓ is the only "Squire" in Massachusetts, & no nobleman ever understood or performed his duties better. I divided my [124] admiration between the landscape of Naushon & him. He is ⟨a m⟩an American to be proud of. Never was such force, good meaning, good sense, good action, combined with such domestic lovely behavior, & such modesty & persistent preference of others. Wherever he moves, he is the benefactor. ⟨How well⟩ It is of course that he should [125] shoot well, ride well, sail well, administer ↑railroads↓ well, carve well, keep house well, but he was the best talker also in the company,—with the perpetual practical wisdom, seeing always the *working*[n] of the thing,— ⟨and⟩ with the multitude & distinction of his facts, (and one detects continually that he has had a hand in every thing that has been done,) and in the [126] temperance with which he parries all offence, & opens the eyes of his interlocutor without contradicting him. I have been proud of many of my countrymen, but I think this is a good country that can breed such a creature as John M. Forbes.[100]

↑[See infra p. ⟨2⟩133↓]

[99] The four names are canceled in pencil.
[100] Pages [124], [125], and [126] are struck through in ink with single vertical use marks, and "Printed" is written at the bottom of each page. "He is . . . John M. Forbes." is used in "Social Aims," *W*, VIII, 103.

There was something dramatic in the conversation of Monday night between Professor [127]¹⁰¹ ⟨↑Goldwin↓ Smith⟩, Forbes, & ⟨Ward⟩, chiefly,—the Englishman being evidently alarmed at the near prospect of the retaliation of America's standing in the identical position soon in which ⟨America⟩England now & lately has stood to us, & playing the same part towards her. Forbes, a year ago, was in Liverpool & London entreating them to respect their own neutrality, & disallow [128] the piracy, & the blockade-running, & hard measure to us in their Colonial ports, &c. And now, so soon, the parts were entirely reversed & Professor Smith was showing us the power & irritability of England & the certainty that war would follow, if we should build & arm a ship in one of our ports[,] send her out to sea & *at sea* sell her to their [129] enemy, which would be a proceeding strictly in accordance with her present proclaimed law of nations. Forbes thinks the Americans are in such a temper toward England, that they will do this, if the opportunity occurs. When the American Govt. urged ⟨them⟩England to make a new treaty to adjust & correct this anomalous rule, English government refused. & 'tis only ignorance that has prevented the ↑Rebel↓ Confederacy from availing themselves of it.

[130] Mr Smith had never heard of J[ames]. J[ohn]. Garth Wilkinson; ↑nor had the Trollopes ↑heard↓ of Elizabeth Shepherd;* nor scarcely any English, 15 years ago, of Browning.↓

History should be written after ideas. The army correspondents write what they see or hear, anecdotes or incidents of the fight. But the man who ⟨knows the⟩ understands the general's plan of the battle, writes all the incidents with the design in his mind, & showing that.

[131] I have often occasion to recall ↑Horace↓ Walpole's ⟨speech⟩ ↑remark↓ that nothing will stay in his memory but the names of men & women. ↑[Equivalent is De Stael's "Mes opinions politiques sont des noms propres."]↓ I look over this desart of Frothingham's metaphysics,¹⁰² & see the names of Carlyle, Ruskin, Emerson, & can

---

¹⁰¹ Page [127] is struck through in ink with a vertical use mark. "Goldwin Smith" and "Ward" are both canceled and circled in pencil.

¹⁰² Probably Ephraim Langdon Frothingham and Arthur Lincoln Frothingham, *Philosophy as Absolute Science, Founded in the Universal Laws of Being, and Including On-*

hope to find some shed & life on the wide prairie at these points.

———

At Naushon, I recall what John Smith said of the Bermudas, & I think as well of Mr Forbes's fences, which are cheap & ⟨deep⟩ steep. "No place known hath better walls or a broader ditch." [VA 130]

[132] What complete men are Forbes, ⟨and⟩ Agassiz, and Rockwood Hoar.

↑Veracity↓
The fault of most of our popular poetry is, that it is not sincere. Talent amuses, but if your verse ⟨is⟩ ↑has↓ not ↑a↓ necessary & autobiographical base, though under what gay poetic veils, it shall not waste my time. It is or must be a chest voice, & not a labial.

↑printed in P. & C. p. 35, 36↓¹⁰³

prior
higher
fire
lyre

[133] I came away ⟨from Naushon⟩ saying to myself of J[ohn]. M[urray]. F[orbes]., how little this man suspects, with his sympathy for men, & his respect for lettered & scientific ⟨m⟩people, that he is not likely ever to meet a man ⟨who is⟩ superior to himself! ↑printed↓¹⁰⁴

[134] The dire, δεινον, is that which I used to long for in orators. I can still remember the imposing march of Otis's eloquence, which, like Burke's, ⟨took⟩ swept into it all styles of address, all varieties of tone & incident, & in its skirts "far flashed the red artillery."¹⁰⁵

———

tology, Theology, and Psychology Made One, as Spirit, Soul and Body (Boston, 1864), in Emerson's library.

   ¹⁰³ "The fault. . . labial.", struck through in ink with a vertical use mark, is used in "Poetry and Imagination," *W*, VIII, 30 and 31.

   ¹⁰⁴ This paragraph, struck through in ink with two wavy vertical use marks, is used in "Social Aims," *W*, VIII, 103. "from Naushon" is canceled and circled in pencil. "printed" is circled in ink.

   ¹⁰⁵ Thomas Campbell, "Hohenlinden," l. 16.

———

In modern eloquence what is more touching or sublime than the first words of Lafayette's speech in the French Assembly in 1815 (?) "When, after so⟨m⟩ many years silence," (the whole consulate & empire) "I raise a voice which the friends of liberty will still ⟨remember," &c⟩ recognize," &c.

[135] Nemesis is that recoil of nature not to be guarded against, which ⟨always⟩ ↑ever↓ surprises the most wary transgressor⟨.⟩ (of the Laws.) Not possibly can you shut up all the issues.   I have written in *FOR*, ↑111,↓ "Always something unexpected leaps from the controversy. Thus the churchmen's attacks upon Bishop Colenso ⟨have more damaged them than he did, through⟩ ↑by↓ the bad morals they have shown⟨.⟩, ↑have damaged them more than he did.↓"

———

Is your neutrality in good faith, or is it ironical?

———

St Beuve notes, in 1838, the charming letters of Lafayette to his wife just published.[106]

[136]   ↑The Age, & the Hour.↓
              ——————————

The party of virility rules the hour, the party of ideas & sentiments ⟨th⟩rules the age.

Oct. 19. Yesterday as I passed Shannon's field, robins, blackbirds, bluebirds & snowbirds (fringilla hiemalis)[n] were enjoying themselves together[.]

———

Bryant has learned where to hang his titles, namely, by tying his mind to autumn woods, winter mornings, rain, brooks, mountains, Evening winds, & ⟨bobolinks⟩ ↑wood-birds↓. Who speaks of these [137] is forced to remember Bryant.
↑American. Never despaired of the Republic. dared name a jay & a gentian, crows.

[106] See "Mémoires du Général La Fayette" in Charles Augustin Sainte-Beuve, *Portraits littéraires,* 2 vols. (Paris, 1852), II, 144 and 148. Emerson withdrew this volume from the Boston Athenaeum April 24–June 8, and June 30–September 4, 1865.

His poetry is sincere. I think of the young poets that they have seen pictures of mountains & seashores but his that he has seen mountains & has the staff in his hand↓[107]
↑New York↓

20 Oct.

It occurred in talking with Henry James yesterday who attached a too exclusive originality to Swedenborg, that he did ↑not↓ seem to recognize the eternal copresence of the revolutionary force. The revolutionary force in intellect is never absent. Such persons as my poor Platonist Taylor in Amesbury; Jones Very; ↑&↓ the shoe-maker   at Berwick; Tufts in ↑Lima, or Cuba,↓ New York; are always appearing in the deadest conservatism;—in an age of anti-quaries [138] representing the most modern times;—in the heart of Papacy & toryism the seed of rebellion;—for the world is ever equal to itself, & centripetence makes centrifugence.[108]

November 1864

Population of Boston, by a recent count by the police of the eight districts of the city, is, 164,788.—families, 34,299.

the count does not include ⟨t⟩persons gone to the army & navy, or otherwise absent from home.

Chicago 169,000 souls

Paris just ten times so many, last year, or, 1,696,151 souls.

↑Cleveland 65,000.↓

[107] "Evening winds, . . . wood-birds." and "I think . . . his hand" are used in Emerson's remarks on November 5, 1864, printed in *The Bryant Festival at "The Century,"* 1865, pp. 16–19. See also pp. [144]–[146] below. "American. . . . hand" is in pencil; "I think . . . hand" is fitted in around "New York", below, which was evidently added in pencil earlier.

[108] Henry Taylor was a correspondent of Emerson's between 1857 and 1865. For Tufts, see Journal FOR, p. [235]. With "the world . . . centrifugence.", cf. "Progress of Culture," *W*, VIII, 213 and 223, and earlier, "Farming," *W*, VII, 146.

[139]　　*American Life.*
　　　　Public & Private Education.
　　　　Social Aims.
　　　　Resources.
　　　　Table-Talk.
　　　　Books.
　　　　Character. ↑Greatness, Moral & religious aspects.↓[109]

↑Population of Boston in 1877⌋ 34⟨0⟩2 000.↓

[140] [blank]
[141]　　　↑America makes its own precedents.↓

The imperial voice of the Age cannot be heard for the tin horns & charivari of the varlets of the hour, such as the London Times, Blackwood, & the Saturday Review⟨,⟩.
But already these *claqueurs* have received their ⟨hint⟩ ↑cue.↓ ⟨that⟩ ↑I suppose it was hinted to them that↓ the American People are not ⟨now in a condition⟩ ↑always↓ to be trifled with⟨:⟩; they are ending their ⟨own⟩ ↑home↓ war, and are ⟨highly⟩ exasperated at English bad behavior, & are in force to destroy English trade. Speak them fair.—ⁿ And "The Times" has just discovered what "temper, valor, constancy, [142] the Union has shown in the War," & what a noble "career of honor & prosperity lies before her," &c.

↑When a lady rallied↓ Adam Smith ⟨said to the lady who rallied him⟩ on his plain dress, he pointed to his well-bound library, & said, "You see Madam, I am a beau in my books." The farmer in this month is very patient of his coarse attire, & thinks, "At least, I am a beau in my woods."

[109] Emerson delivered the six lectures in the "American Life" series (the first was announced as "Education") at the Melodeon in Boston under the auspices of the Parker Fraternity, on successive Sunday evenings from November 27, 1864, to January 1, 1865, and repeated them on a three-week tour to Chicago and Milwaukee in January and February. See *L,* V, 389 and 398–399. For newspaper reports of the Boston lectures, see Gohdes, *Uncollected Lectures,* 1932.

[143] ↑1864. October 25↓ ↑Power of certain States of the sky.↓[110]
There is an astonishing magnificence ⟨in⟩even in this low town, &
within a quarter of a mile of my doors, in the appearance of the Lincoln hills now drest in their colored forest, under the lights & clouds of
morning, as I saw them at 8 o'clock. When I see this spectacle so near,
& so surprising, I think no house should be built quite low, or should
obstruct the prospect by trees.
↑Oct. 25. ⟨Sent word to || . . . || today⟩↓[111]

[144]   native American
        Bryant sincere
              balanced mind had the enthusiasm which perception of
nature inspires but it did not tear him; only enabled him; gave him
twice his power; he did not parade it, but hid it in his verse.
his connection with party usque ad aras.[112]
        simple,   True bard but simple,
I fear he has not escaped the infirmity of fame, like the Presidential
malady, a virus once in, not to be got out of the system: he has this, so
cold & majestic as he sits there,—has this to a heat which has brought
⟨down on⟩ ↑to↓ him the devotion of all the young men & women who
love poetry, & ⟨worse,⟩ of all the old men & women who once were
young. [145] 'Tis a perfect tyranny. Talk of the people[,] shopmen
who advertise their drugs or cosmetics on the walls & on the palisades
& huge rocks along the railways. Why this man more cunning by far
has contrived to levy on all American Nature & subsidized every solitary /forest/grove/ & monument mountain in Berkshire or the Kats-
kills, every waterfowl, every partridge, every gentian & goldenrod,
the prairies, the gardens of the desart, the song of the stars, the Evening wind,—has bribed every one of these to speak for him, so that
there is scarcely a feature of day & night in the [146] ⟨I⟩country which
⟨is not⟩ does not, whether we will or not,—recall the name of Bryant.
This high-handed usurpation ⟨it⟩I charge him with, & on the top of

---

[110] "Power . . . sky." is boxed off in ink on the bottom and both sides.
[111] Added and canceled in pencil.
[112] "All the way to the altars" (Ed.).

this, with persuading us & all mankind to hug our fetters & rejoice in
⟨this⟩ ↑our↓ subjugation[.]¹¹³

[147] ↑Rev.↓ Dr P. talked the other day, ↑at Cambridge↓ as if
he had been much corrupted by society, since I knew him a young
man already much courted, but with his manly simplicity still unspoiled. Now he grimaces, ⟨badly,⟩ & had the pulpit airs of a ⟨worldly⟩
court preacher. Perhaps ⟨his⟩a bad dentist had served him ill, & had
given him ⟨a⟩ fashionable teeth for his own honest grinders. ⟨But⟩
↑Yet↓ I felt, while he spoke, that it was easy, or at least possible, to
open to the [148] audience the thesis which he mouthed upon, how
the Divine Order "pays" the Country for the sacrifices it has made &
makes in the war.—War ennobles the Country; searches it; fires it;
acquaints it with its resources; turns it away from false alliances, vain
hopes, & theatric attitudes; puts it on its mettle; "in ourselves our
safety must be sought"; gives it scope & object; concentrates history
into a year, invents means; systematizes everything. We began the
war in vast confusion⟨,⟩; when we end it↑,↓ all will be in system↑.↓¹¹⁴

[149] 30 Oct. 1864
⟨We⟩At [the Saturday] Club, yesterday, we had a full table, Agassiz,
Hoar, Hedge, Cabot, Holmes, ⟨Cabot,⟩ Appleton, Pierce, Norton,
Forbes, Ward, Sumner, Whipple, Woodman, Dwight, ↑Emerson↓;
Andrew, (who, with Brimmer & Fie↑l↓ds, ⟨were⟩ ↑was↓ elected yes-
terday); and, for guests, Mr C[harles]. G. Loring, Sterry Hunt, & Mr
Godkin, the English correspondent of the "Daily News."

16
 3
——
19

¹¹³ Pages [144], [145], and [146] are in pencil; "balanced mind . . . subjugation" is
struck through in pencil with single vertical use marks on pp. [144], [145], and [146].
"native American . . . sincere" and "simple,   True . . . subjugation" are used in
Emerson's remarks in honor of Bryant on November 5, 1864, printed in *The Bryant Festival at "The Century,"* 1865, pp. 17–18. See also pp. [136]–[137] above.
¹¹⁴ With "War ennobles . . . system.", cf. "Harvard Commemoration Speech, July
21, 1865," *W,* XI, 342. With " 'in ourselves . . . sought' ", cf. Shakespeare, *III King
Henry VI,* IV, i, 43–46. The added punctuation in the last sentence is in pencil.

[150] Before the war, our patriotism was a firework, a salute, ↑a serenade,↓ for holidays & summer evenings, but the reality was cotton thread & complaisance. Now ⟨since⟩ the deaths of thousands & the determination of ⟨all⟩ ↑millions of↓ men & women show it real.

[151]   Rich are the seagods, who gives gifts but they
      ⟨Theirs is⟩ all hidden ↑power↓ gems are theirs
        What power is theirs they give it to the wise
      For every wave is wealth to Daedalus
      Wealth to the cunning artist who can work
      The waves immortal sinew[115]

18 Nov[embe]r.

The way that young woman keeps her school was the best lesson I ⟨attended ↑to↓⟩ ↑received↓ in the Preparatory School today. She knew so much, & carried it so well in her head, & gave it out so well, that the pupils had quite enough to think of, & [152] not an idle moment to waste on noise or disorder. 'Tis the best recipe I know for school discipline.

↑1864↓
Nov. 2⟨4⟩6. Agassiz, Brimmer, Cabot, Holmes, Hoar, Fields, Dana, Norton, Sumner, Whipple, Emerson, at the [Saturday] Club; & Senator Wilson, M Laugel & M Duvergie d'Hauranne guests

I promised Sumner to attend to the question of the Academy[.][116]

[153] J[?]. "was lonesome without ⟨his⟩my tobacco." I suppose, most thoughtful men would agree, that, if they could do their eating by rule,—

Cows are dull sluggish creatures, ⟨w⟩but with ⟨this⟩ ↑a↓ decided talent in one direction—for extracting milk out of ⟨every kind of pas-

---

[115] Cf. "Seashore," ll. 27–32, *W*, IX, 243. The verse, in pencil, is struck through in pencil with a vertical use mark.
[116] "Nov. 2⟨4⟩6. . . . Academy" is in pencil. See *L*, V, 392–393 and 395–397, for the projected "National Academy of Literature and Art."

ture:⟩ ↑meadows:↓— ⟨the best of them⟩ ↑mine↓ have a genius for it, —leaking ⟨milk,⟩ ↑cream,↓ "larding the lean earth as they walk along."[117] ↑Wasps too for making paper.↓ ↑Then what soothing objects are the hens!↓

Dec. 3 sent to Bent[118]

[154] Carry the ball with you,—as I wrote above. ↑*FOR* 60↓ Don't take ⟨so mu⟩ any pains to praise good people. I delight ↑in↓ certain dear persons, that they need no letters of introduction, knowing well, that, wherever they go, they are hung all over with eulogies. If there is any perception in the company, the⟨re⟩se will be found out as fountains of joy.

↑J. A. Harwood　　Littleton↓[119]

[155]　　　O happy town⟨s⟩ /that touch/beside/ the sea⟨!⟩,
　　　　　Whose roads lead everywhere ↑to all↓!
　　　　　⟨A⟩ ↑Than thine no↓ deeper ⟨ditch⟩ ↑moat↓ can ⟨never⟩ be,
　　　　　⟨A⟩ ↑No↓ steeper fence, ⟨a⟩ ↑no↓ /better/haughtier/ wall.

　　　　　O bounteous /ocean without/seas that never/ fail
　　　　　O happy day remembered yet
　　　　　O happy ⟨town⟩ ↑port↓ that spied a sail
　　　　　Which furling landed Lafayette[120]

Lafayette⟨s⟩ arrived in Boston, on his second visit to America in 1780. *St Beuve* ["Mémoires du Général La Fayette,"] *Portraits Litteraire* [1852, II, 153] Come let us have Drake's (?) History of Boston.

---

[117] Cf. Shakespeare, *I Henry IV,* II, ii, 116.

[118] Probably John H. Bent, a farmer who lived on the Walden road not far from Emerson. "Dec 3 . . . Bent" is in pencil.

[119] In pencil.

[120] "Boston," ll. 59–62 and 86–89, *W,* IX, 214 and 215. The verse is struck through in pencil with a vertical use mark. Except for the punctuation, cancellations and revisions in the first stanza are in pencil; "that touch" and "never" are circled in pencil, for cancellation or revision. With "Than thine . . . wall.", cf. p. [131] above.

[156] I read in a paper in Blackwood, "Cornelius O'Dowd," I believe, a dictum maintained at some length, that no superior man had much facility in speaking another language than his own.[121]

Laugel said, the other day, that the French Emperor ↑censures &↓ prohibits ⟨jour⟩ newspapers, but never meddles with books.

↑*Power of Criticism.*↓

But now (May 6) I am glad to see Laboulaye, in his critique on the "Life of Julius Caesar," toss his emperor Napoleon on his horns, & with invulnerable propriety.[122]

[157] Sir Wm Napier says, "For my own part, I would almost sooner quit the army, than go to garrison the Bermudas; not from fear of the climate, but from the knowledge that you are among people whose whole soul is given up to their luxurious appetites, whose enjoyments are founded on cruelty, & whose principles will every moment shock the feelings of a man of honour, wh↑i↓le any abhorrence he expresses of them will engage him in quarrels, or expose him to derision." [Bruce, ed.,] Life of Maj. Gen. Sir W. Napier [1864,] Vol. I. p. 105

[158] The singer can sing ↑either of↓ several parts,—base, tenor, & alto something, and a cultivated person has several social languages to use as occasion requires: the scholastic with clerks; the polite in parlors; &c., ⟨b⟩and⟨,⟩ as a boy with boys in the street⟨,⟩ he learned the coarse English⟨,⟩ which he has not forgotten⟨,⟩ but knows how to use ⟨with effect⟩ ↑like a sharp stick↓ among the rabble↑.↓ ⟨like the stoutest truckman.⟩[123]

---

[121] Charles James Lever, "Cornelius O'Dowd upon Men and Women, and Other Things in General," pt. VI, *Blackwood's Edinburgh Magazine*, XCVI (July 1864), 10–13 ("Linguists").

[122] Auguste L. Laugel, French writer, whose article on Agassiz Emerson had read in 1857 (see *JMN*, XIV, 123), was a guest at the Saturday Club in November 1864; see p. [152] above. Edouard René Lefebvre de Laboulaye (1811–1883), French writer and politician, was the author of several articles and books on the United States. His critique of Emperor Napoleon III's *History of Julius Caesar,* the first volume of which was published in France in late spring, 1865, has not been identified.

[123] With this paragraph, cf. "Eloquence," *W*, VIII, 124.

[159] ↑1865↓ Concord 13 Feb[ruar]y
Home from Chicago & Milwaukee. Chicago grows so fast that one
ceases to respect civic growth: as if all these solid & stately squares,
which we are wont to see as the slow work of a century, had come to
be done by machinery, as cloth & hardware is made, & was therefore
shoddy architecture, without honor.

'Twas tedious the obstructions & squalor of travel. The advantage of their offers at Chicago made it [160] needful to go. It was in
short this dragging a decorous old gentleman out of home, & out of
position, to this juvenile career tantamount to this; "I'll bet you fifty
dollars a day for three weeks, that ⟨I can get your old friend to⟩ ↑you
will not↓ leave ⟨his⟩your library & wade & freeze & ride & run, & ⟨do⟩
↑suffer↓ all manner of indignities, & stand up ⟨still⟩ for an hour each
night reading in a hall:" and I answer, "I'll bet I will," I do it, & win
the $⟨1200⟩900.

[161] People in society like a safe person.

↑1864↓
Victor Cousin said in conversation about the Encyclical Letter, that
"the Pope had missed an opportunity of keeping still, which would
never occur again."
↑As good as the *mot* about Napoleon III's lying.↓

Qu. Do they still use corporal punishment in the English Army? See
what ⟨S⟩ ↑Sir↓ Robert Wilson says of it, in his Diary.[124]

------

[162] Napier quotes Vitellius's observation, that "dead enemies
are pleasant perfumes." [Bruce, ed., *Life of General Sir William Napier*, 1864, I, 108]

A white man in Africa is a fright.

------

[124] See Journal GL, p. [294] above, for Emerson's reading in Wilson's *Private
Diary* . . . , 1861, in the year it was published. The passage Emerson cites has not been
located.

For the *metonomy*,[n] the boys call a hat a tile; a black boy, a snow-ball[.]

[163] Capt. Osborn reckons Grinnell Land, (the extreme northern point of Greenland reached by Mr Morton), ↑to be↓ within 444 miles of the Pole. At Murchison Sound (Greenland) 77.80 n. lat., is a nation of Arctic highlanders purely carnivorous. In 36 years, & 42 explorations, England had lost only 128 men.

[164] "The late good & wise first Lord Ravensworth used to say, 'there was nothing grateful but the earth↑;↓ You cannot do too much for it; it will continue to pay tenfold the pains & labor bestowed upon it.' "
                                                    Bewick's Life.[125] p 212

Every Pericles must have his Creon; Sumner his ⟨Fessenden⟩ ↑Fenton & Conkling↓; & ⟨Bu⟩Dana his Butler. The ⟨only⟩ right remedy is to out-Creon Creon.   Feb. 1869

[165] Even the poor prisoners that starved & perished in the Libby & Andersonville prisons rendered a vast service to their country & mankind, by drawing out into daylight the cruelty & malignity of the Southern people, & showing the corruption that Slavery works on the community in which it exists.   ↑See below, p. 174↓

[166] 10 Apr.
Wilkinson always an affirmative writer; radiant, intellectual, humane, brave as such are.

↑Like some of my trees,↓ I am a "shy bearer."[126]

———

sub rosa or ex cathedra

[167] ↑↑"It is↓ ⟨T⟩the Senate," said Webster, "determines when the Fourth of March ends"↓

[125] *A Memoir of Thomas Bewick, Written by Himself* (Newcastle on Tyne and London, 1862); in Emerson's library.
[126] "10 Apr. . . . bearer.' " and the rule following it are in pencil. For similar praise of Wilkinson, see p. [28] above.

General Hooker, in his order from his head-quarters at Cincinnati, assuming command of the department of the Northwest, says to every officer & soldier, "No one will consider the day as ended, until the duties it brings have been discharged."

———

I value the ↑fortnightly↓ "Publisher⟨'⟩s' Circular,"[127] ⟨as it comes every fortnight,⟩ mainly for its Paris correspondence, containing, as it does, biography of literary men in Paris, & showing the identity of literary life in Paris with our [168] own, scattering the illusion that overhangs Paris in the eyes & reports of frivolous travellers, & showing there just such a coarse & vindictive Bohemia as New York is for dissipated young men of talent.

[169] 'Tis far the best that the rebels have been pounded instead of negociated into a peace. They must remember it, & their inveterate brag will be humbled, if not cured. George Minott ⟨you⟩used to tell me over the wall, when I urged him to go to town meeting & vote, that "votes did no good, what was done so wouldn't last, but what was done by bullets would stay put."[128] General Grant's terms certainly look a little too easy, as foreclosing any action hereafter to convict Lee of treason, and I fear [170] that the high tragic historic justice which the nation ⟨ought⟩ with severest consideration should execute, will be softened & dissipated & toasted away at dinner-tables. But the problems that now remain to be solved are very intricate & perplexing, & men are very much at a loss as to the ri⟨c⟩ght action. If we let the southern States in to Congress, the Northern democrats will join them [171] in thwarting the will of the government. And the obvious remedy is to give the negro his vote. And then the difficult question comes,—what shall be the qualification of voters? We wish to raise the mean white to his right position, that he may withstand the planter. But the negro will learn to ⟨rig⟩write & read, (which should be ↑a↓ required qualification,) before the white will.

[127] *American Literary Gazette and Publisher's Circular*, published in Philadelphia by George W. Childs from 1863 to 1872. See *L*, V, 417–418, and Journal DL, pp. [230] and [260] above.
[128] See *JMN*, XI, 368, and "Courage," *W*, VII, 260.

[172]   ↑"*To be amused.*"↓[129]

People go into the church, as they go into the parlor, to be amused. The frivolous mood takes the most of the time, as the⟨r⟩ frivolous people make the majority. And Cicero said of ⟨his⟩ the Greeks, & eastern provinces, that they gave themselves to Art ⟨as⟩for forgetfulness & the consolation of servitude.   *oblectamenta et solatium servitutis.*[130]

[173] The thunderbolt /falls/strikes/ ⟨but in⟩ on an inch of ground, but the light of it fills the horizon.[131]

———

I should say of Samuel Hoar, ↑Senior↓ what Clarendon writes of Sir Thomas Coventry, that, "he had a strange power of making himself believed, the only justifiable design of eloquence."[132]

———

"The mind of Locke will not always be the measure of the Human Understanding." S[ampson]. Reed
↑See "Literature" in Eng Traits↓[133]

[174] ⟨Booth⟩ The assassin Booth is a type man of a large class of the Southern people.[134] By the destruction of Slavery, we destroy the stove in which the cockatrice eggs are hatched.

———

There is no police so effective as a good hill & wide pasture in the neighborhood of a village, where the boys can run & play & dispose of their superfluous strength & spirits, to their [175] own delight & the annoyance of nobody.

———

[129] Cf. "Character," *W*, X, 109.
[130] "to cheer and console them in their state of subjection." Cicero, *The Verrine Orations*, II, iv, 60.
[131] This sentence is struck through in pencil with two diagonal use marks. Cf. "Fragments on the Poet and the Poetic Gift," XXXII, ll. 3–4, *W*, IX, 334, and *JMN*, X, 368.
[132] See *JMN*, VI, 134. Cf. "Perpetual Forces," *W*, X, 78.
[133] " 'The mind . . . S. Reed" is struck through in pencil with a vertical use mark. "See 'Literature' . . . Traits" is added in pencil; see "Literature," *W*, V, 243.
[134] President Lincoln was assassinated by John Wilkes Booth in Ford's theater in Washington on April 14, 1865.

↑Criticism↓   ↑Illusion of words.↓

There are really few people who distinguish, on reading, a page full of words from a page ⟨full⟩ of /vital records./new experience./ They are satisfied with the first, if it ⟨do not contradict⟩ ↑is in harmony with↓ their habitual ⟨views⟩ opinions. They say it is good, & put it in my hands, or will read it to me, & are discontented if I slight it. But they never take it up again, because it makes no impression on their memory; whilst they do remember[n] [176] & return to the page of real experiences, & thus vindicate the critic.

———

Caddisworm the eclectic architect. The spending of a brook or river vindicates the extreme parsimony of Nature. See above, p 164

———

↑This & next page probably printed in *"Inspiration"*↓[135]
For "inspiration," the experience of writing letters is one of the best keys to the *modus* of it. When we have ceased ⟨to⟩for a long time to have any [177] fulness of thoughts that ⟨make⟩ ↑once made↓ a ⟨journal⟩ ↑diary↓ a ⟨luxury⟩ ↑joy↓, as well as a necessity, & have come to believe that an image or a happy turn of expression is no longer at our command, in writing a letter, we may find that we rise to thought, & to a cordial power of expression that costs ⟨us nothing⟩ no effort, & it seems to us that this facility may be indefinitely applied & resumed. The wealth of the mind in this [178] respect, *of seeing,* is like that of a looking-glass which is never tired or worn by any multitude of ⟨images⟩objects which it reflects. You may carry it all round the world, it is ready & perfect as ever for new millions. So is the mind of Shakspeare.[136]

———

↑Inspiration is like yeast. 'Tis no matter in which of half a dozen odd ways you get the infection of yeast,—you can apply it equally well to your ⟨aim⟩ ↑purpose↓, & get your loaf of bread. When I wish to write on my topic, 'tis of no consequence what kind of book or man

[135] This sentence is added in pencil.
[136] "For 'inspiration', . . . Shakspeare.", struck through in pencil with single vertical use marks on pp. [176] and [177], and on p. [178] with two, is used in "Inspiration," *W,* VIII, 281–282. With "looking-glass . . . millions.", cf. also "Memory," *W,* XII, 93.

gives me a hint⟨,⟩ or a motion, nor how far off that is from my topic.↓[137]

[179] The rise of value in wheat by the famine in Europe ↑in one year↓ enabled us to pay the whole cost of the Mexican War: and ↑now↓ Robert J. Walker affirms that "the additional value of free labor will in one year equal the whole national debt." ↑Apr. 1864↓[138]

——————

↑⟨c⟩*Character.*↓

The right self-subsistency is shown by the man who never mistakes his coat, or ⟨his⟩ coiffure or ⟨his⟩ titles or ⟨his⟩ wealth or power or fame, ⟨as⟩for himself, & so is willing to appear just as he is, whether in his shirt or in his skin, if ⟨you⟩ a visiter surprise him so, with entire composure. But the impostor, if surprised in undress, or ragged, or in some poor & indecorous function, [180] sneaks & hides, ⟨at once⟩ betraying that ⟨it is his⟩ he thinks the greatness is in his clothes, or his grand appearance. M[ary]. M[oody]. E[merson]. used in talking with a companion, tho' a stranger, to take out her teeth, or take off her frisette, to give herself more ease, & could well afford it. She played with all her infirmities.

"The capture of Mobile is one of those events which a few weeks ago would have filled ⟨us⟩ ↑the whole North↓ with joy. But today what is Mobile to us—" says the "Tribune."[139]

——————

↑*Character.*↓ I like not the man who is thinking how to be good, but the man thinking how to accomplish his work.

——————

[181][140] There was a ⟨towered town⟩ ↑city↓ rich & old
⟨And also this I hold⟩

[137] This paragraph, struck through in pencil with a vertical use mark, is used in "Inspiration," *W*, VIII, 271–272.

[138] "in one year", added above "us", is circled in ink and linked to a caret after "Europe." "Apr 1864" is also circled in ink.

[139] Mobile, blockaded since August 5, 1864, was the last Confederate stronghold to surrender, on April 12, 1865.

[140] Pages [181]–[185] are in pencil, p. [181] partially erased.

⟨That⟩ ↑Where↓ⁿ men ⟨who labor⟩ ↑toiled↓ much for little
    gold
In petty ⟨farms⟩ ↑shops↓ & ⟨lit⟩ sultry towns
At their sweat & handicraft
↑If the southwest wind should waft↓
⟨Feel⟩ ↑To these↓ the sweet teachings of the air
Which no ⟨city⟩ ↑town↓ walls can quite exclude
Nor streets of fops nor /din of trade/draymen rude/
⟨And if⟩ ↑One day↓ a Maycart came therein
With ⟨green⟩ sallows cowslips budding boughs
↑With a great cage of singing birds↓
And swains proclaiming Villegiature
A three days' woodland holiday
⟨All children⟩ ↑Half the town↓ would truant play
The men would catch the infection
As when /Hermit/Friar/ Peter preached Crusade
↑The sweetⁿ truth can more persuade↓
And as then the infection ran
To old & young from man to man
The town would ⟨be⟩ empt⟨ied⟩y like a prison
For the fields & ⟨low[?]⟩ ↑broad↓ horizon
Age would limp on his crutch
Uprose the porter & the drudge

[182]   The /pauper/scullion/ creep from his hutch
                                none would stay
  From the festival of May

    ↑I grant,↓ theⁿ woods are well enough,
Nature is sound, and hickory tough;
Ah friend! the covenant needs two,—
The Muse requires both What & Who[141]

[183]   ⟨I⟩W
  & we have trod this path a hundred times
  ↑With idle ↑foot↓steps crooning old rhymes↓

---

[141] These four lines are inscribed opposite "Ah friend ⟨it takes⟩ . . . & who" on p.
[183], and may be a revision.

I know every stick & stone
⟨Every oak⟩ ↑Maple^n & oak↓ the old divan
⟨Twice⟩ ↑Self↓ planted ↑twice↓ like the banian
⟨What's the use⟩ ↑I know not why I come again↓
⟨Of no use till they⟩ ↑Ah but the wood must↓ signify
↑Today↓ they^n will not signify
⟨Wait until they signify⟩
And how ⟨⟨th⟩an⟩ and when will they signify
Ah friend ⟨it takes⟩ ↑the covenant needs↓ two
⟨The green lane⟩ ↑'Tis well enough with stock & stone
The woods are strong & hold their own↓
The Muse requires what & who
Love is the counterpart
↑Terror↓ and ⟨Fear &⟩^n Hope & Remorse
New knowledge   fiery Thought
⟨Duty to sacrifices brought⟩
Duty to grand purpose ⟨brou⟩wrought
I came out t⟨h⟩o this heath by the lake
⟨And heard⟩ ↑Wandering↓ yestermorn I heard
Sharp queries of the sentry bird
The bird sang as if I gave the theme
The bird sang my last night's dream
A brown wren was the Daniel

[184]   That pierced my ⟨dr⟩trance its drift to spell
Knew my secret
Published it to sea & sky
⟨Blabbed all the names⟩
⟨Told every vagabond⟩
Told every ↑word &↓ syllable
In his ⟨profligate musical⟩ ↑flippant chirping↓ babble
All my doubts & all my shames
Nay, God is witness, blabbed the names.[142]

Her passion the shy violet
From Hafiz never hides

[142] Pages [183] and [184] to this point are a draft of "The Miracle," ll. 1–3, 5–7,
11–16, and 23–36, *W*, IX, 368–369.

Lovelongings of the raptured bird
The bird to him confides[143]

[185]   For Lucifer, that ⟨strong⟩ ↑⟨dire⟩↓ ↑old↓ athlete,
Tho' flung from Heaven falls on his feet

Traitors tho' plumed & steel equipped
⟨Are born to be whipped⟩
Are born to be betrayed & whipped
Born to be caught & to be whipped

[186]   ↑⟨P⟩ Immortality.↓
The path of spirits is in silence & hidden from sense.[144] Who
knows where or how the soul has existed, before it was incarnated in
mortal body? Who knows where or how it thinks & works when it
drops its fleshly frame? Like those asteroids which we call shooting
stars which revolve forever ⟨about⟩ in space, but ⟨impinging⟩ ↑⟨cross-
ing⟩↓ ↑sweeping↓ for a moment ↑thro' some ⟨⟨tr⟩arc⟩ arc of↓ our
atmosphere ⟨are⟩ ↑and↓ heated by the friction, ⟨&⟩ give out a ↑daz-
zling↓ gleam↑,↓ ⟨of light,⟩ then pass out of it again on their endless
orbit invisible.

[187]   ↑*President Lincoln.*↓
Why talk of President Lincoln's equality of manners to the elegant or titled men with whom Everett or others saw him? A sincerely
upright & intelligent man as he was, placed in the Chair, has no need
to think of his manners or appearance. His work day by day educates
him rapidly & to the best. He exerts the enormous power of this continent in every hour, in every conversation, in every act;—thinks & decides under this ⟨enormous⟩ [188] pressure, forced to see the vast &
various bearings of the measures he adopts: *he* cannot ⟨trifle⟩ ↑palter↓,
he cannot but carry a grace beyond his own, a dignity, by means of
what he drops, e.g. all ⟨m⟩ pretension & ⟨intrigue⟩ trick,
and arrives, ⟨at⟩of course, at a simplicity, which is the perfection of
manners.

[143] "Hafiz," *W*, IX, 296. See *JMN*, XIII, 423.
[144] This sentence is struck through in ink with two diagonal use marks.

[189] May ⟨5⟩6. 186⟨4⟩5

In reading Mark Antonine, last night,[145] it was pleasant ⟨in⟩to be reminded by some of his precepts, of a living example in a dear person near me.

———

We are such vain peacocks that we read in an English journal with joy, that no house in London or in Paris can compare with the comfort & splendor of Delmonico's in New York.

⟨———⟩↑But I was never in Delmonico's.↓

[190]   "———arces quibus altus Apollo
        Praesidet, horrendae que procul secreta Sibyllae"[146]

———

Sieyes exilé vécut a la lettre, comme le rat de la fable, dans son fromage d'Hollande.   S. Beuve ["Mémoires du Général La Fayette," *Portraits Littéraires,* 1852, II, 181]

———

Lafayette.
"Le bien e↑t↓ le mal de la Revolution paraissaient en général separés par la ligne que j'avais suivie." *Lafayette* [*Ibid.,* p. 176]

↑Mme de Lafayette approaching Olmutz said to her companions the song in *Tobias.* Chap. XIII. v. 2, 3, 4, 5, 6, 7,↓[147] [*Ibid.,* p. 197]

Buonaparte said one day in a sally (sortie) to the Council of State, "Tout le monde en France est corrigé; il n'y a qu⟨e⟩'un seul homme qui ne le soit pas, Lafayette! il n'a jamais reculé d'une ligne. Vous le voyez tranquille; eh bien! je vous dis, moi, qu'il est tout prêt a recommencer." [*Ibid.,* p. 193]

[191] ↑In↓ Saint Beuve, *Portraits Littéraire↑s↓,* [1852,] Vol II. [pp. 143–145] see "Memoires de la Fayette." He vindicates the noble unique fidelity of Lafayette, but finds in him credulity.

---

[145] Perhaps *The Thoughts of the Emperor M. Aurelius Antoninus,* trans. George Long (Boston: Ticknor and Fields, 1864); in Emerson's library, inscribed to him by the publisher.
[146] ". . . the heights, where Apollo sits enthroned, and a vast cavern hard by, hidden haunt of the dread Sibyl." Virgil, *Aeneid,* VI, 9–10.
[147] "Mme de . . . 6, 7," is added in pencil.

In a note, he indicates an important remark of Mirabeau on L., in the correspondence with La Marck, *Vol.* I. p. 62. [Sainte-Beuve, *Portraits littéraires,* 1852, II, 147]

And [Charles] Sumner who read here in Concord a Lecture on Lafayette is ⟨the American⟩ of all Americans the one who is best entitled by his own character & fortunes to read his Eulogy.[148]

Sieyes.   "J'ai vécu⟨,⟩."   in the Terror;

Lafayette. "Je me suis tenu debout⟨,⟩."—in the twelve years of the consulate & Empire. [Sainte-Beuve, *Portraits littéraires,* 1852, II, 191]

[192]   ↑Purity↓
     "La netteté est le vernis des maitres." *Vauvenargues.*

⟨M⟩Boileau asks Molière, "Where the devil do you get your rhyme?"[149] ⟨The⟩ For inspiration has unknown resources, has cunning also.

J'ouvris force livres anciens, mais pas un complet. *Michelet*
                              [*Histoire de France . . .* , 1835–1867, VII, 63]

———

Un cham⟨au⟩eau pliant sous le faix
     "Nul n'est tenu à l'impossible."
—— motto of Jean de Ligny. [*Ibid.,* p. 111]

[193] Alcott thinks there was an infusion of Theodore Parker in Jesus which he could spare.

     Avant, et pendant, et aprés.
Affirmative. ↑"d'aller↓ *toujours en avant, et le plus loin possible,"* said

---

[148] A vertical line is drawn in pencil in the left margin beside "And Sumner . . . all Americans". See p. [279$_h$] below, and *W*, XI, 594. Sumner's Concord Lyceum lecture on Lafayette had been given on November 7, 1860.
[149] This and the preceding quotation are from "Molière," in volume 2 of Sainte-Beuve's *Portraits littéraires,* 1852. " 'La netteté . . . *Vauvenargues.* " is also in "M. de Balzac," *Causeries du lundi,* 1851–1862, II, 357. See *JMN,* XIII, 271.

Napoleon to Lally. [Sainte-Beuve, *Portraits littéraires,* 1852, II, 165]
  de plus en plus fort.
There is ever one who is the second choice of everybody.

It has been impossible to keep the name & fame of John Brown out of
the war from ⟨the⟩ first to ⟨the⟩ last. Governor Wise & Vallandigham
have gone down, Fernando Wood has gone backward, b⟨y⟩ut John
Brown's soul is marching on.[150]

[194] ↑*Scholar a Solitaire.*↓
  If I were successful abroad in talking & dealing with men, I
should not come back to my library & my work, as I do. When the
spirit chooses you for the scribe to ⟨write⟩ ↑publish↓ some commandment, ↑if↓ ⟨to n⟩it makes you odious to men, & men odious to you, ⟨&⟩
you shall accept that loathsomeness with joy.

———

  The moth must fly to the lamp, & ↑t↓he ↑man↓ must solve those
questions though he die.[151]

———

[195]   Talk with Alcott
assured him that Character was the result of pagan morals rel

All the victories of religion belong to the moral sentiment. The
⟨so⟩poor soul sees the Law blazing thro' such impediments as he has, &
they are many, & he yields himself to humility & joy. The parson calls
it Justification by Faith[.]
All the victories, all the convictions, all the anxieties ↑of Revivals↓ are
the old Eternal fact of remorse for wrong, & joy in the Right.
  It is becoming to the Americans to dare in religion to be simple,
as they have been in government, in trade, in social life.

———

[150] Henry Alexander Wise (1806-1876) was governor of Virginia at the time of
John Brown's trial; Clement Laird Vallandigham (1820-1871), an Ohio congressman
from 1858 to 1862, was a Southern sympathizer who had interrogated Brown. For
Wood, see Journal VA, p. [187] above.
  [151] "If I were . . . die.", struck through in pencil with a vertical use mark, is used in
"Inspiration," *W,* VIII, 291-292. With "The moth . . . die.", which occurs in *JMN,* X,
134, cf. also "Inspiration," *W,* VIII, 275.

⟨to⟩They are to break down prisons, capital punishment, slavery, tariff, disfranchisement, caste; and they have rightly [196] pronounced ⟨it⟩Toleration,—that no religious test shall be put. They are to abolish laws against atheism[.]

They are not to allow immorality, they are to be strict in laws of marriage; they are to be just to women, in property, in votes, in personal rights,

And they are to establish the pure religion, ↑Justice,↓ Asceticism, self-devotion, Bounty,

They will lead their language round the globe, & they will lead religion & freedom with them.[152]

[197] Proof of the immorality of the Religions

Assert forever that morals is the test, then these miserable religions that we have known will be exposed. There is no vice that has not skulked behind them. It has been shown the bad morals of the Southern population. It cries to heaven. Yet these poisoning, starving, ↑town burning,↓ f⟨|| . . . ||⟩ever-planting people arrogate to themselves all the Xy[Christianity] of the nation, charge us with plot to kill their Christian President, accuse us of libertinism, reading & writing, slave stealing ⟨an⟩&c[.]

And it is only very lately that our own Churches[,] formerly silent on this crime & notoriously hostile to Abolitionists[,] wheeled into line for Emancipation[.]

[198] Remember Torrey at Park street. It was as all know, the experience of all abolitionists, that the Church was their chief Enemy. The Pope that old impostor↑,—↓what a history is that of the Catholic Church[.]

Now this is the mischief of suffering any doctrine of miracles[,] the immorality of miracles[.]

Put back the emphasis sternly & forever & ever on pure morals[,] al-

---

[152] Pages [195]–[196] are in pencil. "It is becoming . . . life." is overwritten by the same in ink, except that in the pencil version "government" is abbreviated and the punctuation is lacking. "They will . . . with them." is overwritten by the same in ink except for the addition of "& freedom" in the ink version. "All the victories . . . humility & joy." is struck through in pencil with a vertical use mark, which is extended through "The parson . . . Faith"; "All the . . . Faith" is used in "Character," *W*, X, 113. With "They are to break . . . rights.", cf. *ibid.*, p. 114.

ways the same[,] not subject to doubtful interpretation, with no sale of indulgences,—truth-speakers, just dealers, humble & useful[.]^{153}

[199] It was his tender conviction of this power & presence that made Jesus a light in the world, & the spirit that animated him is as swift and puissant today.

Scientific men with their Atheism like the French Savans, appear to me insane men with a talent; and the cure would be the opening of the moral sentiment.

There is far more than bare works; there is faith also: That is, the raptures of goodness are as old as history, & new with this morning's sun. The language & the legends of Arabia & India & Persia are of the same complexion as the Christian. Vishnu⟨,⟩ Purana bear witness. Socrates, Zeno, Menu, ⟨Confucius,⟩ Zertusht, Confucius, Rabbia, are as tender as St. Francis, St. Austin, & Bernard.^{154}

[200]^{155} We say
          There exists a Universal Mind which imparts this perception of duty, opens the interior world to the humble obeyer. This perception is final, sovran:

---

^{153} Pages [197] and [198] are in pencil. "Assert forever . . . behind them.", struck through in pencil with a vertical use mark, "And it . . . Emancipation", struck through in pencil with one vertical and one diagonal use mark, and "Now this . . . miracles" and "Put back . . . useful", struck through in pencil with single vertical use marks, are used or paraphrased in "Character," W, X, 114. With "Assert forever . . . exposed.", cf. the report of the lecture "Public and Private Education" in Gohdes, *Uncollected Lectures*, 1932, p. 15.
^{154} "It was . . . Bernard." is written in ink on p. [199] over a draft of the same in erased pencil which extends onto the top of p. [200]. Variants in the pencil version read: "animated him is ⟨r|| . . . || swift⟩ as puissant" in the first paragraph, and "⟨We sa|| . . . ||⟩ ⟨That⟩ there is faith also: That is, the raptures of ⟨th⟩ good ⟨is are⟩ ↑ness↓ are as old as history ⟨& with⟩ ↑new with this morning's sun↓ The language & the legends of Arabia & India & Persia are of the same complexion as the Christian. Vishnu Purana bear witness. Socrates ⟨also⟩ Zeno, ↑Menu↓ Confucius, Zertusht, Rabbia [200] ↑are as tender as St. Francis, St. Austin, & Bernard.↓" in the third paragraph. "There is . . . Confucius," struck through in pencil with a discontinuous vertical use mark, is used in "Inspiration," W, VIII, 275.
^{155} Pages [200] and [201] are in pencil.

Who has it beholds eternity.
It has been imparted in all ages.

Religion is the homage to this Presence[.]

But religion is corrupted in the very first reception & goes from bad to
worse in the mob[.]¹⁵⁶

The only incorruptible thing is morals. All the religions soon go to
ruin. They get incrusted with miracles, & divert attention from [201]
the rule, the Eternal Presence, to the legend. It is no matter what
Christ did or suffered, or Moses, or John, but of great import how you
stand to your tribunal.¹⁵⁷
But morals must be fresh & perfect every day, they have no memory.

What we call Character is not sectarian ↑virtue↓ but ⟨expresses
the⟩ habitual ⟨respect⟩ selfpossession, habitual respect to interior con-
stitutional motives, so as not to be overset or diverted or at all much
affected by trifles or triflers[.]¹⁵⁸

_____

"Splendid sins" I believe is Scougal's ↑St Augustine's↓ phrase for
Socrates's virtue.

[202] "Well hove, but you are not the one to heave it," said Dr Ripley to that dubious Mrs Foster.

[203]   ↑Southern Morality.↓
I charge the Southerner with starving prisoners of war; with
⟨killing⟩ ↑massacring↓ surrendered men; with the St Albans' raid; with
the plundering railroad passenger-trains ⟨of⟩in peaceful districts; with
plots of burning cities; with advertising a price for the li⟨if⟩fe of Lincoln, Butler, Garrison, & others; with assassination of the President, &

¹⁵⁶ The notes to this point on p. [200] are developed in "Character," _W_, X, 93–97
and 103.
¹⁵⁷ With this paragraph, struck through in pencil with single vertical use marks on
pp. [200] and [201], cf. "Character," _W_, X, 113 and 114.
¹⁵⁸ This sentence, struck through in pencil with a vertical use mark, is used in "Character," _W_, X, 102.

of Seward; with attempts to import the yellow fever into New York; with the cutting up the bones of our soldiers to make ornaments⟨.⟩↑, & drinking-cups of their skulls.↓

[204] [blank]
[205] ↑Mrs Caroline Carson
    149 W. 26th street New York↓[159]

    ↑Forsitan haec spernant↓ Juvenes, quibus arte benignae
    Et meliore luto finxit praecordia Titan.
                        Juvenal   Sat[ires]. XIV. v. 34[-35][160]

I am an old writer, & yet I often meet good English words which I never used once. Thus I met just now the word *wainscot*. ↑pollute↓

[206] We are a little nice about liberties taken with the laws of nature by impatient theologians. Nature is very large & roomy,↑—↓ elastic, plastic, her space prodigal, time without stint, her housekeeping "totally regardless of expense," her chemistry surpassing Proteus or Aladdin; her accumulations of all material likely to be wanted might satisfy the most exigeant quartermaster,—Pennsylvan↑i↓as & Englands of [207] coal, Californias & Australias of gold, ⟨&⟩Russias & Missouris of iron, air enough, water enough, wood at discretion, grass, ↑corn,↓ game, fish, fruit,   ↑Will you go fast? the railroad; will go faster? the balloon: will you send faster? the ↑ocean↓ telegraph.↓ She has a right to be a little particular about ↑being↓ chastiz⟨ing⟩ed↑,↓ ⟨her⟩ "to make two lovers happy." She hints, on such occasions, that there is a right way "within the Constitution" to arrive at the result, if it be anything ⟨within⟩ ↑in↓ reason.[161]

[208] Admirable fairness of Elizabeth Hoar's mind. I think no one who writes or utilizes his opinions, can possibly be so fair. She will see finer *nuances* of equity which you would never see ↑if↓ untold. She

---

[159] The name and address are in pencil.
[160] "Here and there perhaps a youth may decline to follow the bad example: one whose soul the Titan has fashioned with kindlier skill and of finer clay." See *JMN*, IX, 389.
[161] This paragraph is marked with single vertical pencil lines drawn in the left margins of pp. [206] and [207]. The dash after "roomy," is added in pencil.

applied the Napoleon *mot,* "Respect the burden," so well to Lincoln
quoad Wendell Phillips.[162]
And one may say, there is a genius for honesty, as well as for poetry,
and nobody ⟨but⟩ can anticipate the directness & simplicity of the true
man.

[209] The best /⟨of⟩/⟨*in*⟩/ argument is not the accosting in
front the hostile premises, but the *flanking* them by a new generaliza-
tion which incidentally disposes of them.

[210] It should be easy to say what I have always felt, that ⟨En-
field's⟩Stanley's "Lives of the Philosophers"[163] or Marcus Antoninus
are agreeable & suggestive books to me, whilst ⟨S P⟩St Paul or Saint
John are not, & I should never think of taking up these to start me on
my task, as I often have used Plato or Plutarch. It is because the bible
wears black cloth. It comes with a ⟨disagreeable⟩ ↑certain↓ official
[211] claim against which ⟨my⟩ ↑the↓ mind revolts. The book ⟨is well
enough,⟩ ↑has its own nobilities,—↓might well be charming, if it was
⟨new to me, &⟩ ↑left↓ simply on its merits, as the others; but this "you
must,"—"it is your duty"— ⟨makes it loathsome.⟩ ↑repels.↓ 'Tis like
the introduction of martial law into Concord. If you should dot our
farms with picket lines, & I could not go or come across lots without a
pass, I should resist, or else emigrate. [212] If Concord were as beautiful as Paradise, it would be detestable at once.

> ↑And then↓ were[n] Concord ⟨then⟩ ↑plain↓ as fair
> As Eden when high God had blest it,
> I should abandon & detest it.[164]

[213] When divine souls appear, men are compelled by their
own self-respect to distinguish them.[165]

---

[162] For " 'Respect the burden,' " see the anecdote from Emanuel Augustin Dieu-
donné, Comte de Las Cases, *Mémorial de Sainte Hélène. Journal of the Private Life and
Conversations of the Emperor Napoleon at Saint Helena,* 4 vols. (Boston, 1823), I, i,
161–162, in *JMN,* V, 485, and "Napoleon," *W,* IV, 240.

[163] Probably Thomas Stanley, *The History of Philosophy* (London, 1701), which
Emerson had borrowed from the Boston Athenaeum in 1834.

[164] The verse is in pencil. Above it a long rule in pencil has been erased; "And then"
was added in pencil, erased, and added again.

[165] This sentence is used in "Character," *W,* X, 100.

Whenever the Moral Sentiment is ⟨lim[?]⟩affirmed, it must be with dazzling courage.   As long as it is ↑cowardly↓ insinuated, as with the wish to show that it is just what the Church receives today, it is not imparted & cannot be owned.

↑printed in *"Character"*
N[orth]. A[merican]. Rev[iew].↓[166]

————

See Moral Sentiment *ML* 136

————

[214][167]   The Muse
Can at pleasure use
Every ⟨word⟩ syllable men /have heard/preferred/
And can move with every word
⟨She⟩ Need[n] not mimic, ↑plot↓ or veer
But speak right on↑ward↓ without fear
She need not turn aside
Or half convey & half suppress
⟨Her⟩ ↑New↓ meaning in a ⟨current⟩ ↑worn-out↓
        /phrase/dress/
↑She will not walk in crooked ways↓
But bend the language to her
Make the langua⟨n⟩ge bend to her
Not unable   not afraid
To say what ⟨it hath⟩ never ↑yet was↓ said
She need not stray from her path
To find ⟨ornament⟩ ↑the words of love or wrath↓
The world is as rich in ↑nouns &↓ verbs
As in ⟨sand⟩ ↑sea sand↓ or ↑in↓ herbs

[215] [blank]
[216] Quotation
    It seems Columbus must divide with Brunelleschi the story of the egg. See *Michelet*. [*Histoire de France* . . . , 1833–1866,] vol. 7. p. 96 Brunelleschi, whose scholar Michel Angelo is, according to Michelet. [*Ibid.,* pp. 97–98]

————

[166] This paragraph is struck through in ink with two diagonal use marks. "Character" was printed in the *North American Review*, CII (Apr. 1866), 356–373, but this paragraph has not been located there.
    [167] Page [214] is in pencil; "dress" in line 9 of the verse is added in ink.

[217] May 28
In the acceptance that my papers find among ↑my↓ thoughtful countrymen, in these days, I cannot help feeling how limited is their reading. If they read only the books that I do, they would not exaggerate
so wildly.

Select books, select ⟨stories⟩ anecdotes,
Select discoveries, select works of art, select men & women. The most
accomplished man should ⟨teach his⟩ bring his contemporaries to the
high culture by pointing out these with insight & reverence. ⟨At such a
school⟩ [218] The graduate at the University should know ⟨Pythag-
oras's discovery⟩
            "the famed lines Pythagoras devised
            ⟨When⟩ ↑For which↓ a ⟨whole⟩ hecatomb he sacrificed";[168]
Should know Archimedes's Eureka;
Should know Newton's binomial theorem inscribed on his tomb; as
well as his optical,[169] & astronomic, & chemical insights,
Should know Da Vinci's cartoon, & Michel Angelo's Pisan soldiers;
Should know Brunelleschi's dome, and Michel's;
Should know Columbus's guess & its grounds; should know Alfred's
rough hints of English freedom;
[219] Roger Bacon's inventions, &, ⟨if⟩ ↑as far as↓ possible, the his-
tory of the Magnetic Compass;
Should know the Homeric controversy,
Should know the wonderful illumination thrown on all history in our
own day by the scholars of the Sanscrit.
Should know the history of the Mahabarat;
Should know the history of Zoroaster, what, & who, & when was he?
↑(See Nicholas Grimoald's Verses on Zoroas.)↓[170]
Should know how the decimal zero was invented.

---

[168] See *Plutarch's Morals: Translated from the Greek by Several Hands,* 3rd ed., 5 vols.
(London, 1694), II, 194.
[169] A vertical pencil line is drawn in the left margin beside "Should know Newton's
. . . optical,".
[170] Nicholas Grimald's "The death of Zoroas, an Egiptian Astronomer, in the first
fight, that Alexander had with the Persians" was first published in *Tottel's Miscellany,*
1557.

[220] In literature, there are many curiosities of the second or third order which should be known, as the *"Imitation of Christ,"* of A Kempis; or of Gerson; as the *Farce of Patelin;* as the *Song of Roland;* * as the *Mariage de Figaro;* and the *Marseillaise* of Roget. So, in England, the *Sonnets of Shakspeare;* the *Paradise of Dainty Devices;* specially, too, the *Morte d'Arthur.*

[221] Printing is an art of liberty, but it did not hinder Napoleon⟨'s⟩ III's coup d'état, nor the mean despotism of Prussia & Austria, in our time.

I must think that Carlyle's humor & daemonic fun, telling the story in a gale, bantering, scoffing, now at his hero, now at the enemy, always too at the learned reporters⟨,⟩ he has been consulting, will affect all good readers agreeably; for it is a perpetual flattery to the wise reader, a tête à tête with him, ⟨b⟩abusing the whole world as mad dunces,—all but you & I, reader!

↑(Probably in letter to Carlyle)↓[171]

[222] [blank]
[223]–[278] [. . .][172]
[279] [blank]
[279ₐ][173] Clean, self-poised,
      Great-hearted man,
      noble in person
      incorruptible in life
      the friend of the poor,
      the champion of the oppressed

   *see *DL* 241

---

[171] See Emerson's letter of January 7, 1866, *CEC,* p. 546. Emerson is referring to volumes 5 and 6 of Carlyle's *Frederick the Great,* 6 vols. (London, 1862–1865), which Carlyle sent him in the spring of 1865.

[172] Emerson used pp. [223]–[278] for the poetry notebook designated KL[A] by the editors, which runs upside down and backward with respect to KL; see p. 414 above for a description.

[173] Pages [279ₐ]–[279ᵦ] are in pencil. For a description of these notes on Charles Sumner, see pp. 414–415 above. Emerson probably gathered them in 1874 for a brief testimonial printed in Charles Sumner's *Prophetic Voices Concerning America* (Boston and New York, 1874), pp. 4–5 of terminal advertisements. See also *L,* VI, 257–258.

Of course, ⟨in the vast power of⟩ Congress ⟨draws⟩ must draw from every part of the country ⟨multitudes of⟩ swarms of individuals /intent only on their private interests/ [279ᵦ] eager only for private interests/ who could not love his stern justice[.]

⟨Slow & exhaustive training⟩
        ⟨preparation⟩

⟨accomplished man⟩

[279ᵪ] But if they gave him no high employment he made low work high by the ⟨fide⟩ dignity of honesty & truth[.]
But men cannot long do without faculty & perseverance & he rose ⟨by⟩ step by step to the mastery ⟨in⟩of all affairs entrusted to him & by those lights & upliftings with which the Spirit that makes the Universe rewards labor & brave [279ᵈ] truth. He became learned ⟨in⟩ & adequate to the highest questions ⟨In⟩& the counsellor of every ⟨good step⟩ correction of old errors & of every noble reform. How nobly he bore himself in disastrous times. Every reform he led or assisted. In the shock of the war his patriotism never failed⟨;⟩. ⟨fear did not exist for him and ⟨the⟩ in signal instances he⟩[174]

[279ₑ][175] ⟨m⟩Man of varied learning & accomplishment.
He held that every man is to be judged by the horizon of his mind, and Fame he defined as the shadow of excellence, but that which follows him, not which he follows after.
Tragic character, like Algernon Sydney, Man of Conscience & courage, but without humor
Fear did not exist for him

[279ᶠ] ↑In his mind,↓ ⟨T⟩the American idea is no crab, but a man incessantly advancing as the shadow of the dial or the heavenly body that casts it. The American idea is emancipation, to abolish Kingcraft, feudalism, blackletter monopoly, it pulls down the gallows, explodes

---

[174] The period after "failed" is added, and "fear did . . . instances he" is canceled, in pencil.
[175] Page [279ₑ] is in pencil.

priestcraft, opens the doors of the sea to all emigrants, extemporizes government in[176]

[279$_g$] [Journal] N.Y 168

Sumner ⟨his⟩has been collecting his works. They will be the history of the republic for the last 25 years, as told by a brave, perfectly honest & well instructed man with social culture & relation to all eminent persons⟨—⟩a diligent & able workman with rare ability, without genius, without humor but with persevering study, wide reading, excellent memory, high sense of honor (& pure devotion to his country) disdaining any bribe↑,↓ any compliances,[n] & incapable of falsehood.[177] His singular advantages of person, of manners, & a statesman's conversation impress every one favorably. He has the foible of most public men[,] the egotism which seems almost unavoidable at Washington. I sat in his room once at Washington whilst he wrote a weary succession of letters,—he writing without pause as fast as if he were copying. He outshines all his [279$_h$] mates in historical conversation & is so public in his regards that he cannot be relied on to push an office seeker, so that he is no favorite with politicians. But wherever I have met ⟨it⟩with a dear lover of the Country & its moral interests he is sure to be a supporter of Sumner[.]

[279$_i$] ⟨*Sumner*⟩

⟨[Journal] NY 253⟩ It characteri⟨s⟩zes a man for me that he hates Charles Sumner: for it shows that he cannot discriminate between a foible & a vice. Sumner's moral instinct & character are so exceptional⟨,⟩↑ly pure↓ that he must have perpetual magnetism for honest men; his ability & working energy such, that every good friend of the Republic must ⟨vote for⟩ ↑stand by↓ him.[178] Those who come near

---

[176] This entry is struck through in pencil with two vertical use marks. For "⟨T⟩the American . . . casts it.", see *JMN*, XI, 405–406, and "The Fortune of the Republic," *W*, XI, 537.

[177] The comma after "bribe" is in pencil. "Sumner . . . eminent persons" is used in Emerson's testimonial printed in Charles Sumner, *Prophetic Voices Concerning America*, 1874, p. 4 of terminal advertisements.

[178] "*Sumner*" and "NY 253" are canceled in pencil. "vote for" is canceled, and "stand by" inserted, in pencil. The first sentence is struck through in pencil with one diagonal and one discontinuous vertical use mark.

him & are offended by his egotism, or his foible (if you please) of using classic quotations, or other bad taste, easily [279ⱼ] forgive⟨s⟩ these whims, if themselves are good, or magnify them into disgust, if they themselves are incapable of his virtue.

↑KL 191↓ And when he read ⟨in⟩one night in Concord a Lecture on Lafayette we felt that of all Americans he was best entitled by his own character & fortunes to read that Eulogy.

[279ₖ] Every Pericles must have his Creon; Sumner had his adversaries, his wasps & back-biters. We almost wished that he had ⟨scorn⟩ not stooped to answer them. But he condescended to give them truth & patriotism ⟨wh⟩ without ↑asking↓ whether they could appreciate the instruction or not.

[279ₗ] ↑Man of such truth that the
he can be truly described: he needs no exaggerated praise.↓
Not a man of extraordinary genius, but a man of great heart, of a perpetual youth, with the highest sense of honor, incapable of any fraud, little or large, loving his friend & loving his country, ⟨co⟩with ⟨great⟩ perfect steadiness to his purpose, shunning no labor that his aim required, & his works justified him by their scope & ⟨the⟩ thoroughness[.]
He had good masters who quickly found that they had a good scholar[.]

[279ₘ] Talent

He read law with Judge Story who was at the head of the ⟨l⟩Law school ⟨at⟩of Harvard University & who speedily discovered the ⟨rare⟩ value of his pupil & ⟨made him⟩ called him to his assistance in the Law School[.]¹⁷⁹

He had a great ⟨c⟩talent for labor & spared no time & no research to make himself master of his subject. His treatment of every question

---

¹⁷⁹ "Talent", written in pencil between the first two lines, may have been inscribed earlier. "He read . . . School" is struck through in pencil with a vertical use mark.

was faithful & exhaustive & ⟨always⟩ marked ↑always↓ by the noble sentiment[.]

[279ₙ] See Goethe Vol 4, p. 78 for the Romantic poem of "Charon."[180]

Vollziehn   execute
Betracht   /Considered/Concluded/
umschwung   revolution
Sieg   Victory

List of Books, see *KL* 220
and 218
Of Swedenborg see *VS* 175–6,–7,–8,
And Randolph's Letter   *VS* 191
Roger Bacon   *CO* 120,
↑Swedenborg, felicity of devils, *VS* 180↓
P. P. Randolph   *VS* 191

⟨Pond lilies   KL 38⟩   Coombs 42
Indian p 59[181]

[280] [Index material omitted]
[inside back cover] [Index material omitted]

---

[180] See p. [19] above.

[181] "Vollziehn . . . Victory" and "Indian p 59" are in pencil. "Of Swedenborg . . . Randolph *VS* 191" is struck through in pencil with a discontinuous diagonal use mark; "Roger Bacon" and "Coombs" are also struck through in pencil with single diagonal use marks.

Visit to Washington. 79

Disappear 31 January, 1862.

At Washington. 31 January, 1 Feb
2d, + 3d, saw Sumner, who on the
2d, carried me to Mr Chase, Mr
Bates, Mr Staunton, Mr Welles,
Mr Seward, Lord Lyons, and
President Lincoln. The President impressed me more
favorably than I had hoped.
A frank, sincere well meaning
man, with a lawyer's habit
of mind, good clean statement
of his fact, correct enough,
not vulgar, as described;
but with a sort of boyish
cheerfulness, or that kind

10th Henry T. remains erect, calm,
self-subsistent, before me,
and I read him not only
truly in his Journal, but
he is not long out of mind
when I walk, and as today,
row upon the Pond. He
chose wisely no doubt for
himself to be the bachelor
of thought & nature that
he was — how near to the
old monks in their ascetic
religion! He had no talent

Plate II   Journal VA, page 102   Text, page 261
                 Henry T. remains erect, calm

216

Solve senescentem.

Saadi's poem on old age.

Now is the time when weakness comes, & strength goes
The enchant~~ing~~ power of sweet words — quintessence
The harvest ~~and~~ ~~comes~~, & this poem & this light
~~Which the own fragrant garland~~ ~~it~~ departs.

To my foot fails the power — of longer stride;
Happy ~~is he~~ who to his hut — hence goeth.
Saadi's whole power lies — in sweet words
Keep this all the rest & give to may go to blast & bird
Let this remain, — so care I not ~~what~~ goeth.

Saadi

Love's smart is more worth
Than the body's well-being

Saadi No soul has he   who no friend has
       Little joy has he   who no garden has
       Who with a moon face   can refresh his heart
       Enjoys a luck   which has no bound
       A dungeon is that house   which solitude fills
       If ~~the Saadi~~ they have not,   Like Saadi, a rose bed

Plate III   Journal FOR, page 216   Text, pages 384–385
                  Translation of Saadi poem reworked

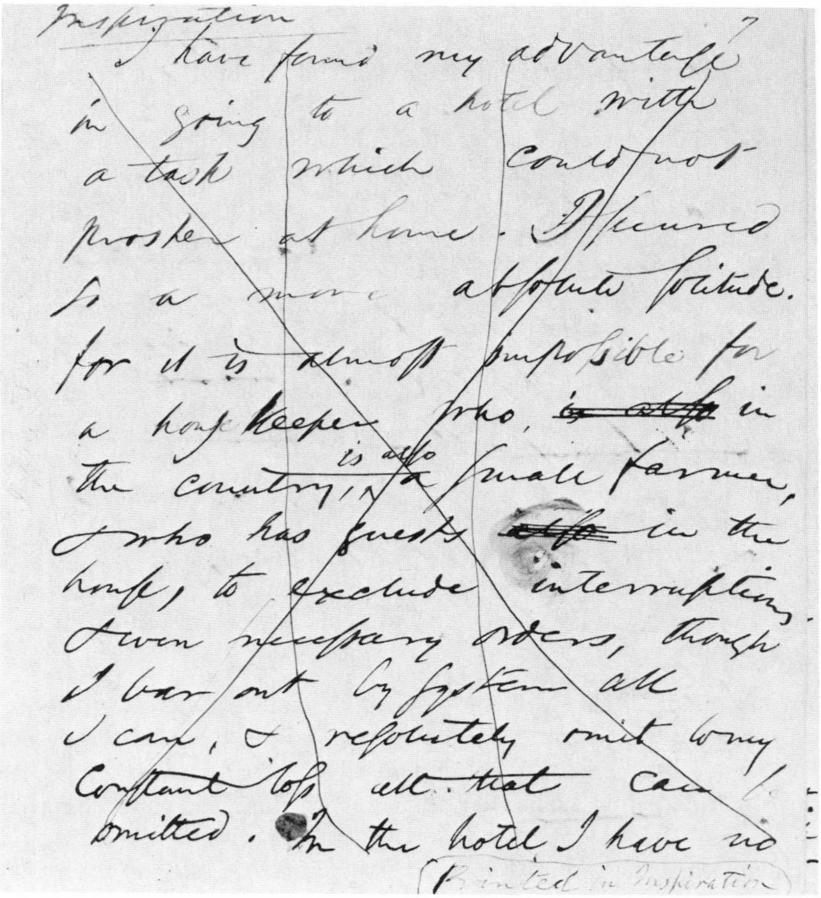

Inspiration

I have found my advantage in going to a hotel with a task which could not prosper at home. I secured so a more absolute solitude. for it is almost impossible for a housekeeper who, ~~is also~~ in the country, is also a small farmer, & who has guests ~~also~~ in the house, to exclude interruptions & even necessary orders, though I bar out by system all I can, & resolutely omit to my constant loss all that can be omitted. In the hotel I have no

(Printed in Inspiration)

Plate IV   Journal KL, page 7   Text, pages 416–417
                A more absolute solitude

PART TWO

Miscellaneous Notebooks

HT

1864–1865?

Emerson began Notebook HT in July 1864 (p. [3]), probably in preparation for his small volume of Thoreau's letters and poems, *Letters to Various Persons,* and may have continued to use it until May 1865, when he sent the copy to Ticknor and Fields.

The covers of the copybook, of marbled tan, black, red, and green paper over boards, measure 17.1 × 21.1 cm. The spine strip and protective corners on front and back covers are of tan leather. "HT" is inscribed in ink, now badly worn, on the spine and upper right front corner.

Including flyleaves (1–2, 283–284), there were 284 unlined pages measuring 17.3 × 20.5 cm; the leaves bearing pages 43–46 have been torn out, but they were discovered filed with lecture manuscripts and have been restored. Twenty pages are numbered in ink: 4, 10–23, 47, and 50–53. Thirty-two are numbered in pencil: 3, 7, 9, 30, 31, 42, 60, 62, 70, 80, 90, 100, 110, 120, 130, 140, 150, 160, 170, 180, 190, 200, 210, 220, 230, 240, 250, 260, 270, 276, 280, and 282. Page 5 is numbered in pencil overwritten in ink. The rest are unnumbered. Pages 1–2, 8, 10, 24–42, 47–50, 54–275, and 277–283 are blank.

Tipped to page 1 is a sheet of striated white paper measuring 20.5 × 25.1 cm, folded once to make four pages; Ellery Channing's "Stanzas: Written to be sung at the funeral of Henry D. Thoreau, of Concord, Massachusetts, Friday, May 9th, 1862" are printed on the third page and revised in pencil, in a hand other than Emerson's; the passage from *Walden* which Emerson copied on page 5 of the notebook, and a note on Rosemary Andromeda growing in Gowan's swamp, are inscribed in ink in another hand, not Emerson's, on pages 1–3.

Laid in between pages 24–25 is a newspaper clipping, a review of Thoreau's *Cape Cod.* Laid in between pages 36–37 is a torn half-sheet of blue-lined paper, measuring roughly 12.5 × 19.6 cm, inscribed at right angles to the lines on both sides, printed as pages 36$_a$–36$_b$ below. Laid in between pages 38–39 is a sheet of blue letter paper torn off along the fold to measure 12.6 × 20.1 cm, inscribed in ink on both sides, printed as pages 38$_a$–38$_b$ below.

[front cover]   HT

[front cover verso]¹ See Extracts from H.T.'s Journals in
                                            VA 127, 170, 172
                                            VA 109
                                            DL
                                            HT

            died 1862
Hawthorn 186

[1]–[2] [blank]
[3] July 1864
            Miscellaneous Notes on H. D. Thoreau—

[4] In ↑Aug.↓ 1843, Henry complains in his letters that it is very difficult for him to keep awake. He was then at Staten Island.²

In 1840, he wrote↑;↓ ⟨in⟩"A good book will not be dropped by its author, but thrown up. It will be so long a promise, that he will not
overtake it soon. He will have slipped the leash of a fleet hound."³

────────────────

            ↑*See next page.* p 5↓

[5] *Poems   to be printed*
            "Sympathy"   Dial Vol 1 p 71
            "Sic Vita."   Dial II p 81
            Friendship   Dial II   204
            Rumors from a Harp ↑Dial↓ III 200
            Smoke   Dial   III, 505
            Haze   III, 506
            Inspiration
            Funeral Bell
            Departure

¹ The front cover verso is inscribed in pencil.
² "Aug." is added in pencil. See Henry D. Thoreau, *Letters to Various Persons,* ed.
Ralph Waldo Emerson (Boston, 1865), p. 27.
³ See Journal DL, p. [140] above.

Travelling
Greece[4]

"I long ago lost a hound, a bay horse, & a turtle-dove, & am still on their trail. Many are the travellers to whom I have spoken concerning them, describing their tracks, & ⟨to⟩what calls they answered to. I have met one or two who had heard the hound, & the tramp of the horse, & even seen the dove disappear behind a cloud, & they seemed as anxious to recover them as if they had lost them themselves." *Walden* [(Boston, 1854),] p. 20[5]

[6] What is the orthography of Tarkiln (?) Hill, New Bedford? Taskila (?)

In letter to D[aniel] R[icketson] Nov. 6, 1858, does the Australian mean Cholmondeley?[6]

[7] ⟨See notice of⟩
Henry resembled Farley. *DL* 61[7]

———

List of books bequeathed to me by Henry D. Thoreau; See *VA* 68.

———

[8] [blank]
[9] *Estabrook Farm*. "There is a tract of pasture, woodland, orchard, & swamp, in the north part of the town, through which the old Carli⟨i⟩sle road runs, which is nearly two miles square, without a single house, & scarcely any cultivated land in it."—4 square miles.
HDT 1853 June [5] p 292 of his Journal[8]

---

[4] *"Poems* . . . Greece" is in pencil; "Funeral Bell . . . Greece" is overwritten in ink by " 'I long . . . have met", printed below. "Sympathy," "Smoke," "Haze," and "Inspiration" are among the poems Emerson included in his edition of Thoreau's *Letters to Various Persons*, 1865.

[5] This quotation is used in "Thoreau," *W*, X, 476.

[6] Page [6] is in pencil. See *Letters to Various Persons*, 1865, pp. 170–171.

[7] "⟨See notice . . . *DL* 61" is in pencil.

[8] See *The Journal* . . . , 1949, V, 225, and Journal VA, p. [172] above.

[10] [blank]

[11] H.D.T. writes to D. Ricketson, March 5, 1856

I was surprised to hear the other day that Channing was in New Bedford. When he was here last in December, I think, he said, like himself, in answer to my inquiry, where he lived? that he did not know the name of the place. So it remained in a degree of obscurity for me. As you have made it certain to me that he is in N.B., perhaps I can return the favor by putting you on the track of his [12] boarding house there. Mrs Arnold told Mrs Emerson where it was, and the latter thinks, ⟨& s⟩though she ma⟨m⟩y be mistaken, that it was at a Mrs Lindsay's. I am rejoiced to hear that you are getting on bravely with him & his verses. He & I, you know, have been old cronies.

> Fed the same flock by fountain, shade, & rill,
> Together both, ere the high lawns appeared,
> Under the opening eyelids of the morn
> We drove afield, & both together heard, &c &c
> —But o the heavy change, now ⟨"thou art gone"⟩ he is gone!

[13] The C. you have seen & described is the real Simon Pure. You have seen him. Many a good ramble may you have together. You will see in him still more *of the same kind*, to attract & puzzle you. How to serve him most effectually has long been a problem with his friends. Perhaps it is left for you to solve it. I suspect that the most that you or any one can do ⟨is⟩for him is to appreciate his genius; to buy & read, & cause others to buy & read [14] his poems. That is the hand which he has put forth to the world,—Take hold by that. Review them, if you can. Perhaps take the risk of publishing something which he may write. Your knowledge of Cowper will help you to know C. He⟨s⟩ will accept sympathy & aid, but he will not bear questioning, unless the aspects of the sky are ⟨sing⟩↑partic↑ularly auspicious. [15] He will ever be "reserved & enigmatic," & you must deal with him at arm's length. I have no secrets to tell you concerning him, & do not wish to call ⟨his⟩obvious excellences & defects by farfetched names. I think I have already spoken to you more & more to the purpose than I am likely to write now, nor need I suggest how witty & poetic he is, & what an inexhaustible fund of good fellowship you will find in him.[9]

---

[9] See *The Correspondence of Henry Thoreau*, ed. Walter Harding and Carl Bode (New York, 1958), p. 413. Emerson printed the beginning and end of this letter in *Letters to Various Persons*, 1865, pp. 131–133, but omitted this section of it.

[16]   Oct. 24, 1847
H.D.T. writes to Sophia T[horeau].

I went to see Perez Blood's telescope, with Mr E. We saw Saturn's ring, the mountains in the moon, ⟨&⟩ the shadows in their craters, & the sunlight on the spurs of their mountains in the dark portion, &c. &c. When I asked him the power of his glass, he said, ↑it was↓ 85.—But what is the power of the Cambridge glass? 2000! The last is about 23 ft. long.[10]

[17] Henry pitched his tone very low in his love of nature,—not on stars⟨,⟩ & suns, nor   but tortoises, crickets, muskrats, suckers, toads & frogs. It was impossible to go lower. Yet it gave him every advantage in conversation: For who ⟨who⟩ ↑that↓ found him always skilled in facts, real experience in objects which made their [18] objects & experiences appear artificial, could tax him with transcendentalism or over-refining: And yet his position was in Nature, & so commanded all its ⟨artilleries⟩ miracles & infinitudes.[n]

[19] In Journal, 1852, August 6, he writes, "Hearing that one with whom I was acquainted had committed suicide, I said, 'I did not know, when I planted the seed of that fact, that I should hear of it.' "

I see the Thoreau poison working today in many valuable lives, in some for good, in some for harm. ↑See *KL 42*↓[11]

[20] "Any excess,—to have drunk too much water, even, the day before,—is fatal to the morning's clarity." Journal July 1852[12]

——————

on p. 8, of his Journal, October 1837, is his account of stooping in his Indian speech, & saying, "here is Tahattawan's arrowhead," and the stone he seized "proved to be a most perfect arrowhead, as sharp as if just from the hands of the Indian fabricator."[13]

[10] See *The Correspondence* . . . , 1958, p. 187, and *JMN*, X, 315.
[11] See *The Journal* . . . , 1949, IV, 280, where the entry is dated August 5, and Journal VA, p. [109] above. "See *KL 42*" is added in pencil; p. [42] is torn out of Journal KL.
[12] See *The Journal* . . . , 1949, IV, 198, and Journal KL, p. [11].
[13] See *ibid.*, I, 7–8; cf. "Thoreau," *W*, X, 463–464.

[21][14] See various Extracts from H D T's Journal in VA 127
      Telegraph harp   VA 131
      Woodfrogs markings   *VA* 136
      Criticism of the gods   VA 135
      Brown thrasher & wood thrush. VA 137
      Beech trees, *VA* 173
      See of his tastes, *FOR* 58

[22] Of a book by Harriet Martineau he said, "Miss Martineau's ↑last↓ book is not so bad as the timidity which fears its influence."[15] "Give me but the eyes to see the things which you possess."

[23] Henry rightly said, the other evening, talking of lightning-rods, that the only rod of safety was in the vertebrae of his own spine. *GO* 22.

[24]–[42] [blank][16]
[36a] ↑H D T↓   ↑*Jan. 1853*↓
      Blue sky at night. 22

———

      Technical Nomenclature   18

———

His hunting & fishing   43

———

      Thundering of the pond

———

diamond window in Hunt-house   ⟨55⟩54
      snow-bird   69

———

      Wild man   46

———

[14] Page [21] is in pencil.
[15] See *The Journal* . . . , 1949, II, 468.
[16] Laid in between pp. [24]–[25] is a newspaper clipping headlined "THOREAU AND HIS WRITINGS.", and signed "SORDELLO", which refers to "Cape Cod" as recently published by Ticknor & Fields and discusses at length Thoreau's writings and his neglect by readers. Laid in between pp. [36]–[37] is a torn half-sheet of lined white paper, inscribed on both sides and printed as pp. [36a]–[36b] below.

Telegraph 3

———

Crowfoot bud 7

———

Echoes 63

His "Night warbler" June 19, 1853 seen & described[17]

[36_b] *1853*
Feb 13. in the driving snowstorm, a dense flock of snowbirds on &
under the pigweed in the garden. (probably tree sparrows),

———

later, corrected thus,

———

Lesser redpoll linnet
    Linaria Minor
having black legs & a ⟨black⟩ crimson crown or frontlet in the male.[18]

[38_a][19] Cornus sericeus
       Vaccinium
       Chiogenes hispidula

[38_b]   Memory
         Fate
         Poet
         Hush

[43][20] Mrs Cynthia Thoreau, Henry's mother, was a woman of
a sharp & malicious wit, and a very entertaining story-teller, I have

[17] "H D T . . . Echoes 63" is in pencil. See *The Journal* . . . , 1949, IV, 469, 467,
480, 439, 487, 493, 482, 458, 460, and 492–493, and V, 281–282.

[18] See *The Journal* . . . ,1949, IV, 493, and V, 3. "⟨black⟩" is fingerwiped.

[19] Laid in between pp. [38]–[39] is a torn half-sheet of blue letter paper inscribed in
ink with botanical names from Thoreau's Journal on the recto, and the titles of four of
Emerson's own poems on the verso, printed here as pp. [38_a]–[38_b].

[20] Pages [43]–[46], two leaves torn out of Notebook HT, are now filed with a
manuscript headed "Prolegomena of Sketch of Thoreau. Rareness of truth of Character.
Sentiment⟨ism⟩alism. Music Hall, June 29, 1862", in Houghton Library.

been told. But my wife repeats two or three passages of her wit. When I first bought a horse in Concord I looked about for a cheap carriage of some kind. Samuel Staples offered to sell me one called a rockaway[n] [44] which would carry four persons, & was decent & convenient. My wife had occasion to speak of it at Mrs Thoreau's, and she replied, "O yes, I know it very well. 'Tis the old one in which Sam Staples always carries his prisoners to jail: they sat right in front of him so they could not get away." a speech quite new to my wife, & which ⟨did⟩ ↑⟨I hop⟩ ↑Mrs Thoreau↓ hoped would↓ not recommend her new carriage ⟨to her⟩ much⟨.⟩ to her imagination.

[45] When Henry was at Staten Is⟨t⟩land, he wrote two or three letters to my wife.⟨.⟩[21] She spoke of them to his family, who eagerly wished to see them. ⟨L⟩She consented, but said, "⟨T⟩She was almost ashamed to show them, because Henry had exalted her by very undeserved praise."—"O yes," said his mother, "Henry is very tolerant."

Mrs Brown ⟨one day⟩ who boarded with the Thoreaus, [46] was one day talking with Mrs T. of the remarks made by ⟨he⟩ many persons on the resemblances between Mr Emerson & Henry ↑in manners, looks, voice, & thought.↓ Henry spoke like Mr E. & walked like him, &c. "O yes," said his mother, "Mr Emerson had been a good deal with David Henry, and it was very natural ⟨he⟩ should catch his ways."

[47]–[50] [blank]
[51]   *Inspiration.*   *By H. D. Thoreau.*

> If with light head erect I sing,
> Though all the muses len⟨t⟩d their force,
> From my poor love of anything,
> The verse is weak & shallow as its source.
>
> But if with bended neck I grope,
> Listening behind me for my wit,
> With faith superior to hope,
> More anxious to keep back, than forward it,

[21] For the letters, dated May 22, June 20, and October 16, 1843, see *Letters to Various Persons*, 1865, pp. 20–26 and 29–30.

Making my soul accomplice there
Unto the flame my heart hath lit,—
Then will the verse forever wear,
Time cannot bend the line which God hath writ.

Always the general show of things
Floats in review before my mind,
And such true love & reverence brings,
That sometimes I forget that I am blind.

[52]   But soon there comes uns⟨u⟩ought, unseen,
Some clear divine electuary,
And I, who had but sensual been,
Grow sensible, & as God is am wary.

I hearing get, who had but ears,
And sight, who had but eyes before,
I moments live, who lived but years,
And truth discern, who knew but learning's lore.

Then chiefly is my natal hour,
And only then my prime of life,
Of manhood's strength it is the flower,
'Tis peace's end, & war's beginning strife.

It comes in summer's broadest noon,
By a gray wall, or some chance place,
Unseasoning time, insulting June,
And vexing day with its presuming face.

[53]   [Such fragrance round my couch it makes,
More rich than are arabian drugs,
That my soul scents its life, & wakes
My body up beneath its perfumed rugs.]

[Such is the Muse, the heavenly maid,
The star that guides our mortal course,
Which shows where ⟨l⟩Life's true kernel's laid,
Its wheats fine flower, & its undying force.]

491

[She with one breath attunes the spheres,
And also my poor human heart;
With one impulse propels the years
Around, & gives my throbbing pulse its start.]

I will then trust the love untold
Which not my worth or want hath bought,
Which wooed me young, & woos me old,
And to this evening hath me brought.[22]

[54]–[275] [blank]
[276] Thoreau like Farley. *DL* 61
His citation & commentary on Herndon. *DL* 97
"Do you read any noble verses?" *DL* 123
Hound. *DL* 140

[277]–[283] [blank]
[284] [Index matter omitted]
[inside back cover] [blank]

[22] Emerson printed the first three stanzas on p. [51], the last three on p. [52], and the last stanza on p. [53] as "Inspiration" in *Letters to Various Persons*, 1865, pp. 218–219. The square brackets around the omitted stanzas on p. [53] are in pencil.

Pocket Diary 13

1861

Pocket Diary 13 is devoted primarily to recording Emerson's lecture engagements for 1861. It also contains miscellaneous addresses, book lists, brief drafts and quotations, and a page of lecture engagements dated from October 12, 1862, to January 6, 1863.

The notebook, bound in stamped black leather, is a commercially published diary entitled "POCKET / DIARY / FOR / 1861, / FOR REGISTERING EVENTS OF / Past or Present Occurrence.", published by Brown & Taggard, Boston. The covers measure 7.8 × 12.4 cm. The back cover extends into a tongue which, when the book is closed, fits into a loop on the front cover; the back cover also contains an expandable pocket. "Diary. 1861." is stamped in gold on the tongue; a paper label fastened to the spine is inscribed "1861. x" in ink.

The white, marble-edged pages, measuring 7.6 × 12.2 cm, are unnumbered. Pages 13–134 are lightly lined in blue; pages 148–172 are ledger-ruled. The inside covers and flyleaves are of yellow paper. The book consists of a front flyleaf (i–ii); a title page (page 1); books published by Brown & Taggard (pages 2–3); a calendar for 1861 (page 4); rates of postage (page 5); eclipses in 1861 (page 6); an almanac for 1861 (pages 7–12); daily appointments for 1861, three to a page (pages 13–134); pages for memoranda (pages 135–147); pages for cash accounts (pages 148–160); pages for bills payable (pages 161–172); and the back flyleaf (pages 173–174).

Entries by Emerson occur on thirty-three pages. Printed matter in Pocket Diary 13 is reproduced here only in the section on daily appointments, in which dates are supplied in brackets where relevant. Otherwise, pages are designated as blank if they bear no inscription by Emerson; the presence or absence of printed matter is not specified.

493

[front cover verso]¹ Life of Eldon Vol I p 117

254 4 Av
212 F St

[i]   R. W. Emerson
                                           Concord, Mass[achuse]tts

Geo. H. Tappan   Colorado Territory

Call at Tappan & McBurney   Summer st²

1861. 14 Nov. pd E. Codman's bill

[ii] 1862
     Oct. 12. Music H[all]

     Dec. 16   Music H[all]
         17   Manchester
         23   Cambridgep[ort]
         30   Cam[bridge]p[or]t

     1863   Ja
     Jan. 6   Toronto (?)

[1]–[12] [blank]³
[13] Roper's Life of Sir T. More.⁴

---

¹ The entries on the front cover verso are in pencil. Emerson's book reference is to Horace Twiss, *The Public and Private Life of Lord Chancellor Eldon*, 2 vols. (Philadelphia, 1844); see *JMN*, XIII, 213.
² "Geo. H. . . . Summer st" is in pencil.
³ Emerson marked the following dates in the almanac for 1861 with short dashes or dots in pencil: on p. [8], March 13, and April 3, 7, 10, 17, and 25; on p. [9], May 1, 2, 4, 8, 9, 11, 16, 18, 23, 25, and 30, and June 1, 6, 8, 13, 15, and 20; on p. [10], July 4, 5, 12, 19, and 26, and August 2, 9, 16, 23, and 30; on p. [11], September 6, 18, 24, and 25, and October 2, 9, 16, 23, and 30; on p. [12], November 5, 6, 13, 20, and 27, and December 4, 11, 18 and 25. "Jan" is written in pencil below the almanac entry for December 31 on p. [12].
⁴ William Roper, *The Life of Sir Thomas More*, ed. Samuel Weller Singer (Chiswick, 1822), which Emerson withdrew from the Boston Athenaeum October 7, 1861–January 8, 1862.

Athenaeum⁵
　　⟨Adams's Lectures.⟩
　　　　Tyrone

———

　⟨Norton's Italy⟩

———

　Sir Rohan

———

　Addison's Italy for St Antony's Speech

———

　Thos. Fuller's, History of Cambridge

　　　"Renowned Chaucer lie a thot more nigh
　　　To rare Beaumont, &c"
a sonnet to Shakspeare ascribed to Donne⁶

[14]⁷ Hippel,—Lebenslaufe

———

Story of the Burnt Nial

———

Hariri　translated by Ruckert

[Sun., Jan. 6] Music Hall　Cause & Effect⁸

---

⁵ Emerson's six citations under this heading are of John Quincy Adams, *Lectures on Rhetoric and Oratory*, 2 vols. (Cambridge, 1810), volume 2 of which Emerson withdrew from the Boston Athenaeum July 17–August 9, 1861; probably "The Story of the First Earl of Tyrone, from Original Sources," *Dublin University Magazine* (Dec. 1861), pp. 732–743; Charles Eliot Norton, *Notes of Travel and Study in Italy* (Boston, 1860); Harriet Prescott Spofford, *Sir Rohan's Ghost. A Romance* (Boston, 1860), quoted on pp. [64]–[65] below; Joseph Addison, *Remarks on Several Parts of Italy, &c. in the Years 1701, 1702, 1703* (London, 1705), pp. 62–74, a lengthy quotation from St. Anthony's "Discourse to an Assembly of Fish" (see *JMN*, XI, 127–128); and Thomas Fuller's *History of the University of Cambridge since the Conquest* (London, 1655).

⁶ The source of Emerson's version of the sonnet, now ascribed to William Basse, has not been ascertained.

⁷ The three items on this page, which may be a continuation of the Athenaeum list on p. [13] above, are probably Theodor Gottlieb von Hipple, *Lebensläufe nach aufsteigender Linie nebst Beilagen A, B, C* (Leipzig, 1859); *Njals Saga, The Story of Burnt Njal*, trans. from the Icelandic by G. W. Dasent, 2 vols. (Edinburgh, 1861); and Abu Muhammad al Kassim al Hariri, *Die Verwandlungen des Abu Seid von Serug oder die Makamen des Hariri von F. Rückert*, 2 vols. (Stuttgart, 1844).

⁸ In pencil.

[15]^9 W E   Mrs Ludlow
260 Green st near 8th

[Wed., Jan. 9] Elmira   Clubs

[16] [Thurs., Jan. 10] Owego.   W. Babcock   Classes of Men
[Fri., Jan. 11] Binghamton   Hornellsville   W R. T. Finch
[Sat., Jan. 12] Cortland

[17] [Mon., Jan. 14] Alfred
[Tues., Jan. 15] Buffalo^{10}

[18] [blank]
[19]^{11} Men have intelligence to read opinions but not intelligence to
see directly facts; as we see objects in nature by reflected light. [FOR
70]

[20] ↑An↓ use^n of the war that it opened Kentucky
Great revolution in favor of S. when ⟨Ar⟩ Christian Art took to plebe-
ian saints [VA 142]
The robin listened for the worm [FOR 70]

[21] C F Dowsett
        At Capt Bottomby   62 Grace Church street   London

[22]–[24] [blank]
[25] [Thurs., Feb. 7] N[ew] Haven ?^{12}

[26] [blank]
[27] [Tues., Feb. 12] So[uth] Danvers ?^{13}
[Wed., Feb. 13] Augusta Maine   "Classes of Men"

---

^{9} The entries on p. [15] are in pencil. "W E" is probably William Emerson. Ellen
apparently accompanied her father to New York early in January, 1861, and stayed at
Mrs. Ludlow's address; see *L*, V, 236.
^{10} "Owego.", "Binghamton", and "Cortland", on p. [16], and "Alfred" and "Buf-
falo", on p. [17], are in pencil.
^{11} The entries on pp. [19] and [20] are in pencil.
^{12} In pencil.
^{13} In pencil.

[28] [blank]
[29] [Wed., Feb. 20] Gloucester

[30] [blank]
[31] [Sun., Feb. 24] Portland[14]

[32]–[62] [blank]
[63] "No great discovery was ever made without a great guess." *Sir I.
Newton* [FOR 70]

[64]   "In the summer even
       While yet the dew was hoar
       I went plucking purple pansies
       Till my love should come to shore

       The fishing lights their dances
       Were keeping out at sea
       And come I sung my true love
       Come hasten home to me

[65]   But the sea it fell a moaning
       And the white gulls rocked thereon
       And the young moon dropt from heaven
       And the lights hid one by one

       All silently their glances
       Slipt down the cruel sea
       And wait cried the night & wind & storm
       Wait till I come to thee."
                             "Sir Rohan's Ghost"[15]

[66]–[75] [blank]
[76] [Wed., July 10] Tufts College

[77]–[101] [blank]
[102] [Fri., Sept. 27] Yarmouth.   W.J. Cross, Jr.

[14] In pencil.
[15] Spofford, *Sir Rohan's Ghost. A Romance,* 1860, pp. 25–26; Emerson printed these
stanzas in *Parnassus,* 1875, p. 448.

[103]-[106] [blank]
[107] [Sat., Oct. 12] Abel Adams & family.[16]

[108] [Mon., Oct. 14] H. James

[109]-[111] [blank]
[112] [Sun., Oct. 27] Music Hall

[113]-[117] [blank]
[118] [Tues., Nov. 12] Fraternity 28th Cong[regatio]n[al] Society.

[119]-[122] [blank]
[123] [Wed., Nov. 27] Salem.

[124] [blank]
[125] [Tues., Dec. 3] Dowse Institute

[126] [blank]
[127] [Tues., Dec. 10] Dowse Institute

[128] [blank]
[129] [Sun., Dec. 15] Portland   M.A. Blanchard
[Tues., Dec. 17] New Bedford   T.G. Hunt

[130][17] [Wed., Dec. 18] Lynn

[131]-[165] [blank]
[166]   30
           100
            20

[167]-[171] [blank]
[172] In 1540, Francesco d'Ollanda[,] miniature painter in service of
King of Portugal[,] visited Rome, & saw there Michel Angelo, as well

[16] See *L*, V, 255, for the planned visit.
[17] The entries on pp. [130] and [166] below are in pencil.

as Vittoria Colonna. His MS. Journal was discovered, by Count Rac-zynsky, in Lisbon. Grimm uses a French Translation of this.[18]

[173] J.L. Lathrop   Hannibal, Mo
Henry Boder   St Josephs
Col Edmund Alexander   Fort Laramie
Gov. Brigham Young   Salt Lake, U.
Hon W H Hooper, Utah
John K Alexander. Utah
A. Comte.   ⎱
O.D. Lombard.⎰ Sacramento
Alsop & Co   San Francisco
Flint, Peabody, & Co   S[an]. F[rancisco].
T.G. Cary, San. F[rancisco].
[174] Fredk. Billings.   San F[rancisco].[19]

[inside back cover] [blank]

---

[18] This entry is struck through in ink with one diagonal and two vertical use marks; see Journal DL, p. [7], and FOR, p. [72] above.

[19] This list of Edward Emerson's contacts during his trip to San Francisco includes: Edmund Brooke Alexander (1800?–1888), a Virginian stationed at Fort Laramie in 1860–1862; Brigham Young (1801–1877), Mormon leader and first governor of the Territory of Utah (1849–1857); W. H. Hooper, a delegate to Congress from the Territory of Utah (see *L*, V, 278), and Frederick Billings (1823–1890), lawyer, president of the Northern Pacific Railroad, and philanthropist. See Journal VA, p. [74] above.

Pocket Diary 14

1863

Pocket Diary 14 is devoted primarily to recording Emerson's lecture engagements for 1863. It also contains miscellaneous addresses, accounts, and memoranda, a calendar of lecture engagements dated November 18–December 26, 1862, and another dated January 1864.

The notebook, bound in black stamped leather, is a commercially published diary entitled "POCKET / DIARY / 1863.", published by Chase & Nichols, Boston. The covers measure 7.8 × 12.5 cm. The back cover extends into a tongue which, when the book is closed, fits into a loop on the front cover; the back cover also contains an expandable pocket. "Diary 1863" is stamped in gold on the tongue; a paper label fastened to the spine, now loose and partly torn off, is inscribed "||18||62. 1863. 1864(.)x" in ink.

The white, marble-edged pages, measuring 7.6 × 12.2 cm, are unnumbered. Pages 135–141 are lightly lined in blue; pages 142–172 are ledger-ruled. The book consists of a front flyleaf (i, ii); a title page (page 1); a table of distances and time by railroad from New York (page 2); a list of Sundays (page 3); a calendar for 1863 (page 4); rates of postage (page 5); eclipses in 1863 (page 6); an almanac for 1863 (pages 7–12); daily appointments for 1863, three to a page (pages 13–134); pages for memoranda (pages 135–141); pages for cash accounts (pages 142–166); pages for memoranda (pages 167–172); and the back flyleaf (pages 173–174).

Entries by Emerson occur on fifty-six pages; the leaf bearing pages 147–148 has been torn out. Printed matter in Pocket Diary 14 is reproduced here only in the section on daily appointments, in which dates are supplied in brackets where relevant. Otherwise, pages are designated as blank if they bear no inscription by Emerson; the presence or absence of printed matter is not specified.

[from cover verso]¹
Oak ¾ pr cord
Soft pine 2 cords
Chestnut 1¾ cords
Hard pine 1½ cord

Athenaeum
Todd's History of Rajasthan
———

Gladiator

[i]   R. W. Emerson
                                                 Concord, Mass[achuse]tts

[ii]² Mrs Sally Sprague
Mr Phinehas S   Town Hall
Mr Richardson   shoe store

[1]–[12] [blank]
[13] [Thurs., Jan. 1] Music Hall Celebration

[14] [Mon., Jan. 5] Toronto   Richd Grahame   "Classes of men"
[Tues., Jan. 6] ⟨Toronto ?⟩   Toronto   Criticism

[15] [Wed., Jan. 7] Toronto
gave a U.S. greenback 5.00 note for 3.75 Canadian currency.
[Thurs., Jan. 8] Rochester   John Bower. "Classes of Men"
This day sent F.C. Browne B[oston] & P[rovidence]. dividend for his
mother^n by mail.
[Fri., Jan. 9] Clyde ⟨?⟩   H.P. Witbeck³

¹ The entries on the front cover verso are in pencil. Emerson's Athenaeum reference
may be to James Tod, *Annals and Antiquities of Rajast'han, of the Central and Western
Rajpoot States of India,* 2 vols. (London, 1829–1832); "Gladiator" probably refers to the
sculpture exhibit for which Emerson had a ticket (see p. 514 below).
² The entries on p. [ii] are in pencil.
³ "Clyde ?" is in pencil; the cancellation is in ink. Emerson did not, however, go to
Clyde, New York; see *L,* V, 306, for this and pp. [17]–[19] below. F. C. Browne is probably Emerson's nephew Francis, the son of Lucy Jackson Brown.

[16] [blank]

[17] [Tues., Jan. 13] Buffalo   David Gray   "Third Estate in Literature"

[Wed., Jan. 14] Cleveland ?   B.F. Peixotto[4]   "Third Estate in Literature"

[Thurs., Jan. 15] ⟨Cleveland?⟩Detroit   R.W. King   "Clubs"[5]

[18] [Fri., Jan. 16] Ann Arbor, Mich.   "Third Estate in Lit[era-
ture]."

———

W B Hendry   x
Wm Mendenhall
Wm A. Ewing

[19] [Mon., Jan. 19] Milwaukee   W G Whipple   Clubs
[Tues., Jan. 20] ⟨Janesville   H.V. Comstock⟩   Racine   Clubs
[Wed., Jan. 21] ⟨Gloucester   B H Corliss⟩Beloit   H.C. Dickenson
Third Estate in Literature[6]

[20] [Thurs., Jan. 22] Chicago.   Perpetual Forces   E[dward]. W.
Russell
[Fri., Jan. 23] ⟨Indianapolis   W B Fletcher⟩

[21] [Tues., Jan. 27] Indianapolis   W B Fletcher   Clubs[7]

[22]–[23] [blank]
[24] [Tues., Feb. 3] Pittsburgh   "Clubs"
W[illiam] H Kincaid   ↑Dr↓ ⟨C⟩G W Weyman   ↑Joseph↓ Albree

---

[4] "Cleveland? . . . Peixotto" is in pencil. Benjamin Franklin Peixotto (1834–1890)
was the editor of the Cleveland *Plain Dealer*. David Gray (1836–1888) was a Buffalo journalist, later the editor of the Buffalo *Courier*.
    [5] "Cleveland?", in pencil, is overwritten by "Detroit" in ink.
    [6] "Clubs", "Racine   Clubs", and "Third . . . Literature" are in pencil; "Janesville
H.V. Comstock" is canceled in pencil. "Gloucester   B H Corliss", in pencil, is overwritten in ink by "Beloit   H.C. Dickenson".
    [7] "Perpetual Forces . . . Fletcher", on pp. [20]–[21], is in pencil. The cancellation
is struck through with three diagonal lines in ink and one in pencil. For Russell's management of the western part of this tour, see *L*, V, 306 and 309.

[Wed., Feb. 4] M.F. Eaton   Pittsburgh[8]
[Thurs., Feb. 5] Pittsburgh   "Classes of Men."

[25] [Sat., Feb. 7] Music Hall[9]

[26] [Wed., Feb. 11] Gloucester ⟨?⟩   B.H. Corliss   Perpetual
    Forces[10]

[27] [Thurs., Feb. 12] ⟨Augusta ?   H S Osgood⟩[11]

[28] [Sun., Feb. 15] Music Hall   ↑Courage↓

[29][12] [Wed., Feb. 18] Agassiz at Concord

2d Avenue   Corner of 13th st   door on 13

[30] [blank]
[31] [Tues., Feb. 24] Edgar Judge   Montreal ? "Classes of Men."
[Wed., Feb. 25] Montreal—"Clubs"
    T.K. Ramsay   J.W. Dawson
    Sheldon Steevens[n]   Leach
       Heavysege
      McLarin[13]
[Thurs., Feb. 26] ⟨Montreal ?⟩[14]

[8] Kincaid, a clerk, served as a member of the lecture committee in Pittsburgh; see *L*, V, 310. "M.F. Eaton   Pittsburgh" is circled in ink.

[9] In pencil.

[10] "Gloucester?" is in pencil; the question mark is canceled in ink.

[11] This entry, in pencil, is canceled by a diagonal line in ink.

[12] The entries on p. [29] are in pencil.

[13] "Edgar Judge   Montreal ?" is in pencil; Judge and W. S. McLarin were directors of the Mercantile Library Association in Montreal (see *L*, V, 350). Thomas Kennedy Ramsay (1826–1886) was a Canadian jurist and author. Sir John William Dawson (1820–1899) was professor of geology at McGill University. Also at McGill, William Turnbull Leach (1805–1866) was a Montreal clergyman and educator. Charles Heavysege (1816–1876) was a Montreal poet and journalist; Emerson had been given one of Heavysege's dramas, *Saul*, in Toronto in 1860, and another, *Count Filippo*, is also in his library.

[14] This entry, in pencil, is canceled in ink.

[32] [blank]
[33] [Tues., Mar. 3] Social Circle

[34]–[45] [blank]
[46] [Sun., Apr. 12] Portland ☞[15]

[47] [⟨Mon., Apr. 13⟩] ⟨Portland⟩   M.A. Blancherd.
Newell A. Foster.   1 Tolman Place
Immortality, sans poeme
Truth & Fontenelle & pp on Temperance from ⟨Essential⟩ Nat[ural].
Religion.[16] & no poetry.

[48]–[79] [blank]
[80] [Wed., July 22] Dartmouth College.

[81]–[82] [blank]
[83]——
Ticknor & Fields
————

Contract for Thoreau's new book
————

Moonlight
& Life without principle
to be first printed
————

Send her Atl[*antic*]. with his pieces
————————

Does Walden sell?
Miss T[horeau]. thinks that $35 or $40 may be due on Articles in the
Atlantic, now.[17]

[15] The hand sign points upward to the entry on p. [47].
[16] See Gohdes, *Uncollected Lectures,* 1932, pp. 47–50, a report of the lecture "Natural Religion," first delivered on February 3, 1861.
[17] Page [83] is in pencil; "Ticknor & . . . his pieces" is struck through with a vertical pencil line. "Thoreau's new book" probably refers to *Excursions,* edited by Emerson and Sophia Thoreau and published in 1863 by Ticknor and Fields of Boston; see *L,* V, 336 and 339. Both "Night and Moonlight" and "Life Without Principle" were printed in the *Atlantic Monthly* in 1863, the first in November, and the second in October.

[84]–[86] [blank]
[87] [Tues., Aug. 11] Waterville College   P Banney   (?)

[88]–[99] [blank]
[100] [Sat., Sept. 19] ⟨Portland⟩
[Sun., Sept. 20] Portland—M.A. Blanchard
"Courage" of Music Hall, with Extracts from "Essential Principles
[of] Nat[ural]. Rel[igion]." and "Fra Cristoforo" and "Classes of
Men" with "Touchstone" snapturtle[18]

[101]–[109] [blank]
[110] [Tues., Oct. 20] ↑Red↓ cow sent to Dakin[19]

[111]–[119] [blank]
[120] [Thurs., Nov. 19] G W Curtis   Salem, "Perpetual Forces"[20]

[121]–[123] [blank]
[124] [Tues., Dec. 1] Fraternity
↑Probably read "The Fortune of the Republic."   RWE 1870↓[21]

[125]–[126] [blank]
[127] [Wed., Dec. 9] Feltonville   W F Brigham   Fortune of Republic[22]
[Fri., Dec. 11] Newburyport   H.A. Tenney   Fortune of Republic

[128] [blank]
[129] [Tues., Dec. 15] ⟨Taunton⟩
[Wed., Dec. 16] Concord   Fortune of Republic

[18] Emerson had delivered the lectures "Essential Principles of Religion" and "Courage" before the Parker Fraternity in Boston on March 16, 1862, and February 15, 1863,
respectively. The story of "Fra Cristoforo" is from Alessandro Manzoni's novel, *I Pro-
messi Sposi*, 3 vols. (Torino, 1827), in Emerson's library. Emerson printed William Al-
lingham's poem "The Touchstone" in *Parnassus*, 1875, pp. 158–159. For the paragraph
on the snapturtle, see "Courage," *W*, VII, 256–257.
[19] This entry is in pencil. Several Dakins lived in Concord.
[20] This entry is in pencil. George William Curtis (1824–1892), once a resident at
Brook Farm, and a prolific writer, was an editor at *Harper's Weekly* in 1863.
[21] The insertion is in pencil; "RWE 1870" is circled in pencil.
[22] "W F Brigham" is in pencil.

[130] [blank]
[131] [Mon., Dec. 21] Brooklyn—N.Y.   S.B. Noyes[23]
am to send subject   Fortune of Republic

[132]–[133] [blank]
[134] [Wed., Dec. 30] ⟨P⟩Manchester   L A Gould   Fortune of Republic

[135][24] 1862

Nov	18	at Music Hall Perpetual Forces
	19	Salem, Perpet. Forces
	26	Concord. Pe⟨p⟩rpet Forces
Dec	9	Charlestown Perpet Force
	10	Lynn Perpet Force
	14	Music Hall Health
	16	New Bedford Perpet For
	17	Manchester Per. For.
	23	Camb[ridge]p[or]t Per. For.
	24	Fall River Per. For.
	25	Worcester Per For
	26	Albany Per For

[136] [blank]
[137][25] W.H. Kincaid, Pittsburg
↑E↓ ⟨E⟩W Russell   Chicago
    J H Patterson   Liberty Ind
    W Whipple   Milwaukee
    W B Fletcher   Indianapolis
    S W McDaniel, Feltonville
    H H Smith   Meadville

[23] Stephen Buttrick Noyes (1833–1885), who had been a librarian at the Boston
Athenaeum for two years after his graduation from Harvard in 1853, was the librarian of
the Mercantile Library Association of Brooklyn.
    [24] Page [135] is in pencil.
    [25] Page [137] is in pencil.

[138] [blank]
[139] Toronto Jan 6
J D Edgar[26]
    Wyman
Robert Sullivan
    Wm Sullivan
        Morse
        McDougal
     R. Grahame
      ↑Wright↓
   Charlton of Hamilton
   Holmes of Hamilton
   ↑Whiton of Hamilton
Saw Mrs Haining at Hamilton, T. Carlyle's sister↓

[140] J.C. Metcalf, Erie, Pa.

[141] Jan	9	Sent to order of L[idian]. E[merson]. a draft of Powers & Co ⟨for⟩on Boston for	93.13
	14	Sent a letter to Edith containing	20.00
	19.	sent a draft to J.M. Cheney, drawn by Alex. H Dey, Detroit on Exchange Bank, Boston, for $50.00	
	20	Draft from B B Wiley on Boston	75[27]
[142][28]	22	Pd B B Wiley say 35. or	45.
		E.W. Russell is to pay him for me	50
		and he should receive from Ann Arbor & Beloit	41
			126.

      to be sent to L[idian]. Emerson

[143] Perpetual Forces
    Classes of Men

---

[26] James David Edgar (1841–1899), later speaker of the Canadian House of Commons, was a young lawyer in Toronto in 1863.

[27] John Milton Cheney, a college classmate of Emerson's, was the cashier of the bank in Concord. "20   Draft . . . 75" is in pencil.

[28] Pages [142] and [143] are in pencil.

Clubs
Third Estate in Lit[erature]
Success

[144] Roch[este]r   93.13
                               20
    19 J.M. C[heney].   50
                               75
        By Wiley   95
                               23
                               18
        to J M C[heney]   50
                              ___100___
                              ↑523
                               61
                              ___584↓[29]___

[145] Toronto   120
      Rochester   50
      Buffalo   50
      Cleveland   50
      Detroit   50
      Ann Arbor   50
      Milwaukee   50
      Racine   30
      Beloit   50
      Chicago   50
      Indianapolis   50
      Pittsburgh   ___100___
                               700

[146] Montreal   100
      In N.Y. Currency $161.

Mrs Haughton   S. Waterford Me
Care Chas E Humphry

[29] The added numbers are in pencil.

Woodman & True   Portland[30]

[147]–[148] [leaf torn out]
[149] Thomas Gavin   Company G 23d Massachusetts
Capt. ↑J.W.↓ Raymond   Col Elwel   Newbern N.C.

John Gavin enlisted 1862 at Beverly   Company G. Regt 41 Mass
Captain Swift
Colonel Chickering   Baton Rouge[31]

[150]–[151] [blank]
[152] [October, 1863]
[Henry] Derby   bbls
    Baldwin^n 2ds   7
        d[itt]o   10
    Baldwin do   11
    ↑rem do   ⟨4⟩3
    Baldwin Firsts,   2
        do   11
    ↑rem do   5↓[32]

──────

Oct. 24.
[Augustus] Adams   2 bbls   Bald[win] ↑1sts↓ 4 50
           2   seconds   2 50
           1   Hubb[ardston].   2.25
           3 bbls at .75   2.25

[30] "Mrs Haughton . . . Portland" is in pencil.
[31] Thomas Edward Chickering (1824–1871) commanded the 41st Massachusetts volunteers when they were sent to New Orleans in December 1862, and was appointed military governor of Opelousas in April 1863.
[32] The insertions on p. [152] are in pencil. The bracketed date and names in this memorandum of apples sold from Emerson's orchard, pp. [152]–[154], are supplied from the more complete record in Account Book 7. Henry Derby and Augustus Adams, below, were Concord residents.

[153]³³   125
          3⟨8⟩1
      ⟨1000⟩125
          375
    ⟨47.50⟩38.75
        40.50   225
        79.25   18
                      1800
                       225
                      40.50

[154]   *Bbls*
    Derby   18 1sts
                           31 2d   49
    Adams   3 1sts
                            3 2d   6
    W[illiam] E[merson]   4 1sts
                            2 2ds   6
    P[atrick]. C[asson].   5 2ds   5
    Coombs   3
    [John] Craig   2
    Bulger³⁴   1
    R.W.E.   7
    Cider apples   50

[155] R.F. Fuller Esq   27 Court St   Boston
        Except Wednesday & Friday

[156] 1864
    Jan
    1 ⟨Jan⟩ Frid
    2 S

³³ This page is in pencil.
³⁴ Patrick Casson and Coombs were local residents who sometimes worked for
Emerson, as did Mrs. Bulger; John Craig was a local woodcutter.

3   S
4   M
5   T   Worcester
6   W
7   Th
8   F
9   S
10 S
11 M
12 T   Dowse [Institute]
13 Wed   Lynn
14th   Augusta   C H True
15 F   ↑Bangor ?↓
16 Sat
17 S
18 M
19 Tu   ↑Middletown↓³⁵
20 W ⎤ No. Bennington
21 Th⎦
22 F
23 S
24 S
25 M
26 Taunton
27 Salem
28
29
30
31

[157] [blank]
[158] Athenaeum   Hepworth Dixon³⁶

³⁵ "Bangor ?" and "Middletown" are in pencil.
³⁶ This entry is in pencil.

511

[159]–[168] [blank]

[169]³⁷ ↑pd↓ ⟨E W E owes C J R   72 24
     ↑pd↓   To Alsop & Co   230⟩

Dials
Nos. 2, 3, 4, 10, 12, 15, 16 ———

[170]³⁸ ———
⟨Carryall⟩
———
Grace shoes
———
⟨bridle at Chisholm's⟩
———
⟨hop poles⟩
———
fencing stuff
———
wood
———
slag & pottery to fill up hole in Minott's.
———
Corn 16 May
cucumbers

[171] ⟨F[rank]. Browne 42.37⟩

trunk & bag
———
Buttrick for fence
———
Go to Barrett's mill
———

---

³⁷ Page [169] is in pencil. "E W E . . . 230" is canceled with two diagonal pencil lines in the shape of an X. "E W E " is Emerson's son Edward; "C J R" is probably Cabot Jackson Russell, who accompanied Edward on his western trip in May 1862, and was killed in action on July 18, 1863.

³⁸ Pages [170]–[171] are in pencil. "⟨Carryall⟩" and "⟨F. Browne 42.37⟩" are written at the top of pp. [170] and [171] respectively over the printed "MEMORANDA." and may have been added. Barrett's Saw and Grist Mills were located in Concord at Barrett's Mill Pond on Spencer Brook.

[172] 2.50
     5 00
     6 40
     4[?]

W. Whitman
Care of Major Hapgood   Paymaster U.S.A.
Corner 15 & F streets   Washington[39]

Wm Emerson Esq 109, 22d Street N.Y.

[173] Mrs Botta   31 West Thirty seventh[40]

[174] Hudson Wisconsin
     Section 17, Township 37, of Range 18.

——

     S.W. quarter of north east quarter

——

     $129\frac{12}{100}$ acres.

Lincoln Sawmill lot   11 a↑c↓res, 147 rods,
Apr 1849, 1850.

[inside back cover] Mrs E.G. Martin
Care of H.D. Martin   Studio Building   15 Tenth st.   N.Y.[41]

[39] The figures, in pencil, are overwritten in ink by "W. Whitman . . . Paymaster". On December 29, 1862, Whitman wrote Emerson that he was in Washington and asked for letters of introduction to Chase and Seward; in February, James Redpath enlisted Emerson's help in raising money to support Whitman's hospital work (see *L*, V, 302–303, 314, and 316).

[40] This entry is in pencil. Emerson planned to call on his brother William in his new house in Manhattan late in May, 1863, en route to West Point (see *L*, V, 328). Anne Charlotte Lynch Botta (1815–1891), a writer herself, was famous among the New York literati for the brilliance of her salon; her *Handbook of Universal Literature, From the Best and Latest Authorities* (Boston, 1864), is in Emerson's library.

[41] Elizabeth Gilbert Davis Martin, a writer and one of the early reviewers for *The Nation*, was the wife of Homer Dodge Martin (1836–1897), American landscape painter, who had a studio in New York in 1863.

Pocket Diary 15

1864

Pocket Diary 15 is devoted primarily to recording Emerson's lecture engagements for 1864. It also contains miscellaneous addresses and memoranda, quotations and notes from his reading, book lists, and a calendar of lecture engagements dated January 1–16, 1865.

The notebook, bound in green stamped leather, is a commercially published diary entitled "POCKET / DIARY / 1864.", published by William Hill, Jr., of Boston. The covers measure 7.8 × 12.5 cm. The back cover extends into a tongue which, when the book is closed, fits into a loop on the front cover; "Diary 1864" is stamped in gold on the tongue. The back cover also contains an expandable pocket containing the following items: a season ticket to "THE EXHIBITION OF THE STATUE OF THE FALLING GLADIATOR" made out to "R. W. Emerson and friend"; a newspaper clipping giving the spring schedule, after April 4, 1864, of the Lexington and West Cambridge Railroad; and a Boston & Maine Railroad ticket, Portland to Kendall's Mills, punched once. A paper label fastened to the spine is inscribed "1864–1865. x" in ink.

The pages, which measure 7.6 × 12.2 cm, are unnumbered. Pages 1–176 are lightly lined in blue; pages 146–176 are ledger-ruled. The book consists of a front flyleaf (i, ii); a title page (page 1); a calendar for 1864 (page 3); postal rates (page 4); "A Table of Stamp Duties as Amended March 3, 1863" (pages 5–9); eclipses and a list of Sundays in 1864 (page 10); an almanac for 1864 (pages 11–16); daily appointments for 1864, three to a page (pages 17–138); pages for memoranda (pages 139–145); pages for cash accounts (pages 146–170); pages for memoranda (pages 171–176); and the back flyleaf (pages 177–178).

Entries by Emerson occur on thirty-nine pages. Printed matter in Pocket Diary 15 is reproduced here only in the section on daily appointments, in which dates are supplied in brackets where relevant. Otherwise, pages are designated as blank if they bear no inscription by Emerson; the presence or absence of printed matter is not specified.

[front cover verso]¹
Wm Munroe, picture
2507   Sunset Scene No 1
2456   Sea View at night
4866   Sea View at Havre

W[illiam] Emerson Esq   23 Washington Place

J[ohn] H[aven] Emerson   24 W. 11th St

[i]   R. W. Emerson.
                                       Concord Mass[achuse]tts

W[illiam] H[enry] Furness   1426 Pine St
P[hilip] Randolph   321 S. 4th
S[amuel]. Bradford   227 S 4th
                      1628 Walnut
J P[eter] Lesley   104 S 5th
     (Lib[raria]n Am[erican] Phil[osophical] Soc[iety])²

[ii] Genuine Poems of Ossian
translated by Patrick Macgregor.
     Under patronage of Highland Soc[iet]y of London
1 vol 12mo   1807³

[1] [blank]
[2]⁴ Stones
     1 ft. high
     11 inches wide
     2 inches thick

¹ The entries on the front cover verso are in pencil. Haven Emerson was the son of
Emerson's brother William.
     ² "W H Furness . . . Phil Soc)" is in pencil. All four Philadelphians were old friends
of Emerson; several books by Lesley are in Emerson's library.
     ³ Emerson owned the Boston, 1857, edition, translated by MacPherson; see Journal
DL, p. [20] above.
     ⁴ Page [2] is in pencil.

[3]–[17] [blank]

[18] [Tues., Jan. 5] Worcester   Chas A. Chase   Fortune of Republic

[Wed., Jan. 6] Lynn ⟨?⟩   ↑5 o'clock↓   Fortune of Republic[5]

[19] [Thurs., Jan. 7] Saltavit et placuit   Inscription d'Antibes[6]

[20] [Tues., Jan. 12] Dowse Institute   Fortune of Republic

[21] [Wed., Jan. 13] ⟨Lynn   Fortune of Republic⟩
[Thurs., Jan. 14] Augusta↑?↓ C.H. True   Fortune of Republic
[Fri., Jan. 15] Bangor↑?↓ Fortune of Republic[7]

[22] [blank]
[23] [Wed., Jan. 20] N. Bennington   Fortune of Republic

[24] [blank]
[25] [Tues., Jan. 26] ⟨Taunton⟩
[Wed., Jan. 27] Salem.   H.J. Cross—   Fortune of Republic[8]

[26]–[29] [blank]
[30] [Tues., Feb. 9] Taunton   ↑Fortune of Republic↓

[31] Macmillan June 1864 advertise
Judas Maccabaeus: an Heroic Poem. By Edmund Peel [(London, 1864)][9]

[32]–[40] [blank]
[41] [Tues., Mar. 15] Social Circle

---

[5] The question mark is canceled and "5 o'clock" added in pencil.

[6] "He danced and found favor" (Ed.). This entry is in pencil. Emerson's source for this phrase, part of an inscription on a tomb at Antibes, has not been ascertained.

[7] The added question marks are in pencil.

[8] H. J. Cross was corresponding secretary of the Salem Lyceum; see *JMN*, XIV, 479.

[9] This entry is in pencil.

[42]–[53] [blank]

[54] "mais, dans les sciences philologiques et historiques, le peu de disposition de l'esprit anglais pour comprende ce qui n'est pas lui—" *Renan*

Eugene Burnouf mettra sa gloire a avoir six ou huit élèves venus des quatres
coins de l'Europe et auxquels il enseigne les textes les plus difficiles   textes
que lui seul sait comprendre et expliquer[10]

[55] Hawes' "Temple of Glass"   Passetyme of Pleas[ure].[11]

[56]–[76] [blank]

[77] [Fri., July 1] Normal School

[78]–[89] [blank]

[90] [Sun., Aug. 7] ⟨⟨Middlebury College⟩
    Philomathesian Soc[iet]y   9 o'c a.m⟩
[Tues., Aug. 9] Middlebury College
    Philomathesian Soc[iet]y   9 a.m.   Ezra Brainerd[12]

[91]–[118] [blank]

[119] [Wed., Nov. 2] West Chester Convention of Teachers.
    W W Woodruff

———

Yarmouth Lecture on Education[13]

———

[Thurs., Nov. 3] ⟨West⟩

---

[10] The entries on pp. [54]–[55] are in pencil. Emerson is quoting from Ernest
Renan, "L'Instruction supérieure en France, son histoire et son avenir," *Revue des Deux
Mondes,* May 1, 1864, pp. 80 and 82.

[11] John Lydgate's "Temple of Glass" is mentioned in Stephen Hawes's *Passetyme of
Pleasure;* Emerson's source has not been ascertained.

[12] "Middlebury College" was struck through horizontally, then "Middlebury . . . 9
o'c a.m" was fingerwiped to cancel it. Ezra Brainerd (1844–1924), a botanist and later the
president of Middlebury College, was a senior there in 1864.

[13] This is the lecture given on September 27, 1861; for an abstract, see Cabot, *A
Memoir* . . . , 1887–1888, II, 782–783. Emerson used a few passages from it in the lecture "Public and Private Education" (see p. [127] below), and Cabot worked parts of it
into the essay "Education," *W,* X, 123–159.

[120] [Sat., Nov. 5] Bryant Festival   New York.
[Sun., Nov. 6] 1 Fraternity[14]

[121] [blank]
[122] [Sun., Nov. 13] ⟨1⟩2 ⟨S⟩Fraternity

[123]–[124] [blank]
[125] [Sun., Nov. 20] ⟨2⟩3 Fraternity

[126] [blank]
[127] [Sun., Nov. 27] ⟨⟨3⟩4 Fraternity⟩1 Fraternity[15]
    Public & Private Education

[128] [blank]
[129] [Sun., Dec. 4] ⟨5 Frater⟩2 Fraternity   Social Aims

[130]–[131] [blank]
[132] [Sun., Dec. 11] ⟨⟨5⟩6 Frater⟩3 Fraternity   "Resources"

[133] [Wed., Dec. 14] Waltham   C.M. Paine   "Social Aims"
[Thurs., Dec. 15] Concord Lyceum   "Resources"

[134] [Sun., Dec. 18] ⟨6⟩4 Fraternity   Table Talk[16]

[135] [blank]
[136] [Sat., Dec. 24] ⟨⟨7⟩5 Fraternity⟩
[Sun., Dec. 25] ↑5.↓ Books (sans Shakspeare)[17]

[137] [Tues., Dec. 27] South Danvers   Social Aims[18]

---

[14] This entry, and those on pp. [122] and [125] below, are in pencil. Emerson probably postponed the start of this series of lectures before the Parker Fraternity until November 27. See p. [127] below.

[15] In this entry and those on pp. [129] and [132] below, the canceled matter is in
pencil, erased, and overwritten in ink. In Account Book 7, Emerson notes the receipt of
$600 from the Parker Fraternity for these six lectures in the "American Life" series, the
last of which, "Character," was given on January 1, 1865.

[16] This entry is in pencil with the "6" overwritten by "4" in ink.

[17] "5" is added and the entry above canceled in pencil.

[18] "South Danvers" is in ink over the same in pencil; the lecture title is in heavier
pencil.

[138] [blank]
[139] Carun, *Karun,*
Coré: cousin german of Moses. vast treasures by chemistry. a miser.
Moses bade the earth open & swallow him & his treasures. Treasure,
tent, family, were sunk, & he ⟨c⟩sunk as far as to the knees: he entreated of Moses four times pardon, who did not yield; which God afterwards reproached Moses with.

Iamschid. Giamschid. King of Persia of the first race built Istakar
(Persepolis) (Chilminar)
under the foundations was a turkoise vase containing a liquor. he
reigned 700 years but claiming divine honors was driven out of his
kingdom.
He built a bridge across the Tigris at Istakhar & learned the art of
guards &c from the bees

[140] 1865

Jan	1	↑Sunday↓	Fraternity
	2	M	
	3	Tues	
	4	W	
	5	Th	
	6	Fri	
	7	Saturday	
	8	S	
	9	M	
	10	t[?]	
	11	W	Norwich. Salem.
	12	Th.	Albany
	13	Fri	Fayetteville
	14		
	15		
	16		Dansville E[dwin] F Sweet[19]

[19] Emerson identifies Edwin F. Sweet as "Secretary of Y. Men's Association" and
the son of a Dansville, New York, banker; see *L*, V, 403.

[141]–[161] [blank]
[162][20] Thos Carlyle born 1795
Wrote in Brewster's Edin[burgh] Encyclopaedia, ↑1823,↓ *Montaigne, Montesquieu, Nelson,* and "the *Two Pitts.*"

[163] ⟨The Prest⟩
Mr L. runs about in a cab to save a convict, but sacrifices the duty of justice in measures, and listens to gossiping visiter[s] all day, instead of ⟨attending⟩ confining attention to his proper function, and writes his own message instead of borrowing the largest understanding as he so easily might[.]

[164]–[167] [blank]
[168] Good vine years
1847, 1851, 1852, '58, '59,

[169]–[172] [blank]
[173] *Athenaeum*
Draper's Civilization

———

Life of Mme Recamier.[21]

———

[174] Dec 12
"Temple Bar"
    article "London Society"
"Fraser"
    Bruce's masterly rendering of "Nala & Damayanti"
"Cornhill"
    Tennyson's hexameter translations

National Review   Article "Criticism" by M. Arnold[22]

[20] Pages [162], [163], and [168] are in pencil.
[21] Probably John William Draper, *History of the Intellectual Development of Europe* (New York, 1863); and Mary Elizabeth Mohl, *Madame Récamier; With a Sketch of the History of Society in France* (London, 1862), which Emerson borrowed from the Boston Athenaeum July 12–September 2, 1864.
[22] The article in the *Temple Bar* has not been identified; the other three articles cited are: " 'The Story of Nala and Damayanti.' Translated from the Sanscrit Text, by Charles

[175] Edinb[urgh]. Evening Courant, Mr James Hannay, Editor.[23]

[176] ⟨‖ . . . ‖⟩0.15
              290
              300

Pay Agassiz for one club dinner for Prof Wilson
Dec 26, ↑1863↓ $5.24

[James?] Tolman 105[24]

Walter Map
author of the Sangraal in Latin[25]
musical trifling

[177][26] ↑Patent office Reports wanted↓ since^n 1849.

⟨You⟩ ↑Lib[rar]y↓ have not
              1858
              1859

[178] [blank]
[inside back cover] 1 ft high
                    11 in broad
                    3   thick

Bruce," *Fraser's Magazine,* LXVIII (Dec. 1863), 754–766, and LXIX (Jan. 1864),
89–100; Alfred Tennyson, "Attempts at Classic Metres in Quantity," *Cornhill Magazine,*
VIII (July–Dec. 1863), 707–709; and Matthew Arnold, "The Function of Criticism at
the Present Time," *National Review,* n. s. I (Nov. 1864), 230–251. "National Review
. . . Arnold" is in pencil.
    [23] This entry is in pencil. James Hannay (1827–1873) was editor of the *Evening
Courant* from 1860 to 1864.
    [24] Page [176] is in pencil to this point. The first numerical notations, inscribed ear-
lier, are partially overwritten by "Pay Agassiz . . . $5.24"; "Tolman 105" may belong to
the earlier inscription. Daniel Wilson (1816–1892), professor of history and English literature at the University of Toronto, was evidently Emerson's guest at the Saturday Club;
see *L,* V, 343.
    [25] See Journal DL, p. [145] above.
    [26] Page [177] and the inside back cover are in pencil. These Reports may have been
among the public documents Emerson received from Charles Sumner, some of which he
sent to the Concord Library; see *L,* V, 362–363. For "1 ft . . . thick", see p. [2] above.

Pocket Diary 16

1865

Pocket Diary 16 is devoted primarily to recording Emerson's lecture engagements for 1865. It also contains miscellaneous addresses, accounts, memoranda, a list of lectures in 1860 and 1863, a list of books, and a calendar of lecture engagements from January 1 to February 15, 1866.

The notebook, bound in blue-black stamped leather, is a commercially published diary entitled "DIARY / AND / MEMORANDUM BOOK / FOR / 1865, / CONTAINING A BLANK SPACE / FOR / Every Day in the Year, / CASH ACCOUNT, / Bills Payable and Receivable, / AND / MEMORANDA.", published by Geo. C. Rand & Avery, Boston. The covers measure 7.9 × 12.0 cm. The back cover extends into a tongue which, when the book is closed, fits into a loop on the front cover; the back cover also contains an expandable pocket, containing a schedule for the Metropolitan Railroad of Boston, valid for March 6 and after. "Diary 1865" is stamped in gold on the tongue; a paper label fastened to the spine is inscribed "1860–1865. x" in ink.

The white, marble-edged pages, measuring 7.8 × 11.5 cm, are unnumbered. Pages 17–168 are blue-lined; pages 139–163 are ledger-ruled. The book consists of a front flyleaf (i–ii); a title page (page 1); a calendar for 1865 (page 2); rates of postage (page 3); 1860 census tables giving population of states and cities (pages 4–5); Federal value of foreign coins (pages 6–7); interest tables (page 8); distances from New York to important U.S. cities (page 9); eclipses in 1865 (page 10); an almanac for 1865 (pages 11–16); daily appointments for 1865, three to a page (pages 17–138); pages for cash accounts (pages 139–151); pages for bills receivable (pages 152–163); pages for memoranda (pages 164–168); and the back flyleaf (pages 169–170).

Entries by Emerson occur on sixty-six pages. Printed matter in Pocket Diary 16 is reproduced here only in the section on daily appointments, in which dates are supplied in brackets where relevant. Otherwise, pages are designated as blank if they bear no inscription by Emerson; the presence or absence of printed matter is not specified.

[front cover verso] [blank]
[i] [blank]
[ii]¹ For Concord 6.50, 11, 4, 5:30, 6

    102 S Pearl
    177 Broadway

[1]–[16] [blank]
[17] [Sun., Jan. 1] Parker Fraternity at Melodeon   Character²
[Mon., Jan. 2] ⟨⟨⟨N[ew] L[ondon] & N[orwich] ?⟩New London⟩ (by
    way of Providence?)   L C Munn
    ⟨Bacon's Hotel⟩⟩³
[Tues., Jan. 3] ⟨⟨N[ew] L[ondon] & N[orwich] ?⟩Norwich⟩ ↑New
    London↓
    New London   Metropolitan Hotel

———

Social Aims⁴

———

[18] [Wed., Jan. 4] Salem   Social Aims
[Thurs., Jan. 5] ? ⟨Fairhaven Vt⟩ ⟨New London & Norwich⟩ ?
[Fri., Jan. 6] ? ⟨Fairhaven Vt⟩ N[ew] L[ondon] & Norwich ?⁵

[19] [blank]
[20] [Wed., Jan. 11] N[ew] L[ondon] & N[orwich] ?
    Fairhaven ⟨Vt⟩ ?
    J.J. [I.T.?] Williams   Social Aims as at Salem⁶
[Thurs., Jan. 12] ⟨Albany⟩

---

¹ The entries on this page are in pencil.
² "Character" is in pencil.
³ "N L & N ?", in pencil, is overwritten by "New London" in ink; "New London" and "Bacon's Hotel" are canceled in ink, and the entire entry is struck through diagonally in pencil.
⁴ "N L & N ?", in pencil, is overwritten by "Norwich" in ink, then canceled and "New London" added in ink. "New London   Metropolitan Hotel" and the rules are in pencil, and "Social Aims" is written in ink over the same in pencil.
⁵ This and the preceding entry are in pencil. "Fairhaven Vt" is canceled horizontally in both entries in pencil, and "New . . . Norwich" diagonally in pencil.
⁶ "N L & N . . . ⟨Vt⟩ ?" is in pencil; "as at Salem" may have been added.

[21] [Fri., Jan. 13] ⟨Fayetteville⟩ Albany   Social Aims as at Salem
C.W. Davis   Mrs Martin

[22] [Mon., Jan. 16] Dansville   E F Sweet   Social Aims as at Salem
[Tues., Jan. 17] ⟨Erie.   ↑did not arrive↓
A H Caughey.   Brown's Hotel
⟨Leave Erie in early train about 4 a.m.   Cleveland 9.40 am
Warren at 1 p.m.⟩⟩[7]
[Wed., Jan. 18] ⟨Cleveland⟩ Warren ?   O. Morgan
    "Social Aims" as read at Salem[8]

[23] [Thurs., Jan. 19] ⟨Warren⟩ Ohio
Cleveland   E R Perkins Esq   "Social Aims" as read at Salem
[Fri., Jan. 20] Pittsburg   Hall Patterson
    Social Aims, as read at Salem
[Sat., Jan. 21] ⟨⟨Oberlin ?⟩Warren ?⟩ Ohio   ⟨Cleveland ?⟩[9]

[24] [Mon., Jan. 23] ⟨⟨Oberlin⟩   Chicago⟩ ↑Mil[waukee]↓ ⟨Education⟩
    Milwaukee   Rev C S Staples ⟨Rev. Robert Collyer⟩
    Education[10]
[Tues., Jan. 24] ⟨⟨Chicago ?⟩ ?
    Milwaukee⟩Milwaukee   Social Aims[11]

[7] "Leave Erie . . . 1 p.m." is canceled in ink with two diagonal lines, and the entire entry with two more. Caughey is probably the Andrew Caughey who arranged a lecture in Erie in 1867; see L, V, 541.

[8] "as read at Salem" may have been added in this and the entries for January 19 and 20 below.

[9] Edwin R. Perkins, assistant cashier of the Commercial National Bank, was corresponding secretary of the Cleveland Library Association; see L, V, 382–383. "Oberlin ?", in pencil, is overwritten by "Warren ?" in ink.

[10] "⟨⟨Oberlin⟩ . . . ⟨Education⟩" is in pencil, overwritten by "Milwaukee . . . Education" in ink; "Oberlin" is canceled in pencil and "Mil" inserted above it. "Rev. Robert Collyer" is canceled in pencil. Carlton Albert Staples, pastor of the Unitarian Church in Milwaukee, arranged Emerson's lecture there (see L, V, 397 and 404); Robert Collyer was the pastor of the Unity Church where Emerson lectured in Chicago (see L, V, 389 and 404).

[11] "Chicago ? ? Milwaukee" is in pencil, overwritten by "Milwaukee . . . Aims" in ink; "Chicago ?" is also canceled in pencil.

[25] [Wed., Jan. 25] ⟨⟨Chicago⟩ ↑Milwaukee↓⟩Milwaukee
    Resources.[12]
[Thurs., Jan. 26] ⟨⟨Milwaukee⟩Chicago⟩Chicago
    ⟨Rev C A Staples⟩ Education[13]
[Fri., Jan. 27] ⟨⟨Milwaukee⟩Chicago⟩Chicago   Social Aims[14]

[26] [Sat., Jan. 28] ⟨⟨Milwaukee⟩Chicago⟩Chicago "Resources"[15]
[Mon., Jan. 30] ⟨⟨Chicago⟩Mil[waukee]⟩Milwaukee "Table-Talk"
    Read "Strangers"[16]

[27] [Tues., Jan. 31] ⟨⟨Chicago⟩Mil[waukee]⟩Milwaukee "Books."
[Wed., Feb. 1] ⟨⟨Chicago⟩Mil[waukee]⟩Milwaukee "Character."[17]
[Thurs., Feb. 2] ⟨⟨Milwaukee⟩Chi[cago]⟩Chicago "Table Talk"
    (omitting Sigurd & Eystein.) Read "Strangers"

[28] [Fri., Feb. 3] ⟨⟨Milwaukee⟩ Chi[cago]⟩Chicago "Books."
[Sat., Feb. 4] ⟨⟨Milwaukee⟩ Chi[cago]⟩Chicago "Character."[18]

[29] [Mon., Feb. 6] ⟨Erie⟩ ⟨Cleveland⟩[19]
[Tues., Feb. 7] ⟨Clevel[and]⟩Erie   Erie[20]
Social Aims ↑as read at Salem↓

[12] The canceled material is in pencil, overwritten in ink.
[13] "Milwaukee", in pencil, is overwritten in pencil by "Chicago", and both are overwritten in ink by "Chicago". "Rev C A Staples" is canceled in pencil and ink.
[14] "Milwaukee", in pencil, is overwritten in pencil by "Chicago", and both are overwritten in ink by "Chicago".
[15] The canceled matter is in pencil ("Milwaukee" is also canceled in pencil), and overwritten in ink.
[16] The canceled matter is in pencil; "Mil" is written over "Chicago", and both are overwritten by "Milwaukee" in ink; "Read 'Strangers' " was probably added. Emerson included Jones Very's poem, "The Strangers," in *Parnassus,* 1875, p. 159.
[17] In this and the preceding entry, "Chicago", in pencil and canceled in pencil, is overwritten by "Mil" in pencil, and both are overwritten by "Milwaukee" in ink.
[18] In this and the two preceding entries, "Milwaukee", in pencil and canceled in pencil, is overwritten by "Chi" in pencil, and both are overwritten by "Chicago" in ink. For "Sigurd & Eystein", see Journal DL, p. [71] above.
[19] This entry is in pencil; "Erie" is canceled diagonally in pencil and "Cleveland" in ink.
[20] "Clevel Erie" was inscribed first in pencil; "Clevel" is canceled in pencil and overwritten by "Erie" in ink.

A.H. Caughey   Left Erie at 3 A.M. Wedn.
[Wed., Feb. 8] Left Buffalo 6 pm

[30] 9th   Reached Syracuse at   8. am
              Left   6 pm
      10th   Arrived at Albany   8 am
              at Concord   7 p.m.
[Fri., Feb. 10] ⟨⟨Worcester ?⟩Worcester⟩[21]

[31] [blank]
[32] [Wed., Feb. 15] Lawrence   Social Aims   Salem Edition
[Thurs., Feb. 16] F↑eltonville↓   Social Aims   Salem Edition
[Fri., Feb. 17] ⟨Worcester ?⟩Worcester   Education[22]

[33] [Mon., Feb. 20] Springfield   Social Aims   C.H. Williams[23]

[34] [Tues., Feb. 21] Springfield.   "Resources"
Dined with Mr George Walker
[Wed., Feb. 22] ⟨Springfield ?   C H Williams⟩"Social Aims"   Salem
Edition[24]
      Hartford   J.S. Robinson   W S Bridgman
[Thurs., Feb. 23] ⟨Springfield ?⟩   Lynn ?[25]

[35] [Fri., Feb. 24] ⟨Worcester ?⟩Worcester   "Social Aims"   ⟨S.⟩[26]
[Sat., Feb. 25] Saturday Club——

[36] [Mon., Feb. 27] Springfield   "Table Talk."
[Tues., Feb. 28] Springfield   "Character"
[Wed., Mar. 1] ⟨Springfield ?⟩ ⟨Lynn ?⟩

[21] "Worcester" is written in ink over "Worcester ?" in pencil and canceled in ink with three diagonal lines.
[22] "eltonville" is added in pencil. "Worcester ?", in pencil, is overwritten by "Worcester" in ink.
[23] "Social . . . Williams" is in pencil.
[24] "Springfield ?   C H Williams", in pencil and canceled diagonally in pencil, is overwritten by " 'Social . . . Edition" in ink.
[25] "⟨Springfield ?⟩ Lynn ?" is in pencil.
[26] "Worcester ?" is in pencil, overwritten in ink; "S." is finger-wiped.

[37] [Thurs., Mar. 2] ⟨Springfield ?⟩
[Fri., Mar. 3] Worcester ? Resources[27]
[Sat., Mar. 4] Inauguration
    W[illiam] H[athaway] F[orbes] and E[dith]. E[merson].[28]

[38] [blank]
[39] [Wed., Mar. 8] ⟨Springf[iel]d ?⟩ Lynn ⟨?⟩ Social Aims[29]
[Thurs., Mar. 9] ⟨Springf[iel]d ?⟩[30]
[Fri., Mar. 10] Worcester Table Talk

[40] [blank]
[41] [Wed., Mar. 15] Lynn Character

[42] [Fri., Mar. 17] Worcester Books

[43] [Tues., Mar. 21] Social Circle
[Wed., Mar. 22] ⟨Haverhill⟩[31]

[44] [Thurs., Mar. 23] ⟨Lynn ?⟩T R Gould[32]
[Fri., Mar. 24] Worcester Character

[45] [Mon., Mar. 27] E.P. Whipple's read "Adirondac"[33]
[Tues., Mar. 28] Harrison Square J B Marvin— "Social Aims."[34]

---

[27] "Worcester ?" and the two preceding entries are in pencil.

[28] On this, the date of Lincoln's second inauguration, Emerson returned home from Boston to learn that his daughter Edith had become engaged to Forbes, then a lieutenant-colonel in the Second Regiment of Cavalry, Massachusetts Volunteers; Forbes was mustered out on May 15th and they were married October 3, 1865, in Concord. See *L*, V, 407–408.

[29] "Springfd ?" is in pencil, canceled in pencil; "Lynn ?" is in pencil, the cancellation in ink.

[30] "Springfd ?" is in pencil, canceled in ink.

[31] This entry is in pencil, canceled in ink.

[32] "Lynn ?", in pencil, is canceled in pencil. Thomas Ridgeway Gould (1818–1881), American sculptor, accepted Emerson's invitation to visit him in Concord on this date; see *L*, V, 410.

[33] Edwin Percy Whipple (1819–1886), an essayist and critic, was an old acquaintance of Emerson and a member of the Saturday Club. Emerson may have read his poem "The Adirondacs," *W*, IX, 182–194, at a meeting of the Ladies' Social Club at Whipple's home; see *L*, V, 411.

[34] According to Account Book 8, this was the first of four lectures at the Harrison Square Church in Boston; Emerson received $35 for each lecture from Rev. J. B. Marvin on March 29 and on April 4, 11, and 18.

[46] [Wed., Mar. 29] Haverhill ?   Rev. S.H. Morse—[35]
"Resources," with Extract on "Manners" from "Social Aims"

[47] [blank]
[48] [Tues., Apr. 4] Go to Milton   Furness at 11   and H James[36]

[49]–[52] [blank]
[53] [Wed., Apr. 19] Funeral Services, at Concord, of Abraham
     Lincoln.

[54]–[68] [blank]
[69] [Tues., June 6] Forceythe Willson[37]

[70]–[74] [blank]
[75] In the "Funeral" of Steele (?) occurs the scene wherein Sable the
undertaker reproaches the too cheerful mute, "Did I not give you ten,
↑then↓ fifteen, & twenty shillings a week to be sorrowful? & the more
I give you, I think, the gladder you are."[38]

[Mon., June 26] Poulteney   Success & ⟨Social⟩Table Talk[39]

[76]–[86] [blank]
[87] [Mon., July 31] Williamstown   ↑Mansion House↓   C[harles]
     T F Spoor
Tell Mr W R Thomas my time of arrival at N. Adams.[40]
[Tues., Aug. 1] ⟨Williams College   C.T.F. Spoor⟩

---

[35] Probably Sidney Henry Morse, who began *The Radical* a few months later; he reprinted Emerson's Divinity School Address in the October 1865 issue. "Haverhill ?" is in
pencil.
   [36] This entry is in pencil.
   [37] Willson had accepted Emerson's invitation to visit him in Concord on this date;
see *L*, V, 415.
   [38] This entry is in pencil; see Journal DL, p. [277] above.
   [39] "Poulteney" is in pencil.
   [40] "Mansion House" and "Tell Mr . . . N. Adams." are in pencil. Emerson gave an
address before the Adelphi Union at Williams College on this date.

[88]–[112] [blank]
[113] [Tues., Oct. 17] Amherst Mass   "Social Aims"   E.H. Bar-
     low[41]
[Wed., Oct. 18] Amherst   E.H. Barlow   "Resources"

[114] [Thurs., Oct. 19] Amherst   "Table Talk"   read "Touch-
     stone"
     ↑did *not* read Sigurd & Eystein.↓
[Fri., Oct. 20] Amherst   "Books, Poetry, Criticism" from "Books"
"Good Books" & "⟨E⟩Third Estate in Literature"

———
     Story of Pytheas[42]
———

[115] [Sun., Oct. 22] Florence, Northampton.
⟨S⟩"Immortality" & ⟨Hist of⟩"Natural Religion."   read Manzoni's
     story
Seth Hunt[43]
[Mon., Oct. 23] "Success" with Conclusion of "Works & Days"
[Tues., Oct. 24] "American Life"   From "Boston", "Anglo Ameri-
can" & "Fortune of Republic"   Read Bunyan

[116]–[119] [blank]
[120] [Tues., Nov. 7] Williamstown   J.H. Stanbrough   ↑"Social
     Aims"↓[44]
[Wed., Nov. 8] W[illia]mstown   "Resources"

[121] [Thurs., Nov. 9] W[illia]mstown   "Table Talk"   enlarged
     from Clubs   omitting Sigurd Crusader   read "Touchstone"

[41] On October 24, Emerson received payment from E. H. Barlow for six lectures
given at Amherst, according to Account Book 8; see *L,* V, 424, for the proposed
"American Life" series.
    [42] For "Touchstone", see Pocket Diary 14, p. [100] above. For "Sigurd & Ey-
stein" and the "Story of Pytheas", see Journal DL, p. [25] above.
    [43] For "Manzoni's story", see Pocket Diary 14, p. [100] above. Seth Hunt ap-
parently arranged the lecture; Emerson notes receipt of payment from him in Account
Book 8. For Emerson's pleased account of the day, see *L,* V, 430.
    [44] See Journal DL, p. [261] above, and *L,* V, 433–434, for the impromptu expan-
sion of this engagement.

[Fri., Nov. 10] W[illia]mstown   "Success"
[Sat., Nov. 11] ⟨W[illia]mstown   Culture⟩

[122] [Mon., Nov. 13] Williamstown   "Culture"   drawn   from
Lecture↑s↓ on "Genius" & "Poetry & Eng. Poetry"
[Tues., Nov. 14] "American Life" compiled from "Boston,"
"Anglo America[n]" & "Fortune of Republic"

[123] [Wed., Nov. 15] North Adams   "Social Aims" & part of
"Table Talk"

[124] [blank]
[125] [Wed., Nov. 22] G.W. Curtis in Concord

[126] [blank]
[127] [Tues., Nov. 28] Concord, N.H.   S.C. Eastman, Esq
    Social Aims ? or Resources ?

[128] [Thurs., Nov. 30] Albany.   E. DeForest   Resources
Passage of Naturalis⟨s⟩t's Methods and of the Willows

[129] [Tues., Dec. 5] Morrisania   Social Aims[45]

[130] [Thurs., Dec. 7] ⟨Albany⟩   E De Forest   ⟨Resources
⟨Passage of the Naturalist's Method; & of the willows.⟩⟩[46]
[Fri., Dec. 8] Rutland   R R Dorr   Social Aims as read at Salem

[131] [Mon., Dec. 11] West Troy, N.Y.   T.W. Jackson
W.T. Exchange Hotel   Resources, like 15 Oct[47]

[132] [Tues., Dec. 12] ⟨Coxsackie ?⟩Coxsackie   N C Bedell
    Resources[48]

---

[45] "Morrisania" is in pencil, over the same in pencil.
[46] "Albany" and "Resources . . . willows." are struck through in ink with three diagonal cancellation lines; "Passage of . . . willows." is also canceled horizontally.
[47] "Resources, . . . Oct" is in pencil.
[48] "Coxsackie" is written in ink over "Coxsackie ?" in pencil.

[133] [Fri., Dec. 15] Brooklyn   Social Aims as read at Salem
[Sat., Dec. 16] Brooklyn   Resources[49]

[134] [Tues., Dec. 19] ⟨↑Williamsburgh↓⟩   Brooklyn
⟨"Classes of Men"⟩   ↑A M Powell↓   Books & Culture drawn from
"Books" 1864 & "Art & Criticism"[50]
[Wed., Dec. 20] ⟨Clinton ?   H C Greeley⟩
⟨Brooklyn ?⟩ ↑Williamsburg↓[51]
25 "Success."   R.H. Huntley

[135] [Thurs., Dec. 21] ⟨Brooklyn.⟩ ↑W[illia]msburgh↓[52]
    ↑W[illia]msburgh↓   "Classes of Men"
[Fri., Dec. 22] ⟨Brooklyn.⟩ ↑Williamsburgh↓   "Clubs"[53] ↑drawing
on "Clubs" & "Table Talk."↓

[136]–[138] [blank]
[139] [Date.] 1865   [Paid.]
     Jan   2 James Tolman   40
               R[ichard] Briggs   6
               J[ohn] ↑H↓ Rogers   45
               knife   60
                  d[itt]o   1 40
               ⟨w⟩hack   50
               waiter   50
               E[llen] T E[merson]   2
               E[llen] T E[merson]   5
          10 Edith [Emerson]   20
          Ticket to Chicago   25 75
               Supper   50

---

[49] "Brooklyn" is in pencil in both entries on p. [133].
[50] "Brooklyn" is in pencil. Aaron M. Powell (1832–?), antislavery and temperance reformer, arranged the three lectures Emerson gave for the Brooklyn Fraternity Course at the Athenaeum there.
[51] "Brooklyn" is canceled, and "Williamsburg" added, in pencil; the question mark is canceled in ink.
[52] "Brooklyn," is canceled, and "Wmsburgh" added, in pencil.
[53] "Brooklyn." is canceled, and "Williamsburgh" added, in pencil.

[140] [blank]

[141] [Date.]   [Received.]   [Paid.]

			Received.	Paid.
↑Jan↓	14	Sent from Albany		50
		Dansbury [Dansville]		50
		Cleveland		50
		Sent to Mrs ⟨P⟩S G Perkins of Fairhaven		10
	24	Sent E[llen] T E[merson].		10
	31	Milwaukee	300	
↑Feb.↓	4	Chicago	346	
		Erie ⟨4⟩55		
		Feltonville 16		
		Lawrence 100[54]		

[142][55] Feb 20   Groton to Sp[ringfiel]d   2.95

Cannibal in literature

[143] [blank]

[144] [Date.] 1866   [Received.]

1 Jan	Mond
2	Tu
3	W
4	Th
5	F
6	Sat
7	S
8	M
9	Tu
10	W
11	Erie, Res[ources]
12	Oberlin People's Books
13	
14	

[54] "Jan 14 . . . E T E.   10" and "Erie . . . Lawrence   100" are in pencil. Emerson records the payment from Dansville in Account Book 7. Mrs. Perkins had evidently loaned Emerson $10 after he lost his purse, probably to a pickpocket, in Vermont; see *L*, V, 401.
[55] The entries on p. [142] are in pencil.

15	Laporte T[able] T[alk]	50
16	Aurora S[ocial] A[ims]	
17	Princeton S[ocial] A[ims]	75
18	Rock Island S[ocial] A[ims]	
19	Davenport. *Res*[ources]	75
20		
21		
22	Lyons Ia S[ocial] A[ims]	
23		
24	Dubuque T[able] T[alk]	
25	Freeport ?	
26	Janesville S[ocial] A[ims]	75

<table>
<tr><td>[145] 1866</td><td></td><td></td></tr>
</table>

↑Jan↓ 27	Delavan Wis. *Res*[ources]	
28		
29		
30	Kalamazoo People's B[oo]ks	75
31	Battle Creek T[able] T[alk]	50
Feb. 1	Jackson	
2	Ann Arbor S[ocial] A[ims]	75
3	Detroit S[ocial] A[ims]	75
4		
5	Toledo T[able] T[alk]	75
6	Cleveland Res[ources]	75
7	Buffalo S[ocial] A[ims]	
8	Dunkirk ? ⟨↑Batavia↓⟩	
9	⟨Lockport⟩Batavia[56]	
10		
11	Dunkirk	
12		
13		
14		
15		

[56] "Dunkirk ? Batavia" is in pencil; "Dunkirk" is partly canceled in ink and the cancellation fingerwiped, and "Batavia" is canceled in ink. "Lockport", in pencil, is overwritten by "Batavia" in ink.

533

[146] [blank]
[147] Harrisburg ↑Pa↓   A T Goodman   care W H Miller
Indianapolis Ind.   Barton D. Jones
Cincinnati.   Wm F. Phillips
Batavia, N.Y.   H.F. Tarbox
↑Dr.↓ A.M. Ross   Toronto Canada
Freeport, Ill.   F.W.S. Brawley
Concord N H   S.C. Eastman, Esq
Coxsackie N.Y.   N.C. Bedell
Lockport N.Y.   Joshua Gaskill
Schenectady ↑N.Y.↓   C G Ellis
Quincy, Ill.   J.M. Bishop
Richmond Ind.   I. Kinley
Youngstown, Ohio   H.B. Case
Monmouth Ill.   J C Gordon[57]

[148]–[156] [blank]
[157] S. 9th St Cong[regational]. Ch[urch]   Rev. Mr Bacon[58]

[158]–[161] [blank]
[162] groundpine at bottom of hickory bank on sawmill brook[59]

[163] Art
     Geology
     Chemistry

[Date.] [December, 1865]	[Dolls.]	[Cts.]
Coxsackie to Hudson	9.	
to Worcester	4	95
to Concord	1	65
To L[idian] E[merson]	10	
To Boston		65
Holmes trunk	3	75

[57] This list, probably of those with whom Emerson corresponded about lectures in late 1865 and early 1866, includes Alfred T. Goodman, probably a reporter in Harrisburg (see *L*, V, 454), and Alexander Milton Ross (1832–1897), Canadian-born naturalist and writer, who served as a surgeon in the Civil War.

[58] This entry is in pencil.

[59] This entry is in pencil.

14   To N[ew]. Y[ork]. 6.
                              65
                              50
                20
                             40   7 85
        St Denis [Hotel]   1.
                            1.75
                            75^{60}

[164] In Jan 1863
Milwaukee
     Clubs
     Success, Feb 9 1860

     In Chicago
Jan 1863   Perpetual Forces
Feb 1860   Manners

In Montreal
     Classes of Men   Feb ↑24↓ 1863
     Clubs   25

Cincinnati
Success ⎤
Manners ⎦ 1860^{61}

[165] Toronto   Jan 5 1863   "Classes of Men,"
"Criticism."   Jan 6 1863

Buffalo   *Criticism*^{n} Jan 63

Cleveland   *Criticism*^{n} Jan. 63

Detroit   *Clubs*^{n} Jan '63

---

^{60} "Coxsackie to . . . 75" is in pencil.
^{61} This entry is in pencil.

535

Pittsburg   Feb 63
   Clubs
   Classes of Men

[166] ——
W.F. Phillips, Box 702   Cincinnati

——
A.M. Ross.   Montreal ?[62]

——
C.H. Williams   Springfield Mass

——
L.C. Munn.   New London

——
E. Sands.   Lewiston, Me.
A H Caughey   Erie Pa
Miss Libbie H. Clarke   577 Michigan Avenue   Chicago
Miss Nina Y. Lunt   171 Michigan Avenue   Chicago
John H. Thompson   Chicago[63]
Thompson & Bishop

[167] Write Ellen[64]

E.G. Reynolds   Hillsdale
C.S. Fraser, Ann Arbor

    S 5th near 4th
  34 ‖ . . . ‖ to 4th along to S. 5th

J. Theron   4⟨1⟩8 W 37 st[65]

[168] Ullman Strong
    Henry ?
    Fanny[66]

---

[62] "Montreal" is circled in ink; the question mark may have been added.

[63] John Howland Thompson, a young Chicago attorney, was corresponding secretary of the Young Men's Association and one of the committee who arranged Emerson's lecture series January 26–February 4, 1865. See *L,* V, 22 and 406.

[64] In pencil.

[65] "J. Theron . . . 37 st" is in pencil; "8 is written in ink over "1" in pencil.

[66] "Ullman . . . Fanny" is in pencil.

March 10   Letter from J.B. Harrison   Kendallville, Noble Co.
    Indiana

[Thomas Hutchinson,] Hutchinson Papers   4.00   Prince Society
                            [(Albany and Boston, 1865)]

[169] [William] Forsyth's Life of [*Marcus Tullius*] Cicero [2 vols.
                            (New York, 1865)]
Bohn's Demosthenes [*The Orations*, trans. C. R. Kennedy (London,
                            1863)]
        Handbook of London
↑Bohn's↓ [John Russell] Hind's Introduction to Astronomy [(London,
                            1863)] 2.25
                    ↑*Scribner*↓

_____

[Matthew] Arnold's Studies [*Essays in Criticism* (Boston, 1865)]

_____

[*Le*] Morte d'Arthur [F. J.] Furnivall, Editor. [(London & Cam-
                    bridge, 1864)] 7↑s↓ 6[d]ⁿ

_____

Muller's [*Lectures on the*] Science of Language   Lectures [*delivered
. . . in . . .*] 1863   [2 vols. (New York, 1865)] 3.50

_____

    [*The*] Rhythm of Bernard de Morlaix[, *Monk of Cluny. On the
    Celestial Country*]. Translated by [Rev. J. M.] Neale
                    20 cts. [(New York:]Durand[, 1865)]

_____

American Weeds & [*Useful*] Plants   By W[illiam]. Darlington
            1.75   [(New York:] O[range]. Judd[, 1865)]

_____

Sydney Smith, Wit & Wisdom [(New York, 1866)]   2.50

_____

Colton's [*Octavo*] Atlas [*of the World* (New York, 1865)]. 8vo 5.00[67]

[67] All of the books Emerson notes on pp. [168]–[169] appear in advertisements or
lists of books recently published in the *American Literary Gazette and Publishers' Circular*,
IV (Feb. 15, 1865), pp. 214–230. The first four books on p. [169] are all advertised for
sale by Chas. Scribner & Co., New York. The "Handbook of London" is not further
identified; it may have been the London, 1863 or 1865 edition of Peter Cunningham's
London As It Is; Emerson owned the 1869 edition.

[170]⁶⁸ Mrs Carson   149 W. 26th st
Mrs Nash   96 E 19th St
Watson & Frank Nash   43 Wall

Charles Brown   47 Kildare St.   ↑Dublin↓

↑office↓   3⟨7⟩0 Bachelors Walk

↑J[oseph]. W[oodward]. Haven   31 Washington Square W.↓

C[hristopher] P[earse] Cranch   Corner 27 & Broadway

[inside back cover]
Old Sergeant   R R   vol. 6
Boy Brittan   vol. 4. p. 62
Kentucky   vol. 2. p. 60
In State   vol. 3 p. 14⁶⁹

I.T. Williams   79 Nassau
J.H.E.   3⟨2⟩19 Broadway
C.E.   50 Broad Street
John S. Rogers   1077 Washington St
Mrs Botta, 31 W. 37th St. N.Y.
E T Rice   41 Wall St
Mrs S.B. Jackson, 77 Remsen   Brooklyn⁷⁰

---

⁶⁸ Except for "J. W. Haven . . . Square W.", which is inserted in ink, p. [170] is in pencil. Mrs. Nash is probably Paulina Tucker Nash, sister of Emerson's first wife, and Frank her son Francis Phillip Nash. Charles Brown married and abandoned Lidian Emerson's sister Lucy. Haven was the brother of Susan Haven Emerson, wife of Emerson's brother William. Cranch, a Unitarian minister, was a lifelong friend of Emerson.

⁶⁹ Emerson found these four poems by Forceythe Willson in the poetry sections of the *The Rebellion Record*, 1861–1868, VI, 32–34; IV, 62; II, 61; and III, 15–16. For Willson and "Old Sergeant", see Journal DL, p. [238] above. Emerson printed "In State" in *Parnassus*, 1875, pp. 255–257.

⁷⁰ "E T Rice . . . Brooklyn" is in pencil. "J.H.E." and "C.E." are undoubtedly Emerson's nephews, John Haven Emerson and Charles Emerson. Edwin T. Rice, a New York lawyer, had apparently been married to Augusta Jackson (d. 1854), a cousin of Lidian's; see *L*, IV, 278 and 436. Susan Bridge Jackson was married to Lidian's brother, C. T. Jackson.

Appendixes

Textual Notes

Index

Appendix I
Journals and Notebooks
in the Harvard Edition

The following table shows which of Emerson's journals and miscellaneous notebooks are already printed in the Harvard University Press edition (*JMN,* I–XIV), and where they may be found, by volume and volume page numbers. Because this edition prints Emerson's manuscript page numbers of the journals and notebooks in the text, the reader should have no difficulty in locating cross-references to previously printed journals or notebooks. These are listed alphabetically, as designated by Emerson or others; the dates are supplied by Emerson, or the editors, or both. Since some passages are undated and some dates are doubtful, scholars should look at individual passages before relying on their dating.

Designation	Harvard edition
A (1833–1834)	IV, 249–387
AB (1847)	X, 3–57
AC (1858–1859)	XIV, 208–290
AZ (1849–1850)	XI, 183–278
B (1835–1836)	V, 3–268
Blotting Book I (1826–1827)	VI, 11–57
Blotting Book II (1826–1829)	VI, 58–101
Blotting Book III (1831–1832)	III, 264–329
Blotting Book IV (1830, 1831? 1833)	III, 359–375
Blotting Book IV[A] (1830, 1832–1834)	VI, 102–114
Blotting Book Psi (1830–1831, 1832)	III, 203–263
Blotting Book Y (1829–1830)	III, 163–202
Blue Book (1826)	III, 333–337
BO (1850–1851)	XI, 279–365
BO Conduct (1851)	XII, 581–599
Books Small [I] (1840?–1856?)	VIII, 442–479
Books Small [II]	VIII, 550–576
C (1837–1838)	V, 277–509
Catalogue of Books Read (1819–1824)	I, 395–399

Designation	Harvard edition
CD (1847)	X, 58–123
Charles C. Emerson (1837)	VI, 255–286
CL (1859–1861)	XIV, 291–369
CO (1851)	XI, 366–452
Collectanea (1825–1828?)	VI, 3–10
College Theme Book (1819–1821, 1822? 1829?)	I, 161–205
Composition (1832?)	IV, 427–438
D (1838–1839)	VII, 3–262
Delta (1837–1841, 1850, 1857, 1862)	XII, 178–268
Dialling (1825? 1841? 1842)	VIII, 483–517
DO (1852–1854, 1856, 1858)	XIII, 3–57
E (1839–1842)	VII, 263–484
ED (1852–1853)	X, 494–568
Encyclopedia (1824–1836)	VI, 115–234
England and Paris (1847–1848)	X, 407–445
F No. 1 (1836–1840)	XII, 75–177
F No. 2 (1840–1841)	VII, 485–547
France and England (1833)	IV, 395–419
G (1841)	VIII, 3–77
Genealogy (1822, 1825, 1828)	III, 349–358
GH (1847–1848)	X, 124–199
GO (1852–1853)	XIII, 58–128
H (1841)	VIII, 78–145
HO (1853–1854)	XIII, 207–289
Index Minor (1843–1847?)	XII, 518–580
IO (1854)	XIII, 290–378
Italy (1833)	IV, 134–162
Italy and France (1833)	IV, 163–208
J (1841–1842)	VIII, 146–197
JK (1843?–1847)	X, 365–404
Journal 1826 (1825, 1826, 1827? 1828)	III, 3–41
Journal 1826–1828 (1824, 1825, 1826–1828)	III, 42–112
Journal at the West (1850–1853)	XI, 510–540
K (1842)	VIII, 198–247
L Concord (1835, 1838)	XII, 3–32
L Literature (1835)	XII, 33–55
LM (1848)	X, 288–362
London (1847–1848)	X, 208–287
Maine (1834)	IV, 388–391
Man (1836)	XII, 56–74
Margaret Fuller Ossoli (1851)	XI, 455–509
Memo St. Augustine (1827)	III, 113–118

Designation	Harvard edition
Meredith Village (1829)	III, 159–162
N (1842)	VIII, 248–308
NO (1855)	XIII, 379–469
No. II (1825)	II, 413–420
No. XV (1824–1826)	II, 272–351
No. XVI (1824–1828?)	II, 396–412
No. XVII (1820)	I, 206–248
No. XVIII (1820–1822)	I, 249–357
No. XVIII[A] (1821?–1829)	II, 355–395
Notebook 1833 (1833–1836)	VI, 235–254
O (1846–1847)	IX, 355–470
Phi (1838–1844? 1847–1851?)	XII, 269–419
Platoniana (1845–1848)	X, 468–488
Pocket Diary 1 (1820–1831)	III, 338–348
Pocket Diary 1 (1847)	X, 405–406
Pocket Diary 2 (1833)	IV, 420–426
Pocket Diary 3 (1848–1849)	X, 446–457
Pocket Diary 4 (1853)	XIII, 473–482
Pocket Diary 5 (1854)	XIII, 483–501
Pocket Diary 6 (1855)	XIII, 502–515
Pocket Diary 7 (1856)	XIV, 431–445
Pocket Diary 8 (1857)	XIV, 446–455
Pocket Diary 9 (1858)	XIV, 456–464
Pocket Diary 11 (1859)	XIV, 465–473
Pocket Diary 12 (1860)	XIV, 474–482
Psi (1839–1842, 1851)	XII, 420–517
Q (1832–1833)	IV, 3–101
R (1843)	VIII, 349–441
RO (1855–1856)	XIV, 3–39
RO Mind (1835)	V, 269–276
RS (1848–1849)	XI, 3–86
Scotland and England (1833)	IV, 209–235
Sea 1833 (1833)	IV, 236–248
Sea-Notes (1847)	X, 200–207
Sermons and Journal (1828–1829)	III, 119–158
Sicily (1833)	IV, 102–133
SO (1856–1857)	XIV, 40–118
T (1834–?)	VI, 317–399
Trees[A:1] (1843–1847)	VIII, 518–533
Trees[A:11]	VIII, 534–549
TU (1849)	XI, 87–182
U (1843–1844)	IX, 3–92

Designation	Harvard edition
Universe 1–7, 7[A], 8 (1820–1822)	I, 358–394
V (1844–1845)	IX, 93–181
VO (1857–1858)	XIV, 119–207
VS (1853–1854)	XIII, 129–206
W (1845)	IX, 182–255
Walk to the Connecticut (1823)	II, 177–186
Warren Lot (1849)	X, 489–493
Wide World 1 (1820)	I, 3–32
Wide World 2 (1820–1821)	I, 33–58
Wide World 3 (1822)	I, 59–90
Wide World 4 (1822)	I, 91–113
Wide World 6 (1822)	I, 114–158
Wide World 7 (1822)	II, 3–39
Wide World 8 (1822)	II, 40–73
Wide World 9 (1822–1823)	II, 74–103
Wide World 10 (1823)	II, 104–143
Wide World 11 (1823)	II, 144–176
Wide World 12 (1823–1824)	II, 187–213
Wide World XIII (1824)	II, 214–271
WO Liberty (1854?–1857?)	XIV, 373–430
Xenien (1848, 1852)	X, 458–467
Y (1845–1846)	IX, 256–354
Z (1831? 1837–1838, 1841?)	VI, 287–316
Z[A] (1842–1843)	VIII, 309–348

Appendix II

Montreal Herald Report
of "Classes of Men"

This clipping, pasted on brown paper and probably cut out of a scrap-book, is laid inside the front cover of Journal GL. "⟨Herald⟩ (24 Feb. 1863) ⟨1863⟩" is inserted in ink above a caret following "On Tuesday evening" at the beginning of the report, and "Ex Herald (Montreal) 26 Feb 1863" is added in ink at the end of it. A note on the back, probably by Edward Emerson, reads "Sent me by David Matheson, Esq.   Hudson Heights   Quebec, Canada." A note on the front by Matheson reads "Memo   Mr Emerson came to Montreal at the request of the Mercantile Literary Society and deliv-ered his lecture on 'Classes of Men.' He remained two days and was the guest of Rev. Dr. Cordner, D.M."

MR. EMMERSON'S LECTURE.

On Tuesday evening this gentleman delivered a lecture in Nord-heimer's Hall, on "Classes of Men," the hall was comfortably filled by a highly respectable audience. About eight o'clock, the lecturer who is an elderly man of a decidedly intellectual cast of countenance, made his appearance, and after being introduced, said that men generally were great classifiers—like children they put things in a row. Each man had his favourite theory, which he generally magnified till it be-came so large that he could not see anything else, for instance one had a taste for music another for war, one for painting, &c, each monoma-niac cherished his favourite whims. This love for each particular whim ran in certain cases into insanity. Again there were the methodical class of men of whose representative Plato said "he shall be as a God to me who can rightly define and divide." These men were classifiers be-cause they were first classified; had method in their mind before they sought to verify their theory of method in the world. But there were always declaimers who would find fault with the best theories simply

545

for the sake of opposition. There were certain well-matched opposing classes in society, the representatives of which—artists, mechanics, men of religious genius—were always sure to manifest themselves. Men of the same taste, liked each other's society—hunters hunters—soldiers soldiers—and from the simple fact that a man was a soldier, many a man with a military turn would vote with a majority of their company; or in other ways labor with toil to effect an object for which before they donned a uniform they would not have spared a shilling. Artificial states of society spring into existence suddenly, but perish and leave no mark behind, but other societies founded on natural distinctions were lasting. The speaker then alluded to the different nations of the earth, and to their beauties and defects one which counteracted the other. The Italians who are a vivacious and delicate people, admirably adapted for works of art, lack that robustness which belonged to some more northern nation. There were four classes of temperments, bilious, phlegmatic, melancholy, sanguine. Under these different kinds were to be found permanent classes, a type of one of which was the public or whole-souled man who could think and feel and act with the crowd—who could, with perfect ease, perform all offices of the day in the street—eat, drink, and if necessary sleep there. Such men were usually of a coarse rather than of a refined cast. They would not stand for trifles, but were inestimable for their right work in society. They were the right men to preside over mass meetings. Such men removed from their proper spheres were as much out of place as a cannon in a pocket. They often received their cast of character when school-boys, and they did not try to swim until they knew how. Close beside the whole-souled class stood that of the lonely man. Solitude to this class was society. There were people upon whom speech made no impression—people upon whom facts made no impression, who could not be made to see that they were in the wrong, and when such people were endowed with genius it widened the chasm between them and others. Dr. Johnson, for instance, a man of truth and piety, clothed with all kinds of culture, was incessantly given to wound in conversation the feelings of those who loved him at the moment they were serving him. The snapping turtle was a strong example of this peevish fretful nervous temperment. If you cut off the head of that animal his teeth will not release the hold of the stick, break its egg and an embryo appears who will still bite furiously. Thus these animals would not only bite when they were dead, but bite before they were born. He was sorry to say that a like propensity could be discovered in man and woman. Contrary to this class was another who were always fretting and whining because they could not realize the most absurd day dreams. When they saw a canary bird immediately they thought of yellow fever, [Laughter]; but there was a period when such nervous people found rest which was in old age, when as they can no longer bite and scratch they say to their opponents meekly "that is not my way of thinking Sir, suit youself." The speaker then alluded to that class of egotists to whom things were consistent according as they harmonized with their peculiar view. Nature cunningly contrived this for the best; had he made each man solicitous for his neighbors welfare, it would have been a very amiable but inconvenient arrangement. Nature provided for each. When some people had nothing else to praise themselves for, they would praise themselves for being alive. The instant a man died no matter how good or how virtuous they said poor John or poor Thomas, at the same time chuckling that they were not dead. Such men inspired pity, mixed with anger, and made us sceptical of a "general resurrection" as it appeared a superfluity to resurrect that particular class of people. But the[r]e was no square foot of land in the world so black and so barren but that life could not be found on it—no swamp but some cultivator would cause it to bear fruit, not an inch of latitude where it might not be feasible to plant cabbages, and so likewise did those apparently selfish characters, bear certain good qualities peculiar to themselves. The speaker after mentioning some of the master minds of the world, stated that recent discoveries were but the result of the past working of such minds, but it was only when theoretical researches took the practical shape of eight per cent, that the people would cry out "it is the voice of God." The merit of genius was too often tasted by the niceties of critics and connoiseurs. Lord Elgin spent fifty thousand pounds, in obtaining ancient Greek statues and bestowed a great amount of labor to fish them out of the OEgean Sea, but after all his expense and labor, the critics looked coldly on them, pronouncing them mere imitations of a late age, and because certain critics did not praise them, they became in the popular esteem of no value. The speaker then spoke of the two classes which we meet in every day life. The motto of one of which is that nobility requires noble action in its possessor and that of the other asserts that Royal blood cannot be base. But who would judge Spartans by Sparta? Men should be judged by their actions. That was the true nobility which magnetized masses by the force of thought and not by luck or chance. Napoleon in France—Washington in America—Demosthenes in Attica, were all types of this class, the greatest and noblest of them all.

Editorial Correspondence of the "Montreal Herald."

Textual Notes

DL

8 &⟨c⟩the   9 ri*v*al   17 Troilus ["T" in pencil]   18 Gen*i*us   36 language,   37 com-[121]pendium | w'*ant*."   41 When | he. | see.   42 *Jesus.*   45 ⟨Howe⟩[?]   52 reiinforces | perchance   53 *the* [underline canceled]   54 *"Por-/* traits   55 also;   56 few, | per-[181]ceives   59 ⟨∧⟩ [caret canceled] | arranged, | ⟨Everything⟩ ↑All was↓ ⟨His death is⟩so | dis-[194]pointment   61 [⟨the good⟩] | situa-[212]tion   65 ⟨y|| . . . ||⟩ [blotted] | ↑↑men↓ whose↓   66 power; | ↑tr.↓ for the present to have customers. [marked for transposition]   67 genius,[?]   68 G⟨rr⟩rand   73 our | *the Vatican*₂ or the *Yosemite Gorge*₁   74 how / how   76 colonel↑s↓cy[?] | him,[?] | themselves. | so ["s" crossed]   79 in,   80 impon-[266]derable | market, that is,   81 We [blotted]   82 b*us*iness,—undertaken ["u" crossed later]   84 a⟨n⟩ [pen ran dry; "n" neither canceled nor retraced]   85 quick

GL

91 rea*l*ity | *sh*all or *sh*an't: | f*r*om,   92 privation.   93 mo-[11]ment   95 th*a*t,   97 evenings,   98 Beccause | At   99 system:[?]   104 they | shovellin[58]ing   106 s*e*lf,   107 *Dre*am.   110 ⟨bag.⟩ ↑⟨bog.⟩↓ [blotted] ↑bog↓ | ⟨⟨to⟩ not to⟩ | caricatures, | ⟨⟨that follow him⟩⟩ | literature,   111 a   113 ⟨l⟩tea⟨rn⟩ch [overwritten in pencil]   116 Let   119 *Autobi*ography   123 wa*v*ed | fr [not canceled]   124 exerc*i*ises,   126 affermative[?]   134 p [not canceled]   136 the↑ir↓ realism [not canceled] | mouth. | [They know everything↑.↓]₂ ⟨in⟩ [There are no secrets from them.]₁ | a ⟨man⟩   138 ⟨to under[170]stand⟩   139 emi-[174₁]grating   141 principle,   143 We   148 subscription?∧ | 264 [blotted]   156 going⟨,⟩.   157 speak   159 y*o*u.   160 second(, or   161 &⟨your   162 Mr— [blotted] | a*l*one;   163 intel[382]lectualist | But   166 nothing.

WAR

173 we   175 Lafayettee[?]   176 sentimentalism. | theatricals, | become ["e" blotted]   178 it ["t" not crossed] | govt.;,   179 climatie[?]   181 ⟨⟨election of a rogue⟩,⟩   184 e|||se|| [obscured by sealing wax]   185 Every | *Effect*↑"↓*s*   188 ⟨i⟩t⟨'⟩↑i↓*s* | I ⟨told him⟩   189 business⟨,⟩?",   190 meantime,   192 writer,— / —She | dem-[112]onstration   196 journey. | under-[134]stood   200 appropri[154]ation   204 & s⟨eas⟩skies, ["& s" left to read "of"]   207 Califor[193]nia, | river,   208 govern-[195]ment | Savan-[198]nah,   210 ⟨they s⟩South   211 the [not canceled] | again. | & ⟨trade⟩   212 of [not canceled] | ⟨c⟩limits[?] | it.   215 Let | And[?] | Will   217 scroll?   218 we | & and   220 Nature.⟨,⟩"[?]   221 re-[248] produce   229 ⟨:⟩ [blotted]   230 *e*very   233 hope₂ & power₁ | can [not canceled]

549

VA

235 of [not canceled] | & [not canceled]   236 that [not canceled]   239 ⟨civ.⟨ⁿ⟩i⟨ti⟩lation we⟩↑civilization we↓ | freedom₂ & [15] exhilaration₃ & security,₁ | handker-[17]chiefs   240 the [not canceled]   245 or ⟨Boston⟩ | ⟨⟨appearing⟩⟩ [parentheses and cancellation in pencil] | ↑profane.↓ | ⟨⟨in nature⟩⟩ [parentheses and cancellation in pencil]   246 apes | ⟨decomposes them⟩₂ & ⟨suffocates their laughter.⟩₁   259 omitted.   260 illustrative ["ll" crossed] | process ["p" blotted]   261 people ["le" blotted]   263 dependences. he [period added in pencil] | Journal   265 a ⟨piece of a mountain⟩ | It   267 misbehave. | rumor⟨e⟨d⟩s⟩s   268 & and   273 this great . . . our [not canceled]   275 it   278 faults. | Ever | What   281 images∧;   284 classifying₂ & seeing₁   287 [⟨I am . . . robbers.⟩]   289 r [not canceled]   291 a | ["facuties" in ink, "faculties" in pencil]   294 The | supply,   296 for   297 ball.   298 A   299 man.   300 of [finger-wiped] | Why   301 th [not canceled or crossed]

FOR

316 Knows   324 among the troops; among the women, [marked for transposition]   326 turned⟩,   327 ages⟩, [comma in pencil] | anschaun⟨g⟩ng ["n" used as "u"]   328 move₂ or drag₁   333 Montesquieu | Montesquieu   334 yes,   335 con-/ duire   338 15. [blotted] | me⟨d⟩iums [?]   341 With   352 And   353 ⟨⟨intellectual⟩⟩ [parentheses in pencil]   355 Came   356 depart-[142]ment | introduction   358 on.   365 When he passed, on the way to the city,₂ the woods₁ [numbered and circumscribed in pencil for transposition]   367 ⟨company⟩ [cancellation finger-wiped] | school↑-keeping↓ | [⟨brutal . . . word,⟩] [brackets in pencil] | A.C.   374 ⟨all⟩ [cancellation canceled]   376 volume↑.↓, | Il⟨l⟩usion.   377 From   384 Solve [?] | to beasts & birds [not canceled]   388 what   389 do   390 Austria, and, and   395 gradually,   396 be- / because   399 words   400 ↑↑gold or↓ with . . . guano,↓   402 ⟨∧⟩ of∧   403 re⟨presen⟩tative.   406 ⟨The Earth⟩, our | anthropized.   410 Ge⟨h⟩alt

KL

416 Every | solitude.   417 what   419 ⟨you   420 per⟨d⟩u   423 ⟨all⟩   424 regi-[35]ment   426 per   427 In⟨s⟩piration   429 Each   430 the   431 him-[67]self | All   436 Na⟨t⟩ure,   438 the ⟨cause⟩   439 interpre-[96]tion   440 Su⟨c⟩cess.   441 lit↑t↓é⟨er⟩rateurs   444 the   445 stru⟨c⟩tural   446 wo⟨r⟩king   449 ⟨hiemalis₂ fringilla₁⟩   451 .— [finger-wiped?]   458 me⟨to⟩nymy   461 remem[176]ber   463 ↑where↓ | great [?] | The   464 maple | They | And ⟨Fear⟩ &   473 Were   474 need   478 compliances.

HT

487 who [could tax . . . over-refining,]₂ [⟨who⟩ ↑that↓ found . . . their [18] objects . . . artificial:]₁ . . . infinitudes.⟨]⟩   490 rocka-[44]way

Pocket Diaries 13, 14, 15, and 16

496 Use   501 mother.   503 St⟨e⟩aevens [?]   509 Baldwin [finger-wiped?]   521 Since   535 Cri⟨t⟩icism | Cri⟨t⟩icism | C⟨l⟩ubs   537 7↑↑s↓ 6

Index

This Index includes Emerson's own index material omitted from the text. His index topics, including long phrases, are listed under "Emerson, Ralph Waldo, INDEX HEADINGS AND TOPICS"; the reader should consult both the general Index and Emerson's. If Emerson did not specify a manuscript page or a date to which his index topic referred, the editors have chosen the most probable passage(s) and added "(?)" to the printed page number(s). If Emerson's own manuscript page number is an obvious error, it has been silently corrected.

References to materials included or to be included in *Lectures* are grouped under "Emerson, Ralph Waldo, LECTURES." References to drafts of unpublished poems are under "Emerson, Ralph Waldo, POEMS." Under "Emerson, Ralph Waldo, WORKS" are references to published versions of poems, to lectures and addresses included in *W* but not in *Lectures,* and to Emerson's essays and miscellaneous publications. Kinds of topics included under "Emerson, Ralph Waldo, DISCUSSIONS" in earlier volumes are now listed only in the general Index.

553

573

574